The Vinson Court Era

AMS STUDIES IN SOCIAL HISTORY, NO. 9
ISSN 0270-6253

Other Titles in this series:

1. Esmond Wright, ed. *Red, White & True Blue: The Loyalists in the Revolution.* 1976.

2. Richard V. Francaviglia. *The Mormon Landscape.* 1978.

3. Taylor Stoehr. *Free Love In America.* 1979.

4. Cynthia Huff. *British Women's Diaries: A Descriptive Bibliography of Selected Nineteenth-Century Women's Manuscript Diaries.* 1985.

5. Nan Hackett. *XIX Century British Working-Class Autobiographies: An Annotated Bibliography.* 1985.

6. Elizabeth Benson-von der Ohe and Valmari M. Mason. *An Annotated Bibliography of U.S. Scholarship on the History of the Family.* 1986.

7. Barbara E. Nolan. *The Political Theory of Beatrice Webb.* 1988.

8. Frederick and Joann Koelln Frankena. *Citizen Participation in Enviromental Affairs, 1970—1986: A Bibliography.* 1988

THE VINSON COURT ERA

The Supreme Court's Conference Votes;
Data and Analysis

Jan Palmer

Ohio University

AMS Press
New York

Libary of Congress Cataloging-in-Publication Data

Palmer, Jan.
    The Vinson court era: the Supreme Court's conference
votes: data and analysis / Jan Palmer.
      p. cm. -- (AMS studies in social history; no. 9)
    Includes bibliographical references.
    ISBN 0-404-61609-7
    1. United States Supreme Court -- History. 2. Vinson, Fred
    M., 1890-1953. 3. Judges -- United States -- Biography. I.
Title. II. Series.
KF8742.P333 1990
347.73'26'09--dc20
[347.3072609]
                                  89-45875
                                     CIP

All AMS books are printed on acid-free paper that meets the
guidelines for performance and durability of the Committee on
Production Guidelines for Book Longevity of the Council on
Library Resources.

AMS PRESS
56 East 13th Street
New York, N.Y. 10003, U.S.A.

Manufactured in the United States of America

Contents

1. Introduction   1

2. The Justices and their Backgrounds   6

3. The Supreme Court's Powers and Procedures   16

4. Dataset Descrition   34

5. Case Selection via Certiori   50

6. Case Selection via Appeals   76

7. Votes on the Merits   97

8. Opinion Assignment   124

References   151

Index   157

Appendix A: Dataset Format   159

Appendix B: U.S. Supreme Court October 1946 Term   161

Appendix C: U.S. Supreme Court October 1947 Term   197

Appendix D: U.S. Supreme Court October 1948 Term   227

Appendix E: U.S. Supreme Court October 1949 Term   259

Appendix F: U.S. Supreme Court October 1950 Term   289

Appendix G: U.S. Supreme Court October 1951 Term   319

Appendix H: U.S. Supreme Court October 1952 Term   351

Appendix I: U.S. Supreme Court October 1953 Term   385

1

Introduction

I. The Vinson Era

This book is an analysis of the U.S. Supreme Court during the tenure of Fred Vinson who served as chief justice of The United States from 1946 to 1953.

During Vinson's chief justiceship, the nation was recovering from the Second World War and experienced the profound social change which often follows great armed conflicts. The economy suffered inflation and strikes, but did not return to the depression that had preceded the war. Jackie Robinson broke the race barrier in major league baseball, but most of U.S. society was characterized by either *de facto* or *de jure* racial segregation. The Marshall Plan helped Europe recover from the ravages of the Second World War, but hopes for a peaceful and cooperative world dimmed with the beginnings of the Cold War and ended with U.S. involvement in the Korean conflict.

Fear of communism permeated American society as China became a communist dictatorship and the Soviet Union developed an atomic bomb. Alger Hiss—a quintessential all-American boy, who had served as a law clerk for Justice Oliver Wendell Holmes—was accused of spying for the Soviet Union. The Rosenbergs were executed as Soviet spies after their trial made them worldwide celebrities. Reckless charges of communist infiltration of the government were taken seriously and resulted in programs requiring that public employees take oaths and otherwise prove their loyalty.

During Vinson's tenure, the Court, like the nation, was sharply divided on several important issues including the rights of labor unions, communists, religious groups, and racial minorities. To a large extent, the history of the Vinson Court is a mirror of U.S. history during the postwar period that encompasses Truman's presidency and the beginning of Eisenhower's.

A few of the best remembered cases of the Vinson era include the following: the Rosenberg spy case, 346 U.S. 273 (1953), which resulted in a minor public outcry when Douglas granted a last minute stay which was lifted by the entire Court in a rare special term; the steel seizure case, 343 U.S. 579 (1952), in which the Court forced the president to return the steel mills to civilian management; *Saia v. New York*, 334 U.S. 558 (1948), which dealt with the proselytizing rights of Jehovah's Witnesses; *Takahashi v. Fish and Game Commission*, 334 U.S. 410 (1948), which involved the rights of aliens; *Joint Anti-Fascist Refugee Committee v. McGrath*, 341 U.S. 123 (1951), which involved free speech claims; *U.S. v. United Mine Workers*, 330 U.S. 258 (1947), which was concerned with whether the Norris-LaGuardia Act protected the mine workers and their leader, John L. Lewis, from a court-imposed back-to-work order; and *Dennis v. U.S.*, 341 U.S. 494 (1951), which dealt with the rights of members of the American Communist Party.

The landmark civil-rights case outlawing segregated public school systems, *Brown v. Board of Education*, 345 U.S. 972 (1953), began during the Vinson Court but was completed after Earl Warren became chief justice. Several precursors to *Brown* were decided by the Vinson Court: *Sipuel v. Board of Regents*, 332 U.S. 631 (1948), and *Sweatt v. Painter*, 339 U.S. 629 (1950), chipped away at state sponsored segregation of higher education; *Shelley v. Kraemer*, 334 U.S. 1 (1948), stopped judicial enforcement of restrictive covenants; *Henderson v. U.S.*, 339 U.S. 816 (1950), dealt with equal accommodations in interstate travel; and *Terry v. Adams*, 345 U.S. 461 (1953), ended the legal exclusion of black voters from primary elections.

II. Apologia

Scores of books and hundreds of articles have been written about the U.S. Supreme Court. It is studied by several different disciplines using many different methodologies. Historians, legal scholars, political scientists, and other social scientists all have their own approaches. But like the blind men who touched and then described an elephant, each explains only a small and atypical part of the whole. No one completely understands the U.S. Supreme Court, partly because it is a complex and ever changing institution and partly because the Court has always used secrecy to enhance its legitimacy.

The secrecy that surrounds the Court has been penetrated by scholars using original sources. The door to the Vinson Court's conferences, originally closed to everyone except the justices, has been opened by Fine (1984) and Berry (1978), who were able to use the justices' papers to reconstruct some of the deliberations that preceded conference votes. Likewise, Ulmer (1972) and Provine (1980) present analyses of certain types of conference votes using Burton's papers.

This book opens the door further by making the secret conference votes available: not just the votes in certain selected or important cases, but rather 44,728 votes cast by the individual justices in 2,500 different cases. Only disbarments, cases on the original docket, and cases unanimously denied review are excluded. Almost all the votes presented are based on multiple sources because each of the surviving collections of the justices' private papers was used to construct the dataset.

The availability of the dataset will allow others to re-examine the many assumptions and speculations about the Court's secret deliberations, which, until now, could not be systematically tested. Much of the information will not surprise those familiar with the Court. For examples, the high level of agreement between Frankfurter and Jackson, Minton's great reluctance and Black's great willingness to grant review, and the small number of opinions assigned to Burton during his first years on the Court are well known.

Other information in the dataset, however, should both interest and surprise Supreme Court scholars. Here is a potpourri of six examples. (1) In the important freedom-of-speech case, *Terminiello v. Chicago*, 337 U.S. 1 (1949), Douglas first voted to affirm the conviction but changed his mind after starting to write the opinion of the Court. (2) Using the final votes in *U.S. Reports* to infer who assigned opinions results in a 16 percent error rate. (3) In *Eisler v. U.S.*, 338 U.S. 189 (1949), a case involving the rights of an alien communist, the Court took seven conference votes before the case was removed from the docket after Eisler, who would have won on-the-merits, fled the country. (4) Reed changed sides in about ten percent of his opinion assignments. (5) He apparently also had an exceptional ability to induce Black and Douglas to change their votes after the conference. (6) In *McLaurin v. Oklahoma State Regents*, 339 U.S. 637 (1950), a case dealing with segregated facilities in higher education, Burton, Reed, and Vinson voted to affirm summarily when the Court was deciding whether to hear the appeal. All three subsequently changed sides and joined a unanimous opinion that outlawed segregated facilities for students attending the same institution.

III. Plan of the Book

Chapter 2 presents brief biographies of the justices and discusses their shared experiences and beliefs. Chapter 3 contains a very detailed explanation of the Vinson Court's procedures, a comprehension of which is essential to understanding and analyzing the Court's votes. Chapter 4 includes descriptions of each justice's private papers, an explanation of how the dataset was gathered and coded, and a discussion of the types and causes of errors. Chapter 5 examines the Court's certiorari decision making and includes analyses of the individual justices' willingness to grant review, the agreement rates between pairings of justices, the connections between the vote on granting review and subsequent votes, and the number of solo dissents by each justice. Chapter 6 contains a very similar analysis of appeals and investigates the differences and similarities between the writs of appeal and certiorari. Chapter 7 explores conference and report votes on-the-merits and contains analyses of the individual justices' reverse rates, agreement rates between pairings of justices, and fluidity between the conference and report votes by the Court and by individual justices. Chapter 8 presents the distribution of signed opinions, examines how the pattern of assignments made by the chief justice differs from that made by the other assigners, and measures the effect of the amount of time taken to complete opinions on the number of opinions assigned to each justice. Appendix A contains a delineation of the dataset format. Finally, appendices B through I contain the individual cases which are grouped according to the Court's terms, beginning with the October 1946 term and ending with the October 1953 term.

Other empirical studies of the Court focus on one type of case or they construct elaborate categories of cases which receive separate analysis. But in my empirical analyses, I have intentionally avoided distinguishing cases according to their type or importance. In this book, a case is a case is a case. Cases are distinguished according to date, type of writ, and disposition but not according to the type of dispute or the nature of the litigants. With the exception of opinion assignments, similar cases that were processed together are not combined into one observation; each is a unique entry in the analysis.

My empirical analyses are simple. Being neither a lawyer nor a political scientist frees me from previous training that would compel the use of specific methodologies or require a search for particular results. I search for relationships that are so strong and so obvious that they emerge clearly from this muddle of cases. Others are encouraged to use the tools of their disciplines on this dataset and they are free to construct subsets of cases dealing only with civil liberties, or with federalism, or some other characteristic.

Hypotheses are tested with statistical methods designed for use with samples drawn from populations. It is possible to argue that the dataset—which contains all the observations for several types of conference votes—is a population rather than a sample and that tests of statistical significance are therefore unnecessary. I have elected, however, to treat the dataset as a sample drawn from a larger population containing additional cases that for various reasons were never reviewed by the Court. All the empirical tests use a five percent confidence level to determine statistical significance.

IV. Limitations of This Book

Although I hope this book is comprehensive enough to stand alone, it does not begin to restate all that is known about the Court. There are so many excellent published works that it is unnecessary to write as if the Court were a complete unknown. Many short explanations, which are adequate to understanding and using the dataset, are supplemented with references to more extensive sources. Thus, the brief portraits of the justices provide enough information to understand the empirical analyses but are minuscule when compared with extensive biographies, e.g., Fine's (1984) three-volume chronicle of Murphy's life. Likewise, no effort is made to recount the drama and turmoil that engulfed the Court or to discuss the emotions that particular decisions evoked from both the justices and the public. Again, others are free to re-attach the justices' passions to the votes presented in my rather sterile dataset.

In the descriptions of the Court's procedures, information that is widely known and readily available elsewhere (e.g., the discussion of the differences between the writs of certiorari and appeal) is presented in adequate but abbreviated form. Other information, especially if it is accessible only through original sources (e.g., descriptions of conference lists), is presented in extensive detail.

The information in the appendices is exhaustive. As stated above, they contain every available vote. My empirical analyses, however, only begins to survey the information. Current and future scholars will explore it, searching for both the obvious and hidden riches that it holds.

2

The Justices and Their Backgrounds

I. Introduction

The United States Supreme Court contains a chief justice and eight associate justices. Although Congress has the power to alter the number of justices, the Court's size has not been changed since 1869 and is apparently fixed at nine members. Like all members of the federal judiciary, Supreme Court justices are nominated by the president and confirmed by the Senate. Once confirmed, they hold office until death, voluntary retirement, or removal via impeachment.

This chapter presents, in section II, brief biographies of the justices on the Vinson Court and, in section III, a short description of their shared experiences and beliefs as well as their ideological differences.

II. The Justices of the Vinson Court

Fred Vinson was nominated as the thirteenth chief justice of the United States on June 6, 1946, by his friend and political ally, Harry Truman, and was confirmed by the Senate on June 20, 1946. He replaced Chief Justice Harlan Stone, who had died on April 22, 1946. Vinson's tenure, which lasted seven and a half years, ended with his unexpected death on September 8, 1953. He was succeeded in office by Earl Warren.

Vinson was born January 22, 1890, in Louisa, Kentucky. He attended Centre College where he received an A.B. in 1909 and an LL.B. in 1911. After joining the bar, he practiced law in Louisa and later in Ashland, Kentucky, became active in local politics, and served as city and later commonwealth attorney. He entered the U.S. House of Representatives in 1924 where he eventually became an important member of the House Ways and Means Committee and gained recognition as an expert on tax legislation. In return for his congressional support for the New Deal, he was appointed by President Roosevelt to the United States Circuit Court of Appeals for the District of Columbia in 1938. After five years of service on the Court of Appeals, he returned to a series of executive posts in the Roosevelt and Truman administrations. He was serving as secretary of the treasury when he was appointed chief justice. While on the Court, Vinson remained a close friend and advisor to Truman who sought the chief justice's counsel on a wide range of issues.

Because of Vinson's ability as a compromiser and conciliator, as well as his wide experience in government, President Truman hoped that Vinson could unify and lead the justices, whose personal and judicial differences were becoming a threat to the institution's prestige. Vinson, however, lacked the requisite skills and was never a dominant actor on the Court. His brethren respected his integrity and decency; but as an intellect, scholar, writer, and leader, he was overshadowed by some of his colleagues.

All eight of the associate justices whom Vinson joined in 1946 had served with Chief Justice Stone, and all but Burton had served with Chief Justice Hughes. Both of these chief justices possessed talents that eclipsed Vinson's. Hughes, in particular, was a skilled legal theorist and a dominant figure on his Court. Vinson was neither a judicial philosopher nor a legal theorist. His beliefs in judicial restraint, pragmatism, common sense, and the beneficence of government led him to defer to the legislative and executive branches whenever possible.

During the Vinson era, ten men served as associate justices. The most senior, Hugo L. Black, was born February 27, 1886, in Harlan, Alabama. After receiving an LL.B. from the University of Alabama in 1906, he practiced law in Ashland and later in Birmingham. He joined the Ku Klux Klan in 1923—an action which later was not only embarrassing but also inconsistent with his subsequent strong support for civil rights. Black entered the U.S. Senate in 1927 as "the poor man's candidate" and became (after Roosevelt's election in 1932) a major supporter of the New Deal. As a senator he was instrumental in the passage of the Fair Labor Standards Act and investigated the lobbying activities of public utilities and abuses of governmental subsidies by the marine and airline industries. Black's nomination on August 12, 1937, was the first Supreme Court appointment made by President Roosevelt. He was confirmed by the Senate on August 17, 1937, and served on the Court until poor health forced his retirement on September 17, 1971.

Black, rated as one of the great justices in the Court's history, was one of the dominant actors on the Vinson Court. He was a determined advocate of the "incorporation doctrine," which holds that the 14th Amendment applied the Bill of Rights to the states. Black believed that the 1st Amendment guarantees of free speech, press, and assembly formed the foundation for democratic government and therefore were paramount and absolute. Although a believer in the literal interpretation of the Constitution, Black was an activist who was unwilling to defer to the other branches of government. His energy, determination, and legal skill made Black the leader of the Court's "liberal" wing which comprised himself, Douglas, Murphy, and Rutledge. The deaths of Murphy and Rutledge reduced his influence during the last four terms of the Vinson Court. During the Warren era, however, Black reached the height of his influence.

Stanley Reed was born December 31, 1884, in Mason County, Kentucky. He received bachelors degrees from Kentucky Wesleyan in 1902 and from Yale in 1906. Although he studied law at the University of Virginia, Columbia, and the Sorbonne, he did not earn a law degree. In 1910 he began a successful law practice in Maysville, Kentucky, which eventually included the Burley Tobacco Growers Cooperative as a client. Reed's knowledge of tobacco marketing led to an appointment in the Hoover administration as counsel to the Federal Farm Board in 1929. After serving in a series of posts in the Hoover and Roosevelt administrations, he was appointed solicitor general in 1935. In this position he argued the constitutionality of New Deal legislation before an often hostile Supreme Court. He was nominated to the Court by Roosevelt on January 15, 1938, and was confirmed by the Senate on January 25, 1938. He served on the Court until his retirement on February 26, 1957.

Reed was a moderate or "center" justice. He accepted as necessary and beneficial the governmental intervention into the economy resulting from the New Deal legislation that he had defended as solicitor general. In the area of civil liberties, he was more likely to support the government against claims of individual rights, especially if the case dealt with the loyalty-security programs.

Felix Frankfurter, whose family immigrated to the U.S. when he was twelve years old, was born on November 15, 1882, in Vienna, Austria. He graduated from the City College of New York in 1902 and the Harvard Law School in 1906. After joining the bar, he became an assistant U.S. attorney and then an assistant to the secretary of war. In 1914 he joined the Harvard Law School faculty where he served as a distinguished scholar and teacher.

He was a founding member of the ACLU and an advisor to the NAACP. Frankfurter became an unofficial advisor to then Governor Franklin Roosevelt in 1928. After Roosevelt became president, Frankfurter—with some success—tried to shape the New Deal with his ideas and his former students, who populated the Washington bureaucracy (Dawson 1980, pp. 169-171). In 1933, he rejected an appointment as solicitor general because the demands of the position would preclude his service as an unofficial presidential advisor on a wide variety of topics. Frankfurter's services were rewarded with a Supreme Court nomination on January 5, 1939. He was confirmed on January 17, 1939, and served until ill health forced his retirement on August 28, 1962.

Although one of the most brilliant men ever to serve on the Court, Frankfurter was also one of the most surprising. His pre-Court liberalism was missing from many of his judicial decisions because his strict adherence to the philosophy of judicial restraint led him to defer to the legislative and executive branches whenever possible. He believed that a judge's greatest responsibility was to avoid substituting his own policies for the erroneous policies of elected officials unless the erroneous policies were clearly proscribed by the Constitution. On the Vinson Court, Frankfurter was often allied with Jackson and had both personal and judicial conflicts with Douglas, Murphy, and Black.

William O. Douglas was born October 16, 1898 in Ottertail County, Minnesota. In 1904, following his father's death, his family moved to Yakima, Washington. His childhood was a struggle against illness and poverty, both of which he ultimately defeated. In 1916, Douglas enrolled in Whitman College from which he graduated in 1920. After teaching school for two years, he left the state of Washington for the Columbia Law School. Following graduation from Columbia in 1925, he practiced law on Wall Street and in Yakima. In 1927 he joined the law faculty at Columbia where he began building a reputation as an expert in corporate law and bankruptcy. In 1929 he moved to Yale where he taught until he joined the staff of the Securities and Exchange Commission in 1934. He was promoted to membership in the SEC in 1936 and to the chairmanship in 1937. Roosevelt nominated him to the Supreme Court on March 20, 1939. He was confirmed on April 4, 1939, and served until failing health forced his retirement on November 12, 1975.

Douglas played a major role in shaping the law during his thirty-six years on the Court. Although he joined the Court as an expert on business law, he is now remembered as a tenacious and impassioned proponent of the freedoms of speech and press. He was a loner who never proselytized. On many important issues he was allied with Black and, to a lesser extent, with Murphy and Rutledge. Douglas was a colorful and controversial justice. He wrote numerous books, had four wives, and survived two serious but feeble attempts at impeachment.

Frank Murphy was born on April 13, 1890, in Harbor Beach, Michigan. He attended the University of Michigan where he received an A.B. in 1912 and an LL.B. in 1914. Following service in Europe during the First World War, Murphy studied law for brief periods at Lincoln's Inn in London and Trinity College in Dublin. He became active in Detroit politics where he served as assistant U.S. attorney (1919-1920), judge on the Detroit Recorder's Court (1923-1930), and mayor (1930-1933). During the 1932 presidential campaign, he actively supported Roosevelt, who appointed him governor-general of the Philippine Islands in 1933. He was elected governor of Michigan in 1936 during a period of labor strife. His handling of the sit-down strikes in the automobile plants was successful but generated controversy which led to his defeat in the 1938 gubernatorial election. Murphy joined the Roosevelt administration as attorney general in 1939. He was nominated associate justice on January 4, 1940, and was confirmed on January 15. He died on July 19, 1949—near the midpoint of Vinson's tenure.

Murphy was a result-oriented justice whose major concern was fairness—as he saw it. Legal formalities and precedents, although important, were secondary to achieving an equitable and compassionate result. His belief that results preceded legal reasoning was strongly opposed by Frankfurter. Murphy frequently voted with Black and Douglas but was closest—both in philosophy and friendship—with Rutledge.

Robert H. Jackson was born February 13, 1892, in Spring Creek, Pennsylvania. He grew up in Jamestown, New York where, at the age of eighteen, he began a legal apprenticeship in a local firm. In addition to his apprenticeship, Jackson received some formal training at the Albany Law School in 1912. He joined the bar in 1913 and quickly established a lucrative and diverse practice. In 1934 he became general counsel to the Internal Revenue Bureau. His talent as an advocate resulted in a rapid series of advancements in the Roosevelt administration. He was assistant attorney general in 1936, solicitor general in 1938, and attorney general in 1940. His service as solicitor general—while Frank Murphy was attorney general—resulted in rivalry and friction between the two that endured during their service on the Court. He was appointed associate justice on June 12, 1941, and confirmed July 7, 1941. His service on the Court, which lasted until his death on October 9, 1954, was interrupted by his temporary assignment as U.S. prosecutor at the Nuremburg war crimes trials in 1945-1946. Although he was one of Roosevelt's closest advisors and supporters, Jackson never saw himself as a "New Dealer." In his own mind, he was a conservative pragmatist who accepted Roosevelt's economic policies as necessary and limited reforms of a democratic and capitalist society.

Chief Justice Stone died while Jackson was serving at the Nuremburg trials. Jackson, who coveted the chief justiceship, was greatly disappointed when the appointment went to Fred Vinson. Believing that his colleagues had conspired to block his appointment, Jackson became enraged at Black and publicly attacked his participation in the *Jewell Ridge* case, 325 U.S. 161 (1945), which had been argued by Black's former partner. The incident demonstrated the deep doctrinal and personal differences between Jackson and Black.

As a justice, Jackson strove for practical and workable solutions, especially when the rights of an individual appeared to compete with the rights of society. On many issues he was allied with Frankfurter. Both were advocates of judicial restraint and believed that the Court should leave economic and social policy to the other branches of government. Jackson was an extremely persuasive advocate and one of the most elegant and powerful writers ever to serve on the Court.

Wiley B. Rutledge was born July 20, 1894, in Cloverport, Kentucky. He attended Marysville College before transferring to the University of Wisconsin. After graduating from Wisconsin in 1914, he taught school in Bloomington, Indiana, while a part-time student at the University of Indiana Law School. Following a nearly fatal bout with tuberculosis, he attended the University of Colorado where he received a law degree in 1922. He practiced law in Boulder for two years before returning to the University of Colorado as a faculty member. Between 1924 and 1939, Rutledge held various academic posts including dean of the University of Iowa College of Law (1935-1939). He publicly criticized the Court's anti-New Deal decisions and, in 1937, supported Roosevelt's proposed "Court-packing plan" which was unpopular in Iowa. In 1939, Roosevelt rewarded him with an appointment to the United States Circuit Court of Appeals for the District of Columbia where he served with Fred Vinson. On January 11, 1943, Rutledge received the last Supreme Court nomination made by Roosevelt. The appointment was confirmed by the Senate on February 8, 1943.

Rutledge died unexpectedly on September 10, 1949. His death, occuring less than two months after Murphy's death, substantially changed the Court's chemistry. Murphy and Rutledge shared a close friendship and similar judicial philosophies. Their deaths made the Court more "conservative" and reduced—for the remainder of the Vinson era—the influence of Black and Douglas.

Rutledge was a "liberal" jurist who believed that economic intervention by the government was necessary and beneficial. The same government, however, was not to be trusted when it intervened in other activities such as speech and religion. Although he was philosophically close to Murphy, Rutledge was more concerned about legal forms and precedents. He produced opinions that were highly regarded for their legal analysis and workmanship. Douglas believed that Rutledge's early death was partially caused by the effort he put into his opinions (Douglas 1980, p.28).

Harold H. Burton was born June 22, 1888, in Jamaica Plain, Massachusetts. He graduated from Bowdoin College in 1909 and the Harvard Law School in 1912. His early legal career included periods of practice in Ohio, Utah, and Idaho. After distinguished service in the First World War, he settled in Cleveland, Ohio, where he held a series of public offices: state legislator, city law director, and mayor. He was elected to the U.S. Senate in 1941. As a senator, he earned the respect and friendship of a fellow senator, Harry Truman. On September 19, 1945, Burton became President Truman's first Supreme Court nominee and was confirmed by his Senate colleagues on the day of his nomination. During his later years on the Court, Burton suffered from Parkinson's disease, which forced his retirement on October 13, 1958.

Burton was a cautious and studious justice who displayed great respect for precedents and felt that important social issues were best decided by the other branches of government. His legal philosophy was close to the that of the chief justice. When he joined the Court, he had limited judicial skills, which made some of his duties, such as opinion writing, difficult and time consuming. His skills improved over time and he eventually became an effective justice, but he was never an important intellectual force on the Court. Burton was well liked by his colleagues and played a major role in maintaining social cohesion during the Vinson era.

Tom C. Clark was born September 23, 1899, in Dallas, Texas. He attended the University of Texas where he received a bachelors degree in 1921 and a law degree in 1922. After joining the bar, he engaged in private practice in Dallas, where he was active in Democratic politics. From 1927 to 1932, he served as civil district attorney for Dallas County. In 1937 he moved to Washington to accept a post in the Justice Department. His various responsibilities included anti-trust enforcement, internment of Japanese-Americans during the Second World War, and prosecution of fraudulent war claims. This last activity brought him into close contact with Senator Harry Truman, who chaired the Senate War Investigation Committee. In 1943, Clark became assistant attorney general in charge of the anti-trust division; later in the year he moved to the criminal division. He supported Truman's vice-presidential bid at the 1944 Democratic National Convention.

When Truman succeeded to the presidency, Clark became his vigorous and powerful attorney general. In addition to being a close presidential advisor, he instituted numerous anti-trust prosecutions, argued important cases before the Supreme Court, and developed an anti-communist program which included the notorious attorney general's list of subversive organizations. Clark's loyalty-security programs, aimed at revealing communists and communist-front organizations, shielded Truman from charges that he was "soft on communism" and helped him win reelection in 1948.

On July 28, 1949, Clark was nominated to fill the vacancy created by Murphy's death. He was confirmed on August 18, 1949, and served until June 12, 1967, when the appointment of his son, Ramsey Clark, as attorney general created the appearance of a conflict-of-interest because the younger Clark would be litigating numerous cases before the Court.

Clark's judicial philosophy changed during his eighteen years on the Court, but during the Vinson era he was ideologically close to the other Truman appointees: Vinson, Burton, and Minton. During this era, he was particularly concerned about protecting the government from communist subversion.

Sherman Minton was born October 20, 1890, in Georgetown, Indiana. He received an LL.B. degree from Indiana University in 1915 and an LL.M. from Yale in 1917. He was named counselor to the Indiana Public Service Commission in 1933, a position that he used to support Indiana's "Little New Deal." In 1934, Minton was elected to the U.S. Senate where he served with fellow Senators Hugo Black and Harry Truman. Minton developed a close friendship with Senator Truman and an active collaboration with Senator Black. Following his defeat in the 1940 election, Minton served for a short time as a presidential counselor. While working as Roosevelt's counselor, Minton supported Senator Truman's successful effort to establish the Senate War Investigation Committee. This "Truman Committee," which included Harold Burton, gave the then Senator Truman national exposure. In 1941, Minton was appointed to the U.S. Circuit Court of Appeals for the Seventh Circuit by Roosevelt. On September 15, 1949, President Truman nominated Minton to fill the vacancy created by Rutledge's death. He was confirmed by the Senate on October 4, 1949. Poor health forced him to retire on October 15, 1956.

Of all the men who served on the Vinson Court, Minton was the most likely to believe in the beneficence of government and was the most willing to defer to decisions of the legislative and executive branches. As a consequence, he was ideologically close to Vinson, Reed, Clark, and Burton. Although intelligent, Minton displayed no great intellectual leadership on the Court. As a senator he had worked for innovation and change, but as a justice he worked for neither. In the Senate, he had collaborated closely with Hugo Black, but on the Court, he and Black were on opposite sides of many important issues. The difference between Senator Minton and Justice Minton resulted from his belief that innovation and change should come from elected legislators rather than appointed judges.

III. Similarities and Differences

The justices of the Vinson Court were born during the 1880s and 90s. By the time they joined the Court in the 1930s and 40s, they had seen profound social and economic changes in U.S. society. They had also observed substantial change in the Supreme Court's role in shaping the law. All were appointed either by Roosevelt or by his successor Truman. Except for Frankfurter, before joining the Court, all had held public positions where they had worked for or with the presidents who appointed them. Frankfurter, the one exception, had served as an informal advisor to Roosevelt.

The justices of Vinson era had vivid memories of recent cataclysmic events which had important and permanent effects on their beliefs about government and the Court's role in government. First, the Great Depression had convinced them of the need for an active governmental role in managing the economy. Except for Burton, all owed their Court appointments, in part, to their service to the New Deal, which they perceived as a needed correction for the flaws of free-market capitalism.

Second, in 1935 and 1936, the Court had invalidated important New Deal legislation as unconstitutional extensions of governmental power. Critics of the Court—who at this time were political liberals—argued that the justices were substituting their own economic beliefs for those of elected officials. These critics called for "judicial restraint" and insisted that the Court could only invalidate legislation when it was clearly proscribed by the Constitution. Frankfurter was a particularly active and effective advocate of judicial restraint.

Third, the Court's rulings during 1935 and 1936 provoked a proposal by Roosevelt that would have allowed him to appoint additional justices. This "Court-packing plan" failed, but not before causing considerable debate about the Court's function. Black, Rutledge, and Minton—none of whom had yet joined the Court—were vocal supporters of the "Court-packing plan."

Fourth, the Second World War, which ended the year before Vinson's appointment, demonstrated the need for a strong central government and the danger of hostile foreign powers. It also ended any respect for fascism's claim of racial superiority, a claim that was disturbingly similar to the state-sponsored racial segregation in the U.S.

Fifth, the Cold War and the spread of communism which followed the Second World War freighted the nation. Many wise and careful people accepted the silly and reckless premise that communist agents possessed almost magical powers to subvert democratic governments and, therefore, represented a real internal threat to the U.S.

The Vinson Court justices often drew different conclusions from these shared experiences. The great constitutional controversy of the 1930s over the legality of governmental intervention in the economy was over. None of the Vinson Court's members had been on the Court during the controversy, and all were subsequently appointed because of their support or at least acceptance of the New Deal. The justices differed greatly, however, on what was to be learned from the controversy. To some, such as Frankfurter, the lesson was the need for judicial restraint because the crisis occurred when earlier justices had confused their own beliefs with constitutional principles and had halted the essential reform efforts of the Congress and the president. To others, such as Black, the controversy marked the end of one era and the beginning of a period of reform which could come from the Court when the other branches failed to act or acted improperly.

Although the constitutionality of governmental intervention in many markets was well established, the function of the government in the market for ideas was still confused. The earlier debate about the government's role in the economy was often couched in terms of individual liberties, such as the right to contract. The new controversy also dealt with personal liberties but sometimes with different results. Some of the justices, such as Black, Douglas, Murphy, and Rutledge, held the modern, schizophrenic view that government had great wisdom when intervening in the market for goods and resources, but was absolutely incompetent in the market for ideas. Others, such as Reed, Clark, and Minton, believed that some ideas were so obviously dangerous, especially communism, that their dissemination could be banned or at least discouraged by the government.

All the justices disliked the racial discrimination that permeated the nation, and was especially prevalent in Washington, D.C. The Vinson Court moved against racial discrimination in a careful and gradual fashion. Although agreeing that it was wrong, the justices differed on the Court's role in its elimination. The landmark case of *Brown v. Board of Education*, 345 U.S. 972 (1953), was begun during Vinson's tenure but was completed after Earl Warren had become chief justice. Warren was the only new justice; the other eight justices participating in the *Brown* decision had served on the Vinson Court.

3

The Supreme Court's Powers and Procedures

I. Introduction

The present chapter is a description of the Supreme Court's powers and procedures as they existed during Vinson's tenure. Much of this discussion also applies to the current Court, e.g., the "rule of four," the secrecy of the conference, and the functions of the chief justice are unchanged. The Court is, however, an evolving institution. Since 1953 several procedures have changed, including the method of assigning docket numbers, the differences between the appellate and miscellaneous dockets, the conference day, and the voting order.

For discussions of the Court's current procedures, see Baum (1985), O'Brien (1986), Stern and Gressman (1978), and Wasby (1988). For a description of the Court's procedures during Vinson's chief justiceship, see Stern and Gressman (1950).

The following discussion is written in the past tense. Although many procedures could—and perhaps should—be described in the present tense, incessant tense-switching would confuse and tire the reader.

II. Seniority

By virtue of his position, the chief justice was always the Court's most senior member. For the associate justices, seniority was determined by length of service. Seniority, an impersonal and automatic ordering process, had numerous purposes. It determined seating order at the secret conference, during public sessions, and when the Court sat for official photographs. Office suites were distributed according to seniority, as were carbon copies of typed memos—with the most junior justice receiving the faintest copy. During the conference, discussions proceeded from senior to junior, voting was in reverse order of seniority, and the most junior justice served as "doorkeeper." After the conference, the responsibility for writing the opinion of the Court was assigned by the senior member of the majority.

This book's tables present information about individual justices in ascending order of seniority, i.e., with the most junior justice at the top of the table and the chief justice at the bottom. This ordering is consistent with the method used by the justices' docket books and with the presentation of the dataset in appendices B through I.

III. Terms

The Court's term began on the first Monday in October and ended during the following June or July. Terms were named according to the year in which they started, resulting in some confusion because a term spanned two calendar years. Thus, most cases adjudicated during the October 1946 term were actually decided and announced during 1947.

At the end of the term, the Court began its recess or vacation which lasted until October. Vacation was a misnomer, though, because preparation for the next term was no less demanding of the justices' time and energy than work done during the term itself.

IV. Natural Courts

A natural Court spanned all the terms during which the Court's membership remained unchanged. There were two natural Courts during Vinson's tenure: the first began in 1946 with the appointment of Vinson and ended in the summer of 1949 with the deaths of Murphy and Rutledge; the second began in 1949 with Clark's and Minton's appointments and ended with the chief justice's death in 1953.

This book's analyses often distinguish the two natural Courts, in part because the memberships are different and in part to provide two tests of the same hypotheses. No effort is made to control for or to determine the existence of a "freshman" effect (Heck and Hall 1981; Brenner 1983) which might have occurred with new justices, i.e., Clark and Minton in 1949.

V. Blocs

The Vinson Court was divided into two identifiable blocs: During the first natural Court, the "liberal" bloc contained Black, Douglas, Murphy, and Rutledge, and the "conservative" bloc contained Vinson, Reed, Frankfurter, Jackson, and Burton. During the second natural Court, the liberal bloc was reduced to Black and Douglas when Clark and Minton joined the conservative bloc. These blocs are a useful but very crude taxonomy of the justices' judicial positions. The members of a bloc frequently voted together, but their votes did not result from an implicit or explicit agreement to cooperate, i.e., the bloc members were not trying to vote as a group. Justices felt no enduring loyalty to one bloc and frequently joined the other for certain types of cases. For example, Black and Frankfurter, who are often seen as leaders of the two blocs, frequently dissented together from the Court's antilibertarian interpretation of federal legislation dealing with civil liberties (Pritchett 1954, pp. 231-238). There were also blocs within blocs. The liberals Rutledge and Murphy were particularly close, as were the conservatives Jackson and Frankfurter.

VI. Cases and Controversies

The Supreme Court decided only specific types of "cases and controversies." A case that was properly before the Court satisfied several conditions: it involved a legal dispute that was real, ripe, non-political, non-moot, and within the Court's jurisdiction; the party bringing the suit had standing to sue; and the issues were important and applicable to similar cases. These terms and characteristics are defined as follows:

Legal Dispute. The Court decided legal rather than factual disputes, i.e., it decided issues of law rather than issues of fact. Settling factual disputes was the function of the state courts and the lower federal courts. The Supreme Court's function was to settle disputes involving constitutional and statutory interpretations.

Real. A case before the Court needed to present a real dispute between two adversaries. Friendly suits or hypothetical disputes were not accepted, cf., Murphy (1964, p.29, fn. 47). Neither did the Court issue advisory opinions, though individual justices often served as unofficial presidential counselors. Vinson, for example, continued to advise Truman while serving as chief justice. This extrajudicial service, although now considered inappropriate, was not uncommon before and during Vinson's tenure (Murphy 1982).

Ripeness. The litigant bringing the case needed to show that the dispute was not subject to further administrative review or non-judicial correction and that all other legal appeals had been exhausted. Despite this restriction, the Court had the rarely used power to accept a case before a decision had been rendered by the circuit court of appeals, see Lindgren and Marshall (1986) and *Youngstown Sheet & Tube v. Sawyer* (51,744A).

Non-Political. The Court did not decide political questions such as whether taxes should be raised or if diplomatic relations should be established with a foreign country. The boundary between political and nonpolitical disputes was set by the Court and has changed considerably since the Vinson era (Strum 1974).

Non-Moot. A case became moot when a real dispute was settled or became hypothetical. If the litigants reached a settlement while their dispute was before the Court, the case was dismissed as moot. Or, if a prisoner died after beginning an appeal of his conviction, his appeal was mooted by his death.

Jurisdiction. The Court's jurisdiction, established by the U.S. Constitution and the various judiciary acts of Congress, excluded most cases from review by the Supreme Court. For example, the state courts had exclusive responsibility for many civil disputes. The Court's modern jurisdiction was established by the Judiciary Act of 1925, commonly called the "Judges Bill," which has been subsequently modified (O'Brien 1986, pp. 149-152) but not substantially changed.

Standing. The litigant bringing the case needed to demonstrate "standing to sue," which required proof of a direct injury to a legally protected interest. Many interests were not protected: a firm lacked standing to sue for the injury caused by a competitor's superior product or lower price, and, in general, one party lacked standing to sue another party for damages done to a third party. Also, when a case was ended by a final and valid judgment, the losing party lacked standing to litigate the case a second time.

Important and applicable to other disputes. By the Vinson era, the Court had evolved into a constitutional court that used cases as resources in its efforts to develop and to clarify the law. The Court was no longer a common law court that settled disputes of interest only to the litigants; resolving these disputes was the function of the lower courts. Neither was it responsible for correcting trial courts' errors, a responsibility that now rested with the circuit courts of appeals and with the state supreme courts. The U.S. Supreme Court's function was to decide those few cases presenting issues that were both important and widely applicable.

These limitations on the Court's powers and responsibilities were real, but they were also nebulous and changing. Political questions could become non-political. The rules of standing could be bent when necessary. The Court's jurisdiction was established by acts of Congress, but the Court was the final interpreter of all legislation. Although it was restricted to settling properly presented disputes between opposing litigants, the restriction did not substantially reduce its ability to shape public policy. Most issues in public policy could eventually be fashioned into law suits that the Court—if it wanted—could properly decide.

VII. Legal Norms

While deciding cases, the Court was obligated to follow norms of judicial behavior. For example, statutory interpretations needed at least to appear consistent with the plain meaning of the statute or with the intent of the enacting legislature. Many statutes and several parts of the Constitution, however, were written with such elastic words that justices could not avoid becoming policy makers when deciding how the law applied in specific situations.

The Court was also obligated to show some respect for its earlier decisions, though this principle of following precedents, *stare decisis*, was less binding on the Supreme Court than it was on lower courts. The justices were usually able to find precedents that supported whatever position they favored. If not, precedents could be distinguished or overruled.

The norms for constitutional interpretation were somewhat different from those of statutory interpretation. The Congress could easily change statutes and thereby overturn the Court's statutory interpretations. Amending the Constitution, however, was a rare and difficult process. Thus, constitutional interpretation was a never-ending endeavor in which earlier decisions were never completely binding. For discussions of the effect of legal norms on Supreme Court decision making and of the differences between statutory and constitutional interpretations, see Spaeth (1979, chapter 3) and Rhode and Spaeth (1976, chapter 2).

VIII. Dockets

The Supreme Court had three dockets: original, appellate, and miscellaneous. Cases on all three dockets were numbered as they were received by the Court. These docket numbers are used in this book to identify and to cite cases that are included in appendices B through I. The docket number is preceded by the term year and is followed by an "A" if the case was on the appellate docket or by an "M" if it was on the miscellaneous docket. Thus (46,3A) refers to *Freeman v. Hewit*, 329 U.S. 249 (1946), which was case number three on the appellate docket during the October 1946 term. *Ex Parte Betz* (46,18M) was case number 18 on the miscellaneous docket during the October 1946 term. It is essential to distinguish the docket because different cases can have the same number. For example, (46,20A) refers to *United Public Workers v. Mitchell*, but (46,20M) refers to *Lavender v. Clark*.

The Court's three dockets corresponded to the various parts of its jurisdiction, some of which was granted by the U.S. Constitution and some of which was granted by the various judiciary acts passed by Congress.

The Original Docket

The original docket contained cases that had not been before a lower court. These cases arose under the Court's original jurisdiction, which was defined by the U.S. Constitution in the second paragraph of Article III, Section 2.

> In all Cases affecting Ambassadors, other public Ministers and Consuls, and those in which a State shall be Party, the supreme Court shall have original Jurisdiction.

Part of this original jurisdiction was nonexclusive and was therefore shared with other federal courts. Cases within this nonexclusive jurisdiction began in the lower courts rather than in the Supreme Court. The original docket contained those very few cases—typically less than ten a term—in which the Court had both original and exclusive jurisdiction. Usually these cases involved boundary or resource use disputes between or among states.

The Court processed cases on the original docket in a manner consistent with how it handled cases on the other dockets: only issues of law rather than issues of fact were decided. To avoid performing a factfinding function, the Court selected a special Master who recommended a disposition for a case on the original docket, which—if unacceptable to one or all of the parties—could be reviewed by the Court.

The justices' papers contain relatively little information about cases on the original docket. Because of their small number and limited information, these cases are excluded from the dataset contained in appendices B through I. Except for the examination of opinion assignments in chapter 8, this book's empirical analyses do not deal with cases on the original docket.

The Appellate Docket

The appellate docket contained the great bulk of cases decided by the Court. Cases arrived on the appellate docket by three routes: certified questions, writs of appeal, and writs of certiorari.

Certified Questions

Certified questions (also known as certificates or as writs of certification) were sent to the Supreme Court by the United States circuit courts of appeals (now known as the courts of appeals) and by the Court of Claims. They allowed the lower courts to ask for rulings on specific and novel issues presented by cases that were still before a lower court. Although common and important in earlier eras, certified questions were now rare, having fallen into disfavor before Vinson's tenure. They were generally discouraged by the Supreme Court, which preferred to hear a case only after the lower courts had decided all issues. The losing party could then request review by the Supreme Court, which—if it decided to hear the case—had the benefit of the lower court's decisions. For examples of certified questions, see *U.S. v. Lauro* (46, 514A) and *C.A.B. v. American Air Transport* (52, 126A).

Certiorari

A writ of certiorari (referred to as certiorari or more commonly as cert) was a discretionary writ granted by the Court as part of its appellate jurisdiction. Originally, the writ was an order to a lower court requesting a true copy of the record, but later, though long before 1946, the Court had stopped actually sending the writ to lower courts and had instead adopted a rule requiring that a cert petition contain a certified copy of the record. By the Vinson era, granting cert served two purposes: it announced that the Court would decide the case on the merits, and it stayed the lower court's decision.

Most cases on the appellate docket resulted from cert requests, but the overwhelming majority of these requests were denied. The party requesting the writ, the "petitioner," was opposed by the "respondent," who could file a counter petition requesting that cert be denied. If the Court denied the petition for cert, the decision of the lower court stood.

The meaning of cert denial was a matter of some controversy and confusion. In theory, it had no precedential value and did not imply that the Supreme Court agreed with the lower court's decision; it meant only that the case was not important enough to warrant review by the Court. In reality, though, cert denial had some—albeit quite limited—meaning especially to those parties and lawyers actively litigating before the Court (Stern and Gressman 1950, pp. 132-135).

Appeals

Writs of appeal (usually referred to as appeals) involved cases in the Court's obligatory appellate jurisdiction, i.e., cases in which a party had a statutory right to review by the Supreme Court. The party taking the appeal, or the "appellant," was opposed by the "appellee." Although guaranteed by law, this right to an appeal was actually nonexistent because the Court disposed of most appeals without granting review. The appellant was required to file a jurisdictional statement explaining why the case was important enough to warrant review by the Court. The appellee could then file a counter motion requesting that the appeal be dismissed or that the decision of the lower court be summarily affirmed.

The Court indicated that it had elected to decide an appeal either by "noting probable jurisdiction" or by postponing further consideration on jurisdiction until the decision on-the-merits. When the Court did not want to review the case, it either summarily affirmed the lower court or dismissed the writ of appeal "for lack of a substantial question" or "for want of jurisdiction." Thus, most obligatory appeals were treated in a fashion quite similar to the discretionary cert petitions. Unlike denied certs, however, appeals summarily affirmed or dismissed by the Court did have some precedential value (Stern and Gressman 1978, pp. 327-338).

The Miscellaneous Docket

The miscellaneous docket had two categories of cases. The first contained all requests for extraordinary writs such as *habeas corpus* and *mandamus*. The second category contained all *in forma pauperis* cert requests, which—beginning with the October 1947 term—were placed on the miscellaneous docket.

Extraordinary writs, which were almost never issued by the Court, included *habeas corpus, mandamus,* prohibition, stay, and bail. Petitions for writs of *habeas corpus* were requested by persons claiming to be unlawfully held in custody, usually prisoners asserting that their imprisonment resulted from an unlawful trial. For an example, see *Reid v Ragen* (48,264M). The writ of *mandamus* was an order compelling a lower court to take some action. For an example, see *Ex parte Collett* (48,206M). Other extraordinary requests include stays, e.g., *McGee v. Mississippi* (48,655M), and bail, e.g., *U.S. (Young) v. Shaughnessy* (51,414M).

In forma pauperis (in the form of a pauper), or IFP, petitions came from persons unable to pay the filing fee. Because these petitions were frequently produced by prison inmates without the aid of an attorney, they were often handwritten and incoherent. In addition to not paying the fees, persons filing IFP petitions often did not provide notification to the opposing party and usually did not include certified copies of the record. In the October 1946 term, IFP petitions were treated the same as paid petitions. But beginning with the October 1947 term, certs that were also IFP were placed first on the miscellaneous docket. If an IFP cert was granted, the case was transferred to the appellate docket, e.g., during the October 1948 term, *Zimmerman v. Maryland* (48,429A) was first docketed as number 118 on the miscellaneous docket and was then re-docketed as number 429 on the appellate docket after cert was granted. Thus, beginning with the October 1947 term, the great majority of cases on the miscellaneous docket were IFP cert petitions. Nevertheless, it is important to remember that the miscellaneous docket contained other requests—especially *mandamus*—which were not IFP and which remained on the miscellaneous docket if the Court granted review. For an example of a non-IFP case on the miscellaneous docket, see *U.S. v. National City Lines* (48,269M).

IX. Procedures

All petitions and appeals received by the Court were docketed by the clerk's office. After the clerk had received the accompanying brief and record as well as the opposing brief filed by the respondent or appellee, a copy of the materials was distributed to each justice. Some IFP petitions did not contain the required number of copies so that only a summarizing memo was sent to every justice. Often, persons filing an IFP request failed to provide the obligatory notification to the opposing counsel, resulting in the absence of opposing briefs.

Before each conference, the chief justice's office distributed a conference list and a special list which served as the agenda. (The word "list" was often synonymous with conference, e.g., "pass to the next list," hold for the next list," or "I would like this taken up on the next list.") Conference lists were organized according to type of vote: statements as to jurisdiction, petitions for cert, petitions for *habeas corpus*, miscellaneous, petitions for rehearing, argued and submitted. Each request, no matter how frivolous, was placed on a conference list.

Most conference lists contained requests that were so completely without merit that they could be rejected without discussion or voting. The chief justice placed these requests on the special lists, which were frequently referred to as "dead lists." Before each conference, the justices marked those cases on the conference list that were also on the special list. Unless a justice asked that the case be removed from the special list, it was automatically rejected without a vote or discussion.

When a justice wanted the Court to consider a case on the dead list, he sent a memo to the chief justice who in turn notified the others that the case was removed from the dead list. Justices apparently changed the marking on their conference list if a case was removed from the special list but had no strong incentive to keep the memos notifying them of the change. Nevertheless, some of these memos have survived. What appears to be a complete set for the October 1951 term in the Felix Frankfurter Papers in the Harvard Law School Library (#55-18) contains requests for a total of twenty-three removals from the dead list. There were undoubtedly other requests that were made orally during the conference. Burton's conference lists for the October 1951 term show that an additional ten dead listed cases were at least discussed during the conference. For an example of a case removed from the dead list during the October 1951 term, see *Perkins v. Benguet Consolidated Mining* (51,85A) which was removed by Burton and was later won on-the-merits by the petitioner.

After the Court decided a case or rejected a petition, the losing party frequently requested a rehearing or filed a second petition. Requests for rehearings, which comprise a large proportion of the conference lists, were automatically rejected unless a member of the original majority moved to grant a rehearing. Granting a rehearing required approval from a majority of the justices who had participated in the preceding disposition. A new justice did not participate in requests for rehearings in cases that were disposed of before he joined the Court. If a rehearing was granted, however, the justice participated in the subsequent disposition, see Clark's votes in *Graver Tank & Manufacturing v. Linde Air* (49,2A).

Second petitions were generally dead listed, but there were no restrictions on participation by new justices or by justices who had dissented from the original disposition. In a memo to Vinson dated April 4, 1953 (Vinson #215), Frankfurter asserted his right to remove from the dead list *On Lee v. U.S.*, 345 U.S. 936 (1953), a second petition in a case in which he had dissented the preceding term (51,543A). In a memo to Frankfurter dated April 4, 1953, the chief justice agreed that because it was a second petition rather than a petition for a rehearing, Frankfurter was not in any way disqualified (Vinson #215).

X. *The Conference*

Conferences were always secret and closed to everyone except the sitting justices. During the first week of the term, there were daily conferences in which the Court considered all the appeals and petitions received during the summer recess. During the remainder of the term, conferences were generally scheduled for three Saturdays per month. If the cases on the conference lists were not disposed of on Saturday, the conference began again the following Monday. For example, the vote on *U.S. v. Alcea Band of Tillamooks* (46,26A) was scheduled for the October 26, 1946 conference, but Burton's docket book shows that the vote took place on October 28. Occasionally a conference was rescheduled to accommodate a justice, e.g., the conference originally scheduled for Saturday, December 30, 1950, was rescheduled for the preceding Friday so that Frankfurter could attend a wedding (memo from Frankfurter to Vinson dated December 26, 1950; memo from Vinson to the conference dated December 27, 1950; Vinson #215). Each justice brought his docket books, conference lists, and memos which had been prepared by his clerks. If a justice was absent or departed early, he typically left his conference list with his intentions marked so that a colleague could cast his votes.

Justices did not participate in cases in which there was the appearance of a conflict of interest. Nonparticipation is referred to as "recusal" (noun) or "to recuse" (verb). The most notorious public dispute during the Vinson Court involved Jackson's criticism of Black's failure to recuse himself in *Jewell Ridge Coal Corporation v. Local 6167, U.M.W.*, 325 U.S. 161 (1945), which was argued by Black's former partner. Each justice had his own standards regarding recusal. When the chief justice was recused, the senior associate performed those administrative tasks normally handled by the chief, e.g., deciding whether a case should be dead listed and opening discussion at the conference.

When the Court considered appeals and petitions for cert, the chief justice briefly outlined the case and stated his views on whether review should be granted. The discussion then proceeded in descending order of seniority from the most senior associate, Black, to the most junior, Burton or Minton. After the discussion, the justices voted in ascending order of seniority, with the chief voting last. Any justice could ask to have a case "re-listed" or "passed to the next list." Granting cert or noting probable jurisdiction required positive votes from four justices. This "rule of four" was relaxed when only six justices participated. For example, cert was granted in *Vanston Bondholders v. Green* (46,42A) based on three votes to grant. The Court's quorum was six; thus, cases with fewer than six justices participating were not considered for lack of a quorum.

With cert petitions, the justices voted to grant or to deny. If the case was an appeal, there were typically four options available to each justice. He could vote (1) to note probable jurisdiction, (2) to postpone further consideration on jurisdiction until the decision on-the-merits, (3) to dismiss, or (4) to affirm. Options 1 and 2 were virtually identical. Options 3 and 4 were similar in that both resulted in a victory for the appellee and were different in that the precedential value of an affirmation exceeded that of a dismissal.

Justices could "pass" during the vote on cert or jurisdiction if they were undecided but did not want the case re-listed. When the number of justices voting for review plus the number passing totaled four or more, the case was automatically re-listed, see *U.S. v. Pevely Dairy Company* (49,592A).

When the Court considered IFP requests in which the respondent or appellee had not been notified, justices could vote to "call for a response" if they were not ready to grant but believed that the request would deserve further consideration after the Court received the opposing brief. For an example of a case in which the Court first called for a response and then granted cert, see *Foster v. Illinois* (46,540A).

The rule of four applied only to cert and jurisdiction. Granting other petitions, such as requests for *habeas corpus* or *mandamus*, required a majority of the sitting justices, as did granting a rehearing, see *Sacher v. U.S.* (51,201A). Currently, petitions for *habeas corpus* can be treated as petitions for cert at the Court's discretion (Stern and Gressman 1978, p. 630). This may not have been the practice during Vinson's tenure because *habeas corpus* petitions were denied when four voted to grant and the denied petitions were not reconsidered as petitions for cert. For an example, see *In The Matter of Dammann* (48,234M).

The Court could summarily reach a decision on-the-merits, based on the litigants' briefs, while it was deciding whether to grant review. Because the Court summarily affirmed when it did not want to note jurisdiction, summary decisions were commonly used with appeals. With certs, summary decisions on-the-merits were much less frequent. For an example of a cert petition that was summarily decided on-the-merits, see *Schroeder's Estate v. C.I.R.* (49,103A).

Usually, when the Court granted review, the case received a plenary or "full dress" disposition. The litigants submitted printed briefs on-the-merits which were generally followed by oral argument before the Court. When a case entailed oral argument, each side was given either a half hour or an hour depending on the importance and complexity of the issues.

The litigants could request that the case "be submitted" for a decision on the printed briefs, i.e., a decision without oral argument. (The case caption in *U.S. Reports* indicates whether the case was argued or submitted on the briefs as well as the date of the argument or submission.) Thus a memo from the clerk of the Court, Harold Willey, to Vinson dated December 2, 1949 (Vinson #216), explains why *Darr v. Burford* (49,51A) was decided without oral argument:

> As I related to you yesterday counsel for petitioner appears to be
> a man 80 years of age, not a member of the bar of this court, and
> represents a party of "limited means". He wired "cannot appear
> for oral argument." We have a wire from Mr. Williamson, the
> Attorney General of Oklahoma, to the effect that if agreeable to the
> Court he waives oral argument. . . .

There was a general belief, however, that important cases should be argued. Frankfurter successfully objected to submitting *Lee v. Mississippi* (47,91A) without oral argument (Frankfurter's memo for the conference dated November 17, 1947; Vinson #215):

> The *Lee* case, it will be recalled, is a capital case involving a Negro
> minor. Disposition of such a case . . . involves a determination
> which may fairly be called among the most important which the
> Court renders. . . . It is, I believe, against good judicial administra-
> tion to dispose of such a case without oral argument and merely
> by reading briefs not always adequately revealing.

Some cases involved special requests such as stays, bail, expedited hearings, permission for special counsels, or additional time for oral argument. These requests required approval from a majority of the Court. Third parties sometimes desired to file *amicus curiae*, or friend of the court, briefs. The federal and state governments could file *amicus* briefs without permission, but others needed the written consent of the litigants or approval from a majority of the Court (Stern and Gressman 1950, pp. 295-297).

After a case was argued and/or submitted, it appeared on the conference list in the "argued and submitted" category. The chief justice opened the discussion, which proceeded in descending order of seniority. Following the discussion, a vote on-the-merits was taken in ascending order of seniority; this was referred to as the conference vote on-the-merits. Usually each justice voted either to affirm or to reverse (or vacate) the lower court, but occasionally a justice was absent, passed, or voted to dismiss as moot, to dismiss as improvidently granted, to remand for further proceedings, or to affirm in part and reverse in part.

Because the chief justice set the order of cases on the conference lists, he might have been able to exploit voting paradoxes or cyclical majorities if he could anticipate his brethren's positions on a series of related cases (Murphy 1964, pp. 85-89). This power, however, was limited by the ability of any associate justice to have a case re-listed, i.e., held for a subsequent conference. Similarly, the chief justice scheduled oral arguments. But, again, the individual associate justices could suggest—but apparently not demand—that related cases be argued in a specific order, e.g., Frankfurter asked that *Musser v. Utah* (47,60A) follow *Winters v. New York* (47,3A) on the argument list (memo from Frankfurter to Vinson dated October 29, 1947; Vinson #215). Likewise, associate justices could request that arguments be delayed or expedited so that complementary cases could be argued consecutively, e.g., Rutledge asked that argument on *American Communications v. Douds* (49,10A) be delayed until the Court considered the cert petition in *United Steelworkers v. N.L.R.B.* (49,13A) (memo from Rutledge to Vinson dated January 12, 1949; Vinson #216).

A judgment on-the-merits required a majority of the participating justices. Occasionally the Court divided four-to-four or three-to-three, which meant that the decision of the lower court was "affirmed by an equally divided Court." For an example of an equally divided Court, see *Doubleday & Company v. New York* (48,11A). An affirmation resulting from an equally divided Court had no precedential value.

Following the conference vote on-the-merits, a member of the majority was assigned the responsibility of writing the opinion of the Court which was either a brief, unsigned *per curiam* (by the Court) announcement or a more detailed, signed opinion. The responsibility for writing the signed opinions was assigned by the chief justice unless he was in the minority, in which event the senior member of the majority made the assignment. If there was no majority, the disposition was stated in a *per curiam* announcement.

A justice writing a signed opinion prepared a preliminary draft which was eventually sent to each member of the Court. Those justices who agreed with the opinion could "join" it or offer comments and criticisms which were frequently incorporated into subsequent drafts. Other justices were free to write concurring and dissenting opinions, which were also distributed to each justice. Because votes could change until the day the opinion was announced, what began as a dissenting or concurring opinion could become the majority opinion. Likewise, what began as the opinion of the Court could become a dissenting or concurring opinion.

When finished, opinions were announced on "Decision Mondays." The authors read or summarized the decision, after which authors of concurring or dissenting opinions announced their views. The opinion of the Court and all the concurring and dissenting opinions were published by the Government Printing Office in *U.S. Reports*. (The votes contained in *U.S. Reports* are hereafter referred to as the report votes on-the-merits.) Before publication, the court reporter suggested editorial changes. For example, in a memo dated May 15, 1952, the reporter, Walter Wyatt, wrote the following to Reed (Reed #175):

> In preparing to publish the bound volume of 342 U.S., we have carefully scrutinized all of the opinions therein in an effort to detect and eliminate any typographical errors. In doing so, we have noted a few minor matters of form in some of your opinions which you may, or may not, wish to change.

XI. Other Actors

There are two additional sets of actors which played important roles in the Court's deliberations: the justices' law clerks and the U.S. government's lawyers, i.e., the solicitor general and the attorney general.

Clerks

Each justice had a secretary, a messenger, and at least one law clerk. (The justices' law clerks should not be confused with the clerk of the Court, who performed certain administrative responsibilities such as docketing cases and notifying litigants of the Court's decisions.) In 1946, the chief justice had three law clerks while the associate justices each had one. In 1947, the associate justices were provided with a second clerk, but Douglas elected to continue with one.

Three current justices served as law clerks during the Vinson era. William Rehnquist clerked for Jackson, Byron White clerked for Vinson, and John Paul Stevens clerked for Rutledge.

Usually a law clerk was a recent law school graduate who served a justice for one term. Occasionally, a clerk served longer. Vinson frequently kept clerks for two years, Burton had the same clerks for the October 1947 and 48 terms, and Eugene Gressman served Murphy for five years (1943-48).

Some justices personally selected their clerks, but others delegated the responsibility to friends or former clerks. Each justice had his own criteria. Frankfurter's clerks were all from Harvard, Murphy's were from the University of Michigan, and Vinson's were usually from Northwestern. Douglas' clerks were from the West. Black preferred southerners who played tennis.

The law clerks' responsibilities varied according to their employers' needs. All justices used clerks for legal research, such as preparing memos on specific topics and checking citations. Most justices had their clerks prepare memos that summarized cert petitions. For a discussion of the drudgery inherent in preparing cert memos, see Chief Justice Rehnquist's (1987) account of his clerkship for Jackson during the October 1951 and 52 terms.

Perhaps the largest variation in how clerks were used occurred in opinion writing. The clerks' roles are sometimes revealed by memos and preliminary drafts of opinions in the justices' papers. Douglas wrote his own opinions with little assistance from anyone and though Clark and Jackson used their clerks as critics, editors, and researchers, they generally did most of the actual writing themselves. Murphy, on the other hand, often delegated substantial responsibility. See Fine (1984, pp. 161-163) for an extensive explanation of Murphy's use of clerks to write opinions.

Solicitor General and Attorney General

When the U.S. government was a litigant, the government's written briefs and oral arguments were presented by the solicitor general or a member of his staff. The solicitor general's relationship with the Court was so close that he was sometimes referred to as the "tenth justice." With few exceptions, an agency of the U.S. government could not request cert or take an appeal to the Court without the solicitor general's approval. Thus, he held a position of trust with the Court which expected his help in eliminating all but the most important request for review from the government. In addition, the Court expected that briefs and arguments presented by the solicitor general would be accurate, objective, and of uniformly high quality (*Yale Law Journal* 1969). Before their appointments to the Court, Reed and Jackson had served as solicitor general and Frankfurter had been offered the position by Roosevelt.

The attorney general, the solicitor general's immediate superior, also interacted with the Court. Although attorneys general rarely argued cases before the Court, attorneys general McGrath and Clark were litigants in numerous cases decided by the Vinson Court. Murphy, Jackson, and Clark served as attorneys general before their appointments to the Court.

XII. Other Parts of Government

Wasby (1988, chapter 9) and Murphy (1964, chapter 2) provide general discussions of the Court's relationships with other parts of government and explain how the Court uses tradition, mutual interest, and public opinion to maintain and enhance its power. Though detailed descriptions of the Court's relationships with the lower courts and with the executive and legislative branches are beyond the scope of this book, certain basic elements in these relationships bear repeating.

As the final arbiter of the Constitution and federal statutes, the Court's power to overrule the lower courts was well settled long before Vinson's tenure. In addition, the lower courts were unquestionably obligated to follow relevant precedents established by the Supreme Court. The judges of the lower federal courts, all of whom were appointed for life and almost none of whom owed any personal loyalty to Supreme Court justices, were hardly subservient vassals. Likewise, members of the state judiciaries were occasionally able to defy or circumvent the Court, which lacked the resources needed to overrule every apparently wrong or defiant decision. In addition, the Court's opinions were sometimes so ambiguous or so inconsistent that obedience by the lower courts was impossible. Murphy provides detailed discussions of lower court defiance (1959) and of how the Supreme Court can discourage defiance (1964, chapter 4). Spaeth (1979, chapter 8) presents a more general analysis of defiance and includes a description of the public resistance to *Zorach v. Clauson* (51,431A).

The division of powers within the federal government caused the relationship between the president and the Court to contain elements of both conflict and interdependence. Although appointed by the president, justices often had no enduring loyalty to either the man or the office. For example, Clark was a major disappointment to Truman (O'Brien 1986, pp. 81-82), who concluded that his nominee's performance on the Court was both inconsistent and disloyal.

Despite its extensive powers of judicial interpretation, the Court was entirely dependent on the executive for enforcement of its decisions. In earlier times presidents had ignored the Court's rulings, but by the Vinson era, defiance was no longer a viable option for presidents. Thus, Truman acquiesced in the steel seizure case, *Youngstown Sheet & Tube v. Sawyer* (51,744A), even though he was bitterly disappointed by the Court's ruling.

The Court had also experienced earlier periods of attack from presidents. One of these, Roosevelt's 1937 Court-packing plan, left an enduring impression on all the justices of the Vinson Court. (Frankfurter, for example, believed that Roosevelt's plan resulted from the mistaken judicial activism of the Hughes Court and was quick to accuse Vinson-era colleagues of the same mistake.) The intricate and shifting relationships between the Court and the presidency are discussed in detail by Scigliano (1971) and by Abraham (1974).

The Court's relationships with the Congress were equally complex. The Congress passed laws, but the Court interpreted them. The Court's interpretation determined the ultimate impact of a statute. In addition, the Court could nullify a law by declaring it unconstitutional. The Congress, on the other hand, could alter the Court's appellate jurisdiction, reduce its budget (but not the justices' salaries), change the number of justices, pass new statutes, and propose constitutional amendments. The Congress also retained the never-used power to remove a justice via the impeachment process. For discussions of "Court-Curbing" by the Congress, see Nagel (1965).

4

Dataset Description

I. Introduction

This chapter describes the dataset and explains how it was constructed. Sections II-IV discuss the justices' private papers. Section V delineates how information was gathered from the various justices' papers and how that information was combined into one dataset. Types and sources of errors are illustrated in section VI.

The dataset contains 2,500 cases in which the Court voted 5,217 times and in which the individual justices cast 44,728 votes. Appendix A explains the dataset format. Appendices B through I contain the cases which are arrange according to the Court's terms (October 1946-53).

Users of this dataset should note the following complementary sources. *U.S. Law Week* contains one-paragraph summaries (in docket number order) of all cases on the appellate docket. The *Harvard Law Review* presents annual reviews of the Court's terms which include aggregate statistics and discussions of important cases. Schubert's (1965 and 1974) dataset contains information on the report votes on-the-merits and distinguishes cases according to categories such as civil liberties and federalism. Entries in Schubert's dataset—which is available from the Inter-university Consortium for Political and Social Research—can be matched with cases in this dataset using docket numbers or *U.S. Reports* citations.

II. Docket Books

Docket books were used by Supreme Court justices to record most of the votes cast during the Court's secret conferences. They reveal how the individual justices voted on cert, jurisdiction, the conference vote on-the-merits, motions for stays, and extraordinary writs such as *mandamus, habeas corpus,* and prohibition. Docket books also contain information on when, to whom, and by whom the opinion assignment was made; the dates of votes; and the docket numbers of related or "vide" cases.

Through the October 1945 term (Chief Justice Stone's last), each justice received a new docket book at the beginning of the term. These books have sewn binding between red leather covers upon which the justice's name and the term date are inlaid with gold lettering. Each has a lock and an individual key. The Reed and Douglas papers contain the best collection of these pre-Vinson era docket books.

The first part of these books contains an alphabetical index with finger tabs for listing case names and docket numbers. The next section contains the opinion assignment pages, each of which has one justice's name printed at the top. These pages are ordered according to seniority, beginning with the chief justice and ending with the most junior member. When an opinion was assigned, the docket number and date were recorded on the page which had the recipient's name at the top.

The next section, which has 31 pages, contains the appellate docket numbers running consecutively from 1 to 1350 (50 per page on 28 pages) followed by miscellaneous docket numbers running consecutively from 1 to 150 (50 per page on three pages). As a case was recorded in the docket book, the case's page number(s) was recorded next to its docket number. Later, when a justice needed to locate the case in his docket book, he found its page number by first finding its docket number in these 31 pages.

Votes are recorded in the next two sections. The first, titled "**Petitions For Certiorari,**" contains four cases per page and was used only to record cert votes. If cert was granted, the subsequent actions were recorded in the next section of the docket book, titled "**Action Taken On Cases, Certificates, Motions, and Miscellaneous Matters.**" In this second section, each case has its own page. The bottom third of the page contains a matrix with the justices' names printed along the left side in ascending order of seniority. Possible actions are printed across the top of the matrix: "Merits," "Dismiss," "Question," "Request For Rule," "Discharge Rule," "S.D.," "P. to M.," "Absent," "Not Voting." The possible votes—"Aff.," "Rev.," "Yes," "No," "Grant," "Refuse"—are printed under each action. A justice recorded votes by placing check marks or X's in the appropriate boxes.

In both of these two sections, cases appear almost randomly because the Court did not process cases in docket number order. Thus, when a justice wanted to look-up the votes for a particular case, he first needed to use the

31-page section which presented page numbers according to docket numbers. Almost all documents and intra-Court correspondence referred to cases according to their docket numbers. If a justice wanted to find a case for which he did not know the docket number, he first used the alphabetical index to find the docket number and then used the 31-page section to find the page number.

These docket books, although beautiful, must have been frustrating to work with for the following reasons. (1) Because they were bound, typing on any of the pages was impossible. All information such as case names and dates had to be entered by hand. (2) Two people could not handle a book simultaneously, making it impossible for a justice to have his secretary record information on some cases while he was recording information on others. (3) Cert votes are on separate pages from the subsequent votes, which necessitated considerable page flipping. (4) The possible actions printed across the top of the matrix did not fulfill the Court's needs. (5) Because the books were bound, they needed a capacity that could accommodate the largest conceivable number of cases. This resulted in docket books that weigh almost six pounds, with many pages that were never used but were nevertheless carried to every conference.

Beginning with the October 1946 term (Chief Justice Vinson's first), docket books are composed of letter-sized, three-hole, loose-leaf sheets, which were pre-printed and added to the book as cases were docketed. Each book's first section contains an alphabetical index where cases' names and docket numbers were entered. The second section holds the opinion assignment pages—one page for each justice. The remainder of the book contains the three dockets: appellate, original, and miscellaneous.

The appellate docket, which is usually first, is printed on white paper. Each sheet is printed on both sides and each side is dedicated to one case. (Some justices' docket books occasionally combined several related cases on one page.) The top of the page contains spaces for entering the lower court and the dates when the case was argued, submitted, voted on, assigned, and announced. The middle of the page contains space for entering the dates and results of the Court's actions as well as other information such as requests by other parties to file *amicus curiae* briefs. Much of this information was typed by the justices' secretaries before and after the conferences. If the case had been held over from the previous term or transferred from the current term's miscellaneous docket, then the earlier docket numbers were usually recorded by the secretaries. Frequently, the docket numbers of related or "vide" cases are also recorded (especially in Burton's docket books). The bottom third of the page contains a matrix used to record votes. The justices' names are printed along the left border, with the most junior justice's name on top and the chief justice's on the bottom. Categories of votes are printed across the top of the matrix: Cert (Grant, Deny); Jurisdictional Statement (Note, Postpone, Dismiss, Affirm); Merits (Reverse, Affirm); Question (No, Yes); Absent; Not Voting.

The original docket, which usually follows the appellate docket, is printed on orange paper. Each case is recorded on one page, but the quantity and quality of information is considerably lower than for cases on the appellate docket.

The miscellaneous docket is on green (sometimes blue-green) sheets, which are usually printed on both sides, though a few are single-sided. A side is divided into fourths, each of which contains one case. For each case, there is a matrix with the justices' names printed along the left side and Grant, Refuse, and Rule printed across the top. The miscellaneous docket contains all requests for extraordinary writs—*habeas corpus, mandamus,* prohibition, etc.

During the October 1946 term, cert requests that were filed *in forma pauperis,* or IFP, were placed on the appellate, rather than the miscellaneous, docket. Because each IFP case was given a complete side of one sheet on the appellate docket, the 1946 docket book weighs eleven pounds. Beginning with the October 1947 term, IFP cases were first placed on the miscellaneous docket where each received only one-fourth of a side. If cert was granted, the case was moved to the appellate docket. Thus, if an IFP cert request was granted, the case has two docket numbers in one term and the cert vote is separated from the subsequent votes.

At the beginning of each term, cases held over from the previous term were given new docket numbers. Frankfurter and Murphy frequently renumbered the old pages and inserted them into the new docket book. Reed, Douglas, Burton, and Clark had the information transferred to new pages, although the amounts and methods of transfer differed.

III. Conference Lists

Conference lists contained the agenda for each conference and often complement and corroborate the information found in docket books. Conference lists were mimeographed on eight-and-one-half by fourteen-inch pages with the conference date printed at the top of the first page. The lists were constructed in the days preceding the conference and were distributed when completed; thus, there can be more than one list for a conference. For example, the conference held on Saturday, December 6, 1947, had three conference lists. The first was printed on one page and was labeled "List 1, Sheet 1." The second was printed on two pages which were labeled "List 2, Sheet 1" and "List 2, Sheet 2." The third was printed on three pages, the last of which was labeled "List 3, Sheet 3." Cases were usually grouped into five categories: Jurisdiction, Petitions for Certiorari, Miscellaneous, Petitions for Rehearing, and Argued and Submitted. Within each category, the docket numbers and case names were entered in docket number order. If the case was not on the appellate docket, then "Misc" or "Org" follows the docket number. The typing was double-spaced, one case to a line.

The special list or "dead list" for each conference was typed on eight-and-one-half by eleven-inch onionskin paper, apparently nine at a time with carbon paper between the onionskins. Thus, some were quite faint, especially those received by the junior justices. The statement "SPECIAL LIST CONFERENCE" followed by the date of the conference was typed at the top of the page. Next, the docket numbers and names of the petitions on the appellate docket that were to be automatically rejected without discussion or voting were listed in docket number order, one case per line. These were sometimes grouped according to the type of petition—jurisdiction, cert, etc.

Petitions on the miscellaneous docket were placed last on the special lists. During the October 1946 through October 1949 terms, miscellaneous cases appearing on the special list were dead listed, i.e., rejected without consideration. Beginning with the October 1950 term, the miscellaneous docket cases that were "To Be Discussed" were listed and all others on the miscellaneous docket were automatically rejected. The different method for handling cases on the appellate and miscellaneous dockets resulted because most cases on the appellate docket were not special listed but most cases on the miscellaneous docket were. This method for handling miscellaneous cases on the special list was not new. Chief Justice Stone had used a similar practice: he listed miscellaneous cases that would be discussed under the caption "TAKE UP" (these cases were referred to as "take ups") (Memo to Murphy from Rutledge dated March 2, 1946, filed with the Rutledge conference lists).

Justices typically transferred the information from the special list to the conference list. Burton drew a box around the docket number of all cases on the conference list that were dead listed. Clark drew a box or an oval around the case name, and Frankfurter placed an X next to the docket number, while Black wrote "list" next to the docket number.

IV. The Justices' Private Papers

The Harold H. Burton collection, at the Library of Congress, presents an accurate and detailed picture of the Court's conferences during the Vinson era. Burton was a compulsive, careful, and systematic record keeper. With the other justices, there was usually a reason for recording and keeping information. But with Burton, recordkeeping was an end in itself. Burton's docket books and conference lists are generally legible, complete, and accurate and their value is increased because they include all seven terms. He dated almost all actions, and his secretary noted each case's previous docket numbers as well as the vide docket numbers. The conference lists are also an excellent source for corroborating the information contained in his docket books. He usually recorded the outcome of a vote on the conference lists, e.g.,"D 8-1," "G 7-2." The votes of the individual justices were occasionally recorded on the conference lists, often when the docket book pages ran out of space. Burton also often noted dissents to dead listing on his conference lists rather than in his docket books. The Burton diaries also contain information which is useful in dating the Court's actions in specific cases.

Burton suffered from Parkinson's disease, which caused his retirement in 1958 and his death in 1964. Micrographia (extremely small handwriting), which is symptomatic of parkinsonism, is apparent in the Burton papers. His handwritten notes on the 1945 conference lists are noticeably larger than those on the 1952 conference lists. For example, on List 1, Sheet 1, for the October 18, 1952, conference, he wrote eight lines of notes on *Crummer Company v. DuPont* (52,107M) in seven-eighths of an inch (#248).

The William O. Douglas collection, located in the Library of Congress, contains complete sets of docket books and conference lists for all seven terms. Douglas recorded almost all votes in his docket books and was particularly diligent with votes on-the-merits. He usually did not date entries, nor did he record information on his conference lists.

When the Court voted more than once, Douglas used a system of check marks for the first vote, X's for the second, and O's for the third. He usually carefully dated and distinguished successive votes so that his docket books are often essential in unscrambling multiple votes, especially on cert or jurisdiction.

There are three limitations in using Douglas' docket books. First, he sometimes stopped recording cert or jurisdiction votes before the voting was finished if the outcome was obvious. Second, he had two prolonged absences: one caused by illness (October 1947 term) and another resulting from an injury (October 1948 term). After these absences, Douglas copied the information from Burton's docket books into his own. The third limitation results from his practice of leaving Washington before the end of the term. For example, his papers (#160) contain a letter dated June 11, 1948, written to him by his secretary, informing him of the Court's expected actions during the second and third weeks of June. (The Court's last conference was June 18 and its last sitting was June 21.) Though the Court did not vote on-the-merits of cases during June, it did dispose of many cert requests and Douglas' absence reduces the number of sources for these end-of-term cert votes.

The Tom Clark collection, at the Tarlton Law Library of the University of Texas, equals the quality of the Burton and Douglas collections. Clark's docket books are accurate and usually complete. The Clark conference lists sometimes contain information that complements his docket books because he typically recorded the Court's action—e.g., "deny," "grant," "reverse"— and occasionally recorded the individual votes. The cert and bench memos are also useful sources of information about the conference.

The value of the Clark collection is limited for the following reasons. Clark did not join the Court until the October 1948 term—the fourth term of Vinson's chief justiceship. He usually did not date votes. He sometimes did not record votes on cases in which he was recused, which were numerous in his first two terms because he had been attorney general before his appointment to the Court. Clark usually recorded in pencil (often colored pencil), and when the Court voted more than once, he sometimes erased the first vote before recording the second. Other times he superimposed the second vote using a different color. The erasings and different colors are lost when photocopied, necessitating special care when coding a case involving multiple votes on one issue.

The papers of Stanley Reed, at the M.I. King Library of the University of Kentucky, contain a complete set of docket books but no conference lists. Reed served during the entire Vinson Court. He typically recorded the conference vote on-the-merits but, with a few exceptions during the October 1946 term, did not record information about votes on cert, jurisdiction, questions, stays, and various other writs. His recording is not as accurate as that of Burton, Douglas, and Clark. Reed's notes on the discussions that preceded the conference vote on-the-merits are typically written (in pencil) on his cert memos.

The M.I. King Library also contains the Fred Vinson collection, which has no docket books or conference lists but does have considerable collegial correspondence as well as the large sheets of butcher paper upon which the chief justice recorded opinion assignments.

The Robert H. Jackson papers at the Library of Congress contain some information on conference votes. Docket book pages begin with the October 1946 term and end with the October 1953 term. Except for a few cases from the beginning of the October 1946 term, Jackson did not record cert and jurisdiction votes on docket book pages, though he did frequently record them on his cert memos. Sometimes each justice's cert vote is shown, while at other times only the names of those voting to grant are listed. These memos are in the individual case files.

The conference vote on-the-merits as well as notes on the discussion that preceded the vote were recorded on docket book pages. After the October 1946 term, these pages were placed in the case files rather than kept in docket books. The overall value of the Jackson collection is limited because case files—many of which no longer exist—were only created if the Court granted review.

The Felix Frankfurter Court papers are divided between two separate collections, one at the Harvard Law School Library, the other at the Library of Congress. The Harvard collection contains Vinson-era docket books and some conference lists. Frankfurter's first docket book, which is from the October 1938 term, is his only surviving pre-1946 docket book. Frankfurter recorded many votes and sometimes wrote extensive comments on the docket book pages. His secretary typed relatively little information, and Frankfurter usually used the same page twice if the case was held over to the next term. The consistency and accuracy of his docket books is decidedly below that of the Burton, Douglas, and Clark docket books.

The Frank Murphy papers, in the Michigan Historical Collection of the University of Michigan, contain docket books for the 1946 and 1947 terms. When cases were held over to the next term, Murphy frequently used the old page in the new docket book with the new docket number handwritten next to the old, which has a line drawn through it. The 1947 docket book was disassembled and filed with the case materials. Murphy's docket books contain only limited information, usually about the conference vote on-the-merits. There are no conference lists, but Murphy's notes on the discussion that preceded the conference vote on-the-merits are often detailed. When Murphy died in August 1949, some of his papers dealing with cases still before the Court were given to Clark and are part of the Clark collection.

The Wiley Rutledge collection and Hugo Black collection at the Library of Congress contain conference lists but no docket books. Both justices wrote the Court's action next to the case name on their conference lists.

More elaborate discussions of these collections are presented by Wigdor (1986) in her description of all the known private papers of Supreme Court justices. Most of the collections discussed above have detailed indices which are available from the individual libraries.

V. How the Dataset Was Gathered

The primary sources used to gather the dataset are the docket books of Burton, Douglas, Clark, and Reed. The secondary sources are the docket books of Murphy, Jackson, and Frankfurter and the conference lists of Rutledge, Burton, Douglas, and Clark. The tertiary sources include case files, cert and bench memos, and conference notes of Vinson, Reed, Douglas, Clark, Burton, and Rutledge.

The Vinson era docket books in the Burton, Douglas, Clark, Reed, and Jackson collections were photocopied, and the photocopies were rearranged so that all entries for a case were placed together. Because many cases began on the miscellaneous docket and were transferred to the appellate docket or began in one term and ended in another, the information for a case is often spread over two or more docket book pages. Therefore, using photocopies of the docket book pages is the only method that allows concurrent viewing of all the pages from the different terms and different justices. The primary disadvantage of using photocopies is the loss of resolution and color. The conference lists and special lists in the Burton, Rutledge, and Clark collections were photocopied and rearranged so that all lists for a conference are together. When necessary, these lists are supplemented with lists from the Douglas collection.

Each justice used his docket books and conference lists for different purposes, and each had his own system of recording information. Whenever possible, multiple sources were used to obtain the votes on a specific case. This is particularly important for difficult cases in which the Court voted several times or for cases that spanned several terms.

For the first natural Court, the Burton and Douglas docket books and the Burton conference lists are the primary sources for all types of votes. For the conference votes on-the-merits, the Reed and Jackson docket books provide additional sources. When Burton and Douglas disagreed or the results were illogical, the Murphy and Frankfurter docket books were used, generally with limited success.

For the second natural Court, there are three consistent sources for all types of votes: Burton, Douglas, and Clark. For conference votes on-the-merits, Reed and Jackson provide additional sources. The Frankfurter docket books provide a sixth source when needed.

The dates of most actions were obtained from Burton's docket books and conference lists. Additional date information was obtained from the conference lists of Rutledge for the first Court and Clark for the second. For both natural Courts, information on opinion assignments is available in all docket books and in assignment sheets in the Douglas and Clark collections.

The dataset includes all cases that were not unanimously rejected by the Court. If there were multiple votes, a case is included if one vote was not a unanimous rejection. For appeals, the case is included if at least one justice voted to note probable jurisdiction, to postpone until the decision on-the-merits, or to affirm. For cert or other writs, the case is included if at least one justice voted to grant, to hold, or to call for a response. The boundaries between cases are occasionally unclear. Related cases were often grouped together and processed as one case, even if the dispositions were different. Information is sometimes spread among these related cases. For example, the vote on cert is recorded on the docket book page of one case, but the conference vote on-the-merits is recorded on the page of another case. In addition, the justices frequently recorded information differently. One justice may have made all entries for both cases on the docket book page of the first case, while another justice made all entries on the page of the second.

A case is a unique entry in the dataset if Burton, Douglas, or Clark recorded at least one of the Court's votes on a docket book page that was assigned exclusively to the case or recorded at least one of the Court's votes on a conference list next to the name of the case. This means that cases that were processed together can be unique entries in the dataset even if they were decided by identical votes.

Each case in the dataset presents all votes even if the information is obtained from other cases and is also presented by these other cases. Thus, scholars using the dataset for empirical analysis may want to delete cases that they consider redundant. The empirical investigations in this book assume that each case is unique. Therefore, all cases are used for the empirical studies. The one exception is the investigation of opinion assignments in which the units of analysis are assignments rather than cases.

VI. Types and Sources of Errors in Conference Votes

There are three categories of errors in the conference votes presented in the dataset. The first category results from my errors in interpreting and coding the justices' entries. The second contains votes that were understood by the recording justice but were incorrectly entered in the docket book or on the conference list. The last category results from instances in which the recording justice either misunderstood his colleague's vote or recorded the vote in a manner that I cannot comprehend.

The extent of the first type of error, those resulting from my coding mistakes, is unknown. Obviously, I have eliminated all the mistakes that I can find but cannot determine the extent of my remaining errors.

The second type of error, those caused by the justices' mistakes, are probably rare. It is unlikely that two or more justices made the same mistake in the same place in their docket books when recording routine votes. Because I used several justices' docket books, errors made by individual justices were usually obvious and did not affect my coding.

With very complex or novel votes, the justices sometimes did not record the information or recorded it in a fashion that only they could discern. The third type of error results either from my failure to understand their entries or because my coding system could not capture the complexity of the Court's actions, particularly when votes did not fit into neat categories such as grant vs. deny or affirm vs. reverse.

These last two categories of errors have five causes: the justices' inability to understand each other's votes; failure to indicate whether the Court voted; erroneous entries; incomplete recordings; and errors in dates, opinion assignments, and report votes. These five causes are explained as follows:

VIa. Understanding Other Justices' Votes

Voting was not always a binary choice between reverse and affirm or between grant and deny. Sometimes a justice stated acceptable alternatives such as reverse if certain precedents were used but affirm if different cases were cited. Other times a justice expressed a preference for one action but voted for another by stating something like, "I would rather reverse but I'll go along if you affirm" or "we should dismiss as improvidently granted; if not, we should reverse." Obviously, the other justices might interpret and record these votes differently.

When the Court voted on jurisdiction, the docket books listed four alternatives: note, postpone the decision on jurisdiction until the decision on-the-merits, affirm, and dismiss. Note and affirm could be combined to create a fifth option. The differences between noting and postponing were subtle, and justices frequently equivocated between the two, leaving their colleagues uncertain as to their actual votes. A comparable situation existed for jurisdiction votes to affirm and to dismiss. Again, the results were so similar that justices were sometimes unclear about their intentions.

With cert votes there were usually two alternatives: grant or deny. Because there were fewer possibilities, there are proportionally fewer disagreements among docket books with cert votes than there are with jurisdiction votes.

With cert or jurisdiction votes in which the opposing litigant had not been notified, a justice could vote to "call for a response brief." Calling for a response—an action that apparently required four votes—involved only IFP cert petitions on the miscellaneous docket because cases on the appellate docket were not processed without the required notification of the opposing party. Because there was no specific place in the docket book to record a vote to call for a response, it was occasionally not recorded or was recorded as a vote to grant. When the Court did call for a response brief, the cert request was re-listed following receipt of the brief. Thus, justices may have left the docket book blank in anticipation of the subsequent vote.

VIb. Determining Whether the Court Voted

It is sometimes difficult to determine whether there was a formal vote or merely a discussion during which positions were announced but no vote was taken. This difficulty occurs most frequently in three situations: cases that were (1) held for the next conference, (2) on the dead lists, and (3) requests for rehearings.

Any justice could ask to have a case held until the next conference or "passed to the next list" or "re-listed." If a justice asked for a re-listing after the discussion but before the vote, the preferences expressed during the discussion may have been recorded as votes, especially if eight justices were prepared to vote and only one wanted a delay. If the request for a re-listing occurred after the voting had begun, at least part of the aborted vote was usually recorded in the docket books.

If a justice wanted the Court to grant a petition that was dead listed, he had two options. First, if there was a chance that the petition would be granted, he could ask to have the case taken off the dead list and put to a vote. For example, Black removed *Ward v. U.S.* (52,390A) from the dead list on October 9, 1952. Second, if there was no chance that the petition would be granted, he could simply note his objection to denial without asking for a vote. For example, in a memo (Black #306; Jackson #165) dated October 3, 1950, Black stated:

> The above cases are on the Special List. I wish my vote to grant noted in each, although I do not ask that the applications be reinstated for consideration by the full Court unless other members of the Court are disturbed by denials.

Sometimes these dead list dissents—particularly if made orally during the conference—were entered as votes in the docket book even though no formal vote was taken and others who favored granting remained silent rather than waste time. Thus, it is occasionally difficult to distinguish these two options, i.e., it is difficult to determine whether "the roll was called on the petition" or a justice simply stated that he would have voted to grant if there had been a vote.

Petitions for a rehearing received formal consideration only if a member of the majority in the first disposition moved for a vote. This did not, however, stop members in the minority from announcing that they favored a rehearing. If these announcements were recorded in a docket book, they can be difficult to distinguish from actual votes.

Some voting occurred outside the conference. Occasionally the chief justice circulated a memo on which each justice in turn recorded his vote. When everyone had voted, the memo was returned to the chief justice. Almost none of these memos are in existence because nearly all the items in Vinson's papers that revealed individual votes were destroyed. Thus, the information remains lost unless one of the justices inquired about the result and recorded the votes in his docket book.

VIc. Erroneous Recording of Votes

There are certain types of errors in docket books that are relatively easily detected. The most obvious occurred when the votes were recorded on the wrong page. Another error involved transposing affirm and reverse. If the Court voted to reverse the circuit court and to affirm or reinstate the decision of the district court, then it is possible that a justice became confused and transposed the votes. This error occurs most frequently in Reed's docket books.

A less obvious error occurred when a justice did not vote. While making docket book entries, it was essential to leave a non-voting justice's square blank and move to the next square before making the next entry. If the square was not left blank, then each justice's vote was recorded in the preceding justice's square. Because the chief justice's vote was always at the bottom of the table, the mistake was usually discovered by the time Vinson voted. The discovery typically resulted in hasty and often inaccurate corrections of the preceding votes. Thus, docket book entries are generally more accurate and consistent when all nine justices voted. Fortunately, Burton and Clark almost never made this type of mistake and Douglas made it only rarely.

VId. Incomplete Recording of Votes

Sometimes a justice recorded only one side of a vote. For example, he may have entered only the votes to reverse, leaving the square blank if a justice voted to affirm. These entries are difficult to interpret because a blank can represent a vote to affirm, or a vote to pass, or no vote if the justice was recused or absent. In addition, the probability of error is much greater because of the care needed to skip the appropriate number of boxes and, as stated above, justices were less likely to err if they recorded nine votes. The practice of recording only one side of a vote was used occasionally by Murphy and Reed and extensively by Frankfurter and Jackson.

When there was more than one vote on granting review or on-the-merits, the docket books had no convenient place for recording the second vote. Sometimes other columns of the matrix were used and the caption at the top was changed. Other times the second vote was recorded over the first in a different color or using a different type of mark. During some votes, the discussion was fluid and minds were being changed. If a justice changed his vote during the voting process, it is sometimes difficult to separate the first from the second or to determine whether there was one or two votes.

If a justice changed his mind after the conference, he could send the chief justice a memo stating his new vote. If he or the chief justice notified his colleagues, then the new vote was generally recorded in docket books, but when the other justices were not informed, their docket books were not changed. This type of omission is probably most common when the vote change had no effect on the Court's action.

With a vote on granting review, it was the Court's action, rather than the individual votes, that was important, unlike a vote on-the-merits, where each justice's vote was important and would eventually be public. Thus, some justices (Murphy, Jackson, and Reed) did not record votes on granting review in their docket books. Others (Frankfurter and Douglas) recorded them with less care than they recorded votes on-the-merits.

Another problem with votes on granting review occurs when the outcome was obvious before voting was completed. Once there were four votes to grant or six to deny review, the remaining votes could not change the result. If the outcome was already determined, the more senior justices (who voted last) may have been equivocal or ambiguous. This is particularly true with Frankfurter, who either confused or bored his colleagues to the point that they sometimes failed to record his vote. Black, on the other hand, was emphatic even when his vote was futile and therefore his vote is less frequently missing in his brethren's docket books.

VIe. Other Types of Errors

There are three remaining types of errors: mistakes in dates, incomplete or inaccurate information regarding opinion assignments, and errors in the report votes.

Errors in dates. Burton almost always dated the Court's votes and actions in his docket book, and his dates are typically corroborated by the conference lists. But if a case was repeatedly re-listed, it can be difficult to determine when the Court voted, a problem that is related to the difficulty, discussed above, of determining *if* the Court voted.

If Burton failed to record the date, and the conference lasted more than one day, it is sometimes difficult to determine exactly when the Court acted. This problem usually occurs when the conference began on Saturday and ended on Monday or when it was held during the first week of the term when the Court held daily conferences.

Errors in opinion assignment information. The dates and recipients of the initial opinion assignments were recorded in the beginning of the docket books, on the individual docket book pages, and on the assignment sheets which were distributed to each justice. Thus, any errors regarding the initial assignment are totally my responsibility. When an opinion was reassigned, however, the information is often limited. For example, I was never able to determine when *Klapprott v. U.S.* (48,42A) was reassigned to Black.

It is important to note that not all opinions were completed and that the dataset records assignments rather than completions. Chapter 8 contains a listing and analysis of opinions that were not completed either because they were reassigned or because they were converted to *per curiam* announcements.

Errors in report votes. The report votes, which are readily available in *U.S. Reports*, are provided as a convenience at the recommendation of early users of the dataset. Unlike the other votes, report votes were not hand recorded by the justices in the matrix on their docket book pages. Instead, they were typed on the pages in abridged form by the secretaries after the conference. Coding the report votes was more difficult and probably resulted in more errors, all of which are solely my responsibility.

Another difficulty with report votes results from the ambiguity of some dissenting opinions. The votes of the majority justices are obvious, but determining the votes of the dissenters can be difficult because dissenting is not always the opposite of assenting. Douglas and Black dissented when the Court reversed in *Albertson v. Millard* (52,384A) because they favored a more sweeping reversal. Jackson dissented when the Court reversed in *U.S. v. Commodities Trading* (49,156A) because he would have reversed and remanded with different instructions. Sometimes the dissenters explicitly stated the action they preferred, e.g., "I would reverse" or "I would remand." Other times the dissenters attacked the majority's action without indicating which of the various alternative actions they preferred.

5

Case Selection Via Certiorari

I. Introduction

The majority of cases decided by the Court arrived via cert petitions, though most cert petitions were denied because they failed to receive the necessary four votes. This chapter analyzes the Court's cert decision making. Section II discusses previous empirical studies of case selection. Section III develops a model of cert voting. The justices' individual grant rates are analyzed in section IV. Sections V through VII examine the relationships between the vote on cert and the conference vote on-the-merits. Complements and substitutes are discussed in section VIII. Sections IX through XII analyze the levels of agreement within pairings of justices, conformity, votes that determined the outcome, and solo dissents. Section XIII contains the conclusions.

In this chapter, votes with fewer than seven justices participating are excluded from the analysis for two reasons. First, cases in which only six justices voted are rare. Second, when only six participated, any justice could have ended the case by recusing himself and thereby depriving the Court of a quorum. Thus, voting strategies might have been different in cases where each justice's participation was essential.

Except for section VII (table 5.3), the following discussion focuses on only nonunanimous votes. Many of the tables, however, present information on two categories: the first category contains all nonunanimous cert votes, the second contains all nonunanimous cert votes as well as all unanimous certs grants. (Certs that were unanimously rejected are excluded from the dataset).

The Court's policies regarding cert were listed in the *Revised Rules* of February 1939, rule 38 (currently rule 19), Paragraph 5 (59 S.Ct. clxi):

> A review on writ of certiorari is not a matter of right, but of sound judicial discretion, and will be granted only where there are special and important reasons therefore.

This statement was followed by a brief listing of the types of cases that might be accepted. The written rule, which was a model of vagueness, was not clarified by the Court's actions, for the Court often avoided important cases while deciding unimportant ones. Frankfurter, for example, complained more or less continuously during the Vinson era that the Court was squandering time on frivolous cases while disposing of important ones after hurried consideration (Felix Frankfurter Papers HLSL #176-4; Provine 1980, p.189, fn.93).

Perhaps the harshest criticism of the Court's case selections comes from Harper and various coauthors in a series of articles (1950, 1951, 1953, and 1954) that identify some of the major cases avoided by the Court. Although not intended to be all-encompassing studies, these articles contain interesting statistics and a wealth of information on some of the important cases that were denied review.

The cert vote was secret and the reasons for granting or denying were not revealed although some justices, particularly Black and Douglas, noted some of their dissents from denial. Scholars have thus needed to construct their own criteria as to what makes a case "certworthy."

II. Previous Empirical Studies

Tanenhaus *et al.* (1963) originated "cue theory" which hypothesizes that justices examine a cert petition to determine whether it possesses certain cues: the federal government as a party, dissension among the justices of lower courts, civil liberties, or economic issues. Petitions with these cues were given more serious consideration and therefore had higher grant rates than those without them. The theory is generally supported by contingency table analysis of data gathered from *U.S. Reports*. Cue theory is also tested and extended by Ulmer *et al.* (1972), Songer (1979), Teger and Kosinski (1980), Armstrong and Johnson (1982), and Ulmer (1984).

These studies have two limitations. First, because docket books are not used, the unit of analysis is the Court rather than the individual justice.

Although the theory explains individual behavior, the empirical tests have been unable to use the individual justices' votes because they were generally unavailable to researchers. Second, cue theory is an explanation of how the justices distinguished frivolous from serious petitions rather than a theory of why the Court granted some serious petitions and denied others. Cue theory is not supported by Provine's examination of special lists and docket books in the Burton papers, i.e., cases possessing the cues were no less likely to be dead listed (Provine 1980, pp. 77-83).

There is no comprehensive study of the relationship between the personnel of the lower courts and the cert votes of the Supreme Court, though lower court judges were not homogeneous in their abilities or in the respect that they received from Supreme Court justices. Rosenzweig (1951) demonstrates that the Court showed exceptional deference toward Judge Edgerton of the United States Circuit Court of Appeals for the District of Columbia and was generally unwilling to grant cert to consider a decision if he wrote the Circuit Court's opinion. Burton, who sometimes wrote lower court judges' names on his conference lists, noted on the third page of his conference list for May 3, 1947 (#164) that Edgerton had written the Circuit Court's opinion in *Potomac Electric v. Public Utilities* (46,1038A). By contrast, Douglas (1980, p. 102) indicates that some lower court judges required close watching by the Supreme Court.

Ulmer (1972) presents a model in which justices vote to grant if they expect to support the petitioner on-the-merits. His hypothesis is supported by a contingency table analysis using the votes of individual justices. The vote data were obtained from Burton's docket books. Subsequent studies by Ulmer (1973, 1978) extend and support his original hypothesis. Baum (1977, 1979) obtains similar results using data from the California Supreme Court.

Brenner (1979A) develops a model in which expected votes on-the-merits impact votes on cert. Using data from Burton's docket books, he shows that when there were four votes to grant cert, justices who voted to grant and wanted to affirm were more successful at the report vote on-the-merits than were justices who voted to grant and wanted to reverse. Provine (1980) finds a positive relationship between voting to grant review and later voting to reverse at the report vote on-the-merits, but she specifically rejects the idea that justices consider the probability of assenting on-the-merits when voting on granting review (Provine 1980, pp. 7,116,125-130).

My earlier study (Palmer 1982) assumes that justices consider both whether they agree with the lower court's decision and whether they expect to vote with the majority on-the-merits. The next section presents an extension of my earlier model.

III. Model of Case Selection

Every case that was processed by the Court changed the law. Some dispositions, such as refusing to grant cert to reconsider a well settled issue, produced very small changes. Others, such as overturning an important precedent, produced profound changes. Let the change in the law resulting from the Court's action in case i be represented by $E(i)$. Let the amount of time that was needed to dispose of case i be represented by $t(i)$. Let the amount of time available to the Court be represented by T, where $T = t(1) + t(2) + \ldots t(n)$. If the Court had been of one mind on-the-merits and on the importance of each request for cert, then it would have spent its limited time to optimize the change in the law. Thus, case i would have been decided by the Court only if $E(i)/t(i)$ equaled or exceeded the marginal product of the Court's time.

For many cases, however, the justices disagreed on whether to grant cert, and if cert was granted, they disagreed on-the-merits. Thus, each cert petition presented a justice with the possibility that the Court would hear an unimportant case or reach the wrong decision in an important case.

Introducing risk into the analysis requires the following simplifying assumptions. Each justice was risk-neutral, and determined *a priori* the following: whether he wanted to affirm or to reverse, the amount of time needed to process the case, and the probability of the Court's affirming, $pa(i)$, and reversing, $pr(i)$, on-the-merits. To simplify further, let $pa(i) + pr(i) = 1$, i.e., the case would not be dismissed as moot or improvidently granted.

Let $d(i)$ = the value of the change that resulted from a denial of cert, i.e., the change from letting the lower court's decision stand.

Let $EA(i)$ = the value of the change in the law that resulted from granting cert and affirming the lower court.

Let $ER(i)$ = the value of the change in the law that resulted from granting cert and reversing the lower court.

Affirming and reversing changed the law in opposite directions. Therefore, $EA(i)$ and $ER(i)$ had opposite signs. The absolute magnitudes of $EA(i)$ and $ER(i)$, however, were not generally equal. The signs of $d(i)$ and $EA(i)$ were the same, but the absolute magnitude of $EA(i)$ exceeded the absolute magnitude of $d(i)$, i.e., denial of cert changed the law in the same direction but by a smaller magnitude than affirming on-the-merits. If a justice preferred to reverse the case, then $ER(i) > 0 > d(i) > EA(i)$. But if a justice wanted to affirm, then $EA(i) > d(i) > 0 > ER(i)$.

When a justice wished to reverse, granting cert had a positive expected return if $pr(i)ER(i) > d(i) - pa(i)EA(i)$. Suppose that $ER(i) = 8$, $EA(i) = -12$, $d(i) = -1$, pr(i) = .6, pa(i) = .4. In this example, pr(i)ER(i) = 4.8 and d(i)-pa(i)EA(i) = 3.8. Therefore, the expected return from granting cert was positive. Although pr(i)ER(i) = -pa(i)EA(i), the expected return from granting was positive because of the certain loss, d(i)< 0, which resulted from denying.

When a justice wanted to affirm, granting cert had a positive expected return if pa(i)EA(i)-d(i)> -pr(i)ER(i). Suppose that EA(i) = 20, d(i) = 6, ER(i) = -30, pa(i) = .7, and pr(i) = .3. In this example, pa(i)EA(i)-d(i) = 8 and -pr(i)ER(i) = 9. Therefore, the expected return from granting cert was negative. Although pa(i)EA(i)> -pr(i)ER(i), the expected return from granting was negative because of the certain gain, d(i)> 0, from denying.

In any event, granting cert had a positive expected return if pa(i)EA(i) -d(i) + pr(i)ER(i)> 0. The expected return divided by the amount of time needed to process the case, t(i), gave the weighted expected return which was used to rank cert requests. Because the Court received a continual flow of cert petitions, it was impossible to rank all the term's petitions simultaneously. Thus, a justice learned to apply a minimum cut-off equal to the marginal product of time and voted to grant only if the petition's weighted expected return exceeded the cut-off. Each justice had his own proclivity toward granting cert because each justice attached his own values to EA(i), ER(i), d(i), pa(i), pr(i), and the marginal productivity of time.

Because the justices had different rankings and because only four votes were needed to grant cert, each justice participated in cases with low or even negative weighted expected returns. Theoretically, a justice in substantial disagreement with most of his colleagues might have voted for cases with low or even negative weighted expected returns (i.e., cases that were either time consuming or unimportant) so as to minimize the Court's impact. There is no evidence, however, that this strategy was used by any of the Vinson Court justices.

IV. Individual Grant Rates

The number and percentage of votes to grant cert for each justice are shown in table 5.1 for the first natural Court and in table 5.2 for the second. For each justice, there are two numbers in each column of tables 5.1 and 5.2. The top number is for nonunanimous cases; the bottom number is for nonunanimous cases plus cases that were granted unanimously. (Cases that were rejected unanimously are not included in the dataset or the analysis.)

The t-value indicates whether there is a statistically significant difference between the grant rate of a justice and the combined grant rate of his eight colleagues. This combined grant rate, which is obtained after dividing the total number of grant votes cast by the eight colleagues by their total number of votes on cert, is different for each justice because the composition of the group of eight colleagues differs.

Table 5.1 shows considerable variation in the justices' grant rates during the first natural Court. Murphy voted to grant in 60 percent of the nonunanimous cases while Jackson voted to grant in only 18 percent. A justice is categorized as grant-prone if his grant rate in nonunanimous votes is greater than his colleagues' combined rate and grant-averse if it is less. Thus, the four liberal justices, Rutledge, Murphy, Douglas, and Black, are all grant-prone, because each has a grant rate that is larger than his eight colleagues' combined rate, and the difference is statistically significant. The five conservatives, Burton, Jackson, Frankfurter, Reed, and Vinson, are all grant-averse, because each has a grant rate that is significantly less than his colleagues' combined rate.

Table 5.2 shows that the differences in grant rates continued into the second Court. Minton voted to grant in only twelve percent of the nonunanimous cert votes while Douglas and Black voted to grant in 59 and 56 percent, i.e., they were five times as likely to grant as was Minton. Burton's and Reed's t-values are not statistically significant, but the other seven justices' t-values are significant. Minton, Clark, Jackson, Frankfurter, and Vinson were grant-averse, while Douglas and Black were grant-prone.

Although there are substantial differences in the individual grant rates, the causes of these differences are unknown. Neither is it certain why the conservatives were grant-averse while the liberals were grant-prone. Douglas and Black, for example, may have had higher grant rates because they were more frequently in disagreement with the lower court, were more likely to think they would assent on-the-merits, could decide cases more quickly than their colleagues, or some combination of these three reasons. Given that both were rapid workers and "activist" justices, their high grant rates probably resulted from their more frequent disagreement with the lower courts and their ability to decide cases quickly.

V. Voting to Grant Cert and Assenting On-The-Merits

Either an increase in pa(i), if the justice wanted to affirm, or an increase in pr(i), if the justice wanted to reverse, increased both the probability of the justice's assenting on-the-merits and the weighted expected return. An increase in the weighted expected return caused an increase in the prob-

Table 5.1

Cert votes — First Natural Court.

Nonunanimous (top) and nonunanimous plus unanimous grants (bottom).
At least seven justices voting.

	Grant	Voted	Grant Rate	t-value
Burton	177	658	27	-5.17*
	264	745	35	-4.54*
Rutledge	305	649	47	6.31*
	392	736	53	5.94*
Jackson	120	653	18	-11.57*
	207	740	28	-9.53*
Murphy	380	633	60	13.46*
	462	715	65	12.78*
Douglas	312	614	51	8.12*
	392	694	56	7.60*
Frankfurter	158	654	24	-7.03*
	246	742	33	-5.99*
Reed	201	655	31	-2.77*
	289	743	39	-2.41*
Black	266	654	41	2.92*
	353	741	48	2.70*
Vinson	142	651	22	-8.73*
	228	737	31	-7.43*

* statistically significant at 5 percent level.

Table 5.2

Cert votes—Second Natural Court

Nonunamious (top) and nonunanimous plus unanimous grants (bottom).
At least seven justices voting.

	Grant	Voted	Grant rate	t-value
Minton	106	905	12	-20.32*
	210	1009	21	-15.69*
Clark	233	890	26	-5.24*
	330	987	33	-4.77*
Burton	300	965	31	-1.75
	410	1075	38	-1.50
Jackson	255	952	27	-4.96*
	366	1063	34	-4.21*
Douglas	525	883	59	16.68*
	614	972	63	15.65*
Frankfurter	286	961	30	-2.72*
	396	1071	37	-2.35*
Reed	343	954	36	1.65
	451	1062	42	1.56
Black	531	952	56	14.78*
	641	1062	60	14.25*
Vinson	246	958	26	-5.86*
	349	1061	33	-5.38*

* statistically significant at 5 percent level.

ability of voting to grant cert. Therefore, there should be a direct relationship, *ceteris paribus*, between having voted to grant cert and having assented on-the-merits. This hypothesis does not require that a justice voted to grant only if he expected to join the majority on-the-merits. A justice who expected to dissent might have voted to grant if a very large gain from converting his brethren offset the small probability of affecting the conversion. Nevertheless, an increase in the likelihood of voting with the majority on-the-merits increases the probability of voting for cert.

There is anecdotal support for this hypothesis. In his autobiography, Douglas explained his rationale for voting to deny cert in a specific case (Douglas 1980, p.94):

> Murphy and Rutledge, joined by Black, voted to grant the petition. If I had done likewise, there would have been four to grant and the Court would have heard the case. It was clear that the majority of five—Stone, Roberts, Reed, Frankfurter, and Jackson—would have voted to affirm; and it seemed to me at that particular point in history unwise to put the Court's seal of approval on that doctrine. Better let the issue be presented at a more auspicious time! . . .
>
> Such a judgment is often made at Conference, and everyone who has been on the Court has succumbed to that influence.

This hypothesis is also supported by Frankfurter's actions in the disposition of *Harding v. U.S.* (50,176A). The case was discussed during the conference of October 4, 1950. The roll was not called, but the discussion revealed that there were four potential votes to grant cert as well as five tentative votes to reverse summarily on-the-merits. On November 2, Frankfurter, who had indicated that he wanted to grant and who was the most senior member of the group that favored reversal, distributed a memo asking his colleagues to state how they intended to vote on-the-merits. When the results showed that there was no longer a majority to reverse, Frankfurter sent a memo (dated November 3) with the following to the chief justice (Vinson #215):

> I thoughtlessly so framed my inquiry regarding No. 176, *Harding v. United States*, as to ask the brethren to state whether they would affirm or reverse instead of whether they would grant or deny certiorari, and if it was to be granted whether they would reverse summarily or after argument. The returns indicate that five of the

Brethren would affirm the case if it came here. That being so, it would require my vote to bring the case here.

In view of the prevailing views of the Court I do not feel warranted in voting to bring the case here. I therefore vote to deny the petition for certiorari.

VI. Voting to Grant Cert and Reversing On-The-Merits

A second hypothesis involves the relationship between voting to grant and disagreeing with the lower court's decision. The result of a cert denial, $d(i)$, had an asymmetric relationship with $EA(i)$ and $ER(i)$. For a justice who wanted to affirm, there was a small but certain gain from denying cert. But for a justice who wanted to reverse, there was a small but certain loss from denying cert. Thus, justices were more likely to vote to grant when they wanted to reverse the lower court. Therefore, there should be a direct relationship, *ceteris paribus*, between having voted to grant cert and having voted to reverse on-the-merits.

VII. Logit Analysis

These two hypotheses regarding the relationships between voting to grant and voting with the majority on-the-merits and voting to reverse on-the-merits can be tested using a maximum-likelihood logistic model. This regression technique estimates the relationship between a binary dependent variable, GRANT (which is one if the justice voted to grant cert and zero if he voted to deny), and the percentage of his brethren that agreed with the justice at the conference vote on-the-merits, %MERIT, and a binary variable, REVERSE (which is one if the justice voted to reverse at the conference vote on-the-merits and zero if he voted to affirm). The model takes the form GRANT = $1/(1+\exp(-(\text{CONSTANT} + b1 \text{ } \%\text{MERIT} + b2 \text{ REVERSE})))$, where $b1$ and $b2$ are regression coefficients.

The percentage of colleagues that voted with the justice on-the-merits at the conference, %MERIT, is used as a proxy for a justice's *a priori* estimated probability of assenting on-the-merits. Obviously, there are problems with this proxy. Occasionally a justice did not know how he or his brethren would vote. Sometimes a justice's position changed between the vote on jurisdiction and the vote on-the-merits. Other times a justice knew how the Court would rule but could not determine whether the decision would be five-to-four or nine-to-zero. Nevertheless, there must have been a positive and strong relationship between %MERIT and the estimated probability of assenting and there is no other proxy available.

The conference rather than the report vote on-the-merits is used in this analysis for two reasons. First, because the cert vote was closer in time to the conference than to the report vote, the conference vote is more likely to reflect the justices' attitudes when they voted on cert. Second, for reasons discussed in chapter 7, the conference vote is more likely to reveal the justices' actual preferences on-the-merits, because it preceded the bargaining that occurred between the conference and report votes. Nevertheless, using the report rather than the conference vote would not substantially change the empirical results presented below.

The observations used in this logit analysis include cases with votes that were unanimous either at cert, or at the conference vote on-the-merits, or at both. Unanimous votes are not excluded for two reasons: first, excluding both types of unanimous votes would substantially reduce the number of observations; second, there is no theoretical rationale for excluding unanimous votes, i.e., there is no reason why the model is more or less applicable to decisions that were unanimous.

Table 5.3 contains the results of the logit analysis. Instead of regression coefficients, the estimated partial derivatives obtained from the regression coefficients are presented because they are much easier to interpret (Landes 1974, p.305). The absolute values of the t-values are in parentheses beneath the partial derivatives.

The first regression shows the results obtained from pooling the data for all eleven justices. The result for REVERSE is statistically significant. The estimated partial derivative, .275, indicates that the probability of a justice having voted to grant cert increases by approximately .275 if he subsequently voted to reverse. The estimated partial derivative for %MERIT, .092, although statistically significant, is small. Thus, a change from dissenting alone on-the-merits to joining a unanimous Court on-the-merits only increases the probability of having voted to grant cert by approximately .092.

The results for the individual justices show that, for each of the eleven justices, there is a positive and statistically significant relationship between having voted to grant cert and having voted to reverse on-the-merits. Vinson has the largest estimated relationship: the probability that he voted to grant cert increases by approximately .401 if he subsequently voted to reverse. Murphy has the smallest estimated relationship, .110. These results show

Table 5.3

Logit analysis of the determinants of the probability of voting to grant cert. Both natural Courts. Includes unanimous votes.

Justice	Sample Size	Log of Liklhood	Votes to GRANT	CONSTANT	%MERIT	REVERSE
ALL	5179	-2797.82	3751	0.002	0.092	0.275
				(0.12)	(3.77)*	(20.62)*
Minton	293	-193.19	160	-.209	0.268	0.171
				(2.62)*	(2.28)*	(2.78)*
Clark	288	-128.81	238	0.136	0.043	0.125
				(1.88)	(0.42)*	(2.72)*
Burton	639	-330.96	468	-.031	0.161	0.305
				(0.65)	(2.19)*	(7.60)*
Rutledge	246	-101.13	202	0.058	0.008	0.273
				(0.77)	(0.08)	(5.36)*
Jackson	584	-355.09	374	-.066	0.120	0.275
				(1.32)	(1.57)	(6.37)*
Murphy	244	-85.04	215	0.192	-.008	0.110
				(3.10)*	(1.04)	(2.68)*
Douglas	511	-234.80	417	0.177	-.069	0.148
				(4.28)*	(1.22)	(4.24)*
Frankfurter	586	-347.40	392	0.046	0.135	0.254
				(0.96)	(1.84)*	(6.08)*
Reed	613	-343.33	447	0.091	0.025	0.195
				(1.93)	(0.35)	(5.08)*
Black	608	-285.33	458	-.059	0.105	0.377
				(1.29)	(1.60)	(9.81)*
Vinson	567	-302.66	380	-.197	0.292	0.401
				(3.20)*	(3.13)*	(8.50)*

*statistically significant at 5 percent level using one-tailed test.

that disagreements with the lower courts' decisions had a much greater impact on Vinson's cert votes than they did on Murphy's.

The estimated relationship between GRANT and %MERIT is statistically significant for four of the eleven justices: Minton, Burton, Frankfurter, and Vinson. Within this group, estimated partial derivatives for Minton (.268) and Vinson (.292) are about twice the size of the estimates for Burton (.161) and Frankfurter (.135). Although statistically significant, these estimated partials are small. For example, for each additional justice who agreed with Vinson on-the-merits, the probability that Vinson had previously voted to grant cert increases by $.292 \times 1/8 = .0365$. Nevertheless, these results do indicate that, when voting on cert, at least four justices gave some consideration to the proportion of their colleagues that would join them at the conference vote on-the-merits.

VIII. Complements and Substitutes

The preceding analysis assumes that each case had an independent effect on the law. It is obvious, however, that some cases were complements to and substitutes for each other. Case q was a substitute for case i if deciding case q reduced $E(i)$. Case q was a complement to case i if deciding case q increased $E(i)$. Because their ideologies and objectives diverged, individual justices evaluated the relationships between cases differently. Thus, cases that were complements for one justice may have been substitutes for another.

It is also likely that the amount of time taken to process case i, $t(i)$ was a function of the amount of time allocated to case q. The relationship could be either positive or negative. Sometimes the factual and legal principles were identical so that the additional time needed to process a complementary case was quite small. Other times the subtle differences between related cases may have required an elaborate and time consuming deliberation and written opinion.

The Court's procedures indicate that it perceived some cases as complements or substitutes: related cases were often listed consecutively on the conference lists, and cert and jurisdiction votes were sometimes delayed until similar cases were decided on-the-merits. If the related cases resulted in a decision unfavorable to the party requesting review, then the petition was rejected. But if the decision favored the petitioner or appellant, then the Court granted review and either combined it with the similar case or reached a summary decision based on the related case. The type of disposition was usually controlled by the justice writing the opinion of the Court. In a memo to Clark dated December 14, 1954, (Felix Frankfurter Papers HLSL #169-11) Frankfurter stated:

> It is, of course, our normal practice that when a petition for certiorari is held to await disposition on the merits of the case raising a kindred question, the writer of the opinion of the controlling case guides the Court in the disposition of the retained petition for certiorari.

Although it is evident that the Court treated some cases as complements or substitutes, it is impossible to quantify the relationships between cases. Many similar cases received different dispositions and not all justices agreed on how cases were related. Thus, this study contains no empirical analysis of the relationship between cases even though political scientists have developed elaborate mechanisms for categorizing them, e.g., Schubert (1965 and 1974) and Spaeth (1979).

IX. Agreement on Cert

The preceding analysis assumes that although a justice's cert vote depended on his colleagues' expected votes on-the-merits, it was independent of his colleagues' cert votes. This section drops the assumption and examines agreements between the justices on the cert decision.

An example of justices influencing a colleague's cert vote is provided by *District Of Columbia v. Little* (49,302A). During the conference of November 5, 1949, Clark first voted to deny cert. He then changed his vote and wrote "I was 4th to vote grant because of strong statements of CJ Reed & Burton" in his docket book, (C67-3). (Reed and Burton subsequently dissented on-the-merits and thus may have later wished that they had saved their "strong statements" for another case.)

Assume that a justice had a unique relationship with each colleague. A justice's effectiveness depended, in part, on these relationships, which changed with every cert vote. Let the impact on a justice's relationship with colleague k resulting from the cert vote on case i be represented by $C(ik)$. A cert vote could have had opposite effects on relationships with different colleagues, i.e., $C(i1)$ was positive while $C(i2)$ was negative. The absolute magnitudes of the effects could have also varied considerably. One colleague, for example, may have believed that granting cert was very important and may have genuinely appreciated others' votes to grant while another colleague may have favored granting but was not disappointed if the petition was denied. The total effect of the cert vote for case i on a justice's relationships with his eight colleagues was the summation over the eight values for k of C(ik). Now, granting cert had a positive expected return if pa(i)EA(i)-d(i) + pr(i)ER(i) + the summation over the eight values for k of C(ik)> 0.

One indication of the relationships between justices on the cert vote is the frequency of agreement in cases in which both voted. Tables 5.4 and 5.5 present the agreement rates in nonunanimous cert votes for each pairing in the first and second natural Courts. The top number is the agreement rate on the cert vote, i.e., the percentage of votes in which both voted to grant or both voted to deny. The bottom number is the agreement-to-grant rate, i.e., the percentage of votes in which both voted to grant.

For example, table 5.4 shows that Burton and Jackson voted together on 74 percent of the nonunanimous cert decisions during the first natural Court. They agreed to grant ten percent, agreed to deny 64 percent (74 minus 10), and disagreed on 26 percent (100 minus 74). The agreement-to-grant rate of ten percent must be interpreted juxtaposed to their individual grant rates on nonunanimous cert decisions. These individual grant rates are shown in table 5.1: 27 percent for Burton and 18 percent for Jackson. Because Jackson voted to grant 18 percent of the cert petitions and agreed with Burton to grant ten percent of the petitions, it follows that Burton voted with Jackson in about half the instances in which Jackson voted to grant in nonunanimous cert decisions.

Table 5.4 shows wide variations in the levels of agreement during the first natural Court, from a high of 78 percent between Jackson and Frankfurter to a low of 45 percent between Jackson and Murphy. The conservatives, Burton, Jackson, Frankfurter, Reed, and Vinson, display strong intra-bloc relationships—the agreement rates for the individual pairings range between 69 and 78 percent. Because members of the conservative bloc were grant-averse, their agreement-to-grant rates are relatively low. For example, Jackson and Vinson voted together in 76 percent of the nonunanimous cert votes, but their agreement-to-grant rate is only eight percent.

When they did vote to grant, members of the conservative bloc were about as likely to vote with the liberals as they were to vote with their fellow conservatives. Provine, who obtains a similar finding from the cert and jurisdiction votes in Burton's 1947 and 1948 docket books, argues that "the pattern indicates the absence of a counter bloc, and it shows the willingness of bloc members to vote with or against anyone for review . . . ." (Provine 1980, p.135).

Table 5.4

Nonunanimous cert votes — First Natural Court.

Percentage of votes in which justices agreed (top) and percentage of votes in which justices agreed to grant (bottom). At least seven justices voting.

	Rutldg	Jacksn	Murphy	Dougls	Frnkfr	Reed	Black	Vinson
Burton	52	74	47	48	71	71	56	75
	13	10	17	13	11	14	12	12
Rutledg		56	60	60	54	53	60	57
		11	34	29	13	15	24	13
Jackson			45	50	78	69	57	76
			12	10	10	9	8	8
Murphy				56	48	50	55	49
				34	16	20	28	15
Douglas					50	50	56	50
					13	15	24	12
Frankfurter						70	54	73
						13	9	09
Reed							56	73
							13	13
Black								62
								13

The liberal bloc contains the grant-prone justices, Rutledge, Murphy, Douglas, and Black. The pairings within the liberal bloc display agreement rates which are weaker than the rates for the conservative bloc. The agreement-to-grant rates within the liberal bloc, however, are about twice the agreement-to-grant rates for pairings within the conservative bloc or for inter-bloc pairings between the liberal and conservative blocs.

Table 5.5 presents the results for the second natural Court. Again, there are wide variations in the levels of agreement. Clark and Minton concurred in 83 percent of the nonunanimous cert votes. By contrast, Reed's agreement rates with Black and with Douglas are both only 39 percent.

The high levels of agreement displayed by Burton, Jackson, Frankfurter, Reed, and Vinson continued during the second Court. This bloc increased to seven when the new justices, Clark and Minton, joined it. Minton's agreement rates with Vinson, 81 percent, and Jackson, 78 percent, are almost double his agreement rates with Douglas, 43 percent, and Black, 44 percent. Clark's agreement rates with Jackson, 78 percent, and Vinson, 81 percent, are substantially higher than his rates with Douglas, 51 percent, and Black, 47 percent.

The deaths of Rutledge and Murphy decreased the liberal bloc to only two justices, Black and Douglas. Their agreement rate on cert, 56 percent, is higher than their individual agreement rates in pairings with the other seven justices. In addition, their agreement-to-grant rate, 35 percent, is the highest agreement-to-grant rate of the second Court, the result of both being grant-prone and frequently agreeing on cert. In contrast, the agreement-to-grant rate between Minton and Vinson is only nine percent. This low rate occurs in spite of their frequent agreement on cert, 81 percent, because both were grant-averse.

The agreement-to-grant rates between members of the conservative and liberal blocs are about the same as those within the conservative bloc. Indeed, Clark and Frankfurter have their highest agreement-to-grant rates with Douglas. These rates support Provine's (1980, p.135) contention that the blocs did not engage in strategic counter-voting.

X. Conformity on Cert

The preceding analysis does not distinguish votes according to whether a justice could control the outcome. If four others voted to grant or six others voted to deny, then an individual justice's vote could not change the result. Because a discussion preceded the vote, the outcome was often obvious

Table 5.5

Nonunanimous cert votes — Second Natural Court.

Percentage of votes in which justices agreed (top) and percentage of votes in which justices agreed to grant (bottom). At least seven justices voting.

	Clark	Burton	Jacksn	Dougls	Frnkfr	Reed	Black	Vinson
Minton	83	76	78	43	74	70	44	81
	10	9	8	8	8	9	5	9
Clark		78	78	51	72	71	47	81
		18	15	18	13	17	14	16
Burton			74	46	66	71	43	76
			16	18	14	19	15	16
Jackson				43	71	71	44	74
				15	14	17	13	13
Douglas					49	39	56	44
					19	18	35	15
Frankfurter						59	51	67
						13	18	11
Reed							39	73
							15	17
Black								43
								12

before voting began. Even if the result was not obvious at this point, it could become obvious before voting ended. The most senior justices (who voted last) often voted after there were already four votes to grant or six to deny.

If the cert decision was a *fait accompli* when a justice voted, then $pa(i)EA(i)-d(i) + pr(i)ER(i) +$ the summation over the eight values for k of $C(ik)> 0$ was not relevant. The justice was concerned solely with whether the summation over the eight values of $C(ik)> 0$. In other words, his vote could not change the Court's decision but it could affect his relationships with his colleagues. In this situation, a justice presumably voted so as to maximize his influence, which meant choosing among several options: voting according to his original intentions, voting with those colleagues who would most appreciate the agreement, conforming with the Court's action, or voting against the Court's action.

When a justice conformed to the Court's action, he typically joined at least four of his brethren and thereby pleased at least as many as he disappointed. Also, conformity may have been appreciated because it demonstrated a willingness to place harmony and cooperation above individual preferences. On the other hand, counter-conformity may have been optimal if conformity was interpreted as weakness or indecisiveness or if it displeased the losers more than it pleased the winners.

This section analyzes a subset of the data containing votes in which a justice could not determine the outcome and therefore might have elected to conform to the Court's action. When all nine justices voted, for example, a justice's vote is included if the cert vote was eight-to-one (i.e., eight to grant and one to deny); seven-to-two; six-to-three; five-to-four; four-to-five (and the justice is one of the five); three-to-six (and the justice is one of the three); two-to-seven, and one-to-eight. Unanimous votes are excluded from this analysis.

Now, in addition to being grant-averse or grant-prone, a justice can be conforming or counter-conforming. A conforming justice's grant rate is significantly larger (smaller) than his colleagues' combined rate for cases in which their votes did not determine the outcome and in which cert was granted (denied). A counter-conforming justice's grant rate is smaller (larger) than his colleagues' combined rate for cases in which their votes did not determine the outcome and in which cert was granted (denied).

Table 5.6, which presents the results for the first natural Court, is divided into two sections: the top section contains the cases in which cert was granted, and the bottom contains those in which it was denied. The table shows the number of votes to grant, the number of votes, the grant rate, and the t-statistic used to test whether the grant rate of a justice is statistically

Table 5.6

Cert votes that could not determine the outcome in nonunanimous decisions —
First Natural Court. At least seven justices voting.

CERT WAS GRANTED BY THE COURT

	Grant Votes	Votes	Grant Rate	t-value
Burton	97	217	45	-2.01*
Rutledge	120	178	67	4.86*
Jackson	74	226	33	-6.23*
Murphy	133	169	79	9.01*
Douglas	107	171	63	3.25*
Frankfurter	83	212	39	-3.78*
Reed	104	217	48	-0.99
Black	106	187	47	1.63
Vinson	97	226	43	-2.65*

CERT WAS DENIED BY THE COURT

	Grant Votes	Votes	Grant Rate	t-value
Burton	50	331	15	-5.06*
Rutledge	118	355	33	3.65*
Jackson	29	324	9	-9.84*
Murphy	172	352	49	9.81*
Douglas	138	332	42	6.69*
Frankfurter	42	328	13	-6.61*
Reed	69	345	20	-2.32*
Black	104	347	30	2.27*
Vinson	30	323	9	-9.49*

* statistically significant at 5 percent level.

different from the combined rate of his eight colleagues when they voted in similar situations.

The results of table 5.6 indicate that none of the justices was conforming or counter-conforming, i.e., those justices whose grant rates were below (or above) their colleagues' when cert was granted were also below (or above) their colleagues' when cert was denied. Those justices whose grant rates were consistently below their colleagues'—Burton, Jackson, Frankfurter, and Vinson—were grant-averse. Those whose rates were consistently above their colleagues'—Rutledge, Murphy, and Douglas—were grant-prone. Reed and Black cannot be categorized because their results when cert was denied are not statistically significant.

Table 5.7, which has the same format as table 5.6, presents the results for the second natural Court. Burton and Clark were conforming. Each has a grant rate when cert was granted that is larger than his colleagues' combined rate and a grant rate when cert was denied that is lower. Minton was grant-averse, while Douglas was grant-prone. The others cannot be categorized because each has at least one t-value that is not statistically significant.

XI. Cases in Which the Justice's Vote Determined the Outcome

This section analyzes votes that determined the outcome: specifically, a vote to grant when there were four to grant or a vote to deny when there were only three to grant. Thus, the justice could have altered the outcome by changing his vote—a not uncommon occurrence. Because the justice determined the outcome, he could be neither conforming nor counter-conforming, though he could be grant-prone or grant-averse.

There are now two possible definitions of grant-prone (averse). The first categorizes a justice as grant-prone (averse) if he was more (less) likely to grant than to deny when he had the opportunity to cast the fourth vote to grant. The second definition labels a justice as grant-prone (averse) if his grant rate—when he could cast the fourth vote to grant—is larger (smaller) than his eight colleagues' combined rate—when they could cast the fourth vote to grant—and the difference is statistically significant.

Table 5.8 presents the results for the first natural Court. For each justice the table shows the number of votes to grant, the number of votes, the grant rate, and the t-statistic used to test whether the justice's grant rate is statistically different from the other eight justices' combined grant rate in those cert

Table 5.7

Cert votes that could not determine the outcome in nonunanimous decisions —
Second Natural Court. At least seven justices voting.

CERT WAS GRANTED BY THE COURT

	Grant Votes	Votes	Grant Rate	t-value
Minton	95	249	38	-7.99*
Clark	163	224	73	4.07*
Burton	172	246	70	3.14*
Jackson	150	239	63	0.53
Douglas	141	208	68	2.13*
Frankfurter	137	241	57	-1.46
Reed	156	232	67	2.07*
Black	122	219	56	-1.73
Vinson	153	248	62	0.17

CERT WAS DENIED BY THE COURT

	Grant Votes	Votes	Grant Rate	t-value
Minton	7	505	1	-30.43*
Clark	40	518	8	-13.74*
Burton	99	576	17	-4.70*
Jackson	75	565	13	-7.89*
Douglas	332	570	58	17.79*
Frankfurter	115	593	19	-3.16*
Reed	148	587	25	0.56
Black	358	632	57	17.94*
Vinson	66	562	12	-9.36*

* statistically significant at 5 percent level.

Table 5.8

Cert votes that determined the outcome — First Natural Court. At least seven justices voting.

	Grant Votes	Votes	Grant Rate	t-value
Burton	30	110	27	-3.03*
Rutledge	67	116	58	4.24*
Jackson	17	103	17	-6.41*
Murphy	75	112	67	6.54*
Douglas	67	111	60	4.77*
Frankfurter	33	114	29	-2.63*
Reed	28	93	30	-2.07*
Black	56	120	47	1.67
Vinson	15	102	15	-7.14*

* statistically significant at 5 percent level.

votes in which his colleagues determined the outcome. The number of votes to deny is not shown but can be computed by subtracting the number to grant from the number of votes. Except for Black, the liberals were generally grant-prone. When Rutledge had the opportunity to cast the fourth vote to grant cert, he was more likely to grant, 67 times, than to deny, 49 times. Thus, he was grant-prone under the first definition. His grant rate, 58 percent, is significantly larger than his colleagues' combined rate, indicating that Rutledge was also grant-prone under the second definition. Murphy and Douglas were also grant-prone under both definitions. Black apparently was neither grant-prone nor grant-averse. His grant rate is not significantly different from his colleagues' combined rate, and he voted to grant about the same number of certs, 56, that he voted to deny, 64.

Burton, Jackson, Frankfurter, Reed, and Vinson are grant-averse under both definitions. When Burton had the opportunity to provide the fourth vote to grant cert, he voted to grant 30 times and to deny 80 times. Jackson voted to grant 17 times and to deny 86. Frankfurter voted to grant 33 certs and to deny 81. Reed voted to grant 28 times and to deny 65 times. Vinson voted to grant 15 times and to deny 87 times. Each has a grant rate that is significantly below his eight colleagues' combined rate.

Table 5.9 presents the results for the second natural Court. The differences between justices are quite dramatic. Minton provided the fourth vote to grant in four of 151 opportunities, while Black provided it in 50 of 101 opportunities, i.e., Black was twelve times as likely as was Minton to provide the fourth vote. Under the first definition, all the justices except Black and Douglas were grant-averse: each cast more votes to deny than to grant when their vote determined the outcome. For Black and Douglas the numbers to grant are almost the same as the numbers to deny. Under the second definition, Minton and Vinson were grant-averse, Black and Douglas were grant-prone, and the other five justices have results that are not statistically significant.

XII. Solo Votes

Table 5.10 presents the results for solo dissents in cert votes during the first natural Court. Each justice cast more solo votes for granting than for denying. The range of solo votes to deny is relatively small (from none by Murphy to five by Jackson). The range for solo votes to grant, however, is quite dramatic (from five by Vinson to 49 by Murphy).

Table 5.11 presents the results for the second Court. Minton and Clark cast more solo votes to deny than they did to grant. The other seven justices cast more solo votes to grant than to deny. The numbers of solo votes to grant cast by Douglas, 93, and Black, 104, are startling. The next closest number of solo grant votes, Reed's 39, is only a third of Black's and less than half of Douglas'. The most surprising finding is that the number of Black's solo grant votes, 104, almost equals *all* of Minton's grant votes, 106, in nonunanimous cases (table 5.2).

XIII. Conclusions

Voting on cert petitions was related to membership in the liberal or conservative blocs in four ways. First, the individual grant rates of the liberals—Rutledge, Murphy, Douglas, and Black—exceed those of the conservatives—Burton, Jackson, Frankfurter, Reed, Vinson, and later Clark and Minton. Second, agreement rates for pairings of justices are greater within

Table 5.9

Cert votes that determined the outcome — Second Natural Court. At least seven justices voting.

	Grant Votes	Votes	Grant Rate	t-value
Minton	4	151	3	-13.18*
Clark	30	148	20	-1.37
Burton	28	143	20	-1.34
Jackson	30	148	20	-1.37
Douglas	51	105	50	5.43*
Frankfurter	33	127	27	0.60
Reed	39	125	29	1.19
Black	50	101	50	5.52*
Vinson	27	148	18	-2.08*

* statistically significant at 5 percent level.

the conservative than within the liberal bloc. Third, the agreement-to-grant rate is highest among pairings of the liberals. Fourth, the agreement-to-grant rates for pairings of a liberal and a conservative are about the same as these rates for pairings of two conservatives.

A model of cert voting generates two hypotheses which are tested using logit regressions. The first hypothesis, that there is a positive relationship between voting to grant cert and subsequently voting to reverse, is supported by the aggregate data and by the individual data for all eleven justices. The second hypothesis, that there is a positive relationship between voting to grant cert and subsequently assenting on-the-merits, is supported by the aggregate data and by individual data for four of the individual justices.

The analysis of votes in which the justice could not control the outcome shows that Burton and Clark were conforming during the second natural Court; all the other justices were grant-prone, grant-averse, or cannot be categorized.

The analysis of votes in which the justice determined the outcome shows wide variations in grant rates, e.g., Black was twelve times as likely as Minton

Table 5.10

Solo cert dissents — First Natural Court. At least seven justices voting.

	Grant Votes	Deny Votes
Burton	13	3
Rutledge	20	4
Jackson	6	5
Murphy	49	0
Douglas	37	4
Frankfurter	8	4
Reed	11	3
Black	29	3
Vinson	5	1

Table 5.11

Solo cert dissents — Second Natural Court. At least seven justices voting.

	Grant Votes	Deny Votes
Minton	1	9
Clark	0	1
Burton	17	3
Jackson	12	4
Douglas	93	8
Frankfurter	22	9
Reed	39	5
Black	104	20
Vinson	11	3

to provide the fourth vote to grant cert. In general, justices who were grant averse (prone) when they could not determine the outcome were also grant averse (prone) when their vote did determine whether cert was granted.

Solo dissents at the cert vote show startling differences. For example, during the second natural Court, Black cast 120 solo cert votes while Minton cast only ten. Like Black, Douglas also cast large numbers of solo dissents, usually when the Court denied cert.

6

Case Selection Via Appeals

I. Introduction

This chapter examines jurisdiction votes using the same theoretical and empirical analyses that were used to examine cert votes in the preceding chapter. In order to facilitate comparisons between certs and appeals, the eleven tables presented in chapter 5 are replicated in this chapter using comparable data for jurisdiction votes. Section II addresses the differences and similarities between appeals and certs. The note rates of individual justices are examined in section III. The model developed (in chapter 5) to analyze cert votes is applied, in section IV, to jurisdiction votes. Section V analyzes agreement on jurisdiction votes. The data are divided between votes in which the justice could not control the outcome (section VI) and those in which his vote determined whether jurisdiction was noted (section VII). Solo jurisdiction dissents are examined in section VIII. Section IX contains the conclusions.

Appeals involved cases within the Court's obligatory jurisdiction. The party taking the appeal, the appellant, had a statutory right to review. This right, however, was substantially limited because the Court dismissed or summarily affirmed most appeals without a plenary hearing.

The Court elected to hear an appeal either by noting probable jurisdiction or by postponing further consideration of jurisdiction until the decision on-the-merits. The former disposition was by far the most common; only occasionally did the Court postpone the decision. For examples of cases in which the jurisdiction decision was postponed, see 48,416A and 49,24A. During the conference vote on jurisdiction, justices favoring plenary review could either vote to note or to postpone the decision on jurisdiction. If the votes to note plus the votes to postpone totaled four or more, then review was granted. For an example, see *U.S. v. Carroll* (52,442A) which had three votes to note and two votes to postpone.

When jurisdiction was noted, the Court retained the option of dismissing the case at a later time. Because there was very little difference between a vote to note and a vote to postpone, the two categories are combined and hereafter referred to as votes to note.

When the Court denied review, it either summarily affirmed the lower court or dismissed the writ of appeal "for lack of a substantial question" or "for want of jurisdiction." Appeals that were summarily affirmed had a greater precedential value than those that were dismissed. The difference, however, was apparently small because justices sometimes equivocated between the two during the conference. In much of the following analysis, votes to dismiss and votes to affirm summarily are combined into one category.

II. Differences and Similarities Between Appeals and Cert

There were important similarities and differences between certs and appeals. The differences had diminished before Vinson's chief justiceship and continued to narrow during and after his tenure because the pressures of a growing case load forced the Court to treat appeals, which were part of its obligatory jurisdiction, in a manner similar to how it treated certs, which were part of its discretionary jurisdiction.

The similarities between cert and appeal include the following. Both required four votes to grant plenary review; this "rule of four" separated certs and appeals from all other writs which were issued only by a majority vote. And, like certs, most appeals were not granted review; if review was granted, both types of cases received similar processing.

The differences include the following. When cert was denied, the precedential value of the Court's action was unclear but quite limited (Stern and Gressman 1950, pp. 132-135). But a vote on jurisdiction had elements of a vote on-the-merits because a dismissal or summary affirmation was an official decision on-the-merits. The precedential value of the decision was uncertain and limited but it unquestionably exceeded that of a cert denial (Stern and Gressman 1978, pp. 327-338). Another difference is that there were numerous IFP cert requests on the miscellaneous docket, but there were no appeals that were IFP nor were there appeals on the miscellaneous docket. In addition, certs were more numerous than appeals: the dataset contains 2,065 cert petitions and 378 appeals. The note rate for appeals in the dataset, 53 percent, is substantially above the grant rate for certs, 36 percent. (The differences between the number of certs and appeals and between the grant rate and the note rate would increase if the dataset included cases that were unanimously denied review because certs were more likely to be unanimously rejected.)

Some cases could be brought to the Court by either cert or appeal. In this event, an appeal was the preferred method because it invoked the Court's obligatory jurisdiction and was more likely to be accepted for plenary review (Stern and Gressman 1978, p. 168). If a case was incorrectly taken as an appeal, the Court could handle it as a petition for cert (28 U.S.C. Section 2103). The dataset contains twelve cases which were treated as both appeals and certs. For example, in *Oklahoma Tax Commission v. Texas Company* (48,40A), which was taken as an appeal, the Court simultaneously dismissed the appeal and granted cert.

III. Note Rates of Individual Justices

Table 6.1 presents the numbers of votes to affirm, to dismiss, to note, and the note rate for the first natural Court. The t-value indicates whether there is a statistically significant difference between the note rate of an individual justice and the combined note rate of his eight brethren.

For each justice, there are two numbers in each column. The top number is for nonunanimous votes. The bottom number contains three categories: cases noted nonunanimously, cases noted unanimously, and cases in which some of the justices voted to affirm summarily while the remainder voted to dismiss. This last category is hereafter treated as appeals that were unanimously denied review. (Appeals that were unanimously dismissed are not included in the dataset.) Except for section IV (table 6.3), the following discussion focuses only on nonunanimous votes.

Three liberal justices—Rutledge, Murphy, and Douglas—have the largest note rates—54, 53, and 72 percent. Three conservative justices—Burton, Frankfurter, and Vinson—have the lowest rates—34, 32, and 29 percent. These results are consistent with those of table 5.1 in the preceding chapter which show that liberals have higher grant rates in cert votes. The conservative-liberal dichotomy, however, lacks an exact correspondence with relative·

Table 6.1

Jurisdiction votes—First Natural Court.

Nonunanimous (top) and nonunanimous plus unanimous notes (bottom). At least seven justices voting.

	Affirm	Dismiss	Note	Note Rate	t-value
Burton	17	35	27	34	-1.78
	25	41	69	51	-1.35
Rutledge	17	19	42	54	2.01*
	25	25	84	63	1.55
Jackson	17	28	31	41	-0.45
	23	34	71	55	-0.27
Murphy	20	15	39	53	1.74
	28	20	80	63	1.46
Douglas	6	15	53	72	5.69*
	15	18	91	73	4.41*
Frankfurter	23	31	25	32	-2.32*
	31	36	67	50	-1.62
Reed	15	31	33	42	-0.27
	24	36	75	56	-0.25
Black	19	32	28	35	-1.52
	24	40	70	52	-1.07
Vinson	24	32	23	29	-2.89*
	33	37	64	48	-2.17*

* statistically significant at 5 percent level.

note rates. Black, a liberal, has a note rate of 35 percent, which is less than those of the conservatives Jackson (41 percent) and Reed (42 percent).

The results of tables 5.1 and 6.1 also show that—except for Murphy and Black—justices have note rates that are larger than their grant rates. This explains why the Court's note rate for appeals exceeds its grant rate for certs.

Table 6.2 presents the results for the second natural Court. The two liberals, Douglas and Black, have the highest note rates, 75 and 60 percent. Douglas' rate is more than four times as large as Minton's, 17 percent. These results are similar to those of table 5.2 which show that Douglas and Black have the highest cert grant rates in the second Court and that their grant rates are five times as large as Minton's. For all nine justices, the note rates in table 6.2 exceed the grant rates in table 5.2, which again explains why the Court's note rate exceeds its grant rate.

IV. Model of Case Selection

The model developed in chapter 5 to analyze cert votes can be applied, after some modifications, to jurisdiction votes. The only difference is that the effect of denying cert was much smaller than the effect of refusing to note jurisdiction. The model generated two hypotheses which are tested in chapter 5: first, that there is a positive relationship between having voted to grant review and later voting to reverse on-the-merits; second, that there is a positive relationship between having voted to grant review and later assenting on-the-merits.

Let $d(i)$ represent the value of a change in the law if the Court denied review. $ER(i)$ represents the value of a change if it reversed on-the-merits. And $EA(i)$ represents the value if it affirmed on-the-merits. Granting review had a positive expected return if $pa(i)EA(i)-d(i) + pr(i)ER(i) > 0$. The expected return divided by the amount of time needed to process the case, $t(i)$, gave the weighted expected return which was used to rank requests for review.

In chapter 5, $d(i)$ represents the effect of cert denial. The signs of $d(i)$ and $EA(i)$ are the same but the absolute size of $EA(i)$ exceeds the absolute size of $d(i)$, i.e., denial of review changed the law in the same direction but by a smaller magnitude than affirming on-the-merits. In this chapter, the absolute magnitude of $d(i)$ increases because the effect of not accepting a case for review was greater for appeals than for certs. This change in the size of $d(i)$ impacts both hypotheses.

The first hypothesis—that there is a positive relationship between voting to grant review and voting to reverse on-the-merits—is affected in the

Table 6.2

Jurisdiction votes — Second Natural Court.

Nonunanimous (top) and nonunanimous plus unanimous notes (bottom). At least seven justices voting.

	Affirm	Dismiss	Note	Note Rate	t-value
Minton	56	60	24	17	-9.28*
	78	63	69	33	-6.20*
Clark	43	50	43	32	-3.83*
	64	53	84	42	-3.09*
Burton	44	35	72	48	0.39
	67	38	119	53	0.37
Jackson	40	38	70	47	0.29
	60	42	115	53	0.32
Douglas	15	21	109	75	8.42*
	29	28	146	72	6.60*
Frankfurter	51	40	60	40	-1.72
	74	43	107	48	-1.34
Reed	34	37	80	53	1.78
	58	39	126	57	1.45
Black	29	31	90	60	3.66*
	48	37	137	62	3.16*
Vinson	42	46	63	42	-1.18
	66	48	109	49	-0.98

* statistically significant at 5 percent level.

following manner: if a justice wished to reverse, then $d(i)$ was negative and an increase in the absolute value of $d(i)$ increased the expected return from granting review. Thus, a justice who disagreed with the lower court's decision would be more likely, *ceteris paribus*, to grant review with appeals than with certs because the certain loss, $d(i)$, that resulted when review was denied was greater with appeals.

If a justice wanted to affirm, then $d(i)$ was positive and an increase in $d(i)$ decreased the expected return from noting probable jurisdiction. Thus, a justice who agreed with the lower court's decision would be less likely, *ceteris paribus*, to grant review with appeals than with certs because the certain gain, $d(i)$, was greater with appeals.

In either event, the greater relative magnitude of $d(i)$ implies that the first hypothesis should apply with appeals. In fact, the relationship between voting for review and voting to reverse on-the-merits should be stronger with appeals than with certs.

It is unclear what effect an increase in the absolute size of $d(i)$ has on the second hypothesis—that there is a positive relationship between voting to grant review and later assenting on-the-merits. If a justice expected to assent on-the-merits and wanted to affirm, then there was less gained, *ceteris paribus*, from noting jurisdiction than from granting cert. But if a justice expected to assent on-the-merits and wanted to reverse, then there was more gained, *ceteris paribus*, from noting jurisdiction than from granting cert. A similar dichotomy exists for cases in which a justice expected to dissent on-the-merits. If he wanted to reverse and expected to dissent, then the expected return from noting jurisdiction in a case taken as an appeal exceeded the expected return of an identical case filed as a cert. The opposite was true if he wanted to affirm and expected to dissent. Thus, it is uncertain how applying the model to appeals rather than to certs affects the second hypothesis.

The two hypotheses regarding the relationships between voting to note and assenting at the conference vote on-the-merits and voting to reverse at the conference vote on-the-merits can be tested using a maximum likelihood logistic model. The specification estimates the relationship between a binary dependent variable, NOTE (which is one if the justice voted to note jurisdiction and zero if he voted to dismiss or summarily affirm); the percentage of his colleagues that voted with the justice at the conference vote on-the-merits, %MERIT; and a binary variable, REVERSE (which is one if the justice voted to reverse at the conference vote on-the-merits and zero if he voted to affirm).

Table 6.3 contains the results of the logit analysis. Instead of regression coefficients, the estimated partial derivatives obtained from the regression

Table 6.3

Logit analysis of the determinants of the probability of voting to note jurisdiction. First natural Court. Includes unanimous votes.

Justice	Sample Size	Log of Liklhood	Votes to NOTE	CONSTANT	%MERIT	REVERSE
ALL	1388	-638.19	1108	0.165	-0.056	0.251
				(5.17)*	(1.38)*	(10.35)*
Minton	94	-55.17	55	0.151	-0.309	0.504
				(0.76)	(1.16)	(3.78)*
Clark	83	-37.78	66	0.007	0.127	0.279
				(0.04)	(0.51)	(2.80)*
Burton	172	-82.08	137	0.033	0.180	0.168
				(0.39)	(1.61)	(2.49)*
Rutledge	61	-23.50	52	0.278	-0.159	0.172
				(1.86)	(0.91)	(1.75)*
Jackson	155	-56.14	134	0.197	-0.072	0.193
				(2.63)*	(0.75)	(2.88)*
Murphy	51	-18.86	42	0.526	-0.563	0.324
				(2.17)*	(1.88)	(2.43)*
Douglas	127	-30.66	118	0.219	-0.104	0.056
				(3.06)*	(1.26)	(1.19)
Frankfurter	158	-81.03	119	0.259	-0.218	0.254
				(2.61)*	(1.72)	(3.34)*
Reed	171	-69.80	145	0.112	0.078	0.135
				(1.39)	(0.75)	(2.32)*
Black	165	-76.11	124	0.072	-0.027	0.448
				(0.84)	(0.24)	(5.17)*
Vinson	151	-72.35	116	0.039	0.050	0.320
				(0.28)	(0.31)	(4.10)*

*statistically significant at 5 percent level using one-tailed test.

coefficients are presented because they are much easier to interpret (Landes 1974, p. 305). The absolute value of the t-values are in parentheses beneath the partial derivatives. The data contains cases with unanimous votes on jurisdiction and/or unanimous votes on-the-merits. The first regression shows the results obtained from pooling the data for all eleven justices. The next eleven regressions present the results for individual justices.

With the pooled data, the result for REVERSE is statistically significant. The estimated partial derivative, .251, indicates that the probability of a justice having voted to note jurisdiction increases by approximately .251 if he later voted to reverse at the conference vote on-the-merits.

The results for the individual justices show that, for ten of the eleven justices, REVERSE is positive and statistically significant. Douglas has the only result that is not significant. Minton has the strongest estimated relationship: the probability that he voted to note increases by approximately .504 if he subsequently voted to reverse. Reed has the smallest statistically significant relationship, .135.

The estimated partial derivatives for REVERSE are not consistently larger than the comparable estimates for cert votes presented in table 5.3. Thus, the prediction that the relationship between voting for review and voting to reverse on-the-merits is stronger for appeals than for certs is not supported by the empirical results.

The estimated partial for %MERIT, with the pooled data, -.056, has the wrong sign and is not statistically significant. Similarly, the estimated relationship between NOTE and %MERIT is not statistically significant in the results for each of the eleven justices and has the wrong sign for seven. Apparently, there was not a positive relationship between voting to note and the proportion of his brethren that a justice joined at the conference vote on-the-merits.

The signs and statistical significance of the estimated partial derivatives for %MERIT are different from the comparable cert votes presented in table 5.3. With certs, %MERIT is positive and significant with the pooled data and with four of the individual justices. For at least some of the justices, therefore, the probability of assenting on-the-merits had an effect on cert votes which was different from its effect on appeals.

The differences in the results for cert (table 5.3) and jurisdiction (table 6.3) show that the individual justices used criteria for jurisdiction votes that were different from the criteria for cert votes. The differences also indicate that the model developed in chapter 5 fails to provide an adequate explanation of jurisdiction votes.

V. Agreement on Jurisdiction Votes

Tables 6.4 and 6.5 present the agreement rates in nonunanimous jurisdiction votes for each pairing in the first and second natural Courts. The top number is the agreement rate on the jurisdiction vote, i.e., the percentage of votes in which they voted together for or against review. The bottom number is the agreement-to-note rate, i.e., the percentage of votes in which both voted to note. The percentage of votes in which both voted *not* to note is not shown but can be computed by subtracting the bottom number from the top. The percentage of votes in which the pairing disagreed is also not shown but can be computed by subtracting the top number from 100.

In this analysis, votes to dismiss and votes to affirm summarily are combined in one category. Placing them in separate categories would have two effects. First, the number of nonunanimous votes would increase because cases in which part of the Court voted to dismiss while the remainder voted to affirm are now treated as unanimous and are excluded from the analysis of this section. Second, agreement rates would change, because instances in which one justice voted to affirm while another voted to dismiss would be treated as a disagreement rather than as an agreement.

Table 6.4 shows that, during the first natural Court, Burton and Jackson voted together on 67 percent of the jurisdiction decisions and voted together to note 20 percent. Thus, they agreed not to note 47 percent (67 minus 20) and disagreed on 33 percent (100 minus 67).

Their agreement-to-note rate of 20 percent must be interpreted juxtaposed to their individual note rates on nonunanimous jurisdiction decisions. These individual note rates are shown in table 6.1—34 percent for Burton and 41 percent for Jackson. Because Jackson voted to note 41 percent of the appeals and agreed with Burton to note 20 percent, it follows that Burton voted with Jackson in about one-half the instances in which Jackson voted to note.

Table 6.4 shows variations in the levels of agreement which are less than the comparable results for cert votes presented in table 5.4. The level of agreement on jurisdiction varies from 85 percent for the Burton-Vinson pairing to 45 percent for the Burton-Murphy pairing. The liberal-conservative dichotomy is muted with jurisdiction votes—especially for pairings containing Black, who is generally regarded as the liberals' leader. For example, the Douglas-Reed pairing has greater agreement than the Douglas-Black pairing. The other three liberals, Rutledge, Murphy, and Douglas, display strong relationships—the agreement-to-note rates for the three pairings range between 37 and 40 percent and are the highest for the first Court.

Table 6.4

Nonunanimous Jurisdiction Votes — First Natural Court.

Percentage of votes in which justices agreed (top) and percentage of votes in which justices agreed to note (bottom). At least seven justices voting.

	Rutldg	Jacksn	Murphy	Dougls	Frnkfr	Reed	Black	Vinson
Burton	58	67	45	54	67	65	61	85
	23	20	16	30	16	20	15	24
Rutldg		65	66	55	68	60	60	60
		29	37	40	27	28	24	22
Jacksn			55	56	72	72	54	67
			25	34	21	26	14	17
Murphy				51	54	51	51	53
				39	20	24	20	18
Dougls					47	58	49	51
					24	35	28	27
Frnkfr						67	61	70
						20	14	15
Reed							58	72
							18	22
Black								61
								13

Table 6.5

Nonunanimous Jurisdiction Votes—Second Natural Court.

Percentage of votes in which justices agreed (top) and percentage of votes in which justices agreed to note (bottom). At least seven justices voting.

	Clark	Burton	Jacksn	Dougls	Frnkfr	Reed	Black	Vinson
Minton	82	63	66	38	69	60	41	73
	15	14	16	15	14	15	8	16
Clark		73	73	46	70	71	45	76
		26	25	27	20	27	18	23
Burton			70	48	55	60	47	69
			33	35	21	30	27	29
Jacksn				52	79	69	38	77
				37	33	34	23	33
Dougls					53	53	52	56
					33	40	44	36
Frnkfr						61	42	71
						27	21	26
Reed							47	68
							30	31
Black								45
								23

Table 6.5 presents the results for the second natural Court. The conservative bloc—which now included Clark and Minton—has generally high agreement rates, with pairings containing the chief justice having the highest. Vinson has agreement rates of 68 percent or more with everyone except the two remaining liberals, Black and Douglas. The two liberals have the highest agreement-to-note rate for the second Court, 44 percent, but their overall agreement rate is almost identical to the Douglas-Jackson, Douglas-Reed, and Douglas-Frankfurter pairings.

VI. Conformity on Jurisdiction Votes

If four others voted to note jurisdiction or six others voted to dismiss or to affirm summarily, then an individual justice's vote could not change the result. This section analyzes a subset of the data containing votes in which a justice could not determine the outcome and therefore might have elected to conform to the Court's action.

Table 6.6, which contains the results for the first Court, is divided into two sections: the top section contains the cases in which jurisdiction was noted, and the bottom contains those in which it was not. The table shows the number of votes to note, the number of votes, the note rate, and the t-statistic used to test whether the note rate of a justice is statistically different from the combined rate of his eight colleagues when they voted in similar situations.

In order to categorize a justice, both of his t-values must be statistically significant. Douglas can be categorized as note-prone, because both when jurisdiction was and was not noted, his note rates are higher than those of his brethren in similar votes. Douglas was also grant-prone in comparable cert votes (table 5.6). The other eight justices cannot be categorized.

Table 6.7 presents the results for the second Court. Jackson was conforming: his note rate was 78 when the Court noted and 16 percent when it dismissed or summarily affirmed. Minton was note-averse while Douglas was again note-prone. These findings can be contrasted to comparable cert votes in table 5.7 which show that Minton was grant-averse, Douglas was grant-prone, and Jackson could not be categorized. Thus, only Douglas and Minton—the two polar extremes in granting review—can be consistently categorized using both cert and jurisdiction votes.

The results in section IV show that Douglas was the only justice without a significant and positive relationship between NOTE and REVERSE, while Minton had the strongest relationship. When combined with the findings in

Table 6.6

Jurisdiction votes that could not determine the outcome in nonunanimous decisions—First Natural Court. At least seven justices voting.

JURISDICTION WAS NOTED BY THE COURT

	Note Votes	Votes	Note Rate	t-value
Burton	19	35	54	-1.12
Rutledge	24	31	77	1.99*
Jackson	19	26	73	1.20
Murphy	19	32	59	-0.45
Douglas	26	29	90	4.60*
Frankfurter	18	33	55	-1.05
Reed	21	30	70	0.87
Black	16	35	46	-2.21*
Vinson	19	36	53	-1.33

JURISDICTION WAS NOT NOTED BY THE COURT

	Note Votes	Votes	Note Rate	t-value
Burton	6	33	18	-1.31
Rutledge	12	35	34	1.02
Jackson	4	31	13	-2.32*
Murphy	15	32	47	2.46*
Douglas	22	36	61	4.60*
Frankfurter	3	31	10	-3.17*
Reed	5	33	15	-1.90
Black	10	37	27	0.05
Vinson	3	32	9	-3.31*

* statistically significant at 5 percent level.

Table 6.7

Jurisdiction votes that could not determine the outcome in nonunanimous decisions—Second Natural Court. At least seven justices voting.

JURISDICTION WAS NOTED BY THE COURT

	Note Votes	Votes	Note Rate	t-value
Minton	24	72	33	-6.30*
Clark	38	60	63	-0.46
Burton	48	69	70	0.67
Jackson	54	69	78	2.56*
Douglas	54	64	84	4.10*
Frankfurter	44	71	62	-0.76
Reed	53	69	77	2.21*
Black	38	67	57	-1.65
Vinson	52	72	72	1.23

JURISDICTION WAS NOT NOTED BY THE COURT

	Note Votes	Votes	Note Rate	t-value
Minton	0	49	0	-14.49*
Clark	0	50	0	-14.49*
Burton	15	61	25	-0.58
Jackson	9	57	16	-2.52*
Douglas	44	65	68	7.48*
Frankfurter	10	59	17	-2.26*
Reed	19	60	32	0.72
Black	43	69	62	6.49*
Vinson	6	59	10	-4.39*

* statistically significant at 5 percent level.

Table 6.8

Jurisdiction votes that determined the outcome — First Natural Court. At least seven justices voting.

	Note Votes	Votes	Note Rate	t-value
Burton	2	11	18	-1.60
Rutledge	6	12	50	1.01
Jackson	8	19	42	0.56
Murphy	5	10	50	0.91
Douglas	5	9	56	1.21
Frankfurter	4	15	27	-0.90
Reed	7	16	44	0.65
Black	2	7	29	-0.47
Vinson	1	11	9	-3.04*

* statistically significant at 5 percent level.

this section, these results indicate the following: Minton was reluctant to note and typically favored granting review only when he disagreed with the lower court's decision; Douglas, on the other hand, was willing to note and was generally unconcerned with whether the lower court was wrong. These differences resulted from their dissimilar perceptions of the Court's functions which are discussed by Provine (1980, chapter 4).

VII. Cases in Which the Justice's Vote Determined the Outcome

This section analyzes votes that determined the outcome: specifically, a vote to note when there were four to note or a vote to dismiss or summarily affirm when there were only three to note. In these situations, the justice could have altered the outcome by changing his vote.

Table 6.8 presents the results for the first Court. For each justice the table shows the number of votes to note, the number of votes, the note rate, and the t-statistic used to test whether the justice's note rate is statistically different from the other eight justices' combined note rates in those jurisdiction votes in which they determined the outcome.

The results for the liberal bloc display no consistent pattern. When Douglas had the opportunity to cast the fourth vote to note jurisdiction, he was more likely to note, five times, than not, four times. Murphy and Rutledge both noted in one-half of their opportunities. The other member of the liberal bloc, Black, noted in only two of seven.

All the members of the conservative bloc have note rates that are less than 50 percent. Differences within the conservative bloc are quite substantial, ranging from 44 percent for Reed to nine percent for the chief justice.

These results are similar to comparable findings on cert votes presented in table 5.8. Rutledge, Douglas, and Murphy have the highest grant rates, while Black's grant rate is the lowest in the liberal bloc. The conservatives have lower rates, with Vinson's the lowest.

Table 6.9 presents the results for the second Court. The differences among justices are quite dramatic. Minton voted against review in each of the 19 opportunities in which his vote determined the outcome. In contrast, Douglas voted to note in eleven of 16 opportunities, and Black voted to note in nine of 14

The findings in table 6.9 are quite similar to those in table 5.9. Douglas and Black have grant rates that are substantially above their colleagues' rates while Minton's is substantially below. When given an opportunity to determine whether cert would be granted, all the members of the conservative bloc were more likely to vote to deny.

━━━━━━━━━━

VIII. Solo Votes

Table 6.10 presents the results for solo dissents in jurisdiction votes during the first natural Court. There were relatively few solo dissents. Douglas cast the most, seven, while Vinson cast none. Except for Douglas, there is little difference between the number of solo votes to note and the number to dismiss or to affirm. These results are different from those of table 5.10 which show that, at the cert vote, most solo dissents were votes to grant.

Table 6.11 presents the results for the second natural Court. The numbers of solo votes cast by Douglas (twelve) and Black (17) are substantially above the numbers cast by Clark (one), Jackson (none), and Vinson (one). Again, except for Douglas, there is little difference between the number of solo votes to note and the number to dismiss or to affirm.

Comparing the results in table 6.11 to solo cert dissents during the second Court (table 5.11) shows the following regarding Black's and Douglas' solo votes. First, Douglas and Black have far more solo cert and jurisdiction dissents than do any of their colleagues. In fact, together they cast more than half of all solo dissents. Second, most of Douglas' solo dissents are votes in favor of granting review, i.e., votes to grant cert or to note jurisdiction. Third, for Black, solo dissents at jurisdiction are almost equally divided between votes to note (eight) and votes to dismiss or to affirm summarily (nine), but his solo dissents at cert (table 5.11) are mostly votes to grant (93) rather than votes to deny (eight).

Together, tables 6.10 and 6.11 contain 71 solo jurisdiction dissents. Solo dissents occurred in about 19 percent of the 378 jurisdiction votes in the dataset. By contrast, the 566 solo cert dissents (tables 5.10 and 5.11) represent 28 percent of the 2,065 cert votes. Therefore, solo dissents were proportionally more common in cert votes than they were in jurisdiction votes. (These percentages of cases involving solo dissents are larger than they would be if the dataset did not exclude cases that were unanimously rejected.)

Table 6.9

Jurisdiction votes that determined the outcome — Second Natural Court. At least seven justices voting.

	Note Votes	Votes	Note Rate	t-value
Minton	0	19	0	-9.76*
Clark	5	26	19	-1.88
Burton	9	21	43	0.96
Jackson	7	22	32	-0.14
Douglas	11	16	69	3.22*
Frankfurter	6	21	29	-0.49
Reed	8	22	36	0.34
Black	9	14	64	2.54*
Vinson	5	20	25	-0.88

* statistically significant at 5 percent level.

Table 6.10

Solo jurisdiction dissents — First Natural Court. At least seven justices voting.

	Note	Dismiss or Affirm
Burton	1	0
Rutledge	1	0
Jackson	1	0
Murphy	3	3
Douglas	7	0
Frankfurter	1	1
Reed	0	2
Black	2	4
Vinson	0	0

Table 6.11

Solo jurisdiction dissents — Second Natural Court. At least seven justices voting.

	Note	Dismiss or Affirm
Minton	0	3
Clark	0	1
Burton	1	3
Jackson	0	0
Douglas	10	2
Frankfurter	0	3
Reed	4	0
Black	8	9
Vinson	0	1

IX. Conclusions

This chapter contrasts jurisdiction votes with the more numerous cert votes discussed in the preceding chapter. The findings can be summarized as follows.

Voting on jurisdiction was related to membership in the liberal or conservative blocs, but the relationship is weaker than the comparable relationship for cert votes.

A justice's jurisdiction note rate is usually higher than his cert grant rate. As a result, the proportion of appeals accepted for review by the Court is larger than the proportion of certs granted review.

There is a positive and statistically significant relationship between voting to note jurisdiction and later voting to reverse at the conference vote on-the-merits. There is not, however, a positive relationship between voting to note and the proportion of his brethren that a justice joined at the conference vote. Thus, the model developed in chapter 5 fails to provide an adequate explanation of jurisdiction votes.

The agreement-to-note rates for pairings of justices are related to bloc membership. Inter-bloc variations, however, are smaller for jurisdiction votes than for cert votes.

The analysis of votes in which a justice could not control the outcome results in the categorization of only three justices. Douglas was note-prone, Minton was note-averse, and Jackson was conforming during the second Court. Douglas' and Minton's behavior on these jurisdiction votes was quite similar to their behavior in comparable cert votes.

Voting patterns in cases in which a justice determined the outcome show wide variations among justices. For example, during the second Court, Minton voted to note in none of the 19 cases where he controlled the outcome, while Douglas voted to note in eleven of 16 cases. The conservatives have note rates that are less than 50 percent, while the liberals generally have rates that equal or exceed 50 percent. These findings are similar to those for comparable cert votes.

The proportion of solo dissents was lower for jurisdiction votes than it was for cert votes, though the patterns of solo dissents are similar. Black and Douglas were responsible for most solo dissents.

7

Votes On-The-Merits.

I. Introduction

This chapter analyzes conference votes on-the-merits, report votes on-the-merits, and changes that occurred between the two. Other studies of conference and report votes are discussed in section II. Sections III and IV examine reverse rates for individual justices and agreement rates for pairings of justices at the conference and report votes on-the-merits. Changes in the Court's disposition that took place between the conference and report votes on-the-merits are analyzed in section V. Changes by individual justices are examined in sections VI through VIII. Section IX contains the conclusions.

In the following analyses, cases are excluded if they were moot or if fewer than seven justices participated. Some of the tables include information on both nonunanimous decisions and all decisions, but (except when noted) the following discussions focus only on the nonunanimous votes.

II. Other Empirical Studies

Until recently, conference votes on-the-merits have been available only in the justices' private papers, and thus have received relatively little attention from scholars. Significant studies include Berry's (1978) analysis of selected conference and final votes, based on Burton's papers, and Fine's (1984) biography of Murphy, based on several justices' papers.

Because they are readily available in *U.S. Reports*, there are numerous studies of final votes on-the-merits. Some deal with a specific case, while others are empirical analyses of larger categories of cases. Four extensive empirical studies merit a brief mention. Pritchett (1954) employs a bloc analysis of the Vinson Court's final votes in civil liberties cases. Sprague (1968) uses a similar method in his examination of federalism votes between 1887 and 1959. Schubert (1965 and 1974) develops elaborate cumulative scales for various categories of cases, e.g., economic liberalism, political liberalism, and federalism. According to Schubert's political scaling for the first natural Court, Murphy and Rutledge were extreme liberals; Douglas and Black were liberals; Jackson and Frankfurter were moderate conservatives; and Burton, Reed, and Vinson were extreme conservatives (Schubert 1965, pp. 103-113). Spaeth utilizes cumulative scaling to develop descriptions of the justices' value systems which he uses to predict subsequent decisions of the Court. For explanations and examples of Spaeth's predictions, see Rhode and Spaeth (1976, chapter 7) and Spaeth (1979, chapter 5).

Because studies of switches made between the conference and report votes on-the-merits require access to conference votes, there are relatively few analyses of vote changes. Murphy (1964) presents a detailed analysis of how justices can induce their colleagues to change positions after the conference vote. As mentioned above, Berry (1978) and Fine (1984) also examine switches between the conference and final votes in selected cases. Howard's (1968) analysis of Murphy's conference notes is the first study to focus specifically on changes between the conference and final votes. Howard refers to these changes as "fluidity." Brenner (1980) presents empirical analyses of fluidity for selected years of the Vinson and Warren Courts using Burton's docket books as a source for conference votes. He distinguishes "strong" or complete changes from "weak" or partial ones and finds that strong fluidity occurred in nine percent and weak fluidity in three percent of the individual justices' votes. Most changes resulted because justices left the minority and joined the majority. The individual justices' strong and weak fluidity caused the Court's decision to change in 14 percent of the cases examined by Brenner.

III. Votes On-The-Merits—First Natural Court

Table 7.1 presents the number of votes to affirm (or dismiss), the number to reverse (or vacate), and the reverse rate at the conference vote on-the-merits for individual justices during the first Court. For each justice there are two numbers in each column. The top number is for nonunanimous decisions, and the bottom is for all decisions. The t-values indicate whether

Table 7.1

Conference Votes On-The-Merits in nonunanimous (top) and unanimous votes (bottom) — First Natural Court. At least seven justices voting.

	Affirm	Reverse	Reverse Rate	t-value
Burton	199	119	37	-5.67*
	222	172	44	-4.94*
Rutledge	104	203	66	5.54*
	127	254	67	4.98*
Jackson	167	131	44	-2.94*
	188	179	49	-2.63*
Murphy	99	200	67	5.78*
	117	248	68	5.46*
Douglas	104	185	64	4.50*
	127	234	65	4.01*
Frankfurter	164	131	44	-2.75*
	188	179	49	-2.63*
Reed	174	142	45	-2.66*
	197	194	50	-2.37*
Black	127	177	58	2.35*
	148	228	61	2.26*
Vinson	177	133	43	-3.41*
	202	184	48	-3.17*

*statistically significant at 5 percent level.

there is a statistically significant difference between the reverse rate of an individual justice and the combined reverse rate of his eight colleagues.

There is considerable variation in the reverse rates, and each justice's rate is significantly different from his brethren's combined rate. Murphy's rate, 67 percent, is almost double Burton's, 37 percent. The liberals, Rutledge, Murphy, Douglas, and Black, all have reverse rates exceeding 50 percent, while the five conservatives all have rates below 50 percent. Thus, the liberals were reverse-prone while the conservatives were affirm-prone. Within the conservative bloc, there is little variation—Jackson, Frankfurter, Reed, and Vinson all have rates between 43 and 45 percent. The one exception, Burton, has the lowest rate, 37 percent.

The levels of agreement within justice pairings for nonunanimous conference votes on-the-merits are presented in table 7.2. For each pairing, the top number shows the overall agreement rate and the bottom shows the agreement-to-reverse rate. The difference between the two, the agreement-to-affirm rate, is not shown.

Within the liberal bloc, the agreement rates range from 69 percent for the Douglas-Black pairing to 78 percent for the Rutledge-Black pairing. Because the liberals were reverse-prone, their agreement-to-reverse rates are also relatively high—ranging from 46 percent for Douglas-Black to 54 percent for Rutledge-Murphy. By contrast, the pairing between the conservative Jackson and the liberal Black shows an agreement rate of 32 percent and an agreement-to-reverse rate of 18 percent.

Within the conservative bloc, the agreement rates range from 76 percent for Reed-Vinson to 57 percent for Jackson-Reed. Because the conservatives were affirm-prone, their agreement-to-reverse rates are low: the highest rate among the conservatives is only 32 percent for the Reed-Vinson pairing, while the lowest is 20 percent for the Burton-Jackson pairing. The Jackson-Frankfurter pairing has the highest agreement rate, 66 percent, for all pairings involving either of these two justices.

Table 7.3, which has the same format as table 7.1, contains the individual results for report votes on-the-merits during the first Court. The raw numbers of these cases are smaller than those of the conference votes (in table 7.1) because some cases were mooted and some justices became recused after the conference vote. Not surprisingly, the reverse rates in table 7.3 are very close to those of table 7.1. The same pattern holds: the liberals are reverse-prone, the conservatives are affirm-prone, and the t-values are statistically significant. Again, Jackson, Reed, and Vinson have very similar rates while Burton has the lowest reverse rate.

In both tables 7.1 and 7.3, each justice has a reverse rate in nonunanimous cases that is lower than his reverse rate in all cases, a difference resulting

Table 7.2

Nonunanimous Conference Votes On-The-Merits.

Percentage of votes in which justices agreed, percentage of votes in which justices agreed to reverse—First Natural Court. At least seven justices voting.

	Rutldg	Jacksn	Murphy	Dougls	Frnkfr	Reed	Black	Vinson
Burton	42	60	40	43	63	68	43	71
	23	20	22	22	23	25	20	26
Rutledge		36	76	71	42	52	78	44
		23	54	52	25	32	51	27
Jackson			35	40	66	57	32	61
			22	24	27	22	18	24
Murphy				68	48	49	70	46
				50	30	31	47	27
Douglas					41	45	69	40
					24	27	46	23
Frankfurter						59	39	65
						24	21	26
Reed							50	76
							27	32
Black								49
								26

Table 7.3

Report Votes On-The-Merits in nonunanimous (top) and unanimous (bottom) votes—First Natural Court. At least seven justices voting.

	Affirm	Reverse	Reverse Rate	t-value
Burton	162	90	36	-5.52*
	210	186	47	-4.17*
Rutledge	81	168	67	5.67*
	131	264	67	4.47*
Jackson	132	105	44	-2.35*
	180	193	52	-2.07*
Murphy	77	168	69	6.05*
	126	262	68	4.75*
Douglas	92	150	62	3.55*
	142	245	63	2.81*
Frankfurter	140	107	43	-2.75*
	189	201	52	-2.21*
Reed	148	101	41	-3.72*
	197	196	50	-2.92*
Black	99	150	60	2.99*
	146	245	63	2.54*
Vinson	145	103	42	-3.37*
	192	197	51	-2.58*

* statistically significant at 5 percent level.

Table 7.4

Nonunanimous Report Votes On-The-Merits.

Percentage of votes in which justices agreed, percentage of votes in which justices agreed to reverse—First Natural Court. At least seven justices voting.

	Rutldg	Jacksn	Murphy	Dougls	Frnkfr	Reed	Black	Vinson
Burton	41	64	37	40	64	73	43	75
	22	22	20	19	22	25	20	26
Rutledge		35	82	68	39	50	79	43
		23	59	48	25	29	53	26
Jackson			36	32	73	62	34	64
			24	18	30	23	20	25
Murphy				70	45	46	82	46
				50	29	28	55	28
Douglas					37	47	70	43
					21	25	46	23
Frankfurter						57	39	64
						21	22	25
Reed							52	79
							27	31
Black								51
								27

from the Court's case selection processes (discussed in chapters 5 and 6). If the justices unanimously agreed that the lower court's decision was correct, then they were most likely to deny review. But if they unanimously agreed that the decision was incorrect, then they were more likely to grant review and reverse on-the merits. Thus, unanimous decisions at either the conference or the report vote on-the-merits were more likely to result in a reversal of the lower court.

Table 7.4, which has the same format as table 7.2, contains the levels of agreement within pairings for report votes on-the-merits. The results are similar to those of table 7.2: the liberals have high agreement rates and were generally reverse-prone, while the conservatives have high agreement rates and were affirm-prone. The Rutledge-Murphy pairing has both the largest agreement rate and the highest agreement-to-reverse rate. Pairings containing Burton, Reed, and the chief justice have agreement rates ranging from 73 to 79 percent. Again, Jackson and Frankfurter agreed with each other more than they agreed with any of their other colleagues.

With intra-bloc pairings, agreement rates are higher for the report votes presented in table 7.4 than for the conference votes reported in 7.2: each bloc exerted a gravitational pull on its members between the conference and report votes. For example, the agreement rate between the conservatives Burton and Jackson increased from 60 to 64 percent while the rate between the liberals Rutledge and Murphy increased from 76 to 82 percent. The only exception is the Rutledge-Douglas pairing which declined from 71 to 68 percent.

With inter-block pairings, however, the agreement rates usually declined between the conference and report votes. For example, the Burton-Murphy pairing declined from 40 to 37 percent and the Douglas-Jackson pairing declined from 40 to 32 percent.

IV. Votes On-The-Merits—Second Natural Court.

The individual results for conference votes during the second Court are presented in table 7.5. Douglas and Black, the two remaining liberals, have reverse rates that exceed 50 percent and both have t-values which are statistically significantly. Although lower than Black's and Douglas' rates, Clark's rate, 53 percent, shows that he was slightly reverse-prone. The remaining six conservatives were all more likely to affirm than to reverse in nonunanimous cases. Burton, Frankfurter, Reed, and Vinson all have reverse

Table 7.5

Conference Votes On The Merits in nonunanimous (top) and unanimous (bottom) votes — Second Natural Court. At least seven justices voting.

	Affirm	Reverse	Reverse Rate	t-value
Minton	194	159	45	-2.20*
	216	220	50	-2.00*
Clark	147	168	53	1.06
	168	226	57	1.02
Burton	186	180	49	-0.55
	210	244	54	-0.55
Jackson	189	150	44	-2.46*
	211	212	50	-2.11*
Douglas	107	176	62	4.24*
	128	228	64	3.74*
Frankfurter	178	166	48	-0.89
	200	229	53	-0.69
Reed	196	168	46	-1.78
	219	233	52	-1.54
Black	138	218	61	4.40*
	160	277	63	3.87*
Vinson	182	164	47	-1.24
	206	227	52	-1.12

* statistically significant at 5 percent level.

Table 7.6

Nonunanimous Conference Votes On-The-Merits.

Percentage of votes in which justices agreed, percentage of votes in which justices agreed to reverse — First Natural Court. At least seven justices voting.

	Clark	Burton	Jacksn	Dougls	Frnkfr	Reed	Black	Vinson
Minton	70	70	55	38	42	67	43	72
	35	32	21	22	18	29	25	32
Clark		69	60	48	49	66	52	76
		36	28	28	23	34	34	39
Burton			55	47	52	60	50	66
			24	27	25	28	30	31
Jackson				42	68	57	44	53
				25	31	23	25	21
Douglas					49	45	66	40
					31	27	44	25
Frankfurter						45	56	42
						20	32	19
Reed							36	69
							21	31
Black								46
								28

rates between 46 and 49 percent. Within the conservative bloc, only Minton and Jackson have rates that are low enough to produce significant t-values.

The levels of agreement within pairings for nonunanimous conference votes on-the-merits are presented in table 7.6. Douglas and Black, the remaining liberals, have an agreement rate of 66 percent and an agreement-to-reverse rate of 44 percent, which is the largest of the second Court. Pairings containing Minton, Clark, and Vinson have agreement rates of 70 percent or more. Again, Jackson and Frankfurter agreed with each other more than they agreed with any of their other colleagues. But, surprisingly, Frankfurter voted with Douglas more than he voted with the chief justice.

Table 7.7 contains the individual results for the report vote during the second Court. As with the first Court, the raw numbers decline between the conference (table 7.5) and report votes (table 7.7) on-the-merits because of mootness and recusals. There is very little overall difference between the rates in tables 7.5 and 7.7. The rates for Minton, Jackson, Reed, and Vinson are almost identical in both, evidence that their close relationship in the first Court continued into the second.

Table 7.8 shows the results of pairings for report votes during the second Court. When compared with the results of table 7.6, they indicate how the agreement rates changed between the conference and report votes. The Douglas-Black agreement rates fell from 66 to 64 percent. With the exception of the Jackson-Frankfurter pairing, the agreement rates for pairings of the seven conservative justices increased. For example, changes between the conference and report votes increased the Minton-Clark agreement rate from 70 to 78 percent. The agreement rates within pairings comprised by Clark, Burton, Reed, and Vinson increased by approximately ten percent between the conference and report votes. Thus, the conservatives continued to reduce their disagreements between the two votes on-the-merits.

Jackson and Frankfurter maintained the high level of agreement mentioned above: their agreement rate, 68 percent, is the highest for any pairing containing Frankfurter. Jackson also had a high agreement rate, 69 percent, with Clark.

In both tables 7.5 and 7.7, the reverse rates in nonunanimous cases are consistently lower than the reverse rates in all cases. These findings, which are similar to those of tables 7.1 and 7.3, result from the Court's case selection processes in which more was gained from granting review if the justices believed that the lower court's decision merited reversal.

Table 7.7

Report Votes On-The-Merits in nonunanimous (top) and unanimous (bottom) votes — Second Natural Court. At least seven justices voting.

	Affirm	Reverse	Reverse Rate	t-value
Minton	168	141	46	-1.89
	212	228	52	-1.66
Clark	132	131	50	-0.30
	174	218	56	0.03
Burton	167	149	47	-1.34
	215	244	53	-1.09
Jackson	165	132	44	-2.29*
	213	223	51	-1.95
Douglas	94	174	65	5.12*
	131	244	65	4.05*
Frankfurter	156	149	49	-0.68
	203	243	54	-0.48
Reed	171	143	46	-1.95
	220	239	52	-1.59
Black	116	199	63	4.87*
	162	293	64	4.17*
Vinson	163	151	48	-0.98
	212	245	54	-0.88

* statistically significant at 5 percent level.

Table 7.8

Nonunanimous Report Votes On-The-Merits.

Percentage of votes in which justices agreed, percentage of votes in which justices agreed to reverse—Second Natural Court. At least seven justices voting.

	Clark	Burton	Jacksn	Dougls	Frnkfr	Reed	Black	Vinson
Minton	78	74	59	34	49	74	42	80
	39	34	24	20	22	33	25	37
Clark		81	69	40	58	76	47	87
		39	30	26	27	38	29	44
Burton			61	41	55	69	44	73
			26	25	25	31	28	34
Jackson				34	68	61	41	61
				23	31	24	25	26
Douglas					44	44	64	39
					30	27	45	25
Frankfurter						47	52	48
						21	32	22
Reed							36	77
							22	35
Black								44
								28

V. Fluidity by the Entire Court.

Vote changes between the conference and report votes are referred to as "fluidity" (Howard 1968) and are categorized using two criteria (Brenner 1980). The first distinguishes "strong" or complete changes (i.e., reverse to affirm, or affirm to reverse) from "weak" or partial changes (i.e., reverse to recused, or reverse in part and affirm in part to affirm). The second criteria distinguishes changes by the Court from changes by an individual justice.

When the unit of analysis is the Court, there are three types of changes: from affirm (or dismiss) to reverse (or vacate), from reverse (or vacate) to affirm (or dismiss), and all other changes. The first two categories contain strong changes, while the last category includes weak ones such as moving from reverse to affirm in part and reverse in part. Cases that became moot between the conference and report votes are excluded from this analysis.

For the first natural Court, there are 16 cases in the first category, (i.e, changes from affirm to reverse), nine in the second category, and 17 in the third. There are 378 cases in which the result is unchanged between the conference and report votes. The total number of changes, 42, is ten percent of the total number of cases, 420.

For the second Court, there are 14 changes from reverse to affirm, 14 changes from affirm to reverse, and 20 weak changes. These three categories total 48, which is approximately ten percent of the 482 cases.

Thus, for both Courts, there is 90 percent agreement between the Court's conference and report actions on-the-merits, and there is no evidence that the Court was more likely to move to any particular outcome when it did change. These results for the Court, however, do not identify changes by the individual justices.

VI. Fluidity by Individual Justices

When analyzing an individual justice's votes, the relevant changes are strong movements from assenting to dissenting or from dissenting to assenting. There were two motivations for switches between the conference and report votes—strategic and sincere. Strategic changes occurred when a justice joined a decision with which he disagreed, either to minimize the damage resulting from the Court's action or to increase his collegial influence. Sincere switches resulted from a genuine change of mind following the conference vote.

Strategic changes to the majority had two advantages and two costs. The first advantage was an increase in collegial influence with the members of the majority. Joining the majority also indicated a willingness to suppress individual preferences for the benefit of the Court, which may have been appreciated by all colleagues, even the dissenters.

The second advantage is that, as a part of the majority, the switching justice gained some control over the Court's opinion and might succeed in making it narrower or more ambiguous. The opinion author wanted, *ceteris paribus*, to minimize the number of dissenters and would make some concessions to obtain additional votes. But the influence of the switching justice was limited by and inversely related to the size of the majority.

The first cost of making a strategic change to the majority was a loss of influence with the minority justices. The second cost of assenting was an inability to write a dissenting opinion which could show that the majority position was illogical, internally inconsistent, or in conflict with previous decisions. Such a dissent could increase the probability that the opinion would be narrowed or overturned in the future. If the author of the Court's opinion needed to answer the dissent, then it also imposed costs on the majority which could increase the dissenter's bargaining power in subsequent and similar cases.

Strategic changes to the minority also had two benefits and two costs. The first benefit was an increase in influence with the dissenters. The second was an improved bargaining position with opinion authors in other cases. It might have been necessary to quit the majority occasionally in order to maintain influence over colleagues' written opinions. A justice who never switched from assenting to dissenting might have found his brethren less willing to make concessions when they wrote the opinion of the Court. This second benefit, however, could also be obtained by writing a concurring opinion which allowed a justice to stay with the majority without joining the opinion of the Court.

The two costs of strategic changes to the minority were a decline in influence with the majority justices and a loss of input into the majority opinion. The first cost was directly related to the size of the majority. The second cost was inversely related to size of the majority, i.e., with a larger majority, the individual assenters had less influence over the opinion.

If the benefits of a strategic switch exceeded the costs, then switching produced a positive net benefit. Thus, an optimizing justice changed sides to obtain the positive net benefit even though he disagreed with his own report vote. There is, however, no method of measuring the relative costs and benefits, the frequency of strategic switches, or whether most strategic changes were to the majority or the minority. Thus, it is impossible to determine if and when joining the majority and thereby trying to alter the opinion of the Court was better than writing a dissent.

In terms of collegial influence, there was probably more gained by joining rather than leaving the majority. Switching to the majority meant that a justice joined more colleagues than he left and the opinion author was particularly pleased by the change. Thus, joining the majority usually had a positive net effect on a justice's collegial influence. But not always. Because each justice evaluated cases differently, occasionally the dissenters—although smaller in number—believed so strongly in their positions that a justice gained more by staying with or joining the dissenters than he lost by leaving or not joining the majority.

A sincere change could have several causes: subsequent research or reflection, the logic presented by a colleague's written opinion, and conversations with law clerks or other justices. Because the majority had more justices, it is likely that conversations with other justices would result in more sincere changes to the majority than to the minority. But again, there is no method for determining which switches were sincere and what proportion of sincere switches were to the majority.

Although the types and causes of vote changes are unknown, it is possible to determine the aggregate number and frequency of changes between the conference and report votes. Table 7.9 presents information on the individual justice's strong switches between the conference and report votes on-the-merits. For each justice, the number and percentage of votes are shown for three categories—votes that did not change after the conference, changes to the majority, and changes to the minority. Cases without a majority at the conference or report votes are excluded from this analysis. The t-value for each justice is used to test whether there is a statistically significant difference between the percentage of his changes to the majority and the percentage of his changes to the minority.

During the first natural Court, the percentage of unchanged votes ranges from a high of 93 for Burton to a low of 83 for Jackson. For each justice, the percentage of changes to the majority exceeds the percentage of changes to the minority and the differences are statistically significant.

During the second Court, the percentage of unchanged votes ranges from a high of 93 for Black to a low of 88 for Clark. The standard deviation of the percentage of unchanged votes declined from 3.7 in the first Court to 1.6 in the second, indicating less variation in the second. Again, for each justice, the percentage of changes to the majority exceeds the percentage of changes to the minority. For all but Douglas, the difference is statistically significant.

Thus, with one exception, most fluidity involved changes to the majority.

Table 7.9

Strong Vote Changes Between the Conference and Report Votes. At least seven justices voting.

First Natural Court

	Un-changed No.	%	To Majority No.	%	To Minority No.	%	t-value
Burton	361	93	24	6	4	1	3.89*
Rutledge	326	89	31	8	10	3	3.40*
Jackson	291	83	48	14	20	3	5.32*
Murphy	301	84	41	11	15	4	3.65*
Douglas	321	93	23	7	3	1	4.04*
Frankfurter	311	88	34	10	9	3	3.98*
Reed	350	92	29	8	1	0	5.31*
Black	341	92	26	7	4	1	4.15*
Vinson	331	89	37	10	4	1	5.40*

Second Natural Court

Minton	378	91	36	9	1	0	6.01*
Clark	329	88	43	12	1	0	6.72*
Burton	396	91	31	7	6	1	4.24*
Jackson	357	89	36	9	9	2	4.19*
Douglas	304	92	18	5	9	3	1.77
Frankfurter	366	92	27	7	6	2	3.77*
Reed	384	89	46	11	1	0	6.94*
Black	384	93	19	5	8	2	2.16*
Vinson	377	91	38	9	0	0	6.47*

* statistically significant at 5 percent level.

But, as stated above, it is impossible to distinguish sincere from strategic changes or to determine which benefit was the most common motivation for joining the majority. It is also impossible to determine why justices did not switch, i.e., which cost was the most common deterrent to fluidity.

VII. Fluidity Influence

A justice switched and joined a colleague for either sincere or strategic reasons, i.e., because he was converted by the colleague or because he wanted to gain or maintain influence with him. In either case, one justice's influence with another depended on several factors—friendship, acknowledged expertise, previous collaboration or disagreement on similar cases, and ideological compatibility or incompatibility. Murphy (1964, chapter 3) presents an extensive and elegant discussion of strategies for influencing colleagues.

One indication of influence was the ability to induce vote changes. If those justices who switched are assumed to have been influenced by those who were consistent, then it is possible to construct a numerical measure of each justice's ability to induce changes.

When a justice changed his vote, those justices (whose votes were unchanged) whom he joined are given equal credit for the switch. For example, on October 22, 1949, at the conference vote in *Brown v. Western Railroad of Alabama* (49,43A), five justices voted to reverse (Clark, Burton, Reed, Black, Vinson), three voted to affirm (Minton, Jackson, Frankfurter), and one did not participate (Douglas).

At the report vote, Minton joined the majority by changing his vote to reverse. His change can be evaluated two ways. First, each of the five justices he joined is credited with one vote change. Hereafter, these are referred to as unweighted changes because they are independent of both the number of justices joined and the number of Minton's switches. Second, the change is divided by the number of justices joined by Minton (five). The result of this division, one-fifth, is the adjusted change. This adjusted change is then divided by the total of Minton's adjusted changes and then multiplied by 100. The result is the weighted change which is measured in percentage terms. Each of the five justices joined by Minton is credited with this weighted change, i.e., each is credited with the percentage of Minton's adjusted fluidity represented by the vote change. The totals of these unweighted and percentage weighted changes credited to a justice serve as measures of his influence over others' fluidity.

The analytical value of these measures is limited for two reasons. First, influence may have been best applied during or before the conference vote rather than after. It is possible, therefore, that by including only those votes that changed, these measures ignore most of a justice's influence and that what is ignored is inversely related to what is included. In other words, it is possible that the most influential justices were the least likely to evoke changes after the conference.

The second limitation results from the lack of systematic information as to why a justice changed positions between the two votes on-the-merits. Although the justices' private papers contain many memos dealing with vote changes, the correspondence is often incomplete and self serving.

In the case discussed above, *Brown v. Western Railroad of Alabama*, it is improbable that the five justices had equivalent influence on Minton and therefore it is unlikely that each deserves equal credit for causing the vote change. Perhaps only one justice influenced Minton, or perhaps his change resulted from his own study of the issue and none of the justices deserves credit.

In spite of these limitations, the numbers do provide some insight into the ability of a justice to influence his brethren's fluidity. The individual justices changed their votes in seven to twelve percent of the cases and many of these changes must have resulted from interactions with colleagues. The careful efforts expended on the laborious task of writing opinions and memos after the conference vote demonstrates that inducing colleagues' fluidity was an important activity.

An alternative approach would control for the percentage of unchanged votes (table 7.9), because the more frequently a justice switched, the less frequently others could join him. An additional modification would adjust for the agreement rates at the conference vote on-the-merits because only justices in disagreement at the conference vote can—in this measure—influence each other after the conference. These adjustments, however, would not substantially alter the empirical results presented below.

Table 7.10 shows, for each justice, the weighted and the unweighted (in brackets) fluidity that resulted from a colleague's joining the position of the justice during the first natural Court. Only strong changes are included. Cases with nonunanimous conference votes that were followed by unanimous report votes are included in this analysis. The names across the top of the table refer to the justices who switched and the names along the left side of the table refer to those whom the switching justice joined.

The leftmost column of numbers presents the total of colleagues' weighted and unweighted switches attributed to each justice. The values in this column are obtained by adding across the table. The total of the weighted changes for all nine justices is 900 percent. Thus, justices who are credited with more than 100 percent (leftmost column) exercised more than proportional influence over their brethren's fluidity.

Burton was joined a total of 213 times by colleagues who changed after the conference vote. These 213 changes yield a total weighted value of 128 percent, which is the largest attributed to any justice and indicates that Burton had the greatest influence—a finding which would astonish Court historians. Other justices who apparently exercised more than proportional influence include Rutledge (103 percent), Douglas (112 percent), Reed (116 percent), and Black (110 percent). The smallest values were obtained by Vinson (74 percent). Others with less than proportional influence include Jackson (86 percent), Murphy (85 percent), and Frankfurter (87 percent).

The sum of a justice's weighted switches to the positions of his eight brethren is 100 percent. (This is obtained by adding down the column under the switching justice's name.) Thus, if a justice's weighted changes to a colleague are more than one-eighth, or 13 percent, then the colleague apparently exercised more than proportional influence over the justice's fluidity. For example, because he is credited with 15 percent of Burton's weighted switches, Rutledge presumably had more than proportional influence over Burton. The result is similar for Reed, who is credited with 18 percent of Burton's weighted fluidity. Vinson, on the other hand, is credited with only eight percent of Burton's weighted switches, i.e., the chief justice had less than proportional influence over Burton's fluidity.

The highest individual weighted value, 21 percent, results from Douglas switching to join Reed. The lowest weighted value, seven percent, was caused by Rutledge switching to join Murphy. Thus, the greatest influence was exercised in an inter-bloc relationship while the least influence was exercised in an intra-bloc pairing.

The individual relationships in table 7.10 are not symmetric. For example, Murphy's weighted switches to Rutledge are twice Rutledge's weighted switches to Murphy. Additional asymmetries exist between Jackson and Burton, Rutledge and Douglas, Murphy and Douglas, Douglas and Reed, and Vinson and Black. Douglas is particularly interesting because 21 percent of his weighted fluidity was to Reed while only twelve percent was to Black. The chief justice's fluidity is also interesting because he has asymmetric relationships with all eight of his brethren—each of whom influenced Vinson more than he was influenced by Vinson.

Table 7.11 presents the weighted and unweighted fluidity for each justice during the second natural Court. The total values (leftmost column) show that four justices had more than proportional influence because they induced a total weighted fluidity that exceeds 100 percent: Burton (112 percent),

Table 7.10

Percentage weighted and unweighted (in brackets) fluidity by a justice (name given horizontally across top of table) that resulted in joining a colleague (name given vertically along left edge). At least seven justices voting.

First Natural Court

	TOTAL	Burton	Rutldg	Jacksn	Murph	Dougls	Frnkfr	Reed	Black	Vinson
Burton	128 [213]		18 [28]	17 [37]	14 [35]	17 [19]	16 [25]	17 [21]	16 [23]	13 [25]
Rutldg	103 [185]	15 [20]		13 [40]	14 [29]	9 [11]	14 [26]	12 [18]	11 [14]	14 [27]
Jacksn	86 [139]	10 [13]	10 [18]		12 [28]	9 [12]	13 [17]	10 [15]	11 [18]	11 [18]
Murphy	85 [159]	12 [19]	7 [13]	11 [37]		9 [10]	11 [22]	10 [16]	13 [17]	12 [25]
Dougls	112 [196]	14 [19]	16 [19]	12 [35]	15 [31]		14 [27]	15 [21]	12 [13]	15 [31]
Frnkfr	87 [150]	12 [15]	10 [19]	10 [30]	9 [21]	11 [13]		13 [17]	12 [17]	10 [18]
Reed	116 [183]	18 [17]	13 [23]	14 [38]	10 [28]	21 [18]	10 [19]		17 [20]	12 [20]
Black	110 [213]	12 [18]	14 [19]	13 [40]	17 [37]	12 [14]	14 [27]	15 [22]		14 [30]
Vinson	74 [149]	8 [12]	11 [22]	9 [31]	9 [24]	13 [17]	8 [17]	8 [12]	8 [14]	

Table 7.11

Percentage weighted and unweighted (in brackets) fluidity by a justice (name given horizontally across top of table) that resulted in joining a colleague (name given vertically along left edge). At least seven justices voting.

Second Natural Court

	TOTAL	Mint	Clark	Burton	Jacksn	Dougls	Frnkfr	Reed	Black	Vinson
Minton	97 [135]		13 [21]	9 [12]	11 [21]	14 [12]	23 [22]	11 [22]	10 [12]	7 [13]
Clark	80 [135]	11 [18]		10 [16]	10 [21]	7 [7]	13 [21]	12 [26]	8 [10]	9 [16]
Burton	112 [175]	14 [22]	18 [31]		15 [27]	10 [10]	14 [20]	14 [29]	15 [15]	13 [21]
Jacksn	91 [140]	15 [23]	10 [19]	11 [17]		5 [6]	10 [13]	11 [24]	14 [14]	15 [24]
Dougls	61 [89]	4 [7]	7 [13]	9 [10]	10 [13]		6 [9]	9 [17]	7 [5]	9 [15]
Frnkfr	120 [167]	19 [27]	14 [25]	19 [23]	11 [16]	10 [9]		15 [30]	13 [11]	18 [26]
Reed	125 [155]	13 [20]	13 [24]	17 [18]	15 [26]	21 [14]	12 [18]		22 [17]	13 [18]
Black	125 [154]	14 [19]	13 [18]	15 [16]	18 [25]	21 [12]	12 [16]	16 [28]		16 [20]
Vinson	90 [144]	11 [18]	12 [22]	9 [14]	12 [23]	13 [12]	11 [17]	12 [26]	10 [12]	

Frankfurter (120 percent), Reed (125 percent), and Black (125 percent). Five justices had less than proportional influence because they are credited with causing a total weighted fluidity that is less than 100 percent: Minton (97 percent), Clark (80 percent), Jackson (91 percent), Douglas (61 percent), and Vinson (91 percent).

Some of the individual relationships presented in table 7.11 display substantial asymmetries. Douglas' weighted fluidity to Minton, 14 percent, is three times as large as Minton's weighted fluidity to Douglas, four percent. Additional asymmetries exist between Clark and Burton, Minton and Burton, and Jackson and Douglas. There is a particularly interesting asymmetry between Douglas and Black: Black's weighted changes to Douglas, seven percent, are a third of Douglas' weighted changes to Black, 21 percent.

Reed apparently exercised considerable influence over both Douglas' and Black's fluidity. In the second Court, 21 percent of Douglas' weighted changes and 22 percent of Black's were to Reed. Table 7.10 presents similar results for the first natural Court—21 percent of Douglas' and 17 percent of Black's weighted changes were to Reed.

Chief Justice Vinson apparently had less than proportional influence over his brethren. For both Courts, the total of his colleagues' weighted fluidity attributed to Vinson is less than 100 percent or less than one-ninth of the total.

Douglas' total influence over his brethren's fluidity declined sharply between the first and second Courts. In the first Court, he is credited with 112 percent (table 7.10) of his colleagues' total weighted changes, but during the second Court, the value falls to 61 percent (table 7.11). The decline was caused by three factors. First, Rutledge and Murphy were replaced by Minton and Clark. Rutledge's (16 percent) and Murphy's (15 percent) weighted switches to Douglas are both substantially above Minton's (four percent) and Clark's (seven percent) weighted switches to Douglas. Second, Douglas spent much of the October 1949 term recuperating from a horse-riding accident and therefore played a minimal role during one of the four terms of the second Court. Third, there were declines in Frankfurter's, Reed's, Black's, and Vinson's weighted fluidity to Douglas that exceed the one-fourth decline that should have resulted from Douglas' absence.

Black, the other member of the liberal bloc, did not suffer a decline in his ability to induce fluidity. He is credited with a total of 110 percent (table 7.10) of his brethren's weighted switches during the first Court and 125 percent (table 7.11) during the second.

Overall, the results in tables 7.10 and 7.11 do not demonstrate that bloc membership was a major determinant of strong switches between the conference and report votes on-the-merits. During the first Court, Rutledge was more likely to switch and join Burton than he was to switch and join Douglas or Black. During the second Court, Jackson was more likely to change to Black's position than he was to change to any of the conservatives' positions. As stated above, the conservative Reed apparently exercised disproportional influence over the fluidity of the liberals Douglas and Black.

These results appear inconsistent with those discussed above in sections III and IV. For example, tables 7.2 and 7.4 show that agreement rates for pairings within blocs increased while those for liberal-conservative pairings decreased between the conference and report votes.

This apparent inconsistency has two causes. First, the differences between the agreement rates presented in tables 7.2 and 7.4 result from both strong and weak changes. Tables 7.10 and 7.11, however, deal only with strong changes. Many weak changes resulted because a justice passed or was absent at the conference vote but participated at the report vote. His report vote usually agreed with the votes of his fellow bloc members. Thus, these weak changes increased agreement rates within blocs. Second, tables 7.2 and 7.4 exclude all unanimous votes, while tables 7.10 and 7.11 do not. Because strong changes to another's position are impossible following a unanimous conference vote, tables 7.10 and 7.11 include only nonunanimous conference votes. However, fluidity did result in some cases becoming unanimous at the report vote. These unanimous report votes are not excluded from tables 7.10 and 7.11. Including them reduces the apparent impact of blocs because unanimous cases are independent of bloc membership.

VIII. Joint Fluidity

Another measure of collegial influence is the ability to induce others to follow one's own changes. If two justices change sides together it is impossible to distinguish the follower from the leader or even to determine if there was a leader. The frequency of joint changes, however, may serve as an indication of mutual influence.

Table 7.12 presents the number (not percent) of times two justices changed together during the first Court. The entries on the diagonal are the number of vote changes for the individual justices. Thus, the first value on the diagonal, 28, at the intersection of Burton with himself, is the number of Burton's switches. (These diagonal values correspond to the results of table 7.9 which show that Burton changed to the majority in 24 cases and changed to the minority in four cases for a total of 28 changes.) Diagonal values allow comparisons between the number of joint changes and the number of

Table 7.12

Number of times two justices changed together between the conference and report vote on the merits. At least seven justices voting.

First Natural Court

	Burton	Rutldg	Jacksn	Murphy	Dougls	Frnkfr	Reed	Black	Vinson
Burton	28	2	9	1	2	7	8	2	9
Rutledge		41	7	18	7	5	6	11	6
Jackson			58	8	2	13	10	4	15
Murphy				56	7	12	9	9	10
Douglas					26	5	4	9	3
Frankfurter						43	7	5	14
Reed							30	4	14
Black								30	6
Vinson									41

individual changes. Thus, Burton and Rutledge changed together in two votes, comprising approximately seven percent (2/28) of Burton's switches and approximately five percent (2/41) of Rutledge's.

Intra-bloc pairings show relatively strong relationships. Murphy and Rutledge changed together 18 times which is almost half of Rutledge's 41 switches. Jackson and Frankfurter often changed together—13 times. The chief justice has relatively large numbers of joint switches with Jackson, 15, Frankfurter, 14, and Reed, 14.

Inter-bloc pairings show relatively few joint changes. For example, Burton has only one joint switch with Murphy and only two each with Rutledge, Douglas, and Black. Douglas has three joint changes with Vinson and two with Jackson.

Table 7.13

Number of times two justices changed together between the conference and report vote on the merits. At least seven justices voting.

Second Natural Court

	Minton	Clark	Burton	Jacksn	Dougls	Frnkfr	Reed	Black	Vinson
Minton	37	10	13	6	5	4	14	6	16
Clark		44	10	11	7	4	12	8	16
Burton			37	8	7	5	15	5	15
Jackson				45	8	10	10	4	10
Douglas					27	5	7	9	6
Frankfurter						33	8	6	7
Reed							47	4	19
Black								27	6
Vinson									38

Table 7.13 presents the number of times two justices changed together during the second Court. Burton and Reed frequently changed together, 15 times, as did Burton and Minton, 13 times. The chief justice had relatively large numbers with Minton, 16, Clark, 16, Burton, 15, and Reed, 19. Douglas and Black, who were the least likely to change, switched with each other more than with any of their other colleagues. Frankfurter, who also had relatively few changes, had the most joint switches with Jackson.

IX. Conclusions

The results of this chapter can be summarized as follows.

When the decision on-the-merits was nonunanimous, the liberal justices were reverse-prone while the conservatives were generally affirm-prone at both the conference and report votes on-the-merits.

Both the conference and the report votes show substantial variations in the agreement rates between pairs of justices—with high agreement rates occurring when the justices belonged to the same bloc. Agreement rates between members of the same bloc generally increased between the conference and report votes.

There is 90 percent agreement between the Court's conference and report actions on-the-merits. The ten percent of cases involving fluidity by the Court showed no consistent tendency toward a particular disposition.

Strong fluidity by individual justices usually involved moving from the minority to the majority position. Certain justices may have been particularly able to induce their colleagues' fluidity, e.g., Reed apparently exercised substantial influence over Douglas and Black. Certain pairings of justices reveal substantially asymmetric relationships. For example, Douglas was much more likely to switch and join Black than Black was to switch and join Douglas.

Measurements of joint fluidity show that justices who usually agreed often changed together. Thus, Murphy and Rutledge frequently changed sides together as did the group of Burton, Reed, and Vinson.

8

Opinion Assignment

I. Introduction

This chapter examines the distribution of signed opinions and presents an analysis of the following topics in opinion assignment: the distribution of assignments made by the chief justice and the distribution made by the associate justices, as well as the differences between the two; reassignments resulting from the author's inability to hold the majority; instances in which the author changed sides and wrote an opinion contrary to his conference vote; the mean number of days needed by each justice to complete opinions; the effect of the mean number of days on the distribution of opinions; and the impact of minimum winning cases (e.g., five-to-four) on the distribution of assignments.

The unit of analysis is an opinion assignment rather than a case. The distinction is important because one assignment can entail multiple cases which were grouped together because they presented similar facts, because the logic of their dispositions was identical, or because the logic was different and the difference required exposition. When an opinion dealt with multiple cases, only one case is used in the analysis. Thus, for example, because *U.S. v. Powell* (46,56A) and *U.S. v. Atlantic Coast Line RR* (46,57A) were handled with one opinion, only the first is used in the empirical analysis.

II. Procedures

Following the conference vote on-the-merits, cases were divided into two categories—those that needed only a brief *per curiam* announcement and those that required a more extensive opinion of the Court signed by its author. *Per curiam* announcements were usually written by the chief justice or a member of his staff. If the chief justice was recused or in dissent, then the senior member of the majority typically wrote the *per curiam*.

A signed opinion of the Court had three purposes. First, it announced the judgment in the particular case. Second, it presented a justification containing the legal reasoning that underlay the Court's action. Third, and most important, it contained an explanation which was essentially a set of instructions to the lower courts as to how they should decide similar cases.

The responsibility for writing a signed opinion of the Court was assigned by the senior member of the conference majority, usually the chief justice. (Vinson assigned 80 percent). When the chief justice was recused or in the minority, the senior associate justice in the majority made the assignment. (Black, Reed, and Frankfurter assigned 15 percent, three percent, and two percent respectively.) If the Court divided four-to-four, the chief justice gave the assignment to whoever appeared able to write an opinion that might gain a majority, see *Alcoa Steamship Company v. U.S.* (49,271A). Cases were usually assigned at the beginning of the week following the conference.

The tradition of having an opinion of the Court written by a member of the majority began with John Marshall who, when he became chief justice, ended the English practice of *seriatim* opinions in which each justice spoke in turn, each presenting his own analysis and decision for the case. By presenting one opinion, the Court muted its disagreements and appeared more united. Marshall also attempted, with less success, to limit dissenting opinions (Jackson 1969, chapter 2).

Vinson did not defer to the opinion assigning expertise of the associate justices when he began his service as chief justice. He came to the Court with five years of prior judicial experience on the Circuit Court of Appeals for the District of Columbia, and his appointment during June of 1946 gave him four months to prepare for the following term. His first opinion assignments, made on October 22, 1946, were cases held over from the previous term (Burton, October 1946 Docket Book). In contrast, his successor, Earl Warren, was much more tentative when he became chief justice. Warren deferred to Black for the first three weeks during the October 1953 term. Black even assigned *Voris v. Eikel* (53,20A) to the new chief justice on November 19, 1953 (Burton, October 1953 Docket Book).

Like his predecessors Hughes and Stone, Vinson did not allow specialization in opinion writing. Thus, it appears that the justices did not generally know, *a priori*, who would receive an assignment. The reasons for the lack of specialization follow from the case selection process. If, at the cert vote, justices could anticipate who would write the opinion, then four justices could pretty much wear out a colleague by selecting numerous complex but unimportant cases in his area of specialization. Brenner (1984) and Brenner and Spaeth (1986) show that specialization developed following the Vinson era. Because of this development, it is likely that justices now have disproportionately greater influence on cert votes in their area of opinion specialization.

After receiving the assignment, the author prepared a preliminary draft which was usually sent to all the other justices, but occasionally the author first obtained responses from those whom he expected would join the opinion. For example, Vinson sent his first draft for *C.I.R. v. Culbertson* (48,313A) only to the conference majority (memo dated May 12, 1949, from Vinson to Reed, Frankfurter, Murphy, Jackson, and Burton; Felix Frankfurter Papers HLSL #24-12). In *Terminiello v. City of Chicago* (48,272A), Douglas received the opinion assignment after voting with the majority to affirm Terminiello's conviction. He changed his mind while writing the draft, which he first sent only to those who had voted to reverse (memo dated March 30, 1949, from Douglas to Black, Reed, Murphy, and Rutledge; Reed #174).

Colleagues unwilling to join the opinion generally notified the author of their intentions or indicated that they preferred to wait until they had seen the dissenting or concurring opinions. Others indicated that they would join only if there were fundamental changes in the opinion. For example, Murphy was assigned the opinion in *U.S. National Bank v. Chase National* (46,371A). His draft opinion contained an evaluation of bankruptcy law that caused some of his colleagues to object to the legal analysis although they agreed with the result. In a memo to Murphy dated March 22, 1947 (Reed #173), Reed indicated his disagreement but stated that "If no one else has the same objection, I shall probably subside . . . ." In a memo to Murphy (Reed #173) sent the same day, Burton raised the same objection and suggested that "you may wish to resubmit it to the conference." On March 27, Reed sent a second memo to Murphy (with a copy to Burton) (Reed #173) containing suggestions for detailed changes. The memo ended with a request that, if Murphy could not accept Reed's suggestions, the opinion be followed with a statement indicating that Reed concurred in the result but not in the opinion. Murphy accepted Reed's suggestions and produced a final opinion that was joined by both Burton and Reed.

Colleagues willing to accept the opinion as written returned it with "join memos," which were often handwritten on the back of the draft. Frequently, join memos contained friendly suggestions or corrections, e.g., a memo from Reed to Black dated February 22, 1949, suggested the following change (accepted by Black) in an opinion dealing with interstate transportation for purposes of prostitution (Reed #174):

Dear Hugo:

Re: No. 143, *Krulewitch v. United States*

I agree.

Why not drop out the names of the women witnesses? It seems too bad to print their names in the books.

The author might revise and re-distribute the draft numerous times as he attempted to write an opinion that would attract a majority. For descriptions of the detailed process of writing an opinion in a difficult case, see the discussions of *Everson v. Board Of Education* (46,52A) in Berry (1978, pp. 54-59) and Fine (1984, pp. 567-574).

The justices' private papers contain numerous preliminary drafts along with the intra-Court correspondence which they generated. It is sometimes possible to trace the evolution of an opinion from first draft to final form. The Jackson collection is particularly interesting because it shows that Jackson's renowned elegance resulted from painstaking and careful rewriting and rewriting. Clark and Douglas, on the other hand, seemed able to write first drafts in long-hand that required few stylistic changes.

While the opinion was being written, other justices were free to write concurring or dissenting opinions. Because votes could be changed until the day the judgment was announced, an opinion could fail to hold the majority. Occasionally, when the author could not hold the majority, the opinion was reassigned to another justice following a second conference vote on-the-merits. For example, *Angel v. Bullington* (46,31A) was transferred from Black to Frankfurter following a conference vote. Most times, however, the author of a dissenting or concurring opinion had obtained a majority and was reassigned the opinion without a conference vote, see *Klapprott v. U.S.* (48,42A).

Sometimes, a majority could agree on a judgment, but could not agree on the justification or explanation. This resulted in the announcement of a judgment of the Court rather than an opinion of the Court. For example, in *Haley v. Ohio* (47,51A), Douglas was joined by Black, Murphy, and Rutledge. Frankfurter wrote a separate opinion, concurring in the result but not in Douglas' opinion. The other four justices dissented. Because he was joined by only three other justices, Douglas announced the judgment rather than the opinion of the Court.

III. Fluidity by Authors

The opinion authors were also free to switch sides. Typically authors changed their votes while conducting the research that preceded the opinion writing. In a memo to the conference, dated November 29, 1949 (Jackson #158), Vinson explained why he changed his position after he began writing the opinion in *U.S. v. Aetna Casualty & Surety Company* (49,35A).

> After considerable study of the question, I have concluded that Nos. 35, 36, 37, and 38 must be affirmed. . . .

> . . . first, I feel that the evidence is overwhelming that R.S. 3477 does not, and was not intended, to bar suits . . . and second, the briefs and arguments were so inadequate that we did not have before us many of the relevant cases and materials when the vote was taken.

Table 8.1 presents the citations for cases in which the author changed sides following receipt of the opinion assignment. The citation is enclosed in parentheses if the author lost the majority and the assignment following his switch. The citation is enclosed in brackets if the author held the majority but the opinion was converted to a *per curiam* announcement. Minton is the only justice who never switched. Reed had nine switches (six resulted in his keeping the assignment), which represent about ten percent of Reed's 89 assignments during the Vinson era. There are many cases in which Reed's attitudes were well known and well established before he began writing the opinion. Thus, the percentage of switches for that undefined set of cases in which he might have changed is higher than ten percent. How the tendency to switch following receipt of the opinion affected the pattern of assignments is unknown, but it must have had some effect, particularly on the type of assignments given to those who were prone to switch.

Table 8.1

Cases in which the opinion author changed sides following receipt of the opinion assignment. Parenthesis indicate that the opinion was lost following the change. Brackets indicate that the opinion was converted to a *per curiam* announcement following the change.

Clark	[51,46A]	51,167A	52,10A	52,374A
Burton	46,89A			
Rutledge	47,54A			
Jackson	47,38A	47,542A	(48,12A)	50,77A 51,17A
Murphy	48,46A	48,56A		
Douglas	48,132A	48,272A	48,522A	(50,287A)
Frankfurter	47,45A	48,63A	48,1389A	49,230A
Reed	46,461A [47,18A] (48,287A) 48,418A 49,46A [49,512A] 50,348A 51,174A 51,143A			
Black	47,121A 48,182A (48,216A) (50,5A) 50,66A [50,169A] (51,6A)			
Vinson	48,313A	49,35A	51,151A	

IV. Bargaining

Justices often disagreed on the judgment; some preferred to reverse while others wanted to affirm. But even within the majority, justices might disagree on the justification because they differed on the relevance or interpretation of precedents and statutes. When justices acceded on the judgment and on its justification, they could still differ on its explanation—some wanting instructions that were so narrow that only virtually identical cases would be affected, others preferring instructions that were broad enough to impact a larger class of similar but different cases.

In general, the author preferred an opinion that was joined by the largest number of justices, showed mastery of the topic, would be understood and respected by the legal community, and contained his personal views regarding the justification and explanation of the judgment. The author also wanted colleagues in the majority to join his opinion rather than publish concurring opinions, and he wanted those in the minority to dissent without publishing a dissenting opinion.

The other justices, however, often had objectives that conflicted with those of the author. Bargains were made when both sides benefited from an exchange, but each exchange dealt with only one opinion, i.e., one justice did not join an opinion in exchange for the author's joining another opinion in an unrelated case.

When bargaining over the content of an opinion, each side had various items it could offer to the other. The author could change the justification—that is, he could base the opinion on precedents and statutes that were acceptable to colleagues. The author could also expand or contract the scope of the explanation and thereby increase or decrease the impact of the judgment.

Colleagues in agreement with the judgment could accept legal analyses and precedents with which they disagreed or instructions that were either too narrow or too broad. Also, they could forego their right to leave the opinion of the Court and write a concurring opinion.

Justices in disagreement with the judgment could join the opinion. They could also offer to dissent without publishing a dissenting opinion to which the opinion of the Court generally needed to respond.

Because various opinions were being written over an entire term, a justice simultaneously played different roles in different negotiations—sometimes asking for changes in another's opinion, while other times being asked to make changes in his own. Although a justice could not expect specific reciprocation when he joined another's opinion, joining (or not joining) affected collegial relationships, which in turn affected his ability to induce others to join his opinions. Thus, bargaining was constrained by the nature of a small, collegial body in which a justice's actions influenced his relationships with each of his eight brethren. In addition, factors such as friendship, ideological compatibility, previous collaboration on similar cases, acknowledged expertise, identification with a specific issue, the importance of the case, the complexity or time involved in writing dissenting or concurring opinions, and the workload had impacts on bargaining.

The size of the majority also had a substantial effect on bargaining. The author's power increased with the size of the majority. If the majority had only five members, then the author needed the support of each of the other four assenters. But as the majority increased, there were diminishing returns to additional votes. In addition, as the majority grew, the potential for conflicting requests from within the majority also increased. For example, if one colleague wanted the opinion narrowed while another wanted it expanded, the author could only satisfy one; thus, the colleague whose request was granted needed to offer more than the colleague whose request was denied. Fine (1984) and Berry (1978) present numerous examples of the opinion bargaining that took place during the Vinson Court. The strategies that could be employed during this process are described and discussed in great detail by Murphy (1964, pp.43-63).

V. Prior Research on Opinion Assignment Patterns

Supreme Court scholars have examined assignment patterns, for various time periods, using the report votes as approximations of the conference votes. See Ulmer (1970); McLaughlan (1972); Rhode (1972); Rathjen (1974); and Slotnick (1978, 1979A, 1979B, 1979C). Brenner (1982A) and Brenner and Spaeth (1988) use conference votes obtained from docket books to examine assignment patterns during the Warren era. Although none of these studies contains a comprehensive theory of opinion assignment, together they pose and test several specific hypotheses.

Two of these hypotheses are important for the present analysis. First, Slotnick (1979B, 1979C) demonstrates that new justices are not given fewer assignments. Therefore, the empirical analyses presented below in sections IX and X do not control for a "freshman" effect or for the length of a justice's service on the Court. Second, Brenner (1982A) shows that, during the Warren era, cases with minimum winning conference votes were disproportionally more likely to be assigned to justices ideologically nearest the dissenters or ideologically furthest from the assigner. This result is extended by Brenner and Spaeth (1988), who find that minimum winning conference majorities were more likely to dissolve before the report vote than were larger majorities. Based on these findings, the analyses presented below examine the differences between the assignment patterns of minimum winning and nonminimum winning cases.

Except for Brenner (1982) and Brenner and Spaeth (1988), other studies use the report vote as recorded in *U.S. Reports* to infer which justices formed the majority at the conference vote, which justice received the assignment, and which justice made the assignment. For an example, see Slotnick (1977).

Using the report vote introduces three inaccuracies into the data. First, this vote reveals nothing about assignments that did not result in an opinion because of reassignments or because the opinions became *per curiam* announcements. This is an important distinction, for during the Vinson era 45 opinions were reassigned and twelve were converted to *per curiam* announcements. Second, there are 60 cases in which Chief Justice Vinson was in the minority at the conference vote but in the majority at the report vote. Using the report vote to infer who made assignments would erroneously attribute these 60 assignments to the chief justice. Third, there are ten cases in which Vinson voted with the majority at the conference and made the opinion assignment but dissented from the final opinion. Using the report vote would erroneously attribute these ten assignments to one of the associate justices. These three types of inaccuracies affect 127 assignments or approximately 16 percent of the total.

VI. Assigners' Objectives

When making an opinion assignment, the chief justice or the senior associate could have several objectives: the opinion would hold or increase the majority, conformed to the views of the assigning justice, was emphatic and unambiguous, was acceptable to the general public, would appeal to legal scholars, fostered an equitable distribution of the workload, and would be completed quickly, or at least before the end of the term.

In addition to these objectives for specific cases, the assigners—particularly the chief justice—had objectives for their overall assignment patterns. Assigners wanted a pattern that maximized their influence with their colleagues, that appeared fair and logical, and that minimized rancor.

There are seven additional factors which have unknown effects on the pattern of opinion assignment: the individual relationships between the assigner and the assignee, the relationships between the author and his other brethren, the number of opinions each justice wanted to write, justices' attitudes toward specific cases, the assignee's public persona, the strategies with minimum winning cases, and methods for handling joint assignments.

The number and type of opinion assignments was a major determinant of the already complex relationships between the assigners and the assignees. An assigner could improve his relationship with a colleague by consistently giving him desired assignments. Likewise, an assigner could display his disfavor by conferring difficult but unimportant or undesired opinions. Assignments could also exploit or modify relationships within the Court. If two justices who normally disagree concurred on a case, then assigning the opinion to one might improve their relationship. Similarly, the relationship between two ideologically-close justices might be weakened if one received the assignment in a case in which they differed.

In cases where there was a serious danger of defections, the assignment might go to whoever was least likely to write an opinion that would be unacceptable to others in the majority. Likewise, if there was a possibility of fluidity toward the majority, the opinion might go to the member of the majority closest to the dissenters.

Some justices produced opinions with great ease, while for others writing was a demanding task. In general, little is known about the percentage or the number that each justice wanted: some may have preferred fewer opinions while others preferred more. Writing was time consuming and, for some, exhausting, but it was the only method of communication with the public. A finished opinion was a source of exhilaration and pride. The justices sent printed copies to friends and associates and seemed to pay close attention to law journal evaluations of their efforts as well as to the mail generated by their opinions. Burton was stung by public criticism of the small number of opinions he wrote during his first two years (Fine 1984, p.195) but there is no evidence that he wanted more assignments. Thus, the extent to which assigners were constrained by the need to give each colleague an equitable, or at least a minimal, number of opinions is unknown.

An example of the justices' differing facilities with words is provided by Vinson's official statement following the death of Black's wife, Elizabeth, in 1951. Tradition required that Vinson release a statement praising her character and expressing the Court's condolences to her family. The statement was actually written by Douglas who sent a rough draft to Vinson who then released it under his own name (handwritten memo dated Dec. 1951 and *DRAFT* from Douglas to Vinson; Vinson #215).

The justices did not perceive cases as perfect substitutes and occasionally revealed their preferences by requesting or refusing assignments. In a memo dated October 9, 1946 (Murphy #71-44), Murphy asked for the assignment in *American Power & Light v. S.E.C.* (46,4A). In a memo dated October 19, 1949 (Vinson #215), Frankfurter refused *McGrath v. Manufacturers Trust Company* (49,11A) and requested *U.S. v. Westinghouse Electric* (49,26A). In general, however, both the justices' preferences and the effect of their preferences on the distribution of assignment are permanent mysteries.

In the public's eye, justices were not perfect substitutes. Each received his appointment because of the successful efforts of various interest groups, and once on the Court, each developed his own positions and constituencies. Thus, an opinion assigner tried to exploit the public persona of each of his brethren (McElwain 1949, p.18; O'Brien 1986, pp.245-247).

Similarly, the chief justice was expected to write more than one-ninth of the important or controversial opinions because the prestige of his office enhanced the public's acceptance of decisions that were either unpopular or had a profound effect on the law (Slotnick 1978). For example, two civil rights cases, *McLaurin v. Oklahoma State Regents* (49,34A) and *Sweatt v. Painter* (49,44A), were transferred from Black to Vinson in order to gain the prestige of the chief justice's office.

When the conference vote on-the-merits was minimum winning, the opinion author needed to write with extra care. The size of the opposition increased the likelihood of a vigorous dissent. Each member of the majority was critical; one defection destroyed the majority. Brenner and Spaeth (1988) demonstrate that Chief Justice Warren's strategy for assigning minimum winning cases was different from his method for assigning cases that had larger majorities. Thus, it is plausible that Vinson also employed one approach with minimum winning and another with nonminimum winning cases.

The assigners often gave a series of related cases to one justice with the apparent expectation that this would result in one opinion. Usually the cases had virtually identical facts and had resulted in the same conference vote. Sometimes, however, one assignment included cases that were related without being identical or that had resulted in different conference votes. For example, *McGrath v. Manufacturers Trust Company* (49,11A) and *Manufacturers Trust Company v. McGrath* (49,15A) were given to Burton as one assignment even though the conference votes had produced different majorities. Occasionally the author wrote multiple opinions for one assignment. Thus, Douglas apparently split the assignment of (50,96A) and (50,205A) into two separate opinions.

The ability to assign similar cases to one or more authors is an overlooked element in the assignment power. Giving similar cases to different justices could magnify the differences between the authors, especially if they agreed on the outcome but differed on the justification or the explanation. In a memo to his brethren dated January 24, 1951 (Reed #175; Black #306), Frankfurter expressed concern that the Court was about to "speak out of three corners of the mouth" in three civil rights opinions—(50,26A), (50,217A), and (50,365A)—each of which was being written by a different justice. Giving related cases to one justice reduced the possibility of inconsistent opinions. Similarly, combining related cases into one assignment resulted in an opinion that was more consistent but perhaps more difficult to write.

Given the large number of objectives and constraints, it is impossible to construct a general theory of opinion assignments or to develop any hypotheses about how Vinson's assignment practices differed from those of other chief justices. Neither is it possible to hypothesize about how Vinson's pattern varied from that of the other assigners on his Court. Although Vinson may have had objectives and faced constraints that were different from those of Black, Reed, and Frankfurter, the relative magnitudes of these differences are unknown. For example, The chief justice's administrative responsibilities could have caused him to favor justices who wrote opinions quickly, resulting in the chief's assignment pattern displaying more inequality than that of the associates. But his leadership role may have caused him to strive for an equitable distribution of the workload, causing the chief's pattern to display more equality than that of the associates.

Although the lack of a model makes it difficult—perhaps improper—to construct hypotheses about opinion assignment patterns, the following sections test for the existence and importance of three factors. The first factor is an inverse relationship between the number of assignments received by a justice and the average number of days he took to complete opinions. It is plausible that the necessity of completing opinions in a timely manner caused assigners to favor those colleagues who wrote most expeditiously. It is also plausible that those who wrote quickly also enjoyed writing and preferred more assignments while those who wrote slowly preferred fewer.

The second factor examined below is the distinction between the chief justice's assignment pattern and the other assigners' pattern. The third factor is the difference between the distributions of minimum and nonminimum winning cases. Although it is impossible to predict *a priori* how these last two factors affect assignments, it is possible to determine *ex post* if they result in different assignment patterns.

VII. Data and Measurements

For each justice the mean number of days, including weekends, between assignment and announcement of an opinion is used as a measure of productivity. This is not, however, a perfect measure of how long it took the various justices to write majority opinions for at least five reasons. First, justices had other important responsibilities which may not have been equally distributed. Second, illness or injury reduced the productivity of some of the justices, e.g., Douglas was injured during much of the October 1949 term and Murphy was in failing health during the October 1948 term. Third, this measure ignores the role that a justice's law clerks played in opinion writing. A justice who delegated substantial opinion writing responsibilities to his law clerks could produce faster than a justice who wrote his own opinions. Fourth, opinion writing was frequently a group, rather than a solo, activity. The author often compromised with other members of the majority and attempted to induce dissenters to join the opinion. The time needed for accommodation and compromise depended as much on the other justices as it did on the opinion writer. In addition, if other justices wrote dissenting or concurring opinions, the majority opinion was usually not released until these other opinions were finished. Fifth, cases that were reassigned or converted to *per curiam* announcements create particular complications, which are discussed below.

This chapter analyzes the actions of both the opinion assigners and the assignees. Assignments were made with the expectation that they would result in completed opinions, even though the assigning justice had only limited influence over the amount of time taken and whether the opinion continued to hold a majority. Therefore, when examining the assigners' behavior, the appropriate variable is assignments rather than completed opinions. However, when computing the mean time taken to complete opinions, only completed opinions are meaningful. Thus, both assignments and completed opinions are used in this analysis, the first to examine the assignment patterns of the assigning justices, the second to estimate the mean number of days each justice took to write opinions.

For reassignments to the same justice, only the last assignment is used. For example, *Winters v. New York* (47,3A) was assigned to Reed on November 11, 1946, and then reassigned to him a year later on November 18, 1947. The case is treated as one assignment, and only the 1947 date is used to compute the mean number of days Reed took to write opinions.

If a case was reassigned to a different justice, both assignments are counted, because both were made with the expectation that they would result in an opinion. However, only a completed assignment can be used to compute the mean number of days, either because the first assignment was not completed or because the date of completion is unknown. For example, *Central Greyhound Lines v. Mealey* (47,14A) was assigned to Murphy by Black on October 22, 1947. Murphy could not hold the majority, so the case was reassigned to Frankfurter by the chief justice on November 14, 1947. Frankfurter delivered the opinion of the Court 213 days later, on June 6, 1948. Both assignments—one by Black and one by Vinson—are used to analyze the justices' assignment behavior, but only the 213 days spent by Frankfurter can be used to estimate the mean number of days taken to complete opinions.

Sometimes, the reassignment cannot be used to estimate the mean number of days taken to complete an assignment because the opinion was transferred just before announcement. For example, *Saia v. New York* (47,504A) was assigned to Frankfurter by the chief justice on April 2, 1948. Frankfurter lost the majority to Douglas on June 1, 1948, when the chief justice changed his vote from affirm to reverse, joined what had been Douglas' dissenting opinion, and assigned the case to Douglas who delivered the opinion of the Court six days later on June 7, 1948. Because Douglas wrote the opinion before he received the assignment, the six-day interval between assignment and announcement is not meaningful. Therefore, cases that were reassigned are not used to compute the mean number of days taken to complete an opinion if there is less than a twenty-day interval between reassignment and announcement of the opinion. The twenty-day minimum—which is obviously arbitrary—results in seven reassignments not being used to compute the mean number of days. Any other minimum would be equally arbitrary and would result in little change in the data and in the empirical results.

When an assignment was converted to a *per curiam* announcement, it is counted as an assignment, but it is not used to compute the mean number of days taken to complete opinions. For example, Black assigned *Dyer v. City Council of Beloit* (47,275A) to Frankfurter on December 17, 1947. The case was subsequently vacated as moot in a brief *per curiam* on February 2, 1948. The case is used to analyze the assignment pattern but it cannot be used to estimate the mean number of days taken by Frankfurter to complete opinions.

Occasionally an assignment was not completed for other reasons. Murphy could not deliver his opinion in *Eisler v. U.S.* (48,255A) because the petitioner (who would have won on-the-merits) had fled the country and thereby mooted the case. Other examples include Clark recusing himself in *Ackermann v. U.S.* (50,35A) after receiving the assignment, and Frankfurter transferring *Trupiano v. U.S.* (47,427A) to Murphy after discovering that Murphy wanted the assignment.

VIII. Method

The relationship between the mean number of days taken to write an opinion and the number of assignments received is measured by the simple correlation between the two variables. The Z-statistic generated by each simple correlation is used to test for statistical significance. The amount of inequality in the number of assignments is measured by a gini coefficient, a number between zero (complete equality) and one (complete inequality). For both natural Courts, the analysis examines two major categories: all assignments and assignments made by the chief justice. The categories are further divided into two different sub-categories: nonminimum winning and minimum winning.

Minimum winning cases were decided by votes of five-to-four, four-to-four, three-to-three, or four-to-three at the conference vote. Cases which were minimum winning at the conference were not always minimum winning in *U.S. Reports*. An example of such a case is *Railway Express Agency v. New York* (48,51A). The conference vote on December 12, 1948, was five-to-four to affirm. On December 18, 1948, Black, the senior member of the majority, assigned the case to Douglas who wrote an opinion that converted the dissenters. The opinion of the Court, announced on January 31, 1949, was nine-to-zero to affirm.

IX. Results for the First Natural Court

The data for the first natural Court contain 373 cases, including two from the original docket. These cases resulted in 365 completed opinions and 398 assignments. The chief justice made 317 assignments, Black made 63, Reed seven, Frankfurter nine, Douglas one, and the assigner of one is unknown. Table 8.2 presents the results obtained for the first natural Court. The first column of numbers shows the number of assignments completed and the number received (in brackets) by each justice. The next column shows the mean number of days taken to complete opinions by each justice.

There are vast differences in the mean number of days taken to write opinions. The range is wide, from 106, 99, and 99 days taken by Frankfurter,

Table 8.2

Opinion assignments completed and received and the mean number of days it took justices to complete majority opinions—First Natural Court.

	ALL ASSIGNMENTS Number Completed [received]	Mean Days	ASSIGNMENTS BY C.J. Number completed [received]	Mean Days
Burton	17 [22]	99	13 [15]	94
Rutledge	29 [30]	75	22 [23]	82
Jackson	41 [42]	61	34 [35]	61
Murphy	35 [39]	55	27 [29]	53
Douglas	70 [71]	43	56 [56]	44
Frankfurter	33 [40]	106	24 [27]	108
Reed	41 [47]	84	33 [37]	82
Black	65 [69]	40	53 [57]	41
Vinson	34 [38]	99	34 [38]	99
TOTAL	365 [398]		296 [317]	
mean	40.6 [44.2]		33.0 [35.2]	
gini	.19		.21	
Correlation mean days and assignments received	-.73 $(Z = -2.30)*$		-.67 $(Z = -2.05)*$	

* statistically significant at 5 percent level.

Burton, and Vinson to 40 and 43 days taken by Black and Douglas. The number of assignments received also varies widely. Douglas and Black obtained 71 and 69, which are more than a standard deviation above the mean. Burton obtained 22, which is more than a standard deviation below the mean. The correlation coefficient between assignments and mean number of days taken to complete opinions (-.73) indicates an inverse relationship which is statistically significant. The distribution of assignments produces a gini coefficient of .19.

The third and fourth columns of table 8.2 show the results for cases assigned by the chief justice. (Information on assignments made by the associate justices is not shown but can be inferred by subtracting the assignments made by the chief justice from all assignments.) The chief justice's assignments also display wide variations. Black and Douglas received 57 and 56, which are more than a standard deviation above the mean, while Burton obtained only 15, which is more than a standard deviation below the mean. The correlation coefficient between assignments and mean number of days (-.67) shows an inverse relationship which is statistically significant.

The gini coefficient for the chief justice's assignments, .21, is very similar to that for all assignments, .19. The chi-square statistic used to test whether the pattern of the chief justice's assignments is independent from the pattern of the other assigners (not shown) is 5.6 with seven degrees of freedom (one less than the number of assignees), which is not statistically significant. Thus, there is no evidence that Vinson's pattern of assignments to the eight associate justices is significantly different from the other assigners' pattern.

Because both distributions are similar and both contain considerable inequality, it is likely that all the assigners confronted similar objectives and constraints. For example, Burton and Rutledge had difficulty writing opinions and may have preferred fewer assignments, while Black and Douglas enjoyed writing and preferred more. In any event, equality in the number of opinion assignments was apparently not a major objective of the assigners.

It is interesting that Chief Justice Vinson favored the justices who wrote most expeditiously (Douglas and Black) even though their judicial ideology was furthest from his own and in spite of the relatively large number of assignments (15 and 12) they received from the other assigners. Burton, on the other hand, was disadvantaged by Vinson even though he was ideologically closest to the chief justice and in spite of the relatively few assignments (seven) he received from the other assigners. The chief justice gave Burton only about a fourth of the number of assignments he gave to Black and Douglas (15 vs. 57 and 56). Reed, Jackson, and Frankfurter, who were philosophically closer to the chief than were Black and Douglas, also received fewer assignments (37, 35, and 27) from Vinson than did Black and Douglas. Thus, the amount of time taken to complete opinions may have motivated Vinson's behavior even though it resulted in a disproportionate number of opinions being written by justices from the liberal bloc who were most often his philosophical opponents.

The gini coefficients for all assignments made by the chief justice decline steadily during the three terms of the first natural Court—.26, .23, and .17 (data not shown)—which indicates that Vinson was moving toward a pattern of more equality in opinion assignments during this period. These results are similar to Slotnick's (1977) findings based on a study that analyzes opinions completed, rather than assignments, and uses the report vote, rather than the conference vote, to determine the opinion assigner.

Tables 8.3a and 8.3b show the results obtained when the dataset for the first natural Court is divided into nonminimum winning and minimum winning cases. For nonminimum winning cases (in table 8.3a), the correlation coefficients between the number of assignments and the mean number of days taken to complete opinions are negative and statistically significant: for all nonminimum winning assignments, -.70, and for nonminimum winning assignments made by the chief justice, -.63. For minimum winning cases (in table 8.3b), however, the correlation coefficients are smaller (-.42 and -.35) and are not statistically significant. The decline in the correlation indicates that the relationship between the amount of time taken to write opinions and the number of assignments was less important when the case was minimum winning.

The chi-square statistics used to determine whether the chief justice's patterns of assignments are independent from the other assigners' patterns are not significant for both nonminimum and minimum winning cases. In addition, the four gini coefficients in tables 8.3a and 8.3b display little variation. Therefore, there is no evidence that the chief justice's pattern resulted in a more or a less equitable distribution.

The chi-square statistics used to determine whether the underlying distributions (to all nine justices) of nonminimum winning and minimum winning cases are independent are both statistically significant. The chi-square statistics (with eight degrees of freedom) are 16.8, for all assignments, and 16.3, for assignments made by the chief justice. Thus, all the assigners apparently used a different strategy when assigning minimum winning cases.

The chief justice, for example, gave more nonminimum winning cases to Black (50) and Douglas (47) than he gave to Reed (24), Jackson (23), and Frankfurter (17). But Vinson assigned more minimum winning cases to Reed (13), Jackson (twelve), and Frankfurter (ten) than he assigned to Douglas

Table 8.3a

Opinion assignments completed and received and the mean number of days it took justices to complete majority opinions — First Natural Court (Nonminimum Winning Cases).

	ALL ASSIGNMENTS Number completed [received]	Mean Days	ASSIGNMENTS BY C.J. Number completed [received]	Mean Days
Burton	12 [15]	94	9 [11]	85
Rutledge	24 [24]	72	19 [19]	77
Jackson	27 [27]	55	23 [23]	53
Murphy	28 [30]	51	23 [24]	50
Douglas	56 [57]	44	47 [47]	43
Frankfurter	21 [22]	112	16 [17]	114
Reed	29 [31]	84	23 [24]	77
Black	52 [55]	39	47 [50]	40
Vinson	29 [32]	98	29 [32]	98
TOTAL	278 [293]		236 [247]	
mean	30.8 [32.6]		26.2 [27.4]	
gini	.22		.25	
Correlation mean days and assignments received	-.70 (Z = -2.15)*		-.63 (Z = -1.81)*	

* statistically significant at 5 percent level.

Table 8.3b

Opinion assignments completed and received and the mean number of days it took justices to complete majority opinions—First Natural Court (Minimum Winning Cases).

	ALL ASSIGNMENTS Number completed [received]	Mean Days	ASSIGNMENTS BY C.J. Number completed [received]	Mean Days
Burton	5 [7]	112	4 [4]	114
Rutledge	5 [6]	90	3 [4]	133
Jackson	14 [15]	72	11 [12]	78
Murphy	7 [9]	70	4 [5]	69
Douglas	14 [14]	42	9 [9]	50
Frankfurter	12 [18]	97	8 [10]	98
Reed	12 [16]	84	10 [13]	93
Black	13 [14]	42	6 [7]	55
Vinson	5 [6]	104	5 [6]	104
TOTAL	87 [105]		60 [70]	
mean	9.7 [11.6]		6.7 [7.8]	
gini	.21		.23	

Correlation mean days and assignments received

$-.42$ $-.35$

$(Z = -1.10)$ $(Z = -0.89)$

Table 8.4

Opinion assignments completed and received and the mean number of days it took justices to complete majority opinions—Second Natural Court

	ALL ASSIGNMENTS Number completed [received]	Mean Days	ASSIGNMENTS BY C.J. Number completed [received]	Mean Days
Minton	42 [42]	38	33 [33]	37
Clark	44 [47]	35	36 [39]	35
Burton	37 [37]	73	27 [27]	73
Jackson	43 [44]	51	38 [38]	50
Douglas	39 [42]	34	35 [36]	29
Frankfurter	37 [38]	77	25 [25]	82
Reed	37 [42]	59	28 [32]	62
Black	46 [57]	40	33 [39]	40
Vinson	41 [41]	75	41 [41]	75
TOTAL	366 [390]		296 [310]	
mean	40.7 [43.3]		32.9 [34.4]	
gini	.06		.09	

Correlation mean days
and assignments received   -.60   -.52
                                       (Z = -1.72)*   (Z = -1.43)

*statistically significant at 5 percent level.

(nine) or Black (seven). Thus, the chief justice favored members of the liberal bloc with nonminimum winning cases but favored his fellow conservatives with minimum winning cases.

X. Results for the Second Natural Court

The dataset for the second natural Court contains 372 cases, including two from the original docket. These cases resulted in 366 completed opinions and 390 assignments. The chief justice made 310 assignments, Black made 57, Reed 18, and Frankfurter five. Table 8.4 presents the results obtained from the data for the second natural Court. The results are also divided into two sections—all assignments and assignments made by the chief justice. Douglas received only four assignments during the October 1949 term because he spent most of the term (the beginning of the second natural Court) recuperating from a serious horse-riding accident. He had written 20 opinions in the preceding term. Thus, the assignment pattern for the second natural Court is distorted by the absence of the most productive writer for most of one of the four terms.

The results for all assignments show differences among the justices in the amount of time taken to complete opinions (e.g., Douglas, Clark, Minton, and Black averaged 34, 35, 38, and 40 days while Burton, Vinson, and Frankfurter averaged 73, 75, and 77), but these differences are smaller than those of the first natural Court. The disparity in the numbers of cases assigned is also smaller during the second Court. The range is from 57 (Black) to 37 (Burton) and the gini coefficient is .06. On the first Court the range is much greater, from 71 (Douglas) to 22 (Burton), and the gini coefficient is three times as large, .19 (table 8.2).

The assignments made by Vinson show much more equality in the second Court. The gini declines from .21 on the first to .09 on the second. The difference between the most, 41 (Vinson), and fewest, 25 (Frankfurter), opinions is also smaller on the second Court. On the first Court the numbers of assignments received by Douglas and Black are a standard deviation above the mean number of assignments made by the chief justice, but on the second, the numbers received by Douglas and Black are much closer to the mean. The trend toward greater equality in Vinson's assignment pattern, which began during the first Court, continued during the second. The gini coefficients for all assignments made by the chief justice declined steadily, .17, .11, .09, and .06 (data not shown) during the four terms.

In table 8.4, the correlation coefficient for all assignments made during

Table 8.5a

Opinion assignments completed and received and the mean number of days it took justices to complete majority opinions—Second Natural Court (Non-minimum winning).

	ALL ASSIGNMENTS Number completed [received]	Mean Days	ASSIGNMENTS BY C.J. Number completed [received]	Mean Days
Minton	36 [36]	39	30 [30]	38
Clark	33 [34]	34	28 [29]	35
Burton	27 [27]	78	22 [22]	74
Jackson	39 [40]	50	35 [35]	48
Douglas	34 [35]	32	32 [33]	30
Frankfurter	28 [28]	71	19 [19]	71
Reed	26 [30]	60	22 [25]	60
Black	35 [44]	40	27 [33]	39
Vinson	40 [40]	73	40 [40]	73
TOTAL	298 [314]		255 [266]	
mean	33.1 [34.9]		28.3 [29.6]	
gini	.09		.12	

Correlation mean days
and assignments received   -.46   -.34
                                              (Z = -1.23)   (Z = -0.88)

the second Court, -.60, is significant and demonstrates the inverse relationship between the number of assignments and the mean number of days taken to complete opinions. But the coefficient for assignments made by the chief justice, -.52, is not significant. Both of these coefficients have lower absolute magnitudes than the comparable coefficients for the first Court (-.73 vs. -.60 for all assignments and -.67 vs. -.52 for assignments made by Vinson). The chi-square statistic used to test for the independence of the chief justice's assignment pattern from that of the associate justices (not shown) is not statistically significant. Thus, although the correlation coefficients in table 8.4 differ, there is no significant evidence that the underlying distributions differ.

The mean number of days taken to complete opinions declined between the first, 66 (data not shown), and second, 53, natural Courts. This two-week decline in the mean had two causes. First, Minton and Clark joined the Court and became relatively rapid opinion writers. Minton wrote opinions in an average of 38 days and Clark in an average of 35. The only faster writer was Douglas, who averaged 34 days. Second, in June of 1949, Douglas became so exasperated that the opinions in *Wolf v. Colorado* (48,17A) and *Lustig v. U.S.* (48,1389A), both of which had been assigned the preceding October, were not finished that he made an effort to force a rule change which would have required a reassignment if the opinion was not finished within three months (Fine 1984, p.254; memo to the conference from Douglas dated June 15, 1949; Vinson #215). Although the rule—which was aimed at Frankfurter, who averaged 106 days during the first Court—was not adopted, it must have had some effect. The three slowest writers on the first Court—Frankfurter, Burton, and Vinson—became two to three weeks faster on the second Court. Frankfurter moved from 106 days to 77, Burton from 99 days to 73, and Vinson from 99 to 75.

Tables 8.5a and 8.5b present the results obtained when the dataset for the second natural Court is divided into nonminimum winning and minimum winning categories. For all nonminimum winning assignments (table 8.5a), the correlation coefficients between the number of assignments and the mean number of days taken to complete assignments are negative, but are not statistically significant: for all assignments, -.46, and for assignments made by the chief, -.34. The results are similar for minimum winning cases (table 8.5b): for all assignments, -.53, and for assignments made by the chief justice, -.30.

The chi-square statistics used to test whether the underlying distributions of nonminimum winning and minimum winning cases are independent are both statistically significant. The chi-square statistics are 18.6, for all assignments, and 15.8, for assignments made by the chief justice. These

Table 8.5b

Opinion assignments completed and received and the mean number of days it took justices to complete majority opinions—Second Natural Court (Minimum Winning).

	ALL ASSIGNMENTS Number completed [received]	Mean Days	ASSIGNMENTS BY C.J. Number completed [received]	Mean Days
Minton	6 [6]	31	3 [3]	29
Clark	11 [13]	35	8 [10]	34
Burton	10 [10]	59	5 [5]	69
Jackson	4 [4]	58	3 [3]	69
Douglas	5 [7]	47	3 [3]	27
Frankfurter	9 [10]	96	6 [6]	118
Reed	11 [12]	58	6 [7]	68
Black	11 [13]	43	6 [6]	43
Vinson	1 [1]	132	1 [1]	132
TOTAL	68 [76]		41 [44]	
mean	7.6 [8.4]		4.6 [4.9]	
gini	.26		.29	

Correlation mean days
and assignments received   -.53   -.30
         $(Z = -1.45)$ $(Z = -0.75)$

statistics indicate that there is a significant difference in the distribution of nonminimum winning and minimum winning assignments during the second Court. These results are quite similar to the results obtained for the first natural Court.

The gini coefficients show that there is considerably more inequality in the distributions of minimum winning than in the distributions of nonminimum winning cases. For all assignments the gini increases from .09 for nonminimum winning to .26 for minimum winning cases. For cases assigned by the chief justice, the gini increases from .12 for nonminimum winning to .29 for minimum winning cases.

The chief justice assigned himself 41 opinions, only one of which was minimum winning. By contrast, he assigned Clark 39 opinions, ten of which were minimum winning. Vinson gave fewer mimimum winning assignments to Black (six) and Douglas (three) than he gave to Clark (ten) and Reed (seven) whose ideological positions were nearer his own. These differences are, however, much smaller than those of the first Court, and the numbers of minimum winning assignments received by Black and Douglas are similar to those received by Frankfurter (six), Burton (five), and Jackson (three). Thus, Vinson's strategy of assigning more nonminimum winning cases to liberals but more minimum winning cases to conservatives was apparently not continued into the second Court.

XI. Conclusions

The major findings of this chapter can be summarized as follows.

There were 40 instances in which the author switched sides following receipt of the opinion assignment. These switches represent about five percent of the total. Minton never changed, while Reed, who switched in about ten percent of his assignments, was the most likely to change.

Using the report vote to infer who assigned the opinion results in inaccuracies in approximately 16 percent of all assignments.

During the first natural Court the average number of days taken by justices to complete opinions ranged from 106 (Frankfurter) to 40 (Black). During the second Court the differences declined: Douglas, who averaged 34 days, was the quickest writer, while Frankfurter, who averaged 77 days, was still the slowest.

Vinson's assignment pattern is not significantly different from that of the other assigners. Both display considerable inequality, but the level of inequality declined steadily during the seven terms.

There is an inverse relationship between the number of assignments received by a justice and the mean number of days he took to complete opinions. This inverse relationship is statistically significant for all assignments in both Courts and for assignments made by Vinson during the first Court.

During the first natural Court, Vinson favored the justices who wrote quickly even though this preference required that he assign proportionally more opinions to colleagues whose ideology was furthest from his own.

The distributions of nonminimum winning and minimum winning cases are different. Vinson followed a strategy of assigning minimum winning cases to colleagues whose ideologies were near his own during the first Court, but there is no evidence that he followed this strategy during the second.

References

Abraham, Henry J. 1974. *Justices And Presidents: A Political History of Appointments to the Supreme Court.* New York: Oxford University Press.

Armstrong, Virginia C. and Charles A. Johnson. 1982. "Certiorari Decisions by the Warren & Burger Courts: Is Cue Theory Time Bound," *Polity.* 15:141-150.

Baum, Lawrence. 1977. "Policy Goals In Judicial Gatekeeping: A Proximity Model Of Discretionary Jurisdiction," *American Journal Of Political Science.* 21:13-35.

Baum, Lawrence. 1979. "Judical Demand-Screening And Decisions On The Merits: A Second Look," *American Politics Quarterly.* 7:109-119.

Baum, Lawrence. 1985. *The Supreme Court: Second Edition.* Washington D.C.: Congressional Quarterly.

Berry, Mary Frances. 1978. *Stability, Security, and Continuity: Mr. Justice Burton and Decision-Making in the Supreme Court 1945-1958.* Westport: Greenwood Press.

Brenner, Saul. 1979A. "The New Certiorari Game, *Journal Of Politics.* 41:649-655.

Brenner, Saul. 1979B. "Minimum Winning Coalitions On The U.S. Supreme Court: A Comparison of the Original Vote on the Merits and the Opinion Vote," *American Politics Quarterly.* 7:384-392.

Brenner, Saul. 1980. "Fluidity on the United States Supreme Court: A Reexamination," *American Journal Of Political Science.* 24:526-535.

Brenner, Saul. 1982A. "Strategic Choice and Opinion Assignment on the U.S. Supreme Court: A Reexamination," *Western Political Quarterly.* 35:204-211.

Brenner, Saul. 1982B. "Fluidity on the Supreme Court: 1956-1967," *American Journal Of Political Science*. 26:388-390.

Brenner, Saul. 1983. "Another Look at Freshman Indecisiveness on the United States Supreme Court," *Polity*. 16:320-328.

Brenner, Saul. 1984. "Issue Specialization as a Variable in Assignment on the U.S. Supreme Court," *Journal of Politics*. 46: 1217-1225.

Brenner, Saul. 1985. "Is Competence Related to Majority Opinion Assignment on the U.S. Supreme Court?" *Capital University Law Review*. 15:1135-1141.

Brenner, Saul. 1986. "Reassigning the Majority Opinion on the United States Supreme Court," *Justice System Journal*. 11:186-195.

Brenner, Saul and Harold J. Spaeth. 1986. "Issue Specialization in Majority Opinion Assignment on the Burger Court," *Western Political Quarterly*. 39:520-527.

Brenner, Saul and Harold J. Spaeth. 1988. "Majority Opinion Assignment and the Maintenance of the Original Coalition on the Warren Court," *American Journal of Political Science*. 32:72-81.

Brigham, John. 1987. *The Cult Of The Court*. Philadelphia: Temple University Press.

Dawson, Nelson L. 1980. *Louis D. Brandeis, Felix Frankfurter And The New Deal*. Hamden, Connecticut: Archon Books.

Douglas, William O. 1980. *The Court Years (1939-1975): The Autobiography of William O. Douglas*. New York: Random House.

Fine, Sidney. 1984. *Frank Murphy: The Washington Years*. Ann Arbor: University of Michigan Press.

Goldman, Sheldon. 1987. *Constitutional Law: Cases and Essays*. New York: Harper & Row.

Harper, Fowler V. and Alan S. Rosenthan. 1950. "What The Supreme Court Did Not Do In The 1949 Term—An Appraisal Of Certiorari," *University Of Pennsylvania Law Review*. 99:293-325.

Harper, Fowler V. and Edwin D. Etherington. 1951. "What The Supreme Court Did Not Do During The 1950 Term," *University Of Pennsylvania Law Review*. 100:354-409.

Harper, Fowler V. and George C. Pratt. 1953. "What The Supreme Court Did Not Do During The 1951 Term," *University Of Pennsylvania Law Review*. 101:439-479.

Harper, Fowler V. and Arnold Leibowitz. 1954. "What The Supreme Court Did Not Do During The 1952 Term," *University Of Pennsylvania Law Review*. 102:427-463.

Heck, Edward V. and Melinda G. Hall. 1981. "Bloc Voting and The Freshman Justice Revisited," *Journal Of Politics*. 43:852-860.

Howard, J. Woodford. 1968. "On The Fluidity of Judicial Choice," *American Political Science Review*, 62:43-56.

Jackson, Percival E. 1969. *Dissent In The Supreme Court: A Chronology*. Norman: University Of Oklahoma Press.

Landes, William. 1974. "Legality and Reality: Some Evidence on Criminal Procedure," *The Journal Of Legal Studies*. 3:287-335.

Lindgren, James and William P. Marshall. 1986. "The Supreme Court's Extraordinary Power To Grant Certiorari Before Judgment In The Court Of Appeals," *The Supreme Court Review*. 1986:259-316.

McElwain, Edwin. 1949. "The Business of the Supreme Court as Conducted by Chief Justice Hughes," *Harvard Law Review*. 63:5-26.

McLauchlan, William. 1972. "Ideology and Conflict In Supreme Court Opinion Assignment, 1946-1962," *Western Political Quarterly*. 25:16-27.

Murphy, Bruce Allen. 1982. *The Brandeis/Frankfurter Connection: The Secret Political Activities of Two Supreme Court Justices*. New York:Oxford University Press.

Murphy, Walter F. 1964. *Elements of Judicial Strategy*. Chicago: University Of Chicago Press.

Murphy, Walter F. 1959. "Lower Court Checks on Supreme Court Power," *American Political Science Review*. 53:1017-1031.

Nagel, Stuart S. 1965. "Court-Curbing Periods in American History," *Vanderbilt Law Review*, 18: 925-944.

O'Brien, David M. 1986. *Storm Center: The Supreme Court in American Politics*. New York: W. W. Norton & Company.

Palmer, Jan S. 1982. "An Economic Analysis of the U.S. Supreme Court's certiorari decisions," *Public Choice*. 39: 387-398.

Pritchett, C. Herman. 1954. *Civil Liberties annd the Vinson Court*. Chicago: University Of Chicago Press.

Provine, Doris Marie. 1980. *Case Selection in the United States Supreme Court*. Chicago: University Of Chicago Press.

Rathjen, Gregory J. 1974. "Policy Goals, Strategic Choice, and Majority Opinion Assignments in the U.S. Supreme Court: A Replication," *American Journal of Political Science*. 18:713-724.

Rathjen, Gregory J. and Harold J. Spaeth. 1983. "Denial Of Access And Ideological Preferences: An Analysis Of The Voting Behavior Of The Burger Court Justices, 1969-1976," *Western Political Quarterly*. 36:71-87.

Rehnquist, William H. 1987. *The Supreme Court: How It Was, How It Is*. New York: William Morrow.

Rhode, David W. 1972. "Policy Goals, Strategic Choices, and Majority Opinion Assignments in the U.S. Supreme Court, *Midwest Journal Of Political Science*. 15:652-82.

Rhode, David W. and Harold J. Spaeth. 1976. *Supreme Court Decision Making*. San Francisco: W.H. Freeman and Company.

Rosenzweig, Simon. 1951. "The Opinions of Judge Edgerton: A Study In The Judicial Process," *Cornell Law Quarterly*. 37:149-205.

Schubert, Glendon. 1965. *The Judicial Mind: The Attitudes and Ideologies of Supreme Court Justices 1946-1963*. Evanston: Northwestern University Press.

Schubert, Glendon. 1974. *The Judicial Mind Revisited, Psychometric Analysis of Supreme Court Ideology*. New York: Oxford University Press.

Scigliano, Robert. 1971. *The Supreme Court and the Presidency*. New York: The Free Press.

Slotnick, Elliott E. 1977. *Who Speaks for the Court? The Chief Justice and the Assignment of Majority Opinions*. Ann Arbor: University Microfilms International.

Slotnick, Elliott E. 1978. "The Chief Justice and the Assignment Majority Opinions: A Research Note," *Western Political Quarterly*. 31: 219-225.

Slotnick, Elliott E. 1979A. "The Equality Principle and Majority Opinion Assignment on the United States Supreme Court," *Polity*. 12: 318-332.

Slotnick, Elliott E. 1979B. "Judicial Career Patterns and Majority Opinion Assignments on the Supreme Court," *Journal of Politics*. 41: 640-648.

Slotnick, Elliott E. 1979C. "Who Speaks for the Court? Majority Opinion Assignment from Taft to Burger," *American Journal of Political Science*. 23: 60-77.

Songer, Donald R. 1979. "Concern for Policy Outputs as a Cue for Supreme Court Decisions on Certiorari," *Journal Of Politics*. 41:1183-1194.

Spaeth, Harold J. 1979. *Supreme Court Policy Making: Explanation and Prediction*. San Francisco: W.H. Freeman.

Spaeth, Harold J. "Distributive Justice: Majority Opinion Assignments in the Burger Court," *Judicature*. 67: 299-304.

Sprague, John D. 1968. *Voting Patterns Of The United States Supreme Court: Cases in Federalism, 1889-1959*. Indianapolis: Bobbs-Merrill.

Steamer, Robert J. 1986. *Chief Justice: Leadership and the Supreme Court*. Columbia SC: University of South Carolina Press.

Stern, Robert and Eugene Gressman. 1950. *Supreme Court Practice*. Washington DC: The Bureau of National Affairs.

Stern, Robert and Eugene Gressman. 1978. *Supreme Court Practice: Fifth Edition*. Washington DC: The Bureau of National Affairs.

Strum, Philippa. 1974. *The Supreme Court And "Political Questions": A Study In Judicial Evasion*. Birmingham: University Of Alabama Press.

Tanenhaus, Joseph, Marvin Schick, Matthew Muraskin, and Daniel Rosen. 1963. "The Supreme Court's Certiorari Jurisdiction: Cue Theory," in *Judicial Decision Making*, (Glenden Schubert, ed.). New York: The Free Press of Glencoe.

Teger, Stuart H. and Douglas Kosinski. 1980. "The Cue Theory of Supreme Court Certiorari Jurisdiction: A Reconsideration," *Journal Of Politics*. 42:834-846.

Ulmer, S. Sidney. 1970. "The Use Of Power in the Supreme Court: The Opinion Assignments of Earl Warren," *Journal Of Public Law*. 19:49-67.

Ulmer, S. Sidney. 1972. "The Deicsion to Grant Certiorari as an Indicator to Decision on the Merits," *Polity* 4:439-447.

Ulmer, S. Sidney. 1973. "Supreme Court Justices as Strict and Not So Strict Constructionists: Some Implications," *Law And Society Review*. 8:13-32.

Ulmer, S. Sidney. 1978. "Selecting Cases for Supreme Court Review: An Underdog Model," *American Political Science Review*. 72:902-910.

Ulmer, S. Sidney. 1984. "The Supreme Court's Certiorari Decisions: Conflict as a Predictive Value," *American Political Science Review*. 78:901-911.

Ulmer, S. Sidney, William Hintze, and Louise Kirklosky. 1972. "The Decision To Grant Or Deny Certiorari: Further Consideration Of Cue Theory," *Law And Society Review*. 6:637-643.

Wasby, Stephen L. 1988. *The Supreme Court In The Federal Judicial System*. 3rd ed. Chicago: Nelson-Hall.

Wigdor, Alexandra. 1986. *The Personal Papers Of Supreme Court Justices: A Descriptive Guide*. New York: Garland Publishing.

Yale Law Journal. 1969. "Government Litigation in the Supreme Court: The Roles of the Solicitor General," *Yale Law Journal*, 78:1442-1481.

Index

amicus curiae 28, 36
Appeals 23
    agreement between justices 85-88
    cases in which a justice determined the
        outcome 92, 93
    case selection via **chapter 6**
    conclusions 95, 96
    conformity 88-92
    differences from certiorari 77, 78
    model of case selection 80, 82-84
    note rates of individual justices 78-80
    noting jurisdiction 27
    solo votes 93-95
Argument of cases 28
Attorney General 9, 13, 31, 32, 40
Black, Hugo 3, 9, 10, 11, 13-15, 18, 26, 31, 47,
    48, 51, 55, 66, 70, 72-75, 80, 85, 88, 92, 93,
    98, 100, 104, 107, 112, 114, 116, 119-121,
    123, 126, 127, 134, 135, 137, 138, 140, 141,
    145, 149
    background 7, 8
    futile votes 47
    private papers 38, 41
    quoted 45
    solo votes 73
Blocs 64
    cert votes **chapter 5**
    jurisdiction votes **chapter 6**
    membership 8, 18
    votes on-the-merits **chapter 7**
Burton, Harold 3, 7, 13, 18, 31, 40, 41, 52, 55,
    63, 64, 70, 72-74, 78, 85, 98, 100, 104, 112,
    116, 119-121, 123, 126, 140, 145, 147, 149
    background 12
    private papers 2, 36, 37, 38, 39, 42, 43, 46,
        48
    quoted 126
Cases and Controversies 18-20
Certiorari 22, 23, 27, 35
    agreement between justices 63-66
    case selection via **chapter 5**
    complementary cases 62, 63
    conclusions 73-75
    conformity 66-70
    differences from appeals 77, 78

    grant rates of individual justices 54, 55
    model of case selection 53-54
    previous studies 51, 52
    relationship with votes on-the-merits 55,
        58, 59-62
    solo votes 73
    written rules 51
Certified Questions 22
Clark, Ramsey 13
Clark, Tom 15, 31, 32, 38, 55, 66, 70, 73, 74,
    88, 93, 107, 112, 114, 119, 127, 137, 145,
    147, 149
    background 12, 13
    opinion writing 31, 127
    private papers 37, 38, 40, 42, 43, 46
    quoted 63
Clerks 30, 31
Conference 17, 25-27, 35
Conference List 25, 29, 37, 38
Court curbing 33
Court-packing plan 11, 14, 33
Cue theory 51, 52
Dataset
    complementary sources 34
    method of gathering 42
    errors 43-49
    format **appendix A**
Dead List *See* Special List
Decision Mondays 30
Docket Books 34-36, 44
Dockets 21
    Original 21, 37
    Appellate 22, 36
    Miscellaneous 23, 37, 38, 77
Douglas, William 2, 8, 9-12, 15, 18, 31, 41,
    48, 51, 52, 55, 66, 70, 72, 73, 75, 78, 80, 85,
    88, 92, 93, 96, 98, 100, 104, 107, 112, 114,
    116, 119, 120, 121, 123, 126, 127, 128, 134,
    136, 137, 138, 140, 141, 145, 147, 149
    background 9, 10
    opinion writing 31, 127
    private papers 37, 39, 40, 42, 43, 46, 47
    quoted 58
Equally divided Court 29
Extraordinary writs 23, 24

Fluidity *See* votes on-the-merits
Frankfurter, Felix 3, 15, 18, 26, 29, 31, 32, 38, 55, 62, 64, 66, 70, 72, 78, 88, 98, 100, 104, 107, 114, 116, 119, 123, 126, 127, 134, 135, 137, 138, 140, 141, 145, 147, 149
  background 8, 9
  complaints about cert 51
  private papers 37, 38, 41, 42, 47
  quoted 28, 58, 63, 135
Freshman effect 18, 131
Gressman, Eugene 31
Habeas corpus 23, 24, 25, 27, 35, 37
Hiss, Alger 1
Hughes, Charles Evans 7, 125
In Forma Pauperis or IFP 23, 24, 27, 37, 77, 78
Jackson, Robert 3, 9, 18, 26, 31, 32, 48, 55, 64, 66, 70, 72, 73, 80, 85, 88, 93, 96, 119, 120, 123, 126, 127, 140, 141, 149
  background 10, 11
  Nuremburg trials 11
  opinion writing 31, 127
  private papers 40, 41, 42, 47
Judges Bill 19
Law clerks *See* clerks
Lewis, John L. 2
Legal Norms 20, 66
Logit Analysis 59-62, 82-84
Mandamus 23, 24, 27, 35, 37
Marshall, John 125
Minton, Sherman 3, 13, 14, 15, 18, 55, 66, 70, 73-75, 80, 88, 92, 96, 107, 114-116, 119, 123, 128, 145, 147
  background 13, 14
Moot 19
Murphy, Frank 5, 8, 9, 11-13, 15, 18, 31, 32, 55, 62, 66, 70, 72, 73, 78, 80, 85, 92, 98, 100, 104, 116, 119, 121, 126, 127, 134, 136, 137, 138
  background 10
  opinion writing 31
  private papers 37, 41, 42, 47
Natural Courts 17
New Deal *See* justices' backgrounds
Opinions
  assignment 29, **chapter 8**
  bargaining 130, 131
  conclusions 149, 150
  fluidity by authors 128, 129
  inaccuracies caused by using report votes 132
  join memos 30, 126
  mimimum winning 131, 132, 134, 138, 141, 147, 149
  objectives of assigners 132-135
  prior research 131, 132
  procedures 124-128
  purpose 125

reassignments 127, 136, 137
  role of clerks 31
  specialization 125, 126
  writing 29, 30
Per Curiam 29, 124, 125, 136, 137
Quorum 50
Recusal 26
Rehearing 25, 46
Reed, Stanley 3, 13, 15, 18, 30, 31, 55, 63, 64, 66, 70, 72, 73, 80, 85, 88, 98, 104, 107, 114, 116, 119, 120, 123, 126, 127, 135, 136, 138, 140, 141, 145
  background 8
  fluidity following receipt of opinion assignments 128
  private papers 37, 40, 42, 46, 47
  quoted 126, 127
Response, Call for 27, 45, 46
Respondent 23, 32, 33
Roosevelt, Franklin 7-11, 13, 14
Rosenberg spy case 1, 2
Rule of four 16, 27, 50, 54, 77
Rutledge, Wiley 8, 9, 10, 13-15, 18, 55, 66, 70, 72, 73, 78, 85, 92, 98, 100, 104, 116, 119, 121, 126, 127, 140
  background 11, 12
  private papers 41, 42
Seniority 16, 17, 27, 29, 125
Solicitor General 8, 9, 10, 31, 32
Special List 25, 38, 45, 46, 52
Statistical significance 5
Stone, Harlan Fiske 7, 11, 35, 125
Summary decisions 23, 27, 28
Terms 17
Truman, Harry 6, 7, 12-14, 19, 32, 33
Vacation 17
Vinson, Fred 1, 3, 12-14, 16, 18, 19, 26, 31, 55, 62, 64, 66, 70, 72, 73, 78, 85, 93, 98, 100, 104, 107, 114, 116, 119, 121, 123, 125, 126, 128, 132, 133, 134, 135, 137, 140, 141, 145, 147, 149, 150
  background 6, 7, 125
  private papers 40, 42, 46
  quoted 128
Votes on-the-merits **chapter 7**
  fluidity by the entire Court 110
  fluidity by individual justices 110-114
  fluidity influence 114-120
  joint fluidity 120-123
  other empirical studies 97, 98
  reverse rates of individual justices 98-109
  sincere or strategic changes 111, 112
Voting paradox 29
Warren, Earl 2, 15, 125, 134
Willey, Harold (Clerk) quoted 28
Wyatt, Walter (Reporter) quoted 30

Appendix A

Dataset Format

The cases are organized according to the terms of their completion. Within each term, cases are presented in docket number order with cases on the appellate docket preceding those on the miscellaneous docket. Cases sometimes have more than one docket number because they were moved from the miscellaneous docket to the appellate docket or because they were begun in one term and completed in another. Cases that span terms are entered in the term of their completion. A case with multiple docket numbers is entered according to the final docket number.

The format for each case is the following:

Case Name (sometimes two line).

Term year (last two digits), docket number, and docket type (A=appellate, M=miscellaneous). If a case has multiple docket numbers, the final term year, docket number, and docket type are first.

U.S. Reports citation followed by term year, docket number, and docket type for any vide (related) cases.

The justice who received the opinion assignment, the date of the assignment, and the lower court. If the opinion was reassigned, the original assignment is first. Most cases were not assigned, and not all assignments were completed. Some request for extraordinary writs did not involve a lower court.

Month and day of the vote.

Year of the vote.

Type of vote. Votes labelled REPORT are available in *U.S. Reports*. All other votes are available only in the justices' private papers.

There are two numbers above each column of votes. The first represents the issue because some cases involve more than one. The second number represents the sequential order of votes on the same issue. Thus, 1 2 represents the second vote on the first issue while 2 1 represents the first vote on the second issue.

Votes. The following code is used to represent various votes: A=affirm, B=no, C=change, D=deny or refuse, F=remove from docket, G=grant, H=hold, I=moot, J=modify or partial, K=hear, L=limit, M=remand, N=note probable jurisdiction, O=reserve judgment, P=postpone, Q=question mark, R=reverse, S=dismiss, T=discharge rule, T1=transfer under 28 U.S.C. 52, 276,2, U=reargue, V=vacate, W=stay, X=pass, Y=yes, Z=without prejudice, @=not final, #=issue rule.

A vote is labelled "QUEST" if it dealt with one of several questions, such as whether to grant additional time or whether a case was premature. The second number above the column of votes represents the sequential order of votes on the same question. The first number represents the type of question according to the following code: 1=unknown, 2=unknown, 3=issue mandate, 4=intervention, 5=competitive bidding, 6=instructions, 7=premature, 8=stay or recall mandate, 9=request brief, 10=expand record, 11=appealable, 12=time extension, 13=vacate stay, 14=special leave to argue, 15=no change in employment, 16=withhold order, 17=proceed on typewritten record, 18=announce today, 20=Norris-LaGuardia stops government for getting injunction, 21=defendants in contempt, 22=civil and criminal improperly blended, 23=Lewis fine excessive, 24=union fine excessive.

Appendix B

U.S. Supreme Court
October 1946 Term

Freeman v Hewit
46 3A 45 4A 44 40A
329 US 249
Rutledg 11/20/44 Frankfr 10/22/44 Indiana

	11/11 1944 MERITS 1 1	10/19 1946 MERITS 1 2	12/16 1946 REPORT 1 1
Burton	R	R	R
Rutledg	R	R	R
Jackson		x	
Murphy	A	A	
Douglas	A	A	
Frankfr	R	R	R
Reed	R	R	
Black	R	R	
Roberts			
Vinson		A	A
Stone	R		

American Power & Light v S.E.C.
46 4A 46 5A 45 6A 45 7A 44 166A
329 US 90
Murphy 11/19/45 Murphy 10/22/46 CCA 1st

	05/26 1945 CERT 1 1	11/19 1945 MERITS 1 1	10/19 1946 MERITS 1 2	11/25 1946 REPORT 1 1
Burton			A	A
Rutledg	G	A	A	A
Jackson				
Murphy	G	A	A	A
Douglas			A	A
Frankfr	G		A	A
Reed			A	A
Black	G	A	A	A
Roberts	G			
Vinson				A
Stone	G	A	A	A

United Brotherhood Carpenters v U.S.
46 6A 45 9A
330 US 395 46 7A 46 10A 45 10A 45 13A 44 666A
Black 03/12/45 Black 05/06/46 Reed 10/22/46 CCA 9th

	12/03 1944 CERT 1 1	03/10 1945 MERITS 1 1	03/10 1945 MERITS 2 1	05/04 1946 MERITS 1 2	05/04 1946 MERITS 2 2
Burton					
Rutledg	D			R	
Jackson					
Murphy	DH		R	R	A
Douglas	G	R		R	A
Frankfr					A
Reed			R		A
Black	G			R	A
Roberts	H				
Vinson	G		R		A
Stone					

Alma Motor v Timken-Detroit Axle
46 11A 44 806A
329 US 129
Vinson 10/28/46 CCA 3rd

	02/03 1945 CERT 1 1	04/28 1945 MERITS 1 1	10/28 1946 MERITS 1 2	12/09 1946 REPORT 1 1
Burton		R	R	>
Rutledg	G	A	R	>
Jackson	G	A	>	>
Murphy	G	A	A	>
Douglas	G	A	R	>
Frankfr	G	A	R	>
Reed	G			
Black	G	R		
Roberts	G	R	R	>
Vinson	G			V
Stone	G			

Cleveland v U.S.
46 12A 45 23A 44 895A 44 896A
329 US 14 46 13A 46 19A 45 24A 45 30A
Douglas 10/22/46 CCA 10th

	03/10 1945 CERT 1 1	10/13 1945 MERITS 1 1	10/19 1946 MERITS 1 2	11/18 1946 REPORT 1 1
Burton		R	R	
Rutledg	G		R	R
Jackson				
Murphy	G	R	R	R
Douglas	G		A	A
Frankfr				A
Reed		R	R	
Black	G			
Vinson			A	A
Stone				

United Public Workers v Mitchell
46 20A 45 34A 44 911A
330 US 75
Stone 04/01/46 Reed 10/28/46 DC DC

	03/10 1945 JURIS 1 1	12/08 1945 MERITS 1 1	10/26 1946 MERITS 1 2	02/10 1947 REPORT 1 1
Burton	P	R	R	R
Rutledg	P		A	A
Jackson	P	X		
Murphy	P	R	R	A
Douglas	P			A
Frankfr		R	R	R
Reed	S			
Black	S		A	A
Roberts	P			
Vinson	P			A
Stone	P			

Champlin Refining Company v U.S.
46 21A 45 75A 44 1269A
329 US 29
Jackson 10/28/46 DC WD Oklahoma

	06/16 1945 JURIS 1 1	11/13 1945 MERITS 1 1	10/26 1946 MERITS 1 2	11/18 1946 REPORT 1 1
Burton	N	R	R	A
Rutledg	N		A	A
Jackson	N			
Murphy	N	R	X	A
Douglas	N	R	R	A
Frankfr	N			A
Reed	N	R	R	
Black	N			
Vinson	N			A
Stone	N			

Levinson v Spector Motor Service
46 22A 45 139A
330 US 649 46 41A
Burton 10/28/46 Illinois

	10/08 1945 CERT 1 1	12/16 1945 MERITS 1 1	10/26 1946 MERITS 3 3	03/31 1947 REPORT 1 1
Burton	G	R	R	R
Rutledg			A	A
Jackson	G			
Murphy	G	D	R	R
Douglas	G		X	X
Frankfr		R	R	R
Reed				
Black		D		A
Vinson	G			A
Stone				

Gibson v U.S.
46 23A 45 221A
329 US 338 46 86A
Rutledg 10/28/46 CCA 8th

Justice	10/20 1945 CERT (1 1)	01/05 1946 MERITS (1 1)	10/26 1946 MERITS (1 2)	12/23 1946 REPORT (1 1)
Burton	GH	R	R	R
Rutledg	GH	R	R	R
Jackson				
Murphy	GH	R	R	R
Douglas	G		X	
Frankfr				
Reed	D	R		R
Black	D		A	R
Vinson	D		A	R
Stone	G			

Halliburton Oil Well v Walker
46 24A 45 290A
329 US 1
Black 10/28/46 CCA 9th

Justice	10/08 1945 CERT (1 1)	01/14 1946 MERITS (1 1)	01/28 1946 REPORT (1 1)	10/26 1946 MERITS (1 2)	11/18 1946 REPORT (1 2)
Burton		R	R	R	R
Rutledg	D		R	R	R
Jackson					R
Murphy		R	R	R	R
Douglas	D	R	R	X	R
Frankfr					R O
Reed		R	R	R	R
Black		A	A	A	R
Vinson	D	A	A	A	R
Stone					A

Unemployment Compensation v Aragon
46 25A 45 309A
329 US 143
Vinson 11/18/46 CCA 9th

Justice	10/08 1945 CERT (1 1)	03/02 1946 MERITS (1 1)	03/30 1946 MERITS (1 2)	11/16 1946 MERITS (1 3)	12/09 1946 REPORT (1 1)
Burton	G	R	R	R	R
Rutledg	G	X	R		R
Jackson	G				R
Murphy	G	R	R	R	R
Douglas	G	R	R	R	R
Frankfr	G				R
Reed	G	R	R	R	R
Black	G				R
Vinson	G				R
Stone					R

U.S. v Alcea Band Of Tillamooks
46 26A 45 387A
329 US 40
Vinson 10/28/46 Ct Cls

Justice	10/20 1945 CERT (1 1)	02/04 1946 MERITS (1 1)	10/28 1946 MERITS (1 2)	11/25 1946 REPORT (1 1)
Burton	G	R	R	R
Rutledg	G	R	R	R
Jackson				
Murphy	D	A	A	A
Douglas	D	A	A	A
Frankfr	D	A	A	A
Reed	G	R SA	R	R
Black			A	A
Vinson	G	R	A	A
Stone	G	R		

Bruce's Juices v American Can Company
46 27A 45 402A
330 US 743
Jackson 11/18/46 Florida

Justice	11/10 1945 CERT (1 1)	02/02 1946 MERITS (1 1)	02/11 1946 REPORT (1 1)	11/16 1946 MERITS (1 2)	04/07 1947 REPORT (1 2)	01/06 1947 REPORT (1 1)
Burton	G	R	R	R	R	R
Rutledg	G	R	R	R	R	R
Jackson						
Murphy	G			AQ		
Douglas	G	R				
Frankfr	G	R	R	A	A	A
Reed	G	R	R	R	R	R
Black	G					
Vinson		A	A	A	A	A
Stone	Q		R	A	R	R

MacGregor v Westinghouse Electric
46 28A 45 410A
329 US 402
Black 11/18/46 Pennsylvania

Justice	11/03 1945 CERT (1 1)	02/04 1946 MERITS (1 1)	02/09 1946 MERITS (1 2)	02/11 1946 REPORT (1 1)	11/16 1946 MERITS (1 3)	01/06 1947 REPORT (1 1)
Burton	G	R	R	R	R	R
Rutledg	G	R X	R	R	R	R
Jackson	G					
Murphy	G	R	R	R	R	R
Douglas	G	R	R	R	R	R
Frankfr	G				X	
Reed	G	R	R	R	R	R
Black						
Vinson	G		A	A	A	A
Stone						

Joseph v Carter & Weekes Stevedoring
46 29A 45 518A
330 US 422 46 30A 45 519A
Douglas 03/05/46 Reed 11/18/46 New York

	11/17 1945 CERT	03/05 1946 MERITS	11/16 1946 MERITS	11/16 1946 MERITS	03/10 1947 REPORT
	1 1	1 1	1 2	2 2	2 1
Burton	G				
Rutledg	G	R		R	R
Jackson			A	A	A
Murphy	G		A	A	A
Douglas	G		A	A	A
Frankfr	G		A	A	A
Reed	G	R		R	R
Black	G		A	A	A
Vinson					
Stone	G	A	A	A	

Angel v Bullington
46 31A 45 540A
330 US 183
Black 04/01/46 Black 11/25/46 Frankfr 01/20/47 CCA 4th

	12/01 1945 CERT	03/09 1946 MERITS	11/23 1946 MERITS	01/18 1947 MERITS	02/17 1947 REPORT	03/10 1947 REPORT
	1 1	1 1	1 2	1 3	1 1	1 1
Burton	G			R		
Rutledg		A	A	R	R	A
Jackson	G		A	A	R	A
Murphy	D					
Douglas			A	A		
Frankfr	G	R		R	R	R
Reed	G		A	A	R	A
Black	G					
Vinson			A	A		A
Stone	G					

Order Of United Commercial v Wolfe
46 32A 45 556A
331 US 586
Stone 03/05/46 Burton 11/18/46 South Dakota

	11/17 1945 CERT	03/04 1946 MERITS	03/30 1946 MERITS	11/16 1946 MERITS	06/09 1947 REPORT
	1 1	1 1	1 2	1 3	1 1
Burton	G				
Rutledg	G	R	R	R	R
Jackson	G	X			
Murphy	G	R	R	R	R
Douglas	G	R			
Frankfr	G	R	R	R	R
Reed	G				
Black	G		A	A	A
Vinson	G				
Stone	G	RM			

Harris v U.S.
46 34A 45 700A
331 US 145
Vinson 12/16/46 CCA 10th

	06/08 1946 CERT	12/16 1946 MERITS	05/05 1947 REPORT
	1 1	1 1	1 1
Burton	G		
Rutledg	G	R	R
Jackson		X	A
Murphy	G	R	R
Douglas	GQ		A
Frankfr	GQ	R	A
Reed			
Black		A	A
Vinson		Q	A

Illinois (Gordon) v Campbell
46 35A 45 750A
329 US 362 45 749A
Rutledg 11/25/46 Illinois

	02/23 1946 CERT	04/01 1946 MERITS	11/23 1946 MERITS	12/23 1946 REPORT
	1 1	1 1	1 2	
Burton	G		R	
Rutledg	G		R	
Jackson		A	A	A
Murphy	G	R		R
Douglas	D	R	R	A
Frankfr	D			A
Reed	G			A
Black		A	A	A
Vinson	G	R		R
Stone				

Carter v Illinois
46 36A 45 764A
329 US 173
Frankfr 11/18/46 Illinois

	05/04 1946 CERT	11/16 1946 MERITS	12/09 1946 REPORT
	1 1	1 1	1 1
Burton	G		
Rutledg	G	R	R
Jackson		A	A
Murphy	G	R	R
Douglas	G	R	R
Frankfr	D		
Reed	G	R	
Black	G		A
Vinson	G		A

Ballard v U.S.
46 37A 45 782A
329 US 187 46 489A
Douglas 10/22/46 CCA 9th

	1946 CERT	10/19 1946 MERITS	10/19 1946 MERITS	12/09 1946 REPORT
	1 1	1 1	2 1	1 1
Burton	G			
Rutledg	G	R	R	R
Jackson	D	R	R	R
Murphy	GQ	R	X	
Douglas	GQ			
Frankfr		R	R	R
Reed	G	R	R	R
Black	D			
Vinson			A	A
Stone	GQ			

N.L.R.B. v Donnelly Garment Company
46 38A 45 786A
330 US 219 46 39A 45 787A
Frankfr 10/28/46 CCA 8th

	04/20 1946 CERT	10/26 1946 MERITS	03/03 1947 REPORT
	1 1	1 1	1 1
Burton	G	R	R
Rutledg	G	R	R
Jackson			
Murphy	G	R	R
Douglas	G		A
Frankfr	G		
Reed	G	R	R
Black	G	R	R
Vinson			A
Stone			A

U.S. v Carmack
46 40A 45 812A
329 US 230
Burton 10/22/46 CCA 8th

	04/20 1946 CERT	10/19 1946 MERITS	12/09 1946 REPORT
	1 1	1 1	1 1
Burton	G		
Rutledg	G	R	R
Jackson	G		A
Murphy	G	R	R
Douglas	G		A
Frankfr	G	R	R
Reed	G		A
Black	G	R	R
Vinson	G		A
Stone			

Pyramid Motor Freight v Ispass
46 41A 45 821A
330 US 695 46 22A
Burton 10/28/46 CCA 2d

	03/23 1946 CERT	10/26 1946 MERITS	03/31 1947 REPORT
	1 1	1 1	1 1
Burton	G	R	✓
Rutledg	G	R	✓
Jackson			✓ A
Murphy		X	✓ A
Douglas	G		✓ AQ
Frankfr	G		✓
Reed	G		✓ AJ
Black	G		✓ A
Vinson	G		✓ A
Stone	G		

Vanston Bondholders v Green
46 42A 45 848A
46 43A 46 45A 46 45A 45 849A 45 851A
329 US 156
Black 10/28/46 CCA 6th

	03/23 1946 CERT	10/26 1946 MERITS	12/09 1946 REPORT	01/11 1947 REHEAR
	1 1	1 1	1 1	1 1
Burton	G	R	R	B
Rutledg	D	R	R	B
Jackson				
Murphy	D	X	R	B
Douglas	X			
Frankfr		A	A	Y
Reed		A	A	
Black	G	A	A	B
Vinson		A	A	B
Stone		A	A	

Richfield Oil v State Board
46 46A 45 864A
329 US 69
Douglas 10/28/46 California

	03/23 1946 JURIS	10/26 1946 MERITS	11/25 1946 REPORT
	1 1	1 1	1 1
Burton	P	R	R
Rutledg	P	R	R
Jackson		R	R
Murphy	D	X	
Douglas	D		
Frankfr		R	R
Reed	P		
Black	D		
Vinson	P	R	R
Stone	P		A

Hickman v Taylor
46 47A 45 885A
329 US 495
Murphy 11/18/46 CCA 3rd

	04/20 1946 CERT	05/25 1946 CERT	11/16 1946 MERITS	01/13 1947 REPORT
	1 1	1 2	1 1	1 1
Burton	D	D	R	A
Rutledg	D			A
Jackson				A
Murphy		G		A
Douglas	D	G	R	A
Frankfr	D			A
Reed	GQ	D	R	A
Black	G	D	R	A
Vinson		G	A	A

Rothensies v Electric Storage Battery
46 48A 45 892A
329 US 296
Jackson 11/25/46 CCA 3rd

	03/23 1946 CERT	11/23 1946 MERITS	11/25 1946 MERITS	12/16 1946 REPORT
	1 1	1 1	1 2	1 1
Burton	G		AQ	
Rutledg	G	R	A	R
Jackson			A	
Murphy	G		A	R
Douglas	G	R		R
Frankfr	G		R	R
Reed	G	R		
Black			AQ	
Vinson	Q		A	R
Stone	Q			

Haupt v U.S.
46 49A 45 900A
330 US 631
Jackson 12/16/46 CCA 7th

	05/25 1946 CERT	12/14 1946 MERITS	03/31 1947 REPORT
	1 1	1 1	1 1
Burton	G	R	R
Rutledg	G	R	A
Jackson		R	A
Murphy	G	X	
Douglas	G	X	A
Frankfr	G		A
Reed	G	R	A
Black			
Vinson			

U.S. v Howard P. Foley Company
46 50A 45 902A
329 US 64
Black 11/08/46 Ct Cls

	04/20 1946 CERT	10/28 1946 MERITS	11/08 1946 MERITS	11/25 1946 REPORT
	1 1	1 1	1 2	1 1
Burton	G	R	R	R
Rutledg		R	R	R
Jackson	D	X		
Murphy			A	A
Douglas	D			
Frankfr	D	R	R	R
Reed				
Black	G			
Vinson			A	A
Stone	GQ		A	A

Fiswick v U.S.
46 51A 45 909A
329 US 211
Douglas 11/25/46 CCA 3rd

	04/20 1946 CERT	11/23 1946 MERITS	12/09 1946 REPORT
	1 1	1 1	1 1
Burton	G	R	R
Rutledg		R	R
Jackson	D		R
Murphy	G	R	R
Douglas	Q	R	R
Frankfr	G	R	R
Reed			R
Black	D		R
Vinson	D	A	R
Stone	G		

Everson v Board Of Education Ewing
46 52A 45 911A
330 US 1
Black 11/25/46 New Jersey

	05/04 1946 JURIS	11/23 1946 MERITS	02/10 1947 REPORT
	1 1	1 1	1 1
Burton	N	R	R
Rutledg			R
Jackson		X	AQ
Murphy	N A		
Douglas	N A		A
Frankfr			A
Reed		R	R
Black			A
Vinson			A

U.S. v Powell
46 56A 45 942A
330 US 238 46 57A 45 943A
Douglas 01/22/47 CCA 4th

	04/27 1946 CERT 1-1	01/18 1947 MERITS 1-1	03/03 1947 REPORT 1-1
Burton	G		
Rutledg	G		
Jackson	G	R	R
Murphy	G	A	A
Douglas	D	A	A
Frankfr	G	A	A
Reed	G	A	A
Black	G	A	A
Vinson	A	A	A

Eagles v U.S. (Samuels)
46 59A 45 948A
329 US 304 46 58A 45 947A
Douglas 11/25/46 CCA 3rd

	05/25 1946 CERT 1-1	11/23 1946 MERITS 1-1	12/23 1946 REPORT 1-1
Burton	G	R	R
Rutledg	G	R	R
Jackson	G		R
Murphy	G	X	R
Douglas	G		R
Frankfr	G	R	R
Reed		R	R
Black		A	R
Vinson		A	R

Morris v Jones
46 62A 45 961A
329 US 545
Douglas 12/16/46 Illinois

	04/27 1946 JURIS 1-1	04/27 1946 CERT 1-1	12/14 1946 MERITS 1-1	01/20 1947 REPORT 1-1
Burton		G	R	R
Rutledg			R	R
Jackson	P	G	R	R
Murphy			A	A
Douglas	P	G	R	R
Frankfr		G	R	R
Reed		G	A	A
Black			S	A
Vinson			A	A

46 53A 45 914A
329 US 379
Rutledg 11/18/46 CCA 6th

	05/11 1946 CERT 1-1	11/16 1946 MERITS 1-1	12/23 1946 REPORT 1-1
Burton		R	R
Rutledg	G D	RQ	R
Jackson		R	R
Murphy	G	A	A
Douglas	GQ D		
Frankfr			A
Reed	G	R	R
Black		R	R
Vinson	G	A	A

U.S. v Ruzicka
46 54A 45 920A
329 US 287
Frankfr 11/25/46 CCA 7th

	04/20 1946 CERT 1-1	11/23 1946 MERITS 1-1	12/16 1946 REPORT 1-1
Burton	G	R	R
Rutledg	G	RQ	R
Jackson	G	R	R
Murphy	G	R	R
Douglas	G	R	R
Frankfr	G	X	R
Reed	G	A	R
Black	G	R	R
Vinson	G		A
Stone	G		A

U.S. v Atlantic Coast Line RR
46 57A 45 943A
330 US 238 46 56A 45 942A
Douglas 01/22/47 CCA 4th

	04/27 1946 CERT 1-1	01/18 1947 MERITS 1-1	03/03 1947 REPORT 1-1
Burton	G	R	R
Rutledg	G		
Jackson	G	R	R
Murphy	G	A	A
Douglas	D	A	A
Frankfr	G	A	A
Reed	G	A	A
Black	G	A	A
Vinson	A	A	A

N.L.R.B. v A.J. Tower Company
46 60A 45 950A
329 US 324
Murphy 11/25/46 CCA 1st

	05/04 1946 CERT 1-1	11/23 1946 MERITS 1-1	12/23 1946 REPORT 1-1
Burton	G	R	R
Rutledg	G	R	R
Jackson	G	R	R
Murphy	G	R	R
Douglas	G	R	R
Frankfr	G	R	R
Reed	G	R	R
Black	D	AQ	A
Vinson			

Order Of Railway Conductors v Swan
46 63A 45 968A
329 US 520 46 64A 45 969A
Murphy 12/16/46 CCA 7th

	04/20 1946 CERT 1-1	12/14 1946 MERITS 1-1	01/13 1947 REPORT 1-1
Burton			R
Rutledg	D		R
Jackson	D	V	R
Murphy		S	R
Douglas	D		R
Frankfr	G	RV	R
Reed	G	S	R
Black	G	A	S
Vinson		A	A
Stone	D	A	A

Bethlehem Steel v New York SLRB
46 55A 45 941A
330 US 767 46 76A 45 1048A
Jackson 01/22/47 New York

	12/21 1946 MERITS 1-1	01/18 1947 MERITS 1-2
Burton	R	R
Rutledg	R A	R
Jackson	R	R
Murphy	R A	R
Douglas	R	R
Frankfr	R A	R
Reed	R	R
Black	RQ	R
Vinson	R	R

Eagles v U.S. (Horowitz)
46 58A 45 947A
329 US 317 46 59A 45 948A
Douglas 11/25/46 CCA 3rd

	05/25 1946 CERT 1-1	11/23 1946 MERITS 1-1	12/23 1946 REPORT 1-1
Burton	G	R	R
Rutledg	G		R
Jackson	G	X	R
Murphy	G		R
Douglas	G	R	R
Frankfr	G	A	R
Reed	G	A	R
Black	G		R
Vinson			R

U.S. v Seatrain Lines
46 61A 45 959A
329 US 424
Black 12/16/46 DC Delaware

	04/20 1946 JURIS 1-1	12/14 1946 MERITS 1-1	01/06 1947 REPORT 1-1
Burton	N	AJ	AJ
Rutledg	N	A	A
Jackson	N	A	A
Murphy	N	A	A
Douglas	N	A	A
Frankfr	N	A	A
Reed		A	A
Black	N	A	A
Vinson		A	A

F.C.C. v WOKO
46 65A 45 972A
329 US 223
Jackson 11/25/46 CCA DC

	04/20 1946 CERT 1-1	11/23 1946 MERITS 1-1	12/09 1946 REPORT 1-1
Burton	G	R	R
Rutledg	G	R	R
Jackson	G	R	R
Murphy	G	RQ	R
Douglas	G	X	R
Frankfr	G	R	R
Reed	G	R	R
Black	G	R	R
Vinson			R
Stone	G		

Board Of Governors v Agnew
46 **66A** 45 973A
329 US 441
Douglas 12/16/46 CCA DC

	04/27 1946 CERT 1 1		12/14 1946 MERITS 1 1		01/06 1947 REPORT 1 1	
Burton	G		R		R	
Rutledg	G		R		R	
Jackson				A	R	
Murphy	G			A	R	
Douglas	G		R		R	
Frankfr	G		R		R	
Reed	G			A	R	
Black	G		R		R	
Vinson				A	R	

U.S. v Bruno
46 **67A** 45 988A
329 US 207
Douglas 11/25/46 CCA 3rd

	05/11 1946 CERT 1 1		11/23 1946 MERITS 1 1		12/09 1946 REPORT 1 1	
Burton	G			A	R	
Rutledg	G			A	R	
Jackson				A	R	
Murphy	G		R		R	
Douglas	G		R		R	
Frankfr	G		R		R	
Reed	G		R		R	
Black	G		R		R	
Vinson				A	R	

Crane v C.I.R.
46 **68A** 45 994A
331 US 1
Vinson 12/16/46 CCA 2d

	04/27 1946 CERT 1 1		12/14 1946 MERITS 1 1		04/14 1947 REPORT 1 1	
Burton	G			A		A
Rutledg	G			A		A
Jackson			R		R	
Murphy		D	R			A
Douglas	G		R		R	
Frankfr	G		R		R	
Reed	GQ			A		A
Black		D		A		A
Vinson				A		A

American Stevedores v Porello
46 **69A** 45 996A
330 US 446 56 514A
Reed 12/16/46 CCA 2d

	05/04 1946 CERT 1 1		12/14 1946 MERITS 1 1		03/10 1947 REPORT 1 1	
Burton	G			A		A
Rutledg	G			A		A
Jackson				A		A
Murphy	G			A		A
Douglas	G			A		A
Frankfr	G		R		R	
Reed	G			A		A
Black		D		A		A
Vinson			R		R	

Edward Katzinger v Chicago Metallic
46 **70A** 45 997A
329 US 402 46 71A 46 28A 45 998A
Black 11/18/46 CCA 7th

	04/27 1946 CERT 1 1		11/16 1946 MERITS 1 1		01/06 1947 REPORT 1 1	
Burton	G			A	R	
Rutledg	G			A		A
Jackson			R		R	
Murphy	G			A		A
Douglas	G			A		A
Frankfr	G		R		R	
Reed	G		R		R	
Black	G			A		A
Vinson				A		A

I.C.C. v Mechling
46 **72A** 45 1010A
330 US 567
Black 02/17/47 DC ND Illinois

	04/27 1946 JURIS 1 1		02/15 1947 MERITS 1 1		03/31 1947 REPORT 1 1	
Burton	N			A		A
Rutledg	N			A		A
Jackson			R		R	
Murphy	N			A		A
Douglas	N			A		A
Frankfr	N		R		R	
Reed	N			A		A
Black	N			A		A
Vinson				A		A

Walling v Halliburton Oil Well
46 **74A** 45 1018A
331 US 17
Vinson 02/17/47 CCA 9th

	05/13 1946 CERT 1 1		02/15 1947 MERITS 1 1		04/14 1947 REPORT 1 1	
Burton		D		A		A
Rutledg	G			A		A
Jackson				A		A
Murphy	G		R		R	
Douglas	G			X		A
Frankfr		D		A		A
Reed	G			A		A
Black	G		R		R	
Vinson				A		A

International Harvester v Evatt
46 **75A** 45 1019A
329 US 416
Black 12/16/46 Ohio

	05/04 1946 JURIS 1 1		12/14 1946 MERITS 1 1		01/06 1947 REPORT 1 1	
Burton	N			A		A
Rutledg	N			AQ		A
Jackson				A		A
Murphy	N			A		A
Douglas	N			A		A
Frankfr	N			A		A
Reed	N			X		A
Black		S		A		A
Vinson				A		A

U.S. v Dickinson
46 **77A** 45 1052A
331 US 745 46 78A 45 1053A
Frankfr 12/16/46 CCA 4th

	05/11 1946 CERT 1 1		12/14 1946 MERITS 1 1		06/16 1947 REPORT 1 1	
Burton	G			A		A
Rutledg		D		A		A
Jackson				A		A
Murphy	G			A		A
Douglas		D		A		A
Frankfr	G			A		A
Reed	G			A		A
Black	G			A		A
Vinson				A		A

Steele v General Mills
46 **79A** 45 1056A
329 US 433
Black 12/23/46 CCA 5th

	05/25 1946 CERT 1 1		12/21 1946 MERITS 1 1		01/06 1947 REPORT 1 1	
Burton	G		R		R	
Rutledg	G		R		R	
Jackson			R		R	
Murphy	G		R		R	
Douglas		D	R		R	
Frankfr	G		R		R	
Reed		D	R		R	
Black	G		R		R	
Vinson			R		R	

Parker v Fleming
46 **80A** 45 1075A
329 US 531
Black 12/23/46 CCA Emergency

	05/11 1946 CERT 1 1		12/21 1946 MERITS 1 1		01/11 1947 MERITS 1 2		01/20 1947 REPORT 1 1	
Burton		D		A		A		A
Rutledg	G		R		R		R	
Jackson				A	R		R	
Murphy	G			A		A	R	
Douglas	G		R		R		R	
Frankfr		D		A		A		A
Reed	G		R		R		R	
Black	G			A	R		R	
Vinson				A		A		A

S.E.C. v Federal Water & Gas
46 **81A** 45 1088A
332 US 194 46 82A 45 1089A
Burton 12/23/46 Murphy 06/03/47 CCA DC

	05/11 1946 CERT 1 1		12/21 1946 MERITS 1 1		06/23 1947 REPORT 1 1	
Burton	G		R		R	
Rutledg	G		R		R	
Jackson				A		A
Murphy	G		R		R	
Douglas						
Frankfr		D		Q		A
Reed	G		R		R	
Black	G		R		R	
Vinson						

Independent Warehouses v Scheele
46 83A 45 1096A
331 US 70
Rutledg 12/23/46 New Jersey

	05/25/1946 JURIS	12/21/1946 MERITS	04/14/1947 REPORT
	1 1	1 1	1 1
Burton	S		A A
Rutledg	NQ		A
Jackson		R	A
Murphy	S		A A
Douglas	N		A A
Frankfr			AQ
Reed	N	R	A A
Black	NQ		A
Vinson	S		R

Oklahoma v U.S. Civil Service
46 84A 45 1098A
330 US 127
Reed 10/28/46 CCA 10th

	10/19/1946 CERT	12/20/1946 MERITS	02/10/1947 REPORT
	1 1	1 1	1 1
Burton	G	R	R
Rutledg	G		R
Jackson			
Murphy	G	R	A
Douglas	G		
Frankfr	G		R
Reed	G		R
Black		X	
Vinson	G	R	R

Trailmobile Company v Whirls
46 85A 45 1099A
331 US 40
Rutledg 12/23/46 CCA 6th

	06/08/1946 CERT	12/21/1946 MERITS	04/14/1947 REPORT
	1 1	1 1	1 1
Burton	G G	R	R R
Rutledg	G		R R
Jackson	G	R	
Murphy	G	X	A
Douglas	G		
Frankfr	G	R	R R
Reed			
Black		R	
Vinson	G	R	R R

Dodez v U.S.
46 86A 45 1103A
329 US 338 46 23A 45 221A
Rutledg 10/28/46 CCA 6th

	05/04/1946 CERT	10/26/1946 MERITS	12/23/1946 REPORT
	1 1	1 1	1 1
Burton	G	R	R
Rutledg	G	R	R
Jackson			R
Murphy	G	R	R
Douglas	G		R
Frankfr	G	X	R
Reed			R
Black	G	R	R A
Vinson		R	R A

Anderson v Yungkau
46 87A 45 1104A
329 US 482
Douglas 12/23/46 CCA 6th

	05/11/1946 CERT	12/21/1946 MERITS	01/13/1947 REPORT
	1 1	1 1	1 1
Burton	G	R	R
Rutledg		RQ	RQ
Jackson	D		
Murphy	G		A
Douglas			A
Frankfr			A A
Reed			A
Black	D		
Vinson	D		A

Jesionowski v Boston & Maine RR
46 88A 45 1129A
329 US 452
Black 12/23/46 CCA 1st

	05/18/1946 CERT	12/21/1946 MERITS	01/13/1947 REPORT
	1 1	1 1	1 1
Burton	G	R	R
Rutledg			A
Jackson	D	R	R
Murphy	G	R	R
Douglas			
Frankfr	D		
Reed			
Black	D	R	R
Vinson	G		A

U.S. v National Lead Company
46 89A 45 1130A
332 US 319 46 90A 46 91A 45 1131A 45 1132A
Burton 03/11/47 DC SD New York

	05/18/1946 JURIS	03/08/1947 MERITS	06/23/1947 REPORT
	1 1	1 1	1 1
Burton		RQ	R
Rutledg	N	RQ	R
Jackson			
Murphy			
Douglas	N		A
Frankfr	N		A
Reed	N		A
Black			
Vinson		A	A

National Lead Company v U.S.
46 90A 45 1131A
332 US 319 46 89A 46 91A 45 1130A 45 1132A
Burton 03/11/47 DC SD New York

	05/18/1946 JURIS	03/08/1947 MERITS	06/23/1947 REPORT
	1 1	1 1	1 1
Burton			A
Rutledg	N		A
Jackson			
Murphy			
Douglas	N		A
Frankfr	N		A
Reed	N		A
Black			
Vinson			A

E.I. Du Pont De Nemours v U.S.
46 91A 45 1132A
332 US 319 46 89A 46 90A 45 1130A 45 1131A
Burton 03/11/47 DC SD New York

	05/18/1946 JURIS	03/08/1947 MERITS	06/23/1947 REPORT
	1 1	1 1	1 1
Burton			A
Rutledg	N		A
Jackson			
Murphy			
Douglas	N		A
Frankfr	N		A
Reed	N		A
Black			
Vinson			A

Gardner v New Jersey
46 92A 45 1143A
329 US 565
Douglas 12/23/46 CCA 3rd

	06/08/1946 CERT	12/21/1946 MERITS	01/20/1947 REPORT
	1 2	1 1	1 1
Burton	G	AM	R
Rutledg		AM	R
Jackson	D		R
Murphy	G	AM	R
Douglas	G	AM	R
Frankfr	D	AM	R
Reed		AM	R
Black	D	AM	R
Vinson	G	AM	R

Gulf Oil v Gilbert
46 93A 45 1148A
330 US 501 46 206A
Jackson 12/23/46 CCA 2d

	05/18/1946 CERT	12/21/1946 MERITS	03/10/1947 REPORT
	1 1	1 1	1 1
Burton	G	R	R
Rutledg	G	R	R
Jackson		R	R
Murphy		X	
Douglas	D		
Frankfr			
Reed	G	R	R
Black	D		
Vinson	D		

U.S. v N.Y. Rayon Importing Company
46 94A
329 US 654 46 96A 46 106A
Murphy 01/11/47 Ct Cls

	10/08/1946 CERT	01/11/1947 MERITS	02/03/1947 REPORT
	1 1	1 1	1 1
Burton	G G	R	R
Rutledg	G G		R
Jackson	G	AJ	R
Murphy	G	R	R
Douglas	D		R
Frankfr		X	R
Reed	G G	R	R
Black	D		
Vinson	G		

Aircraft & Diesel Equipment v Hirsch
46 95A 45 1183A
331 US 752
Rutledg 01/20/47 DC DC

	05/25 1946 JURIS	01/18 1947 MERITS	06/16 1947 REPORT
	1 1	1 1	1 1
Burton		A	A
Rutledg	N	A	A
Jackson	N	MH	A
Murphy		R	R
Douglas		R	
Frankfr	N	MH	A
Reed	N	AQ	A
Black		AQ	A
Vinson		A	A

Adamson v California
46 102A 45 1209A
332 US 46 46 466A
Reed 01/22/47 California

	06/08 1946 JURIS	01/18 1947 MERITS	06/23 1947 REPORT
	1 1	1 1	1 1
Burton		R	
Rutledg	S	A	A
Jackson	N	R	R
Murphy	N		R
Douglas	N	R	R
Frankfr		A	A
Reed		A	A
Black	N	X	A
Vinson		A	A

N.Y. Rayon Importing Company v U.S.
46 96A
329 US 654 46 94A 46 106A
Murphy 01/11/47 Ct Cls

	10/08 1946 CERT	01/11 1947 MERITS	02/03 1947 REPORT
	1 1	1 1	1 1
Burton	G	A	S
Rutledg	G	A	S
Jackson	D		S
Murphy	G	R	S
Douglas	D	R	S
Frankfr	G	X	S
Reed	G	A	S
Black	G	A	S
Vinson	G	A	S

Gospel Army v City Of Los Angeles
46 103A 45 1216A
331 US 543 46 574A
Rutledg 02/11/47 California

	06/01 1946 JURIS	02/08 1947 MERITS	04/12 1947 DISMISS	06/14 1947 REPORT
	1 1	1 1	1 1	1 1
Burton	P	A	Y	S
Rutledg	P	A	Y	S
Jackson			X	S
Murphy	P	X	B	S
Douglas	P	A	Y	S
Frankfr	P	A	Y	S
Reed	P	A	Y	S
Black			B	S
Vinson		A		

Krug v Santa Fe Pacific RR Company
46 97A 45 1192A
329 US 591 46 98A 45 1193A
Black 01/1/47 CCA DC

	06/08 1946 CERT	01/11 1947 MERITS	02/03 1947 REPORT
	1 1	1 1	1 1
Burton	G	R	R
Rutledg	G	R	R
Jackson	D	R	R
Murphy	G	R	R
Douglas	D	X	R
Frankfr	G	A	R
Reed	G	A	R
Black	G	A	R
Vinson	G	R	R

U.S. (Goodman) v Hearn
46 105A 45 1227A
329 US 667
CCA 5th

	06/08 1946 CERT	10/07 1947 REPORT
	1 1	1 1
Burton	G	SI
Rutledg	G	SI
Jackson		SI
Murphy	G	SI
Douglas	G	SI
Frankfr	G	SI
Reed	G	SI
Black	G	SI
Vinson	G	SI

U.S. v Thayer-West Point Hotel
46 106A
329 US 585 46 94A 46 96A
Murphy 12/23/46 Ct Cls

	10/08 1946 CERT	12/21 1946 MERITS	01/20 1947 REPORT
	1 1	1 1	1 1
Burton	G	R	R
Rutledg	G	R	R
Jackson	D		R
Murphy	G	R	R
Douglas	D		R
Frankfr	G	R	R
Reed	G	R	R
Black	G	R	R
Vinson			R

Waller v Northern Pacific Terminal
46 112A
329 US 742
Oregon

	10/11 1946 CERT
	1 1
Burton	
Rutledg	
Jackson	D
Murphy	G
Douglas	D
Frankfr	D
Reed	D
Black	G
Vinson	D

Lewellyn v Fleming
46 113A
329 US 715
CCA 10th

	10/08 1946 CERT
	1 1
Burton	
Rutledg	G
Jackson	
Murphy	G
Douglas	G
Frankfr	G
Reed	
Black	G
Vinson	

Witter v Nikolas
46 117A
329 US 715
CCA 7th

	10/08 1946 CERT
	1 1
Burton	D
Rutledg	D
Jackson	D
Murphy	D
Douglas	D
Frankfr	D
Reed	
Black	?
Vinson	D

California v Edmondson
46 123A
329 US 716
California

	10/08 1946 CERT
	1 1
Burton	
Rutledg	
Jackson	
Murphy	G
Douglas	
Frankfr	
Reed	
Black	
Vinson	

Brooks v U.S. (Bayarsky)
46 125A
329 US 716
CCA 3rd

	10/08 1946 CERT
	1 1
Burton	D
Rutledg	D
Jackson	D
Murphy	D
Douglas	D
Frankfr	D
Reed	G
Black	D
Vinson	D

Liberty Mutual Insurance v Pillsbury
46 128A
329 US 717
CCA 9th

Justice	10/08 1946 CERT
Burton	
Rutledg	G
Jackson	D
Murphy	D
Douglas	D
Frankfr	D
Reed	
Black	G
Vinson	D

Columbia Gas & Electric v U.S.
46 129A
329 US 737 46 130A 46 131A
CCA 6th

Justice	10/08 1946 CERT		
Burton			
Rutledg	G		
Jackson		D	
Murphy		D	
Douglas			D
Frankfr		D	
Reed		D	
Black		D	
Vinson			D

Antonelli Fireworks Company v U.S.
46 134A
329 US 742
CCA 2d

Justice	10/11 1946 CERT
Burton	
Rutledg	D
Jackson	D
Murphy	G
Douglas	D
Frankfr	D
Reed	D
Black	D
Vinson	D

Lloyd v C.I.R.
46 136A
329 US 717
CCA 3rd

Justice	10/08 1946 CERT
Burton	
Rutledg	G
Jackson	D
Murphy	D
Douglas	D
Frankfr	D
Reed	D
Black	D
Vinson	D

Third National Bank v F.S.L.I.C.
46 137A
329 US 718 46 138A
CCA 6th

Justice	10/08 1946 CERT	
Burton		
Rutledg	G	
Jackson		D
Murphy		D
Douglas		D
Frankfr	G	
Reed		
Black	G	
Vinson	G	

De Meerleer v Michigan
46 140A
329 US 663 46 880A
Michigan

Justice	10/19 1946 CERT	01/11 1947 MERITS	02/03 1947 REPORT
Burton	G	R	R
Rutledg	G	R	R
Jackson	G	R	R
Murphy	G	R	R
Douglas	G	R	R
Frankfr	G	R	R
Reed	G	R	R
Black	GR		
Vinson	GR		

Confederated Bands Of Ute v U.S.
46 141A
330 US 169
Black 01/22/47 Ct Cls

Justice	10/08 1946 CERT	01/18 1947 MERITS	02/17 1947 REPORT
Burton			
Rutledg	G		
Jackson		VM	A
Murphy			A
Douglas	D		
Frankfr			
Reed		R	R
Black	D	R	R
Vinson	D	A	A
		A	A

Louisiana (Francis) v Resweber
46 142A 45 1302A
329 US 459
Reed 11/25/46 Louisiana

Justice	06/08 1946 CERT	11/23 1946 MERITS	01/13 1947 REPORT
Burton		R	R
Rutledg	G	R	R
Jackson			
Murphy		R	R
Douglas	D		
Frankfr	G		
Reed		A	A
Black	D	A	A
Vinson	D	A	A

San Geronimo Development v U.S.
46 143A
329 US 718
CCA 1st

Justice	10/08 1946 CERT
Burton	
Rutledg	
Jackson	
Murphy	
Douglas	
Frankfr	G
Reed	
Black	
Vinson	

Uyeki v Styer
46 145A 45 1306A
329 US 689 46 264A
Philippines

Justice	06/08 1946 CERT	12/14 1946 STAY	01/04 1947 MOOT	01/06 1947 REPORT
Burton	G			S1
Rutledg	G	V	B	S1
Jackson		>	Y	
Murphy		>	Y	S1
Douglas	D	>	Y	S1
Frankfr	D	>	Y	S1
Reed		>	Y	S1
Black		>	Y	S1
Vinson	G	>	Y	S1

Albrecht v U.S.
46 148A
329 US 599 46 149A 46 150A 46 151A 46 155A
Black 01/22/47 CCA 8th

Justice	10/08 1946 CERT	01/18 1947 MERITS	02/03 1947 REPORT
Burton	G		A
Rutledg		R	A
Jackson	D	R	A
Murphy		R	A
Douglas	G	A	A
Frankfr		R	R
Reed		A	A
Black	G	R	R
Vinson	G	A	A

Barnes v New York
46 152A
329 US 719
New York

Justice	10/08 1946 CERT
Burton	
Rutledg	G
Jackson	G
Murphy	D
Douglas	D
Frankfr	D
Reed	D
Black	D
Vinson	D

George-Howard v F.D.I.C.
46 156A
329 US 719
CCA 8th

	10/08 1946 CERT 1 1
Burton	
Rutledg	
Jackson	
Murphy	
Douglas	
Frankfr	
Reed	G
Black	
Vinson	

Hedrick v C.I.R.
46 157A
329 US 719
CCA 2d

	10/08 1946 CERT 1 1
Burton	
Rutledg	G
Jackson	
Murphy	
Douglas	
Frankfr	
Reed	
Black	
Vinson	

Haddock v Pillsbury
46 158A
329 US 719
CCA 9th

	10/08 1946 CERT 1 1
Burton	G
Rutledg	
Jackson	
Murphy	
Douglas	
Frankfr	
Reed	
Black	
Vinson	

Ross v Ragen
46 159A
329 US 803
Illinois

	10/11 1946 CERT 1 1
Burton	
Rutledg	E E
Jackson	D
Murphy	
Douglas	E D
Frankfr	
Reed	
Black	E D
Vinson	D

Howard University v District Columbia
46 160A
329 US 739
CCA DC

	10/08 1946 CERT 1 1
Burton	
Rutledg	
Jackson	
Murphy	G
Douglas	
Frankfr	
Reed	
Black	
Vinson	

Moseley v United States Appliance
46 164A
329 US 762
CCA 9th

	11/09 1946 CERT 1 1
Burton	G
Rutledg	
Jackson	
Murphy	G G
Douglas	D
Frankfr	
Reed	D
Black	D
Vinson	D

Sholkin v Judges Superior Court
46 176A
329 US 740
Georgia

	10/08 1946 CERT 1 1	01/04 1947 CERT 1 2
Burton		D
Rutledg		D
Jackson		D
Murphy	G	D
Douglas		D
Frankfr		D
Reed		D
Black		D
Vinson		D

Taylor v Illinois
46 180A
329 US 803
Illinois

	10/11 1946 CERT 1 1
Burton	
Rutledg	E E
Jackson	
Murphy	E
Douglas	D
Frankfr	
Reed	
Black	E D
Vinson	D

Fedora v Illinois
46 181A
329 US 744
Illinois

	10/11 1946 CERT 1 1
Burton	
Rutledg	E
Jackson	
Murphy	
Douglas	D
Frankfr	
Reed	D
Black	D
Vinson	D

Mackey v New York
46 182A
330 US 833
New York

	10/11 1946 CERT 1 1	03/01 1947 CERT 1 2
Burton		
Rutledg	E	D
Jackson	E	G
Murphy	E E	D
Douglas	E	
Frankfr		D
Reed	E	D
Black	E	D
Vinson		D

Cahoon v U.S.
46 183A
329 US 739
CCA 5th

	01/04 1947 CERT 1 2

Cone v West Virginia Pulp & Paper
46 184A
330 US 212
Black 02/11/47 CCA 4th

	10/10 1946 CERT 1 1	02/08 1947 MERITS 1 1	03/03 1947 REPORT 1 1
Burton	GL	R	R
Rutledg			R
Jackson	GL	R	R
Murphy	GL	R	R
Douglas	X D	A	A
Frankfr			R
Reed	GL	R	R
Black	GL	R	R
Vinson	GL	R	R

Anchor Serum v American Cooperative
46 185A   46 186A
329 US 721
CCA 7th

	10/08 1946 CERT 1 1
Burton	
Rutledg	
Jackson	D
Murphy	D
Douglas	D
Frankfr	D
Reed	G
Black	D
Vinson	G

Bozza v U.S.
46 190A
330 US 160
Black 01/11/47 CCA 3rd

	10/08 1946 CERT 1 1	01/11 1947 MERITS 1 1	01/11 1947 MERITS 1 2	02/17 1947 REPORT 1 1	02/17 1947 REPORT 1 2
Burton	G	R	R		R
Rutledg	G	R	R	R	R
Jackson		A	A	R	R
Murphy					R
Douglas	G	A	A	A	R
Frankfr		A	A	A	R
Reed	G				R
Black		A	A	A	R
Vinson					R

Kimler v Ragen
46 192A   46 205A
329 US 745
Illinois

	10/11 1946 CERT 1 1
Burton	
Rutledg	E
Jackson	D
Murphy	E
Douglas	
Frankfr	
Reed	D
Black	D
Vinson	D

Baronia v Ragen
46 202A
329 US 746 46 203A
Illinois

	10/11 1946 CERT	
Burton		
Rutledg	E	D
Jackson		
Murphy	E	
Douglas		D
Frankfr		D
Reed		D
Black		D
Vinson		D

De Viera v Niersheimer
46 205A
329 US 746 46 192A
Illinois

	10/11 1946 CERT	
Burton		
Rutledg	E	D
Jackson		
Murphy	E	
Douglas		D
Frankfr		D
Reed		D
Black		D
Vinson		D

Koster v (American) Lumbermens Mutual
46 206A
330 US 518 46 93A CCA 2d
Jackson 12/23/46

	10/08 1946 CERT	12/21 1946 MERITS	03/10 1947 REPORT
Burton	G		
Rutledg	GH	R	R
Jackson	G	R	R
Murphy	G	A	A
Douglas		A	A
Frankfr	G D	A	A
Reed	G		
Black	G	R	R
Vinson	GH	A	A

Land v Dollar
46 207A
330 US 731
Douglas 02/17/47 CCA DC

	10/08 1946 CERT	02/15 1947 MERITS	04/07 1947 REPORT
Burton			A
Rutledg	G	X	A
Jackson	D		A
Murphy	G	A	A
Douglas		A	A
Frankfr	G	A	A
Reed		A	A
Black		A	A
Vinson	D	A	A

Transparent-Wrap v Stokes & Smith
46 208A
329 US 637
Douglas 01/11/47 CCA 2d

	10/08 1946 CERT	01/11 1947 MERITS	02/03 1947 REPORT
Burton	G		
Rutledg	D	R	A
Jackson	D		
Murphy		R	A
Douglas	G	R	A
Frankfr			
Reed	G	R	R
Black	G		
Vinson	D	R	A

Adams v C.I.R.
46 209A
331 US 737 46 287A
Frankfr 01/11/47 CCA 3rd

	10/08 1946 CERT	01/11 1947 MERITS	06/16 1947 REPORT
Burton	G	R	R
Rutledg	D		
Jackson	D	R	R
Murphy		AQ	AQ
Douglas	G	R	A
Frankfr	G	A	A
Reed		AQ	AQ
Black		A	A
Vinson	G	R	A

Whitmore v Ormsbee
46 210A
329 US 668
DC New Mexico

	10/08 1946 JURIS	10/14 1946 REPORT
Burton		A
Rutledg		A
Jackson		A
Murphy	NP	A
Douglas	NP	A
Frankfr		A
Reed	A	A
Black	A	A
Vinson	A	A

Martin v Ragen
46 215A
329 US 746
Illinois

	10/11 1946 CERT	
Burton		
Rutledg	E	D
Jackson		D
Murphy		D
Douglas		D
Frankfr		D
Reed		D
Black		D
Vinson		D

Bailey v U.S.
46 220A
329 US 670 46 219A
CCA 7th

	10/08 1946 CERT	10/14 1946 REPORT
Burton	GR	R
Rutledg	GR	R
Jackson	GR	R
Murphy	GR	R
Douglas	GR	R
Frankfr	GR	R
Reed	GR	R
Black	GR	R
Vinson	GR	R

Dyer v U.S.
46 226A
329 US 722
CCA DC

	10/08 1946 CERT	
Burton		D
Rutledg		D
Jackson		D
Murphy	G	
Douglas		D
Frankfr		D
Reed		D
Black		D
Vinson	G	

Patterson v Lamb
46 229A
329 US 539
Black 01/11/47 CCA DC

	10/08 1946 CERT	01/11 1947 MERITS	01/20 1947 REPORT
Burton	G	R	R
Rutledg	X	R	R
Jackson	G	R	R
Murphy	G	R	R
Douglas	G	R	R
Frankfr	G	R	R
Reed	G	R	R
Black		R	R
Vinson	G	R	R

Beauchamp v U.S.
46 230A
329 US 723
CCA 6th

	10/08 1946 CERT	
Burton		D
Rutledg		D
Jackson		D
Murphy	G	
Douglas		D
Frankfr		D
Reed		D
Black		D
Vinson	G	

U.S. v Standard Oil Of California
46 235A — 332 US 301 — Rutledg 04/15/47 CCA 9th

	10/08 1946 CERT (1 1)	04/14 1947 MERITS (1 1)	06/23 1947 REPORT (1 1)
Burton	G		
Rutledg	D	R	
Jackson		A	A
Murphy	G	A	A
Douglas	D	A	A
Frankfr	D	A	A
Reed	G	A	A
Black	D	A	A
Vinson	G	A	A

Ladrey v U.S.
46 236A — 329 US 723 — CCA DC

	10/08 1946 CERT (1 1)
Burton	G
Rutledg	D
Jackson	D
Murphy	
Douglas	D
Frankfr	D
Reed	D
Black	D
Vinson	D

Meltzer v C.I.R.
46 239A — 329 US 723 — CCA 2d

	10/10 1946 CERT (1 1)
Burton	G
Rutledg	D
Jackson	D
Murphy	G
Douglas	D
Frankfr	D
Reed	D
Black	D
Vinson	D

Craig v Harney
46 241A — 331 US 367 — Douglas 01/11/47 Texas

	10/10 1946 CERT (1 1)	01/11 1947 MERITS (1 1)	05/19 1947 REPORT (1 1)
Burton	G	A	A
Rutledg	G	R	R
Jackson		A	
Murphy	G	R	R
Douglas	G	R	R
Frankfr		A	A
Reed	G	R	R
Black		R	R
Vinson		R	

Schmoll v U.S.
46 244A — 329 US 724 — Ct Cls

	10/10 1946 CERT (1 1)
Burton	G
Rutledg	
Jackson	
Murphy	G
Douglas	G
Frankfr	
Reed	D
Black	D
Vinson	D

U.S. v Pullman Company
46 253A — 330 US 806 · 46 254A · 46 255A · 46 256A — DC ED Pennsylvania

	10/08 1946 JURIS (1 1)	03/15 1947 MERITS (1 1)	03/29 1947 MERITS (1 2)	03/31 1947 REPORT (1 1)
Burton	N		A	A
Rutledg	N	R	R	R
Jackson	N	R	R	R
Murphy	N		A	
Douglas	N	R	A	A
Frankfr	N	R		
Reed	N		A	A
Black	N	R	A	A
Vinson	N		A	A

Cantos v Styer
46 264A — 329 US 686 · 46 145A — Philippines

	10/10 1946 CERT (1 1)	12/16 1946 REPORT (1 1)
Burton	G	SI
Rutledg	D	SI
Jackson		SI
Murphy	G	SI
Douglas	G	SI
Frankfr		SI
Reed	D	SI
Black	G	SI
Vinson	G	SI

Cardillo v Liberty Mutual Insurance
46 265A — 330 US 469 — Murphy 01/11/47 CCA DC

	10/10 1946 CERT (1 1)	01/11 1947 MERITS (1 1)	03/10 1947 REPORT (1 1)
Burton	G		
Rutledg	G	R	R
Jackson	G		
Murphy	G	R	R
Douglas	G	R	R
Frankfr	G	R	R
Reed	G		
Black	D	R	R
Vinson	G		

Bank Of California National v C.I.R.
46 267A — 329 US 725 — CCA 9th

	10/10 1946 CERT (1 1)
Burton	G
Rutledg	D
Jackson	
Murphy	G
Douglas	D
Frankfr	
Reed	D
Black	D
Vinson	D

Gardner v Griswold
46 269A — 329 US 725 — CCA 7th

	10/10 1946 CERT (1 1)
Burton	D
Rutledg	D
Jackson	
Murphy	D
Douglas	G
Frankfr	
Reed	D
Black	D
Vinson	D

Industrial Commission v McCartin
46 270A — 330 US 622 — Murphy 01/22/47 Wisconsin

	10/10 1946 CERT (1 1)	01/18 1947 MERITS (1 1)	03/31 1947 REPORT (1 1)
Burton	G	R	R
Rutledg	G	R	R
Jackson	G	R	R
Murphy	G	R	R
Douglas	G		
Frankfr	G	A	
Reed	G	R	R
Black	G	R	R
Vinson	G	R	R

Milner Hotels v Porter
46 272A — 329 US 738 · 46 273A — CCA 6th

	10/10 1946 CERT (1 1)
Burton	G
Rutledg	D
Jackson	
Murphy	G
Douglas	D
Frankfr	
Reed	D
Black	D
Vinson	D

[...] Transportation Company v U.S.
46 276A
329 US 668
DC Massachusets

Justice	10/08 1946 JURIS (1 1)	10/14 1946 REPORT (1 1)
Burton	A	A
Rutledg	A	A
Jackson	N	A
Murphy	N	A
Douglas	A	A
Frankfr	A	A
Reed	A	A
Black	A	A
Vinson	A	A

Butz v Niersheimer
46 277A
329 US 804
Illinois

Justice	10/11 1946 CERT (1 1)
Burton	D
Rutledg	E
Jackson	E
Murphy	E
Douglas	E
Frankfr	E
Reed	E
Black	E
Vinson	E

McKay v Nevada
46 281A
329 US 749
Nevada

Justice	10/11 1946 CERT (1 1)
Burton	G
Rutledg	D
Jackson	D
Murphy	E
Douglas	D
Frankfr	D
Reed	D
Black	D
Vinson	D

Codo v International Shoe Company
46 285A
329 US 726
CCA 8th

Justice	10/10 1946 CERT (1 1)
Burton	D
Rutledg	D
Jackson	D
Murphy	D
Douglas	D
Frankfr	D
Reed	D
Black	G
Vinson	D

Hickman v Ragen
46 286A
329 US 750
Illinois

Justice	10/11 1946 CERT (1 1)
Burton	E
Rutledg	D
Jackson	D
Murphy	GE
Douglas	D
Frankfr	D
Reed	D
Black	D
Vinson	D

Bazley v C.I.R.
46 287A
331 US 737
Frankfr 01/11/47 CCA 3rd

Justice	10/10 1946 CERT (1 1)	01/11 1947 MERITS (1 1)	06/16 1947 REPORT (1 1)
Burton	G	R	R
Rutledg		R	
Jackson		R	R
Murphy	G	R	
Douglas		A	R
Frankfr		A	A
Reed		A	A
Black		A	A
Vinson		A	A

Richardson v Kelly
46 288A
329 US 798
Alabama

Justice	01/04 1947 CERT (1 1)
Burton	G
Rutledg	G
Jackson	D
Murphy	G
Douglas	D
Frankfr	D
Reed	D
Black	D
Vinson	D

Kotch v Board Of River Port Pilot
46 291A
330 US 552
Black 02/11/47 Louisiana

Justice	10/08 1946 JURIS (1 1)	02/08 1947 MERITS (1 1)	03/31 1947 REPORT (1 1)
Burton	A	A	A
Rutledg	N	R	R
Jackson	A	A	
Murphy	N	R	R
Douglas	N	R	R
Frankfr	A	A	
Reed	A	A	A
Black	A	A	A
Vinson	A	A	

Evans v U.S.
46 296A
329 US 668
DC WD Virginia

Justice	10/08 1946 JURIS (1 1)	10/14 1946 MERITS (1 1)
Burton	A	A
Rutledg	A	A
Jackson	A	A
Murphy	A	A
Douglas	A	A
Frankfr	A	A
Reed	N	A
Black	A	A
Vinson	A	A

Russell Box Company v Grant Paper Box
46 297A
329 US 741
CCA 1st

Justice	10/11 1946 CERT (1 2)
Burton	D
Rutledg	D
Jackson	D
Murphy	G
Douglas	D
Frankfr	D
Reed	D
Black	G
Vinson	D

Byerly v C.I.R.
46 298A
329 US 727
CCA 6th

Justice	10/10 1946 CERT (1 1)
Burton	G
Rutledg	G
Jackson	G
Murphy	G
Douglas	D
Frankfr	D
Reed	D
Black	G
Vinson	D

Connellan v New York
46 310A
329 US 751
New York

Justice	10/11 1946 CERT (1 1)
Burton	G
Rutledg	G
Jackson	G
Murphy	G
Douglas	D
Frankfr	D
Reed	D
Black	D
Vinson	D

U.S. v Silk
46 312A
331 US 704 46 673A CCA 10th
Reed 03/17/47

Justice	CERT 10/19/1946	MERITS 03/15/1947	REPORT 06/16/1947
Burton	G		A
Rutledg	G D	R	R A
Jackson	G D	R	R A
Murphy	G		A
Douglas	G	R	A
Frankfr	G		R A
Reed	G	R	A
Black	G		A
Vinson	D		A

DeCastro's Estate v C.I.R.
46 317A
329 US 727 CCA 2d

Justice	CERT 10/10/1946	MERITS 03/15/1947
Burton		
Rutledg		R
Jackson		R
Murphy		
Douglas	G	
Frankfr		
Reed		A
Black		
Vinson		

Ellis v Union Pacific RR Company
46 320A
329 US 649
Douglas 01/22/47 Nebraska

Justice	CERT 11/23/1946	MERITS 01/18/1947	REPORT 02/03/1947
Burton	G D	R	R
Rutledg	G D	R	R
Jackson			R
Murphy	G	R	R
Douglas	G D		R
Frankfr			R
Reed	G D	R	R
Black	G D		R
Vinson	G D		R

Buice v Patterson
46 323A
329 US 739 CCA 1st

Justice	CERT 10/10/1946
Burton	
Rutledg	G
Jackson	D
Murphy	G
Douglas	D
Frankfr	D
Reed	D
Black	D
Vinson	D

Coombs v Jersey City
46 328A
329 US 729 CCA 3rd

Justice	CERT 10/10/1946
Burton	G
Rutledg	D
Jackson	D
Murphy	D
Douglas	D
Frankfr	D
Reed	D
Black	D
Vinson	D

Walling v Nashville Chattanooga RR
46 335A
330 US 158 46 336A
Black 01/22/47 CCA 6th

Justice	CERT 10/10/1946	MERITS 01/18/1947	REPORT 02/17/1947
Burton	G	A	A
Rutledg	G	A	A
Jackson	G	X	A
Murphy	G	A	A
Douglas	G	A	A
Frankfr	G	R	A
Reed	G	A	A
Black	G	A	A
Vinson	G	A	A

Piotrowski v New York
46 337A
329 US 752 New York

Justice	CERT 10/11/1946
Burton	
Rutledg	G
Jackson	G D
Murphy	D
Douglas	D
Frankfr	D
Reed	D
Black	D
Vinson	D

Kut v Bureau Of Unemployment Ohio
46 338A
329 US 669 Ohio

Justice	JURIS 10/08/1946
Burton	S
Rutledg	S
Jackson	N
Murphy	S
Douglas	S
Frankfr	S
Reed	S
Black	
Vinson	

McCann v Clark
46 340A
331 US 813 CCA 2d

Justice	CERT 10/11/1946	CERT 04/26/1947
Burton	E	
Rutledg	E	D
Jackson		D
Murphy	E	
Douglas	E	X
Frankfr	E	X
Reed	E	D
Black	E	D
Vinson		D

Sharp & Fellows Contracting v Basler
46 341A
329 US 730
California

Justice	CERT 10/10/1946	REPORT 05/12/1947
Burton	D	A
Rutledg	D	A
Jackson		A
Murphy	G D	A
Douglas		A
Frankfr	D	R
Reed	G	R
Black	G D	A
Vinson	D	A

New York v U.S.
46 343A 46 344A 46 345A
331 US 284
Douglas 03/11/47 DC ND New York

Justice	JURIS 10/08/1946	MERITS 03/08/1947	REPORT 05/12/1947
Burton	N	A	A
Rutledg	N	A	A
Jackson	N	R	R
Murphy	N	A	A
Douglas	N	A	A
Frankfr	N	R	R
Reed	N	A	A
Black	N	A	A
Vinson	N	A	A

Philadelphia Company v Guggenheim
46 359A 46 364A
329 US 731 CCA 3rd

Justice	CERT 10/10/1946
Burton	G
Rutledg	D
Jackson	D
Murphy	D
Douglas	D
Frankfr	D
Reed	
Black	G
Vinson	G

46 367A
331 US 477
Burton 02/11/47 CCA 3rd

	10/10 1946 CERT	02/08 1947 MERITS	06/02 1947 REPORT
	1 1		1 1
Burton	G		R
Rutledg	G	R	R
Jackson	D		R
Murphy	G		R
Douglas	G		R
Frankfr	D		R
Reed			R
Black	G	A	R
Vinson	D		R

v C.I.R.
46 373A
329 US 732
CCA 5th

	10/10 1946 CERT	06/02 1947 REPORT
	1 1	1 1
Burton	G	R
Rutledg	G	R
Jackson	D	R
Murphy	G	R
Douglas	G	R
Frankfr	D	R
Reed		R
Black	G	R
Vinson	D	R

Sioux Tribe v U.S.
46 368A 49 369A
329 US 684
Ct Cls

	10/19 1946 CERT	11/23 1946 CERT	12/07 1946 CERT	12/09 1946 REPORT
	1 1	1 2	1 3	1 1
Burton	D	GVM	GVM	VM
Rutledg	D	GVM	GVM	VM
Jackson				VM
Murphy		GVM	GVM	VM
Douglas				VM
Frankfr				VM
Reed	D			VM
Black	D	GVM	GVM	VM
Vinson	D	GVM	GVM	VM

Patterson v Florida
46 376A
329 US 789
Florida

	12/07 1946 CERT
	1 1
Burton	D
Rutledg	D
Jackson	
Murphy	G
Douglas	G
Frankfr	
Reed	D
Black	D
Vinson	D

U.S. National Bank v Chase National
46 371A
331 US 28
Murphy 02/11/47 CCA 3rd

	10/10 1946 CERT	02/08 1947 MERITS	04/14 1947 REPORT
	1 1		1 1
Burton	G	R	R
Rutledg	G		R
Jackson	D	X	R
Murphy	D		R
Douglas			A
Frankfr		R	R
Reed	G	R	R
Black	G	R	R
Vinson	G	R	R

Fay v New York
46 377A
332 US 261 46 452A
Jackson 04/07/47 New York

	10/10 1946 CERT	04/05 1947 MERITS	06/23 1947 REPORT
	1 1	1 1	1 1
Burton	G		R
Rutledg	G	RQ	R
Jackson	D	R	
Murphy	G		R
Douglas	D	R	A
Frankfr			
Reed	D	R	R
Black	G X	R	A
Vinson	D		A

46 384A
330 US 610
Douglas 02/11/47 New York

	10/10 1946 CERT	02/08 1947 MERITS	03/31 1947 REPORT
	1 1	1 1	1 1
Burton	G		A
Rutledg	G	R	A
Jackson	G		A
Murphy	G		A
Douglas	D		A
Frankfr	D		A
Reed	G		A
Black	G	R	A
Vinson			A

Atlantic Coast Line RR v Phillips
46 385A
332 US 168
Frankfr 04/15/47 Georgia

	10/08 1946 JURIS	04/12 1947 MERITS	06/23 1947 REPORT
	1 1	1 1	1 1
Burton	N		A
Rutledg	A	R	A
Jackson	SA		A
Murphy	N		A
Douglas	N		A
Frankfr	A	R	A
Reed	N		A
Black	A	R	A
Vinson	N		A

Thompson v Illinois
46 386A
329 US 732
Illinois

	10/11 1946 CERT
	1 1
Burton	D
Rutledg	G
Jackson	D
Murphy	G
Douglas	D
Frankfr	D
Reed	D
Black	D
Vinson	D

McLaren v Niersthelmer
46 389A
329 US 685
Illinois

	10/11 1946 CERT 1 1	12/14 1946 CERT 1 2	12/16 1946 REPORT 1 1
Burton	E	GVM	VM
Rutledg	E	GVM	VM
Jackson	D	GVM	VM
Murphy	E	GVM	VM
Douglas	D	GVM	VM
Frankfr	D	GVM	VM
Reed		GVM	VM
Black	E	GVM	VM
Vinson	E	GVM	VM

Conway v Ragen
46 396A
329 US 755
Illinois

	10/11 1946 CERT 1 1	01/18 1947 MERITS 1 1	03/03 1947 REPORT 1 1
Burton	G	A	A
Rutledg	D	A	A
Jackson	D	A	A
Murphy	D	A	A
Douglas	D	A	A
Frankfr	D	A	A
Reed	D	A	A
Black	D	A	A
Vinson	D	A	A

Northern Pacific RR Company v U.S.
46 400A
330 US 248 46 56A 46 57A
Douglas 01/22/47 CCA 7th

	10/11 1946 CERT 1 1
Burton	G
Rutledg	G
Jackson	G
Murphy	G
Douglas	G
Frankfr	G
Reed	G
Black	G
Vinson	G

Brooklyn National v C.I.R.
46 401A
329 US 733
CCA 2d

	10/11 1946 CERT 1 1
Burton	D
Rutledg	D
Jackson	D
Murphy	D
Douglas	G
Frankfr	G
Reed	G
Black	D
Vinson	D

Mexican Light & Power v Texas Mexican
46 404A
331 US 731
Frankfr 02/11/47 Texas

	10/11 1946 CERT 1 1	02/08 1947 MERITS 1 1	06/16 1947 REPORT 1 1
Burton	D	A	A
Rutledg	D	A	A
Jackson	D		A
Murphy	D		A
Douglas	G	R	A
Frankfr	G		A
Reed	G	R	R
Black		R X	R
Vinson	D	R	A

Gayes v New York
46 405A
332 US 145 46 668A
Burton 05/05/47 Frankfr 05/16/47 New York

	10/11 1946 CERT 1 1	12/07 1946 CERT 1 2	12/14 1946 CERT 1 3
Burton	E	G	G
Rutledg	E	G	G
Jackson		D	D
Murphy	E	G	G
Douglas	E	D	D
Frankfr	E	G	G
Reed		D	D
Black	E	D	D
Vinson		D	D

Singer v Ragen
46 415A
329 US 804
Illinois

	10/11 1946 CERT 1 1	01/04 1947 CERT 1 2
Burton	E	D
Rutledg	E	D
Jackson	E	D
Murphy	E	D
Douglas	D	D
Frankfr	D	D
Reed		D
Black		D
Vinson	E	

U.S.D.A. v Remund
46 417A
330 US 539
Murphy 02/11/47 South Dakota

	10/26 1946 CERT 1 1	02/08 1947 MERITS 1 1	03/17 1947 REPORT 1 1
Burton	G	R	R
Rutledg	G	R	R
Jackson	G	R	R
Murphy	G		
Douglas	G		A
Frankfr	G	R	R
Reed	G	R	R
Black	G	R	R
Vinson		A	A

N.L.R.B. v Jones & Laughlin Steel
46 418A
331 US 416 46 419A
Murphy 03/17/47 CCA 6th

	12/21 1946 CERT 1 1	03/15 1947 MERITS 1 1	05/19 1947 REPORT 1 1
Burton	G	R	R
Rutledg	D	R	R
Jackson		R	R
Murphy	D		
Douglas			A
Frankfr	D	R	R
Reed	G	R	R
Black	G	R	R
Vinson		A	A

46 419A
331 US 398   46 418A
Murphy 03/17/47 CCA 7th

Justice	12/21 1946 CERT	03/15 1947 MERITS	05/19 1947 REPORT
Burton	G	R	R
Rutledg	D	R	R
Jackson	D	A	A
Murphy			
Douglas	G	R	R
Frankfr	G	R	R
Reed	D		
Black	D	R	R
Vinson		A	A

Lavender v Kurn
46 427A
329 US 762   46 20M
Missouri

Justice	10/19 1946 CERT
Burton	
Rutledg	K
Jackson	
Murphy	GK
Douglas	
Frankfr	
Reed	G
Black	
Vinson	

C.I.R. v Beck
46 428A
329 US 735   46 298A
CCA 6th

Justice	10/11 1946 CERT
Burton	G
Rutledg	D
Jackson	D
Murphy	
Douglas	D
Frankfr	D
Reed	G
Black	
Vinson	D

U.S. v Pinardi—Leo
46 429A
331 US 256
Reed 02/17/47 CCA 9th

Justice	10/11 1946 CERT	02/15 1947 MERITS	05/12 1947 REPORT
Burton	G		A
Rutledg			A
Jackson	G D		A
Murphy	G	X	A
Douglas	G D		A A
Frankfr			A A
Reed	G	R	
Black	G	R	A A
Vinson	G	R	A A

U.S. v Ogilvie Hardware Company
46 430A
330 US 709
Black 03/11/47 CCA 5th

Justice	10/11 1946 CERT	03/08 1947 MERITS	04/07 1947 REPORT
Burton	G		A A
Rutledg	G		A A
Jackson	G D	R	A
Murphy	G		A A
Douglas	G D		A
Frankfr	G		
Reed	G D	R	A A
Black	G	R	A A
Vinson	G D		A

Testa v Katt
46 431A
330 US 386
Black 02/17/47 Rhode Island

Justice	10/26 1946 CERT	02/15 1947 MERITS	03/10 1947 REPORT
Burton	G	R	R
Rutledg	G	R	R
Jackson	G	R	R
Murphy	G	R	R
Douglas	G	R	R
Frankfr	G	R	R
Reed	G	R	R
Black	G	R	R
Vinson	G	R	R

Aetna Casualty & Surety v Flowers
46 432A
330 US 464
Douglas 02/17/47 CCA 6th

Justice	10/11 1946 CERT	02/15 1947 MERITS	03/10 1947 REPORT
Burton	G	R	R
Rutledg	G	R	R
Jackson	G	R	R
Murphy	G	R	R
Douglas	G	A	
Frankfr	G		
Reed	G	R	R
Black	G	A	
Vinson	G	R	R

Dictheiser v Pennsylvania RR Company
46 435A
329 US 808
CCA 3rd

Justice	01/18 1947 CERT
Burton	D
Rutledg	D
Jackson	D
Murphy	D
Douglas	D
Frankfr	D
Reed	D
Black	D
Vinson	

U.S. v Elchibegoff
46 442A
329 US 694
Ct Cls

Justice	11/09 1946 CERT	02/03 1947 REPORT
Burton	G	SI
Rutledg	D	SI
Jackson	G	SI
Murphy	D	SI
Douglas	G	SI
Frankfr	G	SI
Reed	G	
Black		
Vinson		

Pauly v McCarthy
46 443A
330 US 802
Utah

Justice	10/11 1946 CERT	03/08 1947 MERITS	03/10 1947 REPORT
Burton	G	R	R
Rutledg	G	R	R
Jackson	D	A	
Murphy	G	R	R
Douglas	G	R	R
Frankfr	D	R	R
Reed	G	R	R
Black	D		
Vinson	G	R	R

Bennett v Ragen
46 447A
329 US 804
Illinois

Justice	10/11 1946 CERT	01/04 1947 CERT
Burton	E	D
Rutledg	E	D
Jackson		D
Murphy	E	D
Douglas		D
Frankfr		D
Reed		D
Black	E	D
Vinson		D

Order RR Telegraphers v New Orleans RR
46 449A
329 US 758
CCA 8th

Justice	10/19 1946 CERT	11/16 1946 REHEAR
Burton	D	B
Rutledg	D	Y
Jackson	D	B
Murphy	D	B
Douglas	D	Y
Frankfr	D	Y
Reed	D	
Black	D	B
Vinson	D	B

Penfield Company v S.E.C.
46 453A
330 US 585
Douglas 01/22/47 CCA 9th

	11/09 1946 CERT (1 1)	11/16 1946 REPORT (1 2)
Burton		
Rutledg	D	G
Jackson	D	
Murphy	D	G
Douglas		G
Frankfr		
Reed		
Black	D	D
Vinson	D	D

Fleming v Traphagen
46 454A
329 US 686 46 42A 46 45A
CCA 7th

	12/14 1946 CERT (1 1)	12/16 1946 REPORT (1 1)	01/11 1947 REHEAR (1 1)
Burton	GR	R	B
Rutledg	GR	R	B
Jackson	GR	R	
Murphy	GR	R	B
Douglas	GR	R	Y
Frankfr	GR	R	
Reed	GR	R	B
Black	GR	R	B
Vinson	GR	R	Y

Adams v U.S.
46 457A
330 US 801
Black 02/17/47 CCA 5th

	10/19 1946 CERT (1 1)	03/03 1947 REPORT (1 1)
Burton	G	A
Rutledg	GR	A
Jackson		A
Murphy	GR	A
Douglas		A
Frankfr		A
Reed		A
Black		A
Vinson	GR	A

Davis v Smyth
46 465A
329 US 789
Virginia

	12/07 1946 CERT (1 1)
Burton	D
Rutledg	D
Jackson	D
Murphy	D
Douglas	E
Frankfr	D
Reed	D
Black	D
Vinson	D

Greenberg v California
46 466A
331 US 796 46 102A
California

	06/21 1947 JURIS (1 1)
Burton	A
Rutledg	A
Jackson	A
Murphy	A
Douglas	A
Frankfr	A
Reed	A
Black	A
Vinson	A

Greenough v Tax Assessors Of Newport
46 461A
331 US 486
Reed 03/11/47 Rhode Island

	10/19 1946 JURIS (1 1)	03/08 1947 MERITS (1 1)	03/31 1947 REPORT (1 1)
Burton	N	R	A
Rutledg	N	R	R
Jackson	N		
Murphy	N		
Douglas	N	R	A
Frankfr	N		A
Reed	N		R
Black	N	R	A
Vinson	N	R	A

Baltimore & Ohio RR v Thompson
46 463A
329 US 762 46 552A
CCA 8th

	10/26 1946 CERT (1 1)
Burton	G
Rutledg	D
Jackson	D
Murphy	D
Douglas	D
Frankfr	D
Reed	G
Black	D
Vinson	D

Rice v Santa Fe Elevator
46 470A 46 472A
331 US 218 46 471A 46 473A
Douglas 02/17/47 CCA 7th

	10/19 1946 CERT (1 1)	02/15 1947 MERITS (1 1)	05/05 1947 REPORT (1 1)
Burton	G	R	R
Rutledg	G	R	R
Jackson	G		R
Murphy	G	R	R
Douglas	G	R	R
Frankfr	G	R	R
Reed	G	R	R
Black	G		R
Vinson	G	X	R

Rice v Board Of Trade Of Chicago
46 471A 46 473A
331 US 247 46 470A 46 472A
Douglas 02/17/47 CCA 7th

	10/19 1946 CERT (1 1)	02/15 1947 MERITS (1 1)	05/05 1947 REPORT (1 1)
Burton	G	R	R
Rutledg	G	R	R
Jackson	G		R
Murphy	G	R	R
Douglas	G	R	R
Frankfr	G	R	R
Reed	G	R	R
Black	G		R
Vinson	G	X	R

Murray v Fleming
46 483A
330 US 804 46 512A 46 583A
CCA 1st

	11/09 1946 CERT (1 1)	03/10 1947 REPORT (1 1)
Burton	G	SI
Rutledg	G	SI
Jackson	G	SI
Murphy	G	SI
Douglas	G	SI
Frankfr	G	SI
Reed	G	SI
Black	G	SI
Vinson	G	SI

Ayrshire Collieries v U.S.
46 467A
331 US 132
Murphy 04/15/47 DC SD Indiana

	10/19 1946 JURIS (1 1)	04/12 1947 MERITS (1 1)	04/28 1947 REPORT (1 1)
Burton	N	VM	V
Rutledg	N		V
Jackson	N	VM	V
Murphy	N	AQ	V
Douglas	N	VM	V
Frankfr	N	VM	V
Reed	N		V
Black	N	VM	V
Vinson	NR		A

46 **484A**
329 US 763 46 485A 46 486A
CCA 5th

	10/26 1946 CERT 1 1
Burton	D
Rutledg	D
Jackson	D
Murphy	G
Douglas	GQ
Frankfr	D
Reed	G
Black	D
Vinson	D

Twin Falls Canal Company v Johnson
46 **487A**
329 US 782
Idaho

	11/16 1946 CERT 1 1
Burton	D
Rutledg	G
Jackson	D
Murphy	D
Douglas	D
Frankfr	D
Reed	D
Black	G
Vinson	D

Zap v U.S.
46 **489A** 45 489A
330 US 800 46 37A
Douglas 02/11/46 CCA 9th

	12/08 1945 CERT 1 1	01/05 1946 CERT 1 2	02/11 1946 MERITS 1 1	06/10 1946 REPORT 1 1	03/01 1947 REHEAR 1 1	03/01 1947 MERITS 1 2	03/03 1947 REPORT 1 2
Burton	D	G	A	A	G	R	R
Rutledg	D	D	AQ	R	G	R	R
Jackson							
Murphy	D	G	R	R	G	R	R
Douglas	D	D	A	A	G	R	R
Frankfr	D	G	X	R	G	R	R
Reed	D	D	A	A	G	R	R
Black	D	D	A	A	G	R	R
Vinson							
Stone	D	G	A				

145 Madison Avenue v Asselta
46 **497A**
331 US 199 46 564A 46 74A
Vinson 02/17/47 CCA 2d

	10/26 1946 CERT 1 1	12/07 1946 CERT 1 2	02/15 1947 MERITS 1 1	05/05 1947 REPORT 1 1
Burton	D	G	RQ	A
Rutledg	D	G	A	A
Jackson	D	G	RQ	A
Murphy	D	G	A	A
Douglas	D	G	A	A
Frankfr	D	G	AQ	A
Reed	D	G	R	A
Black	D	G	A	A
Vinson	D	G	A	A

U.S. v Smith
46 **498A**
331 US 469
Jackson 03/17/47 CCA 3rd

	10/26 1946 CERT 1 1	03/15 1947 MERITS 1 1	06/02 1947 REPORT 1 1
Burton	D	R	R
Rutledg	G	A	R
Jackson	G	R	R
Murphy	G	R	R
Douglas	G	R	R
Frankfr	G	A	R
Reed	D	R	R
Black	D	R	R
Vinson	D	A	R

Marr v A.B. Dick Company
46 **504A**
329 US 680
CCA 2d

	11/09 1946 CERT 1 1	11/12 1946 REPORT 1 1
Burton	GVM	VM
Rutledg	GVM	VM
Jackson	GVM	VM
Murphy	GVM	VM
Douglas	GVM	VM
Frankfr	GVM	VM
Reed	GVM	VM
Black	GVM	VM
Vinson	GVM	VM

De La Roi v California
46 **505A**
329 US 761
California

	10/19 1946 CERT 1 1
Burton	D
Rutledg	D
Jackson	D
Murphy	G
Douglas	D
Frankfr	D
Reed	D
Black	D
Vinson	D

Raley v Fleming
46 **512A**
331 US 111 46 483A 46 583A
Douglas 04/07/47 CCA DC

	11/09 1946 CERT 1 1	04/05 1947 MERITS 1 1	04/28 1947 REPORT 1 1
Burton	G	A	A
Rutledg	G	A	A
Jackson	G	A	A
Murphy	G	A	A
Douglas	G	A	A
Frankfr	G	A	A
Reed	G	A	A
Black	G	A	A
Vinson	G	A	A

U.S. v Lauro
46 **514A**
330 US 446 46 69A
Reed 12/16/46 CCA 2d

	12/14 1946 QUEST 1 1	03/10 1947 REPORT 1 1
Burton	Y	Y
Rutledg	Y	Y
Jackson	Y	Y
Murphy	Y	Y
Douglas	Y	Y
Frankfr	Y	Y
Reed	Y	Y
Black	Y	Y
Vinson	Y	Y

Silverman v Osborne Register Company
46 **522A**
329 US 765
CCA DC

	10/26 1946 CERT 1 1
Burton	D
Rutledg	D
Jackson	G
Murphy	D
Douglas	D
Frankfr	D
Reed	D
Black	G
Vinson	D

315 West 97Th Street Realty v Fleming
46 **526A**
329 US 801
CCA Emergency

	01/04 1947 CERT 1 1
Burton	D
Rutledg	D
Jackson	D
Murphy	G
Douglas	D
Frankfr	D
Reed	G
Black	D
Vinson	D

182

Supreme Court Docket Charts

Justice order in each chart: Burton, Rutledg, Jackson, Murphy, Douglas, Frankfr, Reed, Black, Vinson.

Login v Porter
46 528A · 329 US 771 · CCA 9th

Justice	CERT 11/09/1946 (1 1)
Burton	GR
Rutledg	D
Jackson	D
Murphy	D
Douglas	D
Frankfr	D
Reed	D
Black	D
Vinson	D

Cook v Fortson
46 531A · 329 US 675 46 532A · DC ND Georgia

Justice	JURIS 10/19/1946 (1 1)	JURIS 10/26/1946 (1 2)
Burton	N A	
Rutledg	N A	P
Jackson	A	
Murphy	N S A	S
Douglas	A	S
Frankfr	A	S
Reed	A	
Black	N A	S
Vinson	S	S

Turman v Duckworth
46 532A · 329 US 675 46 531A · DC ND Georgia

Justice	JURIS 10/19/1946 (1 1)	JURIS 10/26/1946 (1 2)
Burton	N A	
Rutledg	N A	P
Jackson	A	
Murphy	N S A	S
Douglas	A	S
Frankfr	A	S
Reed	A	
Black	N A	S
Vinson	S	S

Smith v U.S.
46 534A · 329 US 776 · CCA 4th

Justice	CERT 11/09/1946 (1 1)
Burton	D
Rutledg	D
Jackson	
Murphy	G
Douglas	D
Frankfr	D
Reed	D
Black	D
Vinson	D

Sunal v Large
46 535A · 332 US 174 46 840A · Douglas 04/07/47 · CCA 4th

Justice	CERT 01/18/1947 (1 1)	MERITS 04/05/1947 (1 1)	REPORT 06/23/1947 (1 1)
Burton	G	A	A
Rutledg	G	X	R
Jackson	G	X	R
Murphy	G	A	R
Douglas	G	A	R
Frankfr	G	A	A
Reed	G	A	A
Black	G	A	A
Vinson	G	A	A

Eastern Sugar Associates v Puerto Rico
46 537A · 329 US 772 · CCA 1st

Justice	CERT 11/09/1946 (1 1)
Burton	G
Rutledg	D
Jackson	D
Murphy	G
Douglas	D
Frankfr	D
Reed	D
Black	D
Vinson	D

Berman v U.S.
46 538A · 329 US 795 · CCA 9th

Justice	CERT 12/21/1946 (1 1)
Burton	
Rutledg	G D
Jackson	G D
Murphy	D
Douglas	D
Frankfr	D
Reed	D
Black	G D
Vinson	D

Foster v Illinois
46 540A · 332 US 134 · Frankfr 05/14/47 · Illinois

Justice	CERT 11/09/1946 (1 1)	CERT 02/01/1947 (1 2)	MERITS 05/10/1947 (1 1)	REPORT 06/23/1947 (1 1)
Burton	E D	G D	R A	R A
Rutledg	E D	G D	R A	R A
Jackson				
Murphy	E D	G D	R A	R A
Douglas	E D	G D	A	A
Frankfr				
Reed	E D	G D	R A	R A
Black	E D	G D	R A	R A
Vinson				

F.P.C. v Arkansas Power & Light
46 543A · 330 US 802 · CCA DC

Justice	CERT 10/26/1946 (1 1)	MERITS 03/08/1947 (1 1)	REPORT 03/10/1947 (1 1)
Burton	G	R	R
Rutledg	G	R	R
Jackson	G	R	R
Murphy	G	R	R
Douglas	G	R	R
Frankfr	G	R	R
Reed	G	R	R
Black	G	R	R
Vinson	G	R	R

Zayatz v Southern RR Company
46 548A · 329 US 789 · Alabama

Justice	CERT 12/07/1946 (1 1)
Burton	D
Rutledg	D
Jackson	D
Murphy	D
Douglas	D
Frankfr	D
Reed	D
Black	G
Vinson	D

Cities Service Gas Company v F.P.C.
46 556A · 329 US 773 46 733A · CCA 10th

Justice	CERT 11/09/1946 (1 1)
Burton	G
Rutledg	D
Jackson	D
Murphy	G
Douglas	G D
Frankfr	D
Reed	D
Black	D
Vinson	D

Lamont v C.I.R.
46 557A · 329 US 782 · CCA 2d

Justice	CERT 11/09/1946 (1 1)	CERT 11/16/1946 (1 2)
Burton		G
Rutledg	D	
Jackson		
Murphy		G
Douglas	G	G
Frankfr		
Reed		
Black	D	D
Vinson	D	D

Rutherford Food v McComb
46 562A
331 US 722
Reed 04/15/47 CCA 10th

	11/09 1946 CERT	04/14 1947 MERITS	06/16 1947 REPORT
Burton	G	R	A
Rutledg		A	A
Jackson	D	A	A
Murphy	G	A	A
Douglas	D	A	A
Frankfr		A	A
Reed	D	A	A
Black	D	A	A
Vinson	G	A	A

Barlow v Federal Land Bank Of Berkeley
46 563A
329 US 773
CCA 10th

	11/09 1946 CERT
Burton	D
Rutledg	D
Jackson	
Murphy	G
Douglas	
Frankfr	D
Reed	D
Black	D
Vinson	D

Walling v General Industries Company
46 564A
330 US 545
Vinson 02/17/47 CCA 6th

	11/09 1946 CERT	02/15 1947 MERITS	03/31 1947 REPORT
Burton	G	RQ	R
Rutledg	D	R	R
Jackson	D		
Murphy	G	R	R
Douglas		A	A
Frankfr	D	A	A
Reed	D	A	A
Black	D	R	R
Vinson	G	AQ	A

Van Der Loo v Porter
46 567A
329 US 774
CCA Emergency

	11/09 1946 CERT
Burton	D
Rutledg	X
Jackson	D
Murphy	D
Douglas	G
Frankfr	D
Reed	D
Black	D
Vinson	D

John Hancock Mutual Life v U.S.
46 570A
329 US 774
CCA 1st

	11/09 1946 CERT
Burton	D
Rutledg	G
Jackson	G
Murphy	D
Douglas	G
Frankfr	D
Reed	D
Black	D
Vinson	D

Rescue Army v Municipal Court
46 574A
331 US 549 46 103A
Rutledg 02/11/47 California

	10/26 1946 JURIS	02/08 1947 MERITS	06/09 1947 REPORT
Burton	N		S
Rutledg	P	R	S
Jackson	P	X	S
Murphy	N		
Douglas		A	
Frankfr	P	A	S
Reed	P	A	S
Black		A	S
Vinson	N	A	

Fleming v Mohawk Wrecking & Lumber
46 583A
331 US 111 46 512A 46 483A
Douglas 04/07/47 CCA 6th

	11/09 1946 CERT	04/05 1947 MERITS	04/28 1947 REPORT
Burton	G	R	R
Rutledg	G	R	R
Jackson	G	R	R
Murphy	G	R	R
Douglas	G	R	R
Frankfr	G	R	R
Reed	G	R	R
Black	G		
Vinson	G		

Waterman Steamship v Pan-American
46 584A
329 US 774
CCA 2d

	11/09 1946 CERT
Burton	D
Rutledg	D
Jackson	D
Murphy	D
Douglas	
Frankfr	D
Reed	
Black	
Vinson	

U.S. v Hoy
46 585A
330 US 724
Black 03/17/47 DC SD California

	10/26 1946 JURIS	03/15 1947 MERITS	04/07 1947 REPORT
Burton	N	R	R
Rutledg	N	R	R
Jackson	N		
Murphy	N	R	R
Douglas			
Frankfr	N	R	R
Reed		A	A
Black	N	A	A
Vinson		A	A

Reimann v Clark
46 586A
329 US 787 46 587A 46 588A
CCA DC

	12/07 1946 CERT	05/03 1947 MERITS	06/02 1947 REPORT
Burton	D		R
Rutledg	G	R	R
Jackson	D	X	R
Murphy	D		R
Douglas	G	X	R
Frankfr	D	R	R
Reed	D	R	R
Black	D		R
Vinson	D	R	R

Cope v Anderson
46 593A
331 US 461 46 656A
Black 05/05/47 CCA 3rd

	12/07 1946 CERT
Burton	G
Rutledg	G
Jackson	G
Murphy	G
Douglas	G
Frankfr	G
Reed	G
Black	G
Vinson	G

Gotwals v U.S.
46 594A
329 US 781
CCA 10th

	11/16 1946 CERT
Burton	G
Rutledg	D
Jackson	D
Murphy	D
Douglas	G
Frankfr	D
Reed	D
Black	D
Vinson	G

U.S. v Bayer
46 606A
331 US 532
Jackson 04/15/47 CCA 2d

Justice	CERT 12/07 1946 (1 1)	MERITS 04/12 1947 (1 1)	REPORT 06/09 1947 (1 1)
Burton	D	R	R
Rutledg	D		R
Jackson	D	R	R
Murphy			
Douglas	G	R	R
Frankfr	D	A	A
Reed			
Black	G	A	R
Vinson	G	A	R

Chicago Pneumatic Tool v Hughes Tool
46 607A
329 US 781
CCA 3rd

Justice	CERT 11/16 1946 (1 1)
Burton	D
Rutledg	D
Jackson	D
Murphy	D
Douglas	D
Frankfr	D
Reed	D
Black	G
Vinson	D

Kent v U.S.
46 608A
329 US 785
CCA 5th

Justice	CERT 11/23 1946 (1 1)
Burton	D
Rutledg	D
Jackson	D
Murphy	D
Douglas	G
Frankfr	D
Reed	D
Black	D
Vinson	D

Equitable Office Building v Duncan
46 610A
329 US 784   331 US 819   46 609A   46 612A
CCA 2d

Justice	CERT 11/23 1946 (1 1)	CERT 11/23 1946 (2 1)	CERT 05/03 1947 (2 2)
Burton	D	H	D
Rutledg	D	H	D
Jackson	D	H	D
Murphy	D	D	D
Douglas	D	H	D
Frankfr	D	H	D
Reed	D	H	D
Black	D	H	D
Vinson	D	H	D

Granada Apartments v City National Bank
46 613A
329 US 785
CCA 7th

Justice	CERT 11/23 1946 (1 1)
Burton	D
Rutledg	D
Jackson	D
Murphy	D
Douglas	D
Frankfr	D
Reed	D
Black	G
Vinson	D

Fife v Illinois
46 615A
331 US 822
Illinois

Justice	CERT 12/21 1946 (1 1)
Burton	E
Rutledg	E
Jackson	E
Murphy	E
Douglas	E
Frankfr	E
Reed	E
Black	E
Vinson	

Burr's Estate v C.I.R.
46 617A
329 US 785
CCA 2d

Justice	CERT 11/23 1946 (1 1)
Burton	G
Rutledg	D
Jackson	D
Murphy	D
Douglas	G
Frankfr	D
Reed	D
Black	D
Vinson	D

American RR Puerto Rico v Romero
46 624A
329 US 782
CCA 1st

Justice	CERT 11/16 1946 (1 1)
Burton	G
Rutledg	D
Jackson	D
Murphy	D
Douglas	D
Frankfr	D
Reed	D
Black	D
Vinson	D

Caldarola v Eckert
46 625A
332 US 155
Frankfr 04/1/47 New York

Justice	CERT 11/09 1946 (1 1)	MERITS 04/05 1947 (1 1)	MERITS 05/10 1947 (1 2)	REPORT 06/23 1947 (1 1)
Burton	G	R	R	R
Rutledg	G	R	R	A
Jackson	G	R	R	R
Murphy	G		A	A
Douglas	G	X	A	A
Frankfr	G	R	R	R
Reed	G	R	R	A
Black	G		A	A
Vinson	G		A	A

Clark v Allen
46 626A
331 US 503
Douglas 04/15/47 CCA 9th

Justice	CERT 12/07 1946 (1 1)	MERITS 04/15 1947 (1 2)	REPORT 06/09 1947 (1 1)
Burton	G	R	R
Rutledg	G	R	R
Jackson	G	R	R
Murphy	G	X	A
Douglas	G		A
Frankfr	G		A
Reed	G	R	R
Black	G	R	A
Vinson	G	RQ	A

Olson v Ragen
46 628A
329 US 814
Illinois

Justice	CERT 11/09 1946 (1 1)	CERT 02/01 1947 (1 2)
Burton	G	D
Rutledg	E	D
Jackson	G	D
Murphy	E	D
Douglas	G	D
Frankfr	E	D
Reed	G	D
Black	G	D
Vinson	E	D

McDonald v Johnston
46 637A
329 US 795
CCA 9th

Justice	CERT 12/21 1946 (1 1)
Burton	G
Rutledg	D
Jackson	D
Murphy	D
Douglas	D
Frankfr	D
Reed	D
Black	D
Vinson	D

Bailey Farm Dairy Company v Anderson
46 640A
329 US 788
CCA 8th

	12/07 1946 CERT
	1 1
Burton	D
Rutledg	D
Jackson	D
Murphy	
Douglas	G
Frankfr	
Reed	G
Black	D
Vinson	D

Northwestern Mutual Life v Suttles
46 653A
329 US 801
Georgia

	01/04 1947 CERT
	1 1
Burton	G
Rutledg	G
Jackson	
Murphy	G
Douglas	
Frankfr	
Reed	
Black	D
Vinson	D

Anderson v Helmers
46 656A
331 US 461 46 593A
Black 05/05/47 CCA 6th

	05/03 1947 MERITS	06/02 1947 REPORT
	1 1	1 1
Burton		A
Rutledg	X	A
Jackson	X	A
Murphy		A
Douglas		A
Frankfr		A
Reed		A
Black		A
Vinson		A

Packard Motor Car Company v N.L.R.B.
46 658A
330 US 485
Jackson 01/20/47 CCA 6th

	12/07 1946 CERT	01/18 1947 MERITS	03/10 1947 REPORT
	1 1	1 1	1 1
Burton	G	R	R
Rutledg	G	A	A
Jackson	G	A	A
Murphy	G		
Douglas	G		
Frankfr	G	RQ	R
Reed	G	R	R
Black	G	A	A
Vinson	G	R	R

Motorists Mutual v Hendershot
46 670A
329 US 683
Ohio

	11/23 1946 JURIS
	1 1
Burton	
Rutledg	S
Jackson	S
Murphy	S
Douglas	A
Frankfr	
Reed	A
Black	S
Vinson	S

Harrison v Greyvan Lines
46 673A
331 US 704 46 312A
Reed 03/17/47 CCA 7th

	12/14 1946 CERT	03/15 1947 MERITS	06/16 1947 REPORT
	1 1	1 1	1 1
Burton	G	R	A
Rutledg	G	X	M
Jackson	G		
Murphy	G	R	R
Douglas	G		
Frankfr	G	R	R
Reed	G	A	A
Black	G	A	A
Vinson	G	A	A

C.I.R. v Munter
46 674A 46 675A
331 US 210
Black 04/15/47 CCA 3rd

	12/14 1946 CERT	04/15 1947 MERITS	05/05 1947 REPORT
	1 1	1 1	1 1
Burton	G	R	R
Rutledg	G	R	R
Jackson	G	R	R
Murphy	G	R	R
Douglas	G		
Frankfr	G		A
Reed	G	R	R
Black	G	R	R
Vinson	G		

Market Street RR v Railroad Commission
46 679A
329 US 793
California

	12/14 1946 CERT
	1 1
Burton	
Rutledg	
Jackson	G
Murphy	D
Douglas	D
Frankfr	D
Reed	D
Black	D
Vinson	D

Champion Spark Plug Company v Sanders
46 680A
331 US 125
Douglas 04/07/47 CCA 2d

	12/14 1946 CERT	04/05 1947 MERITS	04/28 1947 REPORT
	1 1	1 1	1 1
Burton	G	D	A
Rutledg	G	D	A
Jackson			A
Murphy	G	D	A
Douglas			
Frankfr	G	D	A
Reed			A
Black			A
Vinson			A

W.H. Tompkins Company v U.S.
46 681A
329 US 683
DC MD Tennessee

	12/07 1946 JURIS	12/07 1946 REPORT	12/09 1946 REPORT	01/18 1947 REHEAR
	1 1	1 1	1 1	1 1
Burton		A	A	B
Rutledg		A	A	B
Jackson		A	A	B
Murphy	N			
Douglas				Y
Frankfr	N			B
Reed		A	A	B
Black	N	A	A	B
Vinson		A	A	B

Fleming v Rhodes
46 682A
331 US 100
Reed 04/15/47 DC ND Texas

	12/07 1946 JURIS	04/12 1947 MERITS	04/28 1947 REPORT
	1 1	1 1	1 1
Burton	N		R
Rutledg	N	VM	R
Jackson	N	VM	R
Murphy	N		
Douglas	N		
Frankfr	N	R	R
Reed	N		
Black	N	VM	R
Vinson	N	R	R

Fahey v Mallonee
46 687A
332 US 245 46 133M
Vinson 05/05/47 Jackson 05/16/47 DC SD California

	12/07 1946 JURIS	05/03 1947 MERITS	06/23 1947 REPORT
	1 1	1 1	1 1
Burton	N		R
Rutledg	N	R	R
Jackson	N	R	R
Murphy	N		
Douglas	N		
Frankfr	N	R	R
Reed	N		
Black	N	R	R
Vinson	N	R	R

186

Jordan v New York
46 688A
331 US 861   46 405A
New York

	01/18 1947 CERT (1 1)	06/21 1947 CERT (1 2)
Burton	E	
Rutledg	E	D
Jackson	E	D
Murphy	E	
Douglas	E	G
Frankfr	E	
Reed	E	G
Black	E	
Vinson	E	

Insurance Group v Denver & Rio Grande RR
46 690A
329 US 607   46 63M   CCA 10th
Reed 01/11/47

	12/14 1946 CERT (2 1)	01/11 1947 MERITS (1 1)	02/03 1947 REPORT (1 1)	02/08 1947 QUEST (3 1)
Burton	G	R	>	B
Rutledg	D	R	>	B
Jackson	D		>	B
Murphy	GR	R	>	B
Douglas		A	A	
Frankfr	G		>	B
Reed	GR	R	>	B
Black	GR	R	>	B
Vinson	GR		YQ	YQ

First National Bank v De Korwin
46 696A
329 US 795   CCA 7th

	12/21 1946 CERT (1 1)
Burton	G
Rutledg	G
Jackson	
Murphy	G
Douglas	
Frankfr	D
Reed	D
Black	D
Vinson	D

Broyles v Oklahoma
46 698A
329 US 790
Oklahoma

	12/07 1946 CERT (1 1)
Burton	D
Rutledg	D
Jackson	D
Murphy	G
Douglas	D
Frankfr	D
Reed	D
Black	D
Vinson	D

Swent v C.I.R.
46 699A
329 US 801   CCA 4th

	01/04 1947 CERT (1 1)
Burton	G
Rutledg	D
Jackson	D
Murphy	G
Douglas	G
Frankfr	
Reed	D
Black	D
Vinson	D

Oklahoma v U.S.
46 715A
331 US 788   CCA 10th

	01/18 1947 CERT (1 1)	05/03 1947 MERITS (1 1)	05/19 1947 REPORT (1 1)
Burton	G	A	A
Rutledg	D		A
Jackson	D	X	A
Murphy	G		A
Douglas	D	X	A
Frankfr	G	A	A
Reed	D	A	A
Black	G		A
Vinson	G	A	A

U.S. v Walsh
46 718A
331 US 432
Murphy 05/05/47 DC SD California

	12/14 1946 JURIS (1 1)	05/03 1947 MERITS (1 1)	05/19 1947 REPORT (1 1)
Burton	N	R	R
Rutledg	N	R	R
Jackson	N		
Murphy	N	R	A
Douglas	N		A
Frankfr	N	R	R
Reed	N	R	R
Black	N	R	R
Vinson	N	R	R

Spokane Portland Cement v Swanson
46 719A
329 US 800   CCA 9th

	01/04 1947 CERT (1 1)
Burton	D
Rutledg	D
Jackson	D
Murphy	D
Douglas	G
Frankfr	
Reed	D
Black	D
Vinson	D

Wade v Stimson
46 724A
331 US 793   46 95A
DC DC

	06/14 1947 JURIS (1 1)	06/16 1947 REPORT (1 1)
Burton	A	A
Rutledg	A	A
Jackson		A
Murphy	A	A
Douglas	X	A
Frankfr	A	A
Reed	A	A
Black	A	A
Vinson	A	A

Bartels v Birmingham
46 731A
332 US 126 46 732A
Reed 04/07/47 CCA 8th

	01/04 1947 CERT 1 1	04/05 1947 MERITS 1 1	06/23 1947 REPORT 1 1
Burton	G	R	R
Rutledg	G		R
Jackson	G	R	R
Murphy			
Douglas		X	A
Frankfr			A
Reed	G	R	R
Black			
Vinson	D	R	A

Geer v Birmingham
46 732A
332 US 126 46 731A
Reed 04/07/47 CCA 8th

	01/04 1947 CERT 1 1	04/05 1947 MERITS 1 1	06/23 1947 REPORT 1 1
Burton	G	R	R
Rutledg	G		R
Jackson	G	R	R
Murphy			
Douglas		X	A
Frankfr			A
Reed	G	R	R
Black			
Vinson	D	R	A

Interstate Natural Gas v F.P.C.
46 733A
331 US 682 46 556A
Vinson 05/16/47 CCA 5th

	01/04 1947 CERT 1 1	02/08 1947 CERT 1 2	05/10 1947 MERITS 1 1	06/16 1947 REPORT 1 1
Burton	G	G		A
Rutledg		G		A
Jackson	D	G		A
Murphy		D		A
Douglas	D	D		A
Frankfr		D		A
Reed				A
Black	D	G	R	A
Vinson	D			A

Quinn v U.S.
46 741A
330 US 822
CCA DC

	02/15 1947 CERT 1 1
Burton	G
Rutledg	D
Jackson	G
Murphy	D
Douglas	D
Frankfr	
Reed	G
Black	D
Vinson	D

Cruse v Ragen
46 748A
331 US 839
Illinois

	01/18 1947 CERT 1 1	06/02 1947 CERT 1 2
Burton	E	D
Rutledg	E	D
Jackson		D
Murphy	E	D
Douglas	E	
Frankfr		D
Reed	E	
Black		D
Vinson		D

McCullough v Kammerer
46 755A
331 US 96
Black 04/15/47 CCA 9th

	02/01 1947 CERT 1 1	04/14 1947 MERITS 1 1	04/28 1947 REPORT 1 1
Burton	G	R	R
Rutledg	G		R
Jackson			R
Murphy	D		R
Douglas	D	R	R
Frankfr	D		R
Reed		R	R
Black			R
Vinson	D	R	R

U.S. v United Mine Workers
46 759A 46 760A
330 US 258
Vinson 02/17/47 DC DC

	12/06 1946 CERT 1 1	12/08 1946 CERT 1 2	01/20 1947 QUEST 20 1	01/20 1947 QUEST 21 1	01/20 1947 QUEST 22 1	01/20 1947 QUEST 23 1	01/20 1947 QUEST 24 1
Burton	G	G	B	B	B	B	B
Rutledg	G	G					
Jackson	G	G	B	BQ	B		B
Murphy	G	G	B	Y	Y	Y	Y
Douglas	G	G		B	B		
Frankfr	G	D	BQ	Y	Y	Y	Y
Reed	G		B	Y	B	B	B
Black	G	D		Y			
Vinson	G	D	B	Y	B	B	B

U.S. v United Mine Workers
Continued

	03/06 1947 REPORT 20 1	03/06 1947 REPORT 21 1	03/06 1947 REPORT 22 1	03/06 1947 REPORT 23 2	03/06 1947 REPORT 24 1
Burton	A	R	A	R	A
Rutledg	R	R	R	R	R
Jackson	R	R	R	R	R
Murphy					
Douglas	A	R	A	R	A
Frankfr	R	R	R	R	R
Reed	R	R	A	R	A
Black	A	A	A	R	A
Vinson					

Wabash RR Company v Williamson
46 763A
330 US 824 46 770A
Missouri

	03/01 1947 CERT 1 1
Burton	D
Rutledg	D
Jackson	D
Murphy	D
Douglas	D
Frankfr	D
Reed	
Black	
Vinson	G D

Lincoln Stores v Nashua Manufacturing
46 768A
329 US 811
CCA 1st

Justice	01/18 1947 CERT (1 1)
Burton	D
Rutledg	D
Jackson	
Murphy	
Douglas	D
Frankfr	D
Reed	
Black	
Vinson	D

Cannady v Ragen
46 777A
331 US 839 46 79M
Illinois

Justice	01/18 1947 CERT (1 1)	06/02 1947 CERT (1 2)
Burton	E	D
Rutledg	E	D
Jackson		D
Murphy		
Douglas	E	
Frankfr	E	D
Reed		
Black	E	
Vinson	E	D

Elade Realty v U.S.
46 779A
329 US 810
CCA 2d

Justice	01/18 1947 CERT (1 1)
Burton	G
Rutledg	D
Jackson	D
Murphy	D
Douglas	D
Frankfr	D
Reed	D
Black	D
Vinson	D

Chronicle & Gazette v Attorney General
46 780A
329 US 690
New Hampshire

Justice	01/04 1947 JURIS (1 1)
Burton	S
Rutledg	S
Jackson	N
Murphy	N
Douglas	N
Frankfr	S
Reed	S
Black	S
Vinson	S

U.S. v Michener
46 793A
331 US 789
CCA 8th

Justice	01/18 1947 CERT (1 1)	05/03 1947 MERITS	06/02 1947 REPORT (1 1)
Burton	G	R	R
Rutledg	G	X	
Jackson	G		A
Murphy	G		
Douglas		R	R
Frankfr	G	R	R
Reed	G	R	R
Black	G	R	A
Vinson	G	R	A

Blue v Indiana
46 794A
330 US 840
Indiana

Justice	02/01 1947 CERT (1 1)	03/15 1947 CERT (1 2)
Burton	D	G
Rutledg	D	G
Jackson	D	
Murphy		
Douglas	D	D
Frankfr	D	
Reed	D	
Black	D	
Vinson	D	

U.S. v Balogh
46 800A
329 US 692
CCA 2d

Justice	01/18 1947 CERT (1 1)	01/20 1947 REPORT (1 1)
Burton	GVM	>
Rutledg	GVM	>
Jackson	D	D
Murphy	GVM	>
Douglas	D	>
Frankfr	GVM	>
Reed	D	>
Black	GVM	>
Vinson	GVM	

Mertig v New York
46 804A
330 US 818 46 805A
New York

Justice	02/08 1947 CERT (1 1)
Burton	D
Rutledg	D
Jackson	D
Murphy	D
Douglas	D
Frankfr	
Reed	G
Black	G
Vinson	D

Bisignano v Municipal Court Des Moines
46 809A
330 US 818
Iowa

Justice	02/01 1947 CERT (1 1)	02/08 1947 CERT (1 2)
Burton	G	G
Rutledg	G	G
Jackson	G	
Murphy	G	G
Douglas	G	G
Frankfr		
Reed	G	
Black		
Vinson	G	G

U.S. v Phelps Dodge Mercantile
46 812A
330 US 818
CCA 9th

Justice	02/08 1947 CERT (1 1)
Burton	G
Rutledg	
Jackson	D
Murphy	D
Douglas	G
Frankfr	G
Reed	D
Black	D
Vinson	D

Brummel v L.F. Dietz & Associates
46 826A
329 US 813
New York

Justice	02/01 1947 CERT (1 1)
Burton	D
Rutledg	D
Jackson	D
Murphy	D
Douglas	G
Frankfr	G
Reed	D
Black	D
Vinson	D

Austin v Ragen
46 829A
329 US 815
Illinois

Justice	02/01 1947 CERT (1 1)
Burton	E
Rutledg	E
Jackson	
Murphy	
Douglas	D
Frankfr	D
Reed	D
Black	D
Vinson	D

Amato v Porter
46 833A
329 US 812
CCA 10th

Justice	02/01 1947 CERT (1 1)
Burton	G
Rutledg	D
Jackson	D
Murphy	D
Douglas	D
Frankfr	D
Reed	D
Black	D
Vinson	D

Pennsylvania RR Company v McCarthy
46 838A
329 US 812
CCA 7th

Justice	02/01 1947 CERT (1 1)
Burton	G
Rutledg	D
Jackson	D
Murphy	G
Douglas	D
Frankfr	D
Reed	G
Black	D
Vinson	D

Alexander v U.S. (Kulick)
46 840A
332 US 174   46 535A
Douglas 04/07/47 CCA 2d

Justice	01/18 1947 CERT (1 1)	04/05 1947 MERITS (1 1)	06/23 1947 REPORT (1 1)
Burton	G	R	R
Rutledg	G	X	
Jackson	G	X	A
Murphy	G	R	R
Douglas	G	R	R
Frankfr	G	R	R
Reed	G	R	R
Black	G	R	R
Vinson	G	R	A

Seaboard Surety Company v U.S.
46 846A
330 US 826
Ct Cls

Justice	03/01 1947 CERT (1 1)
Burton	G
Rutledg	D
Jackson	D
Murphy	D
Douglas	D
Frankfr	D
Reed	D
Black	D
Vinson	D

U.S. v Munsey Trust Company
46 847A
332 US 234
Jackson 05/14/47 Ct Cls

Justice	03/01 1947 CERT (1 1)	05/10 1947 MERITS (1 1)	06/23 1947 REPORT (1 1)
Burton	G	A	A
Rutledg	G	AQ	R
Jackson	D	R	R
Murphy	G	R	R
Douglas	D	R	R
Frankfr	G	R	R
Reed	D	R	R
Black	G	R	R
Vinson	D		A

Williams v Austrian
46 850A
331 US 642
Vinson 04/15/47 CCA 2d

Justice	02/08 1947 CERT (1 1)	04/15 1947 MERITS (1 1)	06/16 1947 REPORT (1 1)
Burton	G		
Rutledg	G	A	A
Jackson	G	RQ	R
Murphy	G	A	A
Douglas	G	A	A
Frankfr	G	A	A
Reed	G	R	R
Black	G	A	A
Vinson	G	A	A

U.S. v Illinois Pure Aluminum
46 860A
330 US 834
Ct Cls

Justice	03/08 1947 CERT (1 1)
Burton	D
Rutledg	D
Jackson	D
Murphy	D
Douglas	G
Frankfr	D
Reed	D
Black	D
Vinson	D

C.I.R. v McAllister
46 848A
330 US 826
CCA 2d

Justice	03/01 1947 CERT (1 1)
Burton	G
Rutledg	D
Jackson	D
Murphy	G
Douglas	D
Frankfr	D
Reed	G
Black	D
Vinson	D

Krepper v U.S.
46 876A
330 US 824
CCA 3rd

Justice	03/01 1947 CERT (1 1)
Burton	
Rutledg	
Jackson	D
Murphy	D
Douglas	G
Frankfr	G
Reed	
Black	D
Vinson	D

Fleming v Lee
46 875A
331 US 805
CCA Emergency

Justice	04/12 1947 CERT (1 1)
Burton	G
Rutledg	D
Jackson	D
Murphy	G
Douglas	D
Frankfr	D
Reed	G
Black	D
Vinson	D

Southern Pacific Company v Henwood
46 879A
330 US 836   46 909A   46 936A
CCA 8th

Justice	03/01 1947 CERT (1 1)	03/08 1947 CERT (1 2)
Burton		D
Rutledg		
Jackson	DQ	D
Murphy	DQ	D
Douglas	D	
Frankfr		D
Reed		D
Black	DQ	D
Vinson	DQ	DH

Swem v Michigan
46 880A
330 US 807   46 140A
Michigan

Justice	03/29 1947 CERT (1 1)	03/31 1947 MERITS (1 1)
Burton	GVM	
Rutledg	GVM	>
Jackson	GVM	>
Murphy	GVM	>
Douglas	GVM	>
Frankfr	GVM	>
Reed	GVM	>
Black	GVM	>
Vinson	GVM	

Hudson v U.S.
46 887A
329 US 813
CCA 10th

	02/01 1947 CERT 1 1	
Burton		
Rutledg	G	D
Jackson		
Murphy	G	D
Douglas		D
Frankfr		D
Reed		D
Black		D
Vinson		D

Woods v Illinois
46 894A
330 US 831 46 1136A
Illinois

	03/01 1947 CERT 1 1	
Burton	E	E
Rutledg		
Jackson		
Murphy	E	
Douglas		
Frankfr		
Reed		
Black		
Vinson		

Meyer v Henwood
46 909A
330 US 836 46 879A 46 936A
CCA 8th

	03/01 1947 CERT 1 1		03/08 1947 CERT 1 2	
Burton	DQ	DQ	D	D
Rutledg	DQ	DQ	D	D
Jackson	D	D		
Murphy			G	
Douglas	D	D		
Frankfr			D	
Reed	D	D		
Black				
Vinson	DQ	DQ	D	D

Allen v First National Bank & Trust
46 942A
330 US 828
CCA 5th

	03/01 1947 CERT 1 1	
Burton		D
Rutledg		D
Jackson	G	D
Murphy		D
Douglas		D
Frankfr		D
Reed		D
Black	G	
Vinson		D

Hill Packing v City Of New York
46 940A
331 US 870 46 470A 46 473A
New York

	05/10 1947 JURIS 1 1		05/12 1947 REPORT 1 1	
Burton	N	A		A
Rutledg		A		A
Jackson		A		A
Murphy		A		
Douglas				A
Frankfr				
Reed	N			
Black	N	A		A
Vinson		A		A

Nebraska National Hotel v O'Malley
46 941A
330 US 827
CCA 8th

	03/01 1947 CERT 1 1	
Burton		D
Rutledg		D
Jackson		D
Murphy		D
Douglas		D
Frankfr		D
Reed		D
Black		DHQ
Vinson		DH

McWilliams v C.I.R.
46 945A 46 946A 46 947A
331 US 694
Vinson 06/02/47 CCA 6th

	03/01 1947 CERT 1 1	05/10 1947 MERITS 1 1	06/16 1947 REPORT 1 1
Burton	G		A
Rutledg	G	A	A
Jackson	G		
Murphy	G		A
Douglas	G	A	A
Frankfr	G	A	A
Reed		A	A
Black	G		
Vinson	G		A

Sanitary District v Activated Sludge
46 953A
330 US 834
CCA 7th

	03/08 1947 CERT 1 1	
Burton	G	D
Rutledg		D
Jackson	G	
Murphy		
Douglas		DQ
Frankfr		
Reed	G	
Black		D
Vinson		

U.S. v Petrillo
46 954A
332 US 1
Black 06/02/47 DC ND Illinois

	03/01 1947 JURIS 1 1	05/10 1947 MERITS 1 1	06/23 1947 REPORT 1 1
Burton	N	R	R
Rutledg	N		
Jackson	N	R	R
Murphy	N	AQ	A
Douglas	N	A	
Frankfr	N		
Reed	N	R	R
Black	N	R	R
Vinson	N	A	A

Kaufman v New York
46 960A
330 US 836
New York

	03/08 1947 CERT 1 1	
Burton		D
Rutledg		D
Jackson		
Murphy	G	
Douglas		D
Frankfr		D
Reed		D
Black		D
Vinson		

Brotherhood RR v Baltimore & Ohio
46 970A
331 US 519
Murphy 05/14/47 DC ND Illinois

	03/01 1947 JURIS 1 1	05/10 1947 MERITS 1 1	06/09 1947 REPORT 1 1
Burton	N	R	R
Rutledg	N	R	R
Jackson	N		R
Murphy	N	M	R
Douglas	N	R	R
Frankfr	N	R	R
Reed	N		R
Black	N	X	R
Vinson	N		R

Pioneer Mill Company v Victoria Ward
46 973A
330 US 838
CCA 9th

	03/15 1947 CERT 1 1	
Burton		D
Rutledg	G	
Jackson		D
Murphy		D
Douglas		D
Frankfr		D
Reed		D
Black		
Vinson		D

Allen v U.S.
46 983A
330 US 838
CCA 2d

Justice	03/15 1947 CERT (1 1)
Burton	D
Rutledg	D
Jackson	
Murphy	G
Douglas	D
Frankfr	D
Reed	D
Black	D
Vinson	G

Atlantic Coast Line RR v Moss
46 992A
330 US 839
CCA 2d

Justice	03/15 1947 CERT (1 1) G
Burton	D
Rutledg	D
Jackson	D
Murphy	D
Douglas	D
Frankfr	D
Reed	D
Black	D
Vinson	D

Friedman v Schwellenbach
46 990A
330 US 838
CCA DC

Justice	03/08 1947 CERT (1 2)	04/12 1947 REHEAR (1 1)
Burton	G	B
Rutledg	G	
Jackson	G	Y
Murphy		Y
Douglas	G	
Frankfr		
Reed	G	B
Black	G	B
Vinson		B

Bell v Porter
46 993A
330 US 813
CCA 7th

Justice	03/29 1947 CERT (1 1)	04/05 1947 CERT (1 2)	04/05 1947 REHEAR (1 1)
Burton	D	D	
Rutledg	D	D	Y
Jackson			Y
Murphy	G	G	Y
Douglas	G		
Frankfr	D	G	B
Reed	G	G	Y
Black	G		
Vinson	G	G	Y

Rokey v Day & Zimmermann
46 994A
330 US 842 46 993A 46 995A
CCA 8th

Justice	03/29 1947 CERT (1 1)
Burton	D
Rutledg	D
Jackson	
Murphy	G
Douglas	G
Frankfr	D
Reed	D
Black	D
Vinson	D

Bowers v Remington Rand
46 995A
330 US 843 46 993A 46 994A
CCA 7th

Justice	03/29 1947 CERT (1 1)
Burton	D
Rutledg	D
Jackson	G
Murphy	D
Douglas	D
Frankfr	D
Reed	D
Black	D
Vinson	D

St. Regis Paper Company v Higgins
46 998A
330 US 843
CCA 2d

Justice	03/29 1947 CERT (1 1)
Burton	D
Rutledg	D
Jackson	D
Murphy	D
Douglas	G
Frankfr	D
Reed	G
Black	D
Vinson	D

Mayfair Meat Packing v U.S.
46 1015A
331 US 805
CCA 2d

Justice	04/12 1947 CERT (1 1)
Burton	D
Rutledg	D
Jackson	GV
Murphy	D
Douglas	D
Frankfr	G
Reed	D
Black	D
Vinson	D

Krol v Ragen
46 1020A
331 US 851
Illinois

Justice	06/14 1947 CERT (1 1)
Burton	D
Rutledg	D
Jackson	E
Murphy	D
Douglas	D
Frankfr	D
Reed	D
Black	D
Vinson	D

Utah Junk Company v Fleming
46 1029A
330 US 844
CCA Emergency

Justice	03/29 1947 CERT (1 1)
Burton	D
Rutledg	D
Jackson	D
Murphy	D
Douglas	D
Frankfr	D
Reed	D
Black	G D
Vinson	G D

Colegrove v Barrett
46 1031A
330 US 804
DC ND Illinois

Justice	03/08 1947 JURIS (1 1)
Burton	S
Rutledg	S
Jackson	S
Murphy	N
Douglas	N
Frankfr	
Reed	N
Black	S
Vinson	S

U.S. v Yellow Cab Company
46 1035A
332 US 218
Murphy 05/14/47 DC ND Illinois

Justice	03/15 1947 JURIS (1 1)	05/10 1947 MERITS (1 1) A	06/23 1947 REPORT (1 1) A
Burton	N	R	R
Rutledg	N	R	R
Jackson	N	RQ	R
Murphy	N		
Douglas	N	X	
Frankfr	N		
Reed	N	R	R
Black	N	R	R
Vinson	N	R	R

Smith v Fleming
46 1036A
331 US 816 46 512A 46 583A
CCA 9th
03/29 1947 CERT 1 1

Justice	Vote
Burton	GH
Rutledg	GH
Jackson	GH
Murphy	GH
Douglas	GH
Frankfr	GH
Reed	GH
Black	GH
Vinson	GH

Potomac Electric v Public Utilities
46 1038A
331 US 816 46 1135A
CCA DC
05/03 1947 CERT 1 1 G

Justice	Vote
Burton	D
Rutledg	D
Jackson	D
Murphy	
Douglas	
Frankfr	D
Reed	D
Black	D
Vinson	D

Norfolk Southern Bus v N.L.R.B.
46 1046A
330 US 844
CCA 4th
03/29 1947 CERT 1 1

Justice	Vote
Burton	D
Rutledg	D
Jackson	D
Murphy	D
Douglas	D
Frankfr	D
Reed	G
Black	D
Vinson	D

Smith v Commercial Travelers Mutual
46 1058A
331 US 860 46 32A
CCA 7th
06/14 1947 CERT 1 1

Justice	Vote
Burton	D
Rutledg	X
Jackson	
Murphy	G
Douglas	G
Frankfr	D
Reed	D
Black	D
Vinson	GA

Wilson v Reconstruction Finance
46 1062A
331 US 810
CCA 5th
04/26 1947 CERT 1 1

Justice	Vote
Burton	D
Rutledg	D
Jackson	D
Murphy	D
Douglas	D
Frankfr	D
Reed	
Black	D
Vinson	

Chaney v Stover
46 1065A
330 US 849
CCA 4th
04/05 1947 CERT 1 1

Justice	Vote
Burton	D
Rutledg	D
Jackson	D
Murphy	D
Douglas	D
Frankfr	D
Reed	G
Black	D
Vinson	G

Moss v Pennsylvania RR Company
46 1070A
330 US 849 46 1071A
CCA 7th
04/05 1947 CERT 1 1

Justice	Vote
Burton	D
Rutledg	D
Jackson	D
Murphy	G
Douglas	
Frankfr	D
Reed	D
Black	G
Vinson	DQ

Hook v National Brick Company
46 1071A
330 US 849 46 1070A
CCA 7th
04/05 1947 CERT 1 1

Justice	Vote
Burton	D
Rutledg	D
Jackson	D
Murphy	G
Douglas	
Frankfr	D
Reed	G
Black	
Vinson	DQ

U.S. v Albert & Harrison
46 1075A
331 US 810
Ct Cls
04/26 1947 CERT 1 1

Justice	Vote
Burton	D
Rutledg	D
Jackson	D
Murphy	G
Douglas	
Frankfr	D
Reed	
Black	G
Vinson	D

Fleming v Collins
46 1080A
330 US 850 46 1081A 46 1082A
CCA Emergency
04/15 1947 CERT 1 1

Justice	Vote
Burton	G
Rutledg	D
Jackson	D
Murphy	G
Douglas	D
Frankfr	D
Reed	G
Black	D
Vinson	D

U.S. (Knauer) v Jordan
46 1088A
331 US 810
CCA 7th
04/26 1947 CERT 1 1

Justice	Vote
Burton	D
Rutledg	D
Jackson	D
Murphy	G
Douglas	G
Frankfr	D
Reed	D
Black	D
Vinson	

Falwell v U.S.
46 1091A
330 US 807
DC WD Virginia
03/31 1947 REPORT 1 1

Justice	Vote
Burton	A
Rutledg	A
Jackson	A
Murphy	A
Douglas	A
Frankfr	X
Reed	A
Black	A
Vinson	A

Hayes v New York
46 1099A
330 US 847
New York
03/29 1947 CERT 1 1

Justice	Vote
Burton	D
Rutledg	GE
Jackson	D
Murphy	E
Douglas	D
Frankfr	D
Reed	D
Black	
Vinson	

U.S. v Palletz
46 1100A
330 US 812 46 1101A
DC ED Pennsylvania
03/29 1947 JURIS 1 1

Justice	Vote
Burton	N
Rutledg	R
Jackson	NR
Murphy	R
Douglas	NR
Frankfr	R
Reed	NR
Black	N
Vinson	NR

U.S. v Kromer
46 1101A
330 US 812 46 1100A
DC ED Pennsylvania
03/29 1947 JURIS 1 1

Justice	Vote
Burton	N
Rutledg	R
Jackson	NR
Murphy	R
Douglas	NR
Frankfr	R
Reed	NR
Black	N
Vinson	NR

Trudell v Mississippi
46 1104A
331 US 785 46 1105A
Mississippi

	05/03 1947 CERT 1 1	
Burton		
Rutledg	G	D
Jackson		
Murphy	G	D
Douglas		
Frankfr		
Reed		D
Black		D
Vinson		D

Lewis v Mississippi
46 1105A
331 US 785 46 1104A
Mississippi

	05/03 1947 CERT 1 1	
Burton		
Rutledg	G	D
Jackson		
Murphy	G	D
Douglas		
Frankfr		
Reed		D
Black		D
Vinson		D

Grand Lodge Hall Association v Moore
46 1110A
330 US 808
Indiana

	03/29 1947 JURIS 1 1	03/31 1947 REPORT 1 1
Burton	N	A
Rutledg		A
Jackson	N	A
Murphy		A
Douglas		A
Frankfr	N	A
Reed		A
Black		A
Vinson		A

Calhoun v Niersthelmer
46 1112A
331 US 840
Illinois

	03/31 1947 CERT 1 1
Burton	
Rutledg	E
Jackson	E
Murphy	E
Douglas	E
Frankfr	E
Reed	E
Black	E
Vinson	E

DeFrates v Illinois
46 1116A
331 US 811
Illinois

	04/26 1947 CERT 1 1
Burton	D
Rutledg	D
Jackson	
Murphy	G
Douglas	D
Frankfr	D
Reed	D
Black	D
Vinson	D

Mason & Dixon Lines v Virginia
46 1117A
331 US 807 46 1003A
Virginia

	04/12 1947 CERT 1 1	
Burton	D	
Rutledg	G	D
Jackson	D	
Murphy	G	D
Douglas	D	
Frankfr	D	
Reed	D	
Black	D	
Vinson	D	

Decker v Kann
46 1122A
331 US 807
Pennsylvania

	04/12 1947 CERT 1 1
Burton	
Rutledg	
Jackson	GQ
Murphy	D
Douglas	D
Frankfr	D
Reed	D
Black	D
Vinson	D

Well v H.F. Haessler Hardware Company
46 1126A
331 US 807
Wisconsin

	04/12 1947 CERT 1 1
Burton	D
Rutledg	D
Jackson	D
Murphy	D
Douglas	D
Frankfr	D
Reed	G
Black	D
Vinson	G

Bennion v New York Life Insurance
46 1133A
331 US 811
CCA 10th

	04/26 1947 CERT 1 1
Burton	D
Rutledg	G
Jackson	D
Murphy	G
Douglas	D
Frankfr	D
Reed	D
Black	D
Vinson	D

U.S. v Public Utilities
46 1135A
331 US 816 46 1038A
CCA DC

	05/03 1947 CERT 1 1	
Burton		
Rutledg	G	D
Jackson		D
Murphy		
Douglas		D
Frankfr		D
Reed		D
Black		D
Vinson		D

Heffron v U.S.
46 1139A
331 US 831
CCA 9th

	05/31 1947 CERT 1 1
Burton	D
Rutledg	D
Jackson	
Murphy	D
Douglas	D
Frankfr	
Reed	G
Black	D
Vinson	G

Arenas v U.S.
46 1141A
331 US 842 46 1272A
CCA 9th

	06/07 1947 CERT 1 1
Burton	D
Rutledg	D
Jackson	
Murphy	D
Douglas	G
Frankfr	D
Reed	D
Black	D
Vinson	D

U.S. v Modern Reed & Rattan Company
46 1154A
331 US 831
CCA 2d

	05/31 1947 CERT 1 2	
Burton		D
Rutledg		D
Jackson		
Murphy	G	G
Douglas		
Frankfr		D
Reed	G	G
Black		D
Vinson	G	G

Standard Surety v Plantsville National
46 1157A
331 US 812
CCA 2d

	04/26 1947 CERT 1 1
Burton	D
Rutledg	D
Jackson	D
Murphy	D
Douglas	D
Frankfr	D
Reed	
Black	G
Vinson	G

Times-Mirror Company v N.L.R.B.
46 1161A
331 US 789
CCA 9th

	05/10 1947 CERT 1 2	05/16 1947 CERT 1 2	05/19 1947 REPORT 1 1
Burton		GM	>
Rutledg	GQ	GM	>
Jackson	DQ	GM	>
Murphy		GM	
Douglas	G		>
Frankfr			>
Reed	D	GM	>
Black		GM	
Vinson		GM	

Peterson v California
46 1166A
331 US 861 · 46 102A
California
06/21 1947 CERT · 1 1

Justice	Vote
Burton	D
Rutledg	D
Jackson	D
Murphy	G
Douglas	D
Frankfr	D
Reed	D D
Black	
Vinson	D

New York v Gebhardt
46 1175A
331 US 819
CCA 2d
05/03 1947 CERT · 1 1

Justice	Vote
Burton	D
Rutledg	GQ
Jackson	D
Murphy	
Douglas	D
Frankfr	
Reed	D
Black	G
Vinson	D

Henwood v Wallace
46 1190A
331 US 820
CCA 5th
05/03 1947 CERT · 1 1

Justice	Vote
Burton	G
Rutledg	D
Jackson	D
Murphy	D
Douglas	D
Frankfr	D
Reed	
Black	
Vinson	D

Garlock Packing Company v Walling
46 1191A
331 US 820
CCA 2d
05/03 1947 CERT · 1 1

Justice	Vote
Burton	D
Rutledg	D
Jackson	D
Murphy	
Douglas	D
Frankfr	
Reed	D
Black	D
Vinson	G

Ragen v U.S. (Rooney)
46 1196A
331 US 842
CCA 7th
06/07 1947 CERT · 1 1

Justice	Vote
Burton	G
Rutledg	D
Jackson	D
Murphy	D
Douglas	D
Frankfr	
Reed	
Black	G
Vinson	G

Shapiro Bernstein v Jerry Vogel Music
46 1199A
331 US 820
CCA 2d
05/03 1947 CERT · 1 1

Justice	Vote
Burton	G
Rutledg	D
Jackson	D
Murphy	D
Douglas	D
Frankfr	D
Reed	
Black	D
Vinson	D

Curley v U.S.
46 1211A
331 US 837 · 46 1235A
CCA DC
06/02 1947 CERT · 1 1

Justice	Vote
Burton	D
Rutledg	D
Jackson	D
Murphy	G
Douglas	D
Frankfr	
Reed	D
Black	D
Vinson	

Lagow v U.S.
46 1222A
331 US 858
CCA 2d
06/14 1947 CERT · 1 1 · 06/21 1947 CERT · 1 2

Justice	Vote
Burton	D · D
Rutledg	D
Jackson	X · X
Murphy	G
Douglas	D · G
Frankfr	X
Reed	G · D
Black	G
Vinson	D

Cheltenham & Abington v Pennsylvania
46 1223A
331 US 784
Pennsylvania
04/26 1947 JURIS · 1 1

Justice	Vote
Burton	S
Rutledg	S
Jackson	S
Murphy	S
Douglas	
Frankfr	N
Reed	S
Black	S
Vinson	S

Motor Haulage Company v U.S.
46 1224A
331 US 784
DC ED New York
04/26 1947 JURIS · 1 1 · 04/28 1947 REPORT · 1 1

Justice	JURIS	REPORT
Burton	N	A
Rutledg		A
Jackson	A	A
Murphy	S	A
Douglas	A	A
Frankfr	A	A
Reed	A	A
Black	N	
Vinson	NQ	

Fried v U.S.
46 1231A
331 US 858 · 46 1402A
CCA 2d
06/14 1947 CERT · 1 1 · 06/21 1947 CERT · 1 2

Justice	Vote
Burton	G · D
Rutledg	G
Jackson	G
Murphy	D
Douglas	D
Frankfr	D
Reed	D
Black	D
Vinson	

Smith v U.S.
46 1235A
331 US 837 · 46 1211A
CCA DC
06/02 1947 CERT · 1 1

Justice	Vote
Burton	D
Rutledg	
Jackson	G
Murphy	
Douglas	D
Frankfr	
Reed	
Black	D
Vinson	D

New York v U.S.
46 1237A
331 US 832
CCA 2d
05/31 1947 CERT · 1 1

Justice	Vote
Burton	D
Rutledg	D
Jackson	D
Murphy	D
Douglas	
Frankfr	G
Reed	D
Black	D
Vinson	D

Niewiadomski v U.S.
46 1243A
331 US 850 · 46 1428A
CCA 6th
06/14 1947 CERT · 1 1

Justice	Vote
Burton	D
Rutledg	D
Jackson	D
Murphy	G
Douglas	
Frankfr	
Reed	D
Black	G
Vinson	D

Jimenez v U.S.
46 1251A
331 US 833
CCA 1st
05/31 1947 CERT · 1 1

Justice	Vote
Burton	D
Rutledg	D
Jackson	D
Murphy	G
Douglas	
Frankfr	D
Reed	
Black	D
Vinson	

U.S. v Arenas
46 1272A
331 US 842 46 1141A
CCA 9th

Justice	06/07 1947 CERT 1 1
Burton	D
Rutledg	D
Jackson	
Murphy	G
Douglas	D
Frankfr	D
Reed	D
Black	D
Vinson	D

Chopak (In The Matter Of)
46 1277A
331 US 835
CCA 2d

Justice	05/31 1947 CERT 1 1
Burton	D
Rutledg	D
Jackson	G
Murphy	
Douglas	D
Frankfr	D
Reed	D
Black	D
Vinson	D

Dobbs v Mississippi
46 1294A
331 US 787
Mississippi

Justice	05/10 1947 CERT 1 1	05/10 1947 JURIS 1 1
Burton	D	S
Rutledg	D	S
Jackson		
Murphy	G	
Douglas	D	S
Frankfr	D	
Reed	D	S
Black	D	S
Vinson	D	S

Welsberg v Illinois
46 1301A
331 US 826
Illinois

Justice	05/10 1947 CERT 1 1
Burton	D
Rutledg	D
Jackson	D
Murphy	G
Douglas	
Frankfr	X
Reed	D
Black	D
Vinson	D

Corn Products Refining Company v U.S.
46 1309A
331 US 790
DC ND Illinois

Justice	05/31 1947 JURIS 1 1
Burton	A
Rutledg	A
Jackson	A
Murphy	N
Douglas	A
Frankfr	A
Reed	A
Black	A
Vinson	A

Southern Pacific Company v U.S.
46 1314A
331 US 846
Ct Cls

Justice	06/14 1947 CERT 1 1
Burton	G
Rutledg	GM
Jackson	
Murphy	D
Douglas	D
Frankfr	D
Reed	D
Black	D
Vinson	D

Furman v Ragen
46 1317A
331 US 792
Illinois

Justice	05/16 1947 CERT 1 1
Burton	D
Rutledg	D
Jackson	D
Murphy	
Douglas	
Frankfr	
Reed	D
Black	G
Vinson	D

Davis v Penn Mutual Life Insurance
46 1318A
331 US 829 46 1254A
Georgia

Justice	05/16 1947 CERT 1 1
Burton	D
Rutledg	D
Jackson	D
Murphy	D
Douglas	D
Frankfr	D
Reed	D
Black	G
Vinson	D

Cave v U.S.
46 1320A
331 US 847
CCA 8th

Justice	06/07 1947 CERT 1 1	06/14 1957 CERT 1 2
Burton		D
Rutledg	G	D
Jackson	G	D
Murphy	G	
Douglas		G
Frankfr	G	
Reed		D
Black		D
Vinson	G	D

U.S. v Wheelbarger
46 1334A
331 US 791 46 1100A 46 1336A 46 1341A
DC Oregon

Justice	05/31 1947 MERITS 1 1	06/02 1947 REPORT 1 1
Burton	R	R
Rutledg	R	R
Jackson	R	R
Murphy	R	R
Douglas	R	R
Frankfr	R	R
Reed	R	R
Black	R	R
Vinson	R	R

Humble Oil v Railroad Commission
46 1344A
331 US 791 46 1345A
Texas

Justice	05/31 1947 JURIS 1 1	06/02 1947 REPORT 1 1
Burton	A	A
Rutledg	A	A
Jackson	A	A
Murphy	N	A
Douglas	A	A
Frankfr		A
Reed		A
Black	S	A
Vinson	A	A

Bowker v Hunter
46 1367A
331 US 861
CCA 10th

Justice	06/21 1947 CERT 1 2
Burton	D
Rutledg	G
Jackson	G
Murphy	G
Douglas	G
Frankfr	
Reed	D
Black	D
Vinson	D

Protective Committee v New York RR
46 1368A
331 US 858 46 1369A
CCA 2d

Justice	06/21 1947 CERT 1 1
Burton	D
Rutledg	G
Jackson	
Murphy	D
Douglas	D
Frankfr	G
Reed	G
Black	D
Vinson	D

Mellor v U.S.
46 1361A
331 US 848 46 1362A
CCA 8th

Justice	06/14 1947 CERT 1 1
Burton	D
Rutledg	D
Jackson	D
Murphy	
Douglas	G
Frankfr	D
Reed	D
Black	D
Vinson	D

Institutional Group v New York RR
46 1369A
331 US 859 46 1368A
CCA 2d

Justice	06/21 1947 CERT 1 1
Burton	D
Rutledg	D
Jackson	D
Murphy	D
Douglas	D
Frankfr	
Reed	D
Black	G
Vinson	G

Young v Hawaii
46 1380A
331 US 849
CCA 9th

	06/14 1947 CERT
	1 1
Burton	D
Rutledg	D
Jackson	
Murphy	G
Douglas	D
Frankfr	D
Reed	D
Black	D
Vinson	D

Consumers Home Equipment v U.S.
46 1462A
331 US 860
CCA 6th

	06/21 1947 CERT
	1 1
Burton	D
Rutledg	D
Jackson	D
Murphy	G
Douglas	D
Frankfr	D
Reed	D
Black	D
Vinson	D

Caetano v California
46 1475A
331 US 857
California

	06/14 1947 CERT
	1 1
Burton	D
Rutledg	X
Jackson	
Murphy	G
Douglas	D
Frankfr	D
Reed	D
Black	D
Vinson	X

Betz (Ex Parte)
46 18M
329 US 672 46 19M

	10/11 1946 HABEAS
	1 1
Burton	D
Rutledg	DZ
Jackson	
Murphy	G
Douglas	D
Frankfr	D
Reed	D
Black	DZ
Vinson	D

Durant (Ex Parte)
46 19M
329 US 672 46 18M

	10/11 1946 HABEAS
	1 1
Burton	D
Rutledg	DZ
Jackson	
Murphy	G
Douglas	D
Frankfr	D
Reed	D
Black	DZ
Vinson	D

Lavender v Clark
46 20M
329 US 674 46 427A

	10/19 1946 MNDMUS	
	1 1	
Burton	K	D
Rutledg	K	D
Jackson		
Murphy	K	
Douglas		D
Frankfr		D
Reed		D
Black	K	
Vinson		D

James (Ex Parte)
46 42M
329 US 680

	11/09 1946 CERT
	1 1
Burton	D
Rutledg	G
Jackson	
Murphy	D
Douglas	D
Frankfr	D
Reed	D
Black	D
Vinson	D

Standard Oil Of Indiana (Ex Parte)
46 124M
330 US 809

	03/29 1947 MNDMUS
	1 1
Burton	D
Rutledg	D
Jackson	D
Murphy	D
Douglas	D
Frankfr	G
Reed	D
Black	D
Vinson	D

Fahey (Ex Parte)
46 133M
332 US 258 46 687A
Vinson 05/05/47 Jackson 05/16/47

	05/03 1947 MNDMUS	06/23 1947 REPORT
	1 1	1 1
Burton		D
Rutledg	D	D
Jackson	D	D
Murphy	D	
Douglas	D	
Frankfr		D
Reed	D	D
Black	D	D
Vinson	D	D

Appendix C

U.S. Supreme Court
October 1947 Term

S.E.C. v Engineers Public Service
47 1A 46 2A 45 2A 44 16A 43 635A
332 US 788
Murphy 11/19/45 CCA DC

	11/19 1945 MERITS 1 1	10/18 1947 MERITS 1 2	10/20 1947 REPORT 1 1
Burton	AJ	R	VI
Rutledg	AJ	RQ	VI
Jackson		A	VI
Murphy	AJ	R	VI
Douglas		A	VI
Frankfr	AJ		VI
Reed		A	
Black	AJ	R	VI
Vinson		A	VI
Stone	AJ		

Winters v New York
47 3A 46 33A 45 636A
333 US 507
Reed 11/25/46 Reed 11/18/47 New York

	12/29 1945 JURIS 1 1	03/30 1946 MERITS 1 1	11/23 1946 MERITS 1 2	06/15 1947 REHEAR 1 1	11/15 1947 MERITS 1 3	03/29 1948 REPORT 1 1
Burton			R	B	R	R
Rutledg	P	R	R	Y		
Jackson					A	A
Murphy	P	R	X	Y	R	R
Douglas	S			B		
Frankfr				B	R	R
Reed	P	R	R	B	R	R
Black	S		R	Y	R	R
Vinson	PQ	R	R			
Stone	S		A			

Silesian-American v Clark
47 6A 46 346A
332 US 469 46 934A
Vinson 05/16/47 Reed 11/18/47 CCA 2d

	10/10 1946 CERT 1 1	02/15 1947 CERT 1 2	05/05 1947 MERITS 1 1	11/15 1947 MERITS 1 2	12/08 1947 REPORT 1 1
Burton	G	G			A
Rutledg	D	G	R		A
Jackson	D	G		R	A
Murphy		G			A
Douglas	D	G		A	A
Frankfr		G		A	A
Reed	G	G	RQ	A	A
Black	D	G		A	A
Vinson	D	G		A	A

Morris v McComb
47 7A 46 425A
332 US 422 46 22A 46 41A
Burton 10/22/47 CCA 6th

	04/05 1947 CERT 1 1	10/18 1947 MERITS 1 1	11/17 1947 REPORT 1 1
Burton	GL	R	
Rutledg	GL	R	V
Jackson	GL	R	A
Murphy	GL		A
Douglas	GL	A	A
Frankfr	GL	R	V
Reed	GL	R	V
Black	GL		A
Vinson	GL	R	V

U.S. v Line Material Company
47 8A 46 464A
333 US 287
Reed 05/14/47 Reed 11/25/47 Wisconsin

	10/19 1946 JURIS 1 1	05/10 1947 MERITS 1 1	11/24 1947 MERITS 1 2	03/08 1948 REPORT 1 1
Burton	N			
Rutledg	N	R	R	R
Jackson	N			
Murphy	N	R	R	R
Douglas	N	R	R	R
Frankfr	N		A	A
Reed	N	R	R	R
Black	N	R	R	R
Vinson	N		A	A

N.L.R.B. v Keystone Steel & Wire
47 9A 46 544A
332 US 833
CCA 7th

	11/09 1946 CERT 1 1	12/06 1947 MERITS 1 1	12/08 1947 REPORT 1 1
Burton	G	M	VMI
Rutledg	G	M	VMI
Jackson	G	?	VMI
Murphy	G	M	VMI
Douglas	D	M	VMI
Frankfr	G	M	VMI
Reed	G	M	VMI
Black	G	M	VMI
Vinson	G	M	VMI

Schine Chain Theatres v U.S.
47 10A 46 572A
334 US 110 46 571A
Douglas 12/23/47 DC WD New York

	12/14 1946 JURIS	01/18 1947 MERITS	05/03 1948 REPORT
	1 1	1 2	1 1
Burton	S		A
Rutledg	S		A
Jackson	S		A
Murphy	S	X	A
Douglas	S		A
Frankfr	S	X	A
Reed	S		A
Black	S		A
Vinson			A

U.S. v United States Gypsum Company
47 13A 46 711A
333 US 364
Reed 11/25/47 DC DC

	12/14 1946 JURIS	11/24 1947 MERITS	03/08 1948 REPORT
	1 1	1 1	1 1
Burton	N	R	R
Rutledg	N	R	R
Jackson	N	X	
Murphy	N	R	R
Douglas	N	R	R
Frankfr	N	R	R
Reed	N	R	R
Black	N	R	R
Vinson			

Central Greyhound Lines v Mealey
47 14A 46 745A
334 US 653
Murphy 10/22/47 Frankfr 11/14/47 New York

	12/21 1946 JURIS	10/20 1947 MERITS	06/14 1948 REPORT
	1 1	1 2	1 1
Burton	P		R
Rutledg	P	A	A
Jackson	NP	R	R
Murphy	NP	X	R
Douglas	P	A	A
Frankfr	P		R
Reed	NP	R	R
Black	NP	A	R
Vinson	NP	A	A

U.S. v Evans
47 15A 46 823A
333 US 483
Rutledg 02/13/48 DC SD California

	01/18 1947 JURIS	02/07 1948 MERITS	03/15 1948 REPORT
	1 1	1 1	1 1
Burton	N	R	A
Rutledg	N	AQ	A
Jackson	N	AQ	A
Murphy	N	A	A
Douglas	N	A	A
Frankfr	N	A	A
Reed	N	R	A
Black	N	A	A
Vinson	N	R	A

Priebe & Sons v U.S.
47 16A 46 861A
332 US 407
Douglas 10/22/47 Ct Cls

	03/08 1947 CERT	10/18 1947 MERITS	11/17 1947 REPORT
	1 1	1 1	1 1
Burton	G	R	R
Rutledg	G	R	R
Jackson	G	R	R
Murphy	G		
Douglas	G	R	R
Frankfr	G	R	R
Reed	G	A	R
Black	D	A	A
Vinson	D	A	A

U.S. v John J. Felin & Company
47 17A 46 862A
334 US 624
Frankfr 11/25/47 Ct Cls

	03/01 1947 CERT	05/10 1947 MERITS	11/22 1947 MERITS	06/14 1948 REPORT
	1 1	1 1	1 2	1 1
Burton	G	R	R	R
Rutledg	G	A	RQ	R
Jackson	G	A	R	R
Murphy	G	R		
Douglas	D	X	R	R
Frankfr				
Reed	G	R	R	R
Black	D	A	R	R
Vinson	G	A	R	R

Hunter v Texas Electric Railway
47 18A 46 893A
332 US 827
Reed 10/22/47 Texas

	03/29 1947 CERT	10/20 1947 MERITS	10/20 1947 PER CUR	11/24 1947 REPORT
	1 1		1 1	1 1
Burton				
Rutledg	D	R	Y	R
Jackson	D	A	Y	A
Murphy	G	R	B	
Douglas	G	R	Y	R
Frankfr				
Reed	G	R	B	R
Black	G	R	Y	R
Vinson	G	A	Y	A

Brotherhood Locomotive v Toledo RR
47 21A 46 908A
332 US 748 47 42A 46 1047A
CCA 7th

	03/29 1947 CERT	10/10 1947 MERITS	10/13 1947 REPORT
	1 1		1 1
Burton	G	VMI	VI
Rutledg	G	VMI	VI
Jackson	G	VMI	VI
Murphy	G	VMI	VI
Douglas	G	VMI	VI
Frankfr	G	VMI	VI
Reed	G	VMI	VI
Black	G	VMI	VI
Vinson	G	VMI	VI

F.T.C v Cement Institute
47 23A 46 922A
333 US 683 47 34A 46 933A
Black 10/27/47 CCA 7th

	03/08 1947 CERT	10/25 1947 MERITS	04/26 1948 REPORT
	1 1		1 1
Burton	G	R	R
Rutledg	G	R	R
Jackson	G		
Murphy	G	R	R
Douglas	G	RJ	R
Frankfr			
Reed	G	RJ	R
Black	G	RJ	R
Vinson	G		

Clark v Uebersee Finanz
47 35A 46 934A
332 US 480
Vinson 05/16/47 Douglas 11/18/47 CCA DC

	02/15 1947 CERT 1 1	05/05 1947 MERITS 1 1	05/10 1947 MERITS 1 2	06/04 1947 MERITS 1 3	11/15 1947 MERITS 1 4	12/08 1947 REPORT 1 1
Burton	G					A
Rutledg	G	R	R	R		A
Jackson	G	A	A	A	A	A
Murphy	G					A
Douglas	G				AL	A
Frankfr	G	A	A	A	A	A
Reed	G					A
Black	G	R	R	R		A
Vinson	G	R	R	R		A

Sherrer v Sherrer
47 36A 46 937A
334 US 343
Vinson 10/22/47 Massachusetts

	03/01 1947 CERT 1 1	10/18 1947 MERITS 1 1	06/07 1948 REPORT 1 1
Burton	G	R	R
Rutledg	G	R	R
Jackson	G		
Murphy	G	R	R
Douglas	G		A
Frankfr	G		A
Reed	G	R	R
Black	G	R	R
Vinson	G		

Coe v Coe
47 37A 46 958A
334 US 378
Vinson 10/22/47 Massachusetts

	03/01 1947 CERT 1 1	10/18 1947 MERITS 1 1	06/07 1948 REPORT 1 1
Burton	G	R	R
Rutledg	G	R	R
Jackson	D		
Murphy	G	R	R
Douglas	G		A
Frankfr	G		A
Reed	G	R	R
Black	G	R	R
Vinson	G	R	R

Maggio v Zeitz
47 38A 46 967A
333 US 56
Jackson 10/22/47 CCA 2d

	03/08 1947 CERT 1 1	10/20 1947 MERITS 1 1	02/09 1948 REPORT 1 1
Burton	G		
Rutledg	G	R	R
Jackson	G	A	V
Murphy	G		>
Douglas	G	A	>
Frankfr	G	A	>
Reed	G		
Black	G	R	R
Vinson	G	A	V

Aero Mayflower Transit v Board RR
47 39A 46 1003A
332 US 495
Rutledg 10/22/47 Montana

	03/08 1947 JURIS 1 1	10/15 1947 MERITS 1 1	12/08 1947 REPORT 1 1
Burton	N		A
Rutledg	N	A	A
Jackson	N	A	A
Murphy		A	A
Douglas	N	A	A
Frankfr	N	A	A
Reed	N	A	A
Black		A	A
Vinson	N	A	A

Wade v Mayo
47 40A 46 1024A
334 US 672
Reed 10/22/47 Reed 03/15/48 Murphy 03/17/48 CCA 5th

	04/26 1947 CERT 1 1	06/07 1947 CERT 1 2	10/18 1947 MERITS 1 1	10/20 1947 MERITS 1 2	03/29 1948 CERT 1 3	06/14 1948 REPORT 1 1
Burton	E			R		
Rutledg	E	D	VM			
Jackson		D		R		
Murphy		G	VM	R	R	R
Douglas		G				
Frankfr			VM			
Reed	GE	G	VM	R		R
Black						
Vinson	E	D	VM			

U.S. v Scophony
47 41A 46 1030A
333 US 795
Rutledg 01/19/48 DC SD New York

	03/08 1947 JURIS 1 1	01/17 1948 MERITS 1 1	04/26 1948 REPORT 1 1
Burton	N		R
Rutledg	N	R	R
Jackson	N	R	R
Murphy	N		R
Douglas	N		R
Frankfr	N		R
Reed	N	AQ	R
Black	N		R
Vinson	N	A	R

Farmers Grain v Brotherhood Locomotive
47 42A 46 1047A
332 US 748
CCA 7th

	03/29 1948 CERT 1 1	10/10 1947 MERITS 1 1	10/13 1947 REPORT 1 1
Burton	G	VMI	VI
Rutledg	G	VMI	VI
Jackson	G	VMI	VI
Murphy	G	VMI	VI
Douglas	G	VMI	VI
Frankfr	G	VMI	VI
Reed	G	VMI	VI
Black	G	VMI	VI
Vinson	G	VMI	VI

Oyama v California
47 44A 46 1059A
332 US 633
Vinson 10/27/47 California

Justice	04/05 1947 CERT (1 1)	10/25 1947 MERITS (1 1)	01/19 1948 REPORT (1 1)
Burton	G	R	
Rutledg	D	R	R A
Jackson	G		
Murphy	G	AQ	A
Douglas	D	R	R
Frankfr	D	R	R
Reed	G	R	R
Black			
Vinson	G	R	R A

Federal Crop Insurance v Merrill
47 45A 46 1064A
332 US 380
Frankfr 10/22/47 Idaho

Justice	04/26 1947 CERT (1 1)	10/20 1947 MERITS (1 1)	11/10 1947 REPORT (1 1)
Burton	G	R	R
Rutledg	G		R A
Jackson	G	R	R
Murphy		A	A
Douglas	DQ		
Frankfr			
Reed	G	R	R
Black	GQ	AO	R
Vinson	G	R	R A

International Salt Company v U.S.
47 46A 46 1076A
332 US 392   47 62A 46 1208A
Jackson 10/22/47 DC SD New York

Justice	04/26 1947 JURIS (1 1)	10/20 1947 MERITS (1 1)	11/10 1947 REPORT (1 1)
Burton	N	AJ	AJ
Rutledg	N	A	A
Jackson	N	A	A
Murphy	N	A	A
Douglas	N	AJ	AJ
Frankfr	N S	A	A
Reed	N	AJ	AJ
Black	N	AJ	AJ
Vinson	N	A	A

Williams v Fanning
47 47A 46 1083A
332 US 490
Douglas 11/25/47 California

Justice	04/12 1947 CERT (1 1)	11/08 1947 MERITS (1 1)	12/08 1947 REPORT (1 1)
Burton	GL	R	R
Rutledg	GL	R	R A
Jackson	GL		
Murphy	GL	A	A
Douglas			
Frankfr	GL	R	R
Reed	GL	R	R
Black			
Vinson	GL	R	R A

Mogull v U.S.
47 48A 46 1092A
333 US 424 46 1085A
CCA 5th

Justice	04/12 1947 CERT (1 1)	10/20 1947 MERITS (1 1)	03/08 1948 REPORT (1 1)
Burton	G D	R	R
Rutledg	G D	R	R
Jackson	G D	R	R
Murphy	G D	R	R
Douglas	G	R	R
Frankfr	G D	R	R A
Reed	G	R	R
Black	G	R	R
Vinson	G D	R	R A

Shapiro v U.S.
47 49A 46 1098A
335 US 1
Frankfr 10/27/47 Vinson 01/03/48 CCA 2d

Justice	06/02 1947 CERT (1 1)	10/25 1947 MERITS (1 1)	06/21 1948 REPORT (1 1)
Burton	G	R	R
Rutledg	G	R	R A
Jackson	G	AQ	A
Murphy	G D	R	R
Douglas	G D	R	A
Frankfr	G		
Reed	G	R	R
Black	G		A
Vinson	G	R	R A

Donaldson v Read Magazine
47 50A 46 1108A
333 US 178
Black 10/27/47 Black 01/13/48 CCA DC

Justice	04/26 1947 CERT (1 1)	10/25 1947 MERITS (1 1)	11/08 1947 REHEAR (1 1)	01/10 1948 MERITS (1 2)	03/08 1948 REPORT (1 1)
Burton	G	R	X	R	R
Rutledg	G	R	Y	R	R
Jackson		R	Y	X	R
Murphy	D		Y		
Douglas					
Frankfr		B	B		
Reed	G	R	X	R	R
Black			Y A		R A
Vinson	G	R	Y	R	R A

Haley v Ohio
47 51A 46 1123A
332 US 596
Douglas 11/25/47 Ohio

Justice	06/14 1947 CERT (1 1)	11/22 1947 MERITS (1 1)	01/12 1948 REPORT (1 1)
Burton	G	R	R
Rutledg	G	R	R A
Jackson	G	R	R
Murphy	G		A
Douglas	G	R	R A
Frankfr			
Reed	G	R	R
Black	G		
Vinson	G	R	R A

Local 2680 Lumber Workers v N.L.R.B.
47 53A 46 1147A
332 US 845
CCA 9th

Justice	04/26 1947 CERT (1 1)	05/03 1947 CERT (1 2)	01/05 1948 REPORT (1 1)
Burton	G	D	SI
Rutledg	G	D	SI
Jackson		D	SI
Murphy	G	G	SI
Douglas		D	SI
Frankfr	G		SI
Reed	G	G	SI
Black		D	SI
Vinson	G	G	SI

Blumenthal v U.S.
47 54A 46 1162A
332 US 539 47 55A 46 1163A
Rutledg 10/27/47 CCA 9th

	05/03 1947 CERT	10/25 1947 MERITS	12/22 1947 REPORT
	1 1	1 1	1 1
Burton	G		A
Rutledg	G	AQ	A
Jackson	D	X	A
Murphy	G		A
Douglas			A
Frankfr			A
Reed	G		A
Black	D		A
Vinson	D		A

Rodgers v U.S.
47 58A 46 1176A
332 US 371
Black 10/22/47 CCA 6th

	05/03 1947 CERT	10/20 1947 MERITS	11/10 1947 REPORT
	1 1	1 1	1 1
Burton	GL		
Rutledg	GL		
Jackson	GL		
Murphy	GL	A	A
Douglas		AQ	A
Frankfr			
Reed	GL	R	R
Black	GL	R	R
Vinson	GL	RQ	R

Musser v Utah
47 60A 46 1188A
333 US 95
Jackson 01/13/48 Utah

	04/26 1947 JURIS	12/06 1947 MERITS	01/10 1948 MERITS	02/09 1948 REPORT
	1 1	1 1	1 2	1 1
Burton	N	U	U	V
Rutledg	N	U	V	R
Jackson	N			
Murphy			RV	R
Douglas	S	SQ	V	V
Frankfr	N	U	RV	R
Reed		VM	R	V
Black	S	U	V	V
Vinson	SQ	U	V	V

U.S. v Di Re
47 61A 46 1193A
332 US 581
Jackson 10/27/47 CCA 2d

	05/16 1947 CERT	10/25 1947 MERITS	01/05 1948 REPORT
	1 1	1 1	1 1
Burton	G		A
Rutledg	D		A
Jackson	D		A
Murphy	G		A
Douglas			A
Frankfr	D		A
Reed	G	R	A
Black	G	R	R
Vinson			R

Delgadillo v Carmichael
47 63A 46 1244A
332 US 388
Douglas 10/27/47 CCA 9th

	05/31 1947 CERT	10/25 1947 MERITS	11/10 1947 REPORT
	1 1	1 1	1 1
Burton	G		R
Rutledg		R	R
Jackson	D	R	R
Murphy	G	R	R
Douglas		R	R
Frankfr	D	R	R
Reed	G	R	R
Black	G	R	R
Vinson	G	R	R

U.S. v Griffith
47 64A 46 1249A
334 US 100
Douglas 12/23/47 DC WD Oklahoma

	05/10 1947 JURIS	12/20 1947 MERITS	04/03 1948 REPORT
	1 1	1 1	1 1
Burton	N		
Rutledg	N	R	R
Jackson	N	R	R
Murphy	N		
Douglas			
Frankfr		R	R
Reed	N	X	
Black	N	R	R
Vinson	N	X	A

McCallum & Robinson v Henwood
47 65A 46 1255A
332 US 756
Tennessee

	10/06 1947 CERT
	1 1
Burton	
Rutledg	D
Jackson	D
Murphy	G
Douglas	
Frankfr	D
Reed	G
Black	G
Vinson	D
	D

Cox v U.S.
47 66A 46 1256A
332 US 442 47 67A 57 68A 46 1257A 46 1258A
Reed 10/27/47 CCA 9th

	05/31 1947 CERT	06/07 1947 CERT	10/25 1947 MERITS	11/24 1947 REPORT
	1 1	1 2	1 2	1 1
Burton	GR	G	A	A
Rutledg	G	G	AQ	A
Jackson	G	D		R
Murphy	GR	G	R	
Douglas	GR	D	X	
Frankfr	GR	D	A	A
Reed	GR	G		R
Black	GR	G	A	A
Vinson	GR	G	A	A

Panhandle Eastern v PSC Indiana
47 69A 46 1262A
332 US 507
Rutledg 11/25/47 Indiana

	05/16 1947 JURIS	11/22 1947 MERITS	12/15 1947 REPORT
	1 1	1 1	1 1
Burton	N	A	A
Rutledg		A	A
Jackson	N	A	A
Murphy			
Douglas			A
Frankfr	N	A	A
Reed		A	A
Black	N	A	A
Vinson			A

Kavanagh v Noble
47 70A 46 1264A
332 US 535 47 71A 46 1265A
Murphy 11/25/47 CCA 6th

	06/02 1947 CERT (1 1)	11/22 1947 MERITS (1 1)	12/22 1947 REPORT (1 1)
Burton	G	R	R
Rutledg	G	R	R
Jackson		R A	R
Murphy	D		R
Douglas	D	R A	R A
Frankfr			
Reed	D	R	R
Black	D	R	R
Vinson	G	R	R

Jones v Liberty Glass Company
47 71A 46 1265A
332 US 524 47 70A 46 1264A
Murphy 11/25/47 CCA 10th

	06/02 1947 CERT (1 1)	11/22 1947 MERITS (1 1)	12/22 1947 REPORT (1 1)
Burton	G	R	R
Rutledg	G	R	R
Jackson		R A	R
Murphy	D	R A	R
Douglas	D	R A	R A
Frankfr			R
Reed	G	R	R
Black	D	R	R
Vinson	D	R	R

Shelley v Kraemer
47 72A 46 1268A
334 US 1 47 87A 47 291A 47 153A
Vinson 02/16/48 Missouri

	06/02 1947 CERT (1 2)	06/21 1947 CERT (1 2)	11/15 1947 AMICUS	02/02 1948 MERITS (1 1)	05/03 1948 REPORT (1 1)
Burton	G	G	B	R	R
Rutledg	G	G		R	R
Jackson	G	D		X	
Murphy	G	G D		R	R
Douglas	G	G	Y	R	R
Frankfr					
Reed	G	G	B	R	R
Black	G	G	Y	R	R
Vinson	G	G		R	R

Von Moltke v Gillies
47 73A 46 1285A
332 US 708
Black 11/25/47 CCA 6th

	06/02 1947 CERT (1 1)	11/24 1947 MERITS (1 1)	01/19 1948 REPORT (1 1)
Burton	G	R	R
Rutledg	D	RQ	R
Jackson			
Murphy	G	R	R
Douglas	G	R X	R
Frankfr	G		
Reed			
Black	G D	R A	R A
Vinson	G	R	R

Pownall v U.S.
47 74A 46 1295A
334 US 742 47 105A 46 95A
Burton 11/25/47 CCA 9th

	06/14 1947 CERT (1 1)	11/24 1947 MERITS (1 1)	06/14 1948 REPORT (1 1)
Burton	G	R	R
Rutledg	G	R	R
Jackson			
Murphy	G	R	R A
Douglas	G	A	A
Frankfr	G	R	R
Reed	G	A	A
Black	G	A	A
Vinson	G	A	A

Mandeville Island v American Crystal
47 75A 46 1300A
334 US 219
Rutledg 11/25/47 CCA 9th

	06/02 1947 CERT (1 1)	11/24 1947 MERITS (1 1)	05/10 1948 REPORT (1 1)
Burton	G	R	R
Rutledg	G	R	R
Jackson	G	R	R
Murphy	D		
Douglas	D		
Frankfr		R	R
Reed	D	R	R
Black	G	R A	R A
Vinson	G		

Nathan's Estate v C.I.R.
47 77A 46 1325A
334 US 843 47 52A 47 96A
CCA 10th

	06/14 1947 CERT (1 1)	06/11 1948 CERT (1 2)
Burton	G	D
Rutledg	DH	D
Jackson	D	D
Murphy	D	D
Douglas	DH	D
Frankfr	D	D
Reed	DH	
Black	D	D
Vinson	D	D

Chicago & Southern v Waterman
47 78A 46 1340A
333 US 103 47 88A
Jackson 11/25/47 CCA 5th

	06/14 1947 CERT (1 1)	11/22 1947 MERITS (1 1)	02/09 1948 REPORT (1 1)
Burton	G	R	R
Rutledg	G	R X	R A
Jackson	G	R	R
Murphy	G		R A
Douglas	G		R A
Frankfr	G	A	A
Reed	G	A	A
Black	G D	R	R
Vinson	G	R	R

U.S. v Paramount Pictures
47 79A 46 1348A
334 US 131 47 80A 47 86A
Douglas 02/16/48 DC SD New York

	06/14 1947 JURIS (1 1)	02/16 1948 MERITS (1 1)	02/16 1948 QUEST (4 1)	02/16 1948 QUEST (5 1)	05/03 1948 REPORT (1 1)
Burton	N		B		R
Rutledg	N		B		R
Jackson					
Murphy	N	X	X AJ	Y YQ	R
Douglas	N		B	X	R
Frankfr	N		Y	Y	R
Reed	N			BQ	R
Black	N		B	B	R
Vinson	N				

McLie v Sipes
47 87A 46 1363A
334 US 1 47 72A
Vinson 02/16/48 Michigan

	06/21 1947 CERT (1 1)	02/02 1948 MERITS (1 1) X	05/03 1948 REPORT (1 1) A
Burton	G	R	R
Rutledg	H	X	
Jackson	X		
Murphy	G	R	R
Douglas	G	R	R
Frankfr			
Reed	G	R	R
Black	G	R	R
Vinson	G	R	R

Illinois (McCollum) v Board Education
47 90A 46 1374A
333 US 203
Black 12/16/47 Illinois

	05/31 1947 JURIS (1 1)	12/13 1947 MERITS (1 1) X	03/08 1948 REPORT (1 1) A
Burton	N	R	R
Rutledg	N	R	R
Jackson	N		
Murphy	N		R
Douglas	N P		R
Frankfr			
Reed	N P	R	R
Black	N	R	R
Vinson			

Lee v Mississippi
47 91A 46 1377A
332 US 742
Murphy 11/25/47 Mississippi

	06/14 1947 CERT (1 1)	11/24 1947 MERITS (1 1) A	01/19 1948 REPORT (1 1)
Burton	G	R	R
Rutledg	G	R	R
Jackson			
Murphy	G	R	R
Douglas	G	R	R
Frankfr		R	R
Reed		R	R
Black	G	R	R
Vinson	G	X	R

Van Glahn v New York
47 89A 46 1372A
332 US 842
New York

	06/14 1947 CERT (1 1)	12/13 1947 MERITS (1 2)
Burton	E	R
Rutledg	E	R
Jackson	E	
Murphy	E	R
Douglas	E	
Frankfr	E D	D
Reed	E D	D
Black	E	R
Vinson	E	R

Coger v New York
47 92A 46 1378A
332 US 838
New York

	06/14 1947 CERT (1 1)	12/06 1947 CERT (1 2)
Burton	E	D
Rutledg	E	D
Jackson		D
Murphy	E	D
Douglas	E	D
Frankfr	E	D
Reed	E	D
Black	E	D
Vinson	E	D

Marino v Ragen
47 93A 46 1382A
332 US 561
Illinois

	06/07 1947 CERT (1 1)	12/06 1947 CERT (1 2)	12/22 1947 REPORT (1 1)	03/13 1948 QUEST (6 1) Y
Burton	E	GR	>	B
Rutledg	E D	GR	>	B
Jackson		GR	>	B
Murphy	E D	GR	>	
Douglas	E	GR	>	B
Frankfr		GR	>	
Reed	E D	GR	>	B
Black	E	GR	>	B
Vinson	E D	GR	>	B

Memphis Natural Gas Company v Stone
47 94A 46 1383A
335 US 80
Reed 12/16/47 Mississippi

	06/14 1947 CERT (1 1)	12/13 1947 MERITS (1 1) A	06/21 1948 REPORT (1 1) A
Burton	G	R	R
Rutledg	G	R A	R A
Jackson		R	R
Murphy	G	R A	R A
Douglas	G	R A	R A
Frankfr		R	R
Reed		D	
Black		D	
Vinson	G	R A	R A

Alexander Wool Combing Company v U.S.
47 95A 46 1391A
334 US 742 47 105A 47 74A
Burton 11/25/47 CCA 1st

	11/24 1947 MERITS (1 1) A	06/14 1948 REPORT (1 1) A
Burton		A
Rutledg		A
Jackson	R	A
Murphy		A
Douglas		A
Frankfr		A
Reed		A
Black		A
Vinson		A

U.S. v Hoffman
47 97A 46 1401A
335 US 77
Frankfr 10/27/47 Vinson 01/03/48 DC DC

	10/25 1947 MERITS (1 1)	06/21 1948 REPORT (1 1)
Burton	RQ	R
Rutledg	A	A
Jackson	A	A
Murphy	A	
Douglas	A	R
Frankfr	A	R
Reed	R	R
Black	R	
Vinson	R	

U.S. v Fried
47 98A 46 1402A
332 US 807 46 1231A
CCA 2d

	06/14 1947 CERT (1 1)	06/21 1947 CERT (1 2)	10/27 1947 REPORT (1 1)
Burton	G	G	SI
Rutledg	G X	G	SI
Jackson	G	G	SI
Murphy			SI
Douglas	D	D	SI
Frankfr	D	D	SI
Reed	D	D	SI
Black			SI
Vinson	G	G	SI

Robichaud v Brennan
47 99A 46 1403A
332 US 756
New Jersey

	10/06 1947 CERT (1 1)
Burton	D
Rutledg	D
Jackson	G
Murphy	G
Douglas	
Frankfr	D
Reed	D
Black	D
Vinson	D

U.S. v Brown
47 100A 46 1405A
333 US 18
Rutledg 01/13/48 Vinson 01/03/48 CCA 8th

	10/06 1947 CERT (1 1)	01/10 1948 MERITS (1 1)	02/02 1948 REPORT (1 1)
Burton	G	R	R
Rutledg	G	R	R
Jackson	G	R	R
Murphy	DQ	R A	R A
Douglas			
Frankfr	G	R	R
Reed			
Black	G D	R A	R
Vinson	G	R	R

Eccles v Peoples Bank Of Lakewood
47 101A 46 1414A
333 US 426
Frankfr 12/23/47 CCA DC

	10/06 1947 CERT 1 1	12/13 1947 MERITS 1 1	12/20 1947 QUEST 7 1	12/20 1947 QUEST 7 2	03/15 1948 REPORT 1 1
Burton	G	R	B	Y	R
Rutledg	G DQ	R	B	Y	R
Jackson	D			Y	
Murphy			B	Y	R
Douglas				Y	
Frankfr			B	Y	R
Reed				Y	
Black	G A	R	B A	Y	R A
Vinson				Y	

Lichter v U.S.
47 105A 46 1427A
334 US 742 47 74A 47 95A
Burton 11/25/47 CCA 6th

	06/14 1947 CERT 1 1	11/25 1947 MERITS 1 1	06/14 1948 REPORT 1 1
Burton	G	R A	R A
Rutledg	G		A
Jackson	G	R A	R A
Murphy	G		A
Douglas	G	R A	R A
Frankfr	G		A
Reed	G		A
Black	G	R A	R A
Vinson	G		A

Price v Johnston
47 111A 46 1448A
334 US 266
Murphy 12/23/47 CCA 9th

	06/21 1947 CERT 1 1	12/20 1947 MERITS 1 1	05/24 1948 REPORT 1 1
Burton	G	R A	R A
Rutledg	G D	R A	R A
Jackson	G		
Murphy	G	R A	R A
Douglas	G		
Frankfr	G	R A	R A
Reed	G		
Black	G D	R A	R A
Vinson	G	R A	R A

Lewis v New York
47 117A 46 1460A
332 US 842
New York

	06/14 1947 CERT 1 1
Burton	E
Rutledg	E
Jackson	E
Murphy	E
Douglas	E
Frankfr	E
Reed	E
Black	E D
Vinson	E

U.S. v Sullivan
47 121A 46 1473A
332 US 689
Black 12/16/47 CCA 5th

	10/06 1947 CERT 1 1	12/13 1947 MERITS 1 1	12/31 1947 MERITS 1 2	01/19 1948 REPORT 1 1
Burton	G	RQ	RQ	
Rutledg	G	R AQ	R AQ	R
Jackson	G			
Murphy	G	R A	R A	R
Douglas	G		A	A
Frankfr	G		A A	A
Reed	G	R A	R A	R
Black	G			
Vinson	G	R	R	R

Patton v Mississippi
47 122A 46 1476A
332 US 463
Black 11/25/47 Mississippi

	06/14 1947 CERT 1 1	11/24 1947 MERITS 1 1	12/08 1947 REPORT 1 1
Burton	G X GW	R	R
Rutledg	G	R	R
Jackson	G	R	R
Murphy	G	R	R
Douglas	G EW	R	R
Frankfr	G EW	R	R
Reed	G	R	R
Black	G	R	R
Vinson	G	R	R

Alabama Dry Dock v Caldwell
47 125A 46 1479A
332 US 759 47 126A
CCA 5th

	10/06 1947 CERT 1 1
Burton	D
Rutledg	D
Jackson	D
Murphy	D
Douglas	GQ
Frankfr	D
Reed	D
Black	D
Vinson	D

U.S. v Short Line
47 127A 46 1481A
332 US 753 47 128A
DC Connecticut

	10/06 1947 JURIS 1 1	10/13 1947 REPORT 1 1
Burton	N	SI
Rutledg	N	SI
Jackson	N	SI
Murphy	N	SI
Douglas	N	SI
Frankfr	N	SI
Reed	N	SI
Black	N	SI
Vinson	N	SI

Mitchell v Cohen
47 130A 46 1487A
333 US 411 47 131A
Murphy 01/13/48 CCA DC

	10/06 1947 CERT 1 1	01/10 1948 MERITS 1 1	03/08 1948 REPORT 1 1
Burton	G	R	R
Rutledg	G D	R	R
Jackson	G	R A	R
Murphy	G		
Douglas	G D	R A	R
Frankfr	G		
Reed	G	R	R
Black	G	R	R
Vinson	G	R	R

Nesbitt v Gill
47 132A 46 1489A
332 US 749
North Carolina

Justice	JURIS 10/06 1947 (1 1)	REPORT 10/13 1947 (1 1)
Burton	N	A
Rutledg		A
Jackson		A
Murphy	N	A
Douglas		A
Frankfr	G	A
Reed		A
Black	N	A
Vinson		A

Republic Natural Gas v Oklahoma
47 134A 46 1496A
334 US 62
Frankfr 01/13/48 Oklahoma

Justice	JURIS 10/06 1947 (1 1)	MERITS 01/10 1948 (1 1)	REPORT 05/03 1948 (1 1)
Burton	N	R	A
Rutledg	S	S	A
Jackson			A
Murphy	N	R	SA
Douglas		SA	S
Frankfr	N	R	S
Reed	S	S	S
Black	N	R	S
Vinson	N	R	A

Texas & Pacific RR v Brotherhood
47 136A 46 1500A
332 US 760 47 137A 46 1501A
CCA 5th

Justice	CERT 10/06 1947 (1 1)
Burton	D
Rutledg	D
Jackson	D
Murphy	D
Douglas	
Frankfr	G
Reed	
Black	D
Vinson	D

Adams v Brotherhood
47 137A 46 1501A
332 US 760 47 136A 46 1500A
CCA 5th

Justice	CERT 10/06 1947 (1 1)
Burton	D
Rutledg	D
Jackson	D
Murphy	D
Douglas	D
Frankfr	
Reed	G
Black	D
Vinson	D

Johnson v U.S.
47 138A 46 1502A
333 US 46
Douglas 12/16/47 CCA 9th

Justice	CERT 10/06 1947 (1 1)	MERITS 12/13 1947 (1 1)	REPORT 02/09 1948 (1 1)	QUEST 04/02 1948 (8 1)	REPORT 06/07 1948 (1 1)
Burton	G	R	M	B	R
Rutledg		X	M	Y	A
Jackson	G	R	R	B	A
Murphy			M	Y	M
Douglas	G		M	B	A
Frankfr			R	B	A
Reed	G	AQ	R	B	A
Black		R	R	B	A
Vinson		R	R	B	A

Estin v Estin
47 139A 46 1503A
334 US 541 47 371A *New York*
Douglas 04/26/48

Justice	CERT 10/06 1947 (1 1)	REHEAR 12/13 1947 (1 1)	CERT 12/13 1947 (1 2)	MERITS 02/07 1948 (1 1)
Burton	D	Y	G	
Rutledg	D	Y	G	X
Jackson	D	Y	G	
Murphy	D	Y	G	X
Douglas		Y	G	
Frankfr	G	Y	G	X
Reed		Y	G	
Black	D	Y	G	X
Vinson	D	Y	G	

Selling v Barclay White Company
47 144A
332 US 761
Pennsylvania

Justice	CERT 10/06 1947 (1 1)
Burton	D
Rutledg	D
Jackson	D
Murphy	D
Douglas	G
Frankfr	G
Reed	G
Black	D
Vinson	D

Title Insurance & Guaranty v Hart
47 145A
332 US 761
CCA 9th

Justice	CERT 10/06 1947 (1 1)
Burton	D
Rutledg	D
Jackson	D
Murphy	D
Douglas	G
Frankfr	G
Reed	G
Black	D
Vinson	D

Conrad v Pennsylvania RR Company
47 149A
332 US 762 47 150A
CCA 3rd

Justice	CERT 10/06 1947 (1 1)
Burton	D
Rutledg	D
Jackson	D
Murphy	D
Douglas	GQ
Frankfr	D
Reed	D
Black	DQ
Vinson	D

Trustees Of Monroe Avenue v Perkins
47 153A
334 US 813   47 154A   47 72A
Ohio

	05/07 1948 CERT	05/10 1948 REPORT
Burton		
Rutledg	GR	R
Jackson		
Murphy	GR	R
Douglas	GR	R
Frankfr		
Reed		
Black	GR	R
Vinson	GR	

Massachusetts v U.S.
47 157A
333 US 611
Rutledg 12/23/47 CCA 1st

	10/06 1947 CERT	12/13 1947 MERITS	12/20 1947 MERITS	04/19 1948 REPORT
Burton	G			
Rutledg		R	R	R
Jackson				
Murphy	G			R
Douglas	G	R	R	R
Frankfr		X	A	
Reed				
Black	G	R X	R A	R A
Vinson	G		A	A

Kay v MacCormack
47 158A
332 US 763
New York

	10/06 1947 CERT
Burton	D
Rutledg	D
Jackson	
Murphy	G
Douglas	G
Frankfr	G
Reed	
Black	D
Vinson	D

Wilcox v DeWitt
47 162A
332 US 763
CCA 9th

	10/06 1947 CERT
Burton	D
Rutledg	D
Jackson	
Murphy	G
Douglas	D
Frankfr	D
Reed	D
Black	D
Vinson	D

Madokoro v Del Guercio
47 164A
332 US 764
CCA 9th

	10/06 1947 CERT
Burton	D
Rutledg	G
Jackson	
Murphy	D
Douglas	D
Frankfr	D
Reed	D
Black	G
Vinson	D

Tampa Times Company v City Of Tampa
47 165A
332 US 749   47 166A
Florida

	10/06 1947 JURIS
Burton	S
Rutledg	S
Jackson	S
Murphy	NQ
Douglas	S
Frankfr	S
Reed	S
Black	S
Vinson	S

Jorgensen v York Ice Machinery
47 167A
332 US 764
CCA 2d

	10/06 1947 CERT
Burton	D
Rutledg	G
Jackson	
Murphy	D
Douglas	D
Frankfr	D
Reed	D
Black	D
Vinson	D

Bell v North Carolina
47 168A
332 US 764
North Carolina

	10/06 1947 CERT
Burton	D
Rutledg	G
Jackson	
Murphy	D
Douglas	D
Frankfr	D
Reed	D
Black	G
Vinson	D

King v Order Of United Commercial
47 171A
333 US 153
Vinson 12/16/47 CCA 4th

	10/06 1947 CERT	12/13 1947 MERITS	03/08 1948 REPORT
Burton	G		A
Rutledg	D		A
Jackson		S	A
Murphy	D	SA	A
Douglas	D	X	A
Frankfr	D	S	A
Reed		R	
Black	G		
Vinson	G	R	

Mester v U.S.
47 173A
332 US 749
DC ED New York

	10/06 1947 JURIS	10/13 1947 REPORT
Burton	A	A
Rutledg	A	A
Jackson	A	A
Murphy	A	A
Douglas	A	A
Frankfr	A	
Reed		
Black	A	A
Vinson		

Sealton v U.S.
47 174A
332 US 575
Douglas 12/16/47 CCA 3rd

	10/06 1947 CERT	12/13 1947 MERITS	01/05 1948 REPORT
Burton	G		R
Rutledg	G	R	R
Jackson	G		R
Murphy		R	R
Douglas	G	R	R
Frankfr			R
Reed		AQ	R
Black	G	X	R
Vinson		A	

Pearce v Pennsylvania RR Company
47 176A
332 US 765
CCA 3rd

	10/06 1947 CERT
Burton	D
Rutledg	D
Jackson	DQ
Murphy	D
Douglas	G
Frankfr	D
Reed	
Black	G
Vinson	D

Chase National Bank v Cheston
47 178A
332 US 793 47 179A 47 183A
CCA 7th

Justice	10/10 1947 CERT 1-1	10/11 1947 CERT 1-2	10/18 1947 CERT 1-3	10/18 1947 QUEST 9-1	10/18 1947 CONTMPT 1-1
Burton	D		D		B
Rutledg	D	D	D		B
Jackson	D	G	D		B
Murphy	D	X			B
Douglas			D	Y	B
Frankfr		E	D		Y
Reed	D	D	D		B
Black		D			B
Vinson	D	D	D	Y	B

U.S. v South Buffalo RR Company
47 198A
333 US 771
Jackson 02/13/48 DC WD New York

Justice	10/06 1947 JURIS 1-1	02/07 1948 MERITS 1-1	04/26 1948 REPORT 1-1
Burton	N	R	A
Rutledg	N	AQ	R
Jackson	N	AQ	R
Murphy	N	X	A
Douglas	N		A
Frankfr	A	X	A
Reed	N	R	A
Black		A	
Vinson	A	A	A

Central Nebraska Public Power v F.P.C.
47 199A
332 US 765
CCA 8th

Justice	10/06 1947 CERT 1-1
Burton	D
Rutledg	D
Jackson	D
Murphy	D
Douglas	G
Frankfr	
Reed	D
Black	G
Vinson	D

Globe Liquor v San Roman
47 205A
332 US 571
Black 12/23/47 CCA 7th

Justice	10/06 1947 CERT 1-1	12/20 1947 MERITS 1-1	01/05 1948 REPORT 1-1
Burton	G	R	A
Rutledg		X	A
Jackson	G	R	A
Murphy		X	A
Douglas			A
Frankfr	D	R	A
Reed	G	R	A
Black	G		A
Vinson	G	R	A

Lillie v Thompson
47 206A
332 US 459
CCA 6th

Justice	10/06 1947 CERT 1-1	11/22 1947 PER CUR 1-1	11/24 1947 REPORT 1-1
Burton	G	B	R
Rutledg	D	Y	R
Jackson	G	Y	R
Murphy	D	Y	R
Douglas	D	Y	R
Frankfr	D	Y	R
Reed	G	Y	R
Black	G		
Vinson	G		

Philadelphia Record v O'Donnell
47 207A
332 US 766
Pennsylvania

Justice	10/06 1947 CERT 1-1
Burton	
Rutledg	D
Jackson	D
Murphy	
Douglas	G
Frankfr	DQ
Reed	D
Black	D
Vinson	G

Crowell-Collier Publishing v Caldwell
47 209A
332 US 766
CCA 5th

Justice	10/06 1947 CERT 1-1
Burton	
Rutledg	D
Jackson	D
Murphy	
Douglas	G
Frankfr	
Reed	D
Black	D
Vinson	G

E.J. Stanton & Son v Los Angeles
47 213A
332 US 766
California

Justice	10/08 1947 CERT 1-1
Burton	
Rutledg	D
Jackson	D
Murphy	
Douglas	G
Frankfr	
Reed	G
Black	
Vinson	

Suttle v Reich Brothers Construction
47 214A
333 US 163
Vinson 12/23/47 CCA 5th

Justice	10/06 1947 CERT 1-1	12/20 1947 MERITS 1-1	03/08 1948 REPORT 1-1
Burton	G		R
Rutledg	D	AQ	R
Jackson	D	A	M
Murphy		AQ	M
Douglas	GQ	A	R
Frankfr	G	A	R
Reed	G		R
Black		A	R
Vinson	D	R	R

Oliver (In Re)
47 215A
333 US 257
Black 12/23/47 Michigan

Justice	10/08 1947 CERT 1-1	12/20 1947 MERITS 1-1	01/03 1948 AMICUS 1-1
Burton	G	R	B
Rutledg	D	R	B
Jackson	D	R	B
Murphy		A	Y
Douglas	D	R	B
Frankfr	D	A	Y
Reed	D	R	Y
Black			
Vinson	D	X	Y

Austin v C.I.R.
47 216A
332 US 767 47 227A
CCA 6th

Justice	10/08 1947 CERT 1-1
Burton	G
Rutledg	D
Jackson	D
Murphy	
Douglas	G
Frankfr	GQ
Reed	G
Black	
Vinson	D

Bracey v Luray
47 217A
332 US 790
CCA 4th

Justice	10/08 1947 CERT 1 2
Burton	GRM
Rutledg	GRM
Jackson	GRM D
Murphy	GRM
Douglas	GRM D
Frankfr	
Reed	GRM
Black	D
Vinson	D

U.S. v Baltimore & Ohio RR Company
47 223A
333 US 169
Black 02/13/48 DC ND Ohio

Justice	10/06 1947 JURIS 1 1	12/20 1947 MERITS 1 1	02/09 1948 MERITS 1 1	03/08 1948 REPORT 1 1
Burton	N	R	R	R
Rutledg	N	R	R	R
Jackson	N	R	R	R
Murphy	N	R	R	R A
Douglas	N	R	R	R
Frankfr	N	R	R	R
Reed	N	R	R	R
Black	N	R	R	R A
Vinson	N	R	R	R

Bakery Sales Drivers v Wagshal
47 225A
333 US 437
Frankfr 01/13/48 CCA DC

Justice	10/08 1947 CERT 1 1	12/20 1947 MERITS 1 1	01/03 1948 MERITS 1 2	03/15 1948 REPORT 1 1
Burton	G	R	R A	A
Rutledg	G	R	R A	A
Jackson	G		A	
Murphy	G	R	R A	A
Douglas	G		A	
Frankfr	G	R	R A	A
Reed	G	R	R A	A
Black	G	R	R A	A
Vinson	G	R	R A	A

C.I.R. v Sunnen
47 227A
333 US 591
Murphy 12/23/47 CCA 8th

Justice	10/08 1947 CERT 1 1	12/20 1947 MERITS 1 1	04/05 1948 REPORT 1 1
Burton	G	R	
Rutledg	G	R	
Jackson		R	
Murphy	G	R	
Douglas		R	
Frankfr		R	A
Reed	G	R	
Black		R	A
Vinson	G	R	

Thibaut v Car & General Insurance
47 231A
332 US 751   332 US 828
CCA 5th

Justice	10/08 1947 CERT 1 1
Burton	G
Rutledg	G
Jackson	G
Murphy	G
Douglas	G
Frankfr	
Reed	G
Black	G
Vinson	G

Rice Brothers v Birmingham
47 233A
332 US 768
Iowa

Justice	10/08 1947 CERT 1 1
Burton	GRM
Rutledg	GRM
Jackson	GRM
Murphy	GRM
Douglas	GRM
Frankfr	GRM
Reed	GRM
Black	GRM
Vinson	GRM

Koritz v North Carolina
47 234A
332 US 768
North Carolina

Justice	10/08 1947 CERT 1 1	10/18 1947 HOLD 1 1	11/22 1947 VACATE 1 1	11/22 1947 REHEAR 1 1	11/22 1947 CERT 1 2	11/24 1947 REPORT 1 2
Burton	G		B	BQ	B	G
Rutledg	D	Y	Y	Y	Y	D
Jackson	D	B	X		X	D
Murphy	D	B	Y	Y	Y	D
Douglas	D	B	Y	Y	Y	D
Frankfr	D	B	Y	Y	Y	D
Reed				BQ		
Black	G	B	B	B	B	D
Vinson	D	B	Y	Y	Y	

Bruce v King
47 243A
332 US 769
Texas

Justice	10/10 1947 CERT 1 1
Burton	G
Rutledg	D
Jackson	D
Murphy	D
Douglas	D
Frankfr	D
Reed	G
Black	D
Vinson	D

Caffey v Bereslavsky
47 244A
332 US 770
CCA 2d

Justice	10/08 1947 CERT 1 1
Burton	D
Rutledg	D
Jackson	D
Murphy	D
Douglas	D
Frankfr	D
Reed	G
Black	G
Vinson	D

Mississippi Power v Memphis Gas
47 248A
332 US 770
CCA 5th

Justice	10/08 1947 CERT 1 1
Burton	D
Rutledg	D
Jackson	D
Murphy	D
Douglas	D
Frankfr	D
Reed	G
Black	G
Vinson	D

Cohen v Cauldwell Wingate Company
47 255A
332 US 790
New York

Justice	10/18 1947 CERT 1 1
Burton	D
Rutledg	D
Jackson	D
Murphy	D
Douglas	D
Frankfr	G
Reed	G
Black	D
Vinson	D

211

Peters v U.S.
47 256A
334 US 960 47 49A 47 97A
CCA 8th

Justice	06/18 1948 CERT 1 1
Burton	D
Rutledg	D
Jackson	D
Murphy	D
Douglas	
Frankfr	
Reed	G
Black	D
Vinson	D

Florida (McKeighan) v Sullivan
47 257A
332 US 750
Florida

Justice	10/06 1947 JURIS 1 1
Burton	S
Rutledg	S
Jackson	S
Murphy	
Douglas	S
Frankfr	S
Reed	N
Black	A
Vinson	A

Schwabacher v U.S.
47 258A
334 US 182
Jackson 01/19/48 DC ED Virginia

Justice	10/10 1947 JURIS 1 1	01/10 1948 MERITS 1 1
Burton	N	R
Rutledg	N	RQ
Jackson	N	RQ
Murphy	N	R
Douglas	N	
Frankfr	N	
Reed		
Black	N	X
Vinson	A	A

Bernstein v N.V. Nederlandsche
47 259A
332 US 771 47 277A
CCA 2d

Justice	10/08 1947 CERT 1 1
Burton	
Rutledg	
Jackson	D
Murphy	
Douglas	D
Frankfr	
Reed	D
Black	D
Vinson	D

Allen v Glenn L. Martin Company
47 267A
332 US 749 47 268A 47 269A
Maryland

Justice	10/06 1947 JURIS 1 1
Burton	S
Rutledg	S
Jackson	S
Murphy	S
Douglas	S
Frankfr	
Reed	
Black	S
Vinson	S

Parker v Illinois
47 270A
333 US 571 47 428A
Douglas 02/16/48 Illinois

Justice	12/13 1947 CERT 1 1	12/20 1947 CERT 1 2	01/03 1948 CERT 1 3	02/14 1948 MERITS 1 1	04/05 1948 REPORT 1 1
Burton	G	G	G		
Rutledg	D	D	D	R	A
Jackson					
Murphy	G	G	G	S	A
Douglas	D	D	D	A	A
Frankfr				A	A
Reed					A
Black	G	G	G	A	A
Vinson	D	D	D	R	A

Dyer v City Council Of Beloit
47 275A
333 US 825
Frankfr 12/16/47 Wisconsin

Justice	10/06 1947 JURIS 1 1	12/13 1947 MERITS 1 1	02/02 1948 REPORT 1 1
Burton	N		VI
Rutledg	N	R	VI
Jackson			VI
Murphy	S	R	VS
Douglas	A		VI
Frankfr	S	R	VI
Reed			VI
Black	N	R	VS
Vinson	S		VI

Bernstein v Van Heyghen Freres
47 277A
332 US 772 47 259A
CCA 2d

Justice	10/08 1947 CERT 1 1	10/10 1947 CERT 1 2
Burton	G	D
Rutledg		D
Jackson	D	D
Murphy		
Douglas	D	
Frankfr		G
Reed	G	G
Black	G	D
Vinson	G	D

Touhy v Illinois
47 278A
332 US 791
Illinois

Justice	10/18 1947 CERT 1 1
Burton	
Rutledg	G
Jackson	D
Murphy	G
Douglas	D
Frankfr	
Reed	D
Black	D
Vinson	D

Funk Brothers Seed v Kalo Inoculant
47 280A
333 US 127
Douglas 01/19/48 CCA 7th

Justice	10/08 1947 CERT 1 1	01/17 1948 MERITS 1 1	02/16 1948 REPORT 1 1
Burton	G	R	A
Rutledg	G		
Jackson	G	R	R
Murphy	GQ	X	A
Douglas			
Frankfr		R	R
Reed	G	R	R
Black	G		
Vinson	D		R

Wolfe v Henwood
47 281A
332 US 773
CCA 8th

Justice	10/06 1947 CERT 1 1
Burton	G
Rutledg	
Jackson	G
Murphy	D
Douglas	
Frankfr	D
Reed	D
Black	D
Vinson	D

Lasagna v McCarthy
47 283A
332 US 829 47 321A
Utah

	10/18 1947 CERT 1 1	11/08 1947 CERT 1 2	11/22 1947 CERT 1 3
Burton	G	G D	D
Rutledg			
Jackson			
Murphy	G	G	D
Douglas	G	G	D
Frankfr			
Reed	D	D	D
Black	G		D
Vinson		DQ	D
		DQ	D

Fogel v U.S.
47 285A
332 US 791
CCA 5th

	10/18 1947 CERT 1 1	11/08 1947 CERT 1 2	05/03 1948 REPORT 1 1
Burton	G	G D	R
Rutledg			
Jackson	G	G	
Murphy	G	G	R
Douglas	G		R
Frankfr	G		
Reed		D	
Black	G	D	R
Vinson		D	R
		D	

Hurd v Hodge
47 290A
334 US 24 47 72A 47 87A 47 291A
Vinson 02/16/48 CCA DC

	10/18 1947 CERT 1 1	02/02 1948 MERITS 1 1	05/03 1948 REPORT 1 1
Burton	G	R	R
Rutledg	H	X	
Jackson			
Murphy	G	R	R
Douglas	G	R	R
Frankfr			
Reed	G	R	R
Black			
Vinson	G	R	R

Urciolo v Hodge
47 291A
334 US 24 47 72A 47 87A 47 290A
Vinson 02/16/48 CCA DC

	10/18 1947 CERT 1 1	02/02 1948 MERITS 1 1	05/03 1948 REPORT 1 1
Burton	G	R	R
Rutledg	H	X	
Jackson			
Murphy	G	R	R
Douglas	G	R	R
Frankfr			
Reed	G	R	R
Black			
Vinson	G	R	R

Brunson v North Carolina
47 292A 47 296A
333 US 851 47 122A
North Carolina

	10/08 1947 CERT 1 1	12/13 1947 CERT 1 2	02/09 1948 MERITS 1 1	03/15 1948 REPORT 1 1
Burton	G	G	R	R
Rutledg	G	G	R	R
Jackson	G	G	R	R
Murphy	G	G	R	R
Douglas	G	G	R	R
Frankfr	G	G	R	R
Reed	G	G	R	R
Black	G	G	R	R
Vinson	D	G	A	A
		G	A	R

Hemans v U.S.
47 299A
332 US 801
CCA 6th

	10/18 1947 CERT 1 1
Burton	
Rutledg	
Jackson	D
Murphy	D
Douglas	GQ
Frankfr	
Reed	D
Black	GQ
Vinson	D

Hood v Texas Company
47 300A
332 US 829
CCA 5th

	10/18 1947 CERT 1 1	11/22 1947 CERT 1 2
Burton	GR	D
Rutledg	GR	D
Jackson	GR	D
Murphy		D
Douglas		D
Frankfr		D
Reed		D
Black	GR	D
Vinson	GR	D

Edward G. Budd Manufacturing v N.L.R.B.
47 301A
332 US 840
CCA 6th

	12/13 1947 CERT 1 1	12/13 1947 CERT 2 1	12/15 1947 REPORT 1 1
Burton			
Rutledg		GL	>
Jackson		GL	>
Murphy		GL	>
Douglas			>
Frankfr			>
Reed			>
Black	G	GL	>
Vinson		GL	>

Swift & Company v N.L.R.B.
47 302A
332 US 791
CCA 3rd

	10/18 1947 CERT 1 1
Burton	
Rutledg	
Jackson	D
Murphy	D
Douglas	GQ
Frankfr	
Reed	
Black	GQ
Vinson	

Berman v Levine
47 307A
332 US 792
CCA 7th

	10/18 1947 CERT 1 1 GR
Burton	D
Rutledg	D
Jackson	D
Murphy	
Douglas	
Frankfr	
Reed	G
Black	DQ
Vinson	D

Clark v Kind
47 309A
332 US 808 47 326A
CCA 2d

	10/25 1947 CERT 1 1
Burton	D
Rutledg	D
Jackson	D
Murphy	
Douglas	
Frankfr	
Reed	G
Black	D
Vinson	D

Steinberg v U.S.
47 319A
332 US 808
CCA 5th

	10/25 1947 CERT 1 1
Burton	D
Rutledg	D
Jackson	D
Murphy	
Douglas	
Frankfr	
Reed	G
Black	D
Vinson	D

Lincoln Electric Company v Forrestal
47 320A
334 US 841 47 105A 47 74A 47 95A
DC DC

Justice	10/18 1947 JURIS (1 1)	06/11 1948 MERITS (1 1)	06/14 1948 REPORT (1 1)
Burton	P	AH	A
Rutledg		A	A
Jackson	NH	A	A
Murphy	N	AH	A
Douglas		AH	A
Frankfr		AH	A
Reed		AH	A
Black	G	X	
Vinson			

Benson v Missouri-Kansas-Texas RR
47 321A
332 US 830 47 283A
Texas

Justice	10/25 1947 CERT (1 1)	11/08 1947 CERT (1 2)	11/22 1947 CERT (1 3)
Burton	G		D
Rutledg	GR	G	D
Jackson	G	GR	D
Murphy		G	D
Douglas			D
Frankfr			D
Reed	G		D
Black	G		D
Vinson	X		D

U.S. v Landman
47 325A
332 US 815 47 327A
Ct Cls

Justice	11/08 1947 CERT (1 1)
Burton	G
Rutledg	D
Jackson	
Murphy	G
Douglas	G
Frankfr	D
Reed	D
Black	D
Vinson	

Landman v U.S.
47 327A
332 US 815 47 325A
Ct Cls

Justice	11/08 1947 CERT (1 1)
Burton	G
Rutledg	
Jackson	G
Murphy	G
Douglas	
Frankfr	D
Reed	D
Black	D
Vinson	

Johnson v U.S.
47 329A
333 US 10
Jackson 12/23/47 CCA 9th

Justice	10/25 1947 CERT (1 1)	12/20 1947 MERITS (1 1)	02/02 1948 REPORT (1 1)
Burton	GL	R	R
Rutledg	GL	R	R
Jackson	GL	RQ	R
Murphy	GL	RQ	R
Douglas			A
Frankfr		A	A
Reed			A
Black		A	A
Vinson		A	A

Callen v Pennsylvania RR Company
47 331A
332 US 625
Jackson 12/23/47 CCA 3rd

Justice	10/25 1947 CERT (1 1)	12/20 1947 MERITS (1 1)	01/12 1948 REPORT (1 1)
Burton	G	R	R
Rutledg	D		
Jackson	G	R	R
Murphy	G	X	
Douglas	D		
Frankfr	G	R	R
Reed	G	R	R
Black	D	A	A
Vinson	G	A	A

Connecticut Mutual Life v Moore
47 337A
333 US 541
Reed 12/23/47 New York

Justice	10/18 1947 JURIS (1 1)	12/20 1947 MERITS (1 1)	03/29 1948 REPORT (1 1)
Burton	N	A	A
Rutledg	N	A	A
Jackson	N	R	R
Murphy	N		R
Douglas			
Frankfr		X	A
Reed	N	S	S
Black	A	S	A
Vinson	S	A	A

Knott v Furman
47 339A
332 US 809
CCA 5th

Justice	10/25 1947 CERT (1 1)
Burton	G
Rutledg	G
Jackson	D
Murphy	D
Douglas	D
Frankfr	DQ
Reed	D
Black	
Vinson	

Black v Roland Electric Company
47 340A
333 US 854 47 171A
CCA 4th

Justice	10/25 1947 CERT (1 1)	03/13 1948 CERT (1 2)
Burton	H	D
Rutledg		D
Jackson	H	
Murphy	H	G
Douglas		D
Frankfr		D
Reed	H	D
Black	H	
Vinson	H	D

U.S. v Swiss Confederation
47 342A 47 343A
332 US 815
Ct Cls

Justice	11/08 1947 CERT (1 1)
Burton	D
Rutledg	D
Jackson	D
Murphy	D
Douglas	G
Frankfr	D
Reed	D
Black	D
Vinson	D

F.L. Mendez & Company v General Motors
47 344A
332 US 810
CCA 7th

Justice	10/25 1947 CERT (1 1)
Burton	D
Rutledg	D
Jackson	D
Murphy	D
Douglas	G
Frankfr	D
Reed	D
Black	D
Vinson	D

Watchtower Bible & Tract v Los Angeles
47 346A
332 US 811
California

Justice	10/25 1947 CERT (1 1)
Burton	D
Rutledg	D
Jackson	D
Murphy	D
Douglas	G
Frankfr	D
Reed	D
Black	D
Vinson	D

214

Hermanos v Buscaglia
47 360A
332 US 816
CCA 1st

	11/08 1947 CERT
Burton	
Rutledg	D
Jackson	D
Murphy	D
Douglas	D
Frankfr	
Reed	D
Black	G
Vinson	D

LeMaistre v Lefers
47 362A
333 US 1
Douglas 01/13/48 Florida

	11/08 1947 CERT	01/10 1948 MERITS	02/02 1948 REPORT
Burton	G	R	R
Rutledg	G	R	R
Jackson	G	X	R
Murphy	G		R
Douglas	G	R	R
Frankfr		R	R
Reed	G	R	R
Black	G		
Vinson	G		

Pryor v Craft
47 363A
332 US 816
Oklahoma

	11/08 1947 CERT
Burton	
Rutledg	G
Jackson	D
Murphy	G
Douglas	D
Frankfr	
Reed	D
Black	D
Vinson	D

Downing v Howard
47 365A
332 US 818
CCA 3rd

	11/08 1947 CERT
Burton	
Rutledg	D
Jackson	D
Murphy	D
Douglas	D
Frankfr	
Reed	X
Black	G
Vinson	D

Bay Ridge Operating Company v Aaron
47 366A
334 US 446 47 367A
Reed 01/19/48 CCA 2d

	11/08 1947 CERT	01/17 1948 MERITS	06/07 1948 REPORT
Burton	G	R	R
Rutledg	G	R	Z
Jackson	G	X	Z
Murphy	G	A	
Douglas	G	A	Z
Frankfr		A	R
Reed		A	Z
Black	G		Z
Vinson			

Sipuel v Board Of Regents
47 369A
332 US 631 47 325M
Oklahoma

	11/08 1947 CERT	01/10 1948 MERITS	01/12 1948 REPORT
Burton	G	R	R
Rutledg	G	R	R
Jackson	G	R	R
Murphy	G	R	R
Douglas	G	R	R
Frankfr		R	R
Reed		R	R
Black	G	R	R
Vinson			

Fong Haw Tan v Phelan
47 370A
333 US 6
Douglas 01/13/48 CCA 9th

	11/08 1947 CERT	01/10 1948 MERITS	02/02 1948 REPORT
Burton	G	R	R
Rutledg	G	R	R
Jackson	G	R	R
Murphy	G	R	R
Douglas	G	R	R
Frankfr		R	R
Reed	G	R	R
Black	G	R	R
Vinson	G		

Kreiger v Kreiger
47 371A
334 US 555 47 139A
Douglas 04/26/48 New York

	11/22 1947 CERT	02/07 1948 MERITS	06/07 1948 REPORT
Burton	G		R
Rutledg	G	A	A
Jackson	D	X	
Murphy	G	A	A
Douglas		X	M
Frankfr	D	A	A
Reed	D		A
Black	D	X	A
Vinson	G		

Cole v Arkansas
47 373A
333 US 196
Black 02/13/48 Arkansas

	12/06 1947 CERT	02/09 1948 MERITS	03/08 1948 REPORT
Burton	G	R	R
Rutledg	D	VM	R
Jackson	G	R	R
Murphy	G	R	R
Douglas	G	R	R
Frankfr		R	R
Reed	D	R	R
Black	D		
Vinson	G		

Bob-Lo Excursion v Michigan
47 374A
333 US 28
Rutledg 12/23/47 Michigan

	10/25 1947 JURIS	12/20 1947 MERITS	02/02 1948 REPORT
Burton	N	A	A
Rutledg	N	A	R
Jackson	N		
Murphy	N	A	A
Douglas	N	A	A
Frankfr		A	A
Reed	N	A	A
Black		R	R
Vinson	N		

Miami Tranportation Company v U.S.
47 376A
332 US 803
DC SD Indiana

	10/25 1947 JURIS	10/27 1947 REPORT
Burton	A	A
Rutledg	A	A
Jackson	A	A
Murphy	A	A
Douglas	A	A
Frankfr		A
Reed	A	A
Black	A	A
Vinson	A	

California Apparel Creators v Wieder
47 378A
332 US 816
CCA 2d

	11/08 1947 CERT
Burton	
Rutledg	D
Jackson	D
Murphy	D
Douglas	D
Frankfr	
Reed	G
Black	D
Vinson	G

C.T.H. v South Texas Lumber Company
47 384A
333 US 496
Black 01/19/48 CCA 5th

Justice	CERT 11/22 1947 (1 1)	MERITS 01/17 1948 (1 1)	REPORT 03/29 1948 (1 1)
Burton	G	A	
Rutledg		R	R
Jackson	D	A	R
Murphy			
Douglas	D	X	R
Frankfr		A	
Reed	G	R	R
Black	G	R	R
Vinson	G	R	R

Woods v Stone
47 392A
333 US 472
Jackson 02/13/48 CCA 6th

Justice	CERT 12/06 1947 (1 1)	MERITS 02/09 1948 (1 1)	REPORT 03/15 1948 (1 1)
Burton	GL	R	R
Rutledg	GL	R	R
Jackson	GL	R	R
Murphy	GL	R	R
Douglas	GL	A	R
Frankfr	GL	R	R
Reed	GL	R	R
Black	GL	R	R
Vinson	GL	R	R

Seaboard Air Line RR Company v Daniel
47 390A
333 US 118
Black 01/13/48 South Carolina

Justice	JURIS 10/25 1947 (1 1)	MERITS 01/10 1948 (1 1)	REPORT 02/16 1948 (1 1)
Burton	N	RQ	R
Rutledg	N	R	R
Jackson	N	R	R
Murphy	N	R	R
Douglas	N	R	R
Frankfr	N	R	R
Reed	N	S	R
Black	N	R	R
Vinson	N	R	R

International Teamsters v Denver Milk
47 397A
334 US 809
Colorado

Justice	JURIS 11/08 1947 (1 1)	MERITS 05/01 1948 (1 2)	REPORT 05/03 1948 (1 1)
Burton	N	S	S
Rutledg	N	S	S
Jackson	N	S	S
Murphy	N		
Douglas	N	R	S
Frankfr	N	S	S
Reed	N	S	S
Black	N	R	S
Vinson	N	S	S

Bute v Illinois
47 398A 47 17M
333 US 640
Burton 02/16/48 Illinois

Justice	CERT 10/08 1947 (1 1)	CERT 10/10 1947 (1 2)	MERITS 02/14 1948 (1 1)	REPORT 04/19 1948 (1 1)
Burton	D	G	A	A
Rutledg	D	G	R	R
Jackson	D	G	A	A
Murphy	D	G		
Douglas	D	G	A	A
Frankfr	D	G		
Reed	D	G	A	A
Black	D	G		
Vinson	D	G	A	A

Francis v Southern Pacific Company
47 400A
333 US 445
Douglas 02/13/48 CCA 10th

Justice	CERT 12/06 1947 (1 1)	MERITS 02/09 1948 (1 1)	REPORT 03/15 1948 (1 1)
Burton	G	D	A
Rutledg	G		R
Jackson	G	D	R
Murphy	GO		A
Douglas	G	D	A
Frankfr			A
Reed		D	A
Black	G		A
Vinson		D	

Trust Of Andrus v C.I.R.
47 408A
332 US 830
CCA 2d

Justice	CERT 11/22 1947 (1 1)
Burton	D
Rutledg	D
Jackson	D
Murphy	D
Douglas	D
Frankfr	D
Reed	G
Black	D
Vinson	D

U.S. (Kessler) v Watkins
47 414A
332 US 838
CCA 2d

Justice	CERT 12/06 1947 (1 1)
Burton	D
Rutledg	D
Jackson	D
Murphy	
Douglas	D
Frankfr	
Reed	G
Black	G
Vinson	D

Toomer v Witsell
47 415A
334 US 385
Vinson 01/19/48 DC ED South Carolina

Justice	JURIS 11/22 1947 (1 1)	MERITS 01/17 1948 (1 1)	REPORT 06/07 1948 (1 1)
Burton	N	RQ	R
Rutledg	N	RQ	R
Jackson	N	RQ	R
Murphy	N	R	R
Douglas			R
Frankfr	S		AQ
Reed	N	R	R
Black	N		R
Vinson	N		R

Kuehn v U.S.
47 416A
332 US 837
CCA 9th

Justice	CERT 12/06 1947 (1 1)
Burton	D
Rutledg	G
Jackson	D
Murphy	G
Douglas	D
Frankfr	D
Reed	D
Black	G
Vinson	D

F.W. Woolworth Company v Guerlain
47 419A
332 US 837
New York

Justice	CERT 12/06 1947 (1 1)
Burton	
Rutledg	
Jackson	
Murphy	
Douglas	
Frankfr	
Reed	
Black	
Vinson	G

C.I.R. v Wilson
47 420A
332 US 842
CCA 9th

Justice	CERT 12/13 1947 (1 1)
Burton	D
Rutledg	G
Jackson	D
Murphy	G
Douglas	D
Frankfr	D
Reed	D
Black	G
Vinson	D

C.I.R. v Wiesler
47 421A
332 US 842
CCA 6th

Justice	CERT 12/13 1947 (1 1)
Burton	D
Rutledg	D
Jackson	
Murphy	G
Douglas	D
Frankfr	D
Reed	
Black	G
Vinson	

Texas Company v Montgomery
47 423A
332 US 827
DC ED Louisiana

Justice	JURIS 11/22 1947 (1 1)	REPORT 11/24 1947 (1 1)
Burton	A	A
Rutledg	A	A
Jackson	A	A
Murphy	A	A
Douglas	A	A
Frankfr	A	A
Reed	A	A
Black	S	A
Vinson	A	A

Trupiano v U.S.
47 427A
334 US 699
Frankfr 03/26/48 Murphy 04/14/48 CCA 3rd

Justice	CERT 12/13 1947 (1 1)	MERITS 03/13 1948 (1 1)	REPORT 06/14 1948 (1 1)
Burton	G	R	R
Rutledg	G	R	R
Jackson	G	R	R
Murphy	G	R	R
Douglas	G	R	R
Frankfr	G	R	R
Reed			
Black			
Vinson			

Parker v Illinois
47 428A
334 US 816   47 270A
Illinois
Black 02/16/48

Justice	CERT 12/20 1947 (1 1)
Burton	G D
Rutledg	
Jackson	G D
Murphy	G
Douglas	G D
Frankfr	
Reed	
Black	G D
Vinson	G

Andres v U.S.
47 431A
333 US 740
Reed 02/13/48 CCA 9th

Justice	CERT 12/20 1947 (1 1)	CERT 01/03 1948 (1 2)	MERITS 02/14 1948 (1 1)	MERITS 03/13 1948 (1 2)	REPORT 05/17 1948 (1 1)	REHEAR 06/05 1948 (1 1)
Burton	G	D	R	R	A	
Rutledg	GQ		S			
Jackson	G				R	Y
Murphy	G	D	R	R		Y
Douglas	G	D				
Frankfr		D	R	R	A	B
Reed			A	A	A	B
Black	G	D	A	A	R	Y
Vinson	G		A	A		B

U.S. v Zazove
47 432A
334 US 602
Vinson 04/26/48 CCA 7th

Justice	CERT 12/06 1947 (1 1)
Burton	G A
Rutledg	G
Jackson	G
Murphy	G
Douglas	G
Frankfr	G
Reed	G
Black	A
Vinson	A

Woods v Hills
47 437A
334 US 210
Vinson 01/19/48 CCA 10th

Justice	QUEST 01/17 1948 (1 1)
Burton	B
Rutledg	B
Jackson	B
Murphy	B
Douglas	B
Frankfr	B
Reed	B
Black	B
Vinson	B

Traffic Telephone Workers' v Driscoll
47 438A
332 US 833
DC New Jersey

Justice	JURIS 12/06 1947 (1 1)	REPORT 04/26 1948 (1 1)
Burton	S	R
Rutledg	S	R
Jackson	S	R
Murphy	S	R
Douglas	N	R
Frankfr		R
Reed	N	R
Black	N	R
Vinson	S	

Ahrens v Clark
47 446A
335 US 188
Douglas 04/02/48 CCA DC

Justice	CERT 01/17 1948 (1 1)	MERITS 04/24 1948 (1 1)	REPORT 06/14 1948 (1 1)
Burton	G	R	R
Rutledg	D	R	R
Jackson	D	X	R
Murphy	D	R	R
Douglas	D	AQ	AQ
Frankfr	D		
Reed	D	R	R
Black	D		R
Vinson	D	R	R

Comstock v Group Of Investors
47 451A
335 US 211   47 452A 47 453A 47 454A
Murphy 03/15/48 Jackson 06/14/48 CCA 8th

Justice	CERT 01/03 1948 (1 2)	MERITS 04/02 1948 (1 1)	REPORT 06/21 1948 (1 1)
Burton	X	R	R
Rutledg	D		
Jackson	G		
Murphy	X	R	R
Douglas	G		
Frankfr	G		
Reed	G G		
Black	G	R	R
Vinson	D	R	R

Shade v Downing
47 448A
333 US 586
Douglas 03/15/48 CCA 10th

Justice	QUEST 01/17 1948 (2 1)	REPORT 05/10 1948 (2 1)	QUEST 03/13 1948 (1 1)	REPORT 04/05 1948 (1 1)
Burton	B	B	B	B
Rutledg	B	B	BQ	B
Jackson		B	Y	Y
Murphy	B	B	B X	B
Douglas	S	B	B	B
Frankfr		B		
Reed	B	B	B	B
Black	B	B	B	B
Vinson		B		Y

Marden & Murphy v City Of Lowell
47 449A
332 US 850
Massachusetts

Justice	CERT 01/10 1948 (1 1)	JURIS 01/10 1948 (1 1)	JURIS 01/31 1948 (1 2)	MERITS 04/02 1948 (1 1)	REPORT 06/21 1948 (1 1)
Burton	G	N	G	R	A
Rutledg	D	S	D	R	A
Jackson	D	S	G	R	A
Murphy	D	S	G		
Douglas	D	S	D	R	A
Frankfr	D	S	D		
Reed	D		G		
Black	D		G		
Vinson	D		D		

C.I.R. v California & Hawaiian Sugar
47 455A
332 US 846 47 456A
CCA 9th

	01/03 1948 CERT	
	1	1
Burton		D
Rutledg		D
Jackson		
Murphy	G	D
Douglas		D
Frankfr		D
Reed		
Black	G	D
Vinson		D

U.S. v Columbia Steel Company
47 461A
334 US 495
Reed 05/05/48 DC Delaware

	12/20 1947 JURIS		05/01 1948 MERITS		06/07 1948 REPORT	
	1	1	1	1	1	1
Burton	N			A		A
Rutledg	N		R	A	R	A
Jackson	N		R	A	R	A
Murphy	N			X		
Douglas	N			A		A
Frankfr	N		R	A	R	A
Reed	N					
Black	N		R	A	R	A
Vinson	N			A		A

F.T.C. v Morton Salt
47 464A
334 US 37
Black 03/15/48 CCA 7th

	01/10 1948 CERT		03/13 1948 MERITS		05/03 1948 REPORT	
	1	1	1	1	1	1
Burton	G		R		R	
Rutledg	G		R	A	R	A
Jackson	G		R		R	
Murphy	G		R	A	R	A
Douglas	G		R	X	R	
Frankfr	G		R		R	
Reed	G		R	A	R	A
Black	G		R	A	R	A
Vinson	G		R		R	

Bruszewski v Isthmian Steamship Company
47 475A
333 US 828
CCA 3rd

	01/31 1948 CERT	
	1	1
Burton		D
Rutledg	G	
Jackson		D
Murphy		D
Douglas	G	
Frankfr		D
Reed		D
Black	G	
Vinson		X

Hanson v Triangle Publications
47 478A
332 US 855
CCA 8th

	01/17 1948 CERT	
	1	1
Burton		D
Rutledg		D
Jackson		
Murphy	G	
Douglas		D
Frankfr		D
Reed		D
Black	G	
Vinson		D

S.E.C. v Philadephia Company
47 480A
333 US 828
CCA DC

	01/31 1948 CERT	
	1	1
Burton		
Rutledg		D
Jackson	GQ	
Murphy		D
Douglas	G	
Frankfr		
Reed		
Black	G	
Vinson		D

Moore v New York
47 485A 47 222M
333 US 565
Jackson 02/16/48 New York

	12/20 1947 CERT		02/14 1948 MERITS		03/29 1948 REPORT	
	1	1	1	1	1	1
Burton	G			A		A
Rutledg		D				
Jackson	G		X		R	
Murphy	G			X		
Douglas		D		A		A
Frankfr		D	R	A	R	A
Reed	G			A		A
Black		D		A		A
Vinson			R		R	

Woods v Cloyd W. Miller Company
47 486A
333 US 138
Douglas 02/13/48 DC ND Ohio

	01/10 1948 JURIS		02/09 1948 MERITS		02/16 1948 REPORT	
	1	1	1	1	1	1
Burton	N		R		R	
Rutledg	N		R		R	
Jackson	N		R		R	
Murphy	N		R		R	
Douglas	N		R		R	
Frankfr	N		R		R	
Reed	N		R		R	
Black	N		R		R	
Vinson	N		R		R	

West v Oklahoma Tax Commission
47 489A
334 US 717 47 490A
Murphy 04/02/48 Oklahoma

	01/17 1948 JURIS		04/02 1948 MERITS		06/14 1948 REPORT	
	1	S	1	1	1	1
Burton	N			A		A
Rutledg	N			A		A
Jackson	N		R		R	
Murphy	N			A		A
Douglas	N			A		A
Frankfr	N		R		R	
Reed	N	S				
Black	N			X		
Vinson	N	S		A		A

Flakowicz v Alexander
47 494A
333 US 828
CCA 2d

	01/31 1948 CERT	
	1	1
Burton		D
Rutledg		D
Jackson		D
Murphy	G	
Douglas		D
Frankfr		D
Reed		D
Black		D
Vinson		D

Foremen's Association v L.A. Young
47 502A
333 US 837
CCA DC

	02/14 1948 CERT	
	1	1
Burton		D
Rutledg		D
Jackson		D
Murphy		D
Douglas		D
Frankfr		D
Reed		D
Black	G	D
Vinson		D

Saia v New York
47 504A
334 US 558
Frankfr 04/02/48 Douglas 06/01/48 New York

	01/31 1948 JURIS		04/02 1948 MERITS		06/07 1948 REPORT	
	1	1	1	1	1	1
Burton	N		R	A	R	A
Rutledg				A		A
Jackson			R	A	R	A
Murphy	N			A		A
Douglas	N			A		A
Frankfr	N		R	A	R	A
Reed				A		A
Black	N			A		A
Vinson	N		R	A	R	A

A.B.T. Manufacturing v National Slug
47 506A
333 US 832
CCA 7th

	02/07 1948 CERT 1	1
Burton		D
Rutledg	G	
Jackson		D
Murphy		D
Douglas		D
Frankfr		D
Reed		D
Black	G	
Vinson		D

Randall v U.S.
47 509A
333 US 856 47 555A
CCA 7th

	03/13 1948 CERT 1	1
Burton	G	
Rutledg		D
Jackson		D
Murphy		D
Douglas		D
Frankfr	G	
Reed		D
Black		D
Vinson		D

Williams v Atchison Topeka RR Company
47 512A
333 US 854 47 513A 47 514A
Missouri

	02/14 1948 CERT 1	1	03/13 1948 CERT 1	2
Burton		D		D
Rutledg	G			D
Jackson		D		D
Murphy		D		D
Douglas		D		D
Frankfr		D		D
Reed		D		D
Black		D		D
Vinson		D		D

Fook v U.S.
47 519A
333 US 838
CCA DC

	02/14 1948 CERT 1	1
Burton		D
Rutledg	G	
Jackson		D
Murphy	G	
Douglas		D
Frankfr		D
Reed		D
Black		D
Vinson		D

Shurin v U.S.
47 521A
333 US 837
CCA 4th

	02/14 1948 CERT 1	1
Burton		D
Rutledg	G	
Jackson		D
Murphy		D
Douglas		D
Frankfr		D
Reed		D
Black	G	
Vinson		D

Root v Wolferman
47 522A
333 US 837
Missouri

	02/14 1948 CERT 1	1
Burton		D
Rutledg	G	
Jackson		D
Murphy	G	
Douglas	G	
Frankfr		D
Reed		D
Black		D
Vinson		D

U.S. v Kruszewski
47 526A
333 US 880
CCA 7th

	04/24 1948 CERT 1	1
Burton		D
Rutledg		D
Jackson		D
Murphy	G	
Douglas		D
Frankfr		D
Reed		D
Black		D
Vinson		D

U.S. v U.S. District Court
47 527A 47 303A
334 US 258
Douglas 04/26/48 CCA 2d

	03/06 1948 CERT 1	1	04/24 1948 MERITS 1	1	05/24 1948 REPORT 1	1
Burton	G		R		R	
Rutledg	G		R		R	
Jackson						
Murphy						
Douglas	G		R		R	
Frankfr	G		R		R	
Reed				X	R	
Black	G		R		R	
Vinson	G		R		R	

Joint Council v Southern Pacific
47 528A
333 US 838
CCA 9th

	02/14 1948 CERT 1	1
Burton		D
Rutledg	G	
Jackson		D
Murphy		D
Douglas		
Frankfr		D
Reed		D
Black		D
Vinson		D

Briggs v Pennsylvania RR Company
47 530A
334 US 304
Jackson 04/02/48 CCA 2d

	02/14 1948 CERT 1	1	04/02 1948 MERITS 1	1	05/24 1948 REPORT 1	1
Burton	G			A		A
Rutledg		X		X	R	
Jackson		D		A		A
Murphy	G		R		R	
Douglas	G			A	R	
Frankfr		D		X		A
Reed	G			A		A
Black	G		R		R	
Vinson	G			A		A

Kott v U.S.
47 532A
333 US 858
CCA 5th

	02/14 1948 CERT 1	1	03/13 1948 REHEAR 1	1
Burton		D	B	
Rutledg		D	B	
Jackson		D	B	
Murphy		D	B	
Douglas		D	B	
Frankfr		D		X
Reed		D		Y
Black		D		Y
Vinson		D	B	

Takahashi v Fish & Game Commission
47 533A
334 US 410
Black 05/10/48 California

	03/13 1948 CERT 1	1	04/24 1948 MERITS 1	1	06/07 1948 REPORT 1	1
Burton	G		R		R	
Rutledg	G		R		R	
Jackson	G			AQ		A
Murphy	G		R		R	
Douglas	G		R		R	
Frankfr	G		R		R	
Reed	G			A		A
Black	G		R		R	
Vinson	G		R		R	

Kennedy v Tennessee
47 534A
333 US 846
Tennessee

	02/14 1948 CERT 1	1	03/06 1948 CERT 1	2
Burton		X		D
Rutledg	G		G	
Jackson		D		D
Murphy	G		G	
Douglas		D		D
Frankfr		D		D
Reed		D		D
Black	G		G	
Vinson		D		D

Josephson v U.S.
47 535A
333 US 858
CCA 2d

	02/14 1948 CERT 1	1	03/13 1948 REHEAR 1	1
Burton		D	B	
Rutledg	G		B	
Jackson		D	B	
Murphy	G		B	
Douglas	G			Y
Frankfr		D	B	
Reed		D	B	
Black		D	B	
Vinson		D	B	

Gryger v Burke
47 541A 47 53M
334 US 728 47 542A
Jackson 05/10/48 Pennsylvania

	10/08 1947 CERT 1	1	01/17 1948 CERT 1	2	05/01 1948 MERITS 1	1	06/14 1948 REPORT 1	1
Burton		D		D		A		A
Rutledg	E		G		R		R	
Jackson		D		D		A		A
Murphy	GE		G		R		R	
Douglas	E		G		R		R	
Frankfr		D		D		A		A
Reed		D		D		A		A
Black	GE		G		R		R	
Vinson		D		D		A		A

Townsend v Burke
47 542A 47 55M
334 US 736 47 541A
Jackson 05/10/48 Pennsylvania

Justice	10/08 1947 CERT 1 1	01/17 1948 CERT 1 1	05/01 1948 MERITS 1 1	06/14 1948 REPORT 1 1
Burton				
Rutledg	E	G	R	R
Jackson	E	G	R A	R A
Murphy		G	R	R A
Douglas		D		
Frankfr	E	D	R A	R A
Reed		D		R
Black	E	G	R	
Vinson		D	R A	R A

U.S. v National City Lines
47 544A
334 US 573
Rutledg 05/05/48 DC SD California

Justice	02/07 1948 JURIS 1 1	05/01 1948 MERITS 1 1	06/07 1948 REPORT 1 1
Burton	N	R	R
Rutledg	N	R A	R A
Jackson	N	R	R
Murphy	N	R	R
Douglas	N		
Frankfr	N	R	R
Reed	N	R	R
Black	N		
Vinson	N		

Indiana (Mavity) v Tyndall
47 545A
333 US 834
Indiana

Justice	02/14 1948 JURIS 1 1
Burton	P S
Rutledg	S
Jackson	S
Murphy	
Douglas	P S
Frankfr	S
Reed	S
Black	S
Vinson	S

Hackbusch v U.S.
47 555A
333 US 856 47 509A
CCA 7th

Justice	03/13 1948 CERT 1 1
Burton	
Rutledg	G
Jackson	D
Murphy	D
Douglas	D
Frankfr	
Reed	G
Black	D
Vinson	D

General Motors v Kesling
47 558A
333 US 855
CCA 8th

Justice	03/13 1948 CERT 1 1
Burton	
Rutledg	G
Jackson	D
Murphy	D
Douglas	D
Frankfr	D
Reed	
Black	G
Vinson	G

Hilton v Sullivan
47 560A
334 US 323
Black 04/26/48 CCA DC

Justice	03/06 1948 CERT 1 1	04/24 1948 MERITS 1 1	06/01 1948 REPORT 1 1
Burton	G	RQ A	A
Rutledg	G	R	A
Jackson	G	R	A
Murphy	G		A
Douglas	G	X	A
Frankfr	G		A
Reed	G		A
Black			A
Vinson	G		A

Aspinook v Bright
47 569A
333 US 846 47 347M
CCA 2d

Justice	03/06 1948 CERT 1 1
Burton	D
Rutledg	D
Jackson	D
Murphy	D
Douglas	D
Frankfr	D
Reed	G
Black	D
Vinson	D

Meyer v Hawaii
47 571A
333 US 860
CCA 9th

Justice	03/27 1948 CERT 1 1
Burton	D
Rutledg	D
Jackson	D
Murphy	D
Douglas	D
Frankfr	D
Reed	G
Black	D
Vinson	D

Grimes v Capital Transit Company
47 573A
333 US 845
CCA DC

Justice	03/06 1948 CERT 1 1
Burton	D
Rutledg	G
Jackson	D
Murphy	D
Douglas	G
Frankfr	G
Reed	D
Black	D
Vinson	D

Gottfried v U.S.
47 561A
333 US 860 47 562A
CCA 2d

Justice	03/27 1948 CERT 1 1
Burton	
Rutledg	D
Jackson	D
Murphy	
Douglas	GL
Frankfr	
Reed	G
Black	D
Vinson	D

Sikora Realty v Woods
47 563A
333 US 855
CCA Emergency

Justice	03/06 1948 CERT 1 1	03/13 1948 CERT 1 2	06/05 1948 REHEAR 1 1
Burton	G	G	B YQ
Rutledg	D	D	B
Jackson	D	D	B
Murphy	G	G	B
Douglas	G	G	B
Frankfr	G		B
Reed	D	D	B
Black	D	D	B
Vinson			

Summers v McCoy
47 564A
333 US 855
CCA 6th

Justice	03/13 1948 CERT 1 1
Burton	G
Rutledg	D
Jackson	G
Murphy	D
Douglas	G
Frankfr	D
Reed	D
Black	D
Vinson	D

Bornhurst v U.S.
47 574A
333 US 867
CCA 9th

	04/02 1948 CERT (1 1)
Burton	D
Rutledg	
Jackson	D
Murphy	D
Douglas	
Frankfr	D
Reed	
Black	D
Vinson	

Paterno v Lyons
47 583A 47 233M
334 US 314
Black 05/05/48 New York

	02/07 1948 CERT (1 2)	05/01 1948 MERITS (1 1)	06/03 1948 REPORT (1 1)
Burton	G D	R A	R A
Rutledg	G		
Jackson	G G	R A	R A
Murphy			
Douglas	G	SA A	SA A
Frankfr			
Reed	G	R A	R A
Black		S	S
Vinson	G D	A A	A A

U.S. (Ackermann) v O'Rourke
47 584A
334 US 858 47 585A
CCA 5th

	06/18 1948 CERT (1 1)
Burton	D D
Rutledg	
Jackson	D
Murphy	
Douglas	D
Frankfr	
Reed	D
Black	
Vinson	D

Kosdon v Diversey Hotel
47 587A
333 US 861
CCA 7th

	03/27 1948 CERT (1 1)
Burton	D
Rutledg	
Jackson	D
Murphy	D
Douglas	D
Frankfr	G
Reed	
Black	D
Vinson	D

Steele v Superior Court California
47 589A
333 US 861
CCA 9th

	03/27 1948 CERT (1 1)
Burton	D
Rutledg	
Jackson	D
Murphy	
Douglas	D
Frankfr	G
Reed	D
Black	D
Vinson	D

Baltimore & Ohio RR Company v Plough
47 595A
333 US 861 47 596A 47 597A 47 598A
CCA 2d

	03/27 1948 CERT (1 1)
Burton	D
Rutledg	D
Jackson	D
Murphy	D
Douglas	
Frankfr	
Reed	G
Black	D
Vinson	D

Full Salvation Union v Portage
47 609A
333 US 851
Michigan

	03/13 1948 JURIS (1 1)
Burton	
Rutledg	
Jackson	P S
Murphy	S
Douglas	S
Frankfr	N
Reed	
Black	
Vinson	S

Loew's v William Goldman Theaters
47 611A
334 US 811
CCA 3rd

	04/02 1948 CERT (1 1)	05/01 1948 CERT (1 2)
Burton	D	D
Rutledg	D	D
Jackson	D	D
Murphy	D	
Douglas	D	
Frankfr	G	G
Reed	D	D
Black	D	D
Vinson	D	D

Kennedy v Silas Mason Company
47 590A
334 US 249
Jackson 04/26/48 CCA 5th

	03/06 1948 CERT (1 1)	04/24 1948 MERITS (1 1)	05/17 1948 REPORT (1 1)
Burton	G	RV	V
Rutledg	G	R	V
Jackson	G	RV	V
Murphy	G	R	V
Douglas	G	RV	V
Frankfr	G	RV	V
Reed	G	R	R
Black	G	R	V
Vinson	G	RV	V

Reeder v Banks
47 618A
333 US 858
Oklahoma

	03/27 1948 JURIS (1 1)
Burton	
Rutledg	
Jackson	S
Murphy	S
Douglas	S
Frankfr	N
Reed	S
Black	S
Vinson	S

Anderson v Atchison Topeka RR
47 620A
333 US 821
California

	03/27 1948 CERT (1 1)	04/26 1948 REPORT (1 1)
Burton	GR	R
Rutledg	GR	R
Jackson		R
Murphy	GR	R
Douglas	D	R
Frankfr		R
Reed	GR	R
Black	GR	R
Vinson	D	R

DeLano v Michigan
47 623A
334 US 818
Michigan

	05/15 1948 CERT (1 1)
Burton	D
Rutledg	
Jackson	
Murphy	G
Douglas	G
Frankfr	
Reed	D
Black	D
Vinson	D

King v Priest
47 630A · 333 US 852 · Missouri

Justice	03/13 1948 JURIS (1 1)	(S)
Burton		S
Rutledg	N	
Jackson		S
Murphy	N	
Douglas	X	
Frankfr		
Reed		S
Black		S
Vinson		S

Brown v U.S.
47 632A · 333 US 873 · CCA 3rd

Justice	04/17 1948 CERT (1 1)
Burton	D
Rutledg	D
Jackson	D
Murphy	D
Douglas	D
Frankfr	D
Reed	G
Black	D
Vinson	X

Hunter v Martin
47 643A · 334 US 302 · Jackson 04/26/48 · CCA 2d

Justice	03/13 1948 CERT (1 1)
Burton	G
Rutledg	G
Jackson	G
Murphy	G
Douglas	G
Frankfr	G
Reed	G
Black	G
Vinson	X

Miller v Texas Company
47 646A · 333 US 880 · CCA 5th

Justice	04/24 1948 CERT (1 1)
Burton	D
Rutledg	D
Jackson	D
Murphy	D
Douglas	G
Frankfr	D
Reed	D
Black	D
Vinson	D

National Nugrape Company v Guest
47 654A · 333 US 874 · CCA 10th

Justice	04/17 1948 CERT (1 1)
Burton	D
Rutledg	D
Jackson	D
Murphy	D
Douglas	D
Frankfr	D
Reed	G
Black	D
Vinson	D

Phyle v Duffy
47 655A 47 395M · 334 US 431 · Black 04/26/48 · California

Justice	03/06 1948 CERT (1 1)	05/24 1948 REPORT (1 1)
Burton	G	R
Rutledg	G	R
Jackson	G	R
Murphy	G	R
Douglas		R
Frankfr		R
Reed		R
Black		R
Vinson		

U.S. (Weddeke) v Watkins
47 657A · 333 US 876 · CCA 2d

Justice	04/17 1948 CERT (1 1)
Burton	GO
Rutledg	GO
Jackson	
Murphy	G
Douglas	GO
Frankfr	
Reed	D
Black	D
Vinson	D

Randolph v Missouri-Kansas-Texas RR
47 661A · 334 US 818 47 711A · CCA 8th

Justice	05/07 1948 CERT (1 1)	05/15 1948 (1 2)
Burton	DQ	D
Rutledg		
Jackson	X	
Murphy	G	G
Douglas		
Frankfr	G	G
Reed	D	D
Black	D	D
Vinson	D	D

U.S. v Cold Metal Process Company
47 663A · 334 US 811 · CCA 6th

Justice	04/24 1948 CERT (1 1)	06/07 1948 REPORT (1 1)
Burton	G	S
Rutledg	G	S
Jackson	G	S
Murphy	G	S
Douglas		S
Frankfr		S
Reed		
Black		
Vinson		

Rice v Elmore
47 668A · 333 US 875 · CCA 4th

Justice	04/17 1948 CERT (1 1)
Burton	D
Rutledg	D
Jackson	D
Murphy	G
Douglas	D
Frankfr	G
Reed	D
Black	D
Vinson	D

Cargill v Board Of Trade
47 671A · 333 US 880 · CCA 7th

Justice	04/24 1948 CERT (1 1)
Burton	D
Rutledg	D
Jackson	D
Murphy	D
Douglas	G
Frankfr	D
Reed	D
Black	D
Vinson	D

Hedgebeth v North Carolina
47 674A 47 319M · 334 US 806 47 542A · Frankfr 05/10/48 · North Carolina

Justice	03/13 1948 CERT (1 1)	05/01 1948 MERITS (1 1)	06/14 1948 REPORT (1 1)
Burton	G		S
Rutledg	G	R	R
Jackson	G	R	
Murphy	G		R
Douglas	G	A	S
Frankfr	G	A	S
Reed	G	X	S
Black	G	A	S
Vinson		A	S

Joseph F. Hughes & Company v Machen
47 684A · 333 US 881 · CCA 4th

Justice	04/24 1948 CERT (1 1)
Burton	D
Rutledg	D
Jackson	D
Murphy	D
Douglas	D
Frankfr	D
Reed	D
Black	G
Vinson	D

Betz v Board Of Trade Of Chicago
47 685A · 333 US 881 · CCA 7th

Justice	04/24 1948 CERT (1 1)
Burton	D
Rutledg	D
Jackson	D
Murphy	D
Douglas	D
Frankfr	D
Reed	D
Black	G
Vinson	D

Samett v Reconstruction Finance
47 686A · 334 US 812 · CCA 10th

Justice	05/01 1948 CERT (1 1)
Burton	D
Rutledg	D
Jackson	D
Murphy	D
Douglas	D
Frankfr	D
Reed	D
Black	G
Vinson	D

Chicago Mines Company v C.I.R.
47 691A
333 US 881 47 692A 47 693A
CCA 10th

Justice	04/24 1948 CERT 1 1
Burton	G
Rutledg	D
Jackson	D
Murphy	D
Douglas	
Frankfr	D
Reed	G
Black	G
Vinson	D

Waite v Overlade
47 694A
334 US 812
CCA 7th

Justice	05/01 1948 CERT 1 1
Burton	
Rutledg	G
Jackson	G
Murphy	
Douglas	
Frankfr	G
Reed	
Black	
Vinson	

U.S. v CIO
47 695A
335 US 106
Reed 05/10/48 DC DC

Justice	03/27 1948 JURIS 1 1	06/21 1948 REPORT 1 1
Burton	N	A
Rutledg	N	A
Jackson	N	A
Murphy		A
Douglas		A
Frankfr		A
Reed	N	A
Black	N	A
Vinson	N	A

Burrows v Hagerman
47 705A
334 US 817
Florida

Justice	05/15 1948 JURIS 1 1
Burton	
Rutledg	S
Jackson	S
Murphy	N
Douglas	
Frankfr	
Reed	N
Black	S
Vinson	S

Missouri-Kansas-Texas RR v Randolph
47 711A
334 US 818 47 661A
CCA 8th

Justice	05/07 1948 CERT 1 1	05/15 1948 CERT 1 2
Burton		D
Rutledg	DQ	D
Jackson	X	
Murphy	G	
Douglas	D	G
Frankfr		
Reed	G	G
Black	D	D
Vinson	D	D

Taylor v Alabama
47 721A 47 400M
335 US 252
Burton 05/05/48 Alabama

Justice	04/02 1948 CERT 1 1	05/04 1948 MERITS 1 1	06/21 1948 REPORT 1 1
Burton	G		
Rutledg	G	R	A
Jackson			
Murphy	G	R	R
Douglas	D	R	R
Frankfr	D		
Reed	G	A	A
Black	X		
Vinson	D	A	A

Lovelady v Texas
47 722A 47 415M
333 US 879
Texas

Justice	04/02 1948 CERT 1 1
Burton	
Rutledg	D
Jackson	
Murphy	G
Douglas	G
Frankfr	G
Reed	
Black	D
Vinson	D

U.S. v Sunswick
47 713A
334 US 827
Ct Cls

Justice	05/22 1948 CERT 1 1
Burton	
Rutledg	D
Jackson	D
Murphy	G
Douglas	G
Frankfr	
Reed	
Black	
Vinson	G

Ludecke v Watkins
47 723A 47 147M
335 US 160
Frankfr 05/10/48 CCA 2d

Justice	12/20 1947 CERT 1 1	01/03 1948 CERT 1 2	01/31 1948 STAY 1 1	04/26 1948 REPORT 1 1
Burton	D	D	G	SI
Rutledg	D	D	G	SI
Jackson			G	SI
Murphy	G	G	X	SI
Douglas	G	G	G	SI
Frankfr	D	G	G	SI
Reed	D	G	G	SI
Black	D	D	G	SI
Vinson	D	D	G	SI

Goodwin v U.S.
47 724A
334 US 828
CCA 8th

Justice	05/22 1948 CERT 1 1	06/21 1948 REPORT 1 1
Burton		A
Rutledg	D	A
Jackson		R
Murphy	G	R
Douglas	G	R
Frankfr		A
Reed	D	A
Black	D	A
Vinson	D	A

Cohen Friedlander v Massachusetts Life
47 743A
334 US 820
CCA 6th

Justice	01/31 1948 REHEAR 1 1	04/05 1948 REHEAR 1 2	05/15 1948 CERT 1 1
Burton	B	B	
Rutledg	Y	Y	D
Jackson	Y	Y	
Murphy	B	B	G
Douglas	B	B	G
Frankfr	Y	Y	
Reed	B	B	D
Black	B	B	D
Vinson	B	B	D

Trosclair v Stanolind Oil & Gas
47 744A
334 US 820
CCA 5th

Justice	05/15 1948 CERT 1 1
Burton	
Rutledg	D
Jackson	
Murphy	G
Douglas	D
Frankfr	
Reed	D
Black	D
Vinson	D

Wagner v U.S.
47 749A 47 153M
333 US 870
CCA 5th

Justice	04/17 1948 CERT 1 1	04/19 1948 REPORT 1 1
Burton	GRM	R
Rutledg	GRM	R
Jackson	GRM	R
Murphy	GRM	R
Douglas	GRM	R
Frankfr	GRM	R
Reed	GRM	
Black		
Vinson	GRM	R

Downs v C.I.R.
47 764A
334 US 832 47 765A
CCA 9th

Justice	05/28 1948 CERT 1 1
Burton	
Rutledg	D
Jackson	GO
Murphy	G
Douglas	
Frankfr	G
Reed	
Black	D
Vinson	D

Hoofnel v C.I.R.
47 765A
334 US 833 47 764A
CCA 9th

Justice	05/28 1948 CERT 1 1
Burton	
Rutledg	D
Jackson	GO
Murphy	G
Douglas	
Frankfr	G
Reed	
Black	D
Vinson	D

Barsky v U.S.
47 766A · 339 US 971 · CCA DC

Justice	06/11 1948 CERT 1 1
Minton	
Burton	
Rutledg	G
Jackson	D
Murphy	D
Douglas	D
Frankfr	
Reed	D
Black	D
Vinson	GQ

Eubanks v Thompson
47 775A · 334 US 854 · Arkansas

Justice	06/05 1948 CERT 1 1	06/18 1948 MERITS 1 1	06/21 1948 REPORT 1 1
Burton	GR	R	R
Rutledg	GR	R	R
Jackson	GR	R	R
Murphy	GR	R	R
Douglas	GR	R A	R
Frankfr			R
Reed	GR	R	R
Black	GR	R	R
Vinson	GR	R	R

Land O'Lakes Dairy v Village Of Sebeka
47 777A · 334 US 844 · Minnesota

Justice	06/11 1948 CERT 1 1
Burton	
Rutledg	G
Jackson	D
Murphy	D
Douglas	
Frankfr	
Reed	D
Black	
Vinson	D

Shapero v C.I.R.
47 779A · 334 US 844 · CCA 6th

Justice	06/11 1948 CERT 1 1
Burton	
Rutledg	D
Jackson	D
Murphy	D
Douglas	
Frankfr	
Reed	G
Black	D
Vinson	D

Whitin Machine Works v Reynolds
47 784A · 334 US 844 · CCA 4th

Justice	06/11 1948 CERT 1 1
Burton	
Rutledg	
Jackson	G
Murphy	D
Douglas	D
Frankfr	
Reed	
Black	G
Vinson	

Reynolds Metals Company v Skinner
47 797A · 334 US 858 · CCA 6th

Justice	06/11 1948 CERT 1 1	06/18 1948 CERT 1 2
Burton	G	D
Rutledg	D	D
Jackson	D	D
Murphy	D	D
Douglas		
Frankfr		
Reed	G	G
Black	G	G
Vinson	D	D

DeBardeleben Coal v Ott
47 802A · 334 US 858 47 803A · CCA 5th

Justice	06/18 1948 CERT 1 1
Burton	
Rutledg	D
Jackson	D
Murphy	G
Douglas	
Frankfr	
Reed	D
Black	D
Vinson	D

Glassey v Horrall
47 805A · 334 US 859 · California

Justice	06/18 1948 CERT 1 1
Burton	
Rutledg	
Jackson	G
Murphy	G
Douglas	
Frankfr	
Reed	G
Black	D
Vinson	D

National Maritime Union v Herzog
47 808A · 334 US 854 · DC DC

Justice	06/18 1948 JURIS 1 1	06/21 1948 REPORT 1 1
Burton	A	A
Rutledg	A	A
Jackson	A	A
Murphy	A	A
Douglas		
Frankfr	N	N
Reed		
Black	N	N
Vinson	A	A

Richardson v Ragen
47 66M · 334 US 847 47 141M · Illinois

Justice	10/08 1947 CERT 1 1	06/11 1948 CERT 1 2
Burton		D
Rutledg	E	D
Jackson	E	D
Murphy	E	
Douglas		D
Frankfr		D
Reed	E	D
Black		D
Vinson		D

Krell v Ragen
47 75M · 332 US 847 · Illinois

Justice	10/11 1947 CERT 1 1	01/03 1948 CERT 1 2
Burton		D
Rutledg	E	D
Jackson	E	D
Murphy	E	
Douglas		D
Frankfr		D
Reed	E	D
Black		D
Vinson		D

Ott v Mississippi
47 818A · 334 US 859 47 819A 47 826A · CCA 5th

Justice	06/18 1948 CERT 1 1
Burton	
Rutledg	GQ
Jackson	
Murphy	G
Douglas	
Frankfr	
Reed	D
Black	D
Vinson	D

Milch v U.S.
47 50M · 332 US 789

Justice	10/20 1947 HABEAS 1 1
Burton	
Rutledg	K
Jackson	
Murphy	K
Douglas	K
Frankfr	
Reed	
Black	K
Vinson	D

Bauer v Clark
47 81M · 332 US 839 · CCA 7th

Justice	12/06 1947 CERT 1 1
Burton	D
Rutledg	D
Jackson	D
Murphy	D
Douglas	
Frankfr	
Reed	G
Black	G
Vinson	D

McKay v Foster
47 65M · 332 US 783 · Georgia

Justice	10/08 1947 CERT 1 1
Burton	
Rutledg	D
Jackson	D
Murphy	
Douglas	
Frankfr	
Reed	G
Black	
Vinson	

Maxwell v Hudspeth
47 82M
332 US 752

Justice	10/08 1947 CERT 1 1
Burton	D
Rutledg	D
Jackson	D
Murphy	
Douglas	D
Frankfr	D
Reed	
Black	E
Vinson	D

Bowery v Hartford Accident
47 86M
332 US 838
Missouri

Justice	12/06 1947 CERT 1 1
Burton	D
Rutledg	D
Jackson	D
Murphy	D
Douglas	D
Frankfr	D
Reed	D
Black	
Vinson	D

Chavis v Pennsylvania
47 115M
332 US 811
Pennsylvania

Justice	10/25 1947 CERT 1 1
Burton	
Rutledg	G
Jackson	
Murphy	G
Douglas	D
Frankfr	D
Reed	D
Black	D
Vinson	D

Crist v U.S. War Shipping
47 118M
332 US 852
CCA 3rd

Justice	01/03 1948 CERT 1 1	01/10 1948 CERT 1 2
Burton	G	D
Rutledg		D
Jackson	G	G
Murphy		
Douglas	G	G
Frankfr		D
Reed	G	D
Black		
Vinson	G	D

Morris v Peacock
47 132M
332 US 832
Georgia

Justice	11/08 1947 CERT 1 1	11/22 1947 CERT 1 2
Burton	E	
Rutledg	E	G
Jackson	E	G
Murphy	E	
Douglas	E	G
Frankfr	E	
Reed	E	G
Black	E	
Vinson	E	

Palulis v Ragen
47 141M
334 US 847   47 66M
Illinois

Justice	04/17 1948 CERT 1 1
Burton	E
Rutledg	E
Jackson	E
Murphy	E
Douglas	E
Frankfr	E
Reed	E
Black	E
Vinson	E

Hawkins v Clemmer
47 156M
332 US 812

Justice	10/30 1947 HABEAS 1 1
Burton	D
Rutledg	D
Jackson	D
Murphy	G
Douglas	D
Frankfr	
Reed	D
Black	D
Vinson	D

Thompson v Sanford
47 163M
333 US 856
CCA 5th

Justice	03/13 1948 CERT 1 1
Burton	D
Rutledg	D
Jackson	D
Murphy	G
Douglas	G
Frankfr	
Reed	D
Black	D
Vinson	D

Traffic Telephone Workers' (Ex Parte)
47 172M
332 US 833

Justice	12/06 1947 MNDMUS 1 1
Burton	D
Rutledg	D
Jackson	D
Murphy	Q
Douglas	D
Frankfr	
Reed	D
Black	
Vinson	D

Weiss v Los Angeles Broadcasting
47 180M
333 US 876
CCA 9th

Justice	04/02 1948 CERT 1 1	04/17 1948 CERT 1 2
Burton	G	G
Rutledg	GQ	G
Jackson		GQ
Murphy		
Douglas	D	D
Frankfr	D	D
Reed		
Black	G	G
Vinson	D	D

Richetsky v New York
47 198M
333 US 857
New York

Justice	01/03 1948 CERT 1 1	03/13 1948 CERT 1 2
Burton	E	D
Rutledg	E	D
Jackson	E	
Murphy	E	D
Douglas	E	D
Frankfr	E	
Reed	E	D
Black	E	D
Vinson	E	

Fowler v Hunter
47 229M
333 US 868
CCA 10th

Justice	04/02 1948 CERT 1 1
Burton	G
Rutledg	G
Jackson	
Murphy	
Douglas	D
Frankfr	D
Reed	
Black	D
Vinson	D

Starks v Ragen
47 248M
334 US 821
Illinois

Justice	01/31 1948 CERT 1 1	05/15 1948 CERT 1 2
Burton	E	D
Rutledg	E	G
Jackson	D	
Murphy	E	G
Douglas	E	G
Frankfr	D	
Reed	E	D
Black	E	D
Vinson		D

Hines v Illinois
47 254M
334 US 847
Illinois

Justice	02/14 1948 CERT 1 1	06/11 1948 CERT 1 2
Burton	E	D
Rutledg	E	D
Jackson	D	
Murphy	E	D
Douglas	E	D
Frankfr	D	
Reed		
Black	E	D
Vinson	D	

Brandt v U.S.
47 286M
333 US 836   47 287M   47 299M

Justice	02/14 1948 HABEAS 1 1
Burton	K
Rutledg	
Jackson	K
Murphy	
Douglas	
Frankfr	
Reed	K
Black	
Vinson	

Grimm v Niersheimer
47 310M — 334 US 847 — Illinois

Justice	03/13 1948 CERT (1 1)	06/11 1948 CERT (1 2)
Burton	E	
Rutledg	E	
Jackson	E	GQ
Murphy	E	D
Douglas	E	D
Frankfr	E	
Reed	E	D
Black	E	D
Vinson		D

Fisher v Hurst
47 325M 47 369A — 333 US 147 — Oklahoma

Justice	02/07 1948 MNDMUS (1 1)	02/16 1948 REPORT (1 1)
Burton	D	D
Rutledg	X D	G
Jackson		
Murphy	K	G
Douglas	D	D
Frankfr	D	D
Reed	D	D
Black	K D	D
Vinson	D	D

Mezo v Niersheimer
47 340M — 334 US 817

Justice	05/15 1948 HABEAS (1 1)
Burton	G
Rutledg	D
Jackson	D
Murphy	D
Douglas	D
Frankfr	D
Reed	
Black	G
Vinson	D

Eggers v California
47 351M — 333 US 858 — California

Justice	03/13 1948 CERT (1 1)
Burton	
Rutledg	X D
Jackson	
Murphy	X
Douglas	
Frankfr	G
Reed	D
Black	D
Vinson	D

Mayes v California
47 366M — 333 US 852 — California

Justice	03/13 1948 CERT (1 1)
Burton	
Rutledg	E
Jackson	
Murphy	
Douglas	
Frankfr	
Reed	D
Black	D
Vinson	D

Bennett v Stewart
47 379M — 334 US 848 — Missouri

Justice	04/24 1948 CERT (1 1)
Burton	E
Rutledg	E
Jackson	E
Murphy	E
Douglas	E
Frankfr	
Reed	E
Black	E
Vinson	

Blume (In The Matter Of)
47 407M — 333 US 879

Justice	04/24 1948 PETITN (1 1)
Burton	
Rutledg	E
Jackson	E
Murphy	E
Douglas	
Frankfr	
Reed	E
Black	D
Vinson	

Carmelo v Pennsylvania
47 408M — 334 US 860 — Pennsylvania

Justice	06/18 1948 CERT (1 1)
Burton	E
Rutledg	E
Jackson	D
Murphy	D
Douglas	D
Frankfr	D
Reed	D
Black	D
Vinson	D

Eichel (In The Matter Of)
47 413M — 333 US 865

Justice	04/02 1948 PETITN (1 1)
Burton	E
Rutledg	E
Jackson	D
Murphy	D
Douglas	D
Frankfr	D
Reed	E
Black	D
Vinson	

Peel v Ragen
47 420M — 334 US 838 — Illinois

Justice	06/05 1948 CERT (1 1)
Burton	D
Rutledg	E
Jackson	E
Murphy	D
Douglas	E
Frankfr	
Reed	D
Black	D
Vinson	D

Murray v Mississippi
47 432M — 333 US 869 — Mississippi

Justice	04/02 1948 CERT (1 1)
Burton	D
Rutledg	E
Jackson	D
Murphy	GQ
Douglas	
Frankfr	D
Reed	D
Black	D
Vinson	D

Henry v Baldi
47 436M — 334 US 822 — Pennsylvania

Justice	05/15 1948 CERT (1 1)
Burton	
Rutledg	E
Jackson	
Murphy	
Douglas	
Frankfr	
Reed	
Black	
Vinson	

Haley v Stewart
47 444M
334 US 860
Missouri

	05/28 1948 CERT 1 1
Burton	
Rutledg	E
Jackson	E D
Murphy	X
Douglas	E D
Frankfr	
Reed	E
Black	E
Vinson	E

(top fragment)

	06/18 1948 CERT 1 2
	D D
	D D
	D D D

Gann v Meek
47 451M
334 US 849
CCA 5th

	06/11 1948 CERT 1 1
Burton	
Rutledg	GQ D
Jackson	G
Murphy	
Douglas	D
Frankfr	D
Reed	D
Black	D
Vinson	D

Bodenmiller
(In The Matter Of)
47 490M
334 US 831

	05/28 1948 MNDMUS 1 1
Burton	
Rutledg	G D
Jackson	
Murphy	D
Douglas	D
Frankfr	D
Reed	D
Black	D
Vinson	D

Everett v Truman
47 512M
334 US 824

	05/18 1948 HABEAS 1 1
Burton	
Rutledg	G D
Jackson	
Murphy	G
Douglas	G
Frankfr	
Reed	D
Black	G
Vinson	D

Johnson v Stewart
47 515M
334 US 851
Missouri

	06/11 1948 CERT 1 1
Burton	
Rutledg	E D
Jackson	
Murphy	E D
Douglas	D
Frankfr	D
Reed	D
Black	D
Vinson	D

Asbell v Stewart
47 518M
334 US 851
Missouri

	06/11 1948 CERT 1 1
Burton	
Rutledg	E D
Jackson	
Murphy	E D
Douglas	D
Frankfr	D
Reed	D
Black	D
Vinson	D

Ehlen
(In The Matter Of)
47 526M
334 US 836 47 527M

	06/05 1948 HABEAS 1 1
Burton	
Rutledg	G D
Jackson	
Murphy	G
Douglas	G
Frankfr	
Reed	D
Black	G
Vinson	D

Girke
(In The Matter Of)
47 527M
334 US 836 47 526M

	06/05 1948 HABEAS 1 1
Burton	
Rutledg	G D
Jackson	
Murphy	G
Douglas	G
Frankfr	
Reed	D
Black	G
Vinson	D

Hall v U.S.
47 553M
334 US 853
CCA DC

	06/11 1948 CERT 1 1
Burton	
Rutledg	E D
Jackson	
Murphy	E D
Douglas	E D
Frankfr	
Reed	E
Black	D
Vinson	D

Appendix D

U.S. Supreme Court
October 1948 Term

Ford Motor Company v U.S.
48 1A 47 11A 46 643A
335 US 303 48 2A 47 12A 46 644A
Frankfr 10/19/48 DC ND Indiana

	11/09 1946 JURIS 1 1	10/16 1948 MERITS 1 1	10/16 1948 MERITS 2 1	11/15 1948 REPORT 1 1	11/15 1948 REPORT 2 1
Burton	N	R		R	
Rutledg	N				
Jackson		X	AQ	A	A
Murphy	S				
Douglas	N	R	A	R	A
Frankfr	N	R		R	
Reed	N		A		A
Black	N	R		R	
Vinson	N	R	A	R	A

Commercial Investment v U.S.
48 2A 47 12A 46 644A
335 US 303 48 1A 47 11A 46 643A
Frankfr 10/19/48 DC ND Indiana

	11/09 1946 JURIS 1 1	10/16 1948 MERITS 1 1	10/16 1948 MERITS 2 1	11/15 1948 REPORT 1 1	11/15 1948 REPORT 2 1
Burton	N	R		R	
Rutledg	N				
Jackson		X	AQ	A	A
Murphy	S				
Douglas	N	R	A	R	A
Frankfr	N	R		R	
Reed	N		A		A
Black	N	R		R	
Vinson	N	R	A	R	A

Spiegel's Estate v C.I.R.
48 3A 47 52A 46 1144A
335 US 701
Burton 10/27/47 Black 10/19/48 CCA 7th

	04/26 1947 CERT 1 1	10/25 1947 MERITS 1 1	10/16 1948 MERITS 1 2	01/17 1949 REPORT 1 1
Burton	G	R	R	R
Rutledg	G	R	R	R
Jackson	D			
Murphy				
Douglas	D			
Frankfr	G		A	A
Reed	G		A	A
Black			A	A
Vinson	G		A	A

Loftus v Illinois
48 4A 47 59A 46 1184A
337 US 935 48 50A
Frankfr 05/10/48 Illinois

	04/12 1947 CERT 1 1	02/07 1948 CERT 1 2	05/01 1948 MERITS 1 1	06/20 1949 REPORT 1 1
Burton	E	G		S
Rutledg	E			S
Jackson	E	G	R	S
Murphy	E			S
Douglas	E	G	R	S
Frankfr	E		A	S
Reed				S
Black	E	G	R	S
Vinson		D	A	

C.I.R. v Church's Estate
48 5A 47 96A 46 1395A
335 US 632
Burton 10/27/47 Black 10/19/48 CCA 3d

	06/14 1947 CERT 1 1	10/25 1947 MERITS 1 1	10/16 1948 MERITS 1 2	01/17 1949 REPORT 1 1
Burton	G		R	R
Rutledg	G		R	R
Jackson	D			
Murphy	G			
Douglas	G		R	R
Frankfr	G		RM	VM
Reed	G		R	R
Black	G	R	A	A
Vinson	G		A	A

Grand River Dam v Grand-Hydro
48 6A 47 379A
335 US 359
Burton 10/19/48 Oklahoma

	12/13 1947 CERT 1 1	03/06 1948 REHEAR 1 1	03/13 1948 REHEAR 1 2	10/16 1948 MERITS 1 1	11/22 1948 REPORT 1 1
Burton	D	B	B	R	R
Rutledg	D	B	B	R	R
Jackson				A	A
Murphy					
Douglas	D	B	Y	R	R
Frankfr				A	A
Reed	D		Y	R	R
Black	G	B	Y	R	R
Vinson	G	B	B	A	A

Jungersen v Ostby & Barton Company
48 7A 47 467A
335 US 560 48 8A 47 468A
Reed 11/16/48 CCA 3d

	01/10 1948 CERT 1 1	06/05 1948 CERT 1 2	11/13 1948 MERITS 1 1	01/03 1949 REPORT 1 1
Burton	D	G	R	R
Rutledg	D	G	R	R
Jackson	H	DQ		
Murphy	D	G	RQ	R
Douglas	D	G		
Frankfr	D	G	A	A
Reed		G	A	A
Black	D	G	A	A
Vinson		G	A	A

Ostby & Barton Company v Jungersen
48 8A 47 468A
335 US 560 48 7A 47 48 48A
Reed 11/16/48 CCA 3d

	01/10 1948 CERT 1 1	06/05 1948 CERT 1 2	11/13 1948 MERITS 1 1	01/03 1949 REPORT 1 1
Burton	D	G	R	R
Rutledg	D	G	R	R
Jackson	H	DQ		
Murphy	D	G	R	R
Douglas	D	G	AQ	R
Frankfr	D	G	R	R
Reed		G		
Black	G	G	R	R
Vinson	D	G	R	R

Kovacs v Cooper
48 9A 47 505A
336 US 77 47 504A
Reed 10/19/48 New Jersey

	01/31 1948 JURIS 1 1	04/02 1948 ADVANCE 1 1	06/18 1948 JURIS 1 2	10/16 1948 MERITS 1 1	01/31 1949 REPORT 1 1
Burton	NH		N	R	A
Rutledg	NH	AH	N		
Jackson	N		N	R	A
Murphy	NH		NR	R	A
Douglas		Y	N		
Frankfr	H	B Y		R	A
Reed					
Black	H	B Y	N	R	A
Vinson					

Bellaskus v Crossman
48 10A 47 531A
335 US 840
CCA 5th

	03/06 1948 CERT 1 1	03/13 1948 MERITS 1 2	10/16 1948 MERITS 1 1	10/18 1948 REPORT 1 1
Burton	GRM	GL	R	R
Rutledg	G	G	R	R
Jackson	G	D	R	R
Murphy	G	GL	R	R
Douglas	G	GL	R	R
Frankfr	GRM	G	R	R
Reed	G	G	R	R
Black	G	GL	R	R
Vinson	GRM	GL	R	R

Doubleday & Company v New York
48 11A 47 539A
335 US 848
New York

	03/13 1948 JURIS 1 1	10/23 1948 MERITS 1 1	10/25 1948 REPORT 1 1
Burton	N	R	R
Rutledg	N	RQ	R
Jackson	N	R	R
Murphy	N		
Douglas	N		
Frankfr	N	R	R
Reed			
Black	N		A
Vinson	S		A

Brinegar v U.S.
48 12A 47 551A
338 US 160
Jackson 10/25/48 Rutledg ??/??/4? CCA 10th

	03/06 1948 CERT 1 1	10/23 1948 MERITS 1 1	11/06 1948 MERITS 1 2	06/27 1949 REPORT 1 1
Burton	G			
Rutledg	G	R	R	R
Jackson	G		A	
Murphy	G	R	R	R
Douglas	G	R	R	R
Frankfr	G	R	R	R
Reed				
Black	X		A	A
Vinson	G		A	A

U.S. v Urbuteit
48 13A 47 577A
335 US 355 48 30A 48 640A
Douglas 10/19/48 CCA 5th

	04/17 1948 CERT 1 1	10/16 1948 MERITS 1 1	11/22 1948 REPORT 1 1
Burton	R		
Rutledg	R	AQ	A
Jackson	R		
Murphy	R	R	R
Douglas	R		
Frankfr	R	R	R
Reed	R		
Black	R	R	R
Vinson	R	R	R

International Union UAW v Wisconsin ERB
48 14A 48 15A 47 580A
336 US 245 47 581A
Jackson 11/24/48 Wisconsin

	03/13 1948 CERT 1 1	11/20 1948 MERITS 1 1	02/28 1949 REPORT 1 1
Burton	G		
Rutledg	G	RQ	R
Jackson	X		
Murphy	G	R	R
Douglas	G		
Frankfr	G	R	R
Reed	G		
Black	G	R	R
Vinson	G	R	R

Mandel Brothers v Wallace
48 16A 47 582A
335 US 291
Black 10/19/48 CCA 7th

	03/13 1948 CERT 1 1	10/16 1948 MERITS 1 1	11/08 1948 REPORT 1 1	06/27 1949 REPORT 1 1
Burton	G	R	R	R
Rutledg	G	R	R	R
Jackson	G	R	R	R
Murphy	G		R	R
Douglas	G	R	R	R
Frankfr	G	R	R	R
Reed	G	A	R	R
Black			R	R
Vinson	G	AQ	R	R

Wolf v Colorado
48 17A 48 18A 47 593A
338 US 25 47 594A 48 71A
Frankfr 10/25/48 Colorado

	04/02 1948 CERT 1 1	04/24 1948 MERITS 1 2	10/23 1948 MERITS 1 1	06/27 1949 REPORT 1 1
Burton	G	G	R	R
Rutledg	D	G	R	R
Jackson	G	G	R	R
Murphy		G	R	R
Douglas	D		R	R
Frankfr	D	G	R	R
Reed	D	D	R	R
Black		D	A	A
Vinson	D	G	R	R

Penn v Chicago & North Western RR
48 19A 47 600A
335 US 849
CCA 7th

	04/02 1948 CERT 1 1	10/16 1948 MERITS 1 1	10/25 1948 REPORT 1 1
Burton	G	R	R
Rutledg	D	R	R
Jackson	G	X	R
Murphy	G		R
Douglas	G	X	R
Frankfr		R	R
Reed	G	R	R
Black	G	R	R
Vinson	D		R

Hoiness v U.S.
48 **20A** 47 604A
335 US 297
Douglas 10/25/48 CCA 9th

	03/27 1948 CERT 1 1	10/23 1948 MERITS 1 1	11/08 1948 REPORT 1 1
Burton	GL	R	R
Rutledg	GL	R	R
Jackson	GL	R	R
Murphy	GL	R	R
Douglas		R	R
Frankfr	GL	R	R
Reed	GL	R	R
Black	G	R	R
Vinson	GL	R	R

Callaway v Benton
48 **21A** 47 607A
336 US 132
Vinson 10/25/48 CCA 5th

	03/13 1948 CERT 1 1	10/23 1948 MERITS 1 1	02/07 1949 REPORT 1 1
Burton	D	A	A
Rutledg	G	AQ	R
Jackson	D	A	A
Murphy	D	AQ	A
Douglas	G	R	R
Frankfr	G	A	A
Reed	D	A	A
Black	G	A	A
Vinson	D	A	A

Vermilya-Brown Company v Connell
48 **22A** 47 608A
335 US 377
Reed 10/19/48 CCA 2d

	03/27 1948 CERT 1 1	10/16 1948 MERITS 1 1	12/06 1948 REPORT 1 1
Burton	G	R	R
Rutledg	D	A	A
Jackson	G	R	R
Murphy	G	A	A
Douglas		A	A
Frankfr	G	R	R
Reed	G	A	A
Black	D	A	A
Vinson	D	R	R

Michelson v U.S.
48 **23A** 47 612A
335 US 469
Jackson 10/19/48 CCA 2d

	03/27 1948 CERT 1 1	04/02 1948 CERT 1 2	10/16 1948 MERITS 1 1	12/20 1948 REPORT 1 1
Burton	G	G	A	A
Rutledg	G	G	R	R
Jackson	D	D	A	A
Murphy	D	G	X	R
Douglas		D	X	A
Frankfr	G	G	X	A
Reed	D	D	A	A
Black	D	D	A	A
Vinson	D	D	A	A

Hynes v Grimes Packing Company
48 **24A** 47 613A
337 US 86
Reed 11/09/48 CCA 9th

	04/02 1948 CERT 1 1	11/06 1948 THREAT 1 1	11/06 1948 MERITS 1 1	05/31 1949 REPORT 1 1	05/31 1949 REPORT 2 1
Burton	D	Y	A	V	V
Rutledg	G	B	R	V	R
Jackson	D	Y	A	V	V
Murphy	G		R	V	R
Douglas	G	Y	R	V	R
Frankfr	D	B	R	V	V
Reed	G	Y	AQ	V	V
Black	D	B	R	V	R
Vinson	D	YQ	A	V	V

Ayrshire Collieries v U.S.
48 **25A** 47 619A
335 US 573
Douglas 11/24/48 DC SD Indiana

	03/13 1948 JURIS 1 1	03/27 1948 JURIS 1 2	11/20 1948 MERITS 1 1	01/03 1949 REPORT 1 1
Burton	P	N	A	A
Rutledg	A	A	A	A
Jackson	A	N	R	A
Murphy	A	A	X	A
Douglas	N	N	A	A
Frankfr		A	A	A
Reed	N	N	A	A
Black	A	A	A	A
Vinson	A	A	A	A

AFL v American Sash & Door Company
48 **27A** 47 626A
335 US 538 48 47A 48 34A
Black 11/16/48 Arizona

	03/27 1948 JURIS 1 1	11/13 1948 MERITS 1 1	01/03 1949 REPORT 1 1
Burton	N	A	A
Rutledg	N	A	A
Jackson	N	A	A
Murphy	N	X	R
Douglas		A	A
Frankfr	N	A	A
Reed	N	A	A
Black	N	A	A
Vinson	N	A	A

Eckenrode v Pennsylvania RR Company
48 **28A** 47 628A
335 US 329
CCA 3rd

	04/02 1948 CERT 1 1	10/23 1948 MERITS 1 1	11/15 1948 REPORT 1 1
Burton	D	A	A
Rutledg	G	R	R
Jackson	D	A	A
Murphy	G	R	R
Douglas	G	R	R
Frankfr	D	A	A
Reed	D	A	A
Black	G	R	R
Vinson	D	A	A

National Mutual v Tidewater Transfer
48 **29A** 47 640A
337 US 582 48 43A 48 178A
Jackson 11/16/48 CCA 4th

	03/27 1948 CERT 1 1	11/13 1948 MERITS 1 1	06/20 1949 REPORT 1 1
Burton	G	R	R
Rutledg	G	R	R
Jackson	G	R	R
Murphy	G	R	R
Douglas		R	A
Frankfr	G	A	A
Reed	G	A	A
Black	G	A	R
Vinson	G	R	A

Kordel v U.S.
48 30A 47 645A
335 US 345
Douglas 10/19/48 CCA 7th

	04/17 1948 CERT	10/16 1948 MERITS	11/22 1948 REPORT
Burton	G	A	A
Rutledg	G	A	A
Jackson	G		
Murphy	G	R	R
Douglas	G	R	R
Frankfr	G	A	A
Reed	G	R	R
Black	G	R	R
Vinson	G	R	R

Larson v Domestic & Foreign Commerce
48 31A 47 649A
337 US 682
Vinson 11/16/48 CCA DC

	04/17 1948 CERT	11/13 1948 MERITS	06/27 1949 REPORT
Burton	GQ	R	R
Rutledg	G	R	R
Jackson	G	RQ	AQ
Murphy	G	R	R
Douglas	G	R	R
Frankfr	G	R	R
Reed		R	R
Black	G		A
Vinson	G		A

C.I.R. v Jacobson
48 32A 47 650A
336 US 28 48 33A 47 651A
Burton 11/16/48 CCA 7th

	04/02 1948 CERT	11/13 1948 MERITS	01/17 1949 REPORT
Burton	G	R	R
Rutledg	G	R	R
Jackson	G	R	R
Murphy	G	R	R
Douglas	G	R	R
Frankfr	G	R	R
Reed	G		
Black	G	R	R
Vinson	G	A	A

Whitaker v North Carolina
48 34A 47 660A
335 US 525 48 27A 48 47A
Black 11/16/48 North Carolina

	03/27 1948 JURIS	11/13 1948 MERITS	01/03 1949 REPORT
Burton	N	A	A
Rutledg	N	A	A
Jackson	N		
Murphy	N	X	A
Douglas	N	A	A
Frankfr	N	A	A
Reed	N	A	A
Black	N	A	A
Vinson	N	A	A

Goggin v Division Of Labor Law
48 35A 47 667A
336 US 118
Burton 11/24/48 CCA 9th

	03/27 1948 CERT	11/20 1948 MERITS	01/31 1949 REPORT
Burton	G	R	R
Rutledg	G D	R	R
Jackson	G	R	R
Murphy	G	R	R
Douglas	G D	R	R
Frankfr	G	R	R
Reed	G	R	R
Black			
Vinson	G	R	R

McDonald v U.S.
48 36A 47 678A
335 US 451
Douglas 10/19/48 CCA DC

	04/17 1948 CERT	10/16 1948 MERITS	12/13 1948 REPORT
Burton	G	R	R
Rutledg	G	R	R
Jackson	G	RQ	R
Murphy	G	R	R
Douglas	G	R	R
Frankfr	G		
Reed	G	X	A
Black	G	A	A
Vinson	G		A

U.S. v Women's Sportswear Manufacturers
48 37A 47 683A
336 US 460
Jackson 03/08/49 DC Massachusetts

	04/17 1948 JURIS	03/05 1949 MERITS	03/28 1949 REPORT
Burton	N	R	R
Rutledg	N	R	R
Jackson	N	R	R
Murphy	N	R	R
Douglas	N	R	R
Frankfr		R	R
Reed	N	R	R
Black	N	R	R
Vinson	N	R	R

LaCrosse Telephone v Wisconsin ERB
48 38A 47 701A
336 US 18 48 39A 47 702A
Douglas 11/24/48 Wisconsin

	04/17 1948 JURIS	11/20 1948 MERITS	01/17 1949 REPORT
Burton	P	R	R
Rutledg	N	R	R
Jackson	N	S	R
Murphy	P	R	R
Douglas	P	R	R
Frankfr			
Reed	N	R	R
Black		S	R
Vinson			

Oklahoma Tax Commission v Texas Company
48 40A 47 703A
336 US 342 48 41A 47 704A
Rutledg 11/24/48 Oklahoma

	04/17 1948 JURIS	11/20 1948 MERITS	03/07 1949 REPORT
Burton	S	G	R
Rutledg	S	G	R
Jackson	S	G	RQ
Murphy	S	G	RQ
Douglas	S	G	R
Frankfr		G	R
Reed	S	G	R
Black	S	G	X
Vinson			R

Klappott v U.S.
48 42A 47 732A
335 US 601 336 US 942
Reed 10/25/48 Black ??/??/4? CCA 3rd

Justice	05/15 1948 CERT (1 1)	10/23 MERITS (1 1)	12/04 1948 MERITS (1 2)	01/17 1949 REPORT (1 1)	02/26 1949 MODIFY (1 1)	03/26 1949 MODIFY (1 2)
Burton	D	R	R	R	B	Y
Rutledg	D	R	R	R	B	Y
Jackson		AQ	A			
Murphy	D	R	RM	R	B	Y
Douglas						
Frankfr		R	R	R		
Reed	D					
Black	D	A	A	A	B	Y
Vinson	D	A	A	A	B	Y

Central States v Watson Brothers
48 43A 47 748A
337 US 951 48 29A 48 178A
CCA 7th

Justice	06/24 1949 CERT (1 1)	06/27 1949 REPORT (1 1)
Burton	G	>
Rutledg	G	>
Jackson	GVM	>
Murphy		>
Douglas		>
Frankfr	G	>
Reed	G	>
Black	G	>
Vinson	G	>

Frazier v U.S.
48 44A 47 750A 47 213M
335 US 497
Rutledg 10/19/48 CCA DC

Justice	03/13 1948 CERT (1 1)	04/17 1948 MERITS (1 2)	10/16 1948 MERITS (1 1)	12/20 1948 REPORT (1 1)
Burton	G	G	R	A
Rutledg	G	G	R	A
Jackson				
Murphy	G	G	X	
Douglas		G		
Frankfr				
Reed	D	D	R	A
Black	D	D	R	A
Vinson	D	D		A

Fisher v Pace
48 45A 47 756A
336 US 155
Reed 12/18/48 Texas

Justice	05/22 1948 CERT (1 1)	12/11 1948 MERITS (1 1)	02/07 1949 REPORT (1 1)
Burton	G	R	R
Rutledg	D	R	R
Jackson	D	R	R
Murphy	G		
Douglas	G	X	
Frankfr	G		
Reed	D		R
Black	D	A	A
Vinson	D	A	A

N.L.R.B. v Stowe Spinning Company
48 46A 47 757A
336 US 226 47 676A
Murphy 12/18/48 CCA 4th

Justice	05/28 1948 CERT (1 1)	12/11 1948 MERITS (1 1)	02/28 1949 REPORT (1 1)
Burton	G	R	R
Rutledg	Q	RQ	R J
Jackson		R	
Murphy	G	X	R
Douglas	G		R
Frankfr	G		
Reed	D		R
Black	G	A	A
Vinson	G	A	A

Lincoln Federal v Northwestern Iron
48 47A 47 761A
335 US 525 48 27A 48 34A
Black 11/16/48 Nebraska

Justice	05/22 1948 JURIS (1 1)	11/13 1948 MERITS (1 1)	01/03 1949 REPORT (1 1)
Burton	N	A	A
Rutledg	N	A	A
Jackson	N	A	A
Murphy	N	X	A
Douglas	N		A
Frankfr	N		A
Reed	N	A	A
Black	N	A	A
Vinson	N	A	A

Jungersen v Baden
48 48A 47 776A
335 US 560 48 7A 48 8A
Reed 11/16/48 CCA 2d

Justice	06/05 1948 CERT (1 1)	11/13 1948 MERITS (1 1)	01/03 1949 REPORT (1 1)
Burton	G	R	R
Rutledg	DQ	R	R A
Jackson	G		
Murphy	G		
Douglas	G	RQ	R A
Frankfr	G		
Reed	G	A	A
Black	G	A	A
Vinson	G	A	A

Goesaert v Cleary
48 49A 47 780A
335 US 464
Frankfr 11/24/48 DC ED Michigan

Justice	05/22 1948 JURIS (1 1)	11/20 1948 MERITS (1 1)	12/20 1948 REPORT (1 1)
Burton	N	RL	R
Rutledg	N	X	R
Jackson	N	X	R
Murphy			
Douglas	A		
Frankfr	S		
Reed			
Black	S	A	A
Vinson	S	A	A

Young v Ragen
48 50A 47 195M
337 US 235 48 2M 48 10M
Illinois

Justice	04/24 1948 CERT (1 1)	05/01 1948 MERITS (1 2)	06/06 1949 REPORT (1 1)
Burton	G	G	>
Rutledg	D	D	>
Jackson	D	D	>
Murphy	G	G	>
Douglas	D	D	>
Frankfr			
Reed	G	G	>
Black	D	D	>
Vinson	D	D	>

Railway Express Agency v New York
48 51A 47 786A
336 US 106
Douglas 12/18/48 New York

Justice	06/05/1948 JURIS 1 1	06/11/1948 JURIS 1 2	06/18/1948 JURIS 1 3
Burton	N	S	S
Rutledg		S	SQ
Jackson			
Murphy	N	N	N
Douglas	N	N	N
Frankfr	N	N	N
Reed			
Black	S	S	S
Vinson	S	S	S

Stainback v Mo Hock Ke Lok Po
48 52A 47 789A
336 US 368 48 474A
Reed 01/24/49 DC Hawaii

Justice	05/28/1948 JURIS 1 1	01/17/1949 REPORT 1 1	03/14/1949 REPORT 1 1
Burton	P	S	S
Rutledg	P	S	S
Jackson			
Murphy	S	S	S
Douglas	S	X	S
Frankfr		S	S
Reed	P	S	S
Black	P	S	S
Vinson	P	S	S

Wilkerson v McCarthy
48 53A 47 792A
336 US 53
Black 12/21/48 Utah

Justice	10/05/1948 CERT 1 1	12/11/1948 MERITS 1 1	01/31/1949 REPORT 1 1
Burton	GR	R	R
Rutledg	G	R	R
Jackson			
Murphy	G	R	R
Douglas	G	R	R
Frankfr	D	R	R
Reed			A
Black	G	R	R
Vinson	G	R	R

Coray v Southern Pacific Company
48 54A 47 793A
335 US 520
Black 12/21/48 Utah

Justice	10/05/1948 CERT 1 1	12/11/1948 MERITS 1 1	03/14/1949 REPORT 1 1
Burton	G	RQ	A
Rutledg	G	RQ	A
Jackson	G		A
Murphy	G		A
Douglas	G	R	A
Frankfr	G		A
Reed	G		A
Black	G	R	A
Vinson	G		A

Lawson v Suwannee Fruit & Steamship
48 56A 47 806A
336 US 198
Murphy 12/21/48 CCA 5th

Justice	06/18/1948 CERT 1 1	12/11/1948 MERITS 1 1	01/31/1949 REPORT 1 1
Burton	G	RQ	R
Rutledg	G		R
Jackson	G	RQ	R
Murphy	G		R
Douglas	G		R
Frankfr	G		R
Reed	G		R
Black	G		R
Vinson	G		R

U.S. (Pasela) v Fenno
48 58A 47 811A
335 US 806
CCA 2d

Justice	06/18/1948 CERT 1 1	10/11/1948 REPORT 1 1
Burton	G	SI
Rutledg	G	SI
Jackson	D	SI
Murphy	G	SI
Douglas	D	SI
Frankfr		SI
Reed	G	SI
Black	G	SI
Vinson	D	SI

Marzani v U.S.
48 59A 47 816A
336 US 922
CCA DC

Justice	06/18/1948 CERT 1 1	12/11/1948 MERITS 1 1	01/03/1949 REPORT 1 1
Burton	G	R	R
Rutledg	G		R
Jackson	G		R
Murphy	G	X	R
Douglas	G		R
Frankfr	G		R
Reed	G	R	R
Black	G	R	R
Vinson	G	R	R

Kammerer v McCullough
48 60A 47 817A
335 US 813
CCA 9th

Justice	10/05/1948 CERT 1 1	02/14/1949 REPORT 1 1
Burton	G	A
Rutledg	D	A
Jackson	D	A
Murphy	X	A
Douglas	D	A
Frankfr	D	R
Reed	D	A
Black	D	A
Vinson	D	A

Spina v Ring
48 62A
335 US 813
CCA 2d

Justice	10/05/1948 CERT 1 1	12/18/1948 MERITS 1 2	12/20/1948 REPORT 1 1	01/15/1949 REHEAR
Burton		A	R	B
Rutledg		R	R	
Jackson		R	R	Y
Murphy		R	R	Y
Douglas		R	R	X
Frankfr	G	A	R	Y
Reed		R	R	
Black		R	R	B
Vinson		R	R	

U.S. v C.B. Ross Company
48 64A
335 US 813
Ct Cls

Justice	10/05/1948 CERT 1 1	02/05/1949 REHEAR 1 2	03/05/1949 MERITS 1 3	03/07/1949 REPORT 1 2
Burton		B	R	A
Rutledg			R	R
Jackson		Y	R	R
Murphy		Y	R	R
Douglas		X	R	R
Frankfr		Y	R	R
Reed			R	R
Black	G	B	G	R
Vinson	G		G	A

Kimball Laundry Company v U.S.
48 63A
338 US 1
Frankfr 12/18/48 CCA 8th

Justice	10/05/1948 CERT 1 1	12/11/1948 MERITS 1 1	06/27/1949 REPORT 1 1
Burton	G	R	A
Rutledg	G		R
Jackson	G		R
Murphy	G	D	AQ
Douglas	G	D	A
Frankfr	G	D	A
Reed	G	D	A
Black	G	D	A
Vinson	G		A

Chicago Milwaukee RR v Acme Fast
48 65A
336 US 465
Vinson 12/18/48 CCA 2d

	10/05 1948 CERT	12/11 1948 MERITS	04/04 1949 REPORT
	1 1	1 1	1 1
Burton	G	R	R A
Rutledg	G		R A
Jackson	D	X	A
Murphy			R A
Douglas	G	R	R A
Frankfr			R
Reed	G	R	R A
Black	G	R	R
Vinson	D		

U.S. v Bloedel Donovan Lumber Mills
48 68A
335 US 814
Cl Cls

	10/05 1948 CERT
	1 1
Burton	G
Rutledg	G
Jackson	D
Murphy	D
Douglas	G
Frankfr	D
Reed	G
Black	D
Vinson	D

Fong v Superior Court Of Washington
48 71A
337 US 956 48 17A 48 18A
Washington

	06/24 1949 CERT
	1 1
Burton	D
Rutledg	D
Jackson	
Murphy	
Douglas	
Frankfr	
Reed	
Black	D
Vinson	D

Texas & Pacific RR v Kilpatrick
48 72A
335 US 814 48 73A 48 233M
CCA 2d

	10/08 1948 CERT
	1 1
Burton	D
Rutledg	D
Jackson	
Murphy	G
Douglas	
Frankfr	D
Reed	D
Black	D
Vinson	G

Uveges v Pennsylvania
48 75A 47 201M
335 US 437
Reed 11/24/48 Pennsylvania

	01/03 1948 CERT	06/05 1948 CERT	11/20 1948 MERITS	12/13 1948 REPORT
	1 1	1 2	1 1	1 1
Burton	E	G	R	R S
Rutledg	E	G	R A	
Jackson	E	G	R	R S
Murphy	E	G	S	S
Douglas	E	G	R	R
Frankfr	E	G	R A	R
Reed	E		R	R
Black	E		A	R
Vinson		D		

Harris v South Carolina
48 76A 47 503M
338 US 68
Frankfr 12/07/48 South Carolina

	06/05 1948 CERT	11/20 1948 MERITS	06/27 1949 REPORT
	1 1	1 1	1 1
Burton	G	R	R A
Rutledg	G	R	R
Jackson		R	R A
Murphy	G	R	R
Douglas	G		R
Frankfr	G	R A	R A
Reed	G		R
Black		R A	R A
Vinson	D		

International Teamsters v Dinofria
48 80A
335 US 815
Illinois

	10/05 1948 CERT
	1 1
Burton	D
Rutledg	D
Jackson	
Murphy	DQ
Douglas	
Frankfr	D
Reed	D
Black	D
Vinson	D

C.I.R. v Phipps
48 83A
336 US 410
Murphy 12/18/48 CCA 10th

	10/05 1948 CERT	12/11 1948 MERITS	03/14 1949 REPORT
	1 1	1 1	1 1
Burton	G	R	R
Rutledg	G	R	R
Jackson	G	RQ	R
Murphy			R
Douglas	D	R	R
Frankfr	D	R	R
Reed	D	R	R
Black	G	R	R
Vinson	G	R	R

C.I.R. v Wodehouse
48 84A
337 US 369
Burton 12/21/48 CCA 4th

	10/05 1948 CERT	12/18 1948 MERITS	06/13 1949 REPORT
	1 1	1 1	1 1
Burton	G	R	R
Rutledg	G		
Jackson	G	R	R
Murphy			
Douglas	G	AQ	A
Frankfr	G		
Reed	G	A	A
Black	G	R	R
Vinson	G	AQ	A

Brand v Milwaukee County
48 87A
335 US 802
Wisconsin

	10/05 1948 JURIS	10/05 1948 CERT
	1 1	1 1
Burton	P S	D
Rutledg	S	
Jackson	P S	D
Murphy	P S	
Douglas	S	D
Frankfr	S	D
Reed	S	D
Black		
Vinson		

Leiman v Guttman
48 88A
336 US 1
Douglas 12/21/48 New York

	10/05 1948 CERT	12/20 1948 MERITS	01/17 1949 REPORT
	1 1	1 1	1 1
Burton	G	RV	VM A
Rutledg		D	A
Jackson	G	D	VM A
Murphy	G		A
Douglas	G		A
Frankfr		D	VM A
Reed	G	D	VM A
Black			A
Vinson			

U.S. v Maryland & Virginia Milk
48 89A
335 US 802
DC DC

	10/05 1948 JURIS	10/11 1948 REPORT
	1 1	1 1
Burton	NM	M
Rutledg	NM	M
Jackson	X	
Murphy		M
Douglas	NM	M
Frankfr	NM	M
Reed	NM	M
Black	NM	M
Vinson	NM	M

236

Henslee v Union Planters Bank & Trust
48 90A
335 US 595
Rutledg 12/21/48 CCA 6th

	CERT 10/05 1948	MERITS 12/20 1948	REPORT 01/03 1949
	1 1	1 1	1 1
Burton	GR	R	R
Rutledg	GR	R	R A
Jackson	D		
Murphy	GR	R A	R A
Douglas		R A	R A
Frankfr			
Reed	G	R	R
Black	G	R	R
Vinson	G		

Foley Brothers v Filardo
48 91A
336 US 281
Reed 12/21/48 New York

	CERT 10/05 1948	MERITS 12/20 1948	REPORT 03/07 1949
	1 1	1 1	1 1
Burton	G	R	R
Rutledg	G	R	R A
Jackson	D	R	R
Murphy	G	R A	R A
Douglas	G		
Frankfr	D	R A	R A
Reed	G	R	R
Black	D	R	R
Vinson	D	R	R

H.P. Hood & Sons v Du Mond
48 92A
336 US 525
Jackson 12/21/48 New York

	CERT 10/06 1948	MERITS 12/20 1948	REPORT 04/04 1949
	1 1	1 1	1 1
Burton	G	R	R
Rutledg	G	R	R A
Jackson	G	R	R A
Murphy	G	R M	R A
Douglas	G	R	R A
Frankfr	G	R	R
Reed	G	R X	R
Black	D	R	R
Vinson	D	R	R

Ebensberger v Sinclair Refining
48 93A
335 US 816
CCA 5th

	CERT 10/06 1948
	1 1
Burton	
Rutledg	
Jackson	
Murphy	G
Douglas	
Frankfr	
Reed	
Black	
Vinson	

Iriarte v U.S.
48 94A
335 US 816
CCA 1st

	CERT 10/06 1948
	1 1
Burton	D
Rutledg	D
Jackson	D
Murphy	G
Douglas	D
Frankfr	D
Reed	D
Black	D
Vinson	D

W.E. Hedger v Ira S. Bushey & Sons
48 96A
335 US 816
CCA 2d

	CERT 10/06 1948
	1 1
Burton	
Rutledg	
Jackson	
Murphy	G
Douglas	
Frankfr	
Reed	GQ
Black	GQ
Vinson	D

Upshaw v U.S.
48 98A 47 524M
335 US 410
Black 11/24/48 CCA DC

	CERT 06/11 1948	MERITS 11/13 1948	REPORT 12/13 1948
	1 1	1 1	1 1
Burton	G	R	R
Rutledg	G	R	R
Jackson		R A	R A
Murphy	G	R	R
Douglas	D		
Frankfr	G	R A	R A
Reed		R	R
Black	G	R	R
Vinson	DQ		

McElroy v Pegg
48 99A
335 US 817
CCA 10th

	CERT 10/06 1948
	1 1
Burton	
Rutledg	
Jackson	
Murphy	G
Douglas	
Frankfr	
Reed	
Black	
Vinson	

Turner v Pennsylvania
48 107A 47 567M
338 US 62
Frankfr 12/07/48 Pennsylvania

	CERT 06/18 1948	MERITS 11/20 1948	REPORT 06/27 1949
	1 1	1 1	1 1
Burton	G	R	R A
Rutledg	G	R	R A
Jackson	G	R	R
Murphy	G		
Douglas	G	R	R A
Frankfr	G	R	R A
Reed	G	R	R
Black	G	R	R A
Vinson	G	R	R

F.P.C. v Interstate Natural Gas
48 109A
336 US 577 48 188A 48 209A 48 212A
Douglas 02/12/49 CCA 5th

	CERT 10/06 1948	MERITS 01/15 1949	REPORT 04/18 1949
	1 1	1 1	1 1
Burton	G	R	R
Rutledg	G	R	R
Jackson	G		R AJ
Murphy	G	X	R AJ
Douglas	G		R AJ
Frankfr	G	R	R
Reed	G	R	R
Black	G		R
Vinson	G		R

McComb v Jacksonville Paper Company
48 110A
336 US 187
Douglas 12/21/48 CCA 5th

	CERT 10/06 1948	MERITS 12/20 1948	REPORT 02/21 1949
	1 1	1 1	1 1
Burton	G	R	R
Rutledg	G	R	R
Jackson	G	X	
Murphy	G	R	R
Douglas	G	R A	R A
Frankfr	G		
Reed	G		
Black	G	R A	R A
Vinson	D	AQ	

Ancker v California
48 111A
335 US 852
California

	CERT 10/23 1948
	1 1
Burton	
Rutledg	G
Jackson	G
Murphy	D
Douglas	G
Frankfr	G
Reed	
Black	
Vinson	G

Hightower v U.S.
48 106A
335 US 817
CCA 7th

	CERT 10/06 1948
	1 1
Burton	
Rutledg	
Jackson	
Murphy	G
Douglas	
Frankfr	
Reed	
Black	
Vinson	

Best & Company v Miller
48 114A
335 US 818
CCA 2d

	CERT 10/06 1948
	1 1
Burton	D
Rutledg	D
Jackson	D
Murphy	D
Douglas	G
Frankfr	D
Reed	D
Black	D
Vinson	

Guerrini v U.S.
48 115A · 335 US 843 · CCA 2d

Justice	10/16 1948 CERT (1 1)
Burton	D
Rutledg	D
Jackson	D
Murphy	G
Douglas	G
Frankfr	D
Reed	G
Black	D
Vinson	G

Fogel v U.S.
48 116A · 335 US 865 · CCA 5th

Justice	10/16 1948 CERT (1 1)
Burton	D
Rutledg	D
Jackson	D
Murphy	G
Douglas	G
Frankfr	D
Reed	G
Black	D
Vinson	G

Rice v Rice
48 117A · 336 US 674 · Reed 12/21/48 · Connecticut

Justice	10/06 1948 CERT (1 1)	11/13 1948 MERITS (1 2)	11/15 1948 REPORT (1 1)	12/20 1948 MERITS (1 1)	04/18 1949 REPORT (1 1)
Burton	G	RI	RI	R	A
Rutledg	G Q	RI	RI	R S	R
Jackson	G	RI	RI	R	A
Murphy		RI	RI		
Douglas	G	RI	RI	R	A
Frankfr		RI	RI		
Reed	G	RI	RI	R	A
Black		RI	RI		
Vinson	G	RI	RI		

Petti v U.S.
48 118A · 336 US 916 · CCA 2d

Justice	10/06 1948 CERT (1 1)	02/26 1949 MOOT (1 1)	02/26 1949 VACATE (1 1)	02/29 1949 REPORT (1 1)
Burton	D	B		VI
Rutledg	G	X	Y	VI
Jackson	G		B	VI
Murphy	G	B	Y	VI
Douglas		B	Y	VI
Frankfr			YR	VI
Reed		B	Y	VI
Black	X	B	YR	VI
Vinson	D		Y	VI

Durant v Hironimus
48 119A · 335 US 818 · CCA 4th

Justice	10/06 1948 CERT (1 1)
Burton	D
Rutledg	D
Jackson	D
Murphy	G Q
Douglas	G
Frankfr	D
Reed	D
Black	D Q
Vinson	D

Black Diamond v Robert Stewart & Sons
48 121A · 336 US 386 · 48 130A · Frankfr 01/14/49 · CCA 2d

Justice	10/06 1948 CERT (1 1)	01/08 1949 MERITS (1 1)	03/14 1949 REPORT (1 1)
Burton	G	R	R
Rutledg	G	R	R
Jackson	D Q	R A	A
Murphy	D Q	A	A
Douglas	D Q	R	R
Frankfr		R	R
Reed	G	R	R
Black	G	A	A
Vinson			

Farmers Reservoir v McComb
48 128A · 337 US 755 · 48 196A · Vinson 12/21/48 · CCA 10th

Justice	10/06 1948 CERT (1 1)	10/08 1948 CERT (1 2)	12/20 1948 MERITS (1 1)	06/27 1949 REPORT (1 1)
Burton	D	D	R	
Rutledg	D	D	R	R
Jackson				
Murphy	G	G	R	
Douglas	G	G		
Frankfr				
Reed	X		R	
Black	G	G	R	
Vinson	G	G	R	

Urie v Thompson
48 129A · 337 US 163 · Rutledg 01/14/49 · Missouri

Justice	10/06 1948 CERT (1 1)	01/08 1949 MERITS (1 1)	05/31 1949 REPORT (1 1)
Burton	G	R	R
Rutledg	G	R	R
Jackson	G	R	R
Murphy	G	A	R
Douglas	G	R	R
Frankfr	G	A	R
Reed	G	R	R
Black	G	R	R
Vinson	G		R

U.S. v Cors
48 132A · 337 US 325 · Douglas 02/12/49 · Ct Cls

Justice	10/06 1948 CERT (1 1)	01/15 1949 QUEST (10 1)	02/05 1949 MERITS (1 1)	06/13 1949 REPORT (1 1)
Burton	G	B	R	A
Rutledg	G	B	R	R
Jackson		X		R
Murphy	G	B	R	A
Douglas	D	B	R	R
Frankfr				
Reed	G	B	R Q	A
Black	G	X		A
Vinson	G	B		A

Leeds v U.S.
48 133A
335 US 820
Ct Cls

Justice	CERT 10/06 1948 (1 1)
Burton	D
Rutledg	D
Jackson	D
Murphy	DQ
Douglas	D
Frankfr	D
Reed	D
Black	DQ
Vinson	G

Research Laboratories v U.S.
48 134A
335 US 843
CCA 9th

Justice	CERT 10/08 1948 (1 2)	CERT 10/16 1948 (1 3)
Burton	G	D
Rutledg	G	D
Jackson		
Murphy	G	G
Douglas	G X	G
Frankfr		
Reed	G X	G
Black		D
Vinson	D	D

U.S. v Jones
48 135A
336 US 641 48 198A Ct Cls
Rutledg 02/12/49

Justice	CERT 11/04 1948 (1 1)	MERITS 02/05 1949 (1 1)	REPORT 04/18 1949 (1 1)
Burton	G	RQ	R
Rutledg	G	R	R
Jackson	G	R	R
Murphy	G	R X	R
Douglas	G		
Frankfr	G	AQ	
Reed	G	AQ X	R
Black	G		
Vinson	G	R	

Federal Broadcasting System v ABC
48 140A
335 US 821
CCA 2d

Justice	CERT 10/06 1948 (1 1)
Burton	
Rutledg	D
Jackson	X D
Murphy	
Douglas	G
Frankfr	
Reed	D
Black	D
Vinson	D

Borak v U.S.
48 141A
335 US 821
Ct Cls

Justice	CERT 10/06 1948 (1 1)
Burton	
Rutledg	D
Jackson	D
Murphy	DQ
Douglas	
Frankfr	G
Reed	D
Black	D
Vinson	D

Krulewitch v U.S.
48 143A
336 US 440
Black 01/24/49 CCA 2d

Justice	CERT 10/07 (1 1)	MERITS 01/15 1949 (1 1)	REPORT 03/28 1949 (1 1)
Burton	GL	R	R
Rutledg	GL	R	R
Jackson	GL	R	R
Murphy	GL	R	R
Douglas	GL	R	R
Frankfr	GL	R	R
Reed		A	A
Black			
Vinson	D		

Thompson v Spearman
48 148A
335 US 822
CCA 8th

Justice	CERT 10/06 1948 (1 1)
Burton	
Rutledg	D D
Jackson	D D
Murphy	G
Douglas	G
Frankfr	
Reed	D
Black	D
Vinson	D

Kirkland v Atlantic Coast Line RR
48 150A
335 US 843
CCA DC

Justice	CERT 10/16 1948 (1 1)
Burton	
Rutledg	D D
Jackson	D D
Murphy	G
Douglas	G
Frankfr	
Reed	D
Black	D
Vinson	D

National Carbide v C.I.R.
48 151A 48 152A 48 153A
336 US 422 48 247A CCA 2d
Vinson 01/14/49

Justice	CERT 10/06 1948 (1 1)	MERITS 01/08 1949 (1 1)	REPORT 03/28 1949 (1 1)
Burton	G G	R	A
Rutledg	G	R	A
Jackson	G	R	A
Murphy	G G	V	A
Douglas	G G	A	A
Frankfr		A	A
Reed	D D	A	A
Black	D		
Vinson	D D		

Donovan v Queensboro
48 156A
335 US 804 48 49M
CCA 2d

Justice	CERT 10/06 1948 (1 1)
Burton	D
Rutledg	G D
Jackson	D
Murphy	G D
Douglas	D
Frankfr	D
Reed	D
Black	D
Vinson	D

Excel Auto v Bishop & Babcock
48 162A
335 US 823
CCA 6th

Justice	CERT 10/06 1948 (1 1)
Burton	D
Rutledg	G D
Jackson	D
Murphy	G D
Douglas	D
Frankfr	D
Reed	D
Black	G D
Vinson	G D

Akers v Scofield
48 165A
335 US 823
CCA 5th

Justice	CERT 10/06 1948 (1 1)
Burton	G
Rutledg	G
Jackson	
Murphy	G
Douglas	
Frankfr	
Reed	
Black	
Vinson	

City Of New York v Saper
48 168A
335 US 328 48 200A 48 201A CCA 2d
Jackson 01/14/49

	10/06 1948 CERT (1 1)	01/08 1949 MERITS (1 1)	03/07 1949 REPORT (1 1)
Burton	G		A
Rutledg	G	A	A
Jackson	G	A	A
Murphy	G	A	A
Douglas	G		A
Frankfr	G		A
Reed	G	R	R
Black	G	R	
Vinson	G	R	A

Reinold v U.S.
48 171A
335 US 824
CCA 2d

	10/06 1948 CERT (1 1)
Burton	D
Rutledg	D
Jackson	D
Murphy	D
Douglas	D
Frankfr	D
Reed	G
Black	
Vinson	G

DeWaters v Macklin Company
48 173A
335 US 824
CCA 6th

	10/06 1948 CERT (1 1)
Burton	D
Rutledg	D
Jackson	D
Murphy	D
Douglas	D
Frankfr	D
Reed	G
Black	
Vinson	G

U.S. v Silliman
48 174A
335 US 825
CCA 3rd

	10/06 1948 CERT (1 1)
Burton	D
Rutledg	GQ
Jackson	D
Murphy	G
Douglas	D
Frankfr	D
Reed	D
Black	G
Vinson	D

U.S. (Sutton) v Mulcahy
48 178A
337 US 956 48 29A 48 43A
CCA 2d

	10/08 1948 CERT (1 1)	06/24 1949 CERT (1 2)
Burton	G	
Rutledg	G	
Jackson	D	D
Murphy	D	D
Douglas	D	D
Frankfr	D	D
Reed	G	D
Black	G	G
Vinson	D	D

Weade v Dichmann Wright & Pugh
48 179A
337 US 801
Reed 02/12/49 CCA 4th

	10/06 1948 CERT (1 1)	02/05 1949 MERITS (1 1)	06/27 1949 REPORT (1 1)
Burton	G	R	R
Rutledg	G	R	R
Jackson	G		AJ
Murphy	G	A	
Douglas	G	R	R
Frankfr	G	A	R
Reed		A	
Black	G	A	AJ
Vinson	G		AJ

Giboney v Empire Storage & Ice
48 182A
336 US 490 48 191A Missouri
Black 01/14/49

	10/08 1948 JURIS (1 1)	01/08 1949 MERITS (1 1)	04/04 1949 REPORT (1 1)
Burton			A
Rutledg	N	R	A
Jackson	N		A
Murphy	N	R	A
Douglas	N	R	A
Frankfr	N		A
Reed	N	R	A
Black	N	R	A
Vinson	N	X A	A

Remington Rand v Royal Typewriter
48 183A
335 US 825
CCA 2d

	10/06 1948 CERT (1 1)
Burton	
Rutledg	G
Jackson	D
Murphy	D
Douglas	G
Frankfr	D
Reed	
Black	D
Vinson	D

Watchtower Bible v Metropolitan Life
48 187A
335 US 912 48 400A New York

	11/20 1948 CERT (1 1)	12/04 1948 CERT (1 2)
Burton		
Rutledg	D	D
Jackson	D	D
Murphy		
Douglas	G	G
Frankfr	G	G
Reed		
Black	G	D
Vinson	G	D

Morris v Ford Motor Company
48 189A
335 US 803
Michigan

	10/05 1948 JURIS (1 1)	01/08 1949 MERITS (1 1)	01/10 1949 REPORT (1 1)
Burton	S	S	S
Rutledg	P	S	S
Jackson		SA	S
Murphy	P	A	S
Douglas	S	S	S
Frankfr	S	S	S
Reed	S	S	S
Black	S		
Vinson	S		

Superior Court v Lillefloren
48 191A
335 US 906 48 182A
California

	10/08 1948 CERT (1 1)
Burton	G
Rutledg	D
Jackson	D
Murphy	D
Douglas	
Frankfr	G
Reed	G
Black	D
Vinson	G

Washington v Arkansas
48 193A
335 US 884
Arkansas

	12/04 1948 CERT (1 1)
Burton	
Rutledg	D
Jackson	D
Murphy	
Douglas	G
Frankfr	G
Reed	D
Black	D
Vinson	D

N.L.R.B. v Crompton-Highland Mills
48 197A
337 US 217
Burton 02/12/49 CCA 5th

	10/07 1948 CERT	02/05 1949 MERITS	05/31 1949 REPORT
	1 1	1 1	1 1
Burton	G	R	R
Rutledg	G	R	R
Jackson	G D	R	R
Murphy	G	R X	R A
Douglas	G	R	R
Frankfr			
Reed	X D	R	R
Black		R X	R A
Vinson	G D		R

Jones v U.S.
48 198A
336 US 641 48 135A
Rutledg 02/12/49 Ct Cls

	11/04 1948 CERT	02/05 1949 MERITS
	1 1	1 1
Burton	G	
Rutledg	G	
Jackson	G	A
Murphy	G	A
Douglas	G D	R X
Frankfr		R R
Reed	G	
Black	G	A
Vinson	G	A

Chicago North Western RR v Matsumoto
48 199A
335 US 826
CCA 7th

	10/07 1948 CERT
	1 1
Burton	G
Rutledg	G D
Jackson	D
Murphy	D
Douglas	D
Frankfr	D
Reed	D
Black	D
Vinson	D

New York v Carter
48 200A
336 US 328 48 168A 48 201A CCA 2d
Jackson 01/14/49

	10/07 1948 CERT	01/08 1949 MERITS	03/07 1949 REPORT
	1 1	1 1	1 1
Burton	G		A
Rutledg	G		A
Jackson	G	R	A
Murphy	G		A
Douglas	G	R	A
Frankfr	G	R	R
Reed	G	R	A
Black	G		
Vinson		R	A

Murphey v M.T. Reed
48 206A
335 US 865
CCA 5th

	11/06 1948 CERT	11/15 1948 REPORT
	1 1	1 1
Burton	GV	V
Rutledg		M
Jackson	GV X	V
Murphy	GV	G
Douglas	GV	G V
Frankfr	GV	V
Reed	GV	V
Black	G	G
Vinson	GV	V

Kelley v Union Tank & Supply Company
48 211A
335 US 827
CCA 5th

	10/07 1948 CERT
	1 1
Burton	D
Rutledg	D
Jackson	D
Murphy	
Douglas	GQ
Frankfr	
Reed	D
Black	DQ
Vinson	D

Gantt v Felipe Y. Carlos Hurtado
48 214A
335 US 843
New York

	10/16 1948 CERT	03/07 1949 REPORT
	1 1	1 1
Burton	D	A
Rutledg	D	A
Jackson	D	A
Murphy	D	A
Douglas	D	A
Frankfr	D	A
Reed	D	R A
Black	G	A
Vinson	D	R A

Algoma Plywood v Wisconsin ERB
48 216A
336 US 301 48 283A
Black 11/24/48 Frankfr 03/01/49 Wisconsin

	10/07 1948 CERT	11/20 1948 MERITS	11/20 1948 MERITS
	1 1	1 1	2 1
Burton	G	R	A
Rutledg	G	R	A
Jackson	G		A
Murphy	G		A
Douglas	G	R	A
Frankfr	G		A
Reed	G	R	A
Black	G		A
Vinson	G	R	A

Burns v California
48 219A
335 US 844
California

	10/16 1948 CERT
	1 1
Burton	
Rutledg	
Jackson	
Murphy	G
Douglas	
Frankfr	
Reed	
Black	
Vinson	

Whitney v Madden
48 220A
335 US 828
Illinois

	10/07 1948 CERT
	1 1
Burton	
Rutledg	D
Jackson	D
Murphy	
Douglas	D
Frankfr	D
Reed	D
Black	G
Vinson	D

Joy Oil Company v State Tax Commission
48 223A
337 US 286   48 224A
Frankfr 01/14/49 Michigan

	10/07 1948 CERT	01/08 1949 MERITS	06/13 1949 REPORT	
	1 1	1 1	1 1	
Burton				
Rutledg		R		A
Jackson			A	A
Murphy	G	R	R	
Douglas	G	X	R	A
Frankfr		A		
Reed		A	R	A
Black				A
Vinson	G	R	R	A

Austin v Kelly
48 224A
335 US 828   48 223A
Michigan

	10/07 1948 CERT
	1 1
Burton	
Rutledg	D
Jackson	D
Murphy	G
Douglas	D
Frankfr	D
Reed	D
Black	D
Vinson	D

S.E.C. v Central-Illinois Securities
48 226A
338 US 96   48 243A   48 227A   48 266A
Rutledg 01/24/49 CCA 3rd

	10/23 1948 CERT	01/17 1949 MERITS	06/27 1949 REPORT
	1 1	1 1	1 1
Burton	G	R	R
Rutledg	G	R	R
Jackson	G	RQ	
Murphy	G	R	R
Douglas		X	
Frankfr			
Reed	G	R	R
Black	G	R	R
Vinson		R	R

Nye & Nissen v U.S.
48 228A
336 US 613
Douglas 03/08/49 CCA 9th

	10/23 1948 CERT	03/05 1949 MERITS	03/05 1949 REPORT	
	1 1	1 1	1 1	
Burton	G	RQ	R	A
Rutledg	G	R	R	A
Jackson	G	RQ	R	A
Murphy				A
Douglas	D			A
Frankfr	G	X	X	A
Reed	D			A
Black	D	A	A	A
Vinson	D	A	A	A

U.S. (Hirshberg) v Cooke
48 231A
336 US 210
Black 01/24/49 CCA 2d

	10/16 1948 CERT	01/17 1949 MERITS	02/28 1949 REPORT	
	1 1	1 1	1 1	
Burton	G	R	R	A
Rutledg	G	R	R	A
Jackson		R	R	A
Murphy	G	RQ	R	A
Douglas		R	R	A
Frankfr	D			
Reed		R	R	A
Black	G	R	R	A
Vinson	G			

Simmons v F.C.C.
48 232A
335 US 846
CCA DC

	10/16 1948 CERT
	1 1
Burton	D
Rutledg	D
Jackson	D
Murphy	D
Douglas	D
Frankfr	D
Reed	G
Black	D
Vinson	D

Brodel v Warner Brothers Pictures
48 233A
335 US 844
California

	10/16 1948 CERT	01/15 1949 MERITS	02/14 1949 REPORT	
	1 1	1 1	1 1	
Burton	D	R	R	A
Rutledg				A
Jackson	D			
Murphy	DZ			
Douglas	DZ	R	R	A
Frankfr	D			
Reed	D	R	R	A
Black	D	R	R	A
Vinson	D			

Reynolds v Atlantic Coast Line RR
48 234A
336 US 207
Alabama

	10/16 1948 CERT	10/23 1948 CERT	01/15 1949 MERITS	02/14 1949 REPORT	
	1 1	1 2	1 1	1 1	
Burton	D	G	R	R	A
Rutledg	D				A
Jackson					
Murphy	D	G	R	R	A
Douglas	D	G			A
Frankfr	D		R	R	A
Reed					
Black	D	D	R	R	A
Vinson	D	D			A

Globe Solvents v The California
48 235A
335 US 844
CCA 3rd

Justice	10/16 1948 CERT (1 1)
Burton	D
Rutledg	D
Jackson	D
Murphy	D
Douglas	D
Frankfr	D
Reed	
Black	G
Vinson	G

Wisconsin Electric Power v U.S.
48 237A
336 US 176
Reed 01/14/49 CCA 7th

Justice	01/08 1949 MERITS (1 1)	02/14 1949 REPORT (1 1)
Burton	G	A
Rutledg	G	A
Jackson	G	A
Murphy	G	A
Douglas	R	A
Frankfr	G	A
Reed	G	A
Black	G	A
Vinson	G	A

Blanc v Spartan Tool Company
48 241A
335 US 853
CCA 7th

Justice	10/23 1948 CERT (1 2)
Burton	G
Rutledg	D
Jackson	
Murphy	DQ
Douglas	G
Frankfr	D
Reed	G
Black	D
Vinson	D

Ott v Mississippi Valley Barge
48 244A
336 US 169
Douglas 01/14/49 CCA 5th

Justice	10/05 1948 JURIS (1 1)	01/08 1949 MERITS (1 1)	02/07 1949 REPORT (1 1)
Burton	N	R	R
Rutledg	NP	R	R
Jackson	N	X	
Murphy	N	R	R
Douglas	A	R	R
Frankfr	A	R	R
Reed	A	R	R
Black	N		
Vinson	N	A	A

Railway Express Agency v C.I.R.
48 247A
336 US 944 48 151A 48 152A 48 153A
CCA 2d

Justice	10/16 1948 CERT (1 1)	04/02 1949 CERT (1 2)
Burton	H	D
Rutledg		D
Jackson	H	D
Murphy	D	D
Douglas	H	D
Frankfr	DH	D
Reed	DHQ	D
Black	D	D
Vinson	G	D

Holliday v Governor Of South Carolina
48 249A
335 US 803
DC WD South Carolina

Justice	10/05 1948 JURIS (1 1)	10/08 1948 JURIS (1 2)	10/11 1948 REPORT (1 1)
Burton	S	S	A
Rutledg	S	S	A
Jackson	A		A
Murphy		A	A
Douglas	S	S	A
Frankfr			A
Reed	S	A	A
Black	A	S	A
Vinson	S	A	A

U.S. v Penn Foundry & Manufacturing
48 253A
337 US 198
Douglas 01/24/49 Burton 03/09/49 Ct Cls

Justice	11/06 1948 CERT (1 1)	01/15 1949 MERITS (1 1)	05/31 1949 REPORT (1 1)
Burton		R	R
Rutledg	D	R	RL
Jackson		R	RL
Murphy	D	AQ	
Douglas			
Frankfr	D	A	R
Reed		R	R
Black	G		RL
Vinson	G	A	R

Cascio v Arkansas
48 254A
335 US 845
Arkansas

Justice	10/16 1948 CERT (1 1)
Burton	
Rutledg	
Jackson	
Murphy	G
Douglas	
Frankfr	
Reed	
Black	
Vinson	

McComb v Hunt Foods
48 256A
335 US 845
CCA 9th

Justice	10/16 1948 CERT (1 1)
Burton	D
Rutledg	D
Jackson	D
Murphy	
Douglas	D
Frankfr	G
Reed	
Black	G
Vinson	D

N.L.R.B. v Pittsburgh Steamship
48 258A
337 US 656
Rutledg 05/02/49 CCA 6th

Justice	11/06 1948 CERT (1 1)	04/23 1949 MERITS	06/20 1949 REPORT (1 1)
Burton	G	R	R
Rutledg	D	RL	R
Jackson	G		R
Murphy	D	R	R
Douglas	D	R	R
Frankfr		R	R
Reed	G	R	R
Black	G	R	R
Vinson	D	RQ	R O

Revere Land Company v C.I.R.
48 261A
335 US 853
CCA 3rd

Justice	10/23 1948 CERT (1 1)
Burton	
Rutledg	D
Jackson	
Murphy	D
Douglas	G
Frankfr	DQ
Reed	
Black	G
Vinson	D

Wixman v U.S.
48 263A
335 US 874
CCA 9th

Justice	12/04 1948 CERT (1 1)	12/04 1948 MERITS	12/06 1948 REPORT (1 1)
Burton		R	R
Rutledg	D	R	R
Jackson	D	R	R
Murphy	G	R	R
Douglas	D	R	R
Frankfr		R	R
Reed	G	R	R
Black	D	R	R
Vinson	D	R	R

Eisler v U.S.
48 255A
338 US 189 48 845A 48 0A 48 334A
Murphy 04/05/49 CCA DC

	10/23 1948 CERT 1 1	11/06 1948 CERT 1 2	04/02 1949 MERITS 1 1	05/28 1949 EXTEND 1 1	06/04 1949 MERITS 1 2	06/04 1949 REMOVE 1 1	06/24 1949 DISMISS 1 1	06/27 1949 REPORT 1 1	11/19 1949 DISMISS 1 2
Minton									
Burton	G	D	R	D	R			F	
Rutledg	G			D		B	Y	F	Y
Jackson	G	D	R	D	A	B	Y	R	Y
Murphy	G		R		Y	B	Y	A	Y
Douglas	G	D	R	G				F	
Frankfr					S			S	B
Reed	G		R	G	A	B	Y	F	B
Black	G	D	R	D		B		F	
Vinson	G	D	R	D	S	B	Y	S	Y

North American Company v Koerner
48 265A
335 US 803
Missouri

	10/05 1948 JURIS 1 1
Burton	S
Rutledg	S
Jackson	S
Murphy	N
Douglas	S
Frankfr	S
Reed	S
Black	S
Vinson	S

Farrell v U.S.
48 267A
336 US 511
Jackson 01/24/49 CCA 2d

	11/23 1948 CERT 1 1	01/17 1949 MERITS 1 1	04/04 1949 REPORT 1 1
Burton	D		A
Rutledg	D	x A	R
Jackson			
Murphy	D	RQ	R
Douglas	GQ	R	R
Frankfr			
Reed	D		A
Black	D	R	A
Vinson	D		A

Terminiello v City Of Chicago
48 272A
337 US 1
Douglas 02/25/49 Illinois

	12/04 1948 CERT 1 1	12/11 1948 CERT 1 2	02/05 1949 MERITS 1 1	02/05 1949 DISMISS 1 1	05/16 1949 REPORT 1 1
Burton	G	G	R		A
Rutledg	G	G		B	
Jackson	G	G	R	Y	R
Murphy	G	G		B	R
Douglas	D	G		B	
Frankfr	G	G	R		R
Reed		G	R	B	R
Black				Y	
Vinson	D		D	X Y	A

Brotherhood Of Locomotive v U.S.
48 277A
335 US 867
CCA DC

	11/13 1948 CERT 1 1
Burton	D
Rutledg	G
Jackson	DQ
Murphy	G
Douglas	
Frankfr	D
Reed	D
Black	D
Vinson	D

Standard Oil Company v U.S.
48 279A
337 US 293
Frankfr 03/08/49 DC SD California

	10/16 1948 JURIS 1 1	03/05 1949 MERITS 1 1	06/13 1949 REPORT 1 1
Burton	N	R	
Rutledg	N		R
Jackson	N	x A	A
Murphy	N	x A	
Douglas	N	A	A
Frankfr	N	A	A
Reed	N	A	A
Black	N	x A	
Vinson	N	x	R

Riley v International Teamsters
48 283A
336 US 930 48 216A
New Hampshire

	11/06 1948 CERT 1 1	01/08 1949 CERT 1 2	03/08 1949 CERT 1 3	03/14 1949 REPORT 1 1
Burton	G			VI
Rutledg	H	D	GVI	VI
Jackson	H	D	GVI	VI
Murphy	G		GVI	VI
Douglas	G	D	GVI	VI
Frankfr	H	D	GVI	VI
Reed		D	GVI	VI
Black	H	D	GVI	VI
Vinson	D		GVI	

Whetstone v Washington
48 284A
335 US 858
Washington

	11/06 1948 CERT 1 1
Burton	
Rutledg	
Jackson	
Murphy	G
Douglas	
Frankfr	
Reed	
Black	
Vinson	

Interstate Oil Pipe Line v Stone
48 287A
337 US 662
Reed 01/24/49 Rutledg 05/14/49 Mississippi

	10/16 1948 JURIS	01/17 1949 MERITS	04/30 1949 MERITS	06/20 1949 REPORT
	1 1	1 1	1 2	1 1
Burton	N	A	A	A
Rutledg	N	A	A	A
Jackson	N	R	A	
Murphy	N		A	R
Douglas	N	X	A	A
Frankfr		R	A	A
Reed			A	R
Black	N	A	A	A
Vinson		R	A	A

Minsch v Bailey
48 290A
335 US 854
CCA 1st

	10/23 1948 CERT
	1 1
Burton	D
Rutledg	D
Jackson	D
Murphy	D
Douglas	D
Frankfr	D
Reed	G
Black	D
Vinson	D

McCaffrey v Royall
48 291A 48 131N
335 US 849 335 US 849
CCA DC

	10/23 1948 HABEAS	10/23 1948 CERT
	1 1	1 1
Burton	K	D
Rutledg	D	G
Jackson	D	
Murphy	D	G
Douglas	D	
Frankfr	D	
Reed	D	
Black	K	D
Vinson	D	

Smith v U.S.
48 292A
337 US 137 48 294A
Reed 03/08/49 CCA 2d

	12/04 1948 CERT	03/08 1949 MERITS	03/08 1949 MERITS	05/31 1949 REPORT
	1 1	1 1	2 1	1 1
Burton	G	R	A	R
Rutledg	G	R	R	R
Jackson	G	R	R	R
Murphy	G	R	R	R
Douglas	G	R	R	R
Frankfr	G	R	R	R
Reed	G	R	R	R
Black	G	X	X	R
Vinson	D			R

Daniel v Family Security Life
48 297A
336 US 220
Murphy 02/12/49 DC ED South Carolina

	10/23 1948 JURIS	10/23 1949 MERITS	02/28 1949 REPORT
	1 1	1 1	1 1
Burton	N	R	
Rutledg	N	R	
Jackson	N	R	
Murphy	NR	R	
Douglas	N	R	
Frankfr	N	R	
Reed	N	R	
Black	NR	R	
Vinson	N	R	

Defense Supplies v Lawrence Warehouse
48 298A
336 US 631
Murphy 02/12/49 CCA 9th

	11/06 1948 CERT	02/05 1949 MERITS	04/18 1949 REPORT
	1 1	1 1	1 1
Burton	G	R	>
Rutledg	G	R	>
Jackson	G		>
Murphy	G	R	>
Douglas	G	R	>
Frankfr	G	R	>
Reed	G	R AQ	>
Black	G		>
Vinson	G	R	>

Associated Telephone v Federal Telephone
48 308A
335 US 859
CCA 3rd

	11/06 1948 CERT
	1 1
Burton	D
Rutledg	D
Jackson	D
Murphy	GQ
Douglas	D
Frankfr	G
Reed	D
Black	D
Vinson	

C.I.R. v Culbertson
48 313A
337 US 733 48 509A 48 520A
Vinson 02/12/49 CCA 5th

	11/20 1948 CERT	12/04 1948 CERT	02/11 1949 MERITS	02/11 1949 MERITS	06/27 1949 REPORT
	1 1	1 2	1 1	2 1	1 1
Burton	G	G	R	A	R
Rutledg	D	G	A	A	R
Jackson	D	D	A	A	R
Murphy	D	D	A	A	R
Douglas	D	G			A
Frankfr	D	D	R	A	R
Reed	D	G	A	A	R
Black	G	G	A	A	R
Vinson	G	G	A	A	R

U.S. v Cal-Bay
48 314A
335 US 859
CCA 9th

	11/06 1948 CERT
	1 1
Burton	D
Rutledg	D
Jackson	D
Murphy	D
Douglas	D
Frankfr	D
Reed	D
Black	GQ
Vinson	D

Mulcahy v New York New Haven RR
48 316A
335 US 867
CCA 2d

	11/13 1948 CERT
	1 1
Burton	D
Rutledg	D
Jackson	D
Murphy	D
Douglas	D
Frankfr	D
Reed	G
Black	D
Vinson	D

Benzian v Godwin
48 317A
335 US 886
CCA 2d

	12/04 1948 CERT
	1 1
Burton	
Rutledg	
Jackson	
Murphy	G
Douglas	GQ
Frankfr	
Reed	G
Black	D
Vinson	D

Empresa Siderurgica v County Of Merced
48 327A
337 US 154
Burton 02/12/49 Douglas 04/27/49 California

	11/06 1948 JURIS	02/11 1949 MERITS	05/31 1949 REPORT
	1 1	1 1	1 1
Burton	S	A	A
Rutledg	S	A	A
Jackson	S	A	A
Murphy	N	A	A
Douglas	N	X	M
Frankfr	N	A	A
Reed		S	A
Black	S	A	A
Vinson	A	A	A

Kansas City Terminal RR v Thompson
48 328A
335 US 870
Missouri

	11/20 1948 CERT
	1 1
Burton	D
Rutledg	D
Jackson	D
Murphy	G
Douglas	
Frankfr	
Reed	G
Black	D
Vinson	D

U.S. v I.C.C.
48 330A
337 US 426
Black 03/08/49 DC DC

	11/06 1948 JURIS	03/05 1949 MERITS	06/20 1949 REPORT
	1 1	1 1	1 1
Burton	N	RQ	A
Rutledg	P	A	A
Jackson	N	X	R
Murphy	N	AQ	R
Douglas	N	A	A
Frankfr	N		R
Reed		R	R
Black		R	R
Vinson		R	R

U.S. v Plotzer
48 332A
335 US 885
Ct Cls

	12/04 1948 CERT
	1 1
Burton	D
Rutledg	D
Jackson	D
Murphy	D
Douglas	D
Frankfr	D
Reed	G
Black	D
Vinson	D

Aeronautical Industrial v Campbell
48 333A
337 US 521
Frankfr 02/12/49 CCA 9th

	11/20 1948 CERT	02/05 1949 MERITS	06/20 1949 REPORT
	1 1		1 1
Burton	G	R	R
Rutledg	G		R
Jackson	G	AQ	R
Murphy	G	X	R
Douglas	G	R	R
Frankfr	G	R	R
Reed	G	R	R
Black	G	A	R
Vinson	G	RQ	R

Lawson v U.S.
48 334A
335 US 861 48 255A
CCA DC

	11/06 1948 CERT
	1 1
Burton	D
Rutledg	D
Jackson	D
Murphy	G
Douglas	D
Frankfr	D
Reed	D
Black	D
Vinson	D

Darr v Mutual Life Insurance Company
48 337A
335 US 871
CCA 2d

	11/20 1948 CERT
	1 1
Burton	D
Rutledg	D
Jackson	D
Murphy	G
Douglas	D
Frankfr	D
Reed	D
Black	D
Vinson	

Gross Income Tax Division v Strauss
48 338A
335 US 860
Indiana

	11/06 1948 CERT
	1 1
Burton	D
Rutledg	D
Jackson	
Murphy	
Douglas	G
Frankfr	G
Reed	D
Black	G
Vinson	D

Cingrigrani v B.H. Hubbert & Son
48 340A
335 US 868
CCA 4th

	11/13 1948 CERT
	1 1
Burton	D
Rutledg	D
Jackson	
Murphy	
Douglas	G
Frankfr	
Reed	D
Black	D
Vinson	D

Houston v McCormack
48 345A
335 US 868
California

	11/13 1948 CERT
	1 1
Burton	D
Rutledg	D
Jackson	
Murphy	
Douglas	G
Frankfr	D
Reed	D
Black	D
Vinson	GQ

Josephs' Estate v C.I.R.
48 346A
335 US 871
CCA 8th

Justice	11/20 1948 CERT	
Burton	G	D
Rutledg		D
Jackson	G	
Murphy		D
Douglas		D
Frankfr	G	
Reed		
Black	G	
Vinson		D

Cosmopolitan Shipping v McAllister
48 351A
337 US 783 48 360A 48 102A
Reed 02/12/49 CCA 2d

Justice	11/06 1948 CERT	11/20 1948 CERT	02/05 1949 MERITS	06/27 1949 REPORT
Burton	G	G	R	R
Rutledg	H	G	RQ	R
Jackson	H	G	R	R
Murphy	G DQ	G		
Douglas		G	A	A
Frankfr	H	G	R	R
Reed	D	G		
Black	H	G	R A	R A
Vinson	H		R	R A

California v Zook
48 355A
336 US 725
Murphy 02/12/49 California

Justice	11/20 1948 CERT	02/11 1949 MERITS	04/25 1949 REPORT
Burton	G D	RQ	R
Rutledg	D	R	R
Jackson	D	R	R
Murphy			
Douglas	G D	R A	R A
Frankfr	G	R	R
Reed			
Black	x D		
Vinson	D		

National Bank Of Commerce v Scofield
48 357A
335 US 907 48 90A
CCA 5th

Justice	01/08 1949 CERT	
Burton	G	
Rutledg		D
Jackson	GQ	D
Murphy		
Douglas	x	D
Frankfr		
Reed		D
Black		D
Vinson		D

Fink v Shepard Steamship Company
48 360A
337 US 810 48 351A 48 430A 48 162M
Reed 02/12/49 Oregon

Justice	11/20 1948 CERT	02/05 1949 MERITS	06/27 1949 REPORT
Burton	G		R
Rutledg	G	AQ	R
Jackson	G	A A	R R
Murphy	G		
Douglas	G	A A	R
Frankfr	G	R	R R
Reed	G		
Black	G	A AQ	R A
Vinson	G	A	R A

Bethlehem Steel Company v Moores
48 369A
335 US 874
Massachusetts

Justice	12/04 1948 JURIS	12/06 1948 REPORT	
Burton	N	A	
Rutledg		A	A
Jackson		A	A
Murphy	N	A	
Douglas		A	
Frankfr		A	A
Reed		SA	A
Black		SA	A
Vinson		A	A

Whitney v C.I.R.
48 373A
335 US 892 48 374A 48 385A
CCA 2d

Justice	12/11 1948 CERT	
Burton	G	
Rutledg	G	D
Jackson	G	D
Murphy	G	D
Douglas		
Frankfr		
Reed		D
Black		D
Vinson		D

Transcontinental & Western v C.A.B.
48 387A
336 US 601
Douglas 02/12/49 CCA DC

Justice	12/04 1948 CERT	02/11 1949 MERITS	04/18 1949 REPORT
Burton	G		R A
Rutledg	G		R A
Jackson	G		R
Murphy	G	RQ A	R A
Douglas	G		R
Frankfr	G	RQ A	R
Reed			
Black	D		R A
Vinson	D		R A

Brooks v U.S.
48 388A
337 US 49 48 389A
Murphy 03/08/49 CCA 4th

Justice	12/31 1948 CERT	03/05 1949 MERITS	05/16 1949 REPORT
Burton	G	R	R A
Rutledg	G	R	R A
Jackson	G	R	R
Murphy	G		
Douglas	G	RL	R A
Frankfr	G	R	R
Reed	G		
Black	G	R	R A
Vinson	G	R	R A

Propper v Clark
48 390A
337 US 472
Reed 04/05/49 CCA 2d

	12/31 1948 CERT 1 1	04/02 1949 MERITS 1 1	06/20 1949 REPORT 1 1
Burton	D	A	A
Rutledg	D	A	A
Jackson			
Murphy	GL	R	M
Douglas	GL	A	A
Frankfr	GL	R	A
Reed			
Black	GL	A	A
Vinson		A	A

City Of Morgantown v Royal Insurance
48 396A
337 US 254
Murphy 02/12/49 CCA 4th

	12/11 1948 CERT 1 1	02/11 1949 QUEST 11 1	02/11 1949 MERITS 1 1	06/06 1949 REPORT 1 1
Burton	GQ	Y		A
Rutledg	D	B	R	A
Jackson				
Murphy	GO	B	R	A
Douglas	D	B		A
Frankfr	GO	B		A
Reed				
Black	G	B	Y	A
Vinson	D			A

Brady Transfer & Storage v U.S.
48 397A
335 US 875
DC SD Iowa

	12/04 1948 JURIS 1 1	12/06 1948 REPORT 1 1
Burton	A	A
Rutledg	A	A
Jackson	A	A
Murphy	N	A
Douglas	A	A
Frankfr	A	A
Reed	A	A
Black	A	A
Vinson	A	A

Hall v Virginia
48 400A
335 US 875 48 187A
Virginia

	11/20 1948 JURIS 1 1	12/04 1948 JURIS 1 2
Burton	S	S
Rutledg		S
Jackson		
Murphy	N	N
Douglas	N	N
Frankfr	N	
Reed	NQ	
Black		S
Vinson	S	S

City Bank Farmers Trust v Pedrick
48 401A
335 US 898
CCA 2d

	12/18 1948 CERT 1 1
Burton	D
Rutledg	D
Jackson	D
Murphy	D
Douglas	D
Frankfr	D
Reed	
Black	G
Vinson	D

Guggenheim v U.S.
48 405A
335 US 908
Ct Cls

	12/04 1948 JURIS 1 1	12/06 1948 REPORT 1 1	01/08 1949 CERT 1 1
Burton		A	D
Rutledg		A	D
Jackson		A	D
Murphy	N	A	
Douglas		A	D
Frankfr		A	G
Reed		A	D
Black		A	D
Vinson		A	D

U.S. v Knight
48 406A
336 US 505
Douglas 03/08/49 CCA 3rd

	12/31 1948 CERT 1 1	03/05 1949 MERITS 1 1	04/04 1949 REPORT 1 1
Burton	G	R	R
Rutledg	G	R	
Jackson			
Murphy	D		
Douglas	X		
Frankfr	D	S	S
Reed	G	R	R
Black	G	R	R
Vinson	G		R

Georgia Railroad & Banking v Musgrove
48 413A
335 US 900
Georgia

	12/31 1948 JURIS 1 1	03/05 1949 MERITS 1 1
Burton	S	
Rutledg	S	
Jackson		
Murphy	S	
Douglas	S	
Frankfr	S	S
Reed	N	
Black	S	
Vinson	S	

U.S. v Wallace & Tiernan Company
48 416A
336 US 793
Black 04/05/49 DC Rhode Island

	12/04 1948 JURIS 1 1	04/02 1949 MERITS 1 1	05/02 1949 REPORT 1 1
Burton	P	R	R
Rutledg	P	X	R
Jackson	P	X	R
Murphy	P S		R
Douglas	P S	R	R
Frankfr	P	R	R
Reed	N		R
Black	P	R	R
Vinson	P	A	

Griffin v U.S.
48 417A 48 41M
336 US 704
Murphy 12/21/48 Frankfr 04/22/49 CCA DC

	11/06 1948 CERT 1 1	11/13 1948 CERT 1 2	12/20 1948 MERITS 1 1	04/25 1949 REPORT 1 1
Burton	G	D		
Rutledg	D	G	R	R
Jackson	D			M
Murphy	G	G	A	M
Douglas	D	G	R	R
Frankfr	D		R	
Reed	D	D	M	M
Black	D	D	A	M
Vinson	D	D	A	

Gibbs v Burke
48 418A 48 127M
337 US 773
Reed 04/27/49 Pennsylvania

	11/06 1948 CERT 1 1	11/13 1948 CERT 1 2	04/23 1949 MERITS 1 1	06/27 1949 REPORT 1 1
Burton	G	G	R	R
Rutledg	D	D	A	R
Jackson	D			R
Murphy	G	G	R	R
Douglas	G	G		R
Frankfr	D		A	R
Reed	D	D		
Black	D	D	R	R
Vinson	D	D	A	R

World Publishing Company v U.S.
48 426A
335 US 911
CCA 10th

	01/15 1949 CERT 1 1
Burton	D
Rutledg	D
Jackson	D
Murphy	X
Douglas	D
Frankfr	G
Reed	D
Black	D
Vinson	D

Wade v Hunter
48 427A
336 US 684
Black 03/09/49 CCA 10th

	CERT 01/08 1949	MERITS 03/08 1949	REPORT 04/25 1949
	1 1	1 1	1 1
Burton	G	R	R
Rutledg	D	A	A
Jackson	G	R	R
Murphy	G	R	R
Douglas	G	A	A
Frankfr		A	A
Reed	D	A	A
Black	D		
Vinson	D	A	A

Zimmerman v Maryland
48 429A 48 118M
336 US 901
Maryland

	CERT 11/06 1948	MERITS 11/13 1948	CERT 11/20 1948
	1 1	1 2	1 3
Burton	G	G D	G D
Rutledg	G	G	G
Jackson	G	G	G
Murphy			
Douglas	G	G D	G D
Frankfr			
Reed		G D	G D
Black			
Vinson		G D	G D

Gaynor v Aguillines
48 430A 48 162M
337 US 810 48 351A 48 360A
Reed 02/12/49 CCA 3rd

	CERT 11/20 1948	MERITS 02/05 1949	REPORT 06/27 1949
	1 1	1 1	1 1
Burton	G	R	R
Rutledg	G	AQ	A
Jackson	G	A	A
Murphy	G		
Douglas	G	A	A
Frankfr	G	A	A
Reed		R	R
Black	G	A	A
Vinson	G	A	A

Cohen v Beneficial Industrial Loan
48 442A
337 US 541 48 512A
Jackson 04/25/49 CCA 3rd

	CERT 02/26 1949	MERITS 04/23 1949	REPORT 06/20 1949
	1 1	1 1	1 1
Burton	G	R	R
Rutledg	GVM	A	A
Jackson	G	A	A
Murphy	D		?
Douglas	D	R	?
Frankfr	G	R	R
Reed	G	R	R
Black	G	A	A
Vinson	G	A	A

Wheeling Steel v Glander
48 447A
337 US 562 48 448A
Jackson 04/05/49 Ohio

	JURIS 12/31 1948	MERITS 04/02 1949	REPORT 06/20 1949
	1 1	1 1	1 1
Burton	N	R	R
Rutledg	N	R X	R
Jackson	N	R X	R
Murphy	N		
Douglas	N	R	R
Frankfr	N	R	R
Reed	N		
Black	S	R	R
Vinson	N	A	A

National Distillers v Glander
48 448A
337 US 562 48 447A
Jackson 04/05/49 Ohio

	JURIS 12/31 1948	MERITS 04/02 1949	REPORT 06/20 1949
	1 1	1 1	1 1
Burton	N	R	R
Rutledg	N	R X	R
Jackson	N	R X	R
Murphy	N		
Douglas	N	R	R
Frankfr	N	R	R
Reed	N		
Black	S	R	R
Vinson	N	A	A

Humphrey v Smith
48 457A
336 US 695
Black 04/27/49 CCA 3rd

	CERT 02/05 1949	SUBSTE 02/05 1949	MERITS 04/02 1949	REPORT 04/25 1949
	1 1		1 1	1 1
Burton	G	K	R	R
Rutledg	G	Y	R	R
Jackson	G	Y		
Murphy	G	Y		
Douglas	G	Y	A	AQ
Frankfr	G		R	R
Reed		K	R	R
Black	G		R	R
Vinson		Y	R	R

Carpenter v Rohm & Haas Company
48 458A
336 US 904
CCA 3rd

	CERT 01/29 1949
	1 1
Burton	
Rutledg	
Jackson	
Murphy	
Douglas	G
Frankfr	
Reed	
Black	
Vinson	

Gierens v Illinois
48 462A
336 US 904
Illinois

	CERT 01/29 1949
	1 1
Burton	
Rutledg	
Jackson	
Murphy	
Douglas	G
Frankfr	
Reed	
Black	
Vinson	

Clayton Mark & Company v F.T.C.
48 464A
336 US 956
CCA 7th

	01/29 1948 CERT (1 1)	04/16 1949 MERITS (1 1)	04/23 1949 MERITS (1 2)	04/25 1949 REPORT (1 1)
Burton	G		A	A
Rutledg	G	R		
Jackson	X	A	A	A
Murphy	G			
Douglas	G		A	
Frankfr	G	R	A	A
Reed				
Black	G	R	A	A
Vinson				

Woods v Interstate Realty Company
48 465A
337 US 535
Douglas 04/05/49 CCA 5th

	02/05 1949 CERT (1 1)	04/02 1949 MERITS (1 1)	06/20 1949 REPORT (1 1)
Burton	G	R	R
Rutledg	D	R	R
Jackson	D		
Murphy	G		
Douglas	G	R	R
Frankfr	G	R	R
Reed	G	R	R
Black	G	A	
Vinson	G		

Meyers v U.S.
48 467A
336 US 912
CCA DC

	04/03 1948 BAIL (1 1)	02/11 1949 CERT (1 1)
Burton	B	G
Rutledg		
Jackson		
Murphy	Y	G
Douglas		
Frankfr	B	G
Reed	B	
Black	B	
Vinson		Y

Hill v Atlantic Coast Line RR
48 472A
336 US 911
North Carolina

	02/05 1949 CERT (1 1)	02/05 1949 MERITS (1 1)	02/14 1949 REPORT (1 1)
Burton	G	R	R
Rutledg	D	R	R
Jackson		R	R
Murphy	D	R	R
Douglas	G		
Frankfr	D	S	S
Reed			
Black	G	R	R
Vinson	D	A	

U.S. v Wittek
48 473A
337 US 346
Burton 04/27/49 CCA DC

	03/08 1949 CERT (1 1)	04/23 1949 MERITS (1 1)	06/13 1949 REPORT (1 1)
Burton	G	R	R
Rutledg	G	R	R
Jackson	D	R	R
Murphy	G	R	R
Douglas	G	R	R
Frankfr	D	R	R
Reed	G	R	R
Black	G	R	R
Vinson	X		

Stainback v Mo Hock Ke Lok Po
48 474A
336 US 368 48 52A 47 789A
Reed 01/24/49 CCA 9th

	01/17 1949 CERT (1 1)	01/17 1949 VACATE (1 1)	03/14 1949 REPORT (1 1)
Burton	G	Y	R
Rutledg	D	Y	
Jackson	D		R
Murphy	X	X	R
Douglas	G	B	
Frankfr	G	Y	R
Reed	G	Y	S
Black	G	Y	R
Vinson	G	Y	S

Woods v Durr
48 476A
336 US 941
CCA 3rd

	02/11 1949 CERT (1 1)	04/04 1949 REPORT (1 1)
Burton	G	>
Rutledg	GQ	>
Jackson	D	>
Murphy	G	>
Douglas		>
Frankfr	D	>
Reed	G	>
Black	D	
Vinson	D	

Allied Paper Mills v F.T.C.
48 477A
336 US 918
CCA 7th

	02/26 1949 CERT (1 1)
Burton	G
Rutledg	
Jackson	D
Murphy	D
Douglas	
Frankfr	D
Reed	
Black	D
Vinson	D

Houvardas v Wizon
48 479A
336 US 913
CCA 9th

	02/11 1949 CERT (1 1)
Burton	G
Rutledg	D
Jackson	D
Murphy	D
Douglas	D
Frankfr	D
Reed	
Black	D
Vinson	D

F.C.C. v WJR The Goodwill Station
48 495A
337 US 265
Rutledg 04/27/49 CCA DC

	02/26 1949 CERT (1 1)	04/23 1949 MERITS (1 1)	06/06 1949 REPORT (1 1)
Burton	G	R	R
Rutledg	G	R	R
Jackson	G	R	R
Murphy	G	R	R
Douglas	G	R	R
Frankfr	G	R	R
Reed	G	R	R
Black	G	R	R
Vinson			

American Locomotive v Chemical Research
48 498A
336 US 909 48 499A
CCA 6th

	02/05 1949 CERT (1 1)
Burton	D
Rutledg	D
Jackson	D
Murphy	D
Douglas	D
Frankfr	
Reed	D
Black	D
Vinson	

Union National Bank Of Wichita v Lamb
48 500A
337 US 38
Douglas 04/05/49 Missouri

	01/29 1949 JURIS (1 1)	04/02 1949 MERITS (1 1)	05/16 1949 REPORT (1 1)
Burton	P	R	R
Rutledg	P		
Jackson	P	R	R
Murphy	P	X	
Douglas	P		
Frankfr	P	R	R
Reed	P		
Black	P	R	R
Vinson	P	A	A

250

Kingsland v Barron-Gray Packing
48 504A
336 US 944
CCA DC

Justice	04/02/1949 CERT (1 1)
Burton	G
Rutledg	D
Jackson	
Murphy	D
Douglas	D
Frankfr	D
Reed	D
Black	
Vinson	D

U.S. (Johnson) v Shaughnessy
48 506A
336 US 806
Black 04/27/49 CCA 2d

Justice	03/05/1949 CERT (1 1)	04/23/1949 MERITS (1 1)	05/09/1949 REPORT (1 1)
Burton	G	R	A
Rutledg	G	R	A
Jackson			
Murphy	G	R	A
Douglas	G X	R	A
Frankfr			
Reed	G	R	A
Black			
Vinson			

Kohl v C.I.R.
48 509A
337 US 956 48 313A
CCA 8th

Justice	02/26/1949 CERT (1 1)	06/17/1949 CERT (1 2)	06/24/1949 CERT (1 3)
Burton	H	D	D
Rutledg	H	D	D
Jackson			
Murphy	H	D	D
Douglas			
Frankfr	H	D	D
Reed			
Black			
Vinson			

International Longshoremen's v Wirtz
48 510A
336 US 919
CCA 9th

Justice	02/26/1949 CERT (1 1)
Burton	
Rutledg	D
Jackson	D
Murphy	G
Douglas	G
Frankfr	D
Reed	D
Black	D
Vinson	D

Burnham Chemical v Borax Consolidated
48 513A
336 US 924
CCA 9th

Justice	03/05/1949 CERT (1 1)
Murphy	G
Douglas	G

Poore v Mississippi
48 517A
336 US 922
Mississippi

Justice	03/05/1949 CERT (1 1)
Murphy	G
Douglas	G

Atlantic Freight v Pennsylvania PUC
48 518A
336 US 925
Pennsylvania

Justice	03/05/1949 CERT (1 1)
Burton	
Rutledg	D
Jackson	D
Murphy	D
Douglas	G
Frankfr	D
Reed	D
Black	G
Vinson	D

C.I.R. v Hartz
48 520A
337 US 959 48 313A 48 509A
CCA 8th

Justice	06/17/1949 CERT (1 1)	06/24/1949 CERT (1 2)
Burton	D	D
Rutledg	D	D
Jackson	D	D
Murphy	G	D
Douglas	D	D
Frankfr	D	D
Reed	D	D
Black	GR	G
Vinson	GR	G

Ragan v Merchants Transfer & Warehouse
48 522A
337 US 530
Douglas 04/27/49 CCA 10th

Justice	02/26/1949 CERT (1 1)	04/23/1949 MERITS (1 1)	06/20/1949 REPORT (1 1)
Burton	G	R	A
Rutledg	G DQ	R	A
Jackson			
Murphy	G	R	A
Douglas			
Frankfr			
Reed	G	R	A
Black	G	R	A
Vinson	G	R	A

Moore v C.I.R.
48 525A
337 US 930 48 313A 48 509A 48 520A
CCA 4th

Justice	06/24/1949 CERT (1 1)
Burton	
Rutledg	D
Jackson	D
Murphy	D
Douglas	D
Frankfr	D
Reed	D
Black	G
Vinson	D

Sioux Tribe Of Indians v U.S.
48 526A
337 US 908 48 527A 46 368A 46 369A
Ct Cls

Justice	05/14/1949 CERT (1 1)
Burton	
Rutledg	D
Jackson	D
Murphy	G
Douglas	D
Frankfr	D
Reed	D
Black	D
Vinson	

Christoffel v U.S.
48 528A
338 US 84
Murphy 04/27/49 CCA DC

Justice	03/26/1949 CERT (1 1)	04/23/1949 MERITS (1 1)	06/27/1949 REPORT (1 1)
Burton	G	R	A
Rutledg	G	R	A
Jackson			
Murphy	G		
Douglas	G	R	A
Frankfr	G	R	A
Reed	G	R	A
Black	G	R	A
Vinson	G	R	A

Standard Oil v Superior Court Delaware
48 530A
336 US 930 48 529A 58 531A
Delaware

Justice	03/08/1949 JURIS (1 1)
Burton	
Rutledg	S
Jackson	S X
Murphy	S
Douglas	S
Frankfr	A
Reed	S
Black	S
Vinson	S

Boston RR Holding v Delaware & Hudson
48 533A
336 US 932
Massachusetts

Justice	03/26/1949 JURIS (1 1)
Burton	
Rutledg	S
Jackson	S
Murphy	S
Douglas	S
Frankfr	N
Reed	S
Black	S
Vinson	S

J.D. Richardson Company v U.S.
48 534A
336 US 936
CCPA

Justice	03/26/1949 CERT (1 1)
Burton	
Rutledg	D
Jackson	D
Murphy	D
Douglas	G
Frankfr	G
Reed	G
Black	
Vinson	

Painter v Southern Transportation
48 539A
336 US 931
CCA 4th

Justice	03/08 1949 CERT (1 1)
Burton	D
Rutledg	DQ
Jackson	D
Murphy	
Douglas	
Frankfr	G
Reed	D
Black	D
Vinson	D

Fountain v Filson
48 542A
336 US 681
CCA DC

Justice	03/26 1949 CERT (1 1)	03/26 1949 MERITS	04/18 1949 REPORT (1 1)
Burton	G	R	R
Rutledg	G	R	R
Jackson	G		R
Murphy	G	R	R
Douglas	G	R	R
Frankfr	G	R	R
Reed	G	R	R
Black	G		R
Vinson	G		R

De Meerleer v Michigan
48 544A
336 US 946   48 309M
Michigan

Justice	03/26 1949 CERT (1 1)	
Burton		D
Rutledg	G	D
Jackson		D
Murphy		
Douglas	G	D
Frankfr		D
Reed		D
Black		D
Vinson		D

Brotherhood RR v Baltimore & Ohio RR
48 548A
336 US 944
CCA 7th

Justice	03/26 1949 CERT (1 1)	04/02 1949 CERT (1 2)
Burton	D	D
Rutledg	DQ	D
Jackson		
Murphy	G	D
Douglas		D
Frankfr	X	
Reed		D
Black	G	D
Vinson	X	D

Odom v Mississippi
48 551A
336 US 932
Mississippi

Justice	03/26 1949 CERT (1 1)	03/26 1949 JURIS (1 1)
Burton		S
Rutledg		S
Jackson		S
Murphy	G	N
Douglas	GQ	S
Frankfr	G	N
Reed		S
Black		S
Vinson		S

O'Neill v C.I.R.
48 552A
336 US 937
CCA 2d

Justice	03/26 1949 CERT (1 1)
Burton	D
Rutledg	D
Jackson	D
Murphy	D
Douglas	D
Frankfr	D
Reed	D
Black	D
Vinson	G

Lagemann v Lagemann
48 557A
336 US 932
Nevada

Justice	03/26 1949 JURIS (1 1)
Burton	S
Rutledg	S
Jackson	S
Murphy	N
Douglas	S
Frankfr	S
Reed	S
Black	S
Vinson	S

F.P.C. v Panhandle Eastern Pipe Line
48 558A
337 US 498
Reed 05/06/49   CCA 3rd

Justice	03/26 1949 CERT (1 1)	04/30 1949 MERITS (1 1)	06/20 1949 REPORT (1 1)
Burton	G		A
Rutledg	G	R	A
Jackson			A
Murphy	G	R	A
Douglas		R	A
Frankfr	G		A
Reed			
Black	G		
Vinson	G		

Stemmer v New York
48 567A
336 US 963   48 568A
New York

Justice	04/02 1949 CERT (1 1)	04/26 1949 MERITS (1 1)	04/30 1949 MERITS (1 2)	05/02 1949 REPORT (1 1)
Burton	G	R	R	A
Rutledg	G	R	R	R
Jackson	G	R	R	R
Murphy	G	R	R	R
Douglas	G	A	A	A
Frankfr	G	A	A	A
Reed	D	A	A	A
Black	D	A	A	
Vinson	G			

Metropolis Theatre v Barkhausen
48 572A
336 US 945
CCA 7th

Justice	04/02 1949 CERT (1 1)	
Burton	D	
Rutledg	D	
Jackson	D	
Murphy	D	
Douglas	D	
Frankfr	D	
Reed	G	
Black		
Vinson	G	D

F.C.C. v Broadcasting Service
48 584A
337 US 901
CCA DC

Justice	04/16 1949 CERT (1 1)	05/14 1949 MERITS (1 1)	05/16 1949 REPORT (1 1)
Burton	G	R	R
Rutledg	GR	R	R
Jackson	GR		R
Murphy	G	R	R
Douglas	G	R	R
Frankfr	G	R	R
Reed	GR	R	R
Black	GR	R	R
Vinson	GR	R	R

Ryles v U.S.
48 593A
336 US 949
CCA 10th

Justice	04/16 1949 CERT (1 1)	04/18 1949 REPORT (1 1)
Burton	GVM	VI
Rutledg	GVM	VI
Jackson	GVM	VI
Murphy	GVM	VI
Douglas	GVM	VI
Frankfr	GVM	VI
Reed		
Black	D	
Vinson	D	

Mitchell v White Consolidated
48 599A · 336 US 958 · CCA 7th

Justice	04/16 1949 CERT (1-1)	04/25 1949 REPORT (1-1)
Burton	GV	
Rutledg	GV	>
Jackson	GV	>
Murphy	D	>
Douglas	D	>
Frankfr	D	>
Reed	D	>
Black		>
Vinson	GV	D

Bretagna v New York
48 603A · 336 US 919 · New York

Justice	02/26 1949 CERT (1-1)
Burton	
Rutledg	D
Jackson	D
Murphy	G
Douglas	G
Frankfr	
Reed	D
Black	D
Vinson	D

Ajax Trucking Company v Browne
48 604A · 337 US 951 · 48 287A · New York

Justice	06/24 1949 JURIS (1-1)
Burton	
Rutledg	P S
Jackson	S
Murphy	S
Douglas	S
Frankfr	S
Reed	
Black	
Vinson	PQ

Schnell v Davis
48 606A · 336 US 933 · DC SD Alabama

Justice	03/26 1949 JURIS (1-1)	03/28 1949 REPORT (1-1)
Burton	A	A
Rutledg	A	A
Jackson	A	A
Murphy	A	A
Douglas	N	A
Frankfr		
Reed	N	N
Black	A	A
Vinson	A	A

Capital Airlines v C.A.B.
48 608A · 336 US 961 · CCA DC

Justice	04/16 1949 CERT (1-1)	04/23 1949 CERT (1-2)
Burton	D	D
Rutledg	D	D
Jackson	D	D
Murphy		D
Douglas	H	D
Frankfr		
Reed	D	D
Black	D	D
Vinson	D	D

Watts v Indiana
48 610A · 48 344M · 338 US 49 · Frankfr 04/27/49 · Indiana

Justice	02/26 1949 CERT (1-1)	04/26 1949 MERITS (1-1)	06/27 1949 REPORT (1-1)
Burton	G	R	R
Rutledg	G	A	A
Jackson	G	R	R
Murphy	G	R	R
Douglas	G		
Frankfr			
Reed	G	R	R
Black	G	A	A
Vinson	G	R	R

Great Northern RR Company v U.S.
48 621A · 336 US 933 · DC Delaware

Justice	03/26 1949 JURIS (1-1)	03/28 1949 REPORT (1-1)
Burton		
Rutledg	A	A
Jackson	A	A
Murphy	A	A
Douglas	A	A
Frankfr	A	A
Reed	A	A
Black	A	A
Vinson	A	A

U.S. v Fauber
48 625A · 337 US 906 · Ct Cls

Justice	05/14 1949 CERT (1-1)
Burton	D
Rutledg	D
Jackson	D
Murphy	
Douglas	G
Frankfr	
Reed	D
Black	D
Vinson	D

Tillman v Tillman
48 627A · 336 US 954 · CCA DC

Justice	04/16 1949 CERT (1-1)
Burton	
Rutledg	GR
Jackson	
Murphy	G
Douglas	
Frankfr	
Reed	
Black	
Vinson	

U.S. v Urbuteit
48 640A · 336 US 804 · 48 13A · CCA 5th

Justice	04/23 1949 CERT (1-1)	05/02 1949 REPORT (1-1)
Burton	GR	R
Rutledg	GR	R
Jackson	?	R
Murphy		R
Douglas	GR	R
Frankfr	?	R
Reed	GR	R
Black	?	R
Vinson	GR	R

Becker v Virginia
48 641A · 337 US 956 · Virginia

Justice	06/24 1949 CERT (1-1)
Burton	
Rutledg	
Jackson	
Murphy	
Douglas	G
Frankfr	
Reed	
Black	
Vinson	

Bunn v North Carolina
48 643A · 336 US 942 · North Carolina

Justice	04/02 1949 JURIS (1-1)
Burton	
Rutledg	
Jackson	
Murphy	
Douglas	G
Frankfr	
Reed	
Black	
Vinson	

Maryland Casualty Company v Toups
48 651A · 336 US 967 · CCA 5th

Justice	04/30 1949 CERT (1-1)
Burton	G
Rutledg	D
Jackson	D
Murphy	X
Douglas	D
Frankfr	D
Reed	D
Black	D
Vinson	G

U.S. (Dorfler) v Watkins
48 655A · 337 US 914 · CCA 2d

Justice	05/28 1949 CERT (1-1)
Burton	D
Rutledg	D
Jackson	D
Murphy	D
Douglas	D
Frankfr	
Reed	D
Black	
Vinson	D

Hill v Terminal RR Association
48 665A · 336 US 962 · Missouri

Justice	04/23 1949 CERT (1-1)
Burton	S
Rutledg	S
Jackson	SA
Murphy	S
Douglas	S
Frankfr	SA
Reed	
Black	
Vinson	SA

S.E.C. v Philadelphia Company
48 670A
337 US 901
CCA DC

Justice	05/14/1949 CERT (1 1)	05/16/1949 REPORT (1 1)
Burton	GVI	A
Rutledg	GVI	R A
Jackson	GVI	
Murphy		
Douglas	GVI	VI A
Frankfr	GVI	VI A
Reed	GVI	VI A
Black	GVI	VI A
Vinson	GVI	VI A

Williams v New York
48 671A
337 US 241
Black 04/27/49 New York

Justice	04/23/1949 MERITS (1 1)	06/06/1949 REPORT (1 1)
Burton	X A	A
Rutledg	R A	R A
Jackson	R	R A
Murphy		A
Douglas	A	A
Frankfr	A	A
Reed	A	A
Black	A	A
Vinson	A	A

Vlavianos v S.S. Cypress & Maryland
48 672A
337 US 924 48 752A
CCA 4th

Justice	06/04/1949 CERT (1 1)
Burton	G
Rutledg	D
Jackson	D
Murphy	D
Douglas	D
Frankfr	D
Reed	D
Black	D
Vinson	D

Polizio v New York
48 675A
337 US 957 48 17A 48 18A
New York

Justice	06/24/1949 CERT (1 1)
Burton	D
Rutledg	D
Jackson	
Murphy	G
Douglas	
Frankfr	D
Reed	D
Black	D
Vinson	D

Kennedy v Walker
48 679A
337 US 901
Connecticut

Justice	05/14/1949 JURIS (1 1)	05/14/1949 MERITS (1 1)	05/16/1949 REPORT (1 1)
Burton		R	R
Rutledg	X S	R	R
Jackson			
Murphy	N S	R	R
Douglas			
Frankfr		R	R
Reed		A	A
Black	N	A	A
Vinson	S	A	A

Shaw v Dreyfus
48 681A
337 US 907
CCA 2d

Justice	05/14/1949 CERT (1 1)
Burton	DQ
Rutledg	DQ
Jackson	
Murphy	G
Douglas	D
Frankfr	D
Reed	
Black	GQ
Vinson	DQ

Dunnell v Safeway Stores
48 686A
337 US 907
CCA 9th

Justice	05/14/1949 CERT (1 1)
Burton	
Rutledg	
Jackson	
Murphy	
Douglas	
Frankfr	
Reed	
Black	G
Vinson	

Shepherd v Hunter
48 705A
337 US 916
CCA 7th

Justice	05/28/1949 CERT (1 1)
Burton	D
Rutledg	D
Jackson	
Murphy	G
Douglas	G
Frankfr	
Reed	
Black	D
Vinson	

Updike v West
48 714A
337 US 908
CCA 10th

Justice	05/14/1949 CERT (1 1)
Burton	D
Rutledg	D
Jackson	
Murphy	D
Douglas	D
Frankfr	
Reed	
Black	G
Vinson	D

Frank v Wilson & Company
48 722A
337 US 918 48 723A
CCA 7th

Justice	05/28/1949 CERT (1 1)
Burton	D
Rutledg	G D
Jackson	G D
Murphy	D
Douglas	D
Frankfr	D
Reed	D
Black	GQ D
Vinson	

Grannis v U.S.
48 726A
337 US 918
CCA 4th

Justice	05/28/1949 CERT (1 1)
Burton	D
Rutledg	D
Jackson	
Murphy	G
Douglas	G
Frankfr	
Reed	
Black	D
Vinson	

Midwest Haulers v Glander
48 728A
336 US 963
Ohio

Justice	04/30/1949 JURIS (1 1)
Burton	S
Rutledg	S
Jackson	
Murphy	
Douglas	
Frankfr	
Reed	
Black	N
Vinson	S

Great Lakes Steel v U.S.
48 749A
337 US 952 48 330A
DC ED Michigan

Justice	06/24/1949 MERITS (1 1)	06/27/1949 REPORT (1 1)
Burton	R	A
Rutledg	R	R
Jackson		
Murphy		
Douglas	A	A
Frankfr		
Reed	R	R
Black	R	R
Vinson	A	A

American Surety Company v U.S.
48 750A
337 US 930
CCA 2d

Justice	06/10/1949 CERT (1 1)
Burton	D
Rutledg	D
Jackson	
Murphy	G
Douglas	D
Frankfr	D
Reed	D
Black	D
Vinson	D

Texas v U.S.
48 754A
337 US 911
DC WD Oklahoma

Justice	05/31/1949 REPORT (1 1)
Burton	A
Rutledg	A
Jackson	A
Murphy	A
Douglas	A
Frankfr	N
Reed	A
Black	A
Vinson	A

Roth v Goldman
48 759A
337 US 938
CCA 2d

Justice	06/17/1949 CERT (1 1)
Burton	D
Rutledg	D
Jackson	D
Murphy	D
Douglas	G
Frankfr	D
Reed	D
Black	D
Vinson	D

Kan v Tsang
48 778A
337 US 939
CCA 9th

Justice	06/17/1949 CERT (1 1)
Burton	D
Rutledg	D
Jackson	D
Murphy	D
Douglas	G
Frankfr	D
Reed	D
Black	D
Vinson	D

District Of Columbia v Smoot Sand
48 780A
337 US 939
CCA DC

Justice	06/17/1949 CERT (1 1)
Burton	D
Rutledg	D
Jackson	D
Murphy	D
Douglas	G
Frankfr	G
Reed	D
Black	D
Vinson	D

Campbell v U.S.
48 784A
337 US 957
CCA 5th

Justice	06/24 1949 CERT 1 1
Burton	D
Rutledg	D
Jackson	D
Murphy	
Douglas	
Frankfr	
Reed	D
Black	D
Vinson	G

Graylyn Bainbridge v Woods
48 799A
337 US 958
CCA 8th

Justice	06/24 1949 CERT 1 1
Burton	
Rutledg	G
Jackson	
Murphy	
Douglas	
Frankfr	
Reed	D
Black	D
Vinson	D

Mercury Press v District Of Columbia
48 800A
337 US 931
CCA DC

Justice	06/10 1949 CERT 1 1
Burton	D
Rutledg	D
Jackson	D
Murphy	D
Douglas	D
Frankfr	D
Reed	D
Black	D
Vinson	G

U.S. v 25.406 Acres Of Land
48 803A
337 US 931
CCA 4th

Justice	06/10 1949 CERT 1 1
Burton	D
Rutledg	D
Jackson	
Murphy	G
Douglas	G
Frankfr	
Reed	D
Black	
Vinson	G

Danielly v California
48 807A
337 US 919
California

Justice	05/28 1949 CERT 1 1
Burton	D
Rutledg	D
Jackson	
Murphy	G
Douglas	
Frankfr	
Reed	D
Black	D
Vinson	X

Eisler v U.S.
48 845A 48 0A
337 US 912 337 US 958 48 255A
CCA DC

Justice	05/28 1949 QUEST 12 1	06/17 1949 CERT 1 1	06/24 1949 CERT 1 2
Burton	B		
Rutledg	B		
Jackson	B		D
Murphy	B		
Douglas	B	G	G
Frankfr			
Reed	B	G	D
Black	B		
Vinson	B	H	D

Lustig v U.S.
48 1389A 46 1389A
338 US 74
Frankfr 04/26/48 Frankfr 10/25/48 CCA 3rd

Justice	05/22 1948 CERT 1 1	10/23 1948 MERITS 1 2	04/24 1949 MERITS 1 1	06/27 1949 REPORT 1 1
Burton	G	R	R	R
Rutledg				
Jackson	G	R	R	R
Murphy	G			
Douglas	D	A	A	A
Frankfr	D	A	A	R
Reed		R		R
Black	G		A	
Vinson	D	R	A	R

Adkins v E.I. Du Pont de Nemours
48 1M 47 345M
335 US 331
Black 10/25/48 CCA 10th

Justice	10/23 1948 CERT 1 2	11/22 1948 REPORT 1 1
Burton	GR	
Rutledg		>
Jackson	GR	>
Murphy	GR	>
Douglas		>
Frankfr	GR	>
Reed	GR	>
Black	GR	>
Vinson	GR	>

Thompson v Illinois
48 2M 48 10M 47 475M
337 US 942 48 102M 48 50A
Illinois

Justice	05/15 1948 CERT 1 1
Burton	E
Rutledg	E
Jackson	
Murphy	E
Douglas	E
Frankfr	
Reed	D
Black	D
Vinson	D

Jones v Ragen
48 3M 47 516M
335 US 862
Illinois

Justice	06/11 1948 CERT 1 1	11/06 1948 CERT 1 2
Burton	E	D
Rutledg	E	D
Jackson	E	D
Murphy	E	D
Douglas		D
Frankfr	E	D
Reed	E	D
Black	E	D
Vinson	E	D

Tuthill v California
48 19M
335 US 846
California

Justice	10/16 1948 CERT 1 1
Burton	H D
Rutledg	DO
Jackson	D
Murphy	D
Douglas	D
Frankfr	D
Reed	D
Black	D
Vinson	D

Felton v U.S.
48 27M
335 US 831
CCA DC

Justice	10/07 1948 CERT 1 1
Burton	D
Rutledg	D
Jackson	
Murphy	G
Douglas	D
Frankfr	D
Reed	D
Black	D
Vinson	

Illinois (Marino) v Ragen
48 30M
336 US 969
Illinois

Justice	04/23 1949 CERT (1 1)	04/30 1949 CERT (1 2)
Burton		
Rutledg	X	G
Jackson	D	D
Murphy	X	G
Douglas		G
Frankfr	D	D
Reed	D	D
Black	D	D
Vinson	D	D

Evans v Nierstheimer
48 47M
337 US 235   48 50M   48 106M   48 184M   48 265M
Illinois

Justice	10/07 1948 CERT (1 1)	06/06 1949 REPORT (1 1)
Burton	E	M
Rutledg	E	M
Jackson		M
Murphy	E	M
Douglas		M
Frankfr	E	M
Reed	E	M
Black	E	M
Vinson		M

Garity v New York
48 54M
335 US 909
New York

Justice	01/08 1949 CERT (1 2)
Burton	
Rutledg	D
Jackson	D
Murphy	D
Douglas	X
Frankfr	
Reed	D
Black	D
Vinson	D

U.S. (Parker) v Ragen
48 55M
336 US 920
CCA 7th

Justice	10/07 1948 CERT (1 1)	02/26 1949 CERT (1 2)
Burton		
Rutledg	E	D
Jackson	E	D
Murphy		D
Douglas	E	D
Frankfr	E	D
Reed		D
Black	D	D
Vinson	D	D

Cavallucci v Burke
48 67M
335 US 847
Pennsylvania

Justice	10/16 1948 CERT (1 1)
Burton	D
Rutledg	D
Jackson	
Murphy	D
Douglas	G
Frankfr	D
Reed	D
Black	D
Vinson	D

Roberts v California
48 73M
335 US 847
California

Justice	10/16 1948 CERT (1 1)
Burton	D
Rutledg	D
Jackson	
Murphy	D
Douglas	G
Frankfr	D
Reed	D
Black	D
Vinson	D

Roberts v Memphis Street RR Company
48 86M
335 US 889   48 1M
CCA 6th

Justice	10/08 1948 CERT (1 1)	12/11 1948 MERITS (1 1)	12/13 1948 REPORT (1 1)
Burton		VM	>
Rutledg		VM	>
Jackson	D	VM	>
Murphy	D	VM	>
Douglas	DQ	VM	>
Frankfr		VM	>
Reed	D	VM	>
Black	DH		
Vinson	D	VM	>

Williams v California
48 89M
335 US 835
California

Justice	10/07 1948 CERT (1 1)
Burton	D
Rutledg	G
Jackson	D
Murphy	G
Douglas	G
Frankfr	
Reed	D
Black	D
Vinson	D

Willis v Ragen
48 106M
337 US 235   48 50M   48 47M   48 184M   48 265M
Illinois

Justice	10/07 1948 CERT (1 1)	06/06 1949 REPORT (1 1)
Burton	E	M
Rutledg	E	M
Jackson		M
Murphy	E	M
Douglas		M
Frankfr	E	M
Reed	E	M
Black	D	M
Vinson		M

Taylor v Dennis
48 121M
336 US 907
CCA 5th

Justice	12/11 1948 CERT (1 1)	02/05 1949 MERITS (1 1)	02/07 1949 REPORT (1 1)
Burton	D	A	A
Rutledg	G	R	R
Jackson	G	R	R
Murphy	G	A	A
Douglas		R	R
Frankfr	D	A	A
Reed	G	R	R
Black	D		
Vinson	D		

May v Ragen
48 172M
335 US 893
Illinois

Justice	12/11 1948 CERT (1 1)
Burton	
Rutledg	E
Jackson	D
Murphy	D
Douglas	D
Frankfr	D
Reed	D
Black	D
Vinson	D

Jackson v Illinois
48 177M
335 US 893
Illinois

Justice	12/11 1948 CERT (1 1)
Burton	
Rutledg	E
Jackson	G
Murphy	
Douglas	D
Frankfr	D
Reed	D
Black	D
Vinson	D

Lewis v Ragen
48 184M
337 US 235 48 40M 48 47M 48 106M 48 265M
Illinois

	12/11 1948 CERT (1 1)	06/06 1949 REPORT (1 1)
Burton	E	M
Rutledg	E	M
Jackson		M
Murphy	E	M
Douglas	E	M
Frankfr		M
Reed	D	M
Black	D	M
Vinson		M

Collett (Ex Parte)
48 206M
337 US 55 48 233M 48 269M
Vinson 02/12/49 DC ED Illinois

	12/11 1948 MNDMUS (1 1)	02/11 1949 MNDMUS (1 2)	05/31 1949 REPORT (1 1)
Burton	G	D	D
Rutledg	G	DO	D
Jackson	G	D	D
Murphy	G		
Douglas	G	X	
Frankfr			
Reed	D	G	G
Black	G		
Vinson		D	D

McKay v Aderhold
48 215M
335 US 893
Georgia

	12/11 1948 CERT (1 1)
Burton	D
Rutledg	Q
Jackson	
Murphy	E
Douglas	D
Frankfr	D
Reed	D
Black	D
Vinson	

Nichols v Ohio
48 229M
336 US 910
Ohio

	02/05 1949 CERT (1 1)
Burton	E
Rutledg	E
Jackson	
Murphy	E
Douglas	D
Frankfr	D
Reed	D
Black	D
Vinson	D

Kilpatrick v Texas & Pacific RR
48 233M
337 US 75 48 206M 48 269M
Vinson 02/12/49 CCA 5th

	12/04 1948 MNDMUS (1 1)	12/11 1948 MNDMUS (1 2)	02/11 1949 MNDMUS (1 3)	05/31 1949 REPORT (1 1)
Burton	D	D	D	D
Rutledg	D	G	DO	D
Jackson	D	G		
Murphy	D	G	X	
Douglas				
Frankfr	G	G	D	G
Reed	D	D		
Black	G	D	D	G
Vinson		D	D	D

Dammann (In The Matter Of)
48 234M
336 US 922

	03/05 1949 HABEAS (1 1)
Burton	D
Rutledg	K
Jackson	
Murphy	K
Douglas	K
Frankfr	
Reed	D
Black	K
Vinson	D

Grimm v Stewart
48 247M
336 US 938
Missouri

	01/08 1949 CERT (1 1)	03/26 1949 CERT (1 2)
Burton	D	D
Rutledg	D	D
Jackson		
Murphy	G	
Douglas	D	D
Frankfr	D	D
Reed	D	D
Black	D	
Vinson	D	

McGregor v Ragen
48 262M
336 US 939
CCA 7th

	01/08 1949 CERT (1 1)	03/26 1949 CERT (1 2)
Burton	GE	G
Rutledg	GE	G
Jackson		
Murphy	E	
Douglas	E	
Frankfr		
Reed	D	
Black		
Vinson	D	G

Reid v Ragen
48 264M
335 US 901

	01/08 1949 HABEAS (1 1)
Burton	E
Rutledg	GE
Jackson	
Murphy	E
Douglas	G
Frankfr	
Reed	D
Black	E
Vinson	D

Smith v Ragen
48 265M
337 US 235 48 50M 48 47M 48 106M 48 184M
Illinois

	01/08 1949 CERT (1 1)	04/30 1949 CERT (1 2)	06/06 1949 REPORT (1 1)
Burton	G	G	M
Rutledg	H	G	M
Jackson		D	M
Murphy	G	G	M
Douglas	G	G	M
Frankfr			M
Reed			M
Black			M
Vinson			M

U.S. v National City Lines
48 269M
337 US 78 48 206M 48 233M
Vinson 02/12/49 DC ND Illinois

	12/18 1948 CERT (1 1)	02/11 1949 CERT (1 2)	05/31 1949 REPORT (1 1)
Burton	G	D	D
Rutledg	P	X	D
Jackson			
Murphy	P		D
Douglas	P		D
Frankfr	G		
Reed		G	
Black			
Vinson	G	G	D

McLaren v Niersthimer
48 276M
336 US 969 48 304M
Illinois

	01/08 1949 CERT (1 1)	04/30 1949 CERT (1 2)
Burton	E	D
Rutledg	E	D
Jackson		
Murphy	E	D
Douglas	E	D
Frankfr		
Reed		D
Black	E	D
Vinson	E	D

Pippin v Niersheimer
48 302M
337 US 942 48 50M
Illinois

	02/05 1949 CERT 1 1	D
Burton		
Rutledg	E	
Jackson	E	D
Murphy	E	
Douglas		D
Frankfr	G	
Reed		
Black	GE	
Vinson	E	D

McLaren v Niersheimer
48 304M
336 US 969 48 276M
Illinois

	04/30 1949 CERT 1 1
Burton	D
Rutledg	D
Jackson	
Murphy	GQ
Douglas	D
Frankfr	D
Reed	D
Black	D
Vinson	D

Doelle v Michigan
48 309M
336 US 942 48 544A

	03/26 1949 HABEAS 1 1
Burton	D
Rutledg	D
Jackson	D
Murphy	D
Douglas	
Frankfr	D
Reed	D
Black	D
Vinson	D

Ormsby v Missouri
48 314M
336 US 906
Missouri

	01/29 1949 CERT 1 1	D
Burton	E	
Rutledg	E	
Jackson		D
Murphy		
Douglas		D
Frankfr		
Reed	E	D
Black		D
Vinson		D

Gann v Hiatt
48 338M
337 US 920
CCA 5th

	05/28 1949 CERT 1 1	D
Burton		D
Rutledg	G	D
Jackson		
Murphy		
Douglas		D
Frankfr		D
Reed		D
Black		D
Vinson		D

Blackwell v Nevada
48 356M
336 US 939
Nevada

	03/26 1949 CERT 1 1	D
Burton		D
Rutledg	G	D
Jackson		D
Murphy		D
Douglas		D
Frankfr		D
Reed		D
Black		D
Vinson		D

Koenig v Smith
48 359M
337 US 942
Washington

	02/26 1949 CERT 1 1
Burton	E
Rutledg	E
Jackson	E
Murphy	E
Douglas	E
Frankfr	E
Reed	E
Black	
Vinson	E

Sherman v Ragen
48 372M
337 US 235 48 50M
Illinois

	03/26 1949 CERT 1 1	06/06 1949 REPORT 1 1
Burton	E	M
Rutledg	E	M
Jackson	E	M
Murphy	E	M
Douglas		M
Frankfr	D	M
Reed		M
Black	E	M
Vinson	E	M

Banks v Niersheimer
48 373M 48 374M
337 US 235 48 50M
Illinois

	03/26 1949 CERT 1 1	06/06 1949 REPORT 1 1
Burton	E	M
Rutledg	E	M
Jackson		M
Murphy	E	M
Douglas	E	M
Frankfr		M
Reed		M
Black	E	M
Vinson	E	M

Butler v Clemmer
48 378M
337 US 926
CCA DC

	06/04 1949 CERT 1 1
Burton	
Rutledg	M
Jackson	D
Murphy	G
Douglas	D
Frankfr	
Reed	D
Black	D
Vinson	D

Bush (In The Matter Of)
48 379M
336 US 971

	02/26 1949 HABEAS 1 1	04/02 1949 HABEAS 1 2	05/07 1949 HABEAS 1 3
Burton	EK	G	G
Rutledg			
Jackson	D	D	D
Murphy		G	GK
Douglas	EK	G	GK
Frankfr			
Reed	E		
Black	EK	G	GK
Vinson	D	D	D

Walter v Ragen
48 384M
337 US 235 48 50M
Illinois

	03/26 1949 CERT 1 1	D
Burton	E	
Rutledg	E	D
Jackson		
Murphy	E	
Douglas	E	D
Frankfr		
Reed		D
Black	E	D
Vinson	E	D

Palmer v Arkansas
48 393M
336 US 921
Arkansas

	02/26 1949 CERT 1 1	D
Burton		D
Rutledg		D
Jackson		
Murphy	G	D
Douglas		D
Frankfr		D
Reed		D
Black		D
Vinson		D

Bird v Washington
48 413M
336 US 954
Washington

	04/16 1949 CERT 1 1	D
Burton		
Rutledg	E	D
Jackson		
Murphy	G	
Douglas		
Frankfr		D
Reed		D
Black	X	D
Vinson	E	D

Thomas v Moore
48 414M
337 US 943
Texas

	04/02 1949 CERT 1 1	D
Burton		
Rutledg	E	D
Jackson		D
Murphy		
Douglas	E	
Frankfr	E	D
Reed	E	D
Black		D
Vinson	E	

Weber v Illinois
48 439M
336 US 969
Illinois

	04/30 1949 CERT 1 1
Burton	D
Rutledg	D
Jackson	D
Murphy	
Douglas	G
Frankfr	
Reed	D
Black	D
Vinson	D

Pascal v Burke
48 540M
337 US 944
Pennsylvania

	05/07 1949 CERT 1 1	06/17 1949 CERT 1 2
Burton	E	D
Rutledg	E	D
Jackson	E	D
Murphy	E	
Douglas		D
Frankfr		D
Reed		D
Black		D
Vinson	E	D

Bird v Johnson
48 559M
336 US 950

	04/16 1949 HABEAS 1 1
Burton	D
Rutledg	E
Jackson	D
Murphy	
Douglas	GE
Frankfr	
Reed	D
Black	D
Vinson	D

Keye v Robinson
48 563M
337 US 920
Illinois

	05/28 1949 CERT 1 1
Burton	D
Rutledg	E
Jackson	D
Murphy	E
Douglas	
Frankfr	
Reed	D
Black	D
Vinson	D

Garner v U.S.
48 590M
337 US 945
CCA DC

	06/17 1949 CERT 1 1
Burton	D
Rutledg	G
Jackson	D
Murphy	G
Douglas	
Frankfr	
Reed	D
Black	D
Vinson	D

Federal Security Administrator
48 597M
337 US 902

	05/16 1949 MNDMUS 1 1	05/16 1949 REPORT 1 1
Burton	DT	DT
Rutledg	DT	DT
Jackson	DT	DT
Murphy	G	G
Douglas		
Frankfr	DT	DT
Reed	DT	DT
Black	DT	DT
Vinson		

Electric Power & Light (In The Matter)
48 610M
337 US 903
CCA 2d

	05/14 1949 STAY 1 1
Burton	D
Rutledg	D
Jackson	
Murphy	G
Douglas	
Frankfr	G
Reed	
Black	
Vinson	D

Loper v Texas
48 627M
337 US 946
Texas

	06/17 1949 CERT 1 1
Burton	D
Rutledg	E
Jackson	D
Murphy	E
Douglas	E
Frankfr	
Reed	D
Black	D
Vinson	D

McGee v Mississippi
48 655M
337 US 922

	06/02 1949 STAY 1 1
Burton	D
Rutledg	D
Jackson	
Murphy	G
Douglas	
Frankfr	
Reed	D
Black	D
Vinson	D

Edelman v California
48 666M
337 US 949
California

	06/17 1949 CERT 1 1
Burton	D
Rutledg	X
Jackson	D
Murphy	G
Douglas	
Frankfr	D
Reed	D
Black	D
Vinson	

Dessaure v New York
48 673M
337 US 949
New York

	06/17 1949 CERT 1 1
Burton	D
Rutledg	G
Jackson	D
Murphy	G
Douglas	G
Frankfr	
Reed	DQ
Black	DQ
Vinson	D

Appendix E

U.S. Supreme Court
October 1949 Term

U.S. v Kansas City Life Insurance
49 1A 48 26A 47 621A
339 US 799 49 579A
Rutledg 10/25/48 Burton 04/06/50 Ct Cls

	05/01 1948 CERT 1 1	10/23 1948 MERITS 1 1	04/01 1950 MERITS 1 2	04/05 1950 MERITS 1 3 R	06/05 1950 REPORT 1 1
Minton					
Clark					
Burton		D			A
Rutledg		D	RQ		A
Jackson	G			A	A
Murphy	G			A	A
Douglas	G	R	R	A	A
Frankfr	G	R	R	A	A
Reed	G		R		A
Black	G	R	R	A	A
Vinson	G	RQ		A	A

Graver Tank & Manufacturing v Linde Air
49 2A 48 184A 48 185A
339 US 605
Jackson 01/14/49 Jackson 04/06/50 CCA 7th

	10/08 1948 CERT 1 1	01/08 1949 MERITS 1 1	02/28 1949 REPORT 1 1	05/07 1949 REHEAR 1 1	05/14 1949 REHEAR 1 2	04/01 1950 MERITS 1 2	05/29 1950 REPORT 1 2
Minton							
Clark							
Burton	G	R	R	B	B	R	R
Rutledg	G	R	R	Y	Y	A	A
Jackson			R			A	A
Murphy	D		R	B	B	A	A
Douglas		X	R	B	B	A	A
Frankfr		R	R			A	A
Reed	D	RQ	R	Y	Y	R	R
Black	D	R	R	Y	Y	A	A
Vinson	D	RQ	R	Y	Y	A	A

U.S. (Eichenlaub) v Shaughnessy
49 3A 48 260A
338 US 521 49 82A 48 817A
Burton 11/22/49 CCA 2d

	11/13 1948 CERT 1 1	06/24 1949 CERT 1 2	11/19 1949 MERITS 1 1	01/16 1950 REPORT 1 1
Minton				
Clark				
Burton	D	G		A
Rutledg	D	G		A
Jackson				
Murphy	D	GQ	R	
Douglas	D	G		
Frankfr	D	G		
Reed	D			A
Black	D		R	A
Vinson	D		R	A

U.S. v Gerlach Live Stock Company
49 4A 48 299A
339 US 725 49 5A 49 9A
Jackson 03/08/49 Jackson 04/06/50 Ct Cls

	12/04 1948 CERT 1 1	03/05 1949 MERITS 1 1	04/01 1950 MERITS 1 2 R	06/05 1950 REPORT 1 1
Minton				
Clark				
Burton	G		A	A
Rutledg	G	AQ	A	A
Jackson				
Murphy	G	D	R	A
Douglas	G	D	R	A
Frankfr				
Reed	G		A	A
Black	G		A	A
Vinson	G	AQ	A	A

American Communications v Douds
49 10A 48 336A
339 US 382 49 13A 49 12A 48 404A
Vinson 10/19/49 DC SD New York

	11/06 1948 JURIS 1 1	10/17 1949 MERITS 1 1	05/08 1950 REPORT 1 1
Minton			
Clark			
Burton	N		
Rutledg	N	R	R
Jackson	N		A
Murphy	N		
Douglas	N		M
Frankfr	N		A
Reed	N	R	R
Black	N		A
Vinson	N	R	

McGrath v Manufacturers Trust Company
49 11A 48 386A
338 US 241 49 15A 48 443A
Frankfr 10/19/49 Burton 10/19/49 CCA 2d

	01/15 1949 CERT 1 1	06/24 1949 REHEAR 1 1	10/15 1949 MERITS 1 1 R	11/07 1949 REPORT 1 1
Minton				
Clark				
Burton	D	Y		A
Rutledg	D	Y	R	
Jackson				
Murphy	D	Y		
Douglas	G			A
Frankfr				
Reed	G	Y		A
Black	G	Y	R	A
Vinson	G			A

Osman v Douds
49 12A 48 404A
339 US 846 49 10A 49 13A 48 336A
DC SD New York

	06/10 1949 JURIS	05/27 1950 JURIS	05/27 1950 MERITS	06/05 1950 REPORT
	1 1	1 2	1 1	1 1
Minton				
Clark	G	A	A	A
Burton				
Rutledg	D		NR	R
Jackson	D		NR	R
Murphy				
Douglas	D	A	A	A
Frankfr		A		
Reed	G		NR	R
Black	D	A	A	A
Vinson	D	A	A	A

United Steelworkers v N.L.R.B.
49 13A 48 431A
339 US 382 49 10A 49 12A 48 336A
Vinson 10/19/49 CCA 7th

	01/15 1949 CERT	10/17 1949 MERITS	05/08 1950 REPORT
	1 1	1 1	1 1
Minton			
Clark	G		
Burton	G	A	A
Rutledg	G	R	R
Jackson	G	A	A
Murphy	G	M	
Douglas	G	A	A
Frankfr	G		
Reed	G	R	R
Black	D	A	A
Vinson	D	A	A

Dennis v U.S.
49 14A 48 436A
339 US 162 48 255A
Minton 11/22/49 CCA DC

	01/15 1949 AMICUS	06/24 1949 CERT	11/12 1949 MERITS	03/27 1950 REPORT
	1 1	1 1	1 1	1 1
Minton				
Clark				
Burton				
Rutledg	H	G	D	A
Jackson		G	D	A
Murphy	X	G	D	A
Douglas	DH	G	D	A
Frankfr				
Reed	GH	G	D	A
Black	D	G	D	A
Vinson				

Manufacturers Trust Company v McGrath
49 15A 48 443A
338 US 241 49 11A 48 386A
Frankfr 10/19/49 Burton 10/19/49 CCA 2d

	01/15 1949 CERT	06/24 1949 QUEST	10/15 1949 MERITS	11/07 1949 REPORT
	1 1	2 1	1 1	1 1
Minton				V
Clark				
Burton				
Rutledg	D	Y	A	V
Jackson	D	Y	A	V
Murphy	G	Y	A	V
Douglas	D			
Frankfr		Y		
Reed	D	B	R	V
Black	D	Y		V
Vinson	D	B	R	V

Graham v Brotherhood Of Locomotive
49 16A 48 452A
338 US 232
Jackson 10/19/49 CCA DC

	06/24 1949 CERT	06/24 1949 QUEST	10/17 1949 MERITS	11/07 1949 REPORT
	1 1	13 1	1 1	1 1
Minton				
Clark				
Burton	G	B	R	R
Rutledg	G	B	R	R
Jackson	G	B	RL	R
Murphy	G			
Douglas	G			
Frankfr	G	Y		
Reed	G	B	RM	R
Black	G	B	RM	R
Vinson	G		RM	R

Boyd v Grand Trunk Western RR Company
49 17A 48 486A
338 US 263 48 233M
Michigan

	06/04 1949 CERT	10/17 1949 MERITS	11/07 1949 REPORT
	1 1	1 1	1 1
Minton			
Clark	G	R	R
Burton	G	R	R
Rutledg	G		
Jackson	G	X	R
Murphy	G		
Douglas	G		
Frankfr	G	X	
Reed	G	R	R
Black	G	R	R
Vinson	G	R	R

Standard-Vacuum Oil Company v U.S.
49 18A 48 532A
339 US 157
Minton 10/19/49 Ct Cts

	03/26 1949 CERT	10/15 1949 MERITS	03/27 1950 REPORT	11/07 1949 REPORT
	1 1	1 1	1 1	1 1
Minton				
Clark			V	
Burton	G	A	V	A
Rutledg	D	A	V	A
Jackson	D			
Murphy	D			
Douglas	D	A	V	A
Frankfr	G	A	V	A
Reed	G	A	V	A
Black		A	V	A
Vinson	G			

Faulkner v Gibbs
49 19A 48 537A
338 US 267
CCA 9th

	03/08 1949 CERT	03/26 1949 CERT	10/15 1949 MERITS	11/07 1949 REPORT
	1 1	1 2	1 1	1 1
Minton				
Clark				
Burton	G	D	D	A
Rutledg	G	D	D	A
Jackson				
Murphy				
Douglas	G	D	D	A
Frankfr	G			
Reed	G	D	D	R
Black	G	D	D	A
Vinson	G			

Treichler v Wisconsin
49 20A 48 547A
338 US 251
Clark 10/19/49 Wisconsin

	03/08 1949 JURIS	10/15 1949 MERITS	11/07 1949 REPORT
	1 1	1 1	1 1
Minton			
Clark	N	R	R
Burton	N	R	R
Rutledg	N	R	R
Jackson	N		
Murphy	N		
Douglas	N		
Frankfr	N		
Reed	S	R	R
Black	S	R	R
Vinson	N	R	R

Roth v Delano
49 24A 48 566A
338 US 226 49 21A 48 553A
Jackson 10/19/49 CCA 6th

Justice	03/26/1949 JURIS	10/17/1949 MERITS	11/07/1949 REPORT
Minton			V
Clark		AS	V
Burton	S	A	V
Rutledg			
Jackson	S	RM	V
Murphy			
Douglas			
Frankfr	P S	RM	V
Reed	P S	RM	V
Black	P S	R	V
Vinson	S	A	A

Secretary Of Agriculture v Central Roig
49 27A 48 575A
338 US 604 49 30A 49 32A
Frankfr 10/24/49 CCA DC

Justice	04/16/1949 CERT	04/23/1949 CERT	10/22/1949 MERITS	02/06/1950 REPORT
Minton	G		R	R
Clark	G	D	R	R
Burton		D		
Rutledg		D		
Jackson		D		
Murphy	G	D	R	R
Douglas		D		
Frankfr	G			
Reed	G	D	R	R
Black	G			
Vinson	G	D	A	A

Henderson v U.S.
49 25A 48 570A
339 US 816
Burton 04/10/50 DC Maryland

Justice	03/08/1949 JURIS	01/07/1950 AMICUS	01/07/1950 RIPE	04/08/1950 MERITS	06/05/1950 REPORT
Minton		B	B	R	R
Clark	N	Y	Y	R	R
Burton	N	Y		R	R
Rutledg	N				
Jackson	N	Y	B	R	R
Murphy	N				
Douglas	N	Y		R	R
Frankfr	N		B	R	R
Reed	N	Y		R	R
Black	N	Y	Y	R	R
Vinson	N	Y	Y	R	R

Oakley v Louisville & Nashville RR
49 28A 48 578A
338 US 278 49 29A 48 579A
Burton 10/24/49 CCA 6th

Justice	04/02/1949 CERT	10/22/1949 MERITS	11/14/1949 REPORT
Minton	G	R	R
Clark		R	R
Burton	XQ		
Rutledg	D		
Jackson			
Murphy	G		
Douglas	GQ		
Frankfr			
Reed	D	R	R
Black	D		
Vinson	X		

Reilly v Pinkus
49 31A 48 583A
338 US 269
Black 10/19/49 CCA 3rd

Justice	05/14/1949 CERT	10/17/1949 MERITS	11/14/1949 REPORT
Minton	G	R	R
Clark		R	R
Burton	D		A
Rutledg			A
Jackson		A	A
Murphy			
Douglas	G		
Frankfr	G		
Reed		R	A
Black	GQ		A
Vinson	GQ		A

U.S. v Westinghouse Electric
49 26A 48 574A
339 US 261
Reed 10/19/49 Frankfr 10/19/49 CCA 1st

Justice	04/16/1949 CERT	10/17/1949 MERITS	04/17/1950 REPORT
Minton			
Clark	G	R	R
Burton		R	R
Rutledg	D		
Jackson	D	A	
Murphy			
Douglas	G		
Frankfr	G		
Reed		R	R
Black	GQ	AQ	A
Vinson		R	R

Roth v Delano
49 21A 48 553A
338 US 878 49 24A 48 566A
CCA 6th

Justice	03/26/1949 CERT	11/12/1949 CERT
Minton		
Clark		D
Burton	D	D
Rutledg		
Jackson	G	D
Murphy	G	
Douglas	G	
Frankfr	G	D
Reed		D
Black	D	D
Vinson	D	

U.S. v Yellow Cab Company
49 22A 48 563A
338 US 338
Jackson 11/22/49 DC ND Illinois

Justice	03/05/1949 JURIS	11/19/1949 MERITS	12/05/1949 REPORT
Minton			
Clark	N	A	A
Burton	N	A	A
Rutledg	N	A	A
Jackson	N		
Murphy	N		
Douglas	N	A	A
Frankfr	N	R X	R
Reed	N		R
Black	N	A	A
Vinson		A	A

Carter v Atlanta & Saint Andrews RR
49 23A 48 565A
338 US 430
Clark 11/22/49 CCA 5th

Justice	03/26/1949 CERT	10/17/1949 MERITS	12/19/1949 REPORT
Minton		R	R
Clark	G	R	R
Burton	D	R	R
Rutledg			
Jackson	G	R	R
Murphy	G		
Douglas			
Frankfr	D		S
Reed	D	R	R
Black	D		R
Vinson			

Puerto Rico v Secretary Of Agriculture
49 32A 48 585A
338 US 604 49 27A 49 30A
Frankfr 10/24/49 CCA DC

	CERT 1949	MERITS 10/22 1949	REPORT 02/06 1950
	1 1	1 1	1 1
Minton		A	
Clark	G	A A	S
Burton	D	A A	S
Rutledg			
Jackson		A	S
Murphy	G	A	
Douglas			
Frankfr	G	A A	S
Reed	G		S
Black	G	A A	S
Vinson	D	A	A

Quicksall v Michigan
49 33A 48 609A 48 202M
339 US 660 49 190M 49 48M
Frankfr 02/15/50 Michigan

	CERT 02/26 1950	MERITS 02/11 1950	REPORT 06/05 1950
	1 1	1 1	1 1
Minton		A	A
Clark		A	A
Burton	D	A	A
Rutledg			
Jackson	G	A	A
Murphy			
Douglas	G	A	
Frankfr			
Reed		R	R
Black	G	A A	
Vinson	D	A	A

McLaurin v Oklahoma State Regents
49 34A 48 614A
339 US 637 49 44A 48 614A
Black 04/10/50 Vinson 04/26/50 DC WD Oklahoma

	JURIS 06/24 1949	JURIS 11/05 1949	MERITS 04/08 1950	REPORT 06/05 1950
	1 1	1 2	1 1	1 1
Minton	NL	N	R	R
Clark	A		R	R
Burton	N	N	R	R
Rutledg				
Jackson	N	N	R	R
Murphy				
Douglas	N	N	R	R
Frankfr	NL	N	R	R
Reed	A	N	R	R
Black	N		R	R
Vinson	X A	N	R	R

U.S. v Aetna Casualty & Surety Company
49 35A 48 617A
338 US 366 49 36A 49 37A 49 38A
Vinson 10/24/49 CCA 2d

	CERT 04/23 1949	MERITS 10/22 1949	MERITS 12/03 1949	REPORT 12/12 1949
	1 1	1 1	1 2	1 1
Minton		R	A	A
Clark	G	R	A	A
Burton	G			
Rutledg			A	A
Jackson	G	R		
Murphy				
Douglas	G		A	
Frankfr				
Reed	G	R	A	A
Black	G	R		
Vinson		R	A	A

U.S. v Toronto Hamilton & Buffalo
49 39A 48 624A
338 US 396
Clark 11/15/49 Ct Cls

	CERT 04/30 1949	MERITS 11/12 1949	REPORT 12/12 1949
	1 1	1 1	1 1
Minton		R	R
Clark		R	R
Burton	D	R	R
Rutledg	D		
Jackson	D		
Murphy		A	
Douglas	G		
Frankfr	G	R	R
Reed	G	R	R
Black	G	R	R
Vinson	G		

U.S. v Capital Transit Company
49 40A 48 629A
338 US 286 49 41A 48 630A
Black 10/24/49 DC DC

	JURIS 04/16 1949	MERITS 10/22 1949	REPORT 11/14 1949
	1 1	1 1	1 1
Minton	N	R	R
Clark	N	R	R
Burton	N	R	R
Rutledg			
Jackson	N		
Murphy			
Douglas	N	A	
Frankfr	N		
Reed	N	R	R
Black	N	R X	R
Vinson	N	A	A

U.S. v Spear
49 42A 48 633A
338 US 217
Reed 10/24/49 CCA 2d

	CERT 04/16 1949	MERITS 10/22 1949	REPORT 11/07 1949
	1 1	1 1	1 1
Minton			
Clark		R R	R
Burton	G	D	R R R
Rutledg	D		R
Jackson	D		
Murphy	D		
Douglas			
Frankfr		R R	R R R
Reed			
Black	G	R R	R
Vinson	G	R R	R

Brown v Western RR Of Alabama
49 43A 48 653A
338 US 294
Black 10/24/49 Georgia

	CERT 04/30 1949	MERITS 10/22 1949	REPORT 11/21 1949
	1 1	1 1	1 1
Minton			A
Clark			
Burton	D	R A	R R
Rutledg	D	R	R
Jackson			A
Murphy			
Douglas	D	A	A
Frankfr			
Reed	D	A	A
Black			
Vinson			A

Sweatt v Painter
49 44A 48 667A
339 US 629 49 34A 49 402A 48 614A Texas
Black 04/10/50 Vinson 04/26/50 Texas

	HOLD 06/04 1949	CERT 11/05 1949	AMICUS 02/04 1950	MERITS 04/08 1950	REPORT 06/05 1950
	1 1	1 2	1 1	1 1	1 1
Minton					
Clark	B	G	B		R
Burton	Q	G	B		R
Rutledg					
Jackson	B Y	G Y	Y		R
Murphy					
Douglas	Y	G	B		R
Frankfr	Y	G			
Reed	Y	G	B		R
Black	B Y	G Y	B Y		R R R
Vinson	Y	G	B		R

265

U.S. v Benedict
49 45A 48 668A
338 US 692
Burton 11/22/49 Ct Cls

	04/30 1949 CERT	11/12 1949 MERITS	11/19 1949 MERITS	02/13 1950 REPORT
	1 1	1	1 2	1 1
Minton				
Clark		R	R	R
Burton	G		R	R
Rutledg	G			
Jackson	G	A	A	A
Murphy	G	A		
Douglas	G	A		
Frankfr	G			
Reed	G		R	R
Black	G	A	A	A
Vinson	G	A	A	A

Cassell v Texas
49 46A 48 692A 48 400M
339 US 282
Reed 11/15/49 Texas

	03/05 1949 CERT	11/12 1949 MERITS	04/24 1950 REPORT
	1 1	1 1	1 1
Minton			
Clark		R	R
Burton		R	R
Rutledg		A	A
Jackson	D	A	A
Murphy	G		
Douglas	D	R	R
Frankfr	G	A	A
Reed	D		
Black	D	R	R
Vinson	D	R	R

Colgate-Palmolive-Peet v N.L.R.B.
49 47A 48 694A
338 US 355
Minton 11/22/49 CCA 9th

	05/28 1949 CERT	11/19 1949 MERITS	12/05 1949 REPORT
	1 1	1 1	1 1
Minton		R	R
Clark		R	R
Burton	GL	R	R
Rutledg	GL		
Jackson	G	R	R
Murphy	G	V	
Douglas	GL	X	A
Frankfr			
Reed		R	R
Black	D	A	A
Vinson	D		

Savorgnan v U.S.
49 48A 48 709A
338 US 491
Burton 11/15/49 CCA 7th

	05/28 1949 CERT	11/12 1949 MERITS	01/09 1950 REPORT
	1 1	1 1	1 1
Minton		A	A
Clark	G	A	A
Burton	G		
Rutledg		R	R
Jackson	G	D	
Murphy	G		
Douglas	G		
Frankfr	G		
Reed		R	R
Black		D	R
Vinson		D	R

Parker v County Of Los Angeles
49 49A 48 711A
338 US 327 49 50A 48 712A
Frankf 11/22/49 California

	06/10 1949 CERT	11/19 1949 DISMISS	12/05 1949 REPORT
	1 1	1 1	1 1
Minton		Y	S
Clark		Y	S
Burton	D	Y	S
Rutledg	D		
Jackson	D	Y	S
Murphy	G		
Douglas	G		
Frankfr	G		
Reed		B / Y	S
Black	D	X	S
Vinson	D	Y	S

Darr v Burford
49 51A 48 713A
339 US 200
Reed 12/19/49 CCA 10th

	06/04 1949 CERT	12/17 1949 MERITS	04/03 1950 REPORT
	1 1	1 1	1 1
Minton		R	R
Clark	GM		
Burton	GM	R	R
Rutledg			
Jackson	G	R	R
Murphy	G		
Douglas	G	R	R
Frankfr		A	A
Reed	G		
Black		A	A
Vinson		A	A

Kingsland v Dorsey
49 53A 48 729A
338 US 318
Black 10/24/49 CCA DC

	05/28 1949 CERT	10/22 1949 MERITS	11/21 1949 REPORT
	1 1	1 1	1 1
Minton		R	R
Clark		R	R
Burton	G		
Rutledg	G		A
Jackson	D		
Murphy	G		
Douglas	G		
Frankfr	D	R	R
Reed	G	R	R
Black	G		
Vinson	G	R	R

U.S. (Knauff) v Shaughnessy
49 54A 48 733A
338 US 537
Minton 12/15/49 CCA 2d

	04/30 1949 CERT	12/10 1949 MERITS	01/16 1950 REPORT
	1 1	1 1	1 1
Minton		R	R
Clark		A	A
Burton	G		
Rutledg	G		
Jackson	G	R	R
Murphy	G		
Douglas	G		
Frankfr	G	D	
Reed	G	R	R
Black		R	R
Vinson		R	R

Manufacturers Trust Company v Becker
49 55A 48 742A
338 US 304
Clark 10/24/49 CCA 2d

	06/04 1949 CERT	10/22 1949 MERITS	11/21 1949 REPORT
	1 1	1 1	1 1
Minton		R	R
Clark			
Burton	G		
Rutledg	G		
Jackson	D	A	A
Murphy	G	A	A
Douglas	G	A	A
Frankfr	D	A	A
Reed	D	X	
Black		A	A
Vinson		A	A

266

O'Donnell v Elgin Joliet & Eastern RR
49 56A 48 743A
338 US 384
Jackson 10/24/49 CCA 7th

	CERT 06/10 1949 (1 2)	MERITS 10/22 1949 (1 1)	REPORT 12/12 1949 (1 1)
Minton			
Clark			
Burton	G D	R	R
Rutledg	G D	R	
Jackson	G G	R	
Murphy			
Douglas	D		
Frankfr	G G		
Reed		A	A
Black	G D	R	R
Vinson	G G		

C.I.R. v Connelly
49 57A 48 744A
338 US 258
Minton 10/24/49 CCA DC

	CERT 06/04 1949 (1 1)	MERITS 10/22 1949 (1 1)	REPORT 11/07 1949 (1 1)
Minton			
Clark	G	R	R
Burton	G	R	R
Rutledg		R	R
Jackson			
Murphy		A	
Douglas	D		
Frankfr			
Reed			
Black	G	R	R
Vinson	G	R	R

Creel v Lone Star Defense
49 58A 48 746A
339 US 497   49 79A   49 96A
Burton 12/15/49 CCA 5th

	CERT 06/04 1949 (1 1)	MERITS 12/10 1949 (1 1)	REPORT 05/08 1950 (1 1)
Minton	G	R	R
Clark	G	R	R
Burton			
Rutledg	D		
Jackson	D		A
Murphy	D		
Douglas	D	X	
Frankfr			
Reed	G	R	R
Black	G	R	R
Vinson		X	

Reo Motors v C.I.R.
49 59A 48 751A
338 US 442
Vinson 11/22/49 CCA 6th

	CERT 06/04 1949 (1 1)	MERITS 11/19 1949 (1 1)	REPORT 01/09 1950 (1 1)
Minton	G	A	A
Clark	G	A	A
Burton			
Rutledg	D		
Jackson			
Murphy	G	RQ	
Douglas	G		
Frankfr	G	AQ	A
Reed	G	A	A
Black	G	A	A
Vinson			

Chapman v Sheridan-Wyoming Coal
49 60A 48 755A
338 US 621
Jackson 01/18/50 CCA DC

	CERT 10/04 1949 (1 1)	MERITS 01/14 1950 (1 1)	REPORT 02/06 1950 (1 1)
Minton	G	R	R
Clark	G	R	R
Burton	G	R	R
Rutledg	G	R	R
Jackson			
Douglas	G		
Frankfr	G	A	
Reed	G	R	R
Black	G	R	R
Vinson	G	R	R

Hughes v Superior Court
49 61A 48 761A 48 408M
339 US 460
Franktr 11/15/49 California

	CERT 04/30 1949 (1 1)	MERITS 11/12 1949 (1 1)	REPORT 05/08 1950 (1 1)
Minton	G		A
Clark	GQ	RQ	A
Burton	G		A
Rutledg	G		
Jackson	G		
Murphy			
Douglas	G		
Frankfr			
Reed	D		A
Black	D	R	A
Vinson	X	X	

Cole v Arkansas
49 62A 48 762A
338 US 345
Jackson 11/15/49 Arkansas

	CERT 06/10 1949 (1 1)	MERITS 11/12 1949 (1 1)	REPORT 12/05 1949 (1 1)
Minton			
Clark			
Burton	G D	A	A
Rutledg	G D	A	A
Jackson			
Murphy	G G		A
Douglas			
Frankfr	D D	A	A
Reed	R R	R	A
Black			
Vinson	G D		

Steele's Mills v Robertson
49 63A 48 763A
338 US 848
CCA 4th

	CERT 10/15 1949 (1 1)
Minton	D
Clark	D
Burton	D
Jackson	G
Douglas	D
Frankfr	
Reed	G
Black	
Vinson	D

Banning v Detroit Toledo & Ironton RR
49 68A 48 771A
338 US 815   49 93A
CCA 6th

	CERT 10/04 1949 (1 1)
Minton	D
Clark	D
Burton	G
Jackson	D
Douglas	D
Frankfr	
Reed	G
Black	
Vinson	D

Sinclair v U.S.
49 69A 48 783A
338 US 908
CCA 3rd

Justice	06/17 1949 CERT (1 1)	11/12 1949 MERITS (1 2)	11/19 1949 MERITS	01/09 1950 REPORT (1 1)
Minton		R		R
Clark		R		R
Burton	D		A	
Rutledg	D		A	
Jackson	D	R		R
Murphy				
Douglas	D		A	R
Frankfr	GR	R		R
Reed	G		A	
Black	D		A	R
Vinson	D		A	R

Manning v Seeley Tube & Box Company
49 70A 48 787A
338 US 561
Vinson 11/22/49 CCA 3rd

Justice	06/24 1949 CERT (1 2)	02/06 1950 REPORT (1 1)
Minton		R
Clark		R
Burton	D	R
Rutledg	G D	
Jackson	D	
Murphy		
Douglas	G	
Frankfr	GR	RQ
Reed	D	R
Black	D	R
Vinson	D	R

F.P.C. v East Ohio Gas Company
49 71A 48 789A
338 US 464
Black 11/15/49 CCA DC

Justice	11/12 1949 MERITS (1 1)	01/09 1950 REPORT (1 1)
Minton	R	R
Clark	R	R
Burton		
Rutledg	R	
Jackson		A
Murphy		
Douglas		A
Frankfr		
Reed	G	
Black	G	
Vinson	G	

Wilmette Park District v Campbell
49 75A 48 801A
338 US 411
Clark 1/22/49 CCA 7th

Justice	06/17 1949 CERT (1 1)	11/19 1949 MERITS (1 1)	12/12 1949 REPORT (1 1)
Minton			
Clark			
Burton	D		
Rutledg	G	R	A
Jackson	G		A
Murphy	G		
Douglas	G		
Frankfr	D		A
Reed	D	R	A
Black	G		A
Vinson	D		A

Travelers Health Association v Virginia
49 76A 48 802A
339 US 643
Clark 01/30/50 Black 04/26/50 Virginia

Justice	06/10 1949 JURIS (1 1)	11/19 1949 MERITS (1 1)	04/22 1950 MERITS (1 2)	06/05 1950 REPORT (1 1)
Minton			R	R
Clark				
Burton	S			
Rutledg		R		
Jackson	N		R	R
Murphy	N			
Douglas	N		R	R
Frankfr			A	A
Reed	N	R	A	R
Black	S	R	A	A
Vinson	S		A	A

Solesbee v Balkcom
49 77A 48 806A
339 US 9
Black 11/22/49 Georgia

Justice	06/04 1949 JURIS (1 1)	11/19 1949 MERITS (1 1)	02/20 1950 REPORT (1 1)
Minton			
Clark			
Burton	S		
Rutledg	S	A	A
Jackson	N		A
Murphy	N		
Douglas	N	RK	A
Frankfr	N		
Reed	N		R
Black		A	A
Vinson		A	A

Aaron v Ford Bacon & Davis
49 79A 48 809A
339 US 497 49 58A 49 96A
Burton 12/15/49 CCA 8th

Justice	06/24 1949 CERT (1 1)	12/10 1949 MERITS (1 1)	05/08 1950 REPORT (1 1)
Minton		R	R
Clark			
Burton	G	R	R
Rutledg	G		
Jackson	G		A
Murphy			
Douglas	G		
Frankfr			
Reed	G	R	R
Black	G		R
Vinson	G	X	

U.S. (Willumeit) v Shaughnessy
49 82A 47 817A
338 US 521 49 3A
Burton 11/22/49 CCA 2d

Justice	06/24 1949 CERT (1 1)	11/19 1949 MERITS (1 1)	01/16 1950 REPORT (1 1)
Minton			
Clark			
Burton	G	R	R
Rutledg	G		
Jackson			A
Murphy			
Douglas	D		A
Frankfr			
Reed	D		A
Black	D		R
Vinson	D	X	R

Regents University Of Georgia v Carroll
49 83A 48 820A
338 US 586
Reed 12/15/49 Georgia

Justice	10/15 1949 CERT (1 1)	12/10 1949 MERITS (1 1)	02/06 1950 REPORT (1 1)
Minton		R	R
Clark		R	
Burton	G		A
Rutledg	G		
Jackson	GQ		A
Murphy			
Douglas	G		A
Frankfr	G		A
Reed			
Black	G	R	R
Vinson	G	X	R

Eastern Steamship v Mulligan
49 89A 48 827A
338 US 801
CCA 2d

Justice		10/10 1949 REPORT (1 1)
Minton		
Clark	GVM	>
Burton	GVM	>
Jackson		>
Douglas	GVM	>
Frankfr		>
Reed	GVM	>
Black		>
Vinson	GVM	>

Zarichny v State Board Of Agriculture
49 90A 48 828A
338 US 816
Michigan

Justice	10/04 1949 CERT (1 1)
Minton	
Clark	D DQ
Burton	D
Jackson	
Douglas	D
Frankfr	D
Reed	
Black	D
Vinson	G D

Turner Glass v Hartford-Empire
49 92A
338 US 830
CCA 7th

Justice	10/04 1949 CERT (1 1)
Minton	
Clark	D
Burton	D
Jackson	
Douglas	D
Frankfr	D
Reed	
Black	G D
Vinson	D

Powell v United States Cartridge
49 96A 48 836A
339 US 497 49 58A 49 79A
Burton 12/15/49 CCA 8th

Justice	10/04 1949 CERT (1 1)	12/10 1949 MERITS (1 1)	05/08 1950 REPORT (1 1)
Minton			
Clark	G	R	R
Burton	G		
Jackson	G	A	A
Douglas	G		
Frankfr	G	R	R
Reed	G		
Black	G	R X	R
Vinson	G	X	

U.S. v Moorman
49 97A 48 837A
338 US 457
Black 12/15/49 Ct Cls

Justice	10/04 1949 CERT (1 1)	12/10 1949 MERITS (1 1)	01/09 1950 REPORT (1 1)
Minton			R
Clark	G	R	R
Burton			R
Jackson			R
Douglas	D		
Frankfr	D	S	R
Reed			R
Black	D	R	R
Vinson	D	R	R

U.S. v Fleischman
49 98A 48 838A
339 US 349 49 99A
Vinson 12/19/49 CCA DC

Justice	10/15 1949 CERT (1 1)	12/17 1949 MERITS (1 1)	05/08 1950 REPORT (1 1)
Minton			R
Clark	D	R	R
Burton	D		
Jackson			R
Douglas	D		A
Frankfr	D	R	R
Reed			A
Black	G	R	R
Vinson	G	R	R

U.S. v Bryan
49 99A
339 US 323 49 98A 48 838A
Vinson 12/19/49 CCA DC

Justice	10/15 1949 CERT (1 1)	12/17 1949 MERITS (1 1)	05/08 1950 REPORT (1 1)
Minton			
Clark		R	R
Burton		R	R
Jackson			
Douglas		R	R
Frankfr		R A	R
Reed			
Black		R A	R A
Vinson		R A	R A

Schroeder's Estate v C.I.R.
49 103A
338 US 801
CCA 2d

Justice	10/04 1949 CERT (1 1)	10/10 1949 REPORT (1 1)
Minton	GVM	>
Clark	GVM	>
Burton	GVM	>
Jackson		
Douglas	GVM	>
Frankfr	GVM	>
Reed	GVM	>
Black	GVM	>
Vinson	GVM	>

Adirondack Transit v Hudson Transit
49 104A 48 848A
338 US 802 49 105A
DC SD New York

Justice	10/04 1949 JURIS (1 1)	10/10 1949 REPORT (1 1)
Minton		A
Clark	N	A
Burton	N	A
Jackson		
Douglas	N	A
Frankfr		N
Reed		N
Black	N	A
Vinson	N	A

Freight Forwarders v Pacific Coast
49 114A
338 US 689 49 113A
DC SD California

Justice	10/04 1949 JURIS (1 1)	02/06 1950 REPORT (1 1)
Minton		
Clark	A	A A
Burton	N	A
Jackson	N	A
Douglas	N	A A
Frankfr	N	A A
Reed	N	A A
Black		A
Vinson	A	A

Capital Greyhound Lines v Brice
49 118A
339 US 542
Black 12/15/49 Maryland

Justice	10/04 1949 JURIS (1 1)	10/15 1949 JURIS (1 2)	12/10 1949 MERITS (1 1)	05/15 1950 REPORT (1 1)
Minton	A		A	A
Clark	N	N	R	R
Burton	N	N	R	R
Jackson	A		A	A
Douglas	A	N	A	A
Frankfr	A			
Reed	A			
Black	N			
Vinson	A		A	A

Wissner v Wissner
49 119A
338 US 655
Clark 12/15/49 California

Justice	10/04 1949 JURIS (1 1)	12/10 1949 MERITS (1 1)	02/06 1950 REPORT (1 1)
Minton	N		R
Clark	N	R	R
Burton	N	R	R
Jackson	N	A	A
Douglas	N	A	A
Frankfr	N	A	A
Reed	N		A
Black	N		
Vinson	N	A	A

C.I.R. v Smith
49 120A
338 US 818 49 121A
CCA 5th

Justice	10/04 1949 CERT
	1 1
Minton	
Clark	
Burton	D
Jackson	D
Douglas	
Frankfr	G
Reed	D
Black	D
Vinson	

C.I.R. v Long
49 121A
338 US 818 49 120A
CCA 5th

Justice	10/04 1949 CERT
	1 1
Minton	
Clark	
Burton	D
Jackson	D
Douglas	
Frankfr	G
Reed	D
Black	D
Vinson	

Ball v U.S.
49 122A
338 US 802
DC SD New York

Justice	10/04 1949 JURIS	10/10 1949 REPORT
	1 1	1 1
Minton	A	A
Clark	A	A
Burton	S	A
Jackson	A	A
Douglas		A
Frankfr	A	A
Reed		
Black	D	
Vinson	A	

Fahs v Economy Cab Company
49 123A
338 US 818 49 124A 49 125A
CCA 5th

Justice	10/04 1949 CERT
	1 1
Minton	
Clark	
Burton	D
Jackson	D
Douglas	
Frankfr	G
Reed	D
Black	D
Vinson	D

Fahs v New Deal Cab Company
49 124A
338 US 818 49 123A 49 125A
CCA 5th

Justice	10/04 1949 CERT
	1 1
Minton	
Clark	
Burton	D
Jackson	D
Douglas	
Frankfr	G
Reed	D
Black	D
Vinson	D

U.S. v Party Cab Company
49 125A
338 US 818 49 123A 49 124A
CCA 7th

Justice	10/04 1949 CERT
	1 1
Minton	
Clark	
Burton	D
Jackson	D
Douglas	
Frankfr	G
Reed	D
Black	D
Vinson	D

C.I.R. v Philadelphia Transport
49 126A
338 US 883
CCA 3rd

Justice	10/04 1949 CERT	11/19 1949 MERITS	11/19 1949 MERITS	11/21 1949 REPORT
	1 1	1 1	1 2	1 1
Minton	R	R		A
Clark	R	R		A
Burton	R	R	A	
Jackson			A	R
Douglas		A	A	A
Frankfr	A	A	A	A
Reed	R	R	A	A
Black	A	A	A	A
Vinson	A	A	A	A

Killian v Pennsylvania RR Company
49 130A
338 US 819
Illinois

Justice	10/04 1949 CERT
	1 1
Minton	
Clark	G
Burton	D
Jackson	D
Douglas	
Frankfr	D
Reed	D
Black	
Vinson	D

Beard-Laney v U.S.
49 137A
338 US 803
DC ED South Carolina

Justice	10/04 1949 JURIS	10/10 1949 REPORT
	1 1	1 1
Minton		
Clark	A	A
Burton	A	A
Jackson	A	A
Douglas	N	N
Frankfr		A
Reed	N	A
Black		N
Vinson	A	A

Lee v Mississippi
49 138A
338 US 803
Mississippi

Justice	10/04 1949 CERT	10/04 1949 JURIS
	1 1	1 1
Minton		
Clark		
Burton	D	S
Jackson	D	S
Douglas		S
Frankfr		
Reed	D	S
Black		
Vinson	G	S

New Jersey Realty v Division Of Tax
49 147A
338 US 665
Clark 12/19/49 New Jersey

Justice	10/04 1949 JURIS	12/17 1949 MERITS	02/06 1950 REPORT
	1 1	1 1	1 1
Minton			
Clark	N	R	R
Burton	N	R	R
Jackson	N	R	R
Douglas		A	R
Frankfr			
Reed	N	R	R
Black		R	R
Vinson	N	R	A

Hass v New York
49 148A
338 US 803
New York

Justice	10/04 1949 JURIS
	1 1
Minton	
Clark	S
Burton	S
Jackson	S
Douglas	N
Frankfr	
Reed	N
Black	
Vinson	S

270

The following are Supreme Court voting charts. Each block lists case name, docket number(s), citation, court below, and votes by Justice (Minton, Clark, Burton, Jackson, Douglas, Frankfr, Reed, Black, Vinson) across procedural stages.

U.S. v Colorado & Southern RR
49 149A
338 US 847
DC Colorado

	10/15 1949 CERT
Minton	
Clark	D
Burton	D
Jackson	D
Douglas	G
Frankfr	
Reed	G
Black	G
Vinson	D

Dickinson v Petroleum Conversion
49 150A
338 US 507
Jackson 12/15/49 CCA 2d

	10/04 1949 CERT	12/10 1949 MERITS	01/16 1950 REPORT
Minton			
Clark	G	R	R
Burton	G	R	R
Jackson	G	R	R
Douglas		A	A
Frankfr			
Reed	G	R	R
Black	G	R	R
Vinson	G	R A	R A

Wong Yang Sung v McGrath
49 154A
339 US 33 49 213A
Jackson 12/15/49 CCA DC

	10/04 1949 CERT	12/10 1949 MERITS	02/20 1950 REPORT
Minton			
Clark	G	R	R
Burton	G	R	R
Jackson	G	R	R
Douglas	G		
Frankfr	D	R	R
Reed	G		
Black	G	X	R
Vinson	G	R	R A

U.S. v Commodities Trading
49 156A
339 US 121 49 163A
Black 01/18/50 Ct Cls

	10/22 1949 CERT	01/14 1950 MERITS	03/27 1950 REPORT
Minton			
Clark	G	R	R
Burton	G	R	R
Jackson	G	R	R
Douglas	G		
Frankfr			
Reed	G	R	R
Black	G	R	R
Vinson	G	R	R

C.A.B. v State Airlines
49 157A
338 US 572 49 158A 49 159A
Black 12/19/49 CCA DC

	10/04 1949 CERT	12/17 1949 MERITS	03/27 1950 REPORT
Minton			
Clark	G	R	R
Burton	G	R	R
Jackson	G	R	R
Douglas	D		
Frankfr			
Reed	G	R	R
Black	G	R	R
Vinson	G	R A	R A

Lavender v Illinois Central RR
49 160A
338 US 822
Missouri

	10/04 1949 CERT
Minton	
Clark	
Burton	D
Jackson	D
Douglas	
Frankfr	
Reed	
Black	
Vinson	

Branton v Arkansas
49 162A
338 US 878
Arkansas

	11/12 1949 CERT
Minton	
Clark	
Burton	G
Jackson	D
Douglas	D
Frankfr	D
Reed	D
Black	GO
Vinson	D

Schwenk v U.S.
49 165A
338 US 830
CCA 2d

	10/04 1949 CERT	02/06 1950 REPORT
Minton		
Clark	G	R
Burton	G	R
Jackson	D	R
Douglas	D	
Frankfr		X
Reed		
Black	G	R
Vinson	D	R A

International UMW v U.S.
49 168A
338 US 871 49 169A 48 182A
CCA DC

	10/04 1949 CERT	10/22 1949 CERT	11/05 1949 CERT
Minton			
Clark		D	D
Burton	D		D
Jackson	D	G	G
Douglas	D	G	G
Frankfr			
Reed			
Black			
Vinson	D	G	G

International UMW v U.S.
49 169A
338 US 871 49 168A 48 182A
CCA DC

	10/22 1949 CERT	11/05 1949 CERT	03/13 1950 REPORT
Minton			
Clark	D	D	A
Burton	GL	D	A
Jackson	G	G	A
Douglas	GL	D	A
Frankfr			
Reed	GL	G	A
Black	GL	G	A
Vinson			R

U.S. v Burnison
49 171A
339 US 87 49 188A
Reed 01/03/50 California

	10/04 1949 JURIS	12/17 1949 MERITS
Minton		
Clark	N	R
Burton	N	R
Jackson	N	A
Douglas	N	A
Frankfr		
Reed	N	R
Black	N	R
Vinson	N	

Schuermann v U.S.
49 172A
338 US 831
CCA 8th

	10/05 1949 CERT
Minton	
Clark	G
Burton	G
Jackson	D
Douglas	G
Frankfr	
Reed	
Black	
Vinson	G

U.S. v United States Smelting
49 173A
339 US 186
Minton 02/20/50 DC Utah

	JURIS 10/04 1949 (1 1)	MERITS 02/18 1950 (1 1)	REPORT 03/27 1950 (1 1)
Minton			
Clark	N	R	R
Burton	N	R	R
Jackson	N	A	
Douglas	N	A	A
Frankfr	N	S	
Reed	N	A	R
Black	N	A	R
Vinson	N	A	

Partmar v U.S.
49 175A
338 US 804
DC SD New York

	CERT 10/05 1949 (1 1)	MERITS 02/18 1950 (1 1)	REPORT 03/27 1950 (1 1)
Minton	G		
Clark	G		
Burton	G		
Jackson	G	A	A
Douglas	G		
Frankfr	G		
Reed	G	R	R
Black	G	R	R
Vinson	G		

Bryan v U.S.
49 178A
338 US 552
Minton 12/19/49 CCA 5th

	CERT 10/05 1949 (1 1)	MERITS 12/17 1949 (1 1)	REPORT 01/16 1950 (1 1)
Minton	G	JJ	JJ
Clark	G	A	A
Burton	G	A	A
Jackson	G	A	A
Douglas	G	JJ	JJ
Frankfr	G	A	A
Reed	G	JJ	JJ
Black	G	JJ	JJ
Vinson	G	A	A

U.S. v S.S. Australia Star
49 179A
338 US 823
CCA 2d

	CERT 10/05 1949 (1 1)
Minton	D
Clark	G
Burton	D
Jackson	D
Douglas	D
Frankfr	D
Reed	D
Black	D
Vinson	D

Brotherhood Of Locomotive v U.S.
49 182A
338 US 872 49 168A 49 169A
CCA DC

	CERT 10/15 1949 (1 1)	CERT 11/05 1949 (1 2)
Minton	D	D
Clark		D
Burton	GH	D
Jackson		D
Douglas	DH	D
Frankfr		G
Reed	D	D
Black	GH	D
Vinson		D

Garcia v Pan American Airways
49 184A
338 US 824
New York

	CERT 10/05 1949 (1 1)
Minton	D
Clark	D
Burton	D
Jackson	
Douglas	G
Frankfr	
Reed	G
Black	
Vinson	

U.S. v Gayetty
49 188A
339 US 87 49 171A California
Reed 01/03/50

	JURIS 10/04 1949 (1 1)	MERITS 12/17 1949 (1 1)	REPORT 03/13 1950 (1 1)
Minton	N		
Clark	N	R	A
Burton			A
Jackson	N		A
Douglas	N	R	A
Frankfr			
Reed	N	R	R
Black	N	R	A
Vinson		R	A

Dille v Delaney
49 190A
338 US 824
CCA 10th

	CERT 10/05 1949 (1 1)
Minton	D
Clark	D
Burton	D
Jackson	
Douglas	
Frankfr	G
Reed	D
Black	D
Vinson	

Commission PUC v Lowell Gas Company
49 192A
338 US 825
Massachusetts

	CERT 10/05 1949 (1 1)
Minton	
Clark	
Burton	
Jackson	
Douglas	G
Frankfr	
Reed	
Black	
Vinson	

Marshall v U.S.
49 197A
339 US 933 49 14A 49 236A
CCA DC

	CERT 04/01 1950 (1 1)	MERITS 04/01 1950 (1 1)	CERT 04/08 1950 (1 2)
Minton			D
Clark		R	D
Burton		R	D
Jackson		R	
Douglas	G	R	G
Frankfr		R	G
Reed	G	R	D
Black	G	R	D
Vinson			

Walsh v U.S. (White)
49 199A
338 US 804
CCA 7th

	CERT 10/05 1949 (1 1)	MERITS 10/05 1949 (1 1)	REPORT 10/10 1949 (1 1)
Minton	G	R	R
Clark	G	R	R
Burton			R
Jackson	D		R
Douglas	D	R	R
Frankfr			R
Reed	D	R	R
Black	G	R	
Vinson	G		

Affolder v New York Chicago RR
49 200A
339 US 96
Clark 02/24/50 CCA 8th

	CERT 10/05 1949 (1 1)	MERITS 11/19 1949 (1 1)	REPORT 03/13 1950 (1 1)
Minton	G	R	R
Clark	G	R	R
Burton		A	
Jackson	GQX	AQ	
Douglas	G	SA	SA
Frankfr			
Reed	G	A	A
Black			
Vinson			

U.S., (Lee Wo Shing) v Shaughnessy
49 213A
339 US 906 49 54A 49 154A
CCA 2d

	03/11 1950 CERT (1 1)	03/13 1950 REPORT (1 1)
Minton	GR	R
Clark		
Burton	GR	R
Jackson		A
Douglas	GR	R
Frankfr		A
Reed	GR	R
Black		A
Vinson	GR	R

U.S. v Cumberland Public Service
49 214A
338 US 451
Black 12/19/49 Ct Cs

	10/15 1949 CERT (1 1)	12/17 1949 MERITS (1 1)	01/09 1950 REPORT (1 1)
Minton	G	R	A
Clark	G		A
Burton	D	R	A
Jackson			A
Douglas	G	R	A
Frankfr			A
Reed	G	R	A
Black			A
Vinson	G	R	A

U.S. v Alpers
49 217A
338 US 680
Minton 12/19/49 CCA 9th

	10/05 1949 CERT (1 1)	12/17 1949 MERITS (1 1)	02/06 1950 REPORT (1 1)
Minton	G		R
Clark	G	D	R
Burton	G		R
Jackson	G	D	R
Douglas	G		
Frankfr	G		R
Reed	G	D	R
Black	G		
Vinson	G	D	R

Kentucky Trust Company v Glenn
49 219A
338 US 827
CCA 6th

	10/05 1949 CERT (1 1)
Minton	
Clark	D
Burton	D
Jackson	D
Douglas	D
Frankfr	D
Reed	
Black	G
Vinson	D

Skelly Oil v Phillips Petroleum
49 221A
339 US 667
Frankfr 12/15/49 CCA 10th

	10/15 1949 CERT (1 1)	12/10 1949 MERITS (1 1)	06/05 1950 REPORT (1 1)
Minton		R	RV
Clark	G	R	RV
Burton	G	R	R
Jackson	G		RV
Douglas			
Frankfr			
Reed	G	R	RV
Black		R	RV
Vinson			A

Robinson v U.S.
49 222A
338 US 832 49 223A 338 US 854
CCA 9th

	10/05 1949 CERT (1 1)
Minton	D
Clark	D
Burton	
Jackson	G
Douglas	D
Frankfr	D
Reed	
Black	D
Vinson	D

Baskin v Industrial Accident Commission
49 224A
338 US 854
California

	10/15 1949 CERT (1 1)	10/24 1949 REPORT (1 1)
Minton	GR	>
Clark		>
Burton	GR	>
Jackson	D	
Douglas	GR	>
Frankfr	D	
Reed	GR	>
Black	GR	>
Vinson	GR	>

Montoya v Tide Water Associated Oil
49 226A
338 US 847
CCA 2d

	10/15 1949 CERT (1 1)
Minton	D
Clark	D
Burton	D
Jackson	D
Douglas	G
Frankfr	D
Reed	D
Black	D
Vinson	D

Swift & Company v Compania Colombiana
49 230A
339 US 684
Frankfr 01/09/50 CCA 5th

	10/05 1949 CERT (1 1)	12/17 1949 MERITS (1 1)	01/07 1950 MERITS (1 2)	06/05 1950 REPORT (1 1)
Minton	G	R	R	R
Clark	G	R	R	R
Burton	G	A	A	A
Jackson	G	X		
Douglas	G	A	A	A
Frankfr	G	R	R	R
Reed	G	R	R	R
Black	G	A	A	A
Vinson		AQ	AQ	AQ

Cowher v Pennsylvania RR Company
49 234A
338 US 828
Illinois

	10/05 1949 CERT (1 1)
Minton	
Clark	D
Burton	D
Jackson	
Douglas	G
Frankfr	D
Reed	
Black	G
Vinson	D

Morford v U.S.
49 236A
339 US 258 49 14A 49 197A
CCA DC

Justice	04/1950 CERT 1 1	04/1950 MERITS 1 1
Minton		
Clark	D	R
Burton	D	R
Jackson		R
Douglas	G	R
Frankfr	G	R
Reed		R
Black	G	R
Vinson	D	R

McGee v Mississippi
49 238A
336 US 805 49 46A
Mississippi

Justice	10/04 1949 CERT 1 1	05/13 1950 REHEAR 1 1
Minton		
Clark	D	B
Burton	D	B
Jackson	D	B
Douglas		
Frankfr		Y
Reed	D	B
Black	D	B
Vinson	G	B

Kenosha Motor Coach v PSC Of Wisconsin
49 242A
338 US 805
Wisconsin

Justice	10/04 1949 JURIS 1 1
Minton	S
Clark	N
Burton	S
Jackson	N
Douglas	S
Frankfr	
Reed	N
Black	S
Vinson	N

S.E.C. v Otis & Company
49 244A
338 US 843
CCA DC

Justice	10/15 1949 CERT 1 1	04/08 1950 CERT 1 2	04/10 1950 REPORT 1 1	10/17 1949 REPORT 1 1
Minton	GR	GR	GR	R
Clark	GR		GR	R
Burton	GR		GR	R
Jackson	GR		GR	R
Douglas			GR	R
Frankfr	D		GR	R
Reed	GR			R
Black	GR			R
Vinson				R

Lawson v U.S.
49 248A
339 US 934 49 249A
CCA DC

Justice	10/22 1949 CERT 1 1	04/01 1950 CERT 1 2	04/08 1950 CERT 1 3	05/13 1950 REHEAR 1 1
Minton	H			B
Clark				B
Burton	H		D	
Jackson	H	G	GL	B
Douglas		G	GL	
Frankfr				Y
Reed	G	G	GL	Y
Black	H		D	
Vinson		G	GL	B

Trumbo v U.S.
49 249A
339 US 934 49 248A
CCA DC

Justice	10/22 1949 CERT 1 1	04/01 1950 CERT 1 2	04/08 1950 CERT 1 3	05/13 1950 REHEAR 1 1
Minton	H			B
Clark				B
Burton	H	G	D	
Jackson	H	G	GL	B
Douglas	G	G	GL	
Frankfr				Y
Reed	H	G	GL	Y
Black	G		D	
Vinson	H			B

Cobb v C.I.R.
49 261A
338 US 832
CCA 6th

Justice	10/05 1949 CERT 1 1	11/24 1951 REHEAR 1 1
Minton		B
Clark		B
Burton		
Jackson	G	H
Douglas	GQ	H
Frankfr		H
Reed	G	B
Black		
Vinson		H

Schreiber Trucking v Interstate Common
49 266A
338 US 843 49 265A
DC Maryland

Justice	10/15 1949 JURIS 1 1	05/13 1950 REHEAR 1 1
Minton	D	
Clark	D	
Burton		
Jackson	D	
Douglas		Y
Frankfr		Y
Reed		
Black	D	Y
Vinson		

Sachs v Canal Zone
49 267A
338 US 858
CCA 5th

Justice	10/22 1949 CERT 1 1	04/08 1950 CERT 1 3	05/13 1950 REHEAR 1 1
Minton			B
Clark	D		B
Burton	D	D	
Jackson		GL	
Douglas		GL	Y
Frankfr			Y
Reed		GL	
Black	D		B
Vinson	D		B

Russell v Missouri
49 269A
338 US 849
Missouri

Justice	10/15 1949 CERT 1 1	12/19 1949 REPORT 1 1
Minton	D	A
Clark	D	A
Burton	D	
Jackson	D	A
Douglas		
Frankfr	G	
Reed	D	A
Black	D	A
Vinson	D	A

Alcoa Steamship Company v U.S.
49 271A
338 US 421
Reed 11/22/49 CCA 2d

Justice	10/05 1949 CERT 1 1	11/19 1949 MERITS 1 1
Minton	G	R
Clark		A
Burton	D	R
Jackson	G	R
Douglas	G	
Frankfr	G	R
Reed		A
Black	D	A
Vinson		A

U.S. v Morton Salt Company
49 273A
338 US 632 49 274A
Jackson 12/19/49 CCA 7th

Justice	10/22 1949 CERT 1 1	12/17 1949 MERITS 1 1	02/06 1950 REPORT 1 1
Minton	G	R	R
Clark	G	R	R
Burton	G	R	R
Jackson	D		
Douglas	D	R	R
Frankfr	D		R
Reed		R	R
Black	G	A	R
Vinson	D		

Willapoint Oysters v Ewing
49 280A
338 US 860
CCA 9th

	CERT 10/22 1949	
	1	1
Minton	D	D
Clark		
Burton	G	
Jackson	D	
Douglas		
Frankfr	D	
Reed	D	
Black	D	
Vinson	D	

Lapides v McGrath
49 284A
338 US 888
CCA DC

	CERT 10/22 1949	
	1	1
Minton	D	D
Clark		
Burton	G	
Jackson	G	H
Douglas		
Frankfr	G	
Reed		
Black	G	
Vinson	D	D

Lykes Brothers Steamship v Cannella
49 288A
338 US 859
CCA 2d

	CERT 10/22 1949	
	1	1
Minton	D	D
Clark		
Burton	G	
Jackson		
Douglas		
Frankfr		
Reed		
Black	D	D
Vinson	D	D

U.S. v Rabinowitz
49 293A
339 US 56 49 362A CCA 2d
Minton 01/18/50

	CERT 11/19 1949		MERITS 01/14 1950	REPORT 02/20 1950
	1	1	1 1	1 1
Minton	G		R	R
Clark	D		R	R
Burton	G		R	R
Jackson	D			
Douglas	D		A	A
Frankfr	D			
Reed	G		R	R
Black	G		A	A
Vinson	G		R	R

Maryland v Baltimore Radio Show
49 300A
338 US 912 49 493A
Maryland

	CERT 11/12 1949	MERITS 01/07 1950
	1 1	1 2
Minton	G	D
Clark	D	
Burton	G	G
Jackson	D	
Douglas	D	D
Frankfr	D	
Reed	G	
Black	G	G
Vinson	G	

District Of Columbia v Little
49 302A
339 US 1 CCA DC
Black 01/18/50

	CERT 11/05 1949	MERITS 01/14 1950	REPORT 02/20 1950
	1 1	1 1	1 1
Minton	G	A	A
Clark	G	A	A
Burton		R	R
Jackson	G	A	A
Douglas		A	A
Frankfr	G	A	A
Reed		R	
Black	G	A	A
Vinson	G	A	A

Johnson v Eisentrager
49 306A
339 US 763 49 433M 49 434M CCA DC
Jackson 04/26/50

	CERT 11/12 1949	MERITS 04/22 1950	REPORT 06/05 1950
	1 1	1 1	1 1
Minton	G	R	R
Clark	G	R	R
Burton	G		
Jackson	G	R	R
Douglas		A	A
Frankfr	G	AQ	R
Reed		R	R
Black	D	A	A
Vinson	G	AQ	A

International Teamsters v Hanke
49 309A
339 US 470 49 364A Washington
Frankfr 03/1750

	CERT 12/17 1949	MERITS 02/11 1950	REPORT 05/08 1950
	1 1	1 1	1 1
Minton	G	R	R
Clark	G	R	R
Burton	G	RQ	A
Jackson			A
Douglas	G	A	
Frankfr	G		
Reed	G	R	R
Black	G		
Vinson	G	AQ	A

Sorrentino v U.S.
49 311A
338 US 868 CCA 3rd

	CERT 11/05 1949	
	1	1
Minton	D	
Clark	D	
Burton	D	
Jackson	D	
Douglas	D	
Frankfr	D	
Reed		
Black	G	
Vinson	D	

American Eastern v McCarthy
49 315A
338 US 868 49 452A
CCA 3rd

	CERT 11/05 1949	
	1	1
Minton	D	
Clark	D	
Burton	D	
Jackson	G	
Douglas	D	
Frankfr	D	
Reed		
Black	G	
Vinson	D	

Bernstein v Ems
49 316A
338 US 873
CCA 2d

	CERT 11/05 1949	
	1	1
Minton	D	
Clark	D	
Burton	D	
Jackson	D	
Douglas	D	
Frankfr	D	
Reed	D	
Black	G	
Vinson	D	

Flick v Johnson
49 317A
338 US 879
CCA DC

	CERT 11/12 1949	
	1	1
Minton	D	
Clark	D	
Burton	D	
Jackson		
Douglas	D	
Frankfr	D	
Reed	D	
Black	G	
Vinson	D	

Miller v Wiggins
49 320A
338 US 844
Mississippi

	CERT 10/15 1949	
	1	1
Minton	D	
Clark	D	
Burton	D	
Jackson	D	
Douglas	D	
Frankfr	D	
Reed	D	
Black	G	
Vinson	D	

Moore v Mississippi
49 323A
338 US 844
Mississippi

	CERT 10/15 1949	
	1	1
Minton	D	
Clark	D	
Burton	D	
Jackson	D	
Douglas	D	
Frankfr	D	
Reed	D	
Black	G	
Vinson	D	

Patton v Mississippi
49 324A
338 US 855
Mississippi

	CERT 10/22 1949	
	1	1
Minton	D	
Clark	D	
Burton	D	
Jackson	D	
Douglas	D	
Frankfr	D	
Reed	D	
Black	G	
Vinson	D	

275

49 332A
338 US 864
CCA 3rd

	11/05 1949 CERT (1 1)	11/07 1949 REPORT (1 1)
Minton	GR	R
Clark	GR	R
Burton	GR	R
Jackson	GR	R
Douglas		
Frankfr	GR	R
Reed	GR	R
Black	GR	R
Vinson		

49 333A
338 US 870
CCA 5th — U.S. v Continental-American Bank

	11/05 1949 CERT (1 1)
Minton	D
Clark	D
Burton	D
Jackson	
Douglas	D
Frankfr	
Reed	
Black	G
Vinson	G

U.S. v Shoreline Cooperative
49 334A
338 US 897
DC ND Illinois

	10/15 1949 JURIS (1 1)	12/10 1949 MERITS (1 1)	12/12 1949 REPORT (1 1)
Minton	N	R	R
Clark	N	R	R
Burton	N	R	R
Jackson			
Douglas			
Frankfr	N	R	R
Reed	N	R	R
Black	N	R	R
Vinson	N	R	R

49 335A
338 US 890
Michigan

	12/03 1949 CERT (1 1)
Minton	D
Clark	D
Burton	G
Jackson	D
Douglas	
Frankfr	D
Reed	D
Black	D
Vinson	D

Railway Labor Executives' v U.S.
49 337A
339 US 142
Burton 02/20/50 DC DC

	10/22 1949 JURIS (1 1)	02/18 1950 MERITS (1 1)	03/27 1950 REPORT (1 1)
Minton	N	R	R
Clark	N	R	R
Burton	N	R	R
Jackson	N		
Douglas			
Frankfr	N	A	A
Reed	N		
Black	N	A	A
Vinson	N	A	A

Acme Fast Freight v U.S.
49 338A
338 US 855
DC ND Illinois

	10/24 1949 REPORT (1 1)
Minton	A
Clark	A
Burton	A
Jackson	
Douglas	A
Frankfr	A
Reed	A
Black	A
Vinson	A

49 342A
338 US 863
Arkansas

	11/05 1949 JURIS (1 1)
Minton	S
Clark	N
Burton	N
Jackson	
Douglas	
Frankfr	S
Reed	S
Black	S
Vinson	N

Dexter v Washington
49 344A
338 US 863
Washington

	11/05 1949 JURIS (1 1)	11/07 1949 REPORT (1 1)
Minton		A
Clark	N	A
Burton	N	A
Jackson		A
Douglas		
Frankfr		
Reed		A
Black	N	A
Vinson	N	A

Kaminer v Clark
49 346A
338 US 873
CCA DC

	11/05 1949 CERT (1 1)
Minton	
Clark	D
Burton	D
Jackson	D
Douglas	
Frankfr	
Reed	D
Black	H
Vinson	D

49 350A
338 US 8
CCA 2d

	12/03 1949 CERT (1 1)
Minton	D
Clark	D
Burton	
Jackson	G
Douglas	
Frankfr	
Reed	D
Black	D
Vinson	D

Casselman v Idaho
49 358A
338 US 900
Idaho

	12/03 1949 CERT (1 1)	12/10 1949 CERT (1 2)
Minton	D	
Clark	D	
Burton	G	G
Jackson	D	
Douglas		D
Frankfr		
Reed	D	G
Black	D	G
Vinson	D	D

Hiatt v Brown
49 359A
339 US 103
Clark 02/15/50 CCA 5th

	12/03 1949 CERT (1 1)	02/11 1950 MERITS (1 1)	03/13 1950 REPORT (1 1)
Minton	G	R	R
Clark	G	R	R
Burton	G	R	R
Jackson			
Douglas			
Frankfr	G	R	R
Reed	G	R	R
Black	G	R	R
Vinson	G	R	R

Lynchburg Traffic Bureau v U.S.
49 363A
338 US 864
DC WD Virginia

Justice	11/05 1949 JURIS	11/07 1949 REPORT
Minton	A	A
Clark	A	A
Burton	A	A
Jackson		A
Douglas	A	A
Frankfr	A	A
Reed	A	A
Black	A	A
Vinson	A	A

Automobile Drivers v Cline
49 364A
339 US 470 49 309A
Frankfr 03/17/50 Washington

Justice	12/17 1949 CERT	02/11 1950 MERITS	05/08 1950 REPORT
Minton	G	R	R
Clark	G	R	
Burton	G	RQ	AQ A
Jackson	G		R
Douglas			
Frankfr	G		AQ R
Reed	G		R
Black	G	R	
Vinson	G		A

Potash v Clark
49 366A
338 US 879
CCA DC

Justice	11/12 1949 CERT
Minton	
Clark	D
Burton	D
Jackson	
Douglas	DH
Frankfr	D
Reed	
Black	GH
Vinson	D

U.S. v City Of New York
49 372A
338 US 885
CCA 2d

Justice	11/19 1949 CERT
Minton	
Clark	D
Burton	D
Jackson	D
Douglas	D
Frankfr	D
Reed	D
Black	D
Vinson	D

Cohnstaedt v I.N.S.
49 373A
339 US 901
Kansas

Justice	12/03 1949 CERT	02/11 1950 MERITS	02/20 1950 REPORT
Minton	G	R	R
Clark	G	R	R
Burton	G	A	A
Jackson	G	R	R
Douglas	G		
Frankfr	G	R	R
Reed	G		
Black	G	A	A
Vinson	D		

Western Union Telegraphers' v U.S.
49 375A
338 US 864
DC DC

Justice	11/05 1949 JURIS	11/07 1949 REPORT
Minton	A	A
Clark	A	A
Burton	A	A
Jackson	A	
Douglas	A	A
Frankfr	A	A
Reed	A	A
Black	A	A
Vinson	A	A

U.S. v Winters
49 377A
338 US 903
Ct Cls

Justice	12/17 1949 CERT
Minton	D
Clark	D
Burton	D
Jackson	D
Douglas	D
Frankfr	D
Reed	D
Black	D
Vinson	G

Mullane v Central Hanover Bank
49 378A
339 US 306
Jackson 02/15/50 New York

Justice	11/05 1949 JURIS	02/11 1950 MERITS	04/24 1950 REPORT
Minton	P	R	R
Clark	P	R	R
Burton	P S	R	R
Jackson			
Douglas	P	R	R
Frankfr	P S	R	R
Reed	P	R	R
Black	P	R	R A
Vinson			

Gilson Brothers v Wisconsin ERB
49 383A
338 US 891
Wisconsin

Justice	12/03 1949 CERT
Minton	D
Clark	GR
Burton	D
Jackson	
Douglas	GRM
Frankfr	
Reed	D
Black	
Vinson	G

C.I.R. v Korell
49 384A
339 US 619 49 453A
Vinson 02/15/50 CCA 2d

Justice	12/03 1949 CERT	02/11 1950 MERITS	06/05 1950 REPORT
Minton	G		
Clark	G	R	A A
Burton	G		
Jackson	G		
Douglas			
Frankfr	G	R	R
Reed	G		
Black	G	A	A A
Vinson	G	A	A

District Of Columbia v Hamilton Bank
49 385A
338 US 891
CCA DC

Justice	12/03 1949 CERT
Minton	D
Clark	D
Burton	D
Jackson	D
Douglas	D
Frankfr	
Reed	
Black	D
Vinson	D

Slocum v Delaware Lackawanna RR
49 391A
339 US 239 49 438A
Black 02/15/50 New York

Justice	12/03 1949 CERT	02/11 1950 MERITS	04/10 1950 REPORT
Minton	G	R	R
Clark	G	R	R
Burton	G	R	R
Jackson	G	R	R
Douglas	G		
Frankfr	G	R	R
Reed	G		
Black	G	R	R
Vinson	G	A	A

Pedigo v Celanese
49 393A
338 US 937 49 394A 49 399A
Georgia

Justice	01/07 1950 CERT	
	1	1
Minton	D	D
Clark	G	
Burton	D	D
Jackson		
Douglas	D	D
Frankfr		
Reed		
Black	G	
Vinson		D

Fifth & Walnut v Loew's
49 400A
338 US 894
CCA 2d

Justice	12/03 1949 CERT	
	1	1
Minton	D	D
Clark		
Burton	D	D
Jackson		
Douglas	D	
Frankfr		
Reed	G	G
Black		
Vinson		D

District Of Columbia v Bank Of Commerce
49 401A
338 US 891 49 385A
CCA DC

Justice	12/03 1949 CERT	
	1	1
Minton	D	D
Clark		
Burton	D	D
Jackson		
Douglas	D	
Frankfr		
Reed		
Black	G	G
Vinson		D

Dorsey v Stuyvesant Town
49 402A
339 US 981 49 25A 49 34A 49 44A
New York

Justice	12/03 1949 CERT	04/01 1950 CERT	04/08 1950 CERT	06/03 1950 CERT
	1 1	1 2	1 3	1 4
Minton	D		D	D
Clark				
Burton	G	G	D	D
Jackson		D		
Douglas	G	G / GH		
Frankfr				
Reed				
Black	G	G	G	G
Vinson	D	D	D	D

Reider v Thompson
49 403A
339 US 113
Minton 02/15/50 *CCA 5th*

Justice	12/03 1949 CERT	02/11 1950 MERITS	03/13 1950 REPORT
	1 1	1 1	1 1
Minton	G	R	R
Clark	G	R	R
Burton			
Jackson			A
Douglas		A	
Frankfr	G		
Reed	G	R	R
Black	G	R	R
Vinson	G	R	R

Independence Lead Mines v Kingsbury
49 406A
338 US 900 49 179M
CCA 9th

Justice	12/10 1949 CERT	
	1	1
Minton	D	D
Clark		
Burton	D	D
Jackson		
Douglas	D	
Frankfr		
Reed		
Black	G	
Vinson		D

Papadakis v Maleuris
49 408A
338 US 894 49 389A
CCA 4th

Justice	12/03 1949 CERT	
	1	1
Minton	D	
Clark		
Burton	D	
Jackson	D	
Douglas		
Frankfr	D	
Reed		
Black	G	
Vinson		D

Ryan Stevedoring Company v U.S.
49 410A
338 US 899
CCA 2d

Justice	12/10 1949 CERT	
	1	1
Minton	D	D
Clark		
Burton	D	D
Jackson		
Douglas	D	
Frankfr		
Reed		
Black	G	
Vinson		D

Plankinton Packing v Wisconsin ERB
49 419A
338 US 953
Wisconsin

Justice	12/10 1949 CERT	02/11 1950 MERITS	02/13 1950 REPORT
	1 1	1 1	1 1
Minton	G	R	R
Clark	G	R	R
Burton	G	R	R
Jackson			
Douglas	D		
Frankfr	G	R	R
Reed	G	R	R
Black	G	R	R
Vinson	G	R	R

International Teamsters v Watson
49 426A
338 US 942
Florida

	01/14 1950 CERT 1 1
Minton	D
Clark	D
Burton	D
Jackson	D
Douglas	D
Frankfr	D
Reed	D
Black	D
Vinson	D

Flowers v Mississippi
49 427A
339 US 946 49 46A
Mississippi

	11/12 1949 CERT 1 1	04/29 1950 CERT 1 2
Minton	D	D
Clark	D	D
Burton		D
Jackson	H	
Douglas	HD	G
Frankfr	HD	Q
Reed		
Black	G	G
Vinson	D	D

U.S. v National Association Real Estate
49 428A
339 US 485
Douglas 04/06/50 DC DC

	11/19 1949 JURIS 1 1	04/01 1950 MERITS 1 1	04/01 1950 MERITS 2 1 Q	05/08 1950 REPORT 1 1	05/08 1950 REPORT 2 1
Minton	N	R		R	A
Clark	N	R	A	R	A
Burton			A		A
Jackson	N	R	A	R	A
Douglas					
Frankfr					
Reed	N	R	RQ	R	A
Black	N	R	R	R	A
Vinson	N	RQ		R	A

N.L.R.B. v Atlanta Metallic Casket
49 431A
338 US 910 49 432A
CCA 5th

	01/07 1950 CERT 1 1
Minton	
Clark	D
Burton	D
Jackson	D
Douglas	D
Frankfr	D
Reed	D
Black	G
Vinson	D

N.L.R.B. v Wilson & Company
49 432A
338 US 910 49 431A 49 435A
CCA 5th

	01/07 1950 CERT 1 1
Minton	
Clark	D
Burton	D
Jackson	D
Douglas	D
Frankfr	
Reed	D
Black	D
Vinson	D

N.L.R.B. v Massey Gin & Machine
49 433A
338 US 910 49 434A
CCA 5th

	01/07 1950 CERT 1 1
Minton	
Clark	D
Burton	GM
Jackson	
Douglas	
Frankfr	
Reed	D
Black	G
Vinson	D

N.L.R.B. v Mexia Textile Mills
49 434A
339 US 563 49 435A
Clark 04/26/50 CCA 5th

	01/07 1950 CERT 1 1	04/22 1950 MERITS 1 1	04/24 1950 MERITS 1 2	05/15 1950 REPORT 1 1
Minton				
Clark	G	R	R	>
Burton	G	R	R	>
Jackson	D	A	A	S
Douglas	D	R	R	>
Frankfr				
Reed	G	R	R	v
Black	G	R	R	>
Vinson	G	R	A	S

N.L.R.B. v Pool Manufacturing
49 435A
339 US 577 49 434A
Clark 04/26/50 CCA 5th

	01/07 1950 CERT 1 1	04/22 1950 MERITS 1 1	04/24 1950 MERITS 1 2	05/15 1950 REPORT 1 1
Minton				
Clark	G	R	R	>
Burton	G	R	R	>
Jackson	D	A	A	S
Douglas	D	R	R	>
Frankfr				
Reed	G	R	R	v
Black	G	R	R	>
Vinson	G	R	A	S

Order Of RR Conductors v Southern RR
49 438A
339 US 255 49 391A
Black 02/15/50 South Carolina

	12/10 1949 CERT 1 1	02/04 1950 AMICUS 1 1	02/11 1950 MERITS 1 1	04/10 1950 REPORT 1 1
Minton	H	B	R	R
Clark	H	B	R	R
Burton	G	B	R	R
Jackson				
Douglas				
Frankfr	G	B	R	R
Reed	G	B	R	R
Black	H	Y	B	A
Vinson				

California State Automobile v Smyth
49 444A
338 US 905
CCA 9th

	12/17 1949 CERT
Minton	
Clark	
Burton	D
Jackson	G
Douglas	D
Frankfr	
Reed	D
Black	G
Vinson	D

Brown Shoe Company v C.I.R.
49 445A
339 US 583
Clark 04/10/50 CCA 8th

	01/07 1950 CERT	04/08 1950 MERITS	05/15 1950 REPORT
Minton	G	R	R
Clark	G	R	R
Burton	G	R	R
Jackson	G	R	R
Douglas	G	R	R
Frankfr	G	R	R
Reed	G	R	R
Black	G	R	R
Vinson		R	R

Land O'Lakes Dairy v County Of Wadena
49 447A
338 US 897
Minnesota

	12/10 1949 JURIS	12/12 1949 REPORT
Minton	A	A
Clark	A	A
Burton	A	A
Jackson	S	
Douglas		A
Frankfr	N	A
Reed	N	A
Black		
Vinson	A	

Kamp v U.S.
49 448A
339 US 957
CCA DC

	05/13 1950 CERT
Minton	
Clark	
Burton	D
Jackson	D
Douglas	D
Frankfr	X D
Reed	
Black	D
Vinson	G D

Building Service Employees v Gazzam
49 449A
339 US 532
Minton 03/17/50 Washington

	12/17 1949 CERT	02/11 1950 MERITS	05/08 1950 REPORT
Minton	G		A
Clark	G	R	A
Burton	G		A
Jackson	G	R	A
Douglas	G		A
Frankfr	G		A
Reed	G	R	A
Black	G		A
Vinson	D		A

Shoong v C.I.R.
49 453A
339 US 974 49 384A
CCA 9th

	06/03 1950 CERT
Minton	GR
Clark	GR
Burton	GR
Jackson	GR
Douglas	
Frankfr	GR
Reed	GR
Black	G
Vinson	GR

O.C. Wiley & Sons v U.S.
49 464A
338 US 902
DC WD Virginia

	12/17 1949 JURIS	06/05 1950 REPORT
Minton	A	R
Clark	A	R
Burton	A	R
Jackson	A	R
Douglas		
Frankfr	A	R
Reed	A	R
Black	A	
Vinson	A	R

Automatic Radio v Hazeltine Research
49 455A
339 US 827
Reed 04/10/50 Minton 05/03/50 CCA 1st

	01/14 1950 CERT	03/25 1950 AMICUS	04/08 1950 MERITS	06/05 1950 REPORT
Minton		B	A	A
Clark		B	A	A
Burton	G	B Y		
Jackson				
Douglas		B	A	A
Frankfr		B Y		
Reed			A	A
Black	G	B	A	A
Vinson		B Y	A	A

International UAW v O'Brien
49 456A
339 US 454
Vinson 04/06/50 Michigan

	12/10 1949 JURIS	04/01 1950 MERITS	05/08 1950 REPORT
Minton	N	R	R
Clark	N	R	R
Burton	N	R	R
Jackson		R	R
Douglas	N	R	R
Frankfr	N	R	R
Reed	N	R	R
Black	N	R	R
Vinson		R	R

U.S. v Steffan
49 473A
338 US 902 49 334A
DC ND Illinois

	12/17 1949 JURIS	12/17 1949 MERITS	12/19 1949 REPORT
Minton	N	R	R
Clark	N	R	R
Burton	N	R	R
Jackson	D		
Douglas	D		
Frankfr	N	R	R
Reed	N	R	R
Black	N	R	R
Vinson	D		

Courant v International Photographers
49 471A
338 US 943
CCA 9th

	01/14 1950 CERT
Minton	
Clark	D
Burton	D
Jackson	D
Douglas	D
Frankfr	
Reed	D
Black	
Vinson	D

Warren v U.S.
49 468A
338 US 947
CCA 10th

	02/04 1950 CERT
Minton	D
Clark	D
Burton	
Jackson	G
Douglas	
Frankfr	
Reed	D
Black	D
Vinson	D

United States Smelting v Lowe
49 489A
338 US 954
CCA 9th

Justice	02/04 1950 CERT (1 1)	02/11 1950 CERT (1 2)
Minton	G	GM
Clark	G	GM
Burton	G	GM
Jackson		
Douglas	D	
Frankfr		GM
Reed	G	GM
Black	G	GM
Vinson	G	GM

U.S. v Cotton Valley Operators
49 490A
339 US 972
DC WD Lousiana

Justice	01/07 1950 JURIS (1 1)	04/22 1950 MERITS (1 1)	04/24 1950 REPORT (1 1)
Minton	N		
Clark	N	R	A
Burton	N		
Jackson	N	R	A
Douglas	N		
Frankfr			
Reed	N	R	A
Black	N		
Vinson	N	R	A

Burton v U.S.
49 497A
338 US 946
DC WD Virginia

Justice	02/04 1950 JURIS (1 1)	02/06 1950 REPORT (1 1)
Minton	A	A
Clark	A	A
Burton	A	A
Jackson		
Douglas		
Frankfr		
Reed	A	A
Black	A	A
Vinson	A	A

Washington v Columbia Steel Company
49 500A
339 US 903
Washington

Justice	02/11 1950 CERT (1 1)	02/18 1950 CERT (1 2)
Minton		
Clark	D	D
Burton	D	D
Jackson	G	G
Douglas	D	D
Frankfr		
Reed	D	D
Black	D	D
Vinson	D	D

Tax Commission v Weyerhaeuser Sales
49 501A
339 US 903 49 500A
Washington

Justice	02/11 1950 CERT (1 1)	02/18 1950 CERT (1 2)
Minton		
Clark	D	D
Burton	D	D
Jackson	G	G
Douglas	D	D
Frankfr		
Reed	D	D
Black	D	D
Vinson	D	D

Transport Trading & Terminal v C.I.R.
49 505A
338 US 955
CCA 2d

Justice	02/11 1950 CERT (1 1)
Minton	
Clark	D
Burton	D
Jackson	
Douglas	G
Frankfr	G
Reed	
Black	D
Vinson	D

Lyon v Singer
49 512A
339 US 841 49 513A 49 527A 49 528A
Reed 04/26/50 New York

Justice	02/18 1950 CERT (1 1)	04/22 1950 MERITS (1 1)	06/05 1950 REPORT (1 1)
Minton	G	R	A
Clark	G	R	A
Burton	G	R	A
Jackson	G	RQ	A
Douglas			A
Frankfr	G	R	A
Reed	G		A
Black	G	A	A
Vinson	G	A	A

Lyon v Banque Mellie Iran
49 513A
339 US 841 49 512A 49 527A 49 528A
Reed 04/26/50 New York

Justice	02/18 1950 CERT (1 1)	04/22 1950 MERITS (1 1)	06/05 1950 REPORT (1 1)
Minton	G	R	A
Clark	G	—	A
Burton	G	RV	A
Jackson	G	R	A
Douglas		R	A
Frankfr	G	—	S
Reed	G	RV	A
Black	G	R	A
Vinson	G		A

Cohen v U.S.
49 517A
339 US 920
CCA 2d

Justice	03/11 1950 CERT (1 1)
Minton	
Clark	D
Burton	D
Jackson	D
Douglas	D
Frankfr	
Reed	G
Black	G
Vinson	D

Eleazer v U.S.
49 526A
339 US 903
CCA 4th

Justice	02/18 1950 CERT (1 1)
Minton	
Clark	D
Burton	D
Jackson	D
Douglas	D
Frankfr	
Reed	D
Black	D
Vinson	G

Singer v Yokohama Specie Bank
49 527A
339 US 841 49 512A 49 513A 49 518A
Reed 04/26/50 New York

Justice	02/18 1950 CERT (1 1)	04/22 1950 MERITS (1 1)	06/05 1950 REPORT (1 1)
Minton	G	R	A
Clark	G	R	A
Burton	G	R	A
Jackson	G	R	A
Douglas	G		A
Frankfr	G	RQ	A
Reed	G		A
Black	G	R	S
Vinson		R	A

Banque Mellie Iran v Lyon
49 528A
339 US 841 49 527A 49 512A 49 513A
Reed 04/26/50 New York

Justice	02/18 1950 CERT (1 1)	04/22 1950 MERITS (1 1)	06/05 1950 REPORT (1 1)
Minton	G	R	A
Clark	G	R	A
Burton	G	R	A
Jackson	G	R	A
Douglas	G		A
Frankfr	G	RQ	A
Reed	G		A
Black	G	R	A
Vinson		R	A

United States Graphite v Sawyer
49 532A
339 US 904
CCA DC

	02/18 1950 CERT 1 1
Minton	
Clark	G
Burton	D
Jackson	
Douglas	
Frankfr	
Reed	D
Black	D
Vinson	G

Colonial Airlines v Adams
49 539A
338 US 947
DC DC

	01/14 1950 JURIS 1 1	02/06 1950 REPORT 1 1
Minton		
Clark	A	
Burton	P	SI
Jackson		SI
Douglas		SI
Frankfr	P	SI
Reed	P	SI
Black	P	SI
Vinson	P	SI

Blanchard Machine v R.F.C.
49 540A
339 US 912
CCA DC

	03/11 1950 CERT 1 1
Minton	D
Clark	D
Burton	D
Jackson	
Douglas	
Frankfr	
Reed	D
Black	G
Vinson	D

Gordon v U.S.
49 548A
339 US 935
CCA 6th

	04/08 1950 CERT 1 1
Minton	
Clark	G
Burton	D
Jackson	D
Douglas	
Frankfr	
Reed	D
Black	D
Vinson	G

Local 36 v U.S.
49 562A
339 US 947
CCA 9th

	04/29 1950 CERT 1 1
Minton	D
Clark	D
Burton	D
Jackson	
Douglas	G
Frankfr	G
Reed	
Black	
Vinson	GL

Litton v U.S.
49 564A
339 US 921
CCA 8th

	03/25 1950 CERT 1 1
Minton	D
Clark	D
Burton	D
Jackson	
Douglas	D
Frankfr	
Reed	D
Black	D
Vinson	D

Lyle v Atchison Topeka RR
49 567A
339 US 913
CCA 7th

	03/11 1950 CERT 1 1
Minton	D
Clark	D
Burton	D
Jackson	
Douglas	D
Frankfr	D
Reed	
Black	
Vinson	G

Ewing v Mytinger & Casselberry
49 568A
339 US 594
Douglas 04/26/50 DC DC

	02/18 1950 JURIS 1 1	04/22 1950 MERITS 1 1	05/29 1950 REPORT 1 1
Minton	N	R	R
Clark	N	R	R
Burton	N	R	R
Jackson		A	A
Douglas	N	R	R
Frankfr	N	A	A
Reed	N	R	R
Black		R	R
Vinson			

Beverage v Farm Bureau Mutual
49 569A
339 US 914
CCA 4th

	03/11 1950 CERT 1 1
Minton	D
Clark	D
Burton	D
Jackson	
Douglas	D
Frankfr	
Reed	
Black	
Vinson	D

Lord Manufacturing Company v U.S.
49 570A
339 US 956
Ct Cls

	05/13 1950 CERT 1 1
Minton	D
Clark	
Burton	G
Jackson	
Douglas	D
Frankfr	
Reed	G
Black	
Vinson	D

Winkler v Maryland
49 572A
339 US 919
Maryland

	03/25 1950 CERT 1 1
Minton	D
Clark	D
Burton	D
Jackson	
Douglas	
Frankfr	
Reed	D
Black	G
Vinson	G

Atlantic Coast Line RR v Scarborough
49 573A
339 US 919
CCA 4th

	03/25 1950 CERT 1 1
Minton	D
Clark	
Burton	D
Jackson	
Douglas	G
Frankfr	G
Reed	
Black	
Vinson	X

U.S. v Iowa-Wisconsin Bridge Company
49 579A
339 US 982 49 1A
Ct Cls

	06/03 1950 CERT 1 1
Minton	D
Clark	D
Burton	D
Jackson	
Douglas	G
Frankfr	
Reed	G
Black	G
Vinson	D

U.S. v Union Pacific RR Company
49 580A
339 US 930
Ct Cls

	04/08 1950 CERT 1 1
Minton	D
Clark	D
Burton	D
Jackson	D
Douglas	D
Frankfr	
Reed	
Black	
Vinson	D

U.S. v Pevely Dairy Company
49 592A
339 US 942 49 593A
CCA 8th

	04/15 1950 CERT 1 1	04/22 1950 CERT 1 2
Minton		D
Clark	G	G
Burton	G	G
Jackson	G	G
Douglas		
Frankfr		
Reed		D
Black	X	DQ
Vinson		D

McGrath v Paramount Pictures
49 594A
339 US 953 49 613A
California
05/06 1950 CERT
1 1

Justice	Vote
Minton	
Clark	D
Burton	
Jackson	G
Douglas	
Frankfr	
Reed	D
Black	G
Vinson	D

Atlantic Coast Line RR v St. Joe Paper
49 601A
339 US 929
CCA 5th
04/01 1950 CERT
1 1

Justice	Vote
Minton	
Clark	G
Burton	D
Jackson	D
Douglas	D
Frankfr	
Reed	G
Black	
Vinson	D

Jacobs v Charles Pezkat Manufacturing
49 607A
339 US 915
CCA 7th
03/11 1950 CERT
1 1

Justice	Vote
Minton	
Clark	D
Burton	D
Jackson	
Douglas	
Frankfr	
Reed	D
Black	
Vinson	D

Brock v Solomon
49 614A
339 US 937 49 675A
CCA 7th
04/15 1950 CERT
1 1

Justice	Vote
Minton	D
Clark	D
Burton	D
Jackson	D
Douglas	D
Frankfr	D
Reed	D
Black	G
Vinson	D

Pennsylvania v Curtis Publishing
49 617A
339 US 928
Pennsylvania
04/01 1950 CERT
1 1

Justice	Vote
Minton	
Clark	
Burton	
Jackson	
Douglas	
Frankfr	
Reed	
Black	
Vinson	

Continental Oil Company v Jones
49 618A
339 US 931
CCA 10th
04/08 1950 CERT
1 2

Justice	Vote
Minton	D
Clark	D
Burton	D
Jackson	D
Douglas	D
Frankfr	G
Reed	G
Black	D
Vinson	D

Jackson v Vance
49 641A
339 US 937
CCA 10th
04/08 1950 CERT
1 1

Justice	Vote
Minton	D
Clark	D
Burton	D
Jackson	
Douglas	G
Frankfr	D
Reed	
Black	G
Vinson	D

Allied Oil v Socony-Vacuum Oil
49 643A
339 US 938
CCA 7th
04/15 1953 CERT
1 1

Justice	Vote
Minton	
Clark	
Burton	
Jackson	G
Douglas	
Frankfr	
Reed	
Black	
Vinson	

Stone v Reichman-Crosby Company
49 653A
339 US 917
Mississippi
03/25 1950 CERT — 1 1
03/25 1950 JURIS — 1 1

Justice	CERT	JURIS
Minton		S
Clark	D	S
Burton	D	S
Jackson	G	S
Douglas	D	S
Frankfr		
Reed		
Black	G	N
Vinson	D	S

Holmes v U.S.
49 657A
339 US 927
DC SD New York
04/03 1950 REPORT — 1 1
04/01 1950 JURIS — 1 1

Justice	REPORT	JURIS
Minton	A	A
Clark	A	A
Burton	A	A
Jackson	A	A
Douglas	A	A
Frankfr	A	A
Reed	A	A
Black	A	A
Vinson	A	A

Republic Steel v Farval
49 669A
339 US 938
CCA 6th
04/15 1950 CERT
1 1

Justice	Vote
Minton	
Clark	
Burton	
Jackson	
Douglas	
Frankfr	
Reed	
Black	
Vinson	

United States Gypsum Company v U.S.
49 671A
339 US 959 49 670A
DC DC
05/29 1950 REPORT — 1 1
05/27 1950 JURIS — 1 1

Justice	REPORT	JURIS
Minton	S	A
Clark		
Burton	S	A
Jackson		S
Douglas	S	A
Frankfr		A
Reed	S	
Black	S	S
Vinson	S	A

Becker v Solomon
49 675A
339 US 937 49 614A
CCA 7th
04/15 1950 CERT
1 1

Justice	Vote
Minton	D
Clark	D
Burton	D
Jackson	D
Douglas	D
Frankfr	D
Reed	G
Black	D
Vinson	D

United Artists v Board Of Censors
49 680A
339 US 952
Tennessee
05/06 1950 CERT
1 1

Justice	Vote
Minton	
Clark	
Burton	
Jackson	
Douglas	
Frankfr	
Reed	G
Black	
Vinson	

Randolph Laboratories v Specialties
49 698A
339 US 952
CCA 3rd
05/06 1950 CERT
1 1

Justice	Vote
Minton	D
Clark	D
Burton	
Jackson	
Douglas	
Frankfr	
Reed	G
Black	
Vinson	

Citizens Ice v Atlantic Company
49 706A
339 US 953
CCA 5th
05/06 1950 CERT
1 1

Justice	Vote
Minton	D
Clark	
Burton	G
Jackson	
Douglas	G
Frankfr	D
Reed	D
Black	D
Vinson	D

Safe Harbor Water Power v F.P.C.
49 709A
339 US 957
CCA 3rd
05/13 1950 CERT
1 1

Justice	Vote
Minton	
Clark	
Burton	
Jackson	G
Douglas	
Frankfr	GQ
Reed	
Black	
Vinson	

Beets v Hunter
49 711A
339 US 963 49 241A
CCA 10th
05/27 1950 CERT
1 1

Justice	Vote
Minton	D
Clark	D
Burton	
Jackson	
Douglas	
Frankfr	
Reed	G
Black	D
Vinson	D

U.S. v Martin
49 712A
339 US 957 49 715A
CCA DC

	05/13 1950 CERT 1 1
Minton	D
Clark	D
Burton	D
Jackson	D
Douglas	D
Frankfr	D
Reed	
Black	G
Vinson	D

King v U.S.
49 720A
339 US 964
CCA 5th

	05/27 1950 CERT 1 1
Minton	D
Clark	D
Burton	D
Jackson	D
Douglas	D
Frankfr	DQ
Reed	
Black	G
Vinson	D

Nelson v Johnson
49 721A
339 US 957
CCA DC

	05/13 1950 CERT 1 1
Minton	D
Clark	D
Burton	D
Jackson	
Douglas	D
Frankfr	D
Reed	
Black	G
Vinson	

South v Peters
49 724A
339 US 276
DC ND Georgia

	04/08 1950 JURIS 1 1	04/15 1950 JURIS 1 2	04/17 1950 REPORT 1 1
Minton	S	A	A
Clark	S	A	A
Burton	P S	A	A
Jackson	S	P	R
Douglas	NP S	A	A
Frankfr	S		R
Reed	S	A	A
Black	N		R
Vinson	N S	A	A

Hopkins v Maryland
49 727A
339 US 940
Maryland

	04/22 1950 JURIS 1 1
Minton	S
Clark	S
Burton	S
Jackson	N N
Douglas	S
Frankfr	S
Reed	S
Black	S
Vinson	S

E.B. Kaiser Company v Ric-Wil Company
49 730A
339 US 958
CCA 7th

	05/13 1950 CERT 1 1
Minton	
Clark	
Burton	
Jackson	
Douglas	
Frankfr	
Reed	
Black	G
Vinson	

Alltmont v U.S.
49 734A
339 US 967
CCA 3rd

	05/27 1950 CERT 1 1
Minton	D
Clark	
Burton	G
Jackson	D
Douglas	D
Frankfr	
Reed	G
Black	
Vinson	G

Simonsen v Emmerling
49 740A
339 US 978 49 761A 49 762A
CCA 7th

	05/27 1950 CERT 1 1	06/03 1950 CERT 1 2
Minton	D	D
Clark	D	D
Burton	D	D
Jackson		D
Douglas	D	GM
Frankfr		
Reed	G	G
Black	G	G
Vinson		

U.S. v Knight
49 743A
339 US 978
CCA 3rd

	06/03 1950 CERT 1 1
Minton	D
Clark	D
Burton	D
Jackson	D
Douglas	D
Frankfr	
Reed	D
Black	
Vinson	G

Curtis v U.S.
49 744A
339 US 965
CCA 6th

	05/27 1950 CERT 1 1
Minton	D
Clark	D
Burton	D
Jackson	G
Douglas	D
Frankfr	D
Reed	D
Black	D
Vinson	D

Mahana v U.S.
49 745A
339 US 978
Ct Cls

	06/03 1950 CERT 1 1
Minton	D
Clark	D
Burton	D
Jackson	D
Douglas	D
Frankfr	D
Reed	D
Black	G
Vinson	D

Magidson v Duggan
49 747A
339 US 965
CCA 8th

	05/27 1950 CERT 1 1
Minton	D
Clark	D
Burton	D
Jackson	D
Douglas	D
Frankfr	D
Reed	G
Black	D
Vinson	DQ

Emery Transportion Company v U.S.
49 754A
339 US 955 49 755A
DC SD Ohio

	05/13 1950 JURIS 1 1	05/15 1950 REPORT 1 1
Minton	A	A
Clark	A	A
Burton	A	A
Jackson		
Douglas	N	A
Frankfr		
Reed	A	A
Black	A	A
Vinson	A	A

Hofman v O'Brien
49 755A
339 US 955 49 754A
DC SD New York

	05/13 1950 JURIS 1 1	05/15 1950 REPORT 1 1
Minton	A	A
Clark	A	A
Burton	A	A
Jackson		
Douglas	N	A
Frankfr		
Reed	A	A
Black	A	A
Vinson	A	A

Levine v Berman
49 759A
339 US 982
CCA 7th

	06/03 1950 CERT 1 1
Minton	D
Clark	D
Burton	D
Jackson	D
Douglas	G
Frankfr	D
Reed	D
Black	D
Vinson	D

Pratt v De Korwin
49 771A
339 US 982   49 772A   49 773A
CCA 7th

	06/03 1950 CERT 1 1		
Minton			
Clark	G	D	
Burton			
Douglas	G	D	
Frankfr	GJ	D	
Reed			
Black			
Vinson			

E.I. DuPont De Nemours v U.S.
49 774A
339 US 959
DC ND Illinois

	05/27 1950 JURIS 1 1
Minton	S
Clark	S
Burton	S
Douglas	S
Frankfr	
Reed	N
Black	SQ
Vinson	S

Brooks v St. Louis-San Francisco RR
49 777A
339 US 966
CCA 8th

	06/03 1950 CERT 1 1	
Minton		D
Clark		D
Burton		D
Jackson		D
Douglas		D
Frankfr		D
Reed		D
Black	G	D
Vinson		

Jackson v Ruthazer
49 783A
339 US 980
CCA 2d

	06/03 1950 CERT 1 1	
Minton		D
Clark		D
Burton	D	
Douglas		D
Frankfr		
Reed		D
Black	G	
Vinson		D

Eichenlaub v U.S.
49 788A
339 US 983
CCA 2d

	06/03 1950 CERT 1 1	
Minton		D
Clark		D
Burton		
Douglas		D
Frankfr		D
Reed		D
Black	G	
Vinson		D

Richardson v National Acceptance
49 794A
339 US 981
CCA 7th

	06/03 1950 CERT 1 1	
Minton		D
Clark		D
Burton		D
Jackson		D
Douglas		D
Frankfr		D
Reed		D
Black		D
Vinson	G	

Prichard v U.S.
49 795A
339 US 974
CCA 6th

	06/03 1950 CERT 1 1	
Minton		
Clark		
Burton		M
Jackson		M
Douglas		M
Frankfr		
Reed		
Black		M
Vinson		

Meyers v U.S.
49 802A
339 US 983

	06/03 1950 CERT 1 1	
Minton		D
Clark		D
Burton		
Jackson		D
Douglas		D
Frankfr		D
Reed		D
Black	G	
Vinson		D

Felman v U.S.
49 814A
339 US 973
DC ND Illinois

	06/03 1950 JURIS 1 1	06/05 1950 REPORT 1 1
Minton		A
Clark		A
Burton		A
Jackson		A
Douglas		A
Frankfr		A
Reed		A
Black		A
Vinson		A

Serna v Walters
49 838A
339 US 973
Arizona

	06/03 1950 CERT 1 1	
Minton		D
Clark	E	
Burton	E	D
Jackson	GE	
Douglas		D
Frankfr		D
Reed		D
Black		
Vinson		

Loew's v U.S.
49 844A
339 US 974   49 845A   49 846A   49 847A
DC SD New York

	06/03 1950 JURIS 1 1	10/09 1950 REPORT 1 1	10/14 1950 REHEAR 1 1
Minton	N	N	Y
Clark			
Burton	A	A	BQ
Jackson	A	A	B
Douglas			
Frankfr	N	N	Y
Reed	A	A	B
Black	A	A	B
Vinson			

Roberts v U.S. District Court
49 2M 48 552M
339 US 844
CCA 9th

	06/10 1949 MNDMUS 1 1	04/01 1950 MNDMUS 1 2	06/05 1950 REPORT 1 1
Minton	G		D
Clark	G		D
Burton			D
Rutledg			
Jackson	G		D
Murphy	G		
Douglas	G	G	
Frankfr			D
Reed	G		D
Black			D
Vinson			D

Grayson v Moore
49 3M 48 578M
338 US 873
Texas

	06/17 1949 CERT 1 1	11/05 1949 CERT 1 2
Minton		D
Clark		D
Burton	E	
Rutledg		
Jackson	E	D
Murphy		
Douglas		
Frankfr	E	D
Reed	E	D
Black		D
Vinson		

Gray v Burke
49 4M 48 643M
338 US 834
Pennsylvania

	06/17 1949 CERT 1 1	10/05 1949 CERT 1 2
Minton		D
Clark		D
Burton	E	
Rutledg		
Jackson	E	D
Murphy		
Douglas	E	
Frankfr	E	D
Reed		
Black	E	D
Vinson		

Barrigar v Illinois
49 6M 48 668M
338 US 905
Illinois

	06/24 1949 CERT 1 1	12/17 1949 CERT 1 2
Minton		D
Clark		D
Burton	E	
Rutledg		
Jackson	E	D
Murphy		
Douglas	E	
Frankfr		D
Reed		D
Black		
Vinson		

Evans v Robinson
49 233M
339 US 985
Illinois
02/04 1950 CERT 1 1

Justice	Vote
Minton	
Clark	E
Burton	E
Jackson	E
Douglas	
Frankfr	E
Reed	E
Black	
Vinson	

(above, unnamed — 06/03 1950 CERT 1 2)

Justice	Vote
Minton	D
Clark	D
Burton	D
Jackson	D
Douglas	D
Frankfr	D
Reed	D
Black	D
Vinson	D

Thompson v Robinson
49 255M
338 US 950
Illinois
02/04 1950 CERT 1 1

Justice	Vote
Minton	
Clark	E
Burton	E
Jackson	
Douglas	
Frankfr	
Reed	
Black	E
Vinson	

Carter v Illinois
49 282M
338 US 950
Illinois
02/04 1950 CERT 1 1

Justice	Vote
Minton	
Clark	
Burton	
Jackson	
Douglas	
Frankfr	
Reed	
Black	G
Vinson	

Melanson v Massachusetts
49 190M
339 US 984 49 33A 49 185M 49 195M
Massachusetts
06/03 1950 CERT 1 1

Justice	Vote
Minton	
Clark	D
Burton	D
Jackson	D
Douglas	G
Frankfr	
Reed	D
Black	G
Vinson	D

Crombie v Ragen
49 202M
339 US 921 49 207M
Illinois
03/25 1950 CERT 1 2

Justice	Vote
Minton	D
Clark	
Burton	DZ
Jackson	D
Douglas	DZ
Frankfr	D
Reed	DZ
Black	G
Vinson	D

U.S. v U.S. District Court
49 225M
338 US 889
DC WD Texas
12/03 1949 MNDMUS 1 1

Justice	Vote
Minton	
Clark	D
Burton	
Jackson	
Douglas	G
Frankfr	D
Reed	D
Black	G
Vinson	X

Coggins v Massachusetts
49 189M
338 US 881 49 190M 49 195M
Massachusetts
11/12 1949 CERT 1 1

Justice	Vote
Minton	
Clark	D
Burton	D
Jackson	D
Douglas	G
Frankfr	
Reed	D
Black	D
Vinson	G

Crowe v U.S.
49 90M
338 US 950
CCA 4th
02/04 1950 CERT 1 1

Justice	Vote
Minton	D
Clark	E
Burton	E
Jackson	
Douglas	
Frankfr	
Reed	
Black	E
Vinson	D

Perkins v Cranor
49 151M
338 US 862
Washington
10/22 1949 CERT 1 1

Justice	Vote
Minton	
Clark	D
Burton	D
Jackson	D
Douglas	
Frankfr	
Reed	
Black	G
Vinson	D

Burke v Georgia
49 176M
338 US 941
Georgia
01/07 1950 CERT 1 1

Justice	Vote
Minton	DZ
Clark	DZ
Burton	
Jackson	
Douglas	G
Frankfr	E
Reed	
Black	E
Vinson	

(01/14 1950 CERT 1 2)

Justice	Vote
Minton	DZ
Clark	DZ
Burton	DZ
Jackson	
Douglas	DZ
Frankfr	DZ
Reed	DZ
Black	
Vinson	

Wilson v Texas
49 93M
338 US 838
Texas
10/05 1949 CERT 1 1

Justice	Vote
Minton	
Clark	D
Burton	D
Jackson	
Douglas	
Frankfr	
Reed	
Black	G
Vinson	D

Schneider v Colorado
49 107M
338 US 862
Colorado
10/22 1949 CERT 1 1

Justice	Vote
Minton	
Clark	D
Burton	D
Jackson	
Douglas	
Frankfr	
Reed	
Black	G
Vinson	D

Simmons v Pennsylvania
49 57M
338 US 862
Pennsylvania
10/22 1949 CERT 1 1

Justice	Vote
Minton	
Clark	D
Burton	D
Jackson	D
Douglas	
Frankfr	
Reed	D
Black	G
Vinson	D

Gresham v Texas
49 68M
338 US 937
Texas
01/07 1950 CERT 1 1

Justice	Vote
Minton	
Clark	D
Burton	D
Jackson	D
Douglas	
Frankfr	
Reed	D
Black	G
Vinson	D

Massey v Moore
49 69M
338 US 837
CCA 5th
10/05 1949 CERT 1 1

Justice	Vote
Minton	
Clark	D
Burton	D
Jackson	
Douglas	
Frankfr	
Reed	D
Black	G
Vinson	D

Lovely v U.S.
49 8M
338 US 834
CCA 5th
10/05 1949 CERT 1 1

Justice	Vote
Minton	
Clark	D
Burton	D
Jackson	
Douglas	
Frankfr	G
Reed	D
Black	G
Vinson	D

McClannahan v Michigan
49 48M
339 US 984 49 33A 49 190M
Michigan
06/03 1950 CERT 1 1

Justice	Vote
Minton	
Clark	D
Burton	D
Jackson	
Douglas	
Frankfr	G
Reed	D
Black	G
Vinson	D

Hunter v Madison Avenue
49 54M
338 US 836
CCA 6th
10/05 1949 CERT 1 1

Justice	Vote
Minton	
Clark	D
Burton	D
Jackson	
Douglas	
Frankfr	G
Reed	D
Black	G
Vinson	D

Langford v U.S.
49 291M
339 US 938
CCA 9th
04/15 1950 CERT 1 1

Justice	Vote
Minton	D
Clark	D
Burton	D
Jackson	GR D
Douglas	G
Frankfr	GR D
Reed	
Black	D
Vinson	GR D

Robinson v U.S.
49 305M
339 US 923
CCA 5th
03/25 1950 CERT 1 1

Justice	Vote
Minton	D
Clark	D
Burton	D
Jackson	
Douglas	D
Frankfr	D
Reed	D
Black	D
Vinson	D

Bryan v Georgia
49 307M
339 US 904
Georgia
02/18 1950 CERT 1 1

Justice	Vote
Minton	D
Clark	G
Burton	D
Jackson	
Douglas	D
Frankfr	D
Reed	DZ
Black	G
Vinson	D

Simmons v Hunter
49 332M
339 US 968 49 350M
CCA 10th
05/27 1950 CERT 1 1

Justice	Vote
Minton	D
Clark	D
Burton	D
Jackson	
Douglas	G
Frankfr	
Reed	D
Black	G
Vinson	D

Hart v U.S.
49 334M
339 US 985
CCA 8th
06/03 1950 CERT 1 1

Justice	Vote
Minton	D
Clark	D
Burton	D
Jackson	
Douglas	G
Frankfr	
Reed	D
Black	G
Vinson	D

Thomasson v Missouri
49 336M
339 US 938
Missouri
04/15 1950 CERT 1 1

Justice	Vote
Minton	D
Clark	D
Burton	D
Jackson	
Douglas	G
Frankfr	
Reed	D
Black	D
Vinson	D

Perez v New York
49 345M
338 US 952
New York
02/04 1950 CERT 1 1

Justice	Vote
Minton	D
Clark	D
Burton	D
Jackson	
Douglas	G
Frankfr	
Reed	D
Black	G
Vinson	D

McMahan v Hunter
49 350M
339 US 968 49 332M
CCA 10th
05/27 1950 CERT 1 1

Justice	Vote
Minton	D
Clark	D
Burton	D
Jackson	
Douglas	G
Frankfr	
Reed	D
Black	G
Vinson	D

Darman v New York
49 353M
339 US 968
New York
05/27 1950 CERT 1 1

Justice	Vote
Minton	D
Clark	D
Burton	D
Jackson	
Douglas	G
Frankfr	
Reed	D
Black	D
Vinson	D

Quillian v Sweeney
49 387M
339 US 945 49 388M
Ohio
04/22 1950 CERT 1 1

Justice	Vote
Minton	D
Clark	D
Burton	D
Jackson	
Douglas	G
Frankfr	
Reed	D
Black	D
Vinson	D

Woodall v Sweeney
49 388M
339 US 945 49 387M
Ohio
04/22 1950 CERT 1 1

Justice	Vote
Minton	D
Clark	D
Burton	D
Jackson	
Douglas	G
Frankfr	
Reed	D
Black	D
Vinson	D

Patterson v Georgia
49 393M
339 US 916
Georgia
03/11 1950 CERT 1 1

Justice	Vote
Minton	D
Clark	D
Burton	D
Jackson	
Douglas	D
Frankfr	
Reed	D
Black	GO
Vinson	D

Bridges v North Carolina
49 396M
339 US 939
North Carolina
04/15 1950 CERT 1 1

Justice	Vote
Minton	D
Clark	D
Burton	D
Jackson	G
Douglas	G
Frankfr	
Reed	
Black	D
Vinson	D

Daniels v North Carolina
49 412M
339 US 954
North Carolina
05/06 1950 CERT 1 1

Justice	Vote
Minton	D
Clark	D
Burton	D
Jackson	
Douglas	G
Frankfr	
Reed	D
Black	D
Vinson	D

Arrington v Alabama
49 422M
339 US 950
Alabama
04/29 1950 CERT 1 1

Justice	Vote
Minton	D
Clark	D
Burton	D
Jackson	
Douglas	G
Frankfr	
Reed	D
Black	D
Vinson	D

Hans (In Re)
49 433M
339 US 976 49 434M 49 306A
04/15 1950 HABEAS 1 1

Justice	Vote
Minton	D
Clark	D
Burton	D
Jackson	G
Douglas	G
Frankfr	
Reed	
Black	D
Vinson	D

Schmidt (In Re)
49 434M
339 US 976 49 433M 49 306A
04/15 1950 HABEAS 1 1

Justice	Vote
Minton	D
Clark	D
Burton	D
Jackson	G
Douglas	G
Frankfr	
Reed	
Black	D
Vinson	D

Holt v California
49 441M
339 US 950
California
04/29 1950 CERT 1 1

Justice	Vote
Minton	D
Clark	D
Burton	D
Jackson	
Douglas	G
Frankfr	
Reed	D
Black	E
Vinson	D

Varela v Illinois
49 457M
339 US 936
Illinois
04/08 1950 CERT 1 1

Justice	Vote
Minton	D
Clark	D
Burton	D
Jackson	G
Douglas	G
Frankfr	
Reed	
Black	D
Vinson	D

Seger v Illinois
49 459M
339 US 936
Illinois
04/08 1950 CERT 1 1

Justice	Vote
Minton	D
Clark	D
Burton	D
Jackson	
Douglas	G
Frankfr	
Reed	D
Black	D
Vinson	D

Young v New York Central RR Company
49 466M
339 US 986
Ohio
06/03 1950 CERT 1 1

Justice	Vote
Minton	D
Clark	D
Burton	D
Jackson	
Douglas	G
Frankfr	
Reed	D
Black	G
Vinson	D

Madsen v Johnson
49 491M
339 US 975 49 778A
CCA DC

	05/13 1950 HABEAS 1 1	06/03 1950 HABEAS 1 2
Minton		D
Clark	E	D
Burton	E	D
Jackson		D
Douglas	E	G
Frankfr		
Reed	E	D
Black		G
Vinson	E	D

Chapman v U.S.
District Court
49 546M
339 US 976
DC ND California

	06/03 1950 MNDMUS 1 1
Minton	D
Clark	D
Burton	D
Jackson	
Douglas	G
Frankfr	G
Reed	
Black	D
Vinson	D

Sampsell v
California
49 559M
339 US 990
California

	06/03 1950 CERT 1 1
Minton	D
Clark	G
Burton	D
Jackson	
Douglas	D
Frankfr	D
Reed	D
Black	
Vinson	D

Appendix F

U.S. Supreme Court
October 1950 Term

Standard Oil Company v F.T.C.
50 1A 49 107A 48 851A
340 US 231
Reed 01/18/50 Burton 10/23/50 CCA 7th

	11/05 1949 CERT 1 1	01/14 1950 MERITS 1 1	10/14 1950 MERITS 1 2	01/08 1951 REPORT 1 1
Minton	G			R
Clark	G		R	R
Burton	G	R	R	R
Jackson		AJ	AJ	AJ
Douglas	G		R	R
Frankfr				
Reed	G	R	R	R
Black	G	AJ	AJ	AJ
Vinson	D	AJ	AJ	AJ

Hubsch v U.S.
50 2A 49 379A 49 50M
340 US 804 49 51M
CCA 5th

	10/05 1949 CERT 1 1	10/09 1950 REPORT 1 1
Minton	G	SI
Clark	G	SI
Burton	G	SI
Jackson	D	SI
Douglas	G	SI
Frankfr	G	SI
Reed	G	SI
Black	G	SI
Vinson	G	SI

Compagna v Hiatt
50 5A 49 536A
340 US 880
Black 10/23/50 CCA 5th

	05/13 1950 CERT 1 1	10/14 1950 MERITS 1 1	11/13 1950 REPORT 1 1
Minton	D		A
Clark	G		A
Burton	G D		A
Jackson	G	VJM	
Douglas	G D	VJM	>
Frankfr	G	VJM	>
Reed	G D	AS	>
Black	G	A	A
Vinson	D	A	A

Fogarty v U.S.
50 6A 49 551A
340 US 8
Minton 10/23/50 Burton 10/23/50 CCA 8th

	03/11 1950 CERT 1 1	10/14 1950 MERITS 1 1	11/06 1950 REPORT 1 1
Minton	G		A
Clark	G		A
Burton	G		A
Jackson	G	X	A
Douglas	G		A
Frankfr	G		A
Reed	G		A
Black	GH		A
Vinson	G		A

National Council v McGrath
50 7A 49 554A
341 US 123 50 8A 50 71A
Burton 10/23/50 CCA DC

	04/01 1950 CERT 1 1	05/13 1950 MERITS 1 2	10/16 1950 MERITS 1 1	04/30 1951 REPORT 1 1
Minton	H			A
Clark		D		
Burton	H	G	R	R
Jackson	H	G	R	R
Douglas	G	G	R	A
Frankfr	G			A
Reed	H	D	R	R
Black	G			A
Vinson	G	D	R	A

Joint Anti-Fascist Refugee v McGrath
50 8A 49 556A
341 US 123 50 7A 50 71A 50 229A
Burton 10/23/50 CCA DC

	03/11 1950 CERT 1 1	10/16 1950 MERITS 1 1	04/30 1951 REPORT 1 1
Minton	D		A
Clark	G	R	R
Burton	G	R	R
Jackson	G	R	R
Douglas	D		A
Frankfr			
Reed	G	R	R
Black	D	A	A
Vinson	G	R	A

Feres v U.S.
50 9A 49 558A
340 US 135 50 29A 50 31A
Jackson 10/23/50 CCA 2d

	03/11 1950 CERT 1 1	10/16 1950 MERITS 1 1	12/04 1950 REPORT 1 1
Minton	G		A
Clark	G	R	A
Burton	G	R	A
Jackson	G	A	A
Douglas	G	X	A
Frankfr	G	A	A
Reed	G		A
Black	G	R	A
Vinson	G	A	A

U.S. v Security Trust & Savings
50 10A 49 584A
340 US 47 50 11A 50 12A 50 13A
Minton 10/23/50 California

	04/29 1950 CERT 1 1	10/21 1950 MERITS 1 1	11/13 1950 REPORT 1 1
Minton	D	R	R
Clark	G	R	R
Burton	G	R	R
Jackson	G		R
Douglas	D		R
Frankfr		A	R
Reed	D	R	R
Black	G	R	R
Vinson	D	R	R

Harris v C.I.R.
50 14A 49 596A
340 US 106
Douglas 10/23/50 CCA 2d

	03/25 1950 CERT 1 1	10/21 1950 MERITS 1 1	11/27 1950 REPORT 1 1
Minton	D	R	R
Clark	GL	R	R
Burton	GL	RQ	R
Jackson	GL	R	
Douglas	D		R
Frankfr			
Reed	GL	R	R
Black	D	R	R
Vinson	GL	R	R

Missouri (Southern RR) v Mayfield
50 15A 49 597A
340 US 1 50 16A
Frankfr 10/23/50 Missouri

	CERT 03/25 1950	MERITS 10/21 1950	REPORT 11/06 1950
	1 1	1 1	1 1
Minton	D	RV	A
Clark	D	RV A	> A
Burton	D		
Jackson		RV	>
Douglas	G	RV A	> A
Frankfr	G	RV	>
Reed	G		
Black	G D		A
Vinson	G	A	A

Niemotko v Maryland
50 17A 49 599A
340 US 268 50 18A 49 560A
Vinson 10/23/50 Maryland

	JURIS 03/11 1950	MERITS 10/21 1950	REPORT 01/15 1951
	1 1	1 1	1 1
Minton	NR	R	R
Clark	NR	R	R
Burton	N	R	A
Jackson		R	R
Douglas	N	R A	R
Frankfr	N	R	R
Reed	N	R	R
Black	N	R A	A
Vinson	N	R	A

Gara v U.S.
50 19A 49 609A
340 US 857
CCA 6th

	CERT 04/01 1950	MERITS 10/21 1950	REPORT 10/23 1950
	1 1	1 1	1 1
Minton	D	R	R
Clark	D	R	R
Burton		R	
Jackson	G	R	A
Douglas	G	R A	A
Frankfr	G	R	R
Reed	G	R	R
Black	G	R A	A
Vinson	D	R	A

Rogers v U.S.
50 20A 49 635A
340 US 367 50 21A 50 22A
Black 11/16/50 Vinson 01/16/51 CCA 10th

	CERT 05/13 1950	MERITS 11/11 1950	REPORT 02/26 1951
	1 1	1 1	1 1
Minton			A
Clark	D		AQ
Burton	G	RQ	A
Jackson	G	R	R
Douglas	G	R	R
Frankfr	G	R	R
Reed	G		A
Black	G	A	A
Vinson	G		A

Blau v U.S.
50 21A 49 636A
340 US 332 50 20A 50 22A
Black 11/16/50 CCA 10th

	CERT 05/13 1950	MERITS 11/11 1950	REPORT 01/15 1951
	1 1	1 1	1 1
Minton		R	A
Clark	D	R	R
Burton	G	R	R
Jackson	G	R	R
Douglas	G	R	R
Frankfr	G	R	R
Reed	G	R	R
Black	G	R	R
Vinson	G	R	R

Blau v U.S.
50 22A 49 640A
340 US 159 50 20A 50 21A
Black 11/16/50 CCA 10th

	CERT 05/13 1950	MERITS 11/11 1950	REPORT 12/11 1950
	1 1	1 1	1 1
Minton	G	R	R
Clark			
Burton	G	R	R
Jackson	G	R	R
Douglas	G	R	R
Frankfr	G	R	R
Reed	G	R	R
Black	G	R	R
Vinson	G	R	R

U.S. v Munsingwear
50 23A 49 648A
340 US 36 50 24A 49 649A
Douglas 10/23/50 CCA 8th

	CERT 04/22 1950	MERITS 10/21 1950	REPORT 11/13 1950
	1 1	1 1	1 1
Minton	G	D	A
Clark	G	D	A
Burton			A
Jackson	G	D	A
Douglas	G		A
Frankfr	G		A
Reed	G		
Black	G	D	R A
Vinson	G	R X	A

U.S. v Rock Island Motor Transit
50 25A 49 654A
340 US 419
Reed 11/16/50 DC ND Illinois

	JURIS 03/25 1950	MERITS 11/11 1950	REPORT 02/26 1951
	1 1	1 1	1 1
Minton	N	R	R
Clark	N	R	R
Burton	N	A	
Jackson	N	A	
Douglas	N		
Frankfr	N	R	R
Reed	N	R	
Black	N	A	A
Vinson	N X	R	R

U.S. v Williams
50 26A 49 659A
341 US 70 50 365A 50 134A 50 1M
Frankfr 01/16/51 CCA 5th

	CERT 10/03 1950	CERT 10/14 1950	MERITS 01/13 1951	REPORT 04/23 1951
	1 1	1 2	1 1	1 1
Minton	G	G		A
Clark	G	G	R	R
Burton		G	R	R
Jackson		G		
Douglas	X		R	R
Frankfr	D	D	R	R
Reed	D	D		
Black	D	D	R	R
Vinson	X		R	R

Standard Oil Company v U.S.
50 27A 49 663A
340 US 54 50 28A 49 664A
Black 10/23/50 CCA 2d

	06/03 1950 CERT 1-1	10/16 1950 MERITS 1-1	11/27 1950 REPORT 1-1
Minton	D	A	A
Clark	G		
Burton	D	R	R
Jackson	D	R	R
Douglas		R	
Frankfr			
Reed	D		
Black	D	A	A
Vinson	D	A	A

Jefferson v U.S.
50 29A 49 667A 49 381M
340 US 135 50 9A 50 31A
Jackson 10/23/50 CCA 4th

	03/11 1950 CERT 1-1	10/16 1950 MERITS 1-1	12/04 1950 REPORT 1-1
Minton	G	R	A
Clark	G	R	A
Burton	G		A
Jackson	G	X	A
Douglas			A
Frankfr	G		A
Reed	G		A
Black	G	R	A
Vinson			A

U.S. v United States Gypsum Company
50 30A 49 670A
340 US 76
Reed 11/20/50 DC DC

	-05/27 1950 JURIS 1-1	11/27 1950 REPORT 1-1	12/29 1950 AMEND 1-1
Minton		R	B
Clark	A	R	B
Burton	A		
Jackson		R	B
Douglas	A	R	
Frankfr		R	B
Reed	N	R	
Black	N	A	Y
Vinson	N		Y

U.S. v Griggs
50 31A 49 685A
340 US 135 50 9A 50 29A
Jackson 10/23/50 CCA 10th

	05/16 1950 CERT 1-1	10/16 1950 MERITS 1-1	12/04 1950 REPORT 1-1
Minton	H	A	R
Clark	H	A	R
Burton	G	R	R
Jackson	G		R
Douglas		X	R
Frankfr	H	R	R
Reed	G	R	R
Black	G		R
Vinson	G	A	R

Great Atlantic v Supermarket Equipment
50 32A 49 686A
340 US 147
Jackson 10/23/50 CCA 6th

	04/29 1950 CERT 1-1	10/21 1950 MERITS 1-1	12/04 1950 REPORT 1-1
Minton	G	R	R
Clark		R	R
Burton	D	R	R
Jackson	G	R	R
Douglas	D		R
Frankfr		X	R
Reed	G		R
Black	D	X	R
Vinson	G	R	R

McGrath v Kristensen
50 34A 49 700A
340 US 162 50 301A
Reed 10/23/50 CCA DC

	05/13 1950 CERT 1-1	10/21 1950 MERITS 1	12/11 1950 REPORT 1-1
Minton	G	R	A
Clark	G		A
Burton	D		A
Jackson	D	R	A
Douglas	G		AO
Frankfr	G		A
Reed			A
Black	G		A
Vinson	D		A

Ackermann v U.S.
50 35A 50 36A 49 703A 49 704A
340 US 193
Clark 10/23/50 Minton 10/26/50 CCA 5th

	05/13 1950 CERT 1-1	05/27 1950 CERT 1-2	10/21 1950 MERITS 1-1	12/11 1950 REPORT 1-1
Minton	D		A	A
Clark	D	G	A	
Burton	D		A	A
Jackson	D			
Douglas	G	G		
Frankfr	G	G		
Reed			R	R
Black	D	G	A	A
Vinson	D	G	A	A

Libby McNeill & Libby v U.S.
50 37A 49 710A
340 US 71 50 27A 50 28A
Black 10/23/50 Ct Cls

	06/03 1950 CERT 1-1	10/16 1950 MERITS 1-1	11/27 1950 REPORT 1-1
Minton		G	R
Clark	D	R	R
Burton	D	R	R
Jackson			
Douglas			
Frankfr			
Reed		A	A
Black			
Vinson	A	A	A

U.S. v Texas & Pacific Motor
50 38A 49 713A
340 US 450 50 39A 49 714A
Reed 11/16/50 DC ND Texas

	04/29 1950 JURIS 1-1	11/11 1950 MERITS 1-1	02/26 1951 REPORT 1-1
Minton	N	R	R
Clark	N	R	R
Burton	N		
Jackson	N		
Douglas	N		
Frankfr	N	R	R
Reed	N		
Black	N	A	A
Vinson	N		

294

Regular Common v Texas & Pacific Motor
50 39A 49 714A
340 US 450 50 38A 49 713A
Reed 11/16/50 DC ND Texas

	04/29 1950 JURIS	11/11 1950 MERITS	02/26 1951 REPORT
Minton	N		
Clark	N	R	R
Burton	N	R	R
Jackson	N	A	A
Douglas	N	A	A
Frankfr	N		
Reed	N	R	R
Black	N	A	A
Vinson	N		A

Universal Camera v N.L.R.B.
50 40A 49 723A
340 US 474 50 42A 50 267A
Frankfr 11/16/50 CCA 2d

	05/27 1950 CERT	11/11 1950 MERITS	02/26 1951 REPORT
Minton	G		
Clark	G	RVM	
Burton	G		
Jackson	G	R	V
Douglas	G		V
Frankfr	G	RVM	V
Reed	G		V
Black	G	RVM	V
Vinson	GL	RVM	V

N.L.R.B. v Pittsburg Steamship Company
50 42A 49 732A
340 US 498 50 40A 50 267A
Frankfr 11/16/50 CCA 6th

	05/06 1950 CERT	11/11 1950 MERITS	02/26 1951 REPORT
Minton	G	R	A
Clark	G		A
Burton	G		A
Jackson	G	R	A
Douglas	G	AQ	A
Frankfr	G		A
Reed	G		A
Black	G		A
Vinson	G		A

Littleton v McNeill
50 44A 49 746A
340 US 809 50 58A
CCA 4th

	10/03 1950 CERT
Minton	
Clark	G
Burton	D
Jackson	D
Douglas	
Frankfr	G
Reed	D
Black	G
Vinson	D

Alabama Great Southern RR v U.S.
50 45A 49 748A
340 US 216 50 46A 50 48A
Minton 1/25/50 DC ND Illinois

	05/13 1950 JURIS	11/11 1950 MERITS	01/02 1951 REPORT
Minton		A	A
Clark		A	A
Burton			A
Jackson	N		A
Douglas	N	A	A
Frankfr	N	RQ	R
Reed		X	A
Black	N	A	A
Vinson		X	A

Bailey v Richardson
50 49A 49 766A
341 US 918
CCA DC

	06/03 1950 CERT	10/16 1950 MERITS	04/28 1951 MERITS
Minton	G		1 2
Clark	G	A	
Burton	G	R	R
Jackson	G	R	R
Douglas	G		
Frankfr	G	R	R
Reed	G		
Black	D	R	R
Vinson			

Kunz v New York
50 50A 49 768A
340 US 290 50 17A 50 18A 50 93A
Vinson 10/23/50 New York

	05/13 1950 JURIS	10/21 1950 MERITS	01/15 1951 REPORT
Minton	N	R	R
Clark	N	R	R
Burton	N		R
Jackson	N		R
Douglas	N	A	R
Frankfr	N		R
Reed	N	A	R
Black	N	A	R
Vinson	N		

Prudence-Bonds v Silbiger
50 52A 49 785A
340 US 831 50 78A 49 829A
CCA 2d

	10/03 1950 CERT
Minton	
Clark	G
Burton	G
Jackson	
Douglas	G
Frankfr	
Reed	
Black	
Vinson	

Snyder v Buck
50 64A 49 811A 49 294M
340 US 15
Douglas 10/23/50 CCA DC

	05/06 1950 CERT	10/21 1950 MERITS	11/13 1950 REPORT
Minton	G	G	
Clark	G	RV	
Burton	G	R	
Jackson	G		R
Douglas	G		R
Frankfr	G		R
Reed	G		R
Black	G		R
Vinson	G		R

Dowd v U.S. (Cook)
50 66A
340 US 206
Black 12/13/50 CCA 7th

	10/14 1950 CERT	12/09 1950 MERITS	01/02 1951 REPORT
Minton	G		
Clark	G		
Burton		D	A
Jackson		D	A
Douglas		D	
Frankfr	G		A
Reed	G	R	A
Black		D	
Vinson	G	R	A

U.S. v Five Parcels Of Land
50 68A
340 US 812
CCA 5th

	10/03 1950 CERT
Minton	
Clark	
Burton	
Jackson	
Douglas	G
Frankfr	
Reed	G
Black	
Vinson	G

Shotkin v Colorado (Attorney General)
50 69A
340 US 832
Colorado

	10/03 1950 CERT
Minton	
Clark	
Burton	D
Jackson	D
Douglas	D
Frankfr	
Reed	D
Black	D
Vinson	

International Workers Order v McGrath
50 71A
341 US 123 50 7A 50 8A
Burton 10/23/50 CCA DC

	CERT 10/03 1950	MERITS 10/16 1950	REPORT 04/30 1951
	1 1	1 1	1 1
Minton	H		
Clark	G	R	R
Burton	G	R	R
Jackson	H	R	R
Douglas	G		A
Frankfr	G	R	R
Reed	G		
Black	G	SQ	S
Vinson	H	S	A

Phillips Petroleum Company v Oklahoma
50 73A
340 US 190 50 153A
Clark 11/16/50 Oklahoma

	JURIS 06/03 1950	MERITS 11/11 1950	REPORT 12/11 1950
	1 1	1 1	1 1
Minton	N	S	A
Clark	N	S	A
Burton	N		A
Jackson		X	A
Douglas			A
Frankfr			A
Reed	N		A
Black		SQ	S
Vinson		S	A

Montana-Dakota v Northwestern PSC
50 77A
341 US 246
Jackson 12/13/50 CCA 8th

	CERT 10/03 1950	MERITS 12/09 1950	REPORT 05/07 1951
	1 1	1 1	1 1
Minton	G	R	M
Clark	G		A
Burton	G	R	A
Jackson	G	RVM	M
Douglas	G	R	A
Frankfr	G	RVM	M
Reed			
Black	D	RVM	M
Vinson	D		A

Silbiger v Prudence Bonds
50 78A 49 829A
340 US 813 50 52A
CCA 2d

	CERT 10/03 1950
	1 1
Minton	
Clark	G
Burton	G
Jackson	D
Douglas	D
Frankfr	D
Reed	D
Black	D
Vinson	D

U.S. v Sanchez
50 81A 49 832A
340 US 42
Clark 10/23/50 DC ND Illinois

	JURIS 06/03 1950	MERITS 10/21 1950	REPORT 11/13 1950
	1 1	1 1	1 1
Minton	N	R	R
Clark	N	R	R
Burton	N	R	R
Jackson	NR	R	R
Douglas	N	R	R
Frankfr	N	R	R
Reed	N	R	R
Black	N	X	
Vinson		R	

U.S. (Touhy) v Ragen
50 83A
340 US 462
Reed 12/13/50 CCA 7th

	CERT 10/03 1950	MERITS 12/09 1950	REPORT 02/26 1951
	1 1	1 1	1 1
Minton	G		R
Clark	G	R	
Burton		Q	
Jackson	G		R
Douglas	D		
Frankfr			
Reed	D	R	R
Black	G	A	A
Vinson			A

Local 74 Carpenters v N.L.R.B.
50 85A
341 US 707 50 108A 50 313A 50 393A
Burton 03/15/51 CCA 6th

	CERT 12/09 1950	MERITS 03/03 1951	REPORT 06/04 1951	REPORT 02/26 1951
	1 1	1 1	1 1	1 1
Minton	G			
Clark	G			
Burton	G	R	R	R
Jackson	G	R	R	R
Douglas	G			
Frankfr	G	R	R	RQ
Reed	G			
Black	G			
Vinson	G			

Chenery v S.E.C.
50 86A
340 US 831
CCA 3rd

	CERT 10/03 1950
	1 1
Minton	
Clark	
Burton	GA
Jackson	
Douglas	
Frankfr	
Reed	
Black	
Vinson	

Warren v U.S.
50 87A
340 US 523
Douglas 01/16/51 CCA 2d

	CERT 10/03 1950	AMICUS 12/29 1950
	1 1	B
Minton	G	Y
Clark	G	Y
Burton	G	Y
Jackson	G	Y
Douglas		
Frankfr	G	Y
Reed	G	
Black		
Vinson		

U.S. (Knauff) v McGrath
50 89A 49 842A
340 US 940
CCA 2d

	06/03 1950 CERT 1 1	10/03 1950 CERT 1 2	03/03 1951 CERT 1 3	03/05 1951 REPORT 1 1
Minton	D	D	D	
Clark				
Burton	G	H	GVI	VI
Jackson				
Douglas	G	H	GVI	VI
Frankfr				
Reed	G	D		
Black	G	D	GVI	VI
Vinson			GVI	VI

C.I.R. v Brown
50 90A
340 US 814
CCA 3rd

	10/03 1950 CERT 1 1
Minton	D
Clark	D
Burton	D
Jackson	D
Douglas	D
Frankfr	D
Reed	D
Black	G
Vinson	G

Feiner v New York
50 93A 49 421M
340 US 315 50 17A 50 18A 50 50A
Vinson 10/23/50 New York

	05/27 1950 CERT 1 1	10/21 1950 MERITS 1 1	01/15 1951 REPORT 1 1
Minton	G	A	A
Clark	G	A	A
Burton	G	A	A
Jackson	G		
Douglas	G	R	R
Frankfr			
Reed	G	A	A
Black	G	R	R
Vinson	G	A	A

Canton RR Company v Rogan
50 96A
340 US 511 50 205A
Douglas 12/13/50 Maryland

	10/03 1950 JURIS 1 1	12/09 1950 MERITS 1 1	02/26 1951 REPORT 1 1
Minton		A	A
Clark	N	A	A
Burton		A	A
Jackson	N	R	O
Douglas	N	R	O
Frankfr	N	A	A
Reed		A	A
Black	N	A	A
Vinson	N	A	A

Emmick v Baltimore & Ohio RR Company
50 99A
340 US 831
Illinois

	10/03 1950 CERT 1 1
Minton	D
Clark	
Burton	G
Jackson	D
Douglas	G
Frankfr	D
Reed	D
Black	D
Vinson	D

Visic v Dever
50 104A
340 US 831
CCA 5th

	10/03 1950 CERT 1 1
Minton	D
Clark	
Burton	D
Jackson	
Douglas	G
Frankfr	D
Reed	D
Black	D
Vinson	D

International Electrical v N.L.R.B.
50 108A
341 US 694 50 85A 50 313A 50 393A
Burton 03/15/51 CCA 2d

	12/09 1950 CERT 1 1	03/03 1951 MERITS 1 1	06/04 1951 REPORT 1 1
Minton	G	A	A
Clark	G	A	A
Burton	G	A	A
Jackson	G	R	R
Douglas	G		
Frankfr	G	R	R
Reed	G	A	A
Black	G	A	A
Vinson	G	A	A

Whelchel v McDonald
50 109A 49 429M
340 US 122
Douglas 11/16/50 CCA 5th

	06/03 1950 CERT 1 1	11/11 1950 MERITS 1 1	12/04 1950 REPORT 1 1
Minton	G	A	A
Clark	G	A	A
Burton	G	A	A
Jackson	G	A	A
Douglas	G	AQ	A
Frankfr	G	A	A
Reed	G	A	A
Black	G	A	A
Vinson	G	A	A

Gusik v Schilder
50 110A 49 545M
340 US 128
Douglas 11/16/50 CCA 6th

	06/03 1950 CERT 1 1	11/11 1950 MERITS 1 1	12/04 1950 REPORT 1 1
Minton	G	AJ	R
Clark	G	AJ	R
Burton	G	AJ	R
Jackson	G	AJ	R
Douglas	G	AJ	R
Frankfr	G	AJ	R
Reed	G	AJ	R
Black	G	AJ	R
Vinson	G	AJ	R

Taylor v City Of Birmingham
50 111A
340 US 832
Alabama

	10/03 1950 CERT 1 1
Minton	D
Clark	D
Burton	D
Jackson	
Douglas	G
Frankfr	
Reed	D
Black	G
Vinson	D

Hendricks v Smith
50 114A
340 US 801
Ohio

	10/03 1950 JURIS 1 1
Minton	S
Clark	S
Burton	S
Jackson	S
Douglas	N
Frankfr	S
Reed	S
Black	S
Vinson	S

Ogden v Fielding
50 116A
340 US 817
CCA 2d

	10/03 1950 CERT 1 1
Minton	D
Clark	D
Burton	D
Jackson	D
Douglas	G
Frankfr	D
Reed	D
Black	D
Vinson	D

Benedum v Granger
50 121A
340 US 817
CCA 3rd

Justice	10/03 1950 CERT
Minton	D
Clark	D
Burton	D
Jackson	D
Douglas	D
Frankfr	D
Reed	
Black	G
Vinson	D

N.L.R.B. v Gullett Gin Company
50 122A
340 US 361
Minton 12/13/50 CCA 5th

Justice	10/03 1950 CERT	12/09 1950 MERITS	01/15 1951 REPORT
Minton	G	R	R
Clark	G	R	R
Burton	G	R	R
Jackson	G	R	R
Douglas	G		R
Frankfr	G	A	R
Reed	G	R	R
Black	G	R	
Vinson			

Charles R. Allen v U.S.
50 129A
340 US 818
CCPA

Justice	10/03 1950 CERT
Minton	D
Clark	D
Burton	D
Jackson	D
Douglas	D
Frankfr	D
Reed	
Black	G
Vinson	D

Northwestern Mutual Life v Gilbert
50 130A
340 US 818
CCA 9th

Justice	10/03 1950 CERT
Minton	D
Clark	D
Burton	G
Jackson	D
Douglas	D
Frankfr	D
Reed	D
Black	D
Vinson	D

F.T.C. v Alberty
50 131A
340 US 818
CCA DC

Justice	10/03 1950 CERT
Minton	D
Clark	D
Burton	D
Jackson	D
Douglas	D
Frankfr	D
Reed	
Black	G
Vinson	G

Spector Motor v O'Connor
50 132A
340 US 602
Burton 01/16/51 CCA 2d

Justice	10/03 1950 CERT	01/13 1951 MERITS	03/26 1951 REPORT
Minton	G	A	R
Clark	G	A	R
Burton	G	R	R
Jackson	G	R	R
Douglas	D	R	R
Frankfr	G	A	R
Reed	D	R	R
Black	G	A	R
Vinson	G		

Norton Company v Department Of Revenue
50 133A
340 US 534
Jackson 12/13/50 Illinois

Justice	10/03 1950 CERT	12/09 1950 MERITS	02/26 1951 REPORT
Minton	D	R	V
Clark	G	R	>
Burton	G	R	>
Jackson	D	X	
Douglas	G	R	>
Frankfr	G	R	VR
Reed	G	A	>
Black	D	R	V
Vinson	G		>

U.S. v Williams
50 134A
341 US 58   50 26A   50 365A   50 1M
Reed 01/16/51 DC SD Florida

Justice	10/14 1950 JURIS	01/13 1951 MERITS	04/23 1951 REPORT
Minton	N	R	R
Clark	N	R	R
Burton	N	R	R
Jackson	N	R	R
Douglas	N		
Frankfr	N		
Reed	N	R	R
Black	S	R	R
Vinson	N		

U.S. v Kasinowitz
50 136A
340 US 920   50 22A
CCA 9th

Justice	01/13 1951 CERT
Minton	G
Clark	D
Burton	D
Jackson	D
Douglas	D
Frankfr	D
Reed	
Black	
Vinson	

New Brunswick Trust Company v C.I.R.
50 137A
340 US 819
CCA 3rd

Justice	10/03 1950 CERT
Minton	D
Clark	D
Burton	D
Jackson	D
Douglas	D
Frankfr	D
Reed	
Black	G
Vinson	D

U.S. v Preston
50 138A
340 US 819   50 139A
CCA 9th

Justice	10/03 1950 CERT
Minton	D
Clark	D
Burton	D
Jackson	D
Douglas	D
Frankfr	D
Reed	
Black	G
Vinson	G

U.S. v Preston
50 139A
340 US 819   50 138A
CCA 9th

Justice	10/03 1950 CERT
Minton	D
Clark	D
Burton	D
Jackson	D
Douglas	D
Frankfr	D
Reed	
Black	G
Vinson	G

Rice v Arnold
50 145A
340 US 848
Florida

Justice	10/03 1950 CERT (1 1)	10/14 1950 CERT (1 2)	10/16 1950 REPORT (1 1)
Minton	G	GV	>
Clark	G	GV	>
Burton	G	GV	>
Jackson	G	GV	>
Douglas		GV	>
Frankfr		G	>
Reed	D	GV	>
Black		GV	>
Vinson	D	GV	>

Alabama PSC v Southern RR Company
50 146A
341 US 363   50 395A
Vinson 03/15/51 DC MD Alabama

Justice	10/03 1950 JURIS (1 1)	03/03 1951 MERITS (1 1)	05/21 1951 REPORT (1 1)
Minton	NR	R	R
Clark	NR	R	R
Burton	N	R	R
Jackson	N	R	R
Douglas	N	R	R
Frankfr	N	R	R
Reed	N	R	R
Black	N	R	R
Vinson	N	R	R

West Virginia (Dyer) v Sims
50 147A
341 US 22
Frankfr 12/13/50 West Virginia

Justice	10/04 1950 CERT (1 1)	12/09 1950 MERITS (1 1)	04/09 1951 REPORT (1 1)
Minton	G	R	R
Clark	G	R	R
Burton	G	R	R
Jackson	G	R	R
Douglas	G	R	R
Frankfr	G	R	R
Reed	G	R	R
Black	G	R	R
Vinson	G	R	R

Ohio (Greisiger) v Grand Rapids Board
50 149A
340 US 820
Ohio

Justice	10/04 1950 CERT (1 1)
Minton	
Clark	D
Burton	D
Jackson	D
Douglas	G
Frankfr	
Reed	D
Black	G
Vinson	D

El Dorado Oil Works v McColgan
50 152A
340 US 801
California

Justice	10/03 1950 JURIS (1 1)
Minton	S
Clark	S
Burton	S
Jackson	S
Douglas	S
Frankfr	S
Reed	S
Black	SA
Vinson	SA

Cities Service Gas v Peerless Oil
50 153A
340 US 179   50 73A
Clark 11/16/50 Oklahoma

Justice	10/03 1950 JURIS (1 1)	11/11 1950 MERITS (1 1)	12/11 1950 REPORT (1 1)
Minton	N	A	A
Clark	N	A	A
Burton	N	A	A
Jackson	N	X	A
Douglas	N	A	A
Frankfr	N	A	A
Reed	N	A	A
Black	N	S	S
Vinson	N	A	A

Burt v City Of Pittsburgh
50 157A
340 US 802
DC WD Pennsylvania

Justice	10/03 1950 JURIS (1 1)	10/09 1950 REPORT (1 1)
Minton	A	A
Clark	A	A
Burton	A	A
Jackson		A
Douglas	S	A
Frankfr		A
Reed	A	A
Black	S	A
Vinson		A

Roberts v Missouri-Kansas-Texas RR
50 164A
340 US 832
Texas

Justice	10/04 1950 CERT (1 1)
Minton	D
Clark	D
Burton	D
Jackson	D
Douglas	G
Frankfr	D
Reed	D
Black	G
Vinson	D

Deauville Associates v Murrell
50 165A
340 US 821
CCA 5th

Justice	10/04 1950 CERT (1 1)
Minton	D
Clark	D
Burton	D
Jackson	D
Douglas	G
Frankfr	D
Reed	D
Black	D
Vinson	D

U.S. v Pewee Coal Company
50 168A
341 US 114
Black 01/16/51 Ct Cls

Justice	10/04 1950 CERT (1 1)	01/06 1951 MERITS (1 1)	04/30 1951 REPORT (1 1)	01/13 1951 REHEAR (Y)
Minton	G			
Clark	G	R	R	B
Burton	G	R	R	B
Jackson	G	A	A	B
Douglas	G	A	A	B
Frankfr	G	A	A	B
Reed	G	A	A	B
Black	G	A		B
Vinson	G		R	B

U.S. v Wheelock Brothers
50 169A
341 US 319   50 177A
Black 01/16/51 Vinson ??/??/51 Ct Cls

Justice	10/04 1950 CERT (1 1)	01/06 1951 MERITS (1 1)	05/07 1951 REPORT (1 1)
Minton	G		>
Clark	G	R	>
Burton	G	R	>
Jackson	G	A	>
Douglas	G	A	>
Frankfr	G	A	>
Reed	G	A	>
Black	G	A	>
Vinson	G	R	R

U.S. v Penner Installation
50 170A
340 US 898
Ct Cls

Justice	10/04 1950 CERT (1 1)
Minton	D
Clark	D
Burton	D
Jackson	G
Douglas	D
Frankfr	D
Reed	D
Black	D
Vinson	D

299

Larsson v Coastwise Line
50 171A
340 US 833
CCA 9th

	10/04 1950 CERT
	1 1
Minton	D
Clark	D
Burton	D
Jackson	D
Douglas	G
Frankfr	X
Reed	D
Black	D
Vinson	D

Wheelock Brothers v U.S.
341 US 319 50 169A
Black 01/16/51 Vinson ??/??/51 Ct Cls

	10/04 1950 CERT	05/07 1951 REPORT
	1 1	1 1
Minton	G	>
Clark	G	>
Burton	G	>
Jackson	G	>
Douglas	G	>
Frankfr	G	>
Reed	G	>
Black	G	>
Vinson	G	>

Harding v U.S.
50 176A
340 US 874
CCA 4th

	10/04 1950 MERITS	11/04 1950 CERT
	1 1	1 2
Minton	G	D
Clark	G	R
Burton	G	R
Jackson	G	R A
Douglas		R
Frankfr	D	
Reed	D	A
Black	D	A
Vinson	D	A

Lewyt v Health-Mor
50 182A
340 US 823
CCA 7th

	10/04 1950 CERT
	1 1
Minton	D
Clark	
Burton	D
Jackson	D
Douglas	
Frankfr	D
Reed	D
Black	
Vinson	

Baker-Cammack Hosiery v Davis Company
50 185A
340 US 824
CCA 4th

	10/04 1950 CERT
	1 1
Minton	D
Clark	D
Burton	D
Jackson	D
Douglas	G
Frankfr	
Reed	D
Black	G
Vinson	D

Sims v Iowa
50 186A
340 US 833
Iowa

	10/04 1950 CERT
	1 1
Minton	D
Clark	D
Burton	D
Jackson	D
Douglas	D
Frankfr	D
Reed	D
Black	D
Vinson	D

Willumeit v U.S.
50 191A
340 US 834
CCA 7th

	10/04 1950 CERT
	1 1
Minton	
Clark	D
Burton	
Jackson	D
Douglas	D
Frankfr	H
Reed	D
Black	
Vinson	D

Howard v U.S.
50 195A
340 US 898
CCA 8th

	12/09 1950 CERT	12/11 1950 REPORT
	1 1	1 1
Minton	GVI	VI
Clark	GVI	VI
Burton	GVI	VI
Jackson	GVI	VI
Douglas	GVI	VI
Frankfr	GVI	VI
Reed	GVI	VI
Black	GVI	VI
Vinson	GVI	VI

Jones v New York Central RR Company
50 199A
340 US 850
CCA 6th

	10/14 1950 CERT
	1 1
Minton	D
Clark	D
Burton	
Jackson	G
Douglas	G
Frankfr	
Reed	D
Black	D
Vinson	D

Capital Transit Company v U.S.
50 204A
340 US 543 50 218A
Burton 12/13/50 CCA DC

	10/04 1950 CERT	12/09 1950 MERITS	02/26 1951 REPORT
	1 1	1 1	1 1
Minton	G		
Clark	G	R	R A
Burton	G		R
Jackson	G	R A	R A
Douglas	G		
Frankfr	G	A	R A
Reed	G	A	R
Black		A	R A
Vinson	G	A	R A

Western Maryland RR Company v Rogan
50 205A
340 US 520 50 96A
Douglas 12/13/50 Maryland

	10/03 1950 JURIS	12/09 1950 MERITS	02/26 1951 REPORT
	1 1	1 1	1 1
Minton	N		
Clark	N	R	A
Burton	N		A
Jackson	N	R A	O A
Douglas	N A	A	A
Frankfr	N		O A
Reed	N		
Black	N		R A
Vinson		A	A

U.S. v California
50 206A
340 US 826
CCA 9th

	10/04 1950 CERT
	1 1
Minton	D
Clark	D
Burton	G
Jackson	D
Douglas	G
Frankfr	D
Reed	D
Black	DQ
Vinson	G

Emich Motors v General Motors
50 209A
340 US 558
Clark 01/16/51 CCA 7th

	10/04 1950 CERT	01/06 1951 MERITS	02/26 1951 REPORT
	1 1	1 1	1 1
Minton	GL	R	R
Clark	GL	R	R
Burton	GL	R	R
Jackson			
Douglas	GL D	R A	R
Frankfr			
Reed	GL	RV	R
Black	GL D	R A	R
Vinson			

Niagara Hudson Power v Leventritt
50 211A
340 US 336   50 212A CCA 2d
Burton 12/13/50 CCA 2d

	10/04 1950 CERT	12/09 1950 MERITS	01/15 1951 REPORT
	1 1	1 1	1 1
Minton	G	R	R
Clark	G	R	R
Burton	G	R	R
Jackson			
Douglas	G D	R A	R A
Frankfr			
Reed	G	R	R
Black	G D	R A	R A
Vinson			

S.E.C. v Leventritt
50 212A
340 US 336   50 211A
Burton 12/13/50 CCA 2d

	10/04 1950 CERT	12/09 1950 MERITS	01/15 1951 REPORT
	1 1	1 1	1 1
Minton	G	R	R
Clark	G	R	R
Burton	G	R	R
Jackson			
Douglas	G D	R A	R A
Frankfr			
Reed	G	R	R
Black	G D	R A	R A
Vinson			

United Gas Pipe Line Company v F.P.C.
50 216A
340 US 827
CCA DC

	10/04 1950 CERT
	1 1
Minton	D
Clark	D
Burton	D
Jackson	D
Douglas	D
Frankfr	D
Reed	D
Black	D
Vinson	G

Collins v Hardyman
50 217A
341 US 651
Jackson 01/16/51 CCA 9th

	10/04 1950 CERT	01/13 1951 MERITS	06/04 1951 REPORT
	1 1	1 1	1 1
Minton	G	R A	R A
Clark	G	R A	R
Burton	G	R A	R
Jackson	G	R A	R
Douglas	G	R A	R A
Frankfr	G	R A	R
Reed	G	R A	R
Black	G	R A	R
Vinson	G		

U.S. v Yellow Cab Company
50 218A
340 US 543   50 204A
Burton 12/13/50 CCA 3rd

	10/04 1950 CERT	12/09 1950 MERITS	02/26 1951 REPORT
	1 1	1 1	1 1
Minton	G	R A	R A
Clark	G	R A	R A
Burton	G	R A	R A
Jackson	G	R A	R A
Douglas	G	R A	R A
Frankfr	G	R A	R A
Reed	G	R A	R A
Black	G	R A	R A
Vinson	D		

Byrd v McCready
50 219A
340 US 827
Maryland

	10/04 1950 CERT
	1 1
Minton	D
Clark	D
Burton	D
Jackson	
Douglas	G
Frankfr	D
Reed	D
Black	D
Vinson	D

Johnson v Matthews
50 225A
340 US 828
CCA DC

	10/04 1950 CERT
	1 1
Minton	D
Clark	D
Burton	
Jackson	G
Douglas	G
Frankfr	D
Reed	D
Black	D
Vinson	D

Washington v McGrath
50 229A
341 US 923   50 8A
CCA DC

	05/05 1951 CERT	05/05 1951 MERITS	05/07 1951 REPORT
	1 1	1 1	1 1
Minton	G	R	R
Clark	D		
Burton		R A	R A
Jackson	G	R	R
Douglas	G	R A	R A
Frankfr	D		
Reed	D	R	R
Black		R A	R A
Vinson		R	R

Turner v Alton Banking & Trust
50 232A
340 US 833
CCA 8th

	10/04 1950 CERT
	1 1
Minton	D
Clark	D
Burton	D
Jackson	
Douglas	G
Frankfr	D
Reed	D
Black	G
Vinson	D

Steadman v South Carolina
50 233A
340 US 850
South Carolina

	10/14 1950 CERT
	1 1
Minton	D
Clark	D
Burton	D
Jackson	
Douglas	G
Frankfr	D
Reed	D
Black	D
Vinson	D

Chicago & Southern Air Lines v C.A.B.
50 235A
340 US 829
CCA DC

	10/04 1950 CERT
	1 1
Minton	D
Clark	D
Burton	D
Jackson	
Douglas	G
Frankfr	D
Reed	D
Black	D
Vinson	D

Roberts v Alabama / Great Southern RR — 50 236A — 340 US 829 — Alabama

Justice	10/04 1950 CERT (1 1)
Minton	D
Clark	D
Burton	D
Jackson	
Douglas	D
Frankfr	
Reed	G
Black	D
Vinson	D

Schwarz v West — 50 239A — 340 US 830 — CCA 7th

Justice	10/04 1950 CERT (1 1)
Minton	D
Clark	D
Burton	D
Jackson	D
Douglas	D
Frankfr	D
Reed	G
Black	D
Vinson	D

Ford Motor Company v Ryan — 50 246A — 340 US 851 — CCA 2d

Justice	10/14 1950 CERT (1 1)	10/16 1950 CERT (1 2)
Minton		D
Clark	G	D
Burton	G	
Jackson	G	G
Douglas	G	
Frankfr	G	D
Reed		
Black	G	D
Vinson	G	D

Berg v Schreiber — 50 248A — 340 US 851 — Illinois

Justice	10/14 1950 CERT (1 1)
Minton	D
Clark	D
Burton	D
Jackson	
Douglas	D
Frankfr	
Reed	G
Black	D
Vinson	D

Duisberg v U.S. — 50 251A — 340 US 890 — Ct Cls

Justice	11/25 1950 CERT (1 1)
Minton	D
Clark	D
Burton	
Jackson	G
Douglas	G
Frankfr	
Reed	D
Black	D
Vinson	D

American Fire & Casualty v Finn — 50 252A — 341 US 6 — Douglas 12/13/50 Reed 03/23/51 CCA 5th

Justice	10/14 1950 CERT (1 1)	12/09 1950 MERITS (1 1)	04/09 1951 REPORT (1 1)
Minton	G		
Clark	G	R	R
Burton	G	R	R
Jackson	H	R	A
Douglas	G	R	R
Frankfr			
Reed	G	R	A
Black	D	A	
Vinson	G	R	A

Argonne Company v Hilaffer — 50 253A — 340 US 852 — CCA DC

Justice	10/14 1950 CERT (1 1)
Minton	D
Clark	D
Burton	D
Jackson	D
Douglas	D
Frankfr	
Reed	G
Black	G
Vinson	G

Norfolk Southern Bus v U.S. — 50 254A — 340 US 802 — DC ED Virginia

Justice	10/03 1950 JURIS (1 1)	10/09 1950 REPORT (1 1)
Minton	A	A
Clark	A	A
Burton	A	A
Jackson	A	A
Douglas	A	A
Frankfr	A	A
Reed	A	A
Black	A	A
Vinson		

Rd-Dr v Smith — 50 256A — 340 US 853 — CCA 5th

Justice	10/14 1950 CERT (1 1)
Minton	D
Clark	D
Burton	D
Jackson	D
Douglas	D
Frankfr	
Reed	G
Black	
Vinson	G

Willingham v Home Oil Mill — 50 257A — 340 US 852 — CCA 5th

Justice	10/14 1950 CERT (1 1)	12/09 1950 MERITS (1 1)	01/15 1951 REPORT (1 1)
Minton			
Clark	D	R	RV
Burton	D	R	RV
Jackson	D	R	RV
Douglas	D	R	RV
Frankfr	D	R	RV
Reed	D	R	RV
Black			
Vinson	D	R	RV

Dean Milk Company v City Of Madison — 50 258A — 340 US 349 — Clark 12/13/50 Wisconsin

Justice	10/14 1950 JURIS (1 1)	12/09 1950 MERITS (1 1)
Minton	N	R
Clark	N	R
Burton	N	R
Jackson	N	S
Douglas	N	R
Frankfr	N	R
Reed	N	R
Black	N	S
Vinson		R

Bruszewski v U.S. — 50 260A — 340 US 865 — CCA 3rd

Justice	10/21 1950 CERT (1 1)
Minton	D
Clark	D
Burton	D
Jackson	
Douglas	D
Frankfr	
Reed	G
Black	G
Vinson	D

Carolin v C.I.R.
50 262A
340 US 852
CCA 6th

Justice	10/14 1950 CERT (1 1)
Minton	D
Clark	G
Burton	D
Jackson	D
Douglas	D
Frankfr	D
Reed	D
Black	D
Vinson	

U.S. v Beal
50 266A
340 US 852
CCA 6th

Justice	10/14 1950 CERT (1 1)
Minton	G
Clark	G
Burton	G
Jackson	G
Douglas	G
Frankfr	G
Reed	G
Black	G
Vinson	G

O'Leary v Brown-Pacific-Maxon
50 267A
340 US 504 50 40A 50 42A *CCA 9th*
Frankfr 02/05/51

Justice	10/14 1950 CERT (1 1)	12/29 1950 MERITS (1 1)	02/05 1951 MERITS (1 2)	02/26 1951 REPORT (1 1)
Minton	GR	R	R	A
Clark	D	RQ	RQ	R
Burton	D	R	R	A
Jackson				
Douglas	GR	R	R	A
Frankfr	D	R	R	R
Reed				
Black	GR	R	R	R
Vinson	G			A

Werner v Southern California Newspapers
50 268A
340 US 910
California

Justice	10/03 1950 JURIS (1 1)	10/14 1950 JURIS (1 2)	12/29 1950 JURIS (1 3)
Minton	S	S	SI
Clark	S	S	SI
Burton		N	SI
Jackson	N	N	SI
Douglas	S		SI
Frankfr	S	S	SI
Reed	S		SI
Black	S	N	SI
Vinson	S		SI

Pennsylvania (Master) v Baldi
50 271A
340 US 866
Pennsylvania

Justice	10/21 1950 CERT (1 1)
Minton	D
Clark	D
Burton	D
Jackson	G
Douglas	D
Frankfr	G
Reed	D
Black	G
Vinson	D

Morford v U.S.
50 272A
340 US 878
CCA DC

Justice	11/04 1950 CERT (1 1)
Minton	D
Clark	D
Burton	D
Jackson	G
Douglas	D
Frankfr	G
Reed	D
Black	G
Vinson	D

Brown v Eastern States
50 275A
340 US 864
CCA 4th

Justice	10/14 1950 CERT (1 1)	10/21 1950 CERT (1 2)
Minton	D	D
Clark	D	D
Burton	D	D
Jackson		
Douglas	D	D
Frankfr	G	G
Reed		
Black	G	G
Vinson	G	G

Story v Snyder
50 276A
340 US 866
CCA DC

Justice	10/21 1950 CERT (1 1)
Minton	D
Clark	D
Burton	D
Jackson	
Douglas	Q
Frankfr	G
Reed	
Black	G
Vinson	

Island Creek Fuel v Reeves
50 277A
340 US 853
Kentucky

Justice	10/14 1950 CERT (1 1)
Minton	D
Clark	D
Burton	D
Jackson	G
Douglas	
Frankfr	
Reed	D
Black	
Vinson	

U.S. v Alcea Band Of Tillamooks
50 281A
341 US 48 50 282A
Ct Cls

Justice	11/04 1950 CERT (1 1)	01/06 1951 AMICUS (1 2)	03/03 1951 MERITS (1 1)	04/09 1951 REPORT (1 1)
Minton				
Clark	D	B	R	R
Burton	D	B	R	R
Jackson		B		
Douglas	GL	Y	A	A
Frankfr				
Reed	GL	B	R	R
Black	GL		R	R
Vinson	GL	B	R	R

U.S. v Rogue River Tribe Of Indians
50 282A
341 US 902 50 281A
Ct Cls

Justice	11/04 1950 CERT (1 1)
Minton	
Clark	D
Burton	D
Jackson	
Douglas	H
Frankfr	
Reed	D
Black	GL
Vinson	GL

Gentry v Seaboard Air Line RR Company
50 283A
340 US 853
Florida

Justice	10/14 1950 CERT (1 1)
Minton	
Clark	D
Burton	D
Jackson	
Douglas	G
Frankfr	
Reed	D
Black	
Vinson	D

Potter v Estes
50 286A
340 US 920 50 22A
CCA 5th

Justice	01/13 1951 CERT
Minton	
Clark	G
Burton	D
Jackson	D
Douglas	D
Frankfr	D
Reed	D
Black	D
Vinson	D

Fleischman v U.S.
50 288A
340 US 866
CCA DC

Justice	10/21 1950 CERT
Minton	D
Clark	
Burton	
Jackson	
Douglas	G
Frankfr	
Reed	
Black	G
Vinson	

Molsen v Young
50 292A
340 US 880
CCA 5th

Justice	11/11 1950 CERT	11/13 1950 REPORT
Minton	GVM	VI
Clark	GVM	VI
Burton	GVM	VI
Jackson	GVM	VI
Douglas	GVM	VI
Frankfr	GVM	VI
Reed	GVM	VI
Black	GVM	VI
Vinson	GVM	VI

Wenning v Peoples Bank Company
50 293A
340 US 858
Ohio

Justice	10/21 1950 CERT	10/21 1950 JURIS
Minton	D	
Clark	D	S
Burton	D	S
Jackson	D	S
Douglas		
Frankfr		P
Reed		S
Black	D	P
Vinson		S

Robertson v Chambers
50 295A
341 US 37
Douglas 03/15/51 CCA DC

Justice	11/25 1950 CERT	03/03 1951 MERITS	04/09 1951 REPORT
Minton	G	R	R
Clark	G	R	R
Burton	G	R	R
Jackson		R	R
Douglas		R	R
Frankfr		R	R
Reed		R	R
Black	G	R	R
Vinson		A	A

Johnson v Muelberger
50 296A
340 US 581
Reed 01/16/51 New York

Justice	11/04 1950 CERT	01/06 1951 MERITS	03/15 1951 REPORT
Minton	G	R	R
Clark	G	R	R
Burton		X	
Jackson	D	R	R
Douglas	D		
Frankfr			
Reed	G	R	R
Black	G	R	R
Vinson	G		A

Kiefer-Stewart v Joseph E. Seagram
50 297A
340 US 211 50 294M
Black 12/13/50 CCA 7th

Justice	10/21 1950 CERT
Minton	G
Clark	G
Burton	G
Jackson	G
Douglas	G
Frankfr	D
Reed	G
Black	G
Vinson	G

Zittman v McGrath
50 298A
341 US 446 50 299A 50 314A 50 315A 50 324A
Jackson 03/15/51 CCA 2d

Justice	11/11 1950 CERT	03/03 1951 MERITS	05/28 1951 REPORT
Minton	G	R	R
Clark	X	RQ	
Burton	G	R	R
Jackson	G		
Douglas	G	R	
Frankfr	G		
Reed			
Black	G	A	A
Vinson	G	R	AJ

Zittman v McGrath
50 299A
341 US 471 50 298A 50 314A 50 315A 50 324A
Jackson 03/15/51 CCA 2d

Justice	11/11 1950 CERT	03/03 1951 MERITS	05/28 1951 REPORT
Minton	G	R	A
Clark	X		
Burton	G	R	A
Jackson	G		
Douglas	G	A	A
Frankfr	G	A	A
Reed			
Black	G	A	A
Vinson	G	A	A

Hallinan v U.S.
50 300A
341 US 952 50 201A
CCA 9th

Justice	06/02 1951 CERT	10/03 1951 REHEAR
Minton		B
Clark		B
Burton	D	B
Jackson	D	
Douglas	D	Y
Frankfr	D	B
Reed	D	
Black	D	Y
Vinson	D	B

Moser v U.S.
50 301A
341 US 41 50 34A
Minton 03/15/51

Justice	12/30 1950 CERT	03/12 1951 MERITS	04/09 1951 REPORT
Minton	G	R	R
Clark	G		R
Burton	G	R	R
Jackson	G		R
Douglas	G	R	R
Frankfr	D		R
Reed	G		R
Black	G	R	A
Vinson	Q		A

St. John v Wisconsin ERB
50 302A
340 US 411 50 329A 50 438A
Vinson 01/16/51 DC ED Wisconsin

Justice	10/21 1950 JURIS	02/26 1951 REPORT
Minton	N	A
Clark	N	V
Burton	N	V
Jackson	N	V
Douglas	N	V
Frankfr	N	V
Reed	S	V
Black	N	V
Vinson	N	V

Treichter v Wisconsin
50 304A
340 US 868
Wisconsin

	JURIS 10/21 1950 (1 1)	REPORT 11/06 1950 (1 1)
Minton	A	S
Clark	A	S
Burton	A	S
Jackson	A	S
Douglas	A	S
Frankfr	A	S
Reed	A	S
Black	A	S
Vinson	A	S

Stern v Teeval Company
50 306A
340 US 876   50 307A   50 321A
New York

	CERT 11/04 1950 (1 1)	JURIS 10/21 1950 (2 1)	REPORT 11/06 1950 (1 1)
Minton		A	A
Clark	G	S	A
Burton	D	S	A
Jackson	G	S	A
Douglas	G	S	A
Frankfr		S	A
Reed	G	S	A
Black	D	A	S
Vinson	D	A	A

California State Automobile v Maloney
50 310A
341 US 105
Douglas 03/15/51 California

	JURIS 11/11 1950 (1 1)	MERITS 03/12 1951 (1 1)	REPORT 04/23 1951 (1 1)
Minton	N	S	A
Clark	N	S	A
Burton		A	A
Jackson	N	A	A
Douglas			
Frankfr	N	A	A
Reed	N	S	A
Black		S	S
Vinson		A	A

N.L.R.B. v International Rice Milling
50 313A
341 US 665   50 85A   50 393A
Burton 03/15/51 CCA 5th

	CERT 11/11 1950 (1 1)	CERT 12/09 1950 (1 2)	MERITS 03/03 1951 (1 1)	REPORT 06/04 1951 (1 1)
Minton	D	G	R	R
Clark	D	G	R	R
Burton	D	G	R	R
Jackson	D	G	R	R
Douglas		G	R	R
Frankfr		G	R	R
Reed	D	G	R	R
Black	D	G	R	R
Vinson	D	G	R	R

McCarthy v McGrath
50 314A
341 US 446   50 298A   50 299A   50 315A   50 324A
Jackson 03/15/51 CCA 2d

	CERT 11/11 1950 (1 1)	MERITS 03/03 1951 (1 1)	REPORT 05/28 1951 (1 1)
Minton	G X	R	R
Clark	G	R	R
Burton	G	R	R
Jackson	G	R	R
Douglas	G		
Frankfr	G		A
Reed		A	N
Black	G	R	R
Vinson	G	R	N

McCarthy v McGrath
50 315A
341 US 471   50 298A   50 299A   50 314A   50 324A
Jackson 03/15/51 CCA 2d

	CERT 11/11 1950 (1 1)	MERITS 03/03 1951 (1 1)	REPORT 05/28 1951 (1 1)
Minton	G X		A
Clark	G	A	A
Burton	G	A	A
Jackson	G	A	A
Douglas	G	A	A
Frankfr	G		A
Reed		R	A
Black	G	A	A
Vinson	G	A	A

Moore v Chesapeake & Ohio RR Company
50 318A
340 US 573
Minton 01/16/51 CCA 4th

	CERT 11/04 1950 (1 1)	MERITS 01/06 1951	MERITS 01/13 1951 (1 2)	REPORT 02/26 1951 (1 1)
Minton	GR			
Clark	GR	R	RQ	A
Burton	D	A	A	A
Jackson	D			
Douglas	G	R	R	A
Frankfr	D	S	S	S
Reed				
Black	G X	R	R	A
Vinson	D			

Transamerican v Board Of Governors
50 322A
340 US 883   50 323A
CCA 9th

	CERT 11/11 1950 (1 1)
Minton	D
Clark	D
Burton	D
Jackson	D
Douglas	
Frankfr	G
Reed	D
Black	D
Vinson	

Bank Of America v Board Of Governors
50 323A
340 US 883   50 322A
CCA 9th

	CERT 11/11 1950 (1 1)
Minton	D
Clark	D
Burton	D
Jackson	D
Douglas	
Frankfr	G
Reed	D
Black	D
Vinson	

Gross Income Tax v W.B. Conkey Company
50 328A
340 US 941 50 133A
Indiana

Justice	11/11 1950 CERT (1 1)	03/03 1951 CERT (1 2)
Minton	G	
Clark	H	D
Burton	H	D
Jackson	H	D
Douglas	H	D
Frankfr	H	D
Reed	G	
Black	G	G
Vinson	H	D

Amalgamated Street v Wisconsin ERB
50 329A
340 US 383 50 302A 50 330A 50 438A
Vinson 01/16/51 Wisconsin

Justice	11/04 1950 CERT (1 1)	01/13 1951 MERITS (1 1)	02/26 1951 REPORT (1 1)
Minton	G		
Clark	G	R	R
Burton	G		A
Jackson	G	R A	R
Douglas	G		A
Frankfr	G		
Reed	G	R	R
Black	G	R A	R
Vinson	G		A

Amalgamated Street v Wisconsin ERB
50 330A
340 US 416 50 302A 50 329A 50 438A
Vinson 01/16/51 Wisconsin

Justice	11/04 1950 CERT (1 1)	01/13 1951 MERITS (1 1)	02/26 1951 REPORT (1 1)
Minton	G	DI	
Clark	G	R	VI
Burton	G		VI
Jackson	G	R A	VI
Douglas	G		VI
Frankfr	G		
Reed	G	R	VI
Black	G	R A	VI
Vinson	G		VI

Dennis v U.S.
50 336A
341 US 494
Vinson 12/13/50 CCA 2d

Justice	10/21 1950 CERT (1 1)	11/25 1950 QUEST (14 1)	11/25 1950 POSTPN (1 1)	12/09 1950 MERITS (1 1)	06/04 1951 REPORT (1 1)
Minton	G	Y	B		A
Clark					
Burton	GL		B		A
Jackson	GL	Y	B		A
Douglas	GL	Y	Y	X	
Frankfr	GL	Y		X	R
Reed	GL		Y		A
Black	G		B	R	R
Vinson	GL	Y	B	A	A

Tenney v Brandhove
50 338A
341 US 367 50 388A
Frankfr 03/15/51 CCA 9th

Justice	12/09 1950 CERT (1 1)	03/03 1951 MERITS (1 1)	05/21 1951 REPORT (1 1)
Minton	G	R	R
Clark	G	R	R
Burton	G	R	R
Jackson	G	R	R
Douglas	G	R	R
Frankfr	G	R	R
Reed	G		
Black	G	X	A
Vinson	G D		

Anglin v Bender
50 340A
340 US 878
Georgia

Justice	11/04 1950 CERT (1 1)
Minton	D
Clark	D
Burton	D
Jackson	D
Douglas	X D
Frankfr	G
Reed	
Black	D
Vinson	D

First National Bank v C.I.R.
50 342A
340 US 911 50 416A
CCA 5th

Justice	12/30 1950 CERT (1 1)	03/03 1951 MERITS (1 1)	03/26 1951 REPORT (1 1)
Minton	D	R	R
Clark		R	R
Burton	G	R	R
Jackson	D		
Douglas	D	A	A
Frankfr	D	A	A
Reed	G	R	R
Black		X	R
Vinson	D	A	A

U.S. v Moore
50 344A
340 US 616
Clark 03/15/51 CCA 5th

Justice	11/25 1950 CERT (1 1)	03/03 1951 MERITS (1 1)
Minton	G	R
Clark	G	R
Burton	G	R
Jackson	G	
Douglas	G	X
Frankfr	G	
Reed	D	A
Black	G	A
Vinson	G	A

S.E.C. v Harrison
50 345A
340 US 908
CCA DC

Justice	12/30 1950 CERT (1 1)	01/02 1951 REPORT (1 1)
Minton	GVI	VI
Clark	GVI	VI
Burton	GVI	VI
Jackson	GVI	VI
Douglas	GVI	VI
Frankfr	GVI	VI
Reed	GVI	VI
Black	GVI	VI
Vinson	GVI	VI

U.S. v Lewis
50 347A
340 US 590
Black 03/15/51 Ct Cls

Justice	CERT 12/09/1950	MERITS 03/03/1951	REPORT 03/26/1951
	1 1	1 1	1 1
Minton	G		
Clark	G		
Burton	G		
Jackson	G		
Douglas	G	X	A
Frankfr		D	
Reed	G	R	R
Black	G	R	R
Vinson	G	R	R

Jordan v De George
50 348A
341 US 223
Jackson 03/15/51 Vinson 04/13/51 CCA 7th

Justice	CERT 11/25/1950	MERITS 03/10/1951	REPORT 05/07/1951
	1 1	1 1	1 1
Minton	G	R	R
Clark	G	R	R
Burton	G	R	R
Jackson	G	A	A
Douglas	G	A	A
Frankfr	G	A	A
Reed	G	R	R
Black	G	A	A
Vinson	G	R	R

Timken Roller Bearing Company v U.S.
50 352A
341 US 593
Black 05/01/51 DC ND Ohio

Justice	JURIS 11/04/1950	POSTPN 03/10/1951	MERITS 04/28/1951	REPORT 06/04/1951
	1 1 S	1 1	1 1	1 1
Minton	N	B	R	
Clark	S	B		
Burton		B	R	R
Jackson	N		X	
Douglas		B	Y	AJ
Frankfr	N	B	Y	AJ
Reed	N	B		R
Black		B	A	AJ
Vinson	N	B	A	AJ

Hughes v Fetter
50 355A
341 US 609
Black 03/15/51 Wisconsin

Justice	JURIS 11/11/1950	MERITS 03/03/1951	REPORT 06/04/1951
	1 1	1 1	1 1
Minton		R	R
Clark	S	R	R
Burton			
Jackson	N	R	R
Douglas	N		
Frankfr	N		
Reed			
Black	N	R	R
Vinson	S	A	A

General Steel v Mississippi River Fuel
50 356A
340 US 895 50 357A 50 360A
CCA 5th

Justice	CERT 11/30/1950
	1 1
Minton	D
Clark	D
Burton	D
Jackson	
Douglas	G
Frankfr	D
Reed	
Black	G
Vinson	D

McHugh v Massachusetts
50 359A
340 US 911
Massachusetts

Justice	CERT 12/30/1950
	1 1
Minton	D
Clark	D
Burton	D
Jackson	
Douglas	
Frankfr	
Reed	
Black	G
Vinson	G

Simms v County Of Los Angeles
50 361A
340 US 891 50 362A
California

Justice	CERT 11/25/1950
	1 1
Minton	D
Clark	G
Burton	D
Jackson	G
Douglas	D
Frankfr	D
Reed	D
Black	D
Vinson	D

Security-First v County Of Los Angeles
50 362A
340 US 891 50 361A
California

Justice	CERT 11/25/1950
	1 1
Minton	D
Clark	G
Burton	D
Jackson	G
Douglas	D
Frankfr	D
Reed	D
Black	D
Vinson	D

62 Cases v U.S.
50 363A
340 US 593
Frankfr 03/15/51 CCA 10th

Justice	CERT 11/25/1950	MERITS 03/12/1951	REPORT 03/26/1951
	1 1	1 1	1 1
Minton	G	R	R
Clark		R	R
Burton	D	R	R
Jackson		X	
Douglas	D	R	R
Frankfr			
Reed	G	R	R
Black	G		A
Vinson	G		A

U.S. v Allied Oil
50 364A
341 US 1
Black 03/15/51 CCA 7th

Justice	CERT 11/30/1950 (1 1)	MERITS 03/12/1951 (1 1)	REPORT 04/09/1951 (1 1)
Minton		R	
Clark	D		
Burton	D	R	
Jackson	D	R	
Douglas			
Frankfr	D	R	
Reed	D		
Black	X		
Vinson	D		

Williams v U.S.
50 365A 50 1M 49 354M
341 US 97 50 26A
Douglas 01/16/51 CCA 5th

Justice	CERT 10/14/1950 (1 1)	MERITS 01/13/1951 (1)	MERITS 03/24/1951 (1 2)	REPORT 04/23/1951 (1 1)
Minton	G	R	R	R
Clark	G			AQ A
Burton	G	R A	AO R	R A
Jackson	G		AQ	A
Douglas	G	R	A	R A
Frankfr	G	R A	A R	R A
Reed	G	AO	A AQ	R A
Black	G			R
Vinson	G	R	R	R A

Klapprott v U.S.
50 366A
340 US 896
CCA 3rd

Justice	CERT 11/30/1950 (1 1)
Minton	D
Clark	
Burton	D
Jackson	D
Douglas	
Frankfr	D
Reed	
Black	G
Vinson	D

Martin v U.S.
50 367A
340 US 904
CCA 4th

Justice	CERT 12/09/1950 (1 1)
Minton	D
Clark	D
Burton	D
Jackson	D
Douglas	
Frankfr	G
Reed	
Black	D
Vinson	D

C.I.R. v Tobin
50 368A
340 US 904
CCA 5th

Justice	CERT 12/09/1950 (1 1)
Minton	G
Clark	
Burton	D
Jackson	G
Douglas	
Frankfr	G
Reed	
Black	D
Vinson	D

Larsen v Switzer
50 374A
340 US 911
CCA 8th

Justice	CERT 12/30/1950 (1 1)
Minton	G
Clark	D
Burton	G
Jackson	
Douglas	D
Frankfr	D
Reed	D
Black	D
Vinson	D

Wilson v Louisiana
50 376A 50 140M
341 US 901
Louisiana

Justice	CERT 10/21/1950 (1 1)	MERITS 03/12/1951 (1 1)	REPORT 04/09/1951 (1 1)
Minton	G		
Clark	G		
Burton		R A	R A
Jackson	D	A	
Douglas	G	A	A
Frankfr	G	A	A
Reed	G	R	R
Black		A	A
Vinson	G	A	A

M.H. Jacobs Company v Stahly
50 380A
340 US 896
CCA 7th

Justice	CERT 11/30/1950 (1 1)
Minton	
Clark	D
Burton	D
Jackson	D
Douglas	
Frankfr	D
Reed	D
Black	G
Vinson	D

Standard Oil Company v New Jersey
50 384A
341 US 428
Reed 03/15/51 New Jersey

Justice	JURIS 11/30/1950 (1 1)	MERITS 03/10/1951 (1 1)	REPORT 05/28/1951 (1 1)
Minton	N		
Clark	N	R	R
Burton	N	R A	R A
Jackson	S	RV X	
Douglas	S	R	R
Frankfr	S		
Reed		A	A
Black	N	X	
Vinson		A	A

United Carpenters v N.L.R.B.
50 387A
341 US 947
CCA 10th

Justice	CERT 06/02/1951 (1 1)	REPORT 06/04/1951 (1 1)
Minton	D	R
Clark	D	R
Burton	D	R
Jackson		
Douglas	G	A A
Frankfr	D	
Reed		R
Black	D	R A
Vinson	D	R

N.L.R.B. v Denver Building Trades
50 393A
341 US 675 50 108A 50 313A
Burton 03/16/51 CCA DC

Justice	CERT 12/09/1950 (1 1)	MERITS 03/03/1951 (1 1)
Minton	G	R
Clark	G	R
Burton	G	R
Jackson	G	
Douglas	G	A A
Frankfr	G	A
Reed	G	R
Black	G	R
Vinson	G	R

Alabama PSC v Southern RR Company
50 395A
341 US 341 50 146A
Vinson 03/15/51 DC MD Alabama

Justice	JURIS 11/25/1950 (1 1)	MERITS 03/03/1951 (1 1)	REPORT 05/21/1951 (1 1)
Minton	N	R	R
Clark	N	R	R
Burton	N	R	R
Jackson	N	R A	R A
Douglas	N	A	R
Frankfr	N	R	R
Reed		R	R
Black	N	R	R
Vinson		R	R

Breard v City Of Alexandria
50 **399A**
341 US 622
Reed 03/15/51 Louisiana

	12/09 1950 JURIS 1	1	02/24 1951 AMICUS 1	1	03/12 1951 MERITS 1	1	06/04 1951 REPORT 1	1
Minton		S	B			A		A
Clark	N		B			A		A
Burton		S	B			A		A
Jackson	N		B			A		A
Douglas	N		B		R		R	
Frankfr	N		B			A		A
Reed	N			Y		A		A
Black	N			Y	R		R	
Vinson		S	B		RQ		R	

Kaiser Company v Baskin
50 **402A**
340 US 886
California

	11/25 1950 JURIS 1	1	11/27 1950 REPORT 1	1
Minton		A		A
Clark		A		A
Burton		A		A
Jackson		A		A
Douglas		A		A
Frankfr		A		A
Reed		A		A
Black		A		A
Vinson		A		A

Icenhour v U.S.
50 **406A**
340 US 908
CCA 5th

	12/29 1950 CERT 1	1	01/02 1951 REPORT 1	1
Minton	GVM		VI	
Clark	GVM		VI	
Burton	GVM		VI	
Jackson	GVM		VI	
Douglas	GVM		VI	
Frankfr	GVM		VI	
Reed	GVM		VI	
Black	GVM		VI	
Vinson	GVM		VI	

C.I.R. v Swirin
50 **416A**
340 US 912
CCA 7th

	12/29 1950 CERT 1	1
Minton		D
Clark		D
Burton	G	
Jackson		D
Douglas		D
Frankfr		D
Reed	G	
Black		D
Vinson		D

A.B.T. Manufacturing v National
50 **417A**
340 US 912
CCA 7th

	12/29 1950 CERT 1	1
Minton		
Clark		
Burton		
Jackson		
Douglas		
Frankfr		
Reed		
Black	G	
Vinson		

Shepherd v Florida
50 **420A** 50 189M
341 US 50
Florida

	11/25 1950 CERT 1	1	03/12 1951 MERITS 1	1	04/09 1951 REPORT 1	1
Minton	G		R		R	
Clark	G		R		R	
Burton	G		R		R	
Jackson	G		R		R	
Douglas	G		R		R	
Frankfr	GV		R		R	
Reed	G		R		R	
Black	G		R		R	
Vinson	G		R		R	

Hammerstein v Superior Court
50 **421A**
341 US 491
California

	01/13 1951 CERT 1	1	03/12 1951 MERITS 1	1	05/28 1951 REPORT 1	1
Minton		D	RV			S
Clark	G		RV		G	
Burton		D	RV			S
Jackson	G		RV		G	
Douglas	G		R		G	
Frankfr	G		RV			S
Reed	G		R			S
Black	G		RV		G	
Vinson	G		RV			S

Palermo v Ganey
50 **423A**
340 US 923
CCA 3rd

	02/26 1951 CERT 1	1	02/26 1951 REPORT 1	1
Minton	GVI		VI	
Clark	GVI		VI	
Burton	GVI		VI	
Jackson	GVI		VI	
Douglas	GVI		VI	
Frankfr	GVI		VI	
Reed	GVI		VI	
Black	GVI		VI	
Vinson	GVI		VI	

N.L.R.B. v Highland Park Manufacturing
50 **425A**
341 US 322
Jackson 05/01/51 CCA 4th

	02/26 1951 CERT 1	1	03/24 1951 AMICUS 1	1	04/28 1951 MERITS 1	1	05/14 1951 REPORT 1	1
Minton	G		B			A		A
Clark	G		B			A		A
Burton	G		B			A		A
Jackson	G		B			A		A
Douglas	G			Y	R		R	
Frankfr	G		B		R		R	
Reed	G		B			A		A
Black	G			Y		X		
Vinson	G		B			A		A

City Of Los Angeles v Woods
50 426A
340 US 908
CCA DC

	12/29 1950 CERT	01/02 1951 REPORT
Minton	GVI	VI
Clark	GVI	VI
Burton	GVI	VI
Jackson	GVI	VI
Douglas	GVI	VI
Frankfr	GVI	VI
Reed	GVI	VI
Black	GVI	VI
Vinson	GVI	VI

Healy v Pennsylvania RR Company
50 427A
340 US 935
CCA 3rd

	02/26 1951 CERT
Minton	G D
Clark	D
Burton	D
Jackson	G D
Douglas	
Frankfr	G
Reed	
Black	G D
Vinson	

Sparks v C.A.B.
50 429A
340 US 941
CCA 2d

	03/03 1951 CERT
Minton	
Clark	
Burton	
Jackson	
Douglas	
Frankfr	G GH
Reed	G
Black	G
Vinson	D

U.S. v Champlin Refining Company
50 433A
341 US 290
Clark 03/15/51 DC WD Oklahoma

	12/30 1950 JURIS	03/12 1951 MERITS	05/07 1951 REPORT
Minton	N	A	
Clark	N		
Burton		A	
Jackson	N	X	
Douglas		A	
Frankfr		A	
Reed	N	A	
Black		AQ	R
Vinson		A	

Bowman Dairy Company v U.S.
50 435A
341 US 214
Minton 03/15/51 CCA 7th

	01/13 1951 CERT	03/10 1951 MERITS	04/30 1951 REPORT
Minton	G		R
Clark	G	A	R
Burton	G	A	R
Jackson	G	A	R
Douglas	G		R
Frankfr	G	R	R
Reed	G	R	R
Black	G	X	R
Vinson	G	A	R

Board Of Supervisors LSU v Wilson
50 436A
340 US 909
DC ED Louisiana

	12/30 1950 JURIS	01/02 1951 REPORT
Minton	A	A
Clark	A	A
Burton	A	A
Jackson	A	A
Douglas	A	A
Frankfr	A	A
Reed	A	A
Black	S	A
Vinson	A	A

United Gas Workers v Wisconsin ERB
50 438A
340 US 383 50 302A 50 329A 50 330A
Vinson 01/16/51 Wisconsin

	12/09 1950 CERT	01/13 1951 MERITS	02/26 1951 REPORT
Minton	G		
Clark	G	R A	R A
Burton	G	A	R A
Jackson	G	R	R
Douglas	G	R	R
Frankfr	G	A	A
Reed	G	R	R A
Black	G	A	R A
Vinson	G	R	R A

Schwegmann Brothers v Calvert
50 442A
341 US 384 50 443A 50 538A
Douglas 04/17/51 CCA 5th

	02/26 1951 CERT	04/14 1951 MERITS	05/21 1951 REPORT
Minton	G	R	R
Clark	G D	R	R
Burton	G	R	R
Jackson	G	R	R
Douglas			
Frankfr	G	R	R
Reed	G		
Black		X	
Vinson	G D		R A

Schwegmann Brothers v Seagram
50 443A
341 US 384 50 442A 50 538A
Douglas 04/17/51 CCA 5th

	02/26 1951 CERT	04/14 1951 MERITS	05/21 1951 REPORT
Minton	G	R	R
Clark	G D	R	R
Burton	G	R	R
Jackson	G	R	R
Douglas			
Frankfr	G	R	R
Reed	G		
Black		X	
Vinson	G D		R A

Crest Specialty v Trager
50 446A
341 US 912
CCA 7th

	02/26 1951 CERT	04/14 1951 MERITS	04/23 1951 REPORT
Minton	GR	R	R
Clark	G D	R	R
Burton	GR	R	R
Jackson	GR	R	R
Douglas	GR D	R	R
Frankfr			
Reed	G		R
Black	GR	X	R
Vinson	GR		R

Koons v Kaiser
50 451A
340 US 942 50 452A
CCA 2d

	02/26 1951 CERT	03/03 1951 CERT
Minton	G	G
Clark	G	G
Burton	G	G
Jackson	G	G
Douglas	G	G
Frankfr	G	
Reed	G	G
Black	G	G
Vinson	G D	G D

Garner v Board Of Public Works
50 453A
341 US 716
Douglas 05/01/51 Clark ??/??/51 California

	02/26 1951 CERT	04/28 1951 MERITS	06/04 1951 REPORT
Minton	G	RL	R A
Clark	G D	RL	R A
Burton	G	RL	R A
Jackson	G		R A
Douglas	G		R A
Frankfr	G		R A
Reed	G	R	R A
Black	G	AQ	R A
Vinson	G D		R A

310

Mosser v Darrow
50 461A
341 US 267
Jackson 04/17/51 CCA 7th

	CERT 02/26 1951 1 1	MERITS 04/14 1951 1 1	REPORT 05/07 1951 1 1
Minton	G	R	R
Clark	G	R	R
Burton			
Jackson	G	R	R
Douglas	G	R	R
Frankfr	G	R	R
Reed	G	R	R
Black	D	D	
Vinson		A	A

Pioneer News v Southwestern Bell
50 464A
341 US 929
DC ED Missouri

	JURIS 01/13 1951 1 1	REPORT 05/12 1951 1 1
Minton	S	SI
Clark	S	SI
Burton	S	SI
Jackson		SI
Douglas		SI
Frankfr		SI
Reed		SI
Black		SI
Vinson		SI

Cookingham v U.S.
50 465A
340 US 935
CCA 3rd

	CERT 02/26 1951 1 1
Minton	D
Clark	D
Burton	D
Jackson	
Douglas	G
Frankfr	D
Reed	D
Black	D
Vinson	D

Stebco v Gillmouthe
50 467A
340 US 920
Oregon

	CERT 01/13 1951 1 1
Minton	D
Clark	D
Burton	D
Jackson	G
Douglas	G
Frankfr	
Reed	D
Black	D
Vinson	G

Lafayette Steel Company v Lustron
50 472A
340 US 946
CCA 7th

	CERT 03/10 1951 1 1
Minton	D
Clark	D
Burton	D
Jackson	D
Douglas	D
Frankfr	D
Reed	
Black	G
Vinson	D

Brannan v Elder
50 473A
341 US 277 50 474A
Clark 04/17/51 CCA DC

	CERT 02/26 1951 1 1	MERITS 04/14 1951 1 1	REPORT 05/07 1951 1 1
Minton	D	R	R
Clark	G	R	R
Burton	G		R
Jackson			
Douglas	D	R	R
Frankfr	D	A	R
Reed		X	R
Black	G	A	
Vinson	D	A	A

Elder v Brannan
50 474A
341 US 277 50 473A
Clark 04/17/51 CCA DC

	CERT 02/26 1951 1 1	MERITS 04/14 1951 1 1	REPORT 05/07 1951 1 1
Minton	D	A	A
Clark	D	A	A
Burton			
Jackson	G	A	A
Douglas	D	A	A
Frankfr	D	X	A
Reed	D	A	A
Black	G	R	R
Vinson	G	A	A

Woodward v U.S.
50 476A
341 US 112
CCA 8th

	CERT 02/26 1951 1 1	MERITS 04/14 1951 1 1	REPORT 04/23 1951 1 1
Minton	GL	R	R
Clark	GL	R	R
Burton	GL	R	R
Jackson	GL	R	R
Douglas	GL	R	R
Frankfr	D	R	R
Reed	GL	R	R
Black	GL	R	R
Vinson	GL	R	R

Riss & Company v U.S.
50 479A
341 US 907
DC WD Missouri

	JURIS 02/26 1951 1 1	MERITS 04/14 1951 1 1	REPORT 04/16 1951 1 1
Minton	N	R	R
Clark	N	R	R
Burton	N	R	R
Jackson	N	R	R
Douglas	N	R	R
Frankfr	N	R	R
Reed	N	R	R
Black	N	R	R
Vinson	N	R	R

Panhandle Eastern v Michigan PSC
50 486A
341 US 329 50 479A
Minton 05/01/51 Michigan

	JURIS 02/26 1951 1 1	MERITS 04/28 1951 1 1	REPORT 05/14 1951 1 1
Minton	S	A	A
Clark	S	A	A
Burton			
Jackson	N	X	R
Douglas	S	X	R
Frankfr	N		
Reed	N	R	
Black	S	AQ	A
Vinson	S	A	A

Kemp v South Dakota
50 488A
340 US 923
South Dakota

	JURIS 02/26 1951 1 1
Minton	S
Clark	S
Burton	S
Jackson	S
Douglas	NR
Frankfr	
Reed	S
Black	S
Vinson	S

Hayes v Union Pacific RR Company
50 495A
340 US 942
CCA 9th

	CERT 03/03 1951 1 1
Minton	D
Clark	D
Burton	
Jackson	G
Douglas	
Frankfr	G
Reed	
Black	G
Vinson	D

Fiorella v City Of Birmingham
50 502A
340 US 942
Alabama

Justice	03/03 1951 CERT
	1 1
Minton	D
Clark	D
Burton	
Jackson	
Douglas	D
Frankfr	D
Reed	
Black	D
Vinson	D

Rosecrans v West Edmond Salt Water
50 504A
340 US 924
Oklahoma

Justice	02/26 1951 JURIS
	1 1
Minton	
Clark	
Burton	N
Jackson	
Douglas	N
Frankfr	
Reed	
Black	
Vinson	

Obermeier v U.S.
50 505A
340 US 951 50 557A
CCA 2d

Justice	03/24 1951 CERT
	1 1
Minton	D
Clark	D
Burton	
Jackson	
Douglas	D
Frankfr	D
Reed	
Black	D
Vinson	D

Zimmerman v Chicago Great Western RR
50 506A
340 US 934
CCA 7th

Justice	02/26 1951 CERT
	1 1
Minton	D
Clark	D
Burton	
Jackson	G
Douglas	D
Frankfr	D
Reed	
Black	G
Vinson	D

Reconstruction Finance v Lustron
50 507A
340 US 946
CCA 7th

Justice	03/10 1951 CERT
	1 1
Minton	D
Clark	D
Burton	
Jackson	D
Douglas	D
Frankfr	D
Reed	
Black	D
Vinson	

Consumer Mail Order v McGrath
50 508A
340 US 925
CCA DC

Justice	02/26 1951 JURIS	02/26 1951 REPORT
	1 1	1 1
Minton		A
Clark		A
Burton		A
Jackson	N	
Douglas	N	A
Frankfr		A
Reed		A
Black		A
Vinson		

Sickman v U.S.
50 511A
341 US 939
CCA 7th

Justice	05/26 1951 CERT	11/03 1951 REHEAR
	1 1	1 1
Minton	D	B
Clark	D	B
Burton	G	
Jackson	D	B
Douglas	D	B
Frankfr	D	B
Reed	D	
Black	D	B
Vinson		Y

Hoffman v U.S.
50 513A
341 US 479 50 586A
Clark 05/01/51 CCA 3rd

Justice	03/10 1951 CERT	04/28 1951 MERITS	05/28 1951 REPORT
	1 1	1 1	1 1
Minton	G	R	R
Clark	G	R	R
Burton	G	R	R
Jackson	G	A	R
Douglas	G		R
Frankfr	G	R	R
Reed		A	
Black	G	AQ	R
Vinson	G	A	R

Brooks Transportation Company v U.S.
50 517A
340 US 925
DC ED Virginia

Justice	02/26 1951 JURIS	02/26 1951 REPORT
	1 1	1 1
Minton		A
Clark		A
Burton		A
Jackson		A
Douglas		A
Frankfr		A
Reed		A
Black		A
Vinson		

Hiss v U.S.
50 520A
340 US 948
CCA 2d

Justice	03/10 1951 CERT
	1 1
Minton	D
Clark	D
Burton	D
Jackson	
Douglas	G
Frankfr	
Reed	
Black	G
Vinson	D

Cole v Loew's
50 522A
340 US 954
CCA 9th

Justice	03/24 1951 CERT
	1 1
Minton	D
Clark	D
Burton	D
Jackson	
Douglas	
Frankfr	
Reed	
Black	
Vinson	G

Moffett v Arabian American Oil Company
50 528A
340 US 948
CCA 2d

Justice	03/10 1951 CERT
	1 1
Minton	D
Clark	D
Burton	D
Jackson	D
Douglas	
Frankfr	
Reed	
Black	
Vinson	G

Öttley v St. Louis-San Francisco RR
50 532A
340 US 948
Missouri

Justice	03/10 1951 CERT	06/04 1951 REPORT
	1 1	1 1
Minton	D	
Clark	D	>
Burton	D	>
Jackson		>
Douglas	D	>
Frankfr		>
Reed	D	>
Black		>
Vinson	D	>

Sunbeam v Wentling
50 538A
341 US 944 50 442A 50 443A
CCA 3rd

Justice	06/02 1951 CERT
	1 1
Minton	GV
Clark	GV
Burton	GV
Jackson	GV
Douglas	GV
Frankfr	GV
Reed	
Black	
Vinson	GV

Craven v Atlantic Coast Line RR
50 539A
340 US 952
CCA 4th

Justice	03/24 1951 CERT
	1 1
Minton	D
Clark	D
Burton	D
Jackson	
Douglas	D
Frankfr	D
Reed	
Black	D
Vinson	D

Minkoff v U.S.
50 542A · 340 US 952 · CCA 2d

Justice	03/24/1951 CERT
Minton	D
Clark	D
Burton	D
Jackson	D
Douglas	D
Frankfr	D
Reed	D
Black	G
Vinson	G

Jennings-Watts Oil Company v Gilbert
50 549A · 340 US 953 · CCA 4th

Justice	03/24/1951 CERT
Minton	D
Clark	D
Burton	D
Jackson	D
Douglas	D
Frankfr	D
Reed	D
Black	G
Vinson	G

U.S. v Obermeier
50 557A · 340 US 951 50 505A · CCA 2d

Justice	03/24/1951 CERT
Minton	D
Clark	D
Burton	D
Jackson	D
Douglas	D
Frankfr	D
Reed	D
Black	D
Vinson	D

First National Bank v United Air Lines
50 558A · 341 US 903 · CCA 7th

Justice	04/07/1951 CERT
Minton	D
Clark	D
Burton	D
Jackson	D
Douglas	D
Frankfr	D
Reed	D
Black	H
Vinson	D

Williams v Hughes Tool Company
50 561A · 341 US 934 · CCA 10th

Justice	04/07/1951 CERT
Minton	D
Clark	D
Burton	D
Jackson	D
Douglas	D
Frankfr	D
Reed	G
Black	D
Vinson	D

Radio Corporation Of America v U.S.
50 565A · 341 US 412 · Black 04/17/51 · DC ND Illinois

Justice	03/03/1951 JURIS	04/07/1951 MERITS	05/28/1951 REPORT
Minton	N	A	A
Clark	N	A	A
Burton	N	A	A
Jackson		R	Q
Douglas	N	A	A
Frankfr	N	A	A
Reed	N	A	A
Black	A	A	A
Vinson		A	A

Eastern Air Lines v C.A.B.
50 567A · 341 US 901 · CCA DC

Justice	04/07/1951 CERT	04/09/1951 REPORT
Minton	GVI	VI
Clark	GVI	VI
Burton	GVI	VI
Jackson	G	
Douglas	GVI	VI
Frankfr	GVI	VI
Reed	GVI	VI
Black	GVI	
Vinson	GVI	

Taunah v Jones
50 568A · 341 US 904 · CCA 10th

Justice	04/07/1951 CERT
Minton	D
Clark	D
Burton	G
Jackson	D
Douglas	D
Frankfr	D
Reed	D
Black	G
Vinson	D

Westinghouse Radio Stations v Felix
50 574A · 341 US 909 · CCA 3rd

Justice	04/14/1951 CERT
Minton	D
Clark	D
Burton	G
Jackson	D
Douglas	D
Frankfr	D
Reed	D
Black	G
Vinson	D

Netherlands Ministry v Strika
50 575A · 341 US 904 · CCA 2d

Justice	04/07/1951 CERT
Minton	D
Clark	D
Burton	D
Jackson	D
Douglas	D
Frankfr	D
Reed	D
Black	G
Vinson	D

Gerende v Board Of Supervisors
50 577A · 341 US 56 · Maryland

Justice	03/24/1951 JURIS	04/11/1951 MERITS	04/12/1951 REPORT
Minton	N		A
Clark	N		A
Burton	N		A
Jackson	N	X	A
Douglas	N		A
Frankfr	N		A
Reed	N		A
Black	N	A	A
Vinson	S		

Southern Pacific Company v Guthrie
50 579A · 341 US 904 · CCA 9th

Justice	04/07/1951 CERT
Minton	D
Clark	D
Burton	D
Jackson	D
Douglas	D
Frankfr	D
Reed	D
Black	GQ
Vinson	D

Wheaton Brass Works v Southern Pacific
50 583A · 341 US 904 · New Jersey

Justice	04/07/1951 CERT	06/04/1951 REPORT
Minton	D	>
Clark	D	>
Burton	D	>
Jackson	D	>
Douglas	D	>
Frankfr	D	>
Reed	G	>
Black	G	>
Vinson	D	

Greenberg v U.S.
50 586A · 341 US 944 50 513A · CCA 3rd

Justice	06/02/1951 CERT
Minton	GVM
Clark	GVM
Burton	GVM
Jackson	GVM
Douglas	GVM
Frankfr	GVM
Reed	GVM
Black	GVM
Vinson	GVM

Reiling v Tawes
50 588A · 341 US 901 · DC Maryland

Justice	04/07/1951 JURIS
Minton	S
Clark	S
Burton	A
Jackson	S
Douglas	A
Frankfr	A
Reed	S
Black	S
Vinson	N

National City Lines v U.S.
50 589A
341 US 916
CCA 7th

Justice	04/21/1951 CERT (1 1)	
Minton		
Clark		D
Burton		
Jackson	G	D
Douglas		D
Frankfr		D
Reed		
Black	G	D
Vinson		D

U.S. v Safeway Stores
50 590A
341 US 953   50 591A
Ct Cls

Justice	05/26/1951 CERT (1 1)	06/02/1951 CERT (1 2)	
Minton	G		
Clark			
Burton			D
Jackson	G	G	
Douglas	G	GL	D
Frankfr			
Reed	G		D
Black			D
Vinson			

Chicago Rock Island RR v Acme Brick
50 592A
341 US 920
CCA 5th

Justice	04/28/1951 CERT (1 1)	
Minton		
Clark	G	D
Burton		D
Jackson		
Douglas	G	D
Frankfr		D
Reed		
Black	G	D
Vinson	G	D

Goo v U.S.
50 597A
341 US 916
CCA 9th

Justice	04/21/1951 CERT (1 1)	
Minton		
Clark		D
Burton		D
Jackson		D
Douglas	G	
Frankfr		D
Reed		
Black	G	D
Vinson		

Ross v Texas
50 600A   50 364M
341 US 918
Texas

Justice	03/10/1951 REPORT (1 1)	04/28/1951 MERITS (1 1)
Minton	R	R
Clark	R	R
Burton	R	?
Jackson	R	
Douglas	R	R
Frankfr	R	R
Reed	R	R
Black	R	
Vinson	R	

Atlantic Maritime Company v Rankin
50 607A
341 US 915
CCA 2d

Justice	04/21/1951 CERT (1 1)
Minton	
Clark	
Burton	
Jackson	
Douglas	G
Frankfr	
Reed	
Black	G
Vinson	G

Levinson v Deupree
50 608A
341 US 915
CCA 6th

Justice	04/21/1951 CERT (1 1)	
Minton		
Clark		D
Burton		D
Jackson	G	
Douglas		D
Frankfr		D
Reed		
Black	G	D
Vinson		

Nubar v C.I.R.
50 619A
341 US 925
CCA 4th

Justice	05/05/1951 CERT (1 1)	
Minton		
Clark		D
Burton		D
Jackson	G	D
Douglas		D
Frankfr		D
Reed		
Black	G	D
Vinson		

Ewing v Gardner
50 621A
341 US 321
CCA 6th

Justice	04/28/1951 CERT (1 1)
Minton	G
Clark	G
Burton	G
Jackson	G
Douglas	G
Frankfr	G
Reed	G
Black	G
Vinson	G

Lyon v Compton Union High School
50 627A
341 US 913   50 628A
California

Justice	04/21/1951 JURIS (1 1)
Minton	N
Clark	N
Burton	S
Jackson	N
Douglas	S
Frankfr	S
Reed	N
Black	S
Vinson	S

Roth v Esquire
50 637A
341 US 921
CCA 2d

Justice	04/28/1951 CERT (1 1)
Minton	D
Clark	D
Burton	G
Jackson	D
Douglas	D
Frankfr	D
Reed	D
Black	D
Vinson	

Le Roy Dyal Company v U.S.
50 639A
341 US 926
CCA 3rd

Justice	05/05/1951 CERT (1 1)
Minton	D
Clark	D
Burton	
Jackson	G
Douglas	D
Frankfr	D
Reed	D
Black	D
Vinson	D

Friedman v New York
50 640A
341 US 907
New York

Justice	04/14/1951 JURIS (1 1)
Minton	S
Clark	S
Burton	S
Jackson	N
Douglas	N
Frankfr	N
Reed	S
Black	S
Vinson	S

Warner v U.S.
50 641A
341 US 907
DC WD Tennessee

Justice	04/14/1951 JURIS (1 1)	04/16/1951 REPORT (1 1)
Minton		A
Clark	N	A
Burton	A	A
Jackson	N	A
Douglas	A	A
Frankfr	A	A
Reed	N	A
Black	A	A
Vinson	A	A

Pohl v Acheson
50 643A
341 US 916
CCA DC

Justice	04/21/1951 CERT (1 1)
Minton	D
Clark	D
Burton	
Jackson	G
Douglas	D
Frankfr	D
Reed	
Black	G
Vinson	D

314

Maragon v U.S.
50 650A
341 US 932
CCA DC

Justice	05/12 1951 CERT
Minton	D
Clark	
Burton	D
Jackson	
Douglas	D
Frankfr	D
Reed	D
Black	G
Vinson	D

Mitchell v Flintkote Company
50 651A
341 US 931
CCA 2d

Justice	05/12 1951 CERT
Minton	D
Clark	
Burton	D
Jackson	
Douglas	D
Frankfr	D
Reed	D
Black	G
Vinson	D

Santangelo v Santangelo
50 659A
341 US 927
Connecticut

Justice	05/05 1951 CERT
Minton	D
Clark	
Burton	D
Jackson	
Douglas	D
Frankfr	D
Reed	D
Black	G
Vinson	D

Carlson v U.S.
50 661A
341 US 940
CCA 10th

Justice	05/26 1951 CERT
Minton	D
Clark	
Burton	D
Jackson	G
Douglas	D
Frankfr	G
Reed	D
Black	G
Vinson	D

U.S. v Stewart
50 665A
341 US 940
CCA 7th

Justice	05/26 1951 CERT
Minton	D
Clark	
Burton	D
Jackson	G
Douglas	D
Frankfr	G
Reed	D
Black	G
Vinson	D

Dority v New Mexico (Bliss)
50 670A
341 US 924
New Mexico

Justice	05/05 1951 JURIS
Minton	S
Clark	
Burton	S
Jackson	N
Douglas	S
Frankfr	
Reed	S
Black	N
Vinson	S

Seslar v Union Local 901
50 671A
341 US 940
CCA 7th

Justice	05/26 1951 CERT
Minton	
Clark	
Burton	
Jackson	
Douglas	G
Frankfr	
Reed	G
Black	
Vinson	

City Of Birmingham v Monk
50 673A 11A
341 US 940
CCA 5th

Justice	05/26 1951 CERT
Minton	
Clark	
Burton	
Jackson	G
Douglas	
Frankfr	
Reed	G
Black	
Vinson	

Holmes v U.S.
50 680A
341 US 948
CCA 7th

Justice	06/02 1951 CERT
Minton	D
Clark	D
Burton	D
Jackson	
Douglas	G
Frankfr	
Reed	D
Black	G
Vinson	D

Marshall Drug Company v U.S.
50 671A
341 US 948
Ct Cls

Justice	06/02 1951 CERT
Minton	D
Clark	D
Burton	D
Jackson	
Douglas	G
Frankfr	
Reed	D
Black	D
Vinson	D

Papaliolios v Durning
50 683A
341 US 940
CCA 2d

Justice	05/26 1951 CERT
Minton	
Clark	
Burton	
Jackson	
Douglas	G
Frankfr	
Reed	
Black	
Vinson	

Saucier v Texas
50 691A
341 US 949
Texas

Justice	06/02 1951 CERT
Minton	D
Clark	D
Burton	D
Jackson	
Douglas	G
Frankfr	
Reed	D
Black	G
Vinson	D

Red Rock Company v N.L.R.B.
50 695A
341 US 950
CCA 5th

Justice	06/02 1951 CERT
Minton	D
Clark	D
Burton	D
Jackson	D
Douglas	D
Frankfr	D
Reed	G
Black	D
Vinson	D

Butler v Thompson
50 713A
341 US 937
DC ED Virginia

Justice	05/28 1951 REPORT	05/26 1951 JURIS
Minton	A	
Clark	A	
Burton	A	
Jackson		N
Douglas	A	
Frankfr	A	
Reed	A	
Black	A	
Vinson		

Eastern Air Lines v C.A.B.
50 714A
341 US 901
CCA DC

Justice	06/02 1951 CERT
Minton	D
Clark	D
Burton	D
Jackson	D
Douglas	G
Frankfr	D
Reed	D
Black	
Vinson	

Red Ball Motor Freight v U.S.
50 731A
341 US 938
DC ND Texas

Justice	05/28 1951 REPORT	05/26 1951 JURIS
Minton	A	A
Clark	A	A
Burton	A	A
Jackson		N
Douglas	A	A
Frankfr	A	A
Reed	A	A
Black	A	A
Vinson		

General Motors AC v Commissioner
50 746A
341 US 945
Wisconsin

Justice	06/02 1951 JURIS
Minton	S
Clark	S
Burton	S
Jackson	N
Douglas	S
Frankfr	
Reed	S
Black	S
Vinson	

Simmons v City Of Birmingham
50 752A
341 US 945
Alabama

Justice	06/02 1951 JURIS
Minton	S
Clark	S
Burton	S
Jackson	N
Douglas	S
Frankfr	
Reed	N
Black	S
Vinson	S

Hoskins v Moore
50 2M 49 463M
340 US 804

	10/04 1950 HABEAS 1 1
Minton	D
Clark	D
Burton	D
Jackson	E
Douglas	
Frankfr	
Reed	
Black	G
Vinson	D

Barrett v Hunter
50 3M 49 481M
340 US 897
CCA 10th

	11/30 1950 CERT 1 1
Minton	D
Clark	D
Burton	D
Jackson	D
Douglas	D
Frankfr	D
Reed	D
Black	
Vinson	D

Adkins v E.I. Du Pont de Nemours
50 12M
340 US 835
CCA 10th

	10/04 1950 CERT 1 1
Minton	
Clark	
Burton	
Jackson	
Douglas	
Frankfr	
Reed	
Black	
Vinson	

Agoston v Pennsylvania
50 59M
340 US 844
Pennsylvania

	10/04 1950 CERT 1 1
Minton	D
Clark	D
Burton	D
Jackson	
Douglas	G
Frankfr	G
Reed	
Black	G
Vinson	D

Gallagher v U.S.
50 65M
340 US 913
CCA 3rd

	12/30 1950 CERT 1 1
Minton	D
Clark	D
Burton	D
Jackson	D
Douglas	D
Frankfr	D
Reed	
Black	D
Vinson	D

Bunk v New Jersey
50 69M
340 US 839
New Jersey

	10/04 1950 CERT 1 1
Minton	D
Clark	D
Burton	D
Jackson	
Douglas	G
Frankfr	
Reed	
Black	
Vinson	

Martin v U.S.
50 79M
340 US 892
CCA 5th

	11/25 1950 CERT 1 1
Minton	D
Clark	D
Burton	D
Jackson	
Douglas	G
Frankfr	
Reed	
Black	G
Vinson	D

Gomez v U.S.
50 93M
340 US 897
CCA 1st

	11/30 1950 CERT 1 1
Minton	D
Clark	D
Burton	D
Jackson	
Douglas	G
Frankfr	G
Reed	
Black	G
Vinson	D

Pickett v Texas
50 101M
340 US 867
Texas

	10/21 1950 CERT 1 1
Minton	D
Clark	D
Burton	D
Jackson	
Douglas	
Frankfr	
Reed	
Black	D
Vinson	D

Pennsylvania (Bearringer) v Ashe
50 103M
340 US 913
Pennsylvania

	12/30 1950 CERT 1 1
Minton	D
Clark	D
Burton	D
Jackson	
Douglas	G
Frankfr	
Reed	
Black	G
Vinson	D

Seger v Illinois
50 124M
340 US 867
Illinois

	10/21 1950 CERT 1 1
Minton	D
Clark	D
Burton	D
Jackson	
Douglas	G
Frankfr	G
Reed	
Black	G
Vinson	D

Pennsylvania (Almeida) v Baldi
50 130M
340 US 867
Pennsylvania

	10/21 1950 CERT 1 1
Minton	D
Clark	D
Burton	D
Jackson	
Douglas	G
Frankfr	G
Reed	
Black	D
Vinson	D

Dorsey v U.S.
50 138M
340 US 878
CCA 5th

	11/04 1950 CERT 1 1
Minton	D
Clark	D
Burton	D
Jackson	D
Douglas	D
Frankfr	
Reed	
Black	G
Vinson	D

Woollomes v Heinze
50 157M
340 US 897
California

	11/30 1950 CERT 1 1
Minton	D
Clark	D
Burton	D
Jackson	
Douglas	G
Frankfr	
Reed	
Black	G
Vinson	D

Lapean v Burke
50 159M
341 US 941
Wisconsin

	12/09 1950 CERT 1 1	12/30 1950 CERT 1 2	05/26 1951 CERT 1 3
Minton	D	H	D
Clark	H	H	D
Burton	H	H	D
Jackson	G	G	
Douglas	H	H	
Frankfr	Q	Q	G
Reed	D	D	D
Black			D
Vinson			D

316

Best v U.S.
50 161M
340 US 939
CCA 1st
02/26 1951 CERT · 1 1

Justice	Vote
Minton	D
Clark	
Burton	D
Jackson	D
Douglas	G
Frankfr	D
Reed	
Black	G
Vinson	D

Cooper v Rust Engineering Company
50 162M
340 US 879
CCA 6th
11/04 1950 CERT · 1 1

Justice	Vote
Minton	D
Clark	
Burton	D
Jackson	D
Douglas	G
Frankfr	D
Reed	D
Black	G
Vinson	X

Dowdy v Louisiana
50 174M
340 US 856
Louisiana
10/14 1950 CERT · 1 1

Justice	Vote
Minton	D
Clark	D
Burton	D
Jackson	D
Douglas	G
Frankfr	D
Reed	
Black	D
Vinson	D

Johnson v Pennsylvania
50 161M
340 US 881
Pennsylvania
11/11 1950 CERT · 1 1

Justice	Vote
Minton	GR
Clark	GR
Burton	GR
Jackson	G
Douglas	D
Frankfr	GR
Reed	
Black	GR
Vinson	GR

Marvich v Heinze
50 234M
340 US 902
12/09 1950 HABEAS · 1 1

Justice	Vote
Minton	D
Clark	D
Burton	D
Jackson	
Douglas	G
Frankfr	D
Reed	D
Black	D
Vinson	

Beck v New York
50 239M
340 US 914 50 240M
New York
12/30 1950 CERT · 1 1

Justice	Vote
Minton	D
Clark	D
Burton	D
Jackson	
Douglas	D
Frankfr	D
Reed	D
Black	D
Vinson	D

Fernandez v New York
50 240M
340 US 914 50 239M
New York
12/30 1950 CERT · 1 1

Justice	Vote
Minton	D
Clark	D
Burton	D
Jackson	
Douglas	G
Frankfr	D
Reed	D
Black	D
Vinson	D

Foster v Sheriff Of Los Angeles
50 248M
340 US 921
California
01/13 1951 CERT · 1 1

Justice	Vote
Minton	D
Clark	D
Burton	D
Jackson	
Douglas	G
Frankfr	D
Reed	D
Black	D
Vinson	D

La Coco v Illinois
50 263M
340 US 918
Illinois
01/06 1951 CERT · 1 1

Justice	Vote
Minton	D
Clark	D
Burton	D
Jackson	
Douglas	G
Frankfr	D
Reed	D
Black	D
Vinson	D

Willis v Utecht
50 266M
340 US 915
CCA 8th
12/30 1950 CERT · 1 1

Justice	Vote
Minton	D
Clark	D
Burton	D
Jackson	D
Douglas	D
Frankfr	D
Reed	D
Black	D
Vinson	G

Kumitis v Pennsylvania
50 271M
340 US 922
Pennsylvania
01/13 1951 CERT · 1 1

Justice	Vote
Minton	D
Clark	D
Burton	D
Jackson	
Douglas	G
Frankfr	D
Reed	G
Black	D
Vinson	D

Baker v Atlantic Coast Line RR
50 288M
340 US 939
North Carolina
02/26 1951 CERT · 1 1

Justice	Vote
Minton	D
Clark	D
Burton	D
Jackson	
Douglas	G
Frankfr	D
Reed	D
Black	D
Vinson	D

George v Louisiana
50 291M
340 US 949
Lousiana
03/10 1951 CERT · 1 1

Justice	Vote
Minton	D
Clark	D
Burton	D
Jackson	
Douglas	G
Frankfr	D
Reed	D
Black	D
Vinson	D

Moore v Mead Service Company
50 294M
340 US 944 50 297A
CCA 10th
03/10 1951 CERT · 1 1 · 03/15 1951 REPORT · 1 1

Justice	CERT	REPORT
Minton	GM	>
Clark	GM	>
Burton	GM	>
Jackson	GM	>
Douglas	GM	>
Frankfr	GM	>
Reed	GM	>
Black	GM	>
Vinson	GM	>

DeVane v U.S. Court Of Appeals
50 302M
340 US 941
CCA 5th
02/26 1951 MNDMUS · 1 1 · 03/03 1951 MNDMUS · 1 2

Justice	02/26	03/03
Minton	D	G
Clark		G
Burton		G
Jackson		G
Douglas	D	G
Frankfr		
Reed	D	G
Black		
Vinson	D	G

James v Washington
50 303M
341 US 911 50 304M
Washington
04/14 1951 CERT · 1 1

Justice	Vote
Minton	D
Clark	D
Burton	D
Jackson	D
Douglas	
Frankfr	G
Reed	G
Black	G
Vinson	D

Wells v California
50 324M
340 US 937
California
02/26 1951 CERT · 1 1

Justice	Vote
Minton	D
Clark	D
Burton	D
Jackson	D
Douglas	D
Frankfr	
Reed	G
Black	D
Vinson	D

Mahler v Michigan
50 325M
340 US 949
Michigan
03/10 1951 CERT · 1 1

Justice	Vote
Minton	D
Clark	D
Burton	D
Jackson	D
Douglas	D
Frankfr	
Reed	G
Black	G
Vinson	D

Pennsylvania (Johnson) v Dye
50 334M
341 US 911
Pennsylvania
04/14 1951 CERT — 1 1

Justice	Vote
Minton	D
Clark	D
Burton	D
Jackson	
Douglas	D
Frankfr	G
Reed	G
Black	
Vinson	D

North Dakota (Wright) v Nygaard
50 339M
341 US 921
North Dakota
04/28 1951 CERT — 1 1

Justice	Vote
Minton	D
Clark	D
Burton	D
Jackson	D
Douglas	D
Frankfr	D
Reed	D
Black	
Vinson	G

Marella v Burke
50 341M
341 US 911
Pennsylvania
04/14 1951 CERT — 1 1

Justice	Vote
Minton	D
Clark	D
Burton	
Jackson	G
Douglas	G
Frankfr	D
Reed	D
Black	D
Vinson	D

Paul v Burford
50 372M
341 US 922
Oklahoma
04/28 1951 CERT — 1 1

Justice	Vote
Minton	D
Clark	D
Burton	D
Jackson	D
Douglas	D
Frankfr	D
Reed	
Black	G
Vinson	G

Rowland v Chesapeake & Ohio RR
50 380M
341 US 923
West Virginia
04/28 1951 CERT — 1 1

Justice	Vote
Minton	D
Clark	D
Burton	D
Jackson	D
Douglas	D
Frankfr	G
Reed	
Black	G
Vinson	D

Davis v O'Connell
50 388M
341 US 941
CCA 8th
05/26 1951 CERT — 1 1

Justice	Vote
Minton	D
Clark	D
Burton	
Jackson	G
Douglas	G
Frankfr	
Reed	D
Black	D
Vinson	D

McCarley (Ex Parte)
50 413M
341 US 902
04/07 1951 MNDMUS — 1 1

Justice	Vote
Minton	D
Clark	D
Burton	G
Jackson	D
Douglas	D
Frankfr	D
Reed	
Black	G
Vinson	D

City Of Paducah v Shelbourne
50 415M
341 US 902
West Virginia
04/07 1951 MNDMUS — 1 1

Justice	Vote
Minton	D
Clark	D
Burton	D
Jackson	D
Douglas	D
Frankfr	D
Reed	D
Black	
Vinson	G

McGee v Jones
50 417M
340 US 950
03/24 1951 HABEAS — 1 1

Justice	Vote
Minton	D
Clark	D
Burton	G
Jackson	D
Douglas	D
Frankfr	D
Reed	D
Black	
Vinson	D

Fouquette v Nevada
50 438M
341 US 932
Nevada
05/12 1951 CERT — 1 1

Justice	Vote
Minton	D
Clark	D
Burton	D
Jackson	D
Douglas	G
Frankfr	
Reed	D
Black	D
Vinson	D

Mares v Hill
50 439M
341 US 933
Utah
05/12 1951 CERT — 1 1

Justice	Vote
Minton	D
Clark	D
Burton	D
Jackson	D
Douglas	D
Frankfr	D
Reed	
Black	G
Vinson	D

Chiarella v U.S.
50 447M
341 US 946
CCA 2d
06/02 1951 CERT — 1 1

Justice	Vote
Minton	G
Clark	G
Burton	G
Jackson	G
Douglas	G
Frankfr	G
Reed	G
Black	G
Vinson	G

Babich v Wisconsin
50 451M
341 US 954
Wisconsin
06/02 1951 CERT — 1 1

Justice	Vote
Minton	D
Clark	D
Burton	D
Jackson	D
Douglas	G
Frankfr	G
Reed	
Black	G
Vinson	D

Porch v Georgia
50 458M
341 US 954
Georgia
06/02 1951 CERT — 1 1

Justice	Vote
Minton	D
Clark	D
Burton	D
Jackson	D
Douglas	G
Frankfr	G
Reed	
Black	G
Vinson	D

Daranowich v U.S.
50 466M
341 US 942
CCA 2d
06/04 1951 REPORT — 1 1

Justice	Vote
Minton	V
Clark	V
Burton	V
Jackson	V
Douglas	V
Frankfr	V
Reed	V
Black	
Vinson	

Brown v North Carolina
50 488M
341 US 943
North Carolina
05/26 1951 CERT — 1 1

Justice	Vote
Minton	D
Clark	D
Burton	D
Jackson	D
Douglas	G
Frankfr	G
Reed	
Black	G
Vinson	D

Appendix G

U.S. Supreme Court
October 1951 Term

Georgia Railroad & Banking v Redwine
51 1A 50 4A 49 454A
342 US 299
Vinson 12/12/51 DC ND Georgia

	12/03 1949 JURIS 1 1	02/18 1950 MERITS 1 1	11/03 1951 REARGUE 1 1	12/01 1951 MERITS 1 1	01/28 1952 REPORT 1 1
Minton				R	R
Clark	N A	X	Y	R	R
Burton	N	H	B Y	R	R
Jackson	N	H	Y	R	R
Douglas			Y	R	R
Frankfr	N	H	Y	R	R
Reed	N	H	Y	R	R
Black	N A	H	B	R	R
Vinson	N		Y A	R	A

Stefanelli v Minard
51 2A 50 458A
342 US 117
Frankfr 10/23/51 CCA 3rd

	05/12 1951 CERT 1 1	10/20 1951 MERITS 1 1	12/03 1951 REPORT 1 1
Minton	G	X	A
Clark	G D	A	A
Burton	G D	A	A
Jackson	G	R	R
Douglas	G	A	A
Frankfr	G	A	A
Reed	G D	A	A
Black	G D	R X	R
Vinson	G D	A	A

U.S. v Jeffers
51 3A 50 519A
342 US 48
Clark 10/23/51 CCA DC

	03/24 1951 CERT 1 1	10/20 1951 MERITS 1 1	11/03 1951 REPORT 1 1
Minton	G D	A	A
Clark	G	A	A
Burton	G D	A	A
Jackson	G	A	A
Douglas	G	A	A
Frankfr	G	A	A
Reed	G	R	R
Black	G	R X	R
Vinson	G	A	A

U.S. v Coplon
51 4A 50 529A
342 US 920 51 272A 50 214A
CCA 2d

	01/12 1952 CERT 1 1	01/26 1952 CERT 1 2
Minton	G	
Clark	G	
Burton		
Jackson	G	G
Douglas	D	D
Frankfr	D	D
Reed	G	
Black	G	D
Vinson	G	D

U.S. v Carignan
51 5A 50 530A
342 US 36 51 174A
Reed 10/23/51 CCA 9th

	05/19 1951 CERT 1 1	10/13 1951 MERITS 1 1	11/13 1951 REPORT 1 1
Minton	G	R	R
Clark	G	R	R
Burton	G	R	R
Jackson	G		R
Douglas		D	R
Frankfr			R
Reed	G	R	R
Black	G	R A	R
Vinson	G	A	R

Brannan v Stark
51 6A 50 536A
342 US 451 51 7A 50 537A
Black 10/23/51 Clark 12/26/51 CCA DC

	04/07 1951 CERT 1 1	04/14 1951 CERT 1 2	10/13 1951 MERITS 1 1	03/03 1952 REPORT 1 1
Minton	D			
Clark	D	G		
Burton		G		
Jackson			X	
Douglas	D			
Frankfr	D		A	A
Reed		G	A	R
Black	D	G	A	R
Vinson			A	A

Dairymen's League Co-operative v Stark
51 7A 50 537A
342 US 451 51 6A 50 536A
Black 10/23/51 Clark 12/26/51 CCA DC

	04/07 1951 CERT 1 1	04/14 1951 CERT 1 2	10/13 1951 MERITS 1 1	03/03 1952 REPORT 1 1
Minton	D			
Clark	D	G		
Burton		G		
Jackson			X	
Douglas	D		A	A
Frankfr	D		A	A
Reed		G	A	R
Black	D	G	A	R
Vinson			A	A

Adler v Board Of Education
51 8A 50 541A
342 US 485 51 312A
Minton 01/15/52 New York

	06/02 1951 JURIS 1 1	01/05 1952 MERITS 1 1	03/03 1952 REPORT 1 1
Minton	NR		
Clark	N		A
Burton	N		A
Jackson	N	R	A
Douglas	N		A
Frankfr	N	X	A
Reed	N	R	A
Black	N		A
Vinson	NR		A

Doremus v Board Of Education
51 9A 50 556A
342 US 429
Jackson 02/05/52 New Jersey

	03/10 1951 JURIS 1 1	02/02 1952 JURIS 1 2	03/03 1952 REPORT 1 1
Minton	P S	S	S
Clark	P	S X	S
Burton	P		S
Jackson	P	N	N
Douglas	P S	S	S
Frankfr	P S	S	S
Reed	P	N V	N
Black	P	N	N
Vinson		S	S

U.S. (Giese) v Chamberlin
51 10A 50 564A
342 US 845
CCA 7th

Justice	CERT 04/07 1951	MERITS 10/13 1951	REPORT 10/15 1951	REHEAR 11/10 1951
Minton	G		R	B
Clark	G	A	R	B
Burton	G	A	A	B
Jackson	GV			B
Douglas	GVH	D		B
Frankfr	D			
Reed	G			
Black	G	A	A	Y
Vinson	G	A	A	Y

U.S. v Wunderlich
51 11A 50 584A
342 US 98
Minton 11/13/51 Ct Cls

Justice	CERT 05/05 1951	MERITS 11/10 1951	REPORT 11/26 1951
Minton	G	R	R
Clark	G	R	R
Burton	G		
Jackson	D	X	A
Douglas	D	X	A
Frankfr	D	A	A
Reed			
Black	G	R	R
Vinson	G	R	R

Morissette v U.S.
51 12A 50 593A
342 US 246
Jackson 10/23/51 CCA 6th

Justice	CERT 05/05 1951	MERITS 10/15 1951	REPORT 01/07 1952
Minton	G	R	R
Clark	G	R	R
Burton	G	R	R
Jackson	G	R	R
Douglas	D	A	A
Frankfr	D	A	A
Reed	G	R	R
Black	G	R	R
Vinson	G	R	R

U.S. v Fortier
51 14A 50 602A
342 US 160 51 15A 50 603A
CCA 1st

Justice	CERT 05/05 1951	MERITS 10/13 1951	REPORT 12/11 1951
Minton			A
Clark	G	A	A
Burton	G	A	A
Jackson	G	A	A
Douglas	D	A	A
Frankfr	G	A	A
Reed	G	A	A
Black	D	A	A
Vinson	D	A	A

U.S. v Duvarney
51 15A 50 603A
342 US 902 51 14A 50 602A
CCA 1st

Justice	CERT 05/05 1951	CERT 12/31 1951
Minton	G	D
Clark	G	D
Burton	G	D
Jackson	G	D
Douglas	G	D
Frankfr	G	D
Reed		
Black	D	D
Vinson	D	D

McMahon v U.S.
51 17A 50 606A
342 US 25
Jackson 10/23/51 CCA 3rd

Justice	CERT 05/12 1951	MERITS 10/22 1951	REPORT 11/05 1951
Minton	G	R	R
Clark	G	R	R
Burton	G	RO	
Jackson	G	R	R
Douglas	G		
Frankfr	G		
Reed	G		
Black	G	R	R
Vinson	G	R	R

Bindczyck v Finucane
51 18A 50 612A
342 US 76
Frankfr 11/01/51 CCA DC

Justice	CERT 04/28 1951	MERITS 10/15 1951	REPORT 11/26 1951
Minton	D	D	A
Clark			
Burton	D	R	R
Jackson	G	R	A
Douglas	G		
Frankfr	G		
Reed	G		
Black	G	R	R
Vinson	D	X	A

U.S. v Oregon State Medical Society
51 19A 50 615A
343 US 326
Jackson 01/15/52 DC Oregon

Justice	JURIS 04/07 1951	MERITS 01/12 1952	REPORT 04/28 1952
Minton	P		A
Clark	P	R	A
Burton	P	R	R
Jackson	S	X	A
Douglas	S		
Frankfr			A
Reed	P		A
Black	N	R	R
Vinson	P		A

U.S. v Smith
51 20A 50 630A
342 US 225 51 162A
Douglas 12/12/51 DC WD Texas

Justice	JURIS 04/14 1951	MERITS 12/08 1951	REPORT 01/07 1952
Minton	N		A
Clark	N	R	A
Burton	N	R	R
Jackson	N	X	A
Douglas	N		
Frankfr	N		A
Reed	N	R	R
Black	N		A
Vinson	N		A

Gem Manufacturing v Packard Motor Car
51 21A 50 633A
342 US 802
CCA 7th

	05/12 1951 CERT
	1 1
Minton	G
Clark	G
Burton	G
Jackson	G
Douglas	D
Frankfr	
Reed	G
Black	G
Vinson	G

Gardner v Panama RR Company
51 22A 50 638A
342 US 29
CCA 5th

	05/19 1951 CERT	10/15 1951 MERITS	11/05 1951 REPORT
	1 1	1 1	1 1
Minton	G	R	R
Clark	G	R	R
Burton	G	R	R
Jackson	G D	R	R
Douglas		R	R
Frankfr		R	R
Reed	G	R	R
Black	G	R	R
Vinson	G		

U.S. v Hayman
51 23A 50 642A
342 US 205
Vinson 10/23/51 CCA 9th

	05/12 1951 CERT	10/20 1951 MERITS	01/07 1952 REPORT
	1 1	1 1	1 1
Minton	G	AJ	>
Clark	G	AJ	>
Burton	G	AJ	>
Jackson	G	AJ	>
Douglas	G D		>
Frankfr	G	AJ	>
Reed	G	S AJ	S >
Black	G		
Vinson	G	AJ	>

Sulphen Estates v U.S.
51 25A 50 668A
342 US 19
Douglas 10/23/51 DC SD New York

	05/12 1951 JURIS	10/15 1951 MERITS	11/05 1951 REPORT
	1 1	1 1	1 1
Minton		A	
Clark	A		
Burton	P	A	S
Jackson		A	S
Douglas	P	A	S
Frankfr	A	A	
Reed	P	A	N
Black	P	A	S
Vinson	P		

Lorain Journal Company v U.S.
51 26A 50 669A
342 US 143
Burton 10/23/51 DC ND Ohio

	04/28 1951 JURIS	10/22 1951 MERITS	12/11 1951 REPORT
	1 1	1 1	1 1
Minton		A	A
Clark	A	A	A
Burton	N		A
Jackson		A	A
Douglas	N		A
Frankfr		R	A
Reed	N	R	A
Black	N	A	
Vinson		A	

Fremont Cake & Meal v Wilson & Company
51 28A 50 675A
342 US 812
Nebraska

	10/02 1951 CERT
	1 1
Minton	D
Clark	D
Burton	D
Jackson	
Douglas	G
Frankfr	
Reed	D
Black	G
Vinson	D

Cook v Cook
51 30A 50 688A 50 373M
342 US 126
Douglas 11/13/51 Vermont

	04/14 1951 CERT	04/21 1951 CERT	11/10 1951 MERITS	12/03 1951 REPORT
	1 1	1 2	1 1	1 1
Minton	G		R	R
Clark	G	D	R	R
Burton	G		R	R
Jackson		G	R	R
Douglas	G	D		
Frankfr		G	R	R
Reed	G		R	R
Black	G	D	R	R
Vinson	G	D	A	A

Los Angeles Building Trades v LeBaron
51 31A
342 US 802
CCA 9th

	10/02 1951 CERT	10/08 1951 REPORT
	1 1	1 1
Minton	GVI	VI
Clark	GVI	VI
Burton	GVI	VI
Jackson	GVI	VI
Douglas	GVI	VI
Frankfr	GVI	VI
Reed	GVI	VI
Black	GVI	VI
Vinson	GVI	VI

Carlson v Landon
51 35A 50 703A
342 US 524 51 136A
Reed 12/12/51 CCA 9th

	04/28 1951 BAIL	10/02 1951 CERT	12/01 1951 MERITS	03/10 1952 REPORT	04/26 1952 REHEAR	06/07 1952 STAY
	1 1	1 1	1 1	1 1	1 1	1 1
Minton	Y	G		A		
Clark	Y	G	R	A	B	Y
Burton	Y	G		R	B	Y
Jackson	Y	G	R	R	H	
Douglas	Y	G		A	H	Y
Frankfr	Y	G	R	A		Y
Reed	Y	G		R	B	
Black		G	R	R	H	B
Vinson	Y	G		A		B

Palmer v Ashe
51 38A 50 707A 50 273M
342 US 134 71 7M
Black 11/13/51 Pennsylvania

	04/28 1951 CERT 1 1	11/10 1951 MERITS 1 1	12/11 1951 REPORT 1 1
Minton	G		A
Clark	G	R	
Burton	G	R	A
Jackson	G		
Douglas	G	R	A
Frankfr	G		
Reed	G	R	A
Black	G	R	A
Vinson	G	R	A

Lynn v Lynn
51 40A 50 711A
342 US 849
New York

	10/13 1951 CERT 1 2
Minton	D
Clark	D
Burton	D
Jackson	X D
Douglas	D
Frankfr	D
Reed	G G
Black	G
Vinson	D

Brack v Gross
51 42A 50 715A
342 US 813
CCA 4th

	10/02 1951 CERT 1 1
Minton	D
Clark	G D
Burton	D
Jackson	G D
Douglas	D
Frankfr	D
Reed	D
Black	D
Vinson	D

Harisiades v Shaughnessy
51 43A 50 716A
342 US 580 51 206A 51 264A CCA 2d
Jackson 12/12/51 CCA 2d

	10/02 1951 CERT 1 1	12/08 1951 MERITS 1 1	03/10 1952 REPORT 1 1
Minton	G		A
Clark	G		A
Burton	G		A
Jackson	G	R	R
Douglas	G	X	A
Frankfr	G		A
Reed	G	R	A
Black	G		A
Vinson	G		A

U.S. v Jordan
51 46A 50 720A
342 US 911 50 47A 50 721A CCA 6th
Clark 12/12/51 CCA 6th

	10/02 1951 CERT 1 1	12/01 1951 MERITS 1 1	01/14 1952 REPORT 1 1
Minton			A
Clark	D	R	R
Burton			A
Jackson	GL		
Douglas		R	R
Frankfr		S	S
Reed	GL	R	R
Black	GL	R	R
Vinson			A

U.S. v Shannon
51 47A 50 721A
342 US 288 51 46A 50 720A CCA 4th
Clark 12/12/51 CCA 4th

	10/02 1951 CERT 1 1	12/01 1951 MERITS 1 1	01/14 1952 REPORT 1 1
Minton		R	R
Clark	G	R	R
Burton			A
Jackson			A
Douglas		R	S
Frankfr		S	A
Reed	G	R	R
Black		R	A
Vinson		R	A

U.S. v Loyal Band Of Creek Indians
51 48A 50 722A
342 US 813
Ct Cls

	10/02 1951 CERT 1 1
Minton	D
Clark	D
Burton	
Jackson	G
Douglas	D
Frankfr	D
Reed	
Black	G
Vinson	G

U.S. v Menominee Tribe Of Indians
51 49A 50 723A
342 US 801
Ct Cls

	06/02 1951 JURIS 1 1
Minton	A
Clark	A
Burton	
Jackson	
Douglas	S
Frankfr	
Reed	A
Black	
Vinson	A

Canadian Aviator v U.S.
51 50A 50 724A
342 US 813
CCA 2d

	10/02 1951 CERT 1 1
Minton	D
Clark	D
Burton	D
Jackson	
Douglas	D
Frankfr	D
Reed	G
Black	D
Vinson	D

Haas v Palace Hotel Company
51 51A 50 725A
342 US 813
California

	10/02 1951 CERT 1 1
Minton	D
Clark	D
Burton	D
Jackson	
Douglas	G
Frankfr	D
Reed	D
Black	G
Vinson	G

Parry Navigation v Todd Shipyards
51 54A 50 728A
342 US 918 51 62A
CCA 2d

	10/02 1951 CERT 1 1	01/26 1952 CERT 1 2
Minton		D
Clark	H	D
Burton	H	D
Jackson		D
Douglas		D
Frankfr		D
Reed	GH	D
Black	H	D
Vinson		D

Bates v Batte
51 61A 50 741A
342 US 815
CCA 5th

	10/02 1951 CERT 1 1
Minton	D
Clark	D
Burton	D
Jackson	
Douglas	D
Frankfr	G
Reed	
Black	D
Vinson	D

Halcyon Lines v Haenn Ship Ceiling
51 62A 50 742A
342 US 282 51 197A 51 54A
Black 12/12/51 CCA 3rd

	10/02 1951 CERT 1 1	12/01 1951 MERITS 1 1
Minton	G	A
Clark	G	A
Burton	G	R
Jackson	G	A
Douglas	G	A
Frankfr	G	A
Reed	G	R
Black	G	
Vinson	G	X

Latvian State Cargo v McGrath
51 65A 50 747A
342 US 816
CCA DC

	10/02 1951 CERT 1 1
Minton	D
Clark	D
Burton	G
Jackson	D
Douglas	D
Frankfr	D
Reed	D
Black	D
Vinson	D

North Arlington Bank v Kearny Federal
51 66A 50 748A
342 US 816
CCA 3rd

	10/02 1951 CERT 1 1
Minton	D
Clark	D
Burton	G
Jackson	D
Douglas	D
Frankfr	D
Reed	G
Black	D
Vinson	D

U.S. v Sims
51 68A 50 750A
342 US 816
CCA 3rd

Justice	10/02 1951 CERT 1-1	10/06 1951 CERT 1-2
Minton	D	D
Clark		
Burton		
Jackson	G	G
Douglas	D	D
Frankfr		
Reed	G	G
Black		
Vinson	X	D

Murray v U.S.
51 69A 50 755A
342 US 816
CCA 6th

Justice	10/02 1951 CERT 1-1	10/06 1951 CERT 1-2
Minton	D	D
Clark	G	G
Burton		
Jackson		
Douglas	G	G
Frankfr		
Reed	G	
Black		
Vinson	D	D

Taylor v Hubbell
51 76A
342 US 818
CCA 9th

Justice	10/02 1951 CERT 1-1
Minton	D
Clark	D
Burton	D
Jackson	D
Douglas	D
Frankfr	D
Reed	
Black	G
Vinson	D

Pacific Insurance Company v U.S.
51 77A 50 764A
342 US 857
CCA 9th

Justice	10/02 1951 CERT 1-1	10/20 1951 MERITS 1-1	10/22 1951 REPORT 1-1
Minton	G	SI	SI
Clark	G	SI	SI
Burton	G	SI	SI
Jackson	G	SI	SI
Douglas	G	SI	SI
Frankfr	G	SI	SI
Reed	G	SI	SI
Black	G	SI	SI
Vinson	G	SI	SI

Von Moltke v Gillies
51 78A 50 765A
343 US 922
CCA 6th

Justice	10/02 1951 CERT 1-1	03/01 1952 MERITS 1-1	04/19 1952 MERITS 1-2	04/21 1952 REPORT 1-1
Minton	D			
Clark				
Burton	D	R	R	R
Jackson	G			
Douglas	G			
Frankfr		R	R	R
Reed				
Black	G	R	R	R
Vinson	D			

Keenan v Burke
51 80A 50 767A 50 407M
342 US 881 51 81A 51 82A
Pennsylvania

Justice	05/26 1951 CERT 1-1	11/10 1951 MERITS 1-1	11/26 1951 REPORT 1-1
Minton	G	R	R
Clark	GR	R	R
Burton	G	R	R
Jackson	G	R	R
Douglas	G	R	R
Frankfr	G	R	R
Reed	GR	R	R
Black	G	R	R
Vinson			

Jankowski v Burke
51 81A 50 768A 50 418M
342 US 881 51 80A 51 82A
Pennsylvania

Justice	05/26 1951 CERT 1-1	11/10 1951 MERITS 1-1	11/26 1951 REPORT 1-1
Minton	G	R	R
Clark	G	R	R
Burton	G	R	R
Jackson	G	R	R
Douglas	G	R	R
Frankfr			
Reed	G	R	R
Black	D		
Vinson	D		

Foulke v Burke
51 82A 50 769A 50 419M
342 US 881 50 80A 51 81A
Pennsylvania

Justice	05/26 1951 CERT 1-1	11/10 1951 MERITS 1-1	11/26 1951 REPORT 1-1
Minton	G	R	R
Clark	G	R	R
Burton	G	R	R
Jackson	G	R	R
Douglas	G	R	R
Frankfr			
Reed	G	R	R
Black	D		
Vinson	D		

Rochin v California
51 83A 50 770A 50 450M
342 US 165
Frankfr 10/23/51 California

Justice	05/26 1951 CERT 1-1	10/22 1951 MERITS 1-1	01/02 1952 REPORT 1-1
Minton	G	R	R
Clark	G	R	R
Burton	G	R	R
Jackson	G	R	R
Douglas	G	R	R
Frankfr	G	R	R
Reed	G		
Black	D		
Vinson	D		

Perkins v Benguet Consolidated Mining
51 85A 50 772A
342 US 437
Burton 02/26/52 Ohio

Justice	10/02 1951 CERT 1-1	12/01 1951 MERITS 1-1	03/03 1952 REPORT 1-1
Minton	G	R	R
Clark	G	R	R
Burton	G	R	R
Jackson	G	R	R
Douglas	G	R	R
Frankfr	G		
Reed	G		
Black	G		
Vinson	D		

Hughes v U.S.
51 86A 50 773A
342 US 353
Black 01/15/52 DC SD New York

Justice	10/02 1951 JURIS 1-1	01/12 1952 MERITS 1-1	02/04 1952 REPORT 1-1
Minton	N	R	R
Clark	N		
Burton	N		
Jackson		A	
Douglas	N		
Frankfr		R	R
Reed			
Black		R	R
Vinson		R	R

Alabama PSC v Louisville & Nashville RR
51 89A 50 776A
342 US 802 51 159A
DC MD Alabama

Justice	10/02 1951 JURIS 1-1	10/08 1951 REPORT 1-1
Minton	R	R
Clark	R	R
Burton	R	N
Jackson		
Douglas	R	Z
Frankfr		
Reed	R	R
Black	R	R
Vinson	R	R

U.S. v Halseth
51 91A 50 778A
342 US 277
Minton 12/12/51 DC ED Wisconsin

Justice	JURIS 10/02 1951	MERITS 12/01 1951	REPORT 01/07 1952
Minton	N		A
Clark	N	A	A
Burton	N	R	R
Jackson	N		
Douglas	N	R	R
Frankfr	N	A	A
Reed	N	A	A
Black	N	A	A
Vinson	N	A	A

Thorp v Board Of Trustees
51 92A
342 US 803
New Jersey

Justice	CERT 10/02 1951
Minton	GVI
Clark	GVI
Burton	GVI
Jackson	GVI
Douglas	GVI
Frankfr	GVI
Reed	GVI
Black	GVI
Vinson	GVI

Gallegos v Nebraska
51 94A 50 781A 50 347M
342 US 55
Reed 10/23/51 Nebraska

Justice	CERT 06/02 1951	MERITS 10/13 1951	REPORT 11/26 1951
Minton	G		A
Clark	G	R	A
Burton	G		A
Jackson			
Douglas	G	R	A
Frankfr			
Reed	G		A
Black	G	R	A
Vinson	G		A

Jennings v Illinois
51 95A 50 782A 50 452M
342 US 104 51 96A 51 375A 51 35M
Vinson 11/13/51 Illinois

Justice	CERT 06/02 1951	MERITS 11/10 1951	REPORT 12/03 1951
Minton	G	A	A
Clark	G	A	
Burton			
Jackson	D	v	A
Douglas	G	>	>
Frankfr	G	>	>
Reed		>	
Black	D	>	>
Vinson	G	>	>

La Frana v Illinois
51 96A 50 481A
342 US 104 51 95A 51 375A
Vinson 11/13/51 Illinois

Justice	CERT 06/02 1951	MERITS 11/10 1951	REPORT 12/03 1951
Minton	G	A	A
Clark	G	A	
Burton			
Jackson	D	v	A
Douglas	G	>	>
Frankfr	G	>	>
Reed		>	
Black	D	>	>
Vinson	G	>	>

Baird v Guaranty Trust Company
51 98A
342 US 819
New York

Justice	CERT 10/02 1951
Minton	D
Clark	D
Burton	D
Jackson	D
Douglas	D
Frankfr	D
Reed	
Black	D
Vinson	

U.S. v Bloom
51 100A
342 US 912 51 299A 51 300A
New York

Justice	CERT 11/03 1951	MERITS 01/12 1952	REPORT 01/14 1952
Minton	G		A
Clark	G		A
Burton	G		A
Jackson	G	D	A
Douglas			A
Frankfr	G		A
Reed	G		A
Black	G		A
Vinson	G		A

Thorpe v Landstrom
51 105A
342 US 819
CCA 8th

Justice	CERT 10/02 1951
Minton	D
Clark	D
Burton	D
Jackson	D
Douglas	G
Frankfr	D
Reed	G
Black	G
Vinson	D

Mattox v U.S.
51 110A
342 US 820
CCA 9th

Justice	CERT 10/02 1951
Minton	D
Clark	D
Burton	D
Jackson	D
Douglas	D
Frankfr	
Reed	D
Black	
Vinson	D

Wabash v Ross Electric
51 114A
342 US 820
CCA 2d

Justice	CERT 10/02 1951
Minton	D
Clark	D
Burton	G
Jackson	G
Douglas	D
Frankfr	D
Reed	D
Black	D
Vinson	D

Winn v Pittston Company
51 116A
342 US 803
Virginia

Justice	JURIS 10/02 1951
Minton	S
Clark	S
Burton	S
Jackson	N
Douglas	S
Frankfr	S
Reed	S
Black	S
Vinson	S

Beauharnais v Illinois
343 US 250
Frankfr 12/12/51 Illinois

Justice	CERT 10/02 1951	MERITS 12/01 1951	REPORT 04/28 1952
Minton	G		
Clark	G	A	
Burton	G		
Jackson	G		
Douglas	D	R	R
Frankfr	G		
Reed	G	R	R
Black	D	R	R
Vinson	D		

Gray v Board Of Trustees Tennessee
51 120A 51 159M
342 US 517
DC ED Tennessee

Justice	10/02 1951 JURIS	10/13 1951 MNDMUS	12/01 1951 REHEAR	03/03 1952 REPORT
Minton	S		Y	VI
Clark	P	G	Y	VI
Burton	P	G	Y	VI
Jackson	S	G	Y	VI
Douglas	S		Y	VI
Frankfr	S	D	B	VI
Reed	P		Y	VI
Black	P	G	Y	VI
Vinson	S	G	Y	VI

N.L.R.B. v American National Insurance
51 126A
343 US 395
Vinson 03/18/52 CCA 5th

Justice	10/02 1951 CERT	03/08 1952 MERITS	05/26 1952 REPORT
Minton	G	R	R
Clark	G		A
Burton		A	A
Jackson	D	A	A
Douglas		R	R
Frankfr	D	R	A
Reed	D	X	A
Black	D	A	A
Vinson	D	R	A

Bagsby v Trustees Of Pleasant Grove
51 127A
342 US 821
Texas

Justice	10/02 1951 CERT
Minton	D
Clark	D
Burton	G
Jackson	
Douglas	
Frankfr	
Reed	D
Black	D
Vinson	D

Risberg v Duluth Missabe & Iron Range
51 128A
342 US 832
Minnesota

Justice	10/02 1951 CERT
Minton	D
Clark	D
Burton	D
Jackson	D
Douglas	
Frankfr	D
Reed	G
Black	G
Vinson	D

Georgia v Wenger
51 130A
342 US 822
CCA 7th

Justice	10/02 1951 CERT
Minton	
Clark	
Burton	
Jackson	X
Douglas	
Frankfr	
Reed	
Black	
Vinson	

Kime v U.S.
51 133A
342 US 823
CCA 7th

Justice	10/02 1951 CERT
Minton	D
Clark	D
Burton	
Jackson	D
Douglas	
Frankfr	
Reed	D
Black	
Vinson	D

A/S J. Ludwig Mowinckels v Isbrandtsen
51 134A
342 US 950 51 135A 51 15M
DC SD New York

Justice	10/02 1951 JURIS	02/02 1952 MERITS	02/04 1952 MERITS	03/10 1952 REPORT
Minton	N	R	R	R
Clark	N	R	R	R
Burton	N	R	R	R
Jackson		A		
Douglas	N		A	A
Frankfr	N	R	R	R
Reed		A	A	A
Black	N	A	A	A
Vinson				

Federal Maritime Board v U.S.
51 135A
342 US 950 51 134A 51 15M
DC SD New York

Justice	10/02 1951 JURIS	02/02 1952 MERITS	02/04 1952 MERITS	03/10 1952 REPORT
Minton	N	R	R	R
Clark	N	R	R	R
Burton	N	R	R	R
Jackson		A		
Douglas	N		A	A
Frankfr	N	R	R	R
Reed		A	A	A
Black	N	A	A	A
Vinson				

Butterfield v Zydok
51 136A
342 US 524 51 35A CCA 6th
Reed 12/12/51 CCA 6th

Justice	10/02 1951 CERT	12/01 1951 MERITS	03/10 1952 REPORT
Minton	G	R	>
Clark	G	R	>
Burton	G		A
Jackson	G	R	>
Douglas	G		A
Frankfr	G	R	>
Reed	G		A
Black	G	R	>
Vinson	G		A

Bazzell v U.S.
51 137A
342 US 849 51 138A
CCA 7th

Justice	10/13 1951 CERT
Minton	D
Clark	D
Burton	
Jackson	D
Douglas	D
Frankfr	D
Reed	D
Black	
Vinson	G

Lasby v U.S.
51 138A
342 US 849 51 137A
CCA 7th

Justice	10/13 1951 CERT
Minton	D
Clark	D
Burton	
Jackson	D
Douglas	D
Frankfr	D
Reed	D
Black	
Vinson	G

Marks v U.S.
51 141A
342 US 823
CCA 9th

Justice	10/03 1951 CERT
Minton	D
Clark	D
Burton	
Jackson	D
Douglas	D
Frankfr	D
Reed	D
Black	
Vinson	G

Sutton v Leib
51 143A
342 US 402
Reed 12/12/51 CCA 7th

	CERT 10/13 1951 (1 2)	MERITS 12/08 1951 (1 1)	REPORT 03/03 1952 (1 1)
Minton	D		R
Clark	D		R
Burton	D	S	R
Jackson			R
Douglas		A	R
Frankfr			R
Reed	D		
Black		A	R
Vinson	D	A	A

Muth v Aetna Oil Company
51 147A
342 US 844 51 549A
CCA 7th

	CERT 10/13 1951 (1 2)	REPORT 10/15 1951 (1 1)
Minton	D	>
Clark	D	>
Burton	D	>
Jackson	GV	>
Douglas	D	>
Frankfr	GV	>
Reed	GV	>
Black	D	>
Vinson	D GV	V

U.S. v Great Northern RR Company
51 151A
343 US 562
Vinson 01/15/52 DC Minnesota

	JURIS 10/02 1951 (1 1)	MERITS 01/12 1952 (1 1)	REPORT 06/02 1952 (1 1)
Minton	N		R
Clark	N		R
Burton	N	R	R
Jackson	N		R
Douglas	N		R
Frankfr	N	R	R
Reed	N		R
Black	N		
Vinson	N	A	A

Allen v City Of Long Beach
51 155A
342 US 804
California

	JURIS 10/02 1951 (1 1)
Minton	S
Clark	S
Burton	
Jackson	N
Douglas	S
Frankfr	S
Reed	S
Black	S
Vinson	S

Terrio v U.S.
51 157A
342 US 825
CCA 5th

	CERT 10/13 1951 (1 2)	REPORT 10/15 1951 (1 1)
Minton	D	>
Clark	GV	>
Burton	D	>
Jackson	GV	>
Douglas	D	>
Frankfr	GV	>
Reed	GV	>
Black	D	>
Vinson	GV	V

Lilly v C.I.R.
51 158A
343 US 90
Burton 12/12/51 CCA 4th

	CERT 10/03 1951 (1 1)	MERITS 12/08 1951 (1 1)	REPORT 06/02 1952 (1 1)
Minton	G		R
Clark	G		R
Burton	G		R
Jackson	G		R
Douglas	G	X	R
Frankfr	G		R
Reed	G		R
Black	G		R
Vinson	G	D	R

Florida RPUC v Atlantic Coast Line RR
51 159A
342 US 844 51 89A 51 90A
DC ND Florida

	JURIS 10/02 1951 (1 1)	MERITS 10/13 1951 (1 1)	REPORT 10/15 1951 (1 1)
Minton	R	R	>
Clark	R	VM	>
Burton	R	R	>
Jackson			
Douglas	A	VM	>
Frankfr	A	VM	>
Reed	R	VM	>
Black	R	R	>
Vinson			

Strategical Demolition Torpedo v U.S.
51 160A
342 US 825
Ct Cls

	CERT 10/03 1951 (1 1)
Minton	D
Clark	
Burton	D
Jackson	D
Douglas	G
Frankfr	G
Reed	
Black	D
Vinson	D

U.S. v Dailey
51 162A
342 US 225 51 20A
Douglas 12/12/51 DC DC

	JURIS 10/02 1951 (1 1)	MERITS 12/08 1951 (1 1)	REPORT 01/07 1952 (1 1)
Minton	N	R	R
Clark	N	R	
Burton	N	R	R
Jackson	N		
Douglas	N		
Frankfr	N		
Reed	N	R	R
Black	N	X	
Vinson	N		A

Buck v California
51 165A
343 US 99
Reed 12/12/51 Minton 02/28/52 California

	JURIS 10/02 1951 (1 1)	MERITS 12/01 1951 (1 1)	REPORT 03/10 1952 (1 1)
Minton			
Clark	S		A
Burton	S		A
Jackson	N	R	R
Douglas	N		
Frankfr	N		
Reed			
Black	S S		A
Vinson	N		A

Cates v Haderlein
51 166A
342 US 804
CCA 7th

	CERT 10/03 1951 (1 1)	MERITS 10/08 1951 (1 1)
Minton	GR	RI
Clark	GR	RI
Burton	GR	RI
Jackson	GRI	RI
Douglas	G	
Frankfr	GR	RI
Reed	GR	RI
Black	GR	RI
Vinson	GR	RI

Boyce Motor Lines v U.S.
51 167A
342 US 337
Clark 12/12/51 CCA 3rd

	CERT 10/13 1951 (1 1)	MERITS 12/08 1951 (1 1)	REPORT 01/28 1952 (1 1)
Minton	G	R	
Clark	GQ	R	
Burton	GO		
Jackson			
Douglas	D	R	R
Frankfr			
Reed	D	R	R
Black	D		
Vinson	D	R	R

McGrath v Nagano
51 169A
342 US 916 51 204A
CCA 7th

Justice	CERT 10/03/51 (1 1)	MERITS 12/01/51 (1 1)	MERITS 12/31/51 (1 2)	REPORT 01/28/52 (1 1)
Minton	G			
Clark	G x			
Burton	G		A	A
Jackson	G	A	A	A
Douglas	G	A	A	
Frankfr	G			
Reed	G	R	R	R
Black	G	R		A
Vinson	G	R	A	A

Kaufman v Societe Internationale
51 172A
343 US 156 51 178A
Black 01/15/52 CCA DC

Justice	CERT 10/03/51 (1 1)	CERT 10/13/51 (1 2)	MERITS 01/05/52 (1 1)	REPORT 04/07/52 (1 1)
Minton	D			
Clark	D		R	A
Burton			R	
Jackson	D		R	
Douglas	G	G	R	
Frankfr				
Reed	G	G	R	A
Black	G		R	
Vinson	G	G	R	A

Lykes v U.S.
51 173A
343 US 118
Burton 12/12/51 CCA 5th

Justice	CERT 10/03/51 (1 1)	MERITS 12/01/51 (1 1)	REPORT 03/24/52 (1 1)
Minton	D	D	
Clark	D		A
Burton	D	A	
Jackson		A	A
Douglas	D	A	R
Frankfr	D		R
Reed		A	R
Black	D		
Vinson	D	A	A

Haines v U.S.
51 174A
342 US 888 51 5A
CCA 9th

Justice	CERT 11/24/51 (1 1)
Minton	D
Clark	D
Burton	D
Jackson	G x
Douglas	
Frankfr	
Reed	G
Black	
Vinson	D

Leland v Oregon
51 176A
343 US 790
Clark 02/05/52 Oregon

Justice	JURIS 10/02/51 (1 1)	MERITS 02/02/52 (1 1)	REPORT 06/09/52 (1 1)
Minton	S	A	A
Clark	N	A	A
Burton	S	A	A
Jackson	N	AQ	A
Douglas	N		
Frankfr	S	R	R
Reed	N	A	A
Black	N	R	R
Vinson	S	A	A

Uebersee Finanz v McGrath
51 178A
343 US 205 51 172A
Minton 01/15/52 CCA DC

Justice	CERT 10/13/51 (1 1)	MERITS 01/05/52 (1 1)	REPORT 04/07/52 (1 1)
Minton			J
Clark	D	R	J
Burton	G		J
Jackson	G		J
Douglas	G		J
Frankfr	D		J
Reed	D	R	J
Black			J
Vinson	D	A	J

Kerotest Manufacturing v C-O-Two Fire
51 180A
342 US 180
Frankfr 12/12/51 CCA 3rd

Justice	CERT 10/03/51 (1 1)	MERITS 12/01/51 (1 1)	REPORT 01/02/52 (1 1)
Minton		AS	A
Clark	G	AS	A
Burton	D	AS	A
Jackson	D	AS	A
Douglas	D	AS	A
Frankfr		A	A
Reed	G		
Black	G	AS	A
Vinson	G		
—		R	R
—		R	R

Gandelman v Mercantile Insurance
51 183A
342 US 896
CCA 9th

Justice	CERT 12/08/51 (1 1)
Minton	
Clark	
Burton	
Jackson	
Douglas	
Frankfr	
Reed	
Black	G
Vinson	

Standard Oil Company v Peck
51 184A
342 US 382
Douglas 01/15/52 Ohio

Justice	JURIS 10/02/51 (1 1)	MERITS 01/05/52 (1 1)	REPORT 02/04/52 (1 1)
Minton	N	R	R
Clark	N	R	R
Burton	N	R	R
Jackson	N	X	
Douglas	N	R	R
Frankfr	N	R	R
Reed			
Black	N	R	R
Vinson		S	A

Carson v Roane-Anderson Company
51 186A
342 US 232 51 187A
Douglas 12/12/51 Tennessee

	CERT 10/13/1951 (1 1)	MERITS 12/08/1951 (1 1)	REPORT 01/07/1952 (1 1)
Minton	G	A	A
Clark	D	A	A
Burton	D		A
Jackson	G	R	A
Douglas			A
Frankfr	GH		A
Reed	G	R	A
Black	G	X	
Vinson	G	A	A

Squire v Wheeling-Lake Erie RR
51 189A
342 US 935 51 374A
Ohio

	CERT 10/03/1951 (1 1)	CERT 03/01/1952 (1 2)	REPORT 03/03/1952 (1 1)
Minton	G	GR	R
Clark	G	GR	R
Burton	G	GR	R
Jackson	G	GR	R
Douglas	G	GR	R
Frankfr	G	GR	R
Reed	G	GR	R
Black	G	GR	R
Vinson	G	GR	R

Freidus v U.S.
51 192A
342 US 827
CCA 2d

	CERT 10/03/1951 (1 1)
Minton	D
Clark	D
Burton	D
Jackson	
Douglas	G
Frankfr	
Reed	
Black	G
Vinson	D

Nemours v U.S.
51 193A
342 US 834
CCA 3rd

	CERT 10/03/1951 (1 1)
Minton	D
Clark	D
Burton	D
Jackson	D
Douglas	
Frankfr	D
Reed	D
Black	D
Vinson	D

Rutkin v U.S.
51 195A
343 US 130
Black 12/12/51 Burton 01/17/52 CCA 3rd

	CERT 10/03/1951 (1 1)	MERITS 12/08/1951 (1 1)	REPORT 03/24/1952 (1 1)
Minton		A	A
Clark	G	A	A
Burton		R	A
Jackson	D	A	A
Douglas	D	A	A
Frankfr	D		A
Reed	G		
Black	G		
Vinson	G	A	A

Haenn Ship Ceiling v Halcyon Lines
51 197A
342 US 282 51 62A
Black 12/12/51 CCA 3rd

	CERT 10/02/1951 (1 1)	MERITS 12/01/1951 (1 1)	REPORT 01/14/1952 (1 1)
Minton	G	R	R
Clark	G	R	R
Burton	G	RJ	RJ
Jackson	G	R	R
Douglas	G	R	R
Frankfr	G	R	R
Reed	G	RJ	RJ
Black	G	X	R
Vinson	G	R	R

Sacher v U.S.
51 201A 50 201A
343 US 1 50 336A
Jackson 01/15/52 CCA 2d

	CERT 10/21/1950 (1 1)	MERITS 01/05/1952 (1 2)	REPORT 03/24/1952 (1 1)
Minton		A	A
Clark	H	A	A
Burton	H	A	A
Jackson			
Douglas	H	R	R
Frankfr	GH	R	R
Reed	G	R	R
Black		R	R
Vinson	G	A	A

Koehler v U.S.
51 199A
342 US 852
CCA 5th

	CERT 06/02/1951 (1 2)	REHEAR 10/13/1951 (1 1)	REHEAR 10/20/1951 (1 2)	CERT 10/03/1951 (1 1)	CERT 10/13/1951 (1 2)
Minton					
Clark	D				
Burton	D	B	B		
Jackson				G	
Douglas		Y	Y	GL	D
Frankfr		Y	Y	G	D
Reed	G	Y	Y	GL	D
Black	G	B	B		D
Vinson	G	B	B	G	D

Guessefeldt v McGrath
51 204A
342 US 308 51 169A
Frankfr 01/03/52 CCA DC

	CERT 10/03/1951 (1 1)	MERITS 12/01/1951 (1 1)	MERITS 12/31/1951 (1 2)	MERITS 01/12/1952 (1 1)	REPORT 01/28/1952 (1 1)	REPORT 03/10/1952 (1 1)
Minton	G					
Clark	G	R	R	R	R	A
Burton	G	R	R	R	R	A
Jackson	G	R	R	R	R	
Douglas	G					
Frankfr	X					
Reed	G	R	R	R	R	A
Black	G					
Vinson	G	A	A	A	A	A

Weinmann v McGrath
51 205A
342 US 804
California

	10/02 1951 JURIS
Minton	S
Clark	S
Burton	S
Jackson	N
Douglas	S
Frankfr	S
Reed	N
Black	S
Vinson	S

Mascitti v McGrath
51 206A
342 US 580 51 43A 51 264A
Jackson 12/1/51 DC DC

	10/02 1951 JURIS	12/08 1951 MERITS	03/10 1952 REPORT
Minton	N		
Clark	N	A	A
Burton	N	X	A
Jackson	N		A
Douglas	N	A	A
Frankfr		A	A
Reed	N	R	A
Black	N	R	A
Vinson	N	R	A

U.S. v Kelly
51 209A
342 US 193
Minton 12/12/51 Ct Cls

	10/03 1951 CERT	12/01 1951 MERITS	01/02 1952 REPORT
Minton	G		
Clark	G	R	R
Burton	D		
Jackson			
Douglas	D		
Frankfr	D		
Reed	G	R	R
Black	G	R	R
Vinson	D		

Tucker v New Orleans Laundries
51 210A
342 US 828 51 211A
CCA 5th

	10/03 1951 CERT
Minton	D
Clark	D
Burton	D
Jackson	
Douglas	G
Frankfr	G
Reed	
Black	G
Vinson	D

Tucker v National Linen Service
51 211A
342 US 828 51 210A
CCA 5th

	10/03 1951 CERT
Minton	D
Clark	D
Burton	D
Jackson	
Douglas	G
Frankfr	G
Reed	
Black	G
Vinson	D

Stroud v Swope
51 213A
342 US 829
CCA 9th

	10/03 1951 CERT
Minton	D
Clark	D
Burton	D
Jackson	
Douglas	G
Frankfr	
Reed	
Black	G
Vinson	D

U.S. v Coplon
51 214A
342 US 926 51 4A 51 272A
CCA DC

	01/12 1952 CERT	01/26 1952 CERT
Minton	G	
Clark	G	G
Burton		
Jackson	G	
Douglas	D	D
Frankfr		
Reed	D	
Black	G	G
Vinson	D	D

C.I.R. v Visintainer
51 219A
342 US 858
CCA 10th

	10/20 1951 CERT
Minton	D
Clark	D
Burton	D
Jackson	D
Douglas	D
Frankfr	D
Reed	
Black	G
Vinson	G

Air Line Dispatchers v N.M.B.
51 220A
342 US 849
CCA DC

	10/03 1951 CERT
Minton	D
Clark	D
Burton	D
Jackson	D
Douglas	D
Frankfr	D
Reed	
Black	G
Vinson	G

Railway Express Agency v Kennedy
51 223A
342 US 830
CCA 7th

	10/03 1951 CERT
Minton	D
Clark	D
Burton	D
Jackson	
Douglas	D
Frankfr	
Reed	D
Black	D
Vinson	D

Public Utilities Commission v Pollak
51 224A
343 US 451 51 295A
Burton 03/18/52 CCA DC

	10/13 1951 CERT	03/08 1952 MERITS	05/26 1952 REPORT
Minton	G	R	R
Clark	G	R	R
Burton	G	R	R
Jackson			A
Douglas	D	A	
Frankfr			
Reed	G	RQ	R
Black	G	R	R
Vinson			

Porto Rico Telephone v Puerto Rico CA
51 225A
342 US 830
CCA 1st

	10/03 1951 CERT
Minton	G
Clark	G
Burton	D
Jackson	D
Douglas	D
Frankfr	
Reed	
Black	D
Vinson	D

Pillsbury v United Engineering Company
51 229A
342 US 197
Minton 12/12/51 CCA 9th

Justice	10/13 1951 CERT (1 1)	12/08 1951 MERITS (1 1)	01/02 1952 REPORT (1 1)
Minton	G	A	A
Clark	G	A	A
Burton	G	R	R	A
Jackson	G	R	A
Douglas	G	A	A
Frankfr	G	A	A
Reed	G	R	R	A
Black	G		A
Vinson	G		A

Besser Manufacturing Company v U.S.
51 230A
343 US 444
Jackson 05/06/52 DC ED Michigan

Justice	10/02 1951 JURIS (1 1)	04/26 1952 MERITS (1 1)	05/26 1952 REPORT (1 1)
Minton	N		A
Clark	N	A	A
Burton	N		A
Jackson	N		A
Douglas	N		A
Frankfr	N		A
Reed	N		A
Black	N		A
Vinson	N		A

Desper v Starved Rock Ferry Company
51 231A
342 US 187
Jackson 12/12/51 CCA 7th

Justice	10/13 1951 CERT (1 1)	12/08 1951 MERITS (1 1)	01/02 1952 REPORT (1 1)
Minton	G		
Clark	G		
Burton	G	R	R	
Jackson	G	S	
Douglas	G	A	
Frankfr	G		
Reed	G	R	R	
Black	G	A	
Vinson	G	A	

C. A. Durr Packing v Shaughnessy
51 233A
342 US 850
CCA 2d

Justice	10/13 1951 CERT (1 1)
Minton	
Clark	
Burton	D	D
Jackson	G
Douglas	D	D
Frankfr	G	G
Reed	
Black	
Vinson	D

U.S. v Thomas
51 234A
342 US 850
CCA 6th

Justice	10/13 1951 CERT (1 1)	03/01 1952 REHEAR (1 1)
Minton		H
Clark		H
Burton	D	H
Jackson	D	H
Douglas	D	
Frankfr	D	
Reed		
Black	G	B
Vinson	G	H

Quirk v New York Chicago RR Company
51 238A
342 US 871
CCA 7th

Justice	10/20 1951 CERT (1 2)	11/03 1951 CERT (1 3)
Minton		
Clark	G	D
Burton	X	D	D
Jackson	D	D
Douglas	G	G
Frankfr	G	
Reed	G	G
Black	G	G
Vinson	G	G

Caddel v California
51 242A
342 US 866
California

Justice	10/13 1951 CERT (1 1)	11/03 1951 CERT (1 2)
Minton		
Clark		
Burton		
Jackson	D	D
Douglas	X	D
Frankfr		
Reed		
Black	D	X
Vinson	D	

Bircham v Kentucky
51 243A
342 US 805
Kentucky

Justice	10/13 1951 CERT (1 1)	11/03 1951 CERT (1 2)
Minton		
Clark		
Burton		
Jackson	G	
Douglas	G	G
Frankfr		
Reed		
Black	G	G
Vinson		

International Longshoremen's v Ackerman
51 245A
342 US 859
CCA 9th

Justice	10/02 1951 JURIS (1 1)	(S)
Minton	D	S
Clark	D	S
Burton	D	S
Jackson	D	S
Douglas	D	S
Frankfr	D	
Reed		N
Black		S
Vinson		S

Fruehauf Trailer Company v Gusewelle
51 246A
342 US 866
CCA 8th

Justice	10/20 1951 CERT (1 1)	11/03 1951 CERT (1 2)	(D)
Minton			
Clark	GVM	GVM	D
Burton			D
Jackson	GVM	GVM	D
Douglas			D
Frankfr			
Reed	GVM	GVM	D
Black			D
Vinson			

N.L.R.B. v Illinois Bell Telephone
51 249A
342 US 885
CCA 7th

Justice	11/24 1951 CERT (1 1)
Minton	
Clark	
Burton	
Jackson	
Douglas	G
Frankfr	
Reed	
Black	G
Vinson	

U.S. v New Wrinkle
51 250A
342 US 371
Reed 01/15/52 DC SD Ohio

Justice	10/02 1951 JURIS (1 1)	01/12 1952 MERITS (1 1)	02/04 1952 REPORT (1 1)
Minton			
Clark	N	R	R
Burton	N	R	R
Jackson	N	X	R
Douglas	N	R	R
Frankfr			
Reed	N	R	R
Black	N	R	R
Vinson			

Memphis Steam Laundry Cleaner v Stone
51 253A
342 US 389
Vinson 12/12/51 Mississippi

	10/02 1951 JURIS 1 1	12/08 1951 MERITS 1 1	03/03 1952 REPORT 1 1
Minton	N	S	
Clark	N	R	R
Burton	N	R	R
Jackson	N	R	R
Douglas	N	R	R
Frankfr	N	R	R
Reed	N	R	R
Black	N X	A	A
Vinson	N	R	A

Michel v Louisville & Nashville RR
51 262A
342 US 862
CCA 5th

	10/20 1951 CERT 1 1
Minton	
Clark	
Burton	
Jackson	G
Douglas	
Frankfr	
Reed	
Black	
Vinson	

Coleman v McGrath
51 264A
342 US 580 51 43A 51 206A
Jackson 12/12/51 DC DC

	10/02 1951 JURIS 1 1	12/08 1951 MERITS 1 1	03/10 1952 REPORT 1 1
Minton	N		A
Clark	N	R	A
Burton	N	R	A
Jackson	N	G	A
Douglas	N	R	A
Frankfr	N	X	A
Reed	N	R	A
Black	N	R	A
Vinson	N		A

Maske v Washington Marlboro Lines
51 266A
342 US 834
CCA DC

	10/03 1951 CERT 1 1
Minton	
Clark	D
Burton	D
Jackson	D
Douglas	D
Frankfr	D
Reed	D
Black	G
Vinson	D

Southwest Natural Gas Company v C.I.R.
51 267A
342 US 860
CCA 5th

	10/20 1951 CERT 1 1
Minton	
Clark	
Burton	
Jackson	
Douglas	
Frankfr	
Reed	
Black	G
Vinson	

Moore-McCormack Lines v Foltz
51 271A
342 US 871
CCA 2d

	10/20 1951 CERT 1 1	11/03 1951 CERT 1 2
Minton	G	D
Clark		
Burton	G	D
Jackson		
Douglas	G	D
Frankfr		D
Reed	G	
Black		D
Vinson		D

Coplon v U.S.
51 272A
342 US 926 51 4A 51 214A
CCA DC

	01/12 1952 CERT 1 1	01/26 1952 CERT 1 2
Minton	G	D
Clark	G	
Burton	G	G
Jackson		
Douglas	D	D
Frankfr	D	D
Reed	G	
Black	G	G
Vinson		

Briggs v Elliott
51 273A
342 US 350
DC ED South Carolina

	01/12 1952 JURIS 1 1	01/26 1952 JURIS 1 2	01/28 1952 REPORT 1 1
Minton	NVR	VM	V
Clark	NVR	VM	V
Burton	NVR	VM	V
Jackson	NVR X	N	
Douglas	NVR	VM	V
Frankfr	N	VM	N
Reed	NVR	N	V
Black	N	VM	N
Vinson	NVR	VM	V

U.S. v 88 Cases Of Bireley's
51 274A
342 US 861
CCA 3rd

	10/20 1951 CERT 1 1
Minton	
Clark	
Burton	
Jackson	G
Douglas	
Frankfr	
Reed	
Black	
Vinson	

U.S. (Jaegeler) v Carusi
51 275A
342 US 347
CCA 3rd

	11/03 1951 CERT 1 1	01/12 1952 MERITS 1 1	01/28 1952 REPORT 1 1
Minton	GR	R	V
Clark	GM	R	V
Burton	G	R	V
Jackson	GR	R	V
Douglas	GR	R	V
Frankfr	GR	R	V
Reed	GM	R	V
Black	GR	R	V
Vinson	GM	R	V

Carter (In Re)
51 277A
342 US 862
CCA DC

	10/20 1951 CERT 1 1
Minton	
Clark	
Burton	
Jackson	G
Douglas	
Frankfr	
Reed	
Black	
Vinson	

Peerson v Mitchell
51 278A
342 US 866
Oklahoma

	11/03 1951 CERT 1 1
Minton	D
Clark	D
Burton	D
Jackson	D
Douglas	D
Frankfr	D
Reed	
Black	G
Vinson	D

Rio v Washington
51 279A
342 US 867
Washington

Justice	11/03 1951 CERT
Minton	D
Clark	D
Burton	D
Jackson	
Douglas	G
Frankfr	D
Reed	D
Black	D
Vinson	D

International Longshoremen's v Juneau
51 280A
342 US 237
Douglas 12/12/51 CCA 9th

Justice	10/20 1951 CERT	12/08 1951 MERITS	01/07 1952 REPORT
Minton	G		A
Clark	G		A
Burton		D	A
Jackson		D	A
Douglas	D		A
Frankfr	G		A
Reed	G		A
Black	G	X	A
Vinson	D		A

MacInnis v U.S.
51 281A
342 US 953 51 201A
CCA 9th

Justice	10/20 1951 CERT	03/08 1952 MERITS
Minton		
Clark	G	D
Burton	H	D
Jackson		
Douglas	D	D
Frankfr	H	
Reed	D	D
Black		
Vinson	G	D

Swift & Company v U.S.
51 282A
343 US 373
Minton 03/31/52 DC ND Illinois

Justice	10/13 1951 JURIS	03/08 1952 MERITS	05/05 1952 REPORT
Minton	N	A	A
Clark		R	A
Burton	N		
Jackson	N	R	R
Douglas	N	R	R
Frankfr	N	R	R
Reed	N		
Black	N	X	
Vinson	N	A	A

Guttmann v Illinois Central RR
51 285A
342 US 867
CCA 2d

Justice	11/03 1951 CERT
Minton	D
Clark	D
Burton	G
Jackson	D
Douglas	D
Frankfr	D
Reed	D
Black	D
Vinson	DQ

Mullen v Fitz Simons & Connell Dredge
51 288A
342 US 888
CCA 7th

Justice	11/24 1951 CERT
Minton	GL
Clark	GL
Burton	
Jackson	GL
Douglas	
Frankfr	
Reed	
Black	
Vinson	

Chicago Burlington & Quincy RR v U.S.
51 289A
342 US 845
DC ND Illinois

Justice	10/13 1951 JURIS	10/15 1951 REPORT
Minton	N	A
Clark		A
Burton	N	A
Jackson	N	A
Douglas		A
Frankfr		A
Reed		A
Black	N	A
Vinson	A	A

Cox v U.S.
51 292A
342 US 867
CCA 10th

Justice	11/03 1951 CERT
Minton	
Clark	
Burton	D
Jackson	D
Douglas	D
Frankfr	G
Reed	D
Black	D
Vinson	D

Pollak v Public Utilities Commission
51 295A
343 US 451 51 224A CCA DC
Burton 03/18/52 CCA DC

Justice	10/13 1951 CERT	03/08 1952 MERITS
Minton	G	A
Clark	G	A
Burton	G	R
Jackson	G	
Douglas		D
Frankfr	G	
Reed	G	
Black	G	A
Vinson		AQ A

New York New Haven RR Company v Korte
51 297A
342 US 868
CCA 2d

Justice	11/03 1951 CERT
Minton	
Clark	
Burton	D
Jackson	D
Douglas	G
Frankfr	
Reed	D
Black	D
Vinson	D

U.S. v Edens
51 299A
342 US 912 51 100A 51 300A
CCA 4th

Justice	11/03 1951 CERT	01/12 1952 MERITS	01/14 1952 REPORT
Minton	G	A	A
Clark	G	A	A
Burton	G	A	A
Jackson	G	A	A
Douglas	D	A	A
Frankfr	G	A	A
Reed	G	A	A
Black	G	A	A
Vinson	G	A	A

U.S. v General Engineering
51 300A
342 US 912 51 100A 51 299A
CCA 8th

Justice	11/03 1951 CERT	01/12 1952 MERITS	01/14 1952 REPORT
Minton	G	A	A
Clark	G	A	A
Burton	G	A	A
Jackson	G	A	A
Douglas	D	A	A
Frankfr	G	A	A
Reed	G	A	A
Black	G	A	A
Vinson	G	A	A

Palmer Oil v Amerada Petroleum
51 301A
343 US 390 51 302A
Oklahoma

Justice	01/12 1952 JURIS (1 1)	04/26 1952 MERITS (1 1)	05/12 1952 REPORT (1 1)
Minton	N	A	S
Clark	N	A	S
Burton	N	A	S
Jackson	N	A	S
Douglas	N	A	S
Frankfr	N	A	S
Reed	N	A	S
Black	S	A	S
Vinson	N	A	S

Farwell v Amerada Petroleum
51 302A
343 US 390 51 301A
Oklahoma

Justice	01/12 1952 JURIS (1 1)	04/26 1952 MERITS (1 1)	05/12 1952 REPORT (1 1)
Minton	N	A	S
Clark	N	A	S
Burton	N	A	S
Jackson	N	A	S
Douglas	N	A	S
Frankfr	N	A	S
Reed	N	A	S
Black	S	A	S
Vinson	N	A	S

Lewis v U.S.
51 313A
342 US 869
CCA DC

Justice	11/03 1951 CERT (1 1)
Minton	D
Clark	D
Burton	D
Jackson	D
Douglas	D
Frankfr	D
Reed	D
Black	G
Vinson	D

Cities Service Company v McGrath
51 305A
342 US 330
Clark 01/15/52 CCA 2d

Justice	11/03 1951 CERT (1 1)	01/05 1952 MERITS (1 1)	01/28 1952 REPORT (1 1)
Minton	G	A	A
Clark		R	
Burton	G	A	A
Jackson	G	A	A
Douglas	G	A	A
Frankfr	G	A	A
Reed	G	A	A
Black	G	A	A
Vinson	G	A	A

L'Hommedieu v Board Of Regents
51 312A
342 US 951 51 8A
New York

Justice	10/20 1951 CERT (1 1)	03/08 1952 MERITS (1 1)	03/10 1952 REPORT (1 1)
Minton	G	A	A
Clark	G	A	A
Burton	G	R	R
Jackson	G	R	R
Douglas	G	A	A
Frankfr	G	A	A
Reed	G	A	A
Black	G	A	A
Vinson	G	A	A

Bigelow v California
51 316A
342 US 910 51 83A
California

Justice	01/05 1952 CERT (1 1)
Minton	D
Clark	D
Burton	D
Jackson	D
Douglas	G
Frankfr	D
Reed	D
Black	X
Vinson	D

Day-Brite Lighting v Missouri
51 317A
342 US 421
Douglas 01/15/52 Missouri

Justice	11/03 1951 JURIS (1 1)	01/12 1952 MERITS (1 1)	03/03 1952 REPORT (1 1)
Minton	S	A	A
Clark	S	A	A
Burton		A	A
Jackson	N	A	A
Douglas	N	SA	R
Frankfr		A	A
Reed		A	A
Black	N	A	A
Vinson	N	A	A

Brotherhood Of RR v California
51 320A
342 US 876
California

Justice	11/03 1951 CERT (1 1)	11/10 1951 CERT (1 2)
Minton	G	D
Clark	G	G
Burton		D
Jackson	G	G
Douglas		D
Frankfr		D
Reed		D
Black		D
Vinson	G	D

Utah v Montgomery Ward & Company
51 322A
342 US 869
Utah

Justice	11/03 1951 CERT (1 1)
Minton	D
Clark	D
Burton	D
Jackson	D
Douglas	G
Frankfr	
Reed	D
Black	D
Vinson	D

Crummer Company v Barker
51 323A
342 US 897
CCA 5th

Justice	12/08 1951 CERT (1 1)
Minton	D
Clark	D
Burton	D
Jackson	D
Douglas	D
Frankfr	D
Reed	D
Black	H
Vinson	D

Florida (Hawkins) v Board Of Control
51 325A
342 US 877
Florida

Justice	11/10 1951 CERT (1 1)
Minton	D
Clark	D
Burton	D
Jackson	D
Douglas	D
Frankfr	D
Reed	G
Black	D
Vinson	D

Lassiter v Roos
51 326A
342 US 876
CCA 5th

Justice	11/10 1951 CERT (1 1)
Minton	D
Clark	D
Burton	D
Jackson	D
Douglas	D
Frankfr	D
Reed	G
Black	D
Vinson	D

Mullaney v Anderson
51 329A
342 US 415
Frankfr 01/15/52 CCA 9th

	11/03 1951 CERT 1 1	01/12 1952 MERITS 1 1	03/03 1952 REPORT 1 1
Minton	GR	R	R
Clark	G	R	A
Burton	G		A
Jackson	G	R	A
Douglas	GR		A
Frankfr	D		
Reed	G	R	A
Black	G		A
Vinson	G	R	R

Frisbie v Collins
51 331A
342 US 519
Black 02/05/52 CCA 6th

	11/03 1951 CERT 1 1	02/02 1952 MERITS 1 1	03/10 1952 REPORT 1 1
Minton	G	R	R
Clark	G	R	R
Burton	G	R	R
Jackson	G		R
Douglas	G	R	R
Frankfr	D		R
Reed	G	R	R
Black	G	R	R
Vinson	G		R

Peay v Cox
51 335A
342 US 896
CCA 5th

	12/08 1951 CERT 1 1
Minton	D
Clark	D
Burton	D
Jackson	D
Douglas	G
Frankfr	D
Reed	D
Black	D
Vinson	D

Nabob Oil Company v U.S.
51 337A
342 US 876
CCA 10th

	11/10 1951 CERT 1 1
Minton	D
Clark	D
Burton	D
Jackson	D
Douglas	D
Frankfr	D
Reed	D
Black	G
Vinson	D

Julius Hyman & Company v Velsicol
51 340A
342 US 870
Colorado

	11/03 1951 CERT 1 1
Minton	D
Clark	D
Burton	D
Jackson	D
Douglas	D
Frankfr	D
Reed	G
Black	D
Vinson	G

California v U.S.
51 341A
342 US 885
CCA 9th

	11/24 1951 CERT 1 1
Minton	D
Clark	D
Burton	D
Jackson	D
Douglas	D
Frankfr	G
Reed	D
Black	G
Vinson	D

Warren County Mississippi v Hester
51 342A
342 US 877
Louisiana

	11/10 1951 CERT 1 1
Minton	D
Clark	D
Burton	D
Jackson	D
Douglas	D
Frankfr	D
Reed	D
Black	G
Vinson	D

B.F. Goodrich Company v Washington
51 344A
342 US 876 51 345A
Washington

	11/10 1951 CERT 1 1
Minton	D
Clark	D
Burton	D
Jackson	D
Douglas	D
Frankfr	D
Reed	G
Black	G
Vinson	D

Washington v B.F. Goodrich Company
51 345A
342 US 876 51 344A
Washington

	11/10 1951 CERT 1 1
Minton	D
Clark	D
Burton	D
Jackson	D
Douglas	D
Frankfr	D
Reed	G
Black	G
Vinson	G

New York v U.S.
51 346A
342 US 882
DC ND New York

	11/03 1951 JURIS 1 1	11/24 1951 JURIS 1 2	11/26 1951 REPORT 1 1
Minton	A	A	A
Clark	A	A	A
Burton	A	A	A
Jackson	A	A	A
Douglas			
Frankfr	N	N	R
Reed	A	A	A
Black	N	N	N
Vinson	A	A	A

First National Bank v United Air Lines
51 349A
342 US 396
Black 01/15/52 CCA 7th

	11/03 1951 CERT 1 1	11/10 1951 CERT 1 2	01/12 1952 MERITS 1 1	03/03 1952 REPORT 1 1
Minton	D			R
Clark	G	G	G	R
Burton	D			R
Jackson	G	G	G	R
Douglas	D	D	D	
Frankfr	D			
Reed	G	G	G	R
Black	G			R
Vinson	X	D	D	A

Mogis v Lyman Richey Sand & Gravel
51 350A
342 US 877
CCA 8th

	11/10 1951 CERT 1 1
Minton	D
Clark	D
Burton	D
Jackson	D
Douglas	D
Frankfr	D
Reed	G
Black	G
Vinson	D

U.S. v Osage Nation Of Indians
51 357A
342 US 896
Ct Cls

Justice	12/08/1951 CERT (1 1)	02/02/1952 MERITS (1 1)	03/03/1952 REPORT (1 1)
Minton	D	A	A
Clark	D	A	A
Burton		A	A
Jackson	G	A	A
Douglas	D		
Frankfr	G		
Reed		R	
Black	G	R	A
Vinson	D		A

Kyle v Jones
51 358A
342 US 886
CCA 10th

Justice	11/24/1951 CERT (1 1)
Minton	D
Clark	D
Burton	
Jackson	G
Douglas	
Frankfr	G
Reed	
Black	
Vinson	D

Blackmar v Guerre
51 361A
342 US 512
Minton 02/06/52 CCA 5th

Justice	11/24/1951 CERT (1 1)
Minton	D
Clark	G
Burton	D
Jackson	G
Douglas	G
Frankfr	D
Reed	G
Black	G
Vinson	D

Mead Service Company v Moore
51 362A
342 US 902
CCA 10th

Justice	12/31/1951 CERT (1 1)
Minton	
Clark	D
Burton	D
Jackson	D
Douglas	D
Frankfr	D
Reed	G
Black	D
Vinson	D

U.S. v Branch Banking & Trust Company
51 370A
342 US 893
Ct Cls

Justice	12/01/1951 CERT (1 1)
Minton	
Clark	D
Burton	D
Jackson	D
Douglas	D
Frankfr	D
Reed	
Black	D
Vinson	G

Stroble v California
51 373A 51 5M
343 US 181
Clark 03/18/52 California

Justice	10/03/1951 CERT (1 1)	03/08/1952 MERITS (1 1)	04/07/1952 REPORT (1 1)
Minton	D	R	A
Clark	D	R	A
Burton			
Jackson	G	A	A
Douglas	G	A	A
Frankfr	G	A	A
Reed		A	A
Black	G	A	A
Vinson	G		

Dice v Akron Canton Youngstown RR
51 374A 51 16M
342 US 359 51 189A
Black 12/12/51 Ohio

Justice	10/03/1951 CERT (1 1)	12/08/1951 MERITS (1 1)	02/04/1952 REPORT (1 1)
Minton	G	R	R
Clark	G	R	R
Burton	G		R
Jackson	G	R	R
Douglas	G		R
Frankfr	G	A	A
Reed	G	R	R
Black	G	A	A
Vinson	G	R	R

Sherman v Illinois
51 375A 51 29M
342 US 104 51 95A 51 96A
Vinson 11/13/51 Illinois

Justice	11/10/1951 MERITS (1 1)	12/03/1951 REPORT (1 1)
Minton		
Clark	A	A
Burton	A	A
Jackson	V	V
Douglas	V	V
Frankfr	V	V
Reed		
Black	V	V
Vinson	V	V

Casey v U.S.
51 379A
343 US 808
Frankfr 03/18/52 CCA 9th

Justice	03/08/1952 CERT (1 1)
Minton	RI
Clark	RI
Burton	RI
Jackson	R
Douglas	RI
Frankfr	
Reed	RI
Black	K
Vinson	K

McCoy v Providence Journal Company
51 382A
342 US 894
CCA 1st

Justice	12/01/1951 CERT (1 1)	01/26/1952 CERT (1 1)	03/22/1952 CERT (1 2)
Minton		D	D
Clark	G		
Burton		D	D
Jackson	G	G	G
Douglas		GV	GV
Frankfr		G	G
Reed	G	G	G
Black		D	D
Vinson		D	D

Remington v U.S.
51 387A
343 US 907
CCA 2d

Justice	12/08/1951 DISMISS (1 1)	01/26/1952 CERT (1 1)	03/22/1952 CERT (1 2)
Minton	B		
Clark	H	D	D
Burton	B	H	H
Jackson	B	B	B
Douglas	H	B	B
Frankfr	Q	H	H
Reed	H	Q	Q
Black			
Vinson			

Robertson v U.S.
51 388A
343 US 711
Douglas 05/06/52 CCA 10th

Justice	12/08/1951 CERT (1 1)	04/05/1952 MERITS (1 1)	06/02/1952 REPORT (1 1)
Minton	G		
Clark	G	A	A
Burton	G	A	A
Jackson	G	A	A
Douglas	G	A	A
Frankfr	D	R	R
Reed	G	A	A
Black	G	A	A
Vinson	G	A	A

Broady v Illinois Central RR Company
51 390A
342 US 897
CCA 7th

Justice	CERT 12/08 1951
Minton	D
Clark	D
Burton	D
Jackson	G
Douglas	D
Frankfr	D
Reed	D
Black	G
Vinson	D

Bruner v U.S.
51 391A 51 87M
343 US 112
Vinson 02/05/52 CCA 5th

Justice	CERT 10/20 1951	MERITS 02/02 1952	REPORT 03/24 1952
Minton	G	A	A
Clark	G	A	A
Burton	G		
Jackson	G	A	A
Douglas	G	R	R
Frankfr	G	A	A
Reed	G	R	R
Black	G	A	A
Vinson	D	A	A

Sgitcovich v Sgitcovich
51 394A
342 US 903
Texas

Justice	CERT 12/31 1951
Minton	D
Clark	D
Burton	D
Jackson	D
Douglas	D
Frankfr	D
Reed	D
Black	G
Vinson	G

Richfield Oil v U.S.
51 395A
343 US 922
DC SD California

Justice	JURIS 11/10 1951	MERITS 04/05 1952	REPORT 04/21 1952
Minton	N	A	A
Clark			
Burton	N	A	A
Jackson	N		
Douglas	N	A	A
Frankfr	N		
Reed	N	A	A
Black	N	A	A
Vinson		A	A

Horsman Dolls v UCC Of New Jersey
51 398A
342 US 890
New Jersey

Justice	CERT 11/24 1951	JURIS 11/24 1951	CERT 12/01 1951	JURIS 12/01 1951
Minton	D	S	D	S
Clark	D	S	D	S
Burton	D	S	D	S
Jackson	D	S	D	S
Douglas	D	S	D	S
Frankfr	D	S	D	S
Reed	D		D	
Black		P	G	P
Vinson	D	S		S

Stack v Boyle
51 400A
342 US 1
Vinson 10/26/51 CCA 9th

Justice	QUEST 10/20 1951 (25)	QUEST 10/20 1951 (26)	QUEST 10/20 1951 (27)	BAIL 11/03 1951	REPORT 11/05 1951
Minton	B	B		M	V
Clark	B		Y	M	V
Burton		B	Y	M	V
Jackson	Y	Y		M	V
Douglas	Y	Y	Y	M	V
Frankfr	B	B	B	M	V
Reed	Y	Y	Y	M	V
Black	B	B	B	M	V
Vinson	Y	Y	Y		

Johansen v U.S.
51 401A
343 US 427 51 414A *CCA 2d*
Reed 03/18/52 CCA 2d

Justice	CERT 12/31 1951	MERITS 03/08 1952	REPORT 05/26 1952
Minton	G	R	R
Clark	G		
Burton	G	R	R
Jackson	D		
Douglas	G	R	R
Frankfr	G		
Reed	G	R	R
Black		RQ	R
Vinson			R

Leahy v Canister Company
51 402A
342 US 893
CCA 3rd

Justice	CERT 12/01 1951
Minton	
Clark	
Burton	
Jackson	
Douglas	
Frankfr	
Reed	
Black	G
Vinson	G

Local 333B United Marine v Battle
51 403A
342 US 880
DC ED Virginia

Justice	JURIS 11/24 1951	REPORT 11/26 1951
Minton	D	A
Clark	D	A
Burton	D	A
Jackson	D	A
Douglas	D	A
Frankfr	D	A
Reed		A
Black	S	
Vinson		

Barbee v Capital Airlines
51 405A
342 US 908
CCA DC

Justice	CERT 01/05 1952
Minton	D
Clark	G
Burton	D
Jackson	D
Douglas	D
Frankfr	D
Reed	
Black	G
Vinson	D

Kane v Union Of Soviet Republics
51 407A
342 US 903
CCA 3rd

Justice	CERT 12/31 1951
Minton	D
Clark	G
Burton	D
Jackson	D
Douglas	D
Frankfr	D
Reed	
Black	G
Vinson	G

I.C.C. v New York Central RR Company
51 410A
342 US 890
DC Massachusetts

Justice	JURIS 12/01 1951	REPORT 12/03 1951
Minton	N	A
Clark		A
Burton		A
Jackson		A
Douglas	A	A
Frankfr		A
Reed		
Black	N	A
Vinson		

Madsen v Kinsella
51 411A 51 82M
343 US 341
Burton 01/15/52 CCA 4th

	11/03 1951 CERT	01/12 1952 MERITS	04/29 1952 REPORT
	1 1	1 1	1 1
Minton	D	A	A
Clark	D	A	A
Burton			A
Jackson	D	A	A
Douglas	G	X	A
Frankfr	G	A	A
Reed			A
Black	G	R	R
Vinson	D	R	A

Bondholders v Powell
51 413A
342 US 921
CCA 4th

	12/08 1951 CERT	01/26 1952 CERT
	1 1	1 2
Minton	D	D
Clark	D	D
Burton	D	D
Jackson	D	D
Douglas	D	D
Frankfr	G	
Reed	D	D
Black	D	D
Vinson	G	

Mandel v U.S.
51 414A
343 US 427 51 401A
Reed 03/18/52 CCA 3rd

	12/31 1951 CERT	03/08 1952 MERITS	05/26 1952 REPORT
	1 1	1 1	1 1
Minton	G	R	R
Clark	G		
Burton	G	R	R
Jackson	D	RQ	
Douglas	G		
Frankfr	G		
Reed	G	R	R
Black	G	R	R
Vinson	G		

Ancich v Borcich
51 417A
342 US 905
CCA 9th

	12/31 1951 CERT
	1 1
Minton	D
Clark	D
Burton	D
Jackson	
Douglas	D
Frankfr	D
Reed	
Black	G
Vinson	D

Weberman v Auster
51 418A
342 US 884 51 419A
New York

	11/24 1951 JURIS
	1 1
Minton	S
Clark	S
Burton	S
Jackson	
Douglas	N
Frankfr	
Reed	S
Black	SA
Vinson	SA

Donner v New York (Silverman)
51 419A
342 US 884 51 418A
New York

	11/24 1951 JURIS
	1 1
Minton	S
Clark	S
Burton	S
Jackson	
Douglas	N
Frankfr	
Reed	S
Black	SA
Vinson	SA

H.J. Heinz Company v Owens
51 420A
342 US 905
CCA 9th

	12/31 1951 CERT
	1 1
Minton	D
Clark	D
Burton	D
Jackson	
Douglas	D
Frankfr	D
Reed	
Black	G
Vinson	D

Acheson v Okimura
51 421A
342 US 899
DC Hawaii

	12/31 1951 JURIS	01/02 1952 REPORT
	1 1	1 1
Minton	NVM	VM
Clark	NVM	VM
Burton	NVM	VM
Jackson		
Douglas	NR	R
Frankfr	NVM	VM
Reed	NVM	VM
Black		
Vinson	NVM	VM

(A)

U.S. v Hood
51 426A
343 US 148
Frankfr 03/18/52 DC SD Mississippi

	12/01 1951 JURIS	03/08 1952 MERITS	03/31 1952 REPORT
	1 1	1 1	1 1
Minton	NR	R	R
Clark	N	R	R
Burton	NR	R	R
Jackson	N	RQ	
Douglas	N	R	R
Frankfr			
Reed	N	X	
Black	N		
Vinson	N		

(A / A / A)

Pennsylvania Water & Power v F.P.C.
51 428A
343 US 414 51 429A
Black 04/10/52 CCA DC

	02/02 1952 CERT	03/08 1952 POSTPN	04/05 1952 MERITS	05/26 1952 REPORT
	1 1	1 1	1 1	1 1
Minton	G	B	R	
Clark	G	B	R J	
Burton	G		R J	
Jackson	G	B	R	R
Douglas	G	B		
Frankfr	G	Y		
Reed		Y		
Black	D	B	Q	
Vinson	G	B	A	R

(A A A / A A)

Pennsylvania PUC v F.P.C.
51 429A
343 US 414 41 428A
Black 04/10/52 CCA DC

	02/02 1952 CERT	03/08 1952 POSTPN	04/05 1952 MERITS	05/26 1952 REPORT
	1 1	1 1	1 1	1 1
Minton	G	B	R	
Clark	G	B	R J	
Burton	G		R J	
Jackson	G	B	R	R
Douglas	G	B		
Frankfr	G	Y		
Reed		Y		
Black	D	B	Q	
Vinson	G	B	A	R

(A A A / A A)

Community Services v U.S.
51 430A
342 US 932
CCA 4th

	02/02 1952 CERT
	1 1
Minton	D
Clark	D
Burton	D
Jackson	D
Douglas	D
Frankfr	G
Reed	
Black	D
Vinson	D

Zorach v Clauson
51 431A
343 US 306
Douglas 02/05/52 New York

	12/08 1951 JURIS 1 1	01/12 1952 AMICUS 1 1	02/02 1952 MERITS 1 1	04/28 1952 REPORT 1 1
Minton	N	B		
Clark	N	B		
Burton	N	B	R	R
Jackson	N	B	A	A
Douglas	N	B	A	A
Frankfr	N	B	A	A
Reed	N	B		
Black	NQ	B	RQ	R
Vinson	N	B Y	A	A

Pass v McGrath
51 437A
342 US 910
CCA DC

	01/05 1952 CERT 1 1
Minton	D
Clark	D
Burton	D
Jackson	D
Douglas	D
Frankfr	D
Reed	
Black	
Vinson	G

California State Board v Goggin
51 438A
342 US 909
CCA 9th

	01/05 1952 CERT 1 1
Minton	D
Clark	D
Burton	D
Jackson	D
Douglas	D
Frankfr	D
Reed	D
Black	
Vinson	G

Hammett v U.S.
51 440A
342 US 894 51 441A
CCA 2d

	12/01 1951 CERT 1 1
Minton	D
Clark	D
Burton	D
Jackson	D
Douglas	G
Frankfr	G
Reed	
Black	G
Vinson	D

Field v U.S.
51 441A
342 US 894 51 440A
CCA 2d

	12/01 1951 CERT 1 1
Minton	D
Clark	D
Burton	D
Jackson	D
Douglas	G
Frankfr	G
Reed	
Black	G
Vinson	D

Brunner v U.S.
51 442A
343 US 918
CCA 9th

	01/26 1952 CERT 1 1
Minton	G
Clark	G
Burton	G
Jackson	G
Douglas	G
Frankfr	G
Reed	G
Black	G
Vinson	G

U.S. v Spector
51 443A
343 US 169
Douglas 03/18/52 DC SD California

	12/31 1951 JURIS 1 1	03/08 1952 MERITS 1 1	04/07 1952 REPORT 1 1
Minton	N	R	R
Clark	N	R	R
Burton	N	R	R
Jackson	N	R	R
Douglas	N	A	A
Frankfr	N	A	A
Reed	N		
Black	N A	A	A
Vinson	N	A	A

F.T.C. v Ruberoid Company
51 448A
343 US 470 51 504A
Clark 04/09/52 CCA 3rd

	01/26 1952 CERT 1 1	04/05 1952 MERITS 1 1	05/26 1952 REPORT 1 1
Minton	G	R	R
Clark	G		
Burton	G	R	R
Jackson	G		
Douglas	G	D	D
Frankfr	G	D	A
Reed	G	D	
Black	G	D	R A
Vinson	G	D	A

U.S. v Atlantic Mutual Insurance
51 450A
343 US 236
Black 03/18/52 CCA 2d

	01/12 1952 CERT 1 1
Minton	G
Clark	G
Burton	G
Jackson	G
Douglas	D
Frankfr	G
Reed	D
Black	G
Vinson	D

Rice v Arnold
51 451A
342 US 946
Florida

	01/26 1952 CERT 1 1	03/01 1952 CERT 1 2
Minton		
Clark		
Burton		D
Jackson		D
Douglas	G	G
Frankfr	GA D	G
Reed	G	
Black	G	G
Vinson	G	D

Brotherhood Of RR Trainmen v Howard
51 458A
343 US 768
Black 05/06/52 CCA 8th

	03/01 1952 CERT 1 1	04/26 1952 MERITS 1 1	06/09 1952 REPORT 1 1
Minton	G	R	R
Clark	G	R	R
Burton	G		
Jackson	G		
Douglas	G	A J	A SM
Frankfr	G	A	A
Reed	G	A	A
Black	G	A	A
Vinson	G	R	SM

Greenberg v U.S.
51 461A
343 US 918
CCA 3rd

	01/26 1952 CERT 1 1	04/05 1952 MERITS 1 1	04/07 1952 REPORT 1 1
Minton	GR	R	R
Clark	G	R	R
Burton	GR		
Jackson	GR	R	R
Douglas	G	A	A
Frankfr	G	A	A
Reed	G	A	A
Black	GR	R	R
Vinson	G	A	A

United Air Lines v PUC Of California
51 464A
342 US 908 51 465A
California

Justice	12/31 1951 JURIS 1 1	01/05 1952 JURIS 1 2
Minton	S	S
Clark		S
Burton	N	N
Jackson		S
Douglas	S	S
Frankfr	S	S
Reed	N	N
Black		S
Vinson	S	S

Western Air Lines v PUC Of California
51 465A
342 US 908 51 464A
California

Justice	12/31 1951 JURIS 1 1	01/05 1952 JURIS 1 2
Minton	S	S
Clark		S
Burton	N	N
Jackson		S
Douglas	S	S
Frankfr	S	S
Reed	N	N
Black		S
Vinson	S	S

U.S. v Great Lakes Dredge & Dock
51 466A
342 US 953
Ct Cls

Justice	03/01 1952 CERT 1 1	03/08 1952 CERT 1 2
Minton	GR	G
Clark	GM	G
Burton	GM	
Jackson	GM	
Douglas		
Frankfr		
Reed		
Black	G	
Vinson	G	

Armour & Company v Louisiana Southern
51 467A
342 US 913
CCA 5th

Justice	01/12 1952 CERT 1 1
Minton	D
Clark	D
Burton	D
Jackson	D
Douglas	D
Frankfr	D
Reed	D
Black	D
Vinson	G

Cohen v U.S.
51 468A
342 US 947
CCA 9th

Justice	03/01 1952 CERT 1 1
Minton	D
Clark	D
Burton	D
Jackson	D
Douglas	D
Frankfr	D
Reed	D
Black	D
Vinson	G

Aderman v U.S.
51 470A
342 US 927
CCA 7th

Justice	01/26 1952 CERT 1 1
Minton	D
Clark	D
Burton	D
Jackson	D
Douglas	D
Frankfr	D
Reed	D
Black	D
Vinson	D

Coyne Electrical School v Buckley
51 473A
342 US 927
Illinois

Justice	01/26 1952 CERT 1 1
Minton	D
Clark	
Burton	D
Jackson	D
Douglas	G
Frankfr	
Reed	G
Black	
Vinson	G

Stembridge v Georgia
51 474A
343 US 541
Minton 05/06/52 Georgia

Justice	03/01 1952 CERT 1 1	04/26 1952 MERITS 1 S	05/26 1952 REPORT 1 S
Minton	D		
Clark	D		
Burton		V	G
Jackson	D	V	G
Douglas		V	G
Frankfr	G	A	G
Reed		V	G
Black	G	A	
Vinson	G		

Conference Of Studio Unions v Loew's
51 475A
342 US 919
CCA 9th

Justice	01/26 1952 CERT 1 1
Minton	D
Clark	D
Burton	D
Jackson	D
Douglas	D
Frankfr	D
Reed	D
Black	D
Vinson	D

National Furniture Traffic v U.S.
51 476A
342 US 935
DC Massachusetts

Justice	03/01 1952 JURIS 1 1	03/03 1952 REPORT 1 1
Minton	A	A
Clark	A	A
Burton	A	A
Jackson	A	A
Douglas	A	A
Frankfr	A	A
Reed	A	A
Black	A	A
Vinson	A	A

Geuss v Pennsylvania
51 477A
342 US 912
Pennsylvania

Justice	01/12 1952 JURIS 1 1
Minton	S
Clark	S
Burton	S
Jackson	
Douglas	N
Frankfr	
Reed	N
Black	N
Vinson	S

Barshop v U.S.
51 482A
342 US 920
CCA 5th

Justice	01/26 1952 CERT 1 1
Minton	D
Clark	D
Burton	D
Jackson	D
Douglas	D
Frankfr	D
Reed	D
Black	D
Vinson	D

U.S. v R-B Freight Lines
51 484A
342 US 933
Motor Carrier Claims Commission

Justice	02/02 1952 CERT 1 1
Minton	D
Clark	D
Burton	G
Jackson	D
Douglas	D
Frankfr	D
Reed	
Black	D
Vinson	D

Lee On v Long
51 485A
342 US 947
California

Justice	03/01 1952 CERT 1 1
Minton	D
Clark	D
Burton	D
Jackson	D
Douglas	D
Frankfr	
Reed	G
Black	G
Vinson	D

U.S. v American-Hawaiian Steamship
51 487A
342 US 941
CCA 2d

Justice	03/01 1952 CERT 1 1
Minton	D
Clark	D
Burton	D
Jackson	D
Douglas	D
Frankfr	D
Reed	X
Black	D
Vinson	G

Heagney v Brooklyn Eastern District
51 488A
342 US 920
CCA 2d

	CERT 01/26 1952
Minton	G
Clark	G
Burton	G
Jackson	G
Douglas	D
Frankfr	D
Reed	D
Black	D
Vinson	D

Kuniyuki v Acheson
51 492A
342 US 942
CCA 9th

	CERT 03/01 1952
Minton	D
Clark	D
Burton	D
Jackson	D
Douglas	G
Frankfr	
Reed	G
Black	
Vinson	D

Isbrandtsen Company v Johnson
51 493A
343 US 779
Burton 05/06/52 CCA 3rd

	CERT 03/01 1952	MERITS 04/26 1952	REPORT 06/09 1952
Minton	G	A	A
Clark	G	A	A
Burton	G	R	R
Jackson	G		R
Douglas	G	A	A
Frankfr	G	A	A
Reed		A	A
Black		A	A
Vinson			

Illinois v U.S.
51 497A
342 US 930 51 498A
DC ND Illinois

	JURIS 02/02 1952	REPORT 02/04 1952
Minton	A	A
Clark	A	A
Burton		A
Jackson	N	A
Douglas	A	A
Frankfr		A
Reed	A	A
Black	N	A
Vinson	A	A

City Of Chicago v U.S.
51 498A
342 US 930 51 497A
DC ND Illinois

	JURIS 02/02 1952	REPORT 02/04 1952
Minton	A	A
Clark	A	A
Burton		A
Jackson	N	A
Douglas	A	A
Frankfr		A
Reed	A	A
Black	N	A
Vinson	A	A

Hoskins Coal & Dock v Truax Traer Coal
51 501A
342 US 947
CCA 7th

	CERT 03/01 1952
Minton	D
Clark	G
Burton	D
Jackson	
Douglas	G
Frankfr	
Reed	D
Black	D
Vinson	D

Remmey v Smith
51 503A
342 US 916
DC ED Pennsylvania

	JURIS 01/26 1952
Minton	S
Clark	S
Burton	S
Jackson	N
Douglas	S
Frankfr	SA
Reed	S
Black	
Vinson	S

Ruberoid Company v F.T.C.
51 504A
343 US 470 51 448A
Clark 04/09/52 CCA 2d

	CERT 01/26 1952	MERITS 04/05 1952	REPORT 05/26 1952
Minton	D		A
Clark	D		A
Burton	G	R	A
Jackson	G		R
Douglas		R	A
Frankfr	D	A	A
Reed	D	A	A
Black	G	A	A
Vinson	G	A	A

Central RR Of New Jersey v U.S.
51 506A
342 US 935
DC New Jersey

	JURIS 03/01 1952	REPORT 03/03 1952
Minton	A	A
Clark	A	A
Burton	A	A
Jackson	A	A
Douglas	A	A
Frankfr	A	A
Reed	A	A
Black	A	A
Vinson		

Carroll v Ohio
51 511A
342 US 943
Ohio

	CERT 03/01 1952	REPORT 06/02 1952
Minton		R
Clark		R
Burton		R
Jackson		R
Douglas		R
Frankfr		R
Reed		R
Black	G	
Vinson		

Thompson v U.S.
51 513A
343 US 549
Vinson 05/06/52 DC ED Missouri

	JURIS 03/01 1952	MERITS 04/26 1952	REPORT 06/02 1952
Minton	N	A	R
Clark	N	R	R
Burton	N	R	R
Jackson		A	R
Douglas	N	R	R
Frankfr		R	R
Reed		R	R
Black			
Vinson			

McGee v Ekberg
51 517A
343 US 970 51 191M
CCA 9th

	CERT 03/08 1952	REPORT 06/09 1952
Minton	G	VI
Clark	G	VI
Burton	G	VI
Jackson	G	VI
Douglas	G	VI
Frankfr	G	VI
Reed	G	
Black		
Vinson		

Central RR Of New Jersey v Director
51 520A
342 US 936
New Jersey

Justice	03/01 1952 JURIS
Minton	
Clark	S
Burton	S
Jackson	N
Douglas	N
Frankfr	
Reed	
Black	
Vinson	N

Joseph Burstyn v Wilson
51 522A
343 US 495 51 707A
Clark 05/06/52 New York

Justice	02/02 1952 JURIS	05/26 1952 REPORT
Minton	N	R
Clark	N	R
Burton	N	R
Jackson	N	R
Douglas	N	R
Frankfr	N	R
Reed	N	R
Black	N	
Vinson	N	

Chemical Bank v Group Of Investors
51 524A
343 US 929 51 525A 51 528A
CCA 8th

Justice	03/22 1952 CERT	04/19 1952 CERT
Minton		
Clark	D	D
Burton	D	D
Jackson	D	D
Douglas		
Frankfr	G	G
Reed		
Black	G	G
Vinson	D	D

Farwell v Group Of Investors
51 527A
343 US 929 51 524A 51 528A
CCA 8th

Justice	03/22 1952 CERT	04/19 1952 CERT
Minton		
Clark	D	D
Burton	D	D
Jackson	D	D
Douglas		
Frankfr	G	G
Reed		
Black	G	G
Vinson	D	D

Alleghany v Group Of Investors
51 525A
343 US 929 51 524A 51 528A
CCA 8th

Justice	03/22 1952 CERT	04/19 1952 CERT
Minton		
Clark	D	D
Burton	D	D
Jackson	D	D
Douglas		
Frankfr	G	G
Reed		
Black	G	G
Vinson	D	D

Missouri Pacific v Group Of Investors
51 526A
343 US 929 51 524A 51 528A
CCA 8th

Justice	03/22 1952 CERT	04/19 1952 CERT
Minton		
Clark	D	D
Burton	D	D
Jackson	D	D
Douglas		
Frankfr	G	G
Reed		
Black	G	G
Vinson	D	D

Missouri Pacific v Group Of Investors
51 528A
343 US 929 51 524A 51 527A
CCA 8th

Justice	03/22 1952 CERT	04/19 1952 CERT
Minton		
Clark	D	D
Burton	D	D
Jackson	D	D
Douglas		
Frankfr	G	G
Reed		
Black	G	G
Vinson	D	D

Downey v Beck
51 529A
343 US 912
CCA 9th

Justice	03/29 1952 CERT	03/31 1952 REPORT
Minton	GVM	V
Clark		V
Burton	D	V
Jackson	GVM	V
Douglas	GVM	V
Frankfr		V
Reed	D	V
Black	GVM	
Vinson	GVM	

Buffum v Chase National Bank
51 531A
342 US 944
CCA 7th

Justice	03/01 1952 CERT
Minton	
Clark	D
Burton	D
Jackson	D
Douglas	D
Frankfr	
Reed	D
Black	
Vinson	G

United States Trust Company v Zelle
51 534A
342 US 944
CCA 8th

Justice	03/01 1952 CERT
Minton	
Clark	D
Burton	D
Jackson	D
Douglas	G
Frankfr	D
Reed	
Black	D
Vinson	D

McClelland v Fruco Construction
51 536A
342 US 945
CCA 8th

Justice	03/01 1952 CERT
Minton	
Clark	D
Burton	D
Jackson	D
Douglas	D
Frankfr	
Reed	G
Black	
Vinson	G

Davis v B.F. Avery & Sons Company
51 537A
342 US 945
CCA 5th

Justice	03/01 1952 CERT
Minton	
Clark	D
Burton	D
Jackson	D
Douglas	D
Frankfr	
Reed	G
Black	
Vinson	G

Gregory v Louisville & Nashville RR
51 538A
343 US 903
CCA 6th

Justice	03/22 1952 CERT	03/03 1952 REPORT
Minton		A
Clark	G	A
Burton		A
Jackson	D	A
Douglas	D	
Frankfr	D	A
Reed	G	N
Black		N
Vinson	G	A

Cox v Peters
51 540A
342 US 936
Georgia

Justice	03/01 1952 JURIS
Minton	
Clark	S
Burton	S
Jackson	S
Douglas	N
Frankfr	
Reed	S
Black	
Vinson	S

Riss & Company v U.S.
51 541A
342 US 937
DC WD Missouri

Justice	03/01 1952 JURIS
Minton	
Clark	A
Burton	A
Jackson	A
Douglas	A
Frankfr	
Reed	N
Black	A
Vinson	N

On Lee v U.S.
51 543A
343 US 747
Jackson 05/06/52 CCA 2d

	03/01 1952 CERT	04/19 1952 AMICUS	04/26 1952 MERITS	06/02 1952 REPORT
	1 1	1 1	1 1	1 1
Minton				
Clark	G	B	R	A
Burton	G	B	R	A
Jackson	G	B	R	AQ
Douglas		Y		A
Frankfr	D	Y	R	A
Reed		Y	R	R
Black	G	B	R	A
Vinson	G		R	A

Richards v U.S.
51 544A
342 US 946
CCA DC

	03/01 1952 CERT
	1 1
Minton	
Clark	G
Burton	G
Jackson	
Douglas	G
Frankfr	
Reed	G
Black	
Vinson	G

Century Electric Company v C.I.R.
51 548A
342 US 954
CCA 8th

	03/08 1952 CERT
	1 1
Minton	D
Clark	D
Burton	D
Jackson	D
Douglas	D
Frankfr	D
Reed	G
Black	D
Vinson	

Adamowski v Bard
51 553A
343 US 906
CCA 3rd

	03/22 1952 CERT	06/02 1952 REPORT
	1 1	1 1
Minton	D	
Clark	D	A
Burton	D	A
Jackson	D	R
Douglas	D	A
Frankfr	D	R
Reed	G	A
Black	D	A
Vinson	D	A

Lord v Henderson
51 557A
342 US 937
California

	03/01 1952 JURIS	03/01 1952 JURIS
	1 1	2 1
Minton		
Clark	S	S
Burton	S	S
Jackson	S	S
Douglas	S	S
Frankfr		
Reed	N	N
Black	S A	N
Vinson	A	

Combs v Snyder
51 560A
342 US 939
DC DC

	03/01 1952 JURIS	03/03 1952 REPORT
	1 1	1 1
Minton		
Clark	N	N
Burton	N	N
Jackson		
Douglas		
Frankfr	N	N
Reed		
Black	A	A
Vinson	A	A

Tobin v Alma Mills
51 561A
343 US 933
CCA 4th

	04/26 1952 CERT
	1 1
Minton	D
Clark	D
Burton	D
Jackson	D
Douglas	D
Frankfr	D
Reed	G
Black	D
Vinson	D

Jewell v Davies
51 562A
343 US 904
CCA 6th

	03/22 1952 CERT
	1 1
Minton	D
Clark	D
Burton	D
Jackson	D
Douglas	D
Frankfr	D
Reed	G
Black	D
Vinson	D

Poole Foundry & Machine v N.L.R.B.
51 563A
342 US 954
CCA 4th

	03/08 1952 CERT
	1 1
Minton	D
Clark	G
Burton	G
Jackson	G
Douglas	
Frankfr	
Reed	G
Black	
Vinson	

Rosenblum v F.T.C.
51 566A
343 US 905
CCA 2d

	03/22 1952 CERT
	1 1
Minton	D
Clark	D
Burton	D
Jackson	D
Douglas	D
Frankfr	
Reed	D
Black	G
Vinson	D

Delaware & Hudson v Boston RR Holding
51 567A
343 US 920 51 593A
Massachusetts

	04/05 1952 CERT
	1 1
Minton	D
Clark	D
Burton	D
Jackson	D
Douglas	G
Frankfr	
Reed	G
Black	
Vinson	

S.S.W. v Air Transport Association
51 568A
343 US 955 51 591A
CCA DC

	05/24 1952 CERT
	1 1
Minton	D
Clark	D
Burton	D
Jackson	D
Douglas	
Frankfr	
Reed	G
Black	
Vinson	

Kawakita v U.S.
51 570A 51 220M
343 US 717
Douglas 04/09/52 CCA 9th

	02/02 1952 CERT	04/05 1952 MERITS	06/02 1952 REPORT
	1 1	1 1	1 1
Minton	G	A	A
Clark	G	R	R
Burton	G	A	A
Jackson	G	A	A
Douglas	G	A	A
Frankfr	G	A	A
Reed	G	A	A
Black	G	R	R
Vinson	G	A	A

General American v Indiana Harbor RR
51 576A
343 US 905
CCA 7th

	03/22 1952 CERT
	1 1
Minton	D
Clark	D
Burton	D
Jackson	D
Douglas	D
Frankfr	
Reed	G
Black	D
Vinson	

I.C.C. v James McWilliams Blue Line
51 579A
342 US 951
DC SD New York

	03/08 1952 JURIS	03/10 1952 REPORT
	1 1	1 1
Minton	D	A
Clark	D	A
Burton	D	A
Jackson	D	A
Douglas	D	A
Frankfr	N	A
Reed	D	A
Black		A
Vinson		

345

Pyeatte v Board Of Regents
51 581A
342 US 936
DC WD Oklahoma

Justice	03/01 1952 JURIS	03/03 1952 REPORT
	1 1	1 1
Minton	A	A
Clark	A	A
Burton	A	A
Jackson	A	A
Douglas	A	A
Frankfr	A	A
Reed	A	A
Black	A	A
Vinson	A	A

Maxwell v Arkansas
51 582A
343 US 929
Arkansas

Justice	04/19 1952 CERT
	1 1
Minton	D
Clark	D
Burton	D
Jackson	
Douglas	G
Frankfr	
Reed	D
Black	G
Vinson	D

Seitz v Choctaw & Chickasaw Nations
51 589A
343 US 919
CCA 10th

Justice	04/05 1952 CERT
	1 1
Minton	D
Clark	D
Burton	D
Jackson	
Douglas	G
Frankfr	
Reed	D
Black	G
Vinson	D

Air Transport Association v S.S.W.
51 591A
343 US 955 59 568A
CCA DC

Justice	05/24 1952 CERT
	1 1
Minton	
Clark	
Burton	
Jackson	D
Douglas	D
Frankfr	D
Reed	G
Black	D
Vinson	D

Magenis v Boston RR Holding Company
51 593A
343 US 920 51 567A
Massachusetts

Justice	04/05 1952 CERT
	1 1
Minton	
Clark	
Burton	
Jackson	D
Douglas	D
Frankfr	D
Reed	G
Black	G
Vinson	D

Martini v U.S.
51 598A
343 US 926
CCA 2d

Justice	04/19 1952 CERT
	1 1
Minton	
Clark	
Burton	
Jackson	D
Douglas	D
Frankfr	D
Reed	G
Black	G
Vinson	D

Erie Forge Company v U.S.
51 601A
343 US 930
CCA 3rd

Justice	04/05 1952 CERT	04/19 1952 CERT
	1 1	1 2
Minton		
Clark		
Burton	D	D
Jackson	D	D
Douglas	G	G
Frankfr	G	G
Reed		
Black	D	D
Vinson	D	D

White v U.S.
51 616A
343 US 930
CCA 5th

Justice	04/19 1952 CERT
	1 1
Minton	
Clark	
Burton	
Jackson	D
Douglas	D
Frankfr	
Reed	G
Black	
Vinson	G

Straub v Sampsell
51 627A
343 US 927
CCA 9th

Justice	04/19 1952 CERT
	1 1
Minton	
Clark	
Burton	
Jackson	D
Douglas	D
Frankfr	
Reed	G
Black	
Vinson	G

White v Fitzpatrick
51 633A
343 US 928
CCA 2d

Justice	04/19 1952 CERT
	1 1
Minton	
Clark	
Burton	D
Jackson	D
Douglas	G
Frankfr	G
Reed	
Black	D
Vinson	D

Turek v Pennsylvannia RR Company
51 634A
343 US 928
Pennsylvania

Justice	04/19 1952 CERT
	1 1
Minton	
Clark	
Burton	D
Jackson	D
Douglas	G
Frankfr	
Reed	
Black	G
Vinson	D

Anderson v Jordan
51 635A
343 US 912
California

Justice	03/29 1952 JURIS
	1 1
Minton	S
Clark	S
Burton	S
Jackson	
Douglas	S
Frankfr	N
Reed	S
Black	N
Vinson	S

Bradley Mining Company v Boice
51 648A
345 US 932 52 150A
CCA 9th

Justice	05/03 1952 CERT (1 1)	04/11 1953 REHEAR (1 1)	04/13 1953 REPORT (1 1)
Minton	D	Y	>
Clark	D	Y	>
Burton	D	Y	>
Jackson	D	Y	>
Douglas	D	Y	>
Frankfr	D	Y	>
Reed		Y	>
Black	D	Y	>
Vinson	D	Y	>

Ray v Blair
51 649A
343 US 214
Reed 04/09/52 Alabama

Justice	03/22 1952 CERT (1 1)	03/22 1952 STAY (1 1)	04/02 1952 MERITS (1 1)	04/15 1952 REPORT (1 1)
Minton	G	Y	R	R
Clark	G	Y	R	R
Burton	G	Y	R	R
Jackson	G			
Douglas	G		A	A
Frankfr	G	B	A	A
Reed				
Black	G	Y	R	R
Vinson	G	Y	R	R

Loew's v Milgram
51 653A
343 US 929
CCA 3rd

Justice	04/19 1952 CERT (1 1)
Minton	D
Clark	D
Burton	
Jackson	
Douglas	G
Frankfr	G
Reed	
Black	D
Vinson	D

Stallsworth v U.S.
51 664A
343 US 942
CCA 7th

Justice	05/03 1952 CERT (1 1)
Minton	D
Clark	D
Burton	
Jackson	
Douglas	G
Frankfr	G
Reed	
Black	G
Vinson	G

Auto Transports v U.S.
51 665A
343 US 923
DC WD Oklahoma

Justice	04/19 1952 JURIS (1 1)	04/21 1952 REPORT (1 1)
Minton		A
Clark	N	A
Burton	N	A
Jackson		A
Douglas		A
Frankfr		A
Reed	N	A
Black		A
Vinson		A

Singleton v U.S.
51 666A
343 US 944
CCA 3rd

Justice	05/03 1952 CERT (1 1)	05/10 1952 CERT (1 2)	05/12 1952 REPORT (1 1)
Minton	GR	GR	R
Clark	GR	GR	R
Burton	GR	GR	R
Jackson	G	G	G
Douglas	GR	GR	R
Frankfr	GR	GR	R
Reed			
Black	GR	GR	R
Vinson	GR	GR	A
			A

Baltimore Steam Packet v Virginia
51 671A
343 US 923 51 672A
Virginia

Justice	04/19 1952 JURIS (1 1)
Minton	S
Clark	S
Burton	S
Jackson	SA
Douglas	SA
Frankfr	
Reed	
Black	S
Vinson	S

Choctaw Nation v U.S.
51 679A
343 US 955
Ct Cls

Justice	05/24 1952 CERT (1 1)
Minton	D
Clark	D
Burton	D
Jackson	
Douglas	D
Frankfr	D
Reed	
Black	D
Vinson	G

John Deere Plow v Franchise Tax Board
51 682A
343 US 939
California

Justice	05/03 1952 JURIS (1 1)
Minton	S
Clark	
Burton	S
Jackson	N
Douglas	N
Frankfr	
Reed	N
Black	S
Vinson	S

Heisler v Board Of Review
51 684A
343 US 939
Ohio

Justice	05/03 1952 JURIS (1 1)
Minton	S
Clark	S
Burton	S
Jackson	S
Douglas	
Frankfr	P
Reed	P
Black	N
Vinson	S

Furlong v U.S.
51 685A
343 US 950
CCA 7th

Justice	05/10 1952 CERT (1 1)
Minton	D
Clark	D
Burton	D
Jackson	D
Douglas	D
Frankfr	G
Reed	G
Black	
Vinson	D

Birnbaum v Newport Steel
51 693A
343 US 956
CCA 2d

Justice	05/24 1952 CERT (1 1)
Minton	D
Clark	D
Burton	D
Jackson	D
Douglas	D
Frankfr	D
Reed	
Black	
Vinson	G

Imboden v U.S.
51 699A
343 US 957
CCA 6th

	05/24 1952 CERT 1 1
Minton	
Clark	D
Burton	D
Jackson	G
Douglas	D
Frankfr	
Reed	G
Black	G
Vinson	

Chapman v Santa Fe Pacific RR Company
51 702A
343 US 964
CCA DC

	05/24 1952 CERT 1 2
Minton	D
Clark	D
Burton	D
Jackson	D
Douglas	G D
Frankfr	
Reed	G
Black	G X
Vinson	

Moran v U.S.
51 704A
343 US 965
CCA 2d

	05/29 1952 CERT 1 1
Minton	D
Clark	D
Burton	D
Jackson	D
Douglas	G
Frankfr	
Reed	G
Black	G
Vinson	

Gelling v Texas
51 707A
343 US 960 51 522A
Texas

	05/24 1952 MERITS 1 1	06/02 1952 REPORT 1 1
Minton	R	R
Clark	R	R
Burton	R	R
Jackson	R	R
Douglas	R	R
Frankfr	R	R
Reed	R	R
Black	R	R
Vinson	R	R

American Crystal Sugar v Mandeville
51 711A
343 US 957
CCA 9th

	05/24 1952 CERT 1 1
Minton	
Clark	G
Burton	G
Jackson	
Douglas	D
Frankfr	
Reed	D
Black	D
Vinson	D

Scott v Harman
51 713A
343 US 965
CCA 6th

	05/29 1952 CERT 1 1
Minton	D
Clark	D
Burton	D
Jackson	
Douglas	GR
Frankfr	
Reed	G-X
Black	GR
Vinson	

Brennan v Delaware Lackawanna RR
51 720A
343 US 977 51 728A
New York

	05/24 1952 CERT 1 1
Minton	
Clark	D
Burton	GQ
Jackson	G
Douglas	
Frankfr	D
Reed	D
Black	DH
Vinson	D

Tom's Express v Division Of State
51 722A
343 US 944
DC SD Ohio

	05/10 1952 JURIS 1 1
Minton	S
Clark	S
Burton	S
Jackson	
Douglas	N
Frankfr	N
Reed	
Black	S
Vinson	S

Switchmen's v Delaware Lackawanna RR
51 728A
343 US 977 51 720A
New York

	05/24 1952 CERT 1 1
Minton	
Clark	D
Burton	GQ
Jackson	G
Douglas	
Frankfr	D
Reed	D
Black	DH
Vinson	D

Shein v U.S.
51 731A
343 US 944
DC New Jersey

	05/10 1952 JURIS 1 1	05/12 1952 REPORT 1 1
Minton	A	A
Clark	A	A
Burton	A	A
Jackson	A	A
Douglas	A	A
Frankfr	A	A
Reed	A	A
Black	A	A
Vinson	N	A

Patent Scaffolding v Up-Right
51 738A
343 US 958
CCA 9th

	05/24 1952 CERT 1 1
Minton	D
Clark	D
Burton	D
Jackson	
Douglas	G D
Frankfr	
Reed	G D
Black	
Vinson	

Sholl v Cadwallader
51 743A
343 US 966
CCA DC

	05/29 1952 CERT 1 1	06/07 1952 FEES 1 1
Minton	GM	
Clark		
Burton	D	
Jackson	D	
Douglas	D	
Frankfr	GM	B
Reed		
Black	D	
Vinson	GM D	B

Youngstown Sheet & Tube v Sawyer
51 744A 51 745A
343 US 579
Black 05/16/52 CCA DC

	05/03 1952 STAY 1 1	05/03 1952 CERT 1 1	05/03 1952 QUEST 15 1	05/16 1952 MERITS 1 1	06/02 1952 REPORT 1 1
Minton	Y	G	Y	R	R
Clark	Y	G	Y	A	A
Burton			Y	A	A
Jackson	X	X	Y	A	A
Douglas	Y	G	Y	A	A
Frankfr		D	Y	A	A
Reed	Y	G	Y		
Black	Y	G	Y	R	R
Vinson	Y	G	Y	R	R

Overseas Tankship v Keen
51 749A
343 US 966
CCA 2d

	05/29 1952 CERT 1 1
Minton	D
Clark	D
Burton	D
Jackson	
Douglas	G
Frankfr	D
Reed	D
Black	
Vinson	

Brotherhood Of Locomotive v U.S.
51 759A
343 US 971
CCA 6th

	06/07 1952 CERT 1 1	06/07 1952 FEES 1 1	06/09 1952 REPORT 1 1
Minton	GVI	Y	VI
Clark	GVI	Y	VI
Burton	GVI		VI
Jackson	GVI		VI
Douglas	GVI		VI
Frankfr	GVI	Y	VI
Reed	GVI	Y	VI
Black	GVI		VI
Vinson	GVI		VI

Haidas v Illinois
51 105M
342 US 906 51 113M
Illinois

	12/31 1951 CERT — 1 1
Minton	D
Clark	D
Burton	D
Jackson	
Douglas	GH
Frankfr	
Reed	D
Black	GH
Vinson	D

Touhy v Illinois
51 113M
342 US 905 51 105M
Illinois

	12/31 1951 CERT — 1 1
Minton	D
Clark	D
Burton	D
Jackson	
Douglas	GH
Frankfr	
Reed	D
Black	GH
Vinson	D

McMurrin v Texas
51 123M
342 US 874
Texas

	11/03 1951 CERT — 1 1
Minton	D
Clark	D
Burton	D
Jackson	
Douglas	G
Frankfr	
Reed	D
Black	D
Vinson	D

Nash v MacArthur
51 58M
342 US 838
CCA DC

	10/03 1951 CERT / MNDMUS — 1 1	12/01 1951 CONTIN — 1 1
Minton	G	Y
Clark	G	Y
Burton	G	Y
Jackson	G	
Douglas	G	BK
Frankfr	G	Y
Reed	G	Y
Black	G	BK
Vinson	G	Y

Cogdell (Ex Parte)
51 71M
342 US 163
CCA DC

	12/31 1951 CERT — 1 1
Minton	D
Clark	D
Burton	D
Jackson	D
Douglas	D
Frankfr	
Reed	D
Black	D
Vinson	

Dorsey v Arkansas
51 94M
342 US 851
Arkansas

	10/13 1951 CERT — 1 1
Minton	D
Clark	D
Burton	D
Jackson	D
Douglas	G
Frankfr	G
Reed	G
Black	G
Vinson	G

Geach v Illinois
51 35M
342 US 939 51 95A 51 49M
Illinois

	12/31 1951 CERT — 1 1	03/01 1952 MERITS — 1 1	03/03 1952 REPORT — 1 1
Minton	H	>	>
Clark	H	>	>
Burton	H	>	>
Jackson	H	>	>
Douglas	GVM	>	>
Frankfr	H	>	>
Reed	H	>	>
Black	GVM	>	>
Vinson	GVM	>	>

Thompson v Illinois
51 41M
342 US 906

	12/31 1951 CERT — 1 1
Minton	D
Clark	D
Burton	D
Jackson	D
Douglas	D
Frankfr	
Reed	D
Black	D
Vinson	

Smith v Illinois
51 49M
342 US 939 51 95A 51 35M
Illinois

	12/31 1951 CERT — 1 1	03/01 1952 MERITS — 1 1	03/03 1952 REPORT — 1 1
Minton	H	>	>
Clark	H	>	>
Burton	H	>	>
Jackson	H	>	>
Douglas	GVM	>	>
Frankfr	H	>	>
Reed	H	>	>
Black	GVM	>	>
Vinson	GVM	>	>

Barnes v Hunter
51 9M
342 US 920
CCA 10th

	01/26 1952 CERT — 1 1
Minton	D
Clark	D
Burton	D
Jackson	
Douglas	G
Frankfr	E
Reed	D
Black	D
Vinson	D

Far East Conference v U.S.
51 15M
342 US 570 51 134A 51 135A
Frankfr 02/06/52 DC New Jersey

	10/03 1951 CERT — 1 1	02/02 1952 MERITS — 1 1	03/10 1952 REPORT — 1 1	06/09 1952 REPORT — 1 1
Minton	G	R	R	A
Clark	G	R	R	A
Burton	G	R	R	A
Jackson	G	R	R	A
Douglas	G	A	A	A
Frankfr	G	R	R	A
Reed	G	R	R	A
Black	G	A	A	A
Vinson	G	R	R	A

Middlebrooks v Ross
51 25M
342 US 862
CCA 9th

	10/20 1951 CERT — 1 1
Minton	D
Clark	D
Burton	D
Jackson	
Douglas	G
Frankfr	
Reed	D
Black	D
Vinson	D

County Transportation v New York
51 766A
343 US 961
New York

	05/29 1952 JURIS — 1 1
Minton	S
Clark	S
Burton	S
Jackson	N
Douglas	S
Frankfr	S
Reed	S
Black	S
Vinson	S

Ross v Harris
51 790A
343 US 971
DC SD California

	06/07 1952 JURIS — 1 1	06/09 1952 REPORT — 1 1
Minton	A	A
Clark	A	A
Burton	A	A
Jackson	SQ	A
Douglas	S	A
Frankfr	A	A
Reed	A	A
Black	A	A
Vinson	S	

Smith v Maryland
51 7M
342 US 905 51 38A
Maryland

	10/20 1951 CERT — 1 1	12/31 1951 CERT — 1 2
Minton	D	D
Clark	D	D
Burton	D	D
Jackson		
Douglas	G	G
Frankfr		
Reed	D	D
Black	D	D
Vinson	D	

Taylor v Cranor
51 136M
342 US 878
Washington
11/10 1951 · CERT 1 1

Justice	Vote
Minton	D
Clark	
Burton	G
Jackson	D
Douglas	
Frankfr	D
Reed	D
Black	G
Vinson	D

Scott v U.S.
51 142M
342 US 878
CCA 5th
11/10 1951 · CERT 1 1

Justice	Vote
Minton	G
Clark	D
Burton	D
Jackson	D
Douglas	G
Frankfr	D
Reed	D
Black	G G
Vinson	G

Louisiana (Washington) v Clancy
51 150M
342 US 928
Louisiana
01/26 1952 · CERT 1 2

Justice	Vote
Minton	D
Clark	E
Burton	D
Jackson	D
Douglas	G
Frankfr	E
Reed	D
Black	G G
Vinson	G

Fouquette v Nevada
51 156M
342 US 928
Nevada
01/26 1952 · CERT 1 1

Justice	Vote
Minton	D
Clark	D
Burton	D
Jackson	D
Douglas	G
Frankfr	D
Reed	D
Black	D
Vinson	D

Thomas v Duffy
51 163M
343 US 906
California
11/24 1951 · CERT 1 1

Justice	Vote
Minton	E
Clark	E
Burton	D
Jackson	G
Douglas	G
Frankfr	G
Reed	G
Black	G
Vinson	G

Davis v Illinois
51 167M
342 US 894
Illinois
12/01 1951 · CERT 1 1

Justice	Vote
Minton	D
Clark	G
Burton	G
Jackson	D
Douglas	G
Frankfr	D
Reed	D
Black	D
Vinson	D

Schell v Missouri
51 183M
342 US 933
Missouri
02/02 1952 · CERT 1 1

Justice	Vote
Minton	D
Clark	D
Burton	D
Jackson	G
Douglas	G
Frankfr	D
Reed	G
Black	D
Vinson	D

Roberts v Western Pacific RR
51 193M
342 US 906 · 51 194M
CCA 9th
12/31 1951 · CERT 1 1

Justice	Vote
Minton	D
Clark	G
Burton	D
Jackson	D
Douglas	D
Frankfr	D
Reed	D
Black	D
Vinson	D

U.S. (Roberts) v Western Pacific RR
51 194M
342 US 906 · 51 193M
CCA 9th
12/31 1951 · CERT 1 1

Justice	Vote
Minton	D
Clark	D
Burton	G
Jackson	D
Douglas	D
Frankfr	D
Reed	G
Black	G
Vinson	D

Reeves v Heinze
51 201M
342 US 955
California
03/08 1952 · CERT 1 1

Justice	Vote
Minton	D
Clark	D
Burton	D
Jackson	G
Douglas	D
Frankfr	D
Reed	D
Black	D
Vinson	D

Braasch v Utah
51 205M
342 US 910
Utah
01/05 1952 · CERT 1 1

Justice	Vote
Minton	D
Clark	D
Burton	D
Jackson	G
Douglas	G
Frankfr	D
Reed	D
Black	D
Vinson	D

Lewis v McDaniel
51 223M
342 US 933
Tennessee
02/02 1952 · CERT 1 1

Justice	Vote
Minton	DO
Clark	D
Burton	D
Jackson	D
Douglas	GQ
Frankfr	D
Reed	D
Black	DO
Vinson	D

Buckowski v California
51 224M
342 US 928
California
01/26 1952 · CERT 1 1

Justice	Vote
Minton	D
Clark	D
Burton	D
Jackson	D
Douglas	D
Frankfr	D
Reed	D
Black	G
Vinson	D

Whitehead v Henry
51 234M
342 US 933
Georgia
02/02 1952 · CERT 1 1

Justice	Vote
Minton	D
Clark	G
Burton	D
Jackson	G
Douglas	G
Frankfr	D
Reed	G
Black	G
Vinson	D

Williams v Illinois
51 235M
343 US 972 · 51 95A
Illinois
06/07 1952 · CERT 1 1

Justice	Vote
Minton	GVM
Clark	GVM
Burton	GVM
Jackson	D
Douglas	GVM
Frankfr	GVM
Reed	GVM
Black	GVM
Vinson	GVM

Eaton v Eidson
51 246M
343 US 979
Missouri
06/07 1952 · CERT 1 1

Justice	Vote
Minton	D
Clark	D
Burton	D
Jackson	G
Douglas	G
Frankfr	D
Reed	G
Black	D
Vinson	D

Williams v Illinois
51 247M
342 US 934
Illinois
01/26 1952 · CERT 1 1

Justice	Vote
Minton	D
Clark	D
Burton	D
Jackson	G
Douglas	G
Frankfr	D
Reed	G
Black	D
Vinson	D

Shotkin v Atchison Topeka RR
51 252M
343 US 906
Colorado
03/22 1952 · CERT 1 1

Justice	Vote
Minton	
Clark	
Burton	
Jackson	
Douglas	G
Frankfr	
Reed	
Black	
Vinson	

Docket voting chart. Justice order in each block: Minton, Clark, Burton, Jackson, Douglas, Frankfr, Reed, Black, Vinson.

Beale v Mississippi
51 267M — 342 US 948 — Mississippi

Justice	CERT 03/01/1952 (1 1)
Minton	D
Clark	D
Burton	D
Jackson	D
Douglas	G
Frankfr	D
Reed	D
Black	D
Vinson	D

Patterson v U.S.
51 282M — 343 US 951 — CCA 5th

Justice	CERT 05/10/1952 (1 1)
Minton	D
Clark	D
Burton	D
Jackson	D
Douglas	G
Frankfr	D
Reed	D
Black	D
Vinson	D

Alexander v New Jersey
51 284M — 343 US 908 — New Jersey

Justice	CERT 03/22/1952 (1 1)
Minton	D
Clark	D
Burton	D
Jackson	D
Douglas	G
Frankfr	D
Reed	D
Black	D
Vinson	D

Anthony v Kaufman
51 290M — 342 US 955 — CCA 2d

Justice	CERT 03/08/1952 (1 1)
Minton	D
Clark	D
Burton	D
Jackson	D
Douglas	D
Frankfr	D
Reed	D
Black	G
Vinson	D

Tyler v U.S.
51 291M — 343 US 908 — CCA DC

Justice	CERT 03/22/1952 (1 1)
Minton	D
Clark	D
Burton	D
Jackson	D
Douglas	G
Frankfr	D
Reed	D
Black	D
Vinson	D

Preston v Texas
51 321M — 343 US 933 — Texas

Justice	CERT 03/29/1952 (1 1)
Minton	D
Clark	D
Burton	DZ
Jackson	D
Douglas	D
Frankfr	D
Reed	D
Black	DZ
Vinson	D

Levinton v U.S.
51 326M — 343 US 946 — CCA 2d

Justice	CERT 05/10/1952 (1 1)
Minton	D
Clark	D
Burton	D
Jackson	D
Douglas	G
Frankfr	G
Reed	D
Black	G
Vinson	D

Hurley v City Of Atlanta Georgia
51 351M — 343 US 917 — Georgia

Justice	CERT 03/29/1952 (1 1)
Minton	D
Clark	D
Burton	D
Jackson	D
Douglas	G
Frankfr	G
Reed	D
Black	G
Vinson	D

Chessman v California
51 371M — 343 US 915 — California

Justice	REHEAR 04/26/1952 (1 1)	CERT 04/26/1952 (1 2)
Minton	B	D
Clark	B	D
Burton	B	D
Jackson	Y	D
Douglas	Y	D
Frankfr	Y	D
Reed	Y	D
Black	B	
Vinson		G

U.S. (Jellison) v Warden Of New Jersey
51 372M — 343 US 916 51 378M 51 379M — CCA 3rd

Justice	CERT 03/29/1952 (1 1)
Minton	D
Clark	D
Burton	D
Jackson	D
Douglas	G
Frankfr	D
Reed	D
Black	G
Vinson	D

U.S. (Smith) v Warden Of New Jersey
51 378M — 343 US 916 51 372M 51 379M — CCA 3rd

Justice	CERT 03/29/1952 (1 1)
Minton	D
Clark	D
Burton	D
Jackson	D
Douglas	G
Frankfr	D
Reed	D
Black	G
Vinson	D

U.S. (Bunk) v Warden Of New Jersey
51 379M — 343 US 916 51 372M 51 378M — CCA 3rd

Justice	CERT 03/29/1952 (1 1)
Minton	D
Clark	D
Burton	D
Jackson	D
Douglas	G
Frankfr	D
Reed	D
Black	G
Vinson	D

Wilson v Washington
51 401M — 343 US 950 — Washington

Justice	CERT 05/10/1952 (1 1)
Minton	D
Clark	D
Burton	D
Jackson	D
Douglas	G
Frankfr	D
Reed	D
Black	D
Vinson	D

U.S. (Young) v Shaughnessy
51 414M — 343 US 913

Justice	BAIL 03/29/1952 (1 1)
Minton	B
Clark	B
Burton	B
Jackson	B
Douglas	Y
Frankfr	B
Reed	B
Black	Y
Vinson	B

Ross v Texas
51 483M — 343 US 969 — Texas

Justice	CERT 05/29/1952 (1 1)
Minton	D
Clark	D
Burton	D
Jackson	D
Douglas	G
Frankfr	D
Reed	D
Black	D
Vinson	D

Hoffman v Circuit Court Of Winnebago
51 485M — 343 US 972 — Illinois

Justice	CERT 06/07/1952 (1 1)	REPORT 06/09/1952 (1 >)
Minton		>
Clark		>
Burton	D	GVM
Jackson		>
Douglas	D	GVM
Frankfr		GVM
Reed		GVM
Black		GVM
Vinson		GVM

Liquor Control Commission (In Matter)
51 510M — 343 US 975

Justice	MNDMUS 05/29/1952 (1 1)	MNDMUS 06/07/1952 (1 2)
Minton		
Clark	D	D
Burton	D	D
Jackson	D	D
Douglas	G	G
Frankfr	G	G
Reed	G	G
Black	G	G
Vinson	G	G

Appendix H

U.S. Supreme Court
October 1952 Term

Land v Dollar
52 1A 51 32A 50 353A 50 552A 50 697A
344 US 806 51 247A 52 2A 52 5A
CCA DC

	11/11 1950 CERT (1 1)	03/10 1951 CERT (1 2)	05/26 1951 CERT (1 3)	04/21 1951 QUEST (13 1)	10/06 1952 MERITS (1 1)	10/13 1952 REPORT (1 1)
Minton						
Clark						
Burton		D	G	B		
Jackson	D	D	G	B K	SI	SI
Douglas	D	D		B	SI	SI
Frankfr		H	G	B Y	SI	SI
Reed	G	D	G		SI	SI
Black						
Vinson	G	H	G	B	SI	SI

Killion (In The Matter Of)
52 2A 52 6A 51 248A 50 702A
344 US 806 52 1A 52 5A
CCA DC

	11/10 1951 CERT (1 1)	10/06 1952 DISMISS (1 1)	10/13 1952 REPORT (1 1)
Minton	G		SI
Clark	G	Y	SI
Burton	G	Y	SI
Jackson	G	Y	
Douglas	G D	Y	SI
Frankfr	G H	Y	
Reed	G	Y	
Black	G		
Vinson	G	Y	SI

Kedroff v Saint Nicholas Cathedral
52 3A 51 44A 50 717A
344 US 94
Reed 02/05/52 New York   Reed 10/28/52 New York

	06/02 1951 JURIS (1 1)	02/02 1952 MERITS (1 1)	10/18 1952 MERITS (1 2)	11/24 1952 REPORT (1 1)
Minton	N	RM A	R	R
Clark	S N	R	R A	R
Burton	N	A	R	R A
Jackson	N	R	R	R
Douglas	N	RM	R	R
Frankfr	N		R	R
Reed			AQ	
Black				
Vinson				

Dixon v Duffy
52 4A 51 79A 50 766A 50 328M
344 US 143
Vinson 04/26/52 California

	05/12 1951 CERT (1 1)	05/26 1951 CERT (1 2)	10/22 1951 CLARIFY (1 1)	04/19 1952 MERITS (1 1)	11/14 1952 MERITS (1 2)	12/08 1952 REPORT (1 1)
Minton						
Clark	H D	G D	Y	S A	>	>
Burton						
Jackson	H	G	Y	S A	>	>
Douglas	H	G	Y	S A	> S	> S
Frankfr	H D	G D	Y	S	>	>
Reed	H	G	Y	S	>	>
Black	H D	G D	Y	S	>	>
Vinson	H	G	Y	S	>	>

Sawyer v Dollar
52 5A 51 247A
344 US 806 52 1A 52 2A 52 6A
CCA DC

	11/03 1951 CERT (1 1)	11/10 1951 CERT (1 2)	10/06 1952 MERITS (1 1)	10/13 1952 REPORT (1 1)
Minton	GH	GH	VI	VI
Clark	GH	GH	VI	VI
Burton				
Jackson	G D	G D	VI	VI
Douglas				
Frankfr	G H	G H	VI	VI
Reed	GH	GH	VI	VI
Black				
Vinson	GH	GH	VI	VI

Gordon v Heikkinen
52 7A 51 334A
344 US 870
CCA 8th

	03/22 1952 CERT (1 1)	05/10 1952 VACATE (1 1)	11/08 1952 CERT (1 1)	11/10 1952 REPORT (1 1)
Minton	GV	B	VI	VI
Clark	G	B	VI	VI
Burton	G	B	VI	VI
Jackson	G	B	VI	VI
Douglas	G D	B	VI	VI
Frankfr	G	B		
Reed	G D	B	VI	VI
Black	GV	B	VI	VI
Vinson	GV	B	VI	VI

King v U.S.
52 9A 51 444A
344 US 254 52 455A
Burton 10/28/52 DC ND Florida

	12/31 1951 JURIS	05/24 1952 AMICUS	10/09 1952 ARGUE	10/18 1952 MERITS	12/22 1952 REPORT
	1 1	1 1	1 1	1 1	1 1
Minton	N	B	B		A
Clark	N		B	R	A
Burton	A	B	B		A
Jackson		Y	B		A
Douglas	N	B	B		A
Frankfr				R	
Reed	A	Y			A
Black	A	Y	Y	R	A
Vinson	N	B	B	R	A

U.S. v Henning
52 10A 51 456A
344 US 66 52 39A
Clark 10/28/52 CCA 1st

	01/26 1952 CERT	04/05 1952 MERITS	11/17 1952 REPORT
	1 1	1 1	1 1
Minton	G	R	R
Clark	G	R	R
Burton	G	R	R
Jackson	G	R A	R
Douglas	G	R A	R
Frankfr	G	R	R
Reed	G	R	R A
Black	G	R	R
Vinson	G	R	R

F.T.C. v Minneapolis-Honeywell
52 11A 51 479A
344 US 206 52 248A
Vinson 10/28/52 CCA 7th

	03/01 1952 CERT	10/18 1952 DISMISS	12/22 1952 REPORT
	1 1	1 1	1 1
Minton	G	Y	S
Clark	G D	Y	S
Burton	D	Y	S
Jackson	G D	Y	S
Douglas	G D	B Y	S
Frankfr			
Reed	G	B Y	G
Black	G	Y	GR
Vinson	G	B Y	S

F.P.C. v Idaho Power Company
52 12A 51 483A
344 US 17
Douglas 10/28/52 CCA DC

	03/01 1952 CERT	10/25 1952 MERITS	11/10 1952 REPORT
	1 1	1 1	1 1
Minton	G	R	R
Clark	G		
Burton	G	R	R
Jackson	G	R	R
Douglas	G	R	R
Frankfr	G	R S	R
Reed	G		
Black	G		
Vinson	G		

U.S. v Bell Aircraft
52 13A 51 559A
344 US 860
Ct Cls

	03/29 1952 CERT	10/25 1952 MERITS	10/27 1952 REPORT
	1 1	1 1	1 1
Minton	G	R	R
Clark	G D		
Burton	D		
Jackson	D	R A	R A
Douglas	D		
Frankfr			
Reed	G	R A	R A
Black	G		
Vinson	G D	R A	R A

Wieman v Updegraff
52 14A 51 590A
344 US 183
Clark 10/28/52 Oklahoma

	03/08 1952 JURIS	10/18 1952 MERITS	12/15 1952 REPORT
	1 1	1 1	1 1
Minton	N	R	R
Clark	N	R	R
Burton	N	R	R
Jackson	N		
Douglas	N	R	R
Frankfr	N		
Reed	N	R	R
Black	N	R	R
Vinson	N	R	R

Mandoli v Acheson
52 15A 51 597A
344 US 133 51 570A
Jackson 10/28/52 CCA DC

	04/19 1952 CERT	06/07 1952 CERT	10/18 1952 MERITS	11/24 1952 REPORT
	1 1	1 2	1 1	1 1
Minton	H	G	RVM	R
Clark	H	G	RVM AS	R A
Burton	G	G	RVM A	R A
Jackson				
Douglas	H	G D	RVM AS	R A
Frankfr				
Reed	G		RVM A	R A
Black	G D	G D		
Vinson	D	D		

U.S. v Caltex (Philippines)
52 16A 51 610A
344 US 149
Vinson 10/28/52 Ct Cls

	05/24 1952 CERT	10/25 1952 MERITS	12/08 1952 REPORT
	1 1	1 1	1 1
Minton	G	R	R
Clark	G	R	R
Burton	G	R	R
Jackson	G		
Douglas	G	R A	R A
Frankfr			
Reed	G	R	R
Black	G D	R	R
Vinson	G D	R	R

Kwong Hai Chew v Colding
52 17A 51 617A
344 US 590
Burton 10/28/52 CCA 2d

	04/26 1952 CERT	10/18 1952 MERITS	02/09 1953 REPORT
	1 1	1 1	1 1
Minton	G	R	R
Clark	G D	R	R
Burton	G	R	R
Jackson	G	R A	R A
Douglas	G D		
Frankfr			
Reed	G	R A	R A
Black	G D	R	R
Vinson	G D	R A	R A

U.S. v L.A. Tucker Truck Lines
52 18A 51 621A
344 US 33 52 17A 52 77A
Jackson 10/28/52 DC ED Missouri

Justice	03/22 1952 JURIS (1 1)	10/25 1952 MERITS (1 1)	11/10 1952 REPORT (1 1)
Minton	N	R	R
Clark	N	R	R
Burton	N	R	R
Jackson	N	X	
Douglas	A	A	A
Frankfr	N	R	R
Reed	N	R	R
Black	A	A	A
Vinson	N	R	R

Perez v California
52 19A 51 623A
344 US 903 52 4A
California

Justice	12/13 1952 CERT (1 1)
Minton	D
Clark	D
Burton	D
Jackson	D
Douglas	
Frankfr	D
Reed	D
Black	
Vinson	D

Daniels v Allen
52 20A 51 626A 51 271M
344 US 443 52 22A 52 32A
Reed 10/28/52 CCA 4th

Justice	03/01 1952 CERT (1 1)	06/07 1952 MERITS (1 1)	10/27 1952 MERITS (1 2)	02/09 1953 REPORT (1 1)
Minton	G	R	R	A
Clark	G	R	R	AQ
Burton				A
Jackson				A
Douglas	G	S		
Frankfr		R	R	A
Reed				
Black	G		R	A
Vinson	G			

U.S. v Reynolds
52 21A 51 638A
345 US 1
Vinson 10/28/52 CCA 3rd

Justice	04/05 1952 CERT (1 1)	10/25 1952 MERITS (1 1)	03/09 1953 REPORT (1 1)
Minton	G	R	R
Clark	G	R	R
Burton	G	R	R
Jackson			
Douglas	D	A	A
Frankfr	D	R	R
Reed			
Black	D	A	A
Vinson	G	R	R

Speller v Allen
52 22A 51 643A 51 274M
344 US 443 52 20A 52 32A
Reed 10/28/52 CCA 4th

Justice	03/08 1952 CERT (1 1)	10/25 1952 MERITS (1 1)	02/09 1953 REPORT (1 1)
Minton	G	R	R
Clark	G	R	R
Burton	G	A	A
Jackson	G	A	A
Douglas	G	A	A
Frankfr	G	R	R
Reed	G		
Black	G	A	A
Vinson	G	A	A

City Of Chicago v Willett Company
52 23A 51 644A 50 493A
344 US 574
Frankfr 10/28/52 Illinois

Justice	04/21 1951 CERT (1 1)	10/20 1951 CLARIFY (1 1)	05/03 1952 CERT (1 2)	10/18 1952 MERITS (1 1)	02/09 1953 REPORT (1 1)
Minton	GVM	Y	G	R	R
Clark	GVM D	Y	G	R	R
Burton	GVM	Y	G	R	R
Jackson	GVM	Y	G		
Douglas	GVM	Y			
Frankfr	GVM	Y	G	R	R
Reed	GVM	Y	G		
Black	GVM D	Y	G	X	
Vinson	GVM D		G		

Gulf Research & Development v Leahy
52 24A 51 645A
344 US 861
CCA 3rd

Justice	04/19 1952 CERT (1 1)	10/25 1952 MERITS (1 1)	10/27 1952 REPORT (1 1)
Minton	G	A	A
Clark	G	R	R
Burton	G	R	R
Jackson	G	R	R
Douglas	G		
Frankfr	G	R	R
Reed	G	A	A
Black	D	A	A
Vinson			

Cardox v C-O-Two Fire Equipment
52 25A 51 646A
344 US 861
CCA 7th

Justice	04/19 1952 CERT (1 1)	10/25 1952 MERITS (1 1)	10/27 1952 REPORT (1 1)
Minton	G	A	A
Clark	G	R	R
Burton	G	R	R
Jackson	G	R	R
Douglas	DH		
Frankfr	G	R	R
Reed	G	A	A
Black	D	A	A
Vinson			

American Trucking Associations v U.S.
52 26A 51 647A
344 US 298 52 35A 52 36A
Reed 11/25/52 DC ND Alabama

Justice	04/19 1952 JURIS (1 1)	11/21 1952 MERITS (1 1)	01/12 1953 REPORT (1 1)
Minton		A	A
Clark		A	A
Burton			
Jackson	N		
Douglas	N	R	R
Frankfr	N		
Reed	N		
Black		A	A
Vinson		R	R

U.S. v Cardiff
52 27A 51 652A
Douglas 11/25/52 CCA 9th

	05/03 1952 CERT	11/21 1952 MERITS	12/08 1952 REPORT
Minton	G		A
Clark	G		A
Burton		R	
Jackson	D		A
Douglas	D		A
Frankfr	G		A
Reed			A
Black	G		A
Vinson	G		A

U.S. (Chapman) v F.P.C.
52 28A 51 658A
345 US 153 52 29A
Frankfr 10/28/52 CCA 4th

	05/03 1952 CERT	10/25 1952 MERITS	03/16 1953 REPORT
Minton	G		A
Clark	G		A
Burton		R	R
Jackson	D		A
Douglas	D		A
Frankfr	D	A	A
Reed			A
Black	G	R	R
Vinson	G	R	R

Virginia Rea Association v F.P.C.
52 29A 51 659A
345 US 153 52 28A
Frankfr 10/28/52 CCA 4th

	05/03 1952 CERT	10/25 1952 MERITS	03/16 1953 REPORT
Minton	G		A
Clark	G		A
Burton		R	R
Jackson	D		A
Douglas	D		A
Frankfr	D	A	A
Reed			A
Black	G	R	R
Vinson	G	R	R

U.S. v Beacon Brass Company
52 30A 51 662A
344 US 43
Minton 10/28/52 DC Massachusetts

	04/19 1952 JURIS	10/25 1952 MERITS	11/10 1952 REPORT
Minton	N	R	R
Clark	N	R	R
Burton	N	R	R
Jackson	N	X	R
Douglas	N	R	R
Frankfr	N	R	R
Reed	N		R
Black	N	X	R
Vinson	N	R	A

U.S. (Smith) v Baldi
52 31A 51 669A 51 300M
344 US 561 52 20A 52 22A 52 32A
Reed 10/28/52 CCA 3rd

	03/22 1952 CERT	10/27 1952 MERITS	02/09 1953 REPORT
Minton	G		A
Clark	G		A
Burton	G	R	R
Jackson	G	R	R
Douglas	D		A
Frankfr	G	R	R
Reed	G		A
Black	D	R	R
Vinson	D	R	R

Brown v Allen
52 32A 51 670A 52 20A 52 22A 52 31A
344 US 443 52 20A 52 22A 52 31A
Reed 10/28/52 CCA 4th

	03/22 1952 CERT	10/27 1952 MERITS	02/09 1953 REPORT
Minton	GH		A
Clark	GH		A
Burton	GH	X	A
Jackson	G	DH	A
Douglas	H		A
Frankfr	G	R	R
Reed	G	R	R
Black	G		A
Vinson	G	R	R

Secretary Of Agriculture v U.S.
52 36A 51 710A
344 US 298 52 35A 52 26A
Reed 11/25/52 DC SD Indiana

	05/10 1952 JURIS	11/21 1952 MERITS	01/12 1953 REPORT
Minton	N		A
Clark	N	R	A
Burton	N	R	A
Jackson	N	A	A
Douglas	N		A
Frankfr	N		
Reed	N	R	R
Black	N		
Vinson	N	R	R

Lloyd A. Fry Roofing Company v Wood
52 37A 51 721A
344 US 157
Black 11/25/52 Arkansas

	05/29 1952 CERT	11/14 1952 MERITS	12/08 1952 REPORT
Minton		R	R
Clark	D	SA	A
Burton	D	S	A
Jackson			A
Douglas	D	S	A
Frankfr		SA	A
Reed			A
Black		R	R
Vinson			A

Steele v Bulova Watch Company
52 38A 51 725A
344 US 280
Clark 11/25/52 CCA 5th

	05/29 1952 CERT	11/14 1952 MERITS	12/22 1952 REPORT
Minton	G		A
Clark	G		A
Burton	G	R	A
Jackson	G		A
Douglas	G		A
Frankfr	G		A
Reed	G		A
Black	G	R	R
Vinson	G		A

Nathanson v N.L.R.B.
52 33A 51 677A
344 US 25
Douglas 11/25/52 CCA 1st

	05/29 1952 CERT	10/25 1952 MERITS	11/10 1952 REPORT
Minton	G	R	R
Clark	G	R	R
Burton	G	R	R
Jackson	G		
Douglas	G		A
Frankfr	G	R	R
Reed	G	R	R
Black	D		A
Vinson	D	X	A

Brock v North Carolina
52 34A 51 681A 51 324M
344 US 424
Minton 10/28/52 North Carolina

	03/29 1952 CERT	10/25 1952 MERITS	02/03 1953 REPORT
Minton	G		A
Clark	G		A
Burton	G		A
Jackson	G	R	R
Douglas	G		A
Frankfr	G	R	R
Reed	G		A
Black	G	R	R
Vinson	G		A

Eastern Motor Express v U.S.
52 35A 51 709A
344 US 298 52 36A 52 26A
Reed 11/25/52 DC SD Indiana

	05/10 1952 JURIS	11/21 1952 MERITS	01/12 1953 REPORT
Minton	N		A
Clark	N	R	A
Burton	N	R	A
Jackson	N	A	A
Douglas	N		A
Frankfr	N		
Reed	N	R	R
Black	N		
Vinson	N	R	R

Baumet v U.S.
52 39A 51 726A 51 203M
344 US 82 52 10A
Clark 10/28/52 CCA 2d

Justice	04/19 1952 CERT	10/18 1952 MERITS	11/17 1952 REPORT
Minton	G		R
Clark	G	RJ	R
Burton	G		R
Jackson	G	RJ	A
Douglas	G		R
Frankfr	G	RJ	A
Reed	G		A
Black	G	RJ	R
Vinson	G		R

Johnson v New York New Haven RR
52 40A 51 729A
344 US 48
Black 10/28/52 CCA 2d

Justice	05/29 1952 CERT	10/25 1952 MERITS	11/17 1952 REPORT
Minton			A
Clark			A
Burton		R	V
Jackson	GL		A
Douglas		R	V
Frankfr	GL		
Reed		R	V
Black	GL	R	V
Vinson	GL		V

Schwartz v Texas
52 41A 51 730A
344 US 199 52 102A
Minton 11/25/52 Texas

Justice	06/07 1952 CERT	11/14 1952 MERITS	12/15 1952 REPORT
Minton		D	A
Clark	G	D	A
Burton		D	A
Jackson	G		A
Douglas	G	AO	A
Frankfr		A	
Reed	G	A	A
Black	G	A	A
Vinson	G	A	A

F.W. Woolworth v Contemporary Arts
52 42A 51 734A
344 US 228
Jackson 11/25/52 CCA 1st

Justice	05/29 1952 CERT	11/21 1952 MERITS	12/22 1952 REPORT
Minton	GL		A
Clark	GL		A
Burton	GL		A
Jackson	GL		A
Douglas	GL		A
Frankfr		D	
Reed			A
Black	GL	R	A
Vinson	GL	R	A

Montgomery Building Trades v Ledbetter
52 43A 51 736A
344 US 178
Minton 11/25/52 Alabama

Justice	05/29 1952 CERT	10/09 1952 AMICUS	11/14 1952 FINAL	12/22 1952 REPORT
Minton	G		B	R
Clark	G	B	B	R
Burton	G		BQ	R
Jackson				
Douglas	G	Y	B	R
Frankfr	G	Y		
Reed		Y		R
Black	G	Y	B	R
Vinson	G	Y	Y	A

PSC Of Utah v Wycoff Company
52 44A 51 741A
344 US 237
Jackson 11/25/52 CCA 10th

Justice	06/06 1952 CERT	11/14 1952 MERITS	12/22 1952 REPORT
Minton		D	R
Clark	D	D	R
Burton	G		R
Jackson	G	R	
Douglas	G		R
Frankfr		D	R
Reed	G	R	R
Black	G	R	R
Vinson	G	RQ	R

Sanford v Kepner
52 46A 51 746A
344 US 13
Black 10/28/52 CCA 3rd

Justice	06/07 1952 CERT	10/25 1952 MERITS	11/10 1952 REPORT
Minton	G	A	A
Clark	G	A	A
Burton	G	A	A
Jackson	G		A
Douglas	G		A
Frankfr	D		A
Reed	G		A
Black	G	A	A
Vinson	G	A	A

U.S. v Universal C.I.T. Credit
52 47A 51 747A
344 US 218
Frankft 11/25/52 DC WD Missouri

Justice	05/24 1952 JURIS	11/21 1952 MERITS	12/22 1952 REPORT
Minton	N		
Clark	N	R	
Burton	N	R	R
Jackson	N		
Douglas	N		
Frankfr	N		
Reed	N	R	
Black	N	X	R
Vinson	N		

Arrowsmith v C.I.R.
52 51A 51 753A
344 US 6
Black 10/28/52 CCA 2d

Justice	06/07 1952 CERT	10/25 1952 MERITS	11/10 1952 REPORT
Minton	G		A
Clark	G	R	A
Burton	G	R	A
Jackson	G		
Douglas	G		
Frankfr	G		R
Reed	G	A	R
Black	G		
Vinson	G		

Terry v Adams
52 52A 51 754A
345 US 461
Black 03/31/53 CCA 5th

	11/14 1952 CERT	03/14 1953 MERITS	05/04 1953 REPORT
	1 1	1 1	1 1
Minton	G	R	R
Clark	G	R	R
Burton		A	A
Jackson	G	R	R
Douglas		A	A
Frankfr	G	R	R
Reed	G	A	A
Black		R	R
Vinson	G	A	A

American Newspaper v N.L.R.B.
52 53A 51 755A
345 US 100 52 56A
Burton 11/25/52 CCA 7th

	10/07 1952 CERT	11/21 1952 MERITS	03/09 1953 REPORT
	1 1	1 1	1 1
Minton	GL	R	R
Clark	GL	A	A
Burton	GL	A	A
Jackson	GL	AQ	R
Douglas	GL	A	A
Frankfr	GL	A	A
Reed	GL		A
Black	GL	R	A
Vinson	GL	A	A

Ruddy Brook Clothes v British & Foreign
52 55A
344 US 816
CCA 7th

	10/07 1952 CERT
	1 1
Minton	D
Clark	D
Burton	D
Jackson	D
Douglas	G
Frankfr	D
Reed	D
Black	G
Vinson	D

Providence Fruit & Produce v Gamco
52 58A 51 764A
344 US 817
CCA 1st

	10/07 1952 CERT
	1 1
Minton	D
Clark	D
Burton	D
Jackson	D
Douglas	D
Frankfr	D
Reed	D
Black	D
Vinson	G

Pennsylvania RR Company v O'Rourke
52 60A 51 767A
344 US 334
Reed 12/23/52 CCA 2d

	10/07 1952 CERT	12/13 1952 MERITS	01/12 1953 REPORT
	1 1	1 1	1 1
Minton	G	R	R
Clark	G	R	R
Burton	G	RQ	R
Jackson		A	A
Douglas	D	RQ	R
Frankfr	G		
Reed	G		
Black		A	A
Vinson	G	A	A

Yanish v Barber
52 61A
344 US 817
CCA 9th

	10/07 1952 CERT
	1 1
Minton	D
Clark	D
Burton	D
Jackson	D
Douglas	G
Frankfr	D
Reed	D
Black	G
Vinson	D

Lutwak v U.S.
52 66A
344 US 604
Minton 12/23/52 CCA 7th

	10/07 1952 CERT	12/13 1952 MERITS	02/09 1953 REPORT
	1 1	1 1	1 1
Minton	G	A	A
Clark	G	A	A
Burton		A	A
Jackson	G	A	A
Douglas	D	R	R
Frankfr	D	A	A
Reed	G	R	R
Black	G	R	R
Vinson	G	A	A

Algonquin Gas v Northeastern Gas
52 70A
344 US 850 52 172A
CCA 3rd

	10/07 1952 CERT	10/18 1952 QUEST
	1 1	16 1
Minton	D	B
Clark	D	B
Burton	D	B
Jackson	D	B
Douglas	D	B
Frankfr		Y
Reed	D	B
Black		
Vinson		

H.B. Zachry Company v Terry
52 73A
344 US 819
CCA 5th

	10/07 1952 CERT
	1 1
Minton	D
Clark	D
Burton	D
Jackson	D
Douglas	G
Frankfr	D
Reed	
Black	G
Vinson	D

Independent Broadcasting v F.C.C.
52 74A
344 US 837
CCA DC

	10/07 1952 CERT
	1 1
Minton	D
Clark	D
Burton	D
Jackson	D
Douglas	G
Frankfr	D
Reed	
Black	G
Vinson	D

F.T.C. v Motion Picture Advertising
52 75A
344 US 392
Douglas 12/23/52 CCA 5th

	10/07 1952 CERT	12/13 1952 MERITS	02/02 1953 REPORT
	1 1	1 1	1 1
Minton	G	R	R
Clark		R	R
Burton	G	A	A
Jackson	D		
Douglas	G	R	R
Frankfr		A	A
Reed	D	R	R
Black	G	R	R
Vinson	D	R	R

Healy v C.I.R.
52 76A
345 US 278 51 138A
Vinson 12/23/52 CCA 2d

	10/07 1952 CERT	12/13 1952 MERITS	04/06 1953 REPORT
	1 1	1 1	1 1
Minton	G		A
Clark	G		A
Burton	G	R	R
Jackson	G		A
Douglas	G		A
Frankfr	G	R	R
Reed	X		A
Black	X	R	R
Vinson	G		A

W.J. Dillner Transfer Company v U.S.
52 77A 51 789A
344 US 883 52 18A
DC WD Pennsylvania

	06/07 1952 JURIS	11/14 1952 JURIS	11/17 1952 REPORT
	1 2	1	1
Minton	H	A	A
Clark	H	A	A
Burton	H	A	A
Jackson	H	A	A
Douglas	H	A	A
Frankfr	H	A	A
Reed	H	A	A
Black	H	A	A
Vinson	H	A	A

Alison v U.S.
52 79A 51 792A
344 US 167 52 80A 51 793A
Black 11/25/52 CCA 3rd

	06/07 1952 CERT	11/14 1952 MERITS	12/08 1952 REPORT
	1 1	1 1	1 1
Minton	K	R	R
Clark	G	R	R
Burton	G		
Jackson	X	RQ	R
Douglas	K		
Frankfr	G	R	R
Reed	K	R	R
Black	G	R	R
Vinson	G	R	R

U.S. v Stevenson-Chislett
52 80A 51 793A
344 US 167 52 79A 51 792A
Black 11/25/52 CCA 3rd

	06/07 1952 CERT	11/14 1952 MERITS	12/08 1952 REPORT
	1 1	1 1	1 1
Minton	K	R	R
Clark	G	R	R
Burton	G		
Jackson	X	R	R
Douglas	K		
Frankfr	G	R	R
Reed	K	R	R
Black	G	R	R
Vinson	G	R	R

Edelman v California
52 85A 51 799A 51 306M
344 US 357
Clark 11/25/52 California

	05/03 1952 CERT	05/24 1952 CERT	11/21 1952 MERITS	01/12 1953 REPORT
	1 1	1 2	1 1	1 1
Minton		D	S	S
Clark		D	S	S
Burton		D	S	S
Jackson		D	X	
Douglas	G	D	S	S
Frankfr		D		
Reed	G		R	R
Black	G	D	S	S
Vinson	G	D	S	S

Local Union No. 10 v Graham
52 86A
345 US 192 52 446A
Burton 12/23/52 Virginia

	10/07 1952 CERT	12/13 1952 MERITS	03/16 1953 REPORT
	1 1	1 1	1 1
Minton	G	A	A
Clark	G	A	A
Burton		A	A
Jackson	D	A	A
Douglas	D	R	R
Frankfr	D	A	A
Reed	G	A	A
Black	D	R	R
Vinson	G	A	A

U.S. v Rumely
52 87A
345 US 41
Douglas 12/23/52 Frankfr 03/04/53 CCA DC

	10/07 1952 CERT	12/20 1952 MERITS	03/09 1953 REPORT
	1 1	1 1	1 1
Minton	G	A	A
Clark	G	R	A
Burton	G	A	A
Jackson	G	A	A
Douglas	G	A	A
Frankfr	G	A	A
Reed	G	R	A
Black	G	A	A
Vinson	X	A	A

Automatic Canteen Company v F.T.C.
52 89A
346 US 61
Frankfr 12/23/52 CCA 7th

	10/07 1952 CERT	12/06 1952 AMICUS	12/20 1952 MERITS	06/08 1953 REPORT
	1 1	1 1	1 1	1 1
Minton	G	B	R	R
Clark	G	B	R	R
Burton	G	Y	R	R
Jackson				
Douglas	D	B	R	R
Frankfr	G	B		
Reed				
Black	G	B	A	A
Vinson	D	Y	A	A

58th Street Plaza Theatre v C.I.R.
52 91A
344 US 820
CCA 2d

	10/07 1952 CERT
	1 1
Minton	D
Clark	D
Burton	D
Jackson	D
Douglas	D
Frankfr	D
Reed	
Black	G
Vinson	D

Wottle v Atchison Topeka RR Company
52 95A 51 809A 51 405M
344 US 850
CCA 10th

	05/29 1952 CERT	10/20 1952 REPORT
	1 1	1 1
Minton	G	SI
Clark	D	SI
Burton	G	SI
Jackson	G	SI
Douglas	D	SI
Frankfr	G	SI
Reed	D	
Black	G	SI
Vinson	G	SI

Jefferson v Chronicle Publishing
52 96A
344 US 803
California

Justice	10/07 1952 JURIS (1 1)
Minton	
Clark	S S
Burton	
Jackson	N N
Douglas	
Frankfr	S S
Reed	S S
Black	
Vinson	N S

N.L.R.B. v Dant
52 97A
344 US 375 52 459A 52 460A *CCA 9th*
Reed 12/23/52

Justice	10/07 1952 CERT (1 1)	12/20 1952 MERITS (1 1)	02/02 1953 REPORT (1 1)
Minton	G	R	R
Clark	G	R	R
Burton	G	R	R
Jackson		A	A
Douglas		RQ	
Frankfr	G	R	R
Reed		R	R
Black	G	R	R
Vinson	G	R	R

Sweeney v Woodall
52 100A
344 US 86
CCA 6th

Justice	10/07 1952 CERT (1 1)
Minton	G
Clark	G
Burton	G
Jackson	G
Douglas	G
Frankfr	G
Reed	G
Black	G
Vinson	G

Bratburd v Maryland
52 102A
344 US 908 52 41A
Maryland

Justice	12/30 1952 CERT (1 1)
Minton	D
Clark	D
Burton	D
Jackson	
Douglas	G
Frankfr	
Reed	D
Black	D
Vinson	D

Arnall v Safeway Stores
52 103A
344 US 803
CCA Emergency

Justice	10/07 1952 CERT (1 1)	10/13 1952 MERITS (1 1)
Minton	GVM	
Clark	GVM	>
Burton	GVM	>
Jackson	GVM	>
Douglas	GVM	>
Frankfr	GVM	>
Reed	GVM	>
Black	GVM	>
Vinson	GVM	>

Jones v Harper
52 104A
344 US 821
CCA 10th

Justice	10/07 1952 CERT (1 1)
Minton	D
Clark	D
Burton	
Jackson	G
Douglas	D
Frankfr	
Reed	G
Black	D
Vinson	

Chapman v U.S.
52 105A
344 US 821
CCA 5th

Justice	10/07 1952 CERT (1 1)
Minton	D
Clark	D
Burton	
Jackson	G
Douglas	DO
Frankfr	D
Reed	D
Black	D
Vinson	

Williams v Steele
52 110A
344 US 822
CCA 8th

Justice	10/07 1952 CERT (1 1)
Minton	D
Clark	D
Burton	D
Jackson	
Douglas	G
Frankfr	G
Reed	
Black	D
Vinson	D

Rosenberg v U.S.
52 111A
344 US 889 52 112A 52 687A *CCA 2d*

Justice	10/07 1952 CERT (1 1)	11/14 1952 REHEAR (1 1)
Minton	D	
Clark	D	
Burton	G	Y
Jackson	D	
Douglas	D	
Frankfr	G	Y
Reed		
Black	D	Y
Vinson	D	

Sobell v U.S.
52 112A
344 US 889 52 111A 52 719A *CCA 2d*

Justice	10/07 1952 CERT (1 1)	11/14 1952 REHEAR (1 1)
Minton	D	
Clark	D	
Burton	G	Y
Jackson	D	
Douglas	D	
Frankfr	G	Y
Reed		
Black	G	Y
Vinson	D	

Tinder v U.S.
52 113A 51 828A 51 305M
345 US 565
Reed 04/15/53 CCA 4th

Justice	05/03 1952 CERT (1 1)	06/07 1952 CERT (1 2)	04/11 1953 MERITS (1 1)	05/25 1953 REPORT (1 1)
Minton	D	D		
Clark	D	D	A	A
Burton			A	A
Jackson			A	A
Douglas	H	G	R	R
Frankfr	G	G	R	R
Reed	G	G	R	R
Black			R	R
Vinson	D	D		

U.S. v Crescent Amusement Company
52 120A
344 US 901
DC MD Tennessee

Justice	10/07 1952 JURIS (1 1)	12/15 1952 REPORT (1 1)
Minton	S	SI
Clark	N	SI
Burton		
Jackson	A	SI
Douglas	N	SI
Frankfr		
Reed	S	
Black	N	SI
Vinson	N	

Kaiser-Frazer v Otis & Company
52 123A
344 US 855
CCA 2d

	10/08 1952 CERT	10/18 1952 CERT	
	1 1	1 2	
Minton			D
Clark			
Burton			
Jackson	G		
Douglas	G		D
Frankfr	G		
Reed	G		D
Black			
Vinson	X		D

C.A.B. v American Air Transport
52 126A
344 US 4
CCA DC

	10/09 1952 DISMISS	10/20 1952 REPORT	
	1 1	1 1	
Minton	Y	S	
Clark	Y	S	
Burton	Y	S	
Jackson	Y	S	A
Douglas	Y		A
Frankfr	Y	S	
Reed	Y	S	
Black	Y	S	
Vinson	G		

C.I.R. v Smith
52 138A
345 US 278 52 76A
Vinson 12/23/52 CCA 6th

	10/08 1952 CERT	12/13 1952 MERITS	04/06 1953 REPORT	
	1 1	1 1	1 1	
Minton	G	R	R	
Clark	G	R	R	
Burton	G	R	R	
Jackson	G			
Douglas	G	A		A
Frankfr	G	A	R	
Reed	G	R	R	
Black	G	R	R	
Vinson	G	R	R	

Tide Water Associated Oil v Robison
52 148A
344 US 804
California

	10/07 1952 JURIS	10/13 1952 REPORT	
	1 1	1 1	
Minton	N	A	
Clark	SA	A	
Burton	A	A	
Jackson			
Douglas			
Frankfr	N	N	
Reed			
Black	S	A	
Vinson	A	A	A

Jaroszewski v Central RR New Jersey
52 143A
344 US 839
New Jersey

	10/08 1952 CERT
	1 1
Minton	D
Clark	G
Burton	D
Jackson	D
Douglas	D
Frankfr	D
Reed	D
Black	D
Vinson	D

Shaughnessy v U.S. (Mezei)
52 139A
345 US 206
Clark 01/22/53 CCA 2d

	10/08 1952 CERT	01/10 1953 MERITS	03/16 1953 REPORT	
	1 1	1 1	1 1	
Minton	G	R	R	
Clark				
Burton	G	R	R	
Jackson				
Douglas	D	A	A	A
Frankfr	D	A	A	A
Reed				A
Black	G	R	R	
Vinson	G	R	R	A

Mondakota Gas v Montana-Dakota
52 152A
344 US 827 349 US 969
CCA 9th

	10/08 1952 CERT	06/03 1955 REHEAR	
	1 1	1 1	
Harlan		B	
Minton	D	B	
Clark	D	B	
Burton	D	B	
Jackson			
Douglas	G	Y	
Frankfr			
Reed	G	B	
Black	G	B	
Warren		B	Y
Vinson	D		

Western Pacific RR v Western Pacific
52 150A
345 US 247 52 160A 52 266A
Vinson 12/23/52 CCA 9th

	10/08 1952 CERT	12/20 1952 MERITS	04/06 1953 REPORT	
	1 1	1 1	1 1	
Minton	GL	R	>	
Clark	GL	R	>	
Burton	G		>	
Jackson	GL	X	>	A
Douglas	G		>	
Frankfr	G		>	
Reed	GL	R	>	
Black	G	R	>	
Vinson		AQ		

Mills v U.S.
52 149A
344 US 826
CCA DC

	10/08 1952 CERT
	1 1
Minton	
Clark	
Burton	
Jackson	
Douglas	
Frankfr	G
Reed	
Black	
Vinson	

Spencer v U.S.
52 164A
344 US 828
Ct Cls

	10/08 1952 CERT	
	1 1	
Minton		D
Clark		D
Burton		D
Jackson		
Douglas		D
Frankfr	G	
Reed		D
Black	G	
Vinson		

Metzger v Western Pacific RR
52 160A
345 US 247 52 150A 52 266A
Vinson 12/23/52 CCA 9th

	10/08 1952 CERT	12/20 1952 MERITS	04/06 1953 REPORT	
	1 1	1 1	1 1	
Minton	GL	R	>	
Clark	GL	R	>	
Burton	G		>	A
Jackson	GL	X	>	
Douglas	G		>	A
Frankfr	G		>	
Reed	GL	R	>	
Black	G	R	>	
Vinson		AQ		A

Ochs v C.I.R.
52 158A
344 US 827
CCA 2d

	10/08 1952 CERT
	1 1
Minton	D
Clark	D
Burton	G
Jackson	D
Douglas	G
Frankfr	D
Reed	D
Black	G
Vinson	D

All States Freight v U.S.
52 166A
344 US 804
DC ND Ohio

	10/07 1952 JURIS	10/13 1952 REPORT
	1 1	1 1
Minton	A	A
Clark	A	A
Burton	A	A
Jackson	A	A
Douglas	A	A
Frankfr	A	A
Reed	A	A
Black	A	A
Vinson		

U.S. v Kahriger
52 167A
345 US 22
Reed 01/22/53 DC ED Pennsylvania

	10/07 1952 JURIS	11/08 1952 AMICUS	12/20 1952 MERITS	03/09 1953 REPORT
	1 1	1 1	1 1	1 1
Minton	N	B	R	R
Clark	N	B	R	R
Burton	N	B	R	R
Jackson	N	B		
Douglas	N	B	A	A
Frankfr	N	B	A	A
Reed	N	B		
Black	N	B	X	R
Vinson			A	A

Johnson v U.S.
52 168A
344 US 839
Ct Cls

	10/08 1952 CERT
	1 1
Minton	D
Clark	
Burton	D
Jackson	D
Douglas	D
Frankfr	G
Reed	
Black	D
Vinson	G

McGrath v National Association
52 174A
344 US 804
DC DC

	10/07 1952 JURIS	10/13 1952 REPORT	11/14 1952 REHEAR
	1 1	1 1	1 1
Minton	VI	VI	B
Clark			
Burton	VI	VI	B
Jackson	VI	VI	
Douglas	VI	VI	B
Frankfr	VI	VI	B
Reed	VI	VI	
Black	VI	VI	B
Vinson	VI	VI	Y

Gage v U.S.
52 177A
344 US 829
Ct Cls

	10/08 1952 CERT
	1 1
Minton	D
Clark	D
Burton	D
Jackson	D
Douglas	G
Frankfr	D
Reed	
Black	G
Vinson	D

South Buffalo RR Company v Ahern
52 179A
344 US 367
Clark 12/23/52 New York

	10/07 1952 JURIS	12/20 1952 MERITS	01/19 1953 REPORT
	1 1	1 1	1 1
Minton	S	S	A
Clark	S	S	A
Burton		R	R
Jackson	N		A
Douglas	N	SA	A
Frankfr	N	SA	A
Reed		A	A
Black	N	SA	SA
Vinson	S	A	A

Clements v Gospodonovich
52 181A
344 US 911 52 187A 52 258A 52 197A
DC ED Louisiana

	10/07 1952 JURIS	01/03 1953 JURIS	01/05 1953 REPORT
	1 1	1 2	1 1
Minton	A		SJ
Clark	A		SJ
Burton		A	SJ
Jackson	N		SJ
Douglas	N	A	SJ
Frankfr			SJ
Reed	N		SJ
Black		A	SJ
Vinson	A		SJ

Gordon v U.S.
52 182A
344 US 414
Jackson 12/23/52 CCA 7th

	10/08 1952 CERT	12/20 1952 MERITS	02/02 1953 REPORT
	1 1	1 1	1 1
Minton	D		A
Clark	D	R	R
Burton		R	R
Jackson	GL	R	R
Douglas	GL	R	R
Frankfr	GL	R	R
Reed			R
Black	GL		R
Vinson	D		

Bode v Barrett
52 187A
344 US 583 52 274A 52 181A 52 197A
Douglas 01/22/53 Illinois

	10/07 1952 JURIS	01/10 1953 MERITS	02/09 1953 REPORT
	1 1	1 1	1 1
Minton	S	A	A
Clark	S	A	A
Burton		A	A
Jackson	N	A	A
Douglas	N	R	R
Frankfr	N	A	A
Reed		A	A
Black	S		
Vinson	S		

Brooks Transportation Company v U.S.
52 190A
344 US 804
DC ED Virginia

Justice	10/07 1952 JURIS	10/13 1952 REPORT
Minton	A	A
Clark	A	A
Burton	A	A
Jackson	A	A
Douglas	A	A
Frankfr	A	A
Reed	A	A
Black	A	A
Vinson	A	A

Ford Motor Company v Huffman
52 193A
345 US 330 52 194A
Burton 12/23/52 CCA 6th

Justice	10/08 1952 CERT	12/20 1952 MERITS	04/06 1953 REPORT
Minton	G	R	R
Clark	G	R	R
Burton	G	R	R
Jackson	G	R	R
Douglas	D	R	R
Frankfr		R	R
Reed		R	R
Black	G	R	R
Vinson	D	R	R

International Union UAW v Huffman
52 194A
345 US 330 52 193A
Burton 12/23/52 CCA 6th

Justice	10/08 1952 CERT	12/20 1952 MERITS	04/06 1953 REPORT
Minton	G	R	R
Clark	G	R	R
Burton	G	R	R
Jackson	G	R	R
Douglas	D	R	R
Frankfr		R	R
Reed		R	R
Black	G	R	R
Vinson	D	R	R

T.M. Duche & Sons v U.S.
52 195A
344 US 830
CCPA

Justice	10/08 1952 CERT
Minton	D
Clark	D
Burton	
Jackson	G
Douglas	D
Frankfr	D
Reed	D
Black	D
Vinson	D

U.S. v Wilson
52 197A
344 US 923 52 181A 52 258A 52 198A
DC ED Louisiana

Justice	10/07 1952 JURIS	01/10 1953 MERITS	02/02 1953 REPORT
Minton		A	A
Clark	S		
Burton	S	R	R
Jackson			
Douglas	N	R	R
Frankfr	N	A	A
Reed	N	A	A
Black	N	A	A
Vinson	N	A	A

U.S. v Purchasing Corporation
52 198A
344 US 923 52 197A 52 181A 52 258A
DC ED Louisiana

Justice	10/07 1952 JURIS	01/10 1953 MERITS	02/02 1953 REPORT
Minton		A	A
Clark	S		
Burton	S	R	R
Jackson			
Douglas	N	R	R
Frankfr	N	A	A
Reed	N	A	A
Black	N	A	A
Vinson	N	A	A

Crolich v U.S.
52 199A
344 US 830
CCA 5th

Justice	10/08 1952 CERT
Minton	D
Clark	D
Burton	
Jackson	
Douglas	D
Frankfr	D
Reed	D
Black	D
Vinson	D

California v U.S.
52 202A
344 US 831
CCA 9th

Justice	10/08 1952 CERT
Minton	D
Clark	D
Burton	
Jackson	G
Douglas	G
Frankfr	
Reed	G
Black	D
Vinson	D

City Of New York v New York RR
52 203A
344 US 293
Black 12/23/52 CCA 2d

Justice	10/08 1952 CERT	12/20 1952 MERITS	01/12 1953 REPORT
Minton	D	R	R
Clark		R	R
Burton	D	R	R
Jackson		R	R
Douglas	G	R	R
Frankfr	G	R	R
Reed		R	R
Black	G		
Vinson	G		AQ

U.S. v PUC Of California
52 205A
345 US 295 52 206A 52 291A
Reed 01/22/53 California

Justice	10/08 1952 CERT	01/17 1953 MERITS	04/06 1953 REPORT
Minton	H	R	R
Clark	H	R	R
Burton	G		R
Jackson	GH	X	R
Douglas	G	X	R
Frankfr	H	A	R
Reed	G	R	R
Black	G	R	R
Vinson	G	R	R

County Of Mineral v PUC Of California
52 206A
345 US 295 52 205A 52 291A
Reed 01/22/53 California

Justice	10/08 1952 CERT	01/17 1953 MERITS	04/06 1953 REPORT
Minton	H	R	R
Clark	H	R	R
Burton	G		R
Jackson	GH	X	R
Douglas	G	X	R
Frankfr	H	A	R
Reed	G	R	R
Black	G	R	R
Vinson	G	R	R

Division 26 v City Of Detroit
52 207A
344 US 805
Michigan

Justice	10/07 1952 JURIS
Minton	S
Clark	S
Burton	
Jackson	N
Douglas	NP
Frankfr	
Reed	S
Black	N
Vinson	S

A. Gusmer v McGranery
52 212A
344 US 831
CCA DC

	10/08 1952 CERT
	1 1
Minton	D
Clark	D
Burton	
Jackson	GQ
Douglas	D
Frankfr	D
Reed	D
Black	D
Vinson	D

N.L.R.B. v Seven-Up Bottling Company
52 217A
344 US 344
Frankfr 12/23/52 CCA 5th

	10/08 1952 CERT	12/20 1952 MERITS	01/12 1953 REPORT
	1 1	1 1 A	1 1 A
Minton	G		
Clark	G	R	R A
Burton	G	R	R A
Jackson		X	
Douglas	G	R	R A
Frankfr			
Reed	G	R	R A
Black	G		
Vinson	G	R A	R A

Martinez v Neely
52 218A
344 US 916
CCA 7th

	10/08 1952 CERT
	1 1
Minton	G
Clark	G
Burton	G
Jackson	
Douglas	G D
Frankfr	
Reed	G D
Black	G D
Vinson	G D

Goldberger v U.S.
52 223A
344 US 833
CCA 3rd

	10/08 1952 CERT
	1 1
Minton	D
Clark	D
Burton	D
Jackson	D
Douglas	D
Frankfr	G
Reed	D
Black	D
Vinson	D

Lauritzen v Larsen
52 226A
345 US 571
Jackson 01/22/53 CCA 2d

	10/08 1952 CERT	01/10 1953 MERITS	02/07 1953 AMICUS	05/25 1953 REPORT
	1 1	1 1		1 1
Minton	G	R	B	R
Clark	G	R	B	R
Burton	G	R	B	R
Jackson	G	R	B	R
Douglas	G	R	B	R
Frankfr	G	R	B	R
Reed				
Black	G	R	B	R
Vinson		A	B	Y	R

Creek Nation v McGhee
52 227A
344 US 856, 52 245A, 52 247A
Ct Cls

	10/08 1952 CERT
	1 1
Minton	D
Clark	D
Burton	D
Jackson	D
Douglas	D
Frankfr	
Reed	
Black	G
Vinson	G

U.S. v Schaeffer
52 232A
344 US 854
Ct Cls

	10/18 1952 CERT
	1 1
Minton	D
Clark	D
Burton	D
Jackson	D
Douglas	D
Frankfr	D
Reed	D
Black	D
Vinson	G

Burns v Carolina Power & Light Company
52 233A
344 US 863
CCA 4th

	10/25 1952 CERT
	1 1
Minton	D
Clark	G
Burton	D
Jackson	D
Douglas	D
Frankfr	D
Reed	D
Black	G
Vinson	A

N.L.R.B. v Gamble Enterprises
52 238A
345 US 117, 52 53A
Burton 11/25/52 CCA 6th

	10/08 1952 CERT	11/21 1952 MERITS	03/09 1953 REPORT
	1 1	1 1 A	1 1 A
Minton	G		
Clark	G	R	R A
Burton	G	R	R A
Jackson	G		
Douglas	G	R	R A
Frankfr	G	R	R A
Reed	G		
Black	G	R	R A
Vinson	G	R A	R A

Aeration Processes v Lange
52 239A
344 US 834
CCA 8th

	10/08 1952 CERT
	1 1
Minton	D
Clark	D
Burton	D
Jackson	D
Douglas	G
Frankfr	D
Reed	D
Black	D
Vinson	D

Crummer Company v DuPont
52 240A
344 US 856, 52 107M
CCA 5th

	10/18 1952 CERT
	1 1
Minton	D
Clark	D
Burton	D
Jackson	D
Douglas	D
Frankfr	
Reed	D
Black	D
Vinson	D

Bailess v Paukune
52 242A
344 US 171
Douglas 11/25/52 Oklahoma

	10/08 1952 CERT	11/14 1952 MERITS	12/08 1952 REPORT
	1 1	1 1	1 1
Minton	D	R	R
Clark	D	R	R
Burton	G	R	R
Jackson		R	R
Douglas	G	X	R
Frankfr	G	R	R
Reed	D	R	R
Black	D	R	R
Vinson	G	R	R

Sanson Hosiery Mills v N.L.R.B.
52 243A
344 US 863
CCA 5th

Justice	10/08/1952 CERT (1 1)	10/25/1952 CERT (1 2)
Minton	D	D
Clark		
Burton	G	G
Jackson		
Douglas	G	
Frankfr		
Reed	D	D
Black	D	
Vinson		X

May v Anderson
52 244A
345 US 528
Burton 01/22/53 Ohio

Justice	10/07/1952 JURIS (1 1)	11/14/1952 QUEST (17 1)	01/10/1953 MERITS (1 1)	05/18/1953 REPORT (1 1)
Minton	N	B		A
Clark	N		R	R
Burton	N	Y	A	A
Jackson	N		R	R
Douglas	N	Y	A	A
Frankfr	N		R	R
Reed		B	R	R
Black		Y	R	R
Vinson	N	B	A	A

U.S. v Thompson
52 245A
344 US 856 52 227A 52 246A 52 247A
Ct Cls

Justice	10/18/1952 CERT (1 1)
Minton	D
Clark	D
Burton	D
Jackson	D
Douglas	D
Frankfr	
Reed	
Black	G
Vinson	G

U.S. v Ristling
52 246A
344 US 856 52 227A 52 245A 52 247A
Ct Cls

Justice	10/18/1952 CERT (1 1)
Minton	D
Clark	D
Burton	D
Jackson	D
Douglas	D
Frankfr	D
Reed	
Black	G
Vinson	G

U.S. v McGhee
52 247A
344 US 856 52 227A 52 245A 52 246A
Ct Cls

Justice	10/18/1952 CERT (1 1)
Minton	D
Clark	D
Burton	D
Jackson	D
Douglas	D
Frankfr	D
Reed	
Black	G
Vinson	G

U.S. v Price
52 248A
344 US 911 52 11A
Ct Cls

Justice	10/18/1952 CERT (1 1)	01/03/1953 CERT (1 2)
Minton	G	D
Clark	G	G
Burton		D
Jackson		D
Douglas		D
Frankfr		D
Reed	G	
Black	G	D
Vinson		

McGuire v Todd
52 252A
344 US 835
CCA 5th

Justice	10/08/1952 CERT (1 1)
Minton	D
Clark	D
Burton	G
Jackson	G
Douglas	D
Frankfr	D
Reed	G
Black	G
Vinson	D

U.S. v Certain Parcels Of Land
52 253A
345 US 344
Clark 01/22/53 CCA 4th

Justice	10/08/1952 CERT (1 1)	01/17/1953 MERITS (1 1)	04/06/1953 REPORT (1 1)
Minton	D	R	R
Clark	D	R	R
Burton		R	R
Jackson	D	X	
Douglas	D	R	R
Frankfr		R	R
Reed	G		
Black	G	R	R
Vinson	D	A	A

Baltimore & Ohio RR Company v U.S.
52 258A
345 US 146 52 181A 52 274A 52 197A
Black 01/22/53 DC ED Missouri

Justice	10/07/1952 JURIS (1 1)	01/10/1953 MERITS (1 1)	03/16/1953 REPORT (1 1)
Minton		A	A
Clark	A	A	A
Burton	N	R	R
Jackson	N	R	
Douglas	E	A	A
Frankfr	N	RQ	
Reed		A	A
Black	N	A	R
Vinson		A	A

Calmar Steamship v U.S.
52 262A
345 US 446   52 303A
Frankfr 01/22/53 CCA 2d

	10/18 1952 CERT	01/17 1953 MERITS	04/27 1953 REPORT
	1 1	1 1	1 1
Minton	G	R	>
Clark		R	>
Burton	D	R	>
Jackson	D	R	>
Douglas	G	R	>
Frankfr	G	R	>
Reed		R	>
Black	X D	R	>
Vinson	G	R	>

Baldi v U.S. (Almeida)
52 264A
345 US 904   52 20A   52 22A   52 32A
CCA 3rd

	10/18 1952 CERT	03/07 1953 REPORT
	1 1	1 2
Minton	GH	D
Clark		D
Burton	H	D
Jackson	G	D
Douglas	D	D
Frankfr	D	D
Reed	D	D
Black	H	D
Vinson		D

William H. Banks Warehouses v Watt
52 266A
345 US 932   52 160A   52 150A
CCA 9th

	04/11 1953 MERITS	04/13 1953 REPORT
	1 1	1 1
Minton	>	>
Clark	>	>
Burton	>	>
Jackson	>	>
Douglas	>	>
Frankfr	>	>
Reed	>	>
Black	>	>
Vinson	>	

Paris v Texas
52 267A
344 US 888
Texas

	10/18 1952 CERT
	1 1
Minton	D
Clark	D
Burton	D
Jackson	
Douglas	G
Frankfr	
Reed	D
Black	D
Vinson	D

Kobe v Dempsey Pump Company
52 270A
344 US 837
CCA 10th

	10/09 1952 CERT
	1 1
Minton	D
Clark	D
Burton	D
Jackson	
Douglas	G
Frankfr	G
Reed	D
Black	D
Vinson	D

Co-ordinated Transport v Barrett
52 274A
344 US 583   52 187A   *Illinois*
Douglas 01/22/53

	10/07 1952 JURIS	01/10 1953 MERITS	02/09 1953 REPORT
	1 1	1 1	1 1
Minton	N	A	A
Clark	N	A	A
Burton	N	A	R
Jackson	N	A	A
Douglas	N	A	R
Frankfr	N	A	A
Reed	N	A	A
Black	N	A	A
Vinson	N	A	A

Carter v Simpson
52 275A
344 US 837
CCA 7th

	10/09 1952 CERT
	1 1
Minton	D
Clark	D
Burton	D
Jackson	
Douglas	G
Frankfr	
Reed	G
Black	D
Vinson	D

Pennsylvania RR Company v Donnelly
52 276A
344 US 855
Illinois

	10/18 1952 CERT
	1 1
Minton	D
Clark	D
Burton	D
Jackson	D
Douglas	D
Frankfr	D
Reed	D
Black	G
Vinson	D

U.S. v Abrams
52 277A
344 US 855
CCA 6th

	10/18 1952 CERT
	1 1
Minton	D
Clark	D
Burton	
Jackson	G
Douglas	G
Frankfr	G
Reed	
Black	D
Vinson	D

Ramspeck v Federal Trial Examiners
52 278A
345 US 128
Minton 01/22/53 CCA DC

	10/18 1952 CERT	01/17 1953 MERITS	03/09 1953 REPORT
	1 1	1 1	1 1
Minton	G	R	R
Clark	G	R	R
Burton	G	R	R
Jackson	D	A	A
Douglas	DQ		
Frankfr	G	R	R
Reed			
Black	G	R	R
Vinson	G	A	A

R.H. Johnson & Company v S.E.C.
52 285A
344 US 855
CCA 2d

	10/18 1952 CERT
	1 1
Minton	D
Clark	D
Burton	D
Jackson	D
Douglas	D
Frankfr	D
Reed	G
Black	D
Vinson	D

Polizzi v Cowles Magazines
52 287A
345 US 663
Black 03/17/53 Minton 04/11/53 CCA 5th

	10/18 1952 CERT	03/14 1953 MERITS	06/04 1953 REPORT
	1 1	1 1	1 1
Minton	G	R	R
Clark	G	R	R
Burton	G	RM	R
Jackson		R	R
Douglas	D		
Frankfr	D		
Reed			
Black	GQ	A	R
Vinson	D	A	R

Watson v C.I.R.
52 290A
345 US 544
Burton 02/12/53 CCA 9th

	12/06 1952 CERT 1-1	02/07 1953 MERITS 1-1	05/18 1953 REPORT 1-1
Minton	G		
Clark	G	R	R
Burton	G		
Jackson	G		A
Douglas	G		A
Frankfr	G	R	A
Reed	G	R	A
Black	G		AQ
Vinson	G		A

Wisconsin Michigan Power v F.P.C.
52 291A
345 US 934 52 205A 52 206A
CCA 7th

	10/25 1952 CERT 1-1	04/11 1953 MERITS 1-2
Minton	H	D
Clark	H	D
Burton	H	D
Jackson	H	D
Douglas	H	D
Frankfr	H	D
Reed	H	D
Black	H	D
Vinson	H	D

Unexcelled Chemical v U.S.
52 293A
345 US 59
Douglas 01/22/53 CCA 3rd

	10/25 1952 CERT 1-1	01/10 1953 MERITS 1-1	03/09 1953 REPORT 1-1
Minton	G	R	R
Clark	G	R	R
Burton	G	R	R
Jackson	G	R	R
Douglas	G	R	R
Frankfr	G	R	R
Reed	G	R	R
Black	G	R	R
Vinson	G	R	R

Howard v Commissioners Sinking Fund
52 295A
344 US 624
Minton 01/22/53 Kentucky

	10/25 1952 JURIS 1-1	01/17 1953 MERITS 1-1	02/09 1953 REPORT 1-1
Minton	S		A
Clark	S		A
Burton	S		A
Jackson			A
Douglas	N	R	A
Frankfr	N	R	
Reed	N	R	A
Black	N	R	A
Vinson	S		A

Alstate Construction Company v Durkin
52 296A
345 US 13 52 336A
Black 02/12/53 CCA 3rd

	12/06 1952 CERT 1-1	02/07 1953 MERITS 1-1	03/09 1953 REPORT 1-1
Minton	G		A
Clark	G		A
Burton	G		A
Jackson	G	R	A
Douglas	G	R	A
Frankfr	G		A
Reed	G		A
Black	G		A
Vinson	G	D	A

Jacoby v New York
52 299A
344 US 864
New York

	10/25 1952 CERT 1-1
Minton	D
Clark	D
Burton	D
Jackson	
Douglas	G
Frankfr	G
Reed	
Black	
Vinson	

Brannan v Kass
52 300A
344 US 891
CCA 2d

	11/21 1952 CERT 1-1
Minton	D
Clark	D
Burton	D
Jackson	D
Douglas	D
Frankfr	D
Reed	G
Black	D
Vinson	D

Dameron v Brodhead
52 302A
345 US 322
Reed 02/12/53 Colorado

	11/21 1952 CERT 1-1	02/07 1953 MERITS 1-1	04/06 1953 REPORT 1-1
Minton	G	R	R
Clark	G	R	R
Burton	G	R	R
Jackson	G	A	A
Douglas	G	A	A
Frankfr	G		
Reed	G		
Black	G	A	A
Vinson	G	A	A

Calmar Steamship v Scott
52 303A
345 US 427 52 262A
Frankfr 01/22/53 CCA 2d

	10/18 1952 CERT 1-1	01/17 1953 MERITS 1-1	04/27 1953 REPORT 1-1
Minton	G	R	
Clark	G	R	R
Burton	G		
Jackson	G		A
Douglas	G	R	>
Frankfr	X	R	>
Reed	D		>
Black			>
Vinson	G	A	A

Dalehite v U.S.
52 308A
346 US 15
Reed 04/27/53 CCA 5th

	11/08 1952 CERT 1-1	04/11 1953 MERITS 1-1	04/25 1953 MERITS 1-2	06/08 1953 REPORT 1-1
Minton	G			A
Clark				A
Burton	G	R	R	R
Jackson	G		R	R
Douglas	D			
Frankfr	G	R	R	R
Reed	D			
Black	G	Q		
Vinson	D		A	A

Etier v Cincinnati New Orleans RR
52 309A
344 US 864
CCA 6th

	10/25 1952 CERT 1-1
Minton	D
Clark	D
Burton	D
Jackson	D
Douglas	D
Frankfr	D
Reed	
Black	
Vinson	D

N.L.R.B. v Rockaway News Supply
52 318A
345 US 71
Jackson 01/22/53 CCA 2d

	10/25 1952 CERT 1-1	01/17 1953 MERITS 1-1	03/09 1953 REPORT 1-1
Minton	G	R	R
Clark	G		
Burton	G	R	R
Jackson			
Douglas	G	R	R
Frankfr	G		
Reed	G	A	A
Black	G	A	A
Vinson	G	AQ	A

Stone v New York Chicago RR Company
52 320A
344 US 407
Douglas 01/22/53 Missouri

Justice	CERT 10/25 1952 (1 1)	MERITS 01/17 1953 (1 1)	REPORT 02/02 1953 (1 1)
Minton		R	R
Clark	G	R	R
Burton	D	R	R
Jackson	D	A	A
Douglas	D	A	A
Frankfr		A	A
Reed	G	A	A
Black	G	R	R
Vinson	G	R	R

Kornfeind v U.S.
52 321A
344 US 862
DC ND Illinois

Justice	REPORT 10/27 1952 (1 1)
Minton	A
Clark	A
Burton	A
Jackson	A
Douglas	A
Frankfr	A
Reed	A
Black	A
Vinson	A

Pope v Atlantic Coast Line RR Company
52 322A
345 US 379
Vinson 01/22/53 Georgia

Justice	CERT 10/25 1952 (1 1)	MERITS 01/17 1953 (1 1)	REPORT 04/27 1953 (1 1)
Minton		R	R
Clark	G	R	R
Burton	D	R	R
Jackson	D	R	R
Douglas	D	A	A
Frankfr		A	A
Reed	N	R	R
Black	G	R	R
Vinson	G	R	R

Centracchio v Garrity
52 328A
344 US 866
CCA 1st

Justice	CERT 10/25 1952 (1 1)
Minton	D
Clark	D
Burton	D
Jackson	D
Douglas	G
Frankfr	G
Reed	
Black	G
Vinson	D

Costello v U.S.
52 329A
344 US 874
CCA 2d

Justice	CERT 11/08 1952 (1 1)
Minton	D
Clark	D
Burton	D
Jackson	D
Douglas	D
Frankfr	D
Reed	G
Black	G
Vinson	G

Esso Standard Oil Company v Evans
52 330A
345 US 495 52 378A
Reed 03/17/53 Tennessee

Justice	JURIS 11/08 1952 (1 1)	MERITS 03/14 1953 (1 1)	REPORT 05/04 1953 (1 1)
Minton	N		
Clark	N		
Burton	N	R	R
Jackson	N	A	A
Douglas	N		
Frankfr	N	AQ	R
Reed	N	A	A
Black	N	A	A
Vinson			

Gasway v Texas
52 335A
344 US 874
Texas

Justice	CERT 11/08 1952 (1 1)
Minton	D
Clark	D
Burton	D
Jackson	
Douglas	G
Frankfr	G
Reed	
Black	G
Vinson	G

A.M. Collins & Company v Panama RR
52 338A
344 US 875
CCA 5th

Justice	CERT 11/08 1952 (1 1)
Minton	D
Clark	D
Burton	D
Jackson	D
Douglas	D
Frankfr	D
Reed	G
Black	G
Vinson	G

Fowler v Rhode Island
52 340A
345 US 67 52 341A
Douglas 02/12/53 Rhode Island

Justice	JURIS 11/08 1952 (1 1)	MERITS 02/07 1953 (1 1)	REPORT 03/09 1953 (1 1)
Minton		R	R
Clark	S	R	R
Burton	N	R	R
Jackson	N	R	R
Douglas	N	R	R
Frankfr	N	R	R
Reed	N	R	R
Black		R	R
Vinson	S		

Poulos v New Hampshire
52 341A
345 US 395 52 340A
Reed 02/12/53 New Hampshire

Justice	JURIS 11/08 1952 (1 1)	MERITS 02/07 1953 (1 1)	REPORT 04/27 1953 (1 1)
Minton	S	A	A
Clark	P	A	A
Burton	P	A	A
Jackson	S	A	A
Douglas	S	A	A
Frankfr	P	A	A
Reed	SH	R	R
Black	S	R	R
Vinson	P	A	A

Marr v A.B. Dick Company
52 344A
344 US 878
CCA 2d

Justice	CERT 11/08 1952 (1 1)
Minton	
Clark	
Burton	D
Jackson	
Douglas	
Frankfr	
Reed	G
Black	G
Vinson	

Isserman v Ethics Committee Essex
52 348A
345 US 927 52 5M
New Jersey

Justice	CERT 11/21 1952 (1 1)	CERT 12/13 1952 (1 2)	CERT 04/04 1953 (1 3)
Minton	D	D	D
Clark	D	DH	D
Burton	D	DH	D
Jackson	D	DH	D
Douglas	D	DH	D
Frankfr	D	D	D
Reed			
Black	G	G	G
Vinson	D	G	G

Chicago & North Western RR v U.S.
52 353A
344 US 871
DC ND Illinois

Justice	11/08/1952 JURIS (1 1)	11/10/1952 REPORT (1 1)
Minton	A	A
Clark	A	A
Burton	A	A
Jackson	A	A
Douglas	A	A
Frankfr	A	A
Reed	A	A
Black	A	A
Vinson	A	A

Cooper v Cooper
52 355A
344 US 876
Kentucky

Justice	01/17/1953 RETAX (1 1)	(Y)
Minton		
Clark		
Burton	B	Y
Jackson	G	
Douglas	B	Y
Frankfr		
Reed	G / B	Y
Black		
Vinson	G / B	Y

Gordon Woodroffe v U.S.
52 357A
344 US 908
Ct Cls

Justice	12/20/1952 CERT (1 1)
Minton	D
Clark	D
Burton	D
Jackson	D
Douglas	D
Frankfr	D
Reed	G
Black	
Vinson	D

Copperweld Steel Company v U.S.
52 358A
344 US 871
DC WD Pennsylvania

Justice	11/08/1952 JURIS (1 1)	11/10/1952 REPORT (1 1)
Minton	A	A
Clark	A	A
Burton	A	A
Jackson	A	A
Douglas	N	A
Frankfr	A	A
Reed	A	A
Black	A	A
Vinson	A	A

Eunice Rice Milling v Employers Mutual
52 359A
344 US 876
CCA 5th

Justice	11/08/1952 CERT (1 1)
Minton	D
Clark	D
Burton	D
Jackson	D
Douglas	
Frankfr	G
Reed	
Black	G
Vinson	G / D

Dragna v California
52 365A
344 US 921
California

Justice	01/17/1953 CERT (1 1)
Minton	D
Clark	D
Burton	D
Jackson	D
Douglas	D
Frankfr	
Reed	G
Black	X
Vinson	D

Springfield Institution v Worcester
52 367A
344 US 884
Massachusetts

Justice	11/14/1952 CERT (1 1)
Minton	D
Clark	D
Burton	D
Jackson	D
Douglas	D
Frankfr	G
Reed	D
Black	D
Vinson	D

De La Rama Steamship Company v U.S.
52 368A
344 US 886
Frankfr 01/22/53 CCA 2d

Justice	11/14/1952 CERT (1 1)	01/17/1953 MERITS (1 1)	02/02/1953 REPORT (1 1)
Minton	GL	R	R
Clark	GL	R	R
Burton	GL	R	R
Jackson	GL	R	R
Douglas	GL	R	R
Frankfr	GL	R	R
Reed	GL	R	R
Black	GL	R	R
Vinson	GL	R	R

U.S. v McConville
52 369A
344 US 877
CCA 2d

Justice	11/08/1952 CERT (1 1)
Minton	D
Clark	D
Burton	D
Jackson	D
Douglas	D
Frankfr	
Reed	G
Black	
Vinson	D

Tisneros v Chicago & North Western RR
52 370A
344 US 885
CCA 7th

Justice	11/14/1952 CERT (1 1)
Minton	
Clark	
Burton	
Jackson	
Douglas	G
Frankfr	
Reed	
Black	G
Vinson	

Kemble v U.S.
52 373A
344 US 893
CCA 3rd

Justice	11/14/1952 CERT (1 1)	11/21/1952 CERT (1 1)
Minton		
Clark	D	
Burton	D	
Jackson	D	
Douglas		G
Frankfr		G
Reed		
Black		
Vinson		

Times-Picayune Publishing v U.S.
52 374A 52 375A
345 US 594
Clark 03/17/53 DC ED Louisiana

Justice	11/08/1952 JURIS (1 1)	03/14/1953 MERITS (1 1)	05/25/1953 REPORT (1 1)
Minton	N	A	A
Clark	N	A	A
Burton	N	A	A
Jackson	N	AQ	AQ
Douglas	N	RQ	A
Frankfr	N	RQ	R
Reed	N	R	R
Black	N	R	R
Vinson	N	R	R

Olney v U.S.
52 376A
344 US 898
Ct Cls

Justice	CERT 12/06 1952
Minton	D
Clark	D
Burton	D
Jackson	G
Douglas	D
Frankfr	
Reed	G
Black	D
Vinson	D

U.S. v Evans
52 378A
345 US 495 52 330A
Reed 03/17/53 Tennessee

Justice	JURIS 11/08 1952	MERITS 03/14 1953	REPORT 05/04 1953
Minton	N		
Clark	N	A	A
Burton		A	A
Jackson	A		
Douglas	N	R	R
Frankfr	N	AQ	A
Reed	N		
Black	N	R	R
Vinson	N	R	R

Albertson v Millard
52 384A
345 US 242
DC ED Michigan

Justice	JURIS 11/08 1952	MERITS 02/07 1953	REPORT 03/16 1953
Minton	N	VM	R
Clark	N	VM	R
Burton	N	VM	R
Jackson	N	N	R
Douglas	N	VM	R
Frankfr	N	VM	N
Reed	N	VM	R
Black	N	VM	R
Vinson	N	VM	R

United Fruit v W.E. Hedger
52 388A
344 US 896
CCA 2d

Justice	CERT 12/06 1952
Minton	D
Clark	D
Burton	D
Jackson	G
Douglas	D
Frankfr	
Reed	G
Black	D
Vinson	G

Ward v U.S.
52 390A 52 9M
344 US 924
CCA 5th

Justice	CERT 10/09 1952	MERITS 01/17 1953	REPORT 02/02 1953
Minton	G	R	R
Clark	G	R	R
Burton		R	R
Jackson	D	R	R
Douglas	G	R	R
Frankfr	G	R	R
Reed		R	R
Black	D	R	R
Vinson	G	R	R

Stein v New York
52 391A 52 15M
346 US 156 52 392A 52 393A
Jackson 12/23/52 New York

Justice	CERT 10/09 1952	MERITS 12/20 1952	REPORT 06/15 1953
Minton	G	R	R
Clark	G	R	R
Burton	G	R	R
Jackson	G	R	R
Douglas	G	A	A
Frankfr	G	R	R
Reed	G	R	R
Black	D	A	A
Vinson	D	A	A

Wissner v New York
52 392A 52 16M
346 US 156 52 391A 59 393A
Jackson 12/23/52 New York

Justice	CERT 10/09 1952	MERITS 12/20 1952	REPORT 06/15 1953
Minton	D	A	A
Clark	D	A	A
Burton	D	A	A
Jackson	D		
Douglas		R	R
Frankfr			
Reed		R	R
Black		A	A
Vinson	D	A	A

Cooper v New York
52 393A 52 24M
346 US 156 52 391A 52 392A
Jackson 12/23/52 New York

Justice	CERT 10/09 1952	MERITS 12/20 1952	REPORT 06/15 1953
Minton	G	R	R
Clark	G	R	R
Burton	G	R	R
Jackson	G	R	R
Douglas	G	A	A
Frankfr	G	R	R
Reed	G	R	R
Black	D	A	A
Vinson	D	A	A

Wells v Simonds Abrasive Company
52 394A 52 52M
345 US 514
Vinson 01/22/53 CCA 3rd

Justice	CERT 10/09 1952	MERITS 01/10 1953	REPORT 05/18 1953
Minton	D	R	R
Clark	D		
Burton	D		
Jackson	G		
Douglas	G	A	A
Frankfr	G	A	A
Reed	G	A	A
Black	D	R	R
Vinson	D	A	A

Creamer v Ogden Union RR & Depot
52 396A
344 US 912
Utah

Justice	CERT 01/03 1953
Minton	D
Clark	D
Burton	D
Jackson	G
Douglas	D
Frankfr	D
Reed	D
Black	D
Vinson	D

Local 333B v Virginia (Virginia Ferry)
52 398A
344 US 893
Virginia

Justice	CERT 11/21 1952
Minton	D
Clark	D
Burton	D
Jackson	G
Douglas	D
Frankfr	D
Reed	D
Black	D
Vinson	G

Vitari (In Re)
52 399A
344 US 896
Louisiana

Justice	CERT 12/06 1952
Minton	D
Clark	D
Burton	D
Jackson	G
Douglas	D
Frankfr	D
Reed	D
Black	D
Vinson	G

Western Union Telegraph v Lesesne
52 402A
344 US 896
CCA 4th

	CERT 12/06 1952
Minton	D
Clark	D
Burton	D
Jackson	D
Douglas	D
Frankfr	D
Reed	
Black	G
Vinson	G

Orvis v Brownell
52 404A
345 US 183
Jackson 02/12/53 CCA 2d

	CERT 12/13 1952	MERITS 02/07 1953	REPORT 03/16 1953
Minton			A
Clark	G	R	A
Burton	G	R	A
Jackson			
Douglas	G	A	A
Frankfr			
Reed	G	A	A
Black	G	A	A
Vinson			A

Kross v California
52 407A
344 US 908
California

	CERT 12/20 1952
Minton	D
Clark	D
Burton	D
Jackson	D
Douglas	D
Frankfr	D
Reed	
Black	G
Vinson	G

Thomas v Hempt Brothers
52 410A
345 US 19
Black 02/12/53 Pennsylvania

	CERT 12/06 1952	MERITS 02/07 1953	REPORT 03/09 1953
Minton	G	R	R
Clark	G	R	R
Burton	G	R	R
Jackson	G		
Douglas	G	A	A
Frankfr	G		
Reed	G	R	R
Black	G	R	R
Vinson	G		

United Electrical Workers v Oliver
52 414A
344 US 897
CCA 8th

	CERT 12/06 1952
Minton	D
Clark	D
Burton	D
Jackson	D
Douglas	D
Frankfr	D
Reed	
Black	G
Vinson	G

Westwood Pharmacal v Fielding
52 417A
344 US 897
California

	CERT 12/06 1952
Minton	D
Clark	D
Burton	D
Jackson	D
Douglas	D
Frankfr	D
Reed	
Black	G
Vinson	G

United Brick & Clay v Deena Artware
52 419A
344 US 897
CCA 6th

	CERT 12/06 1952
Minton	D
Clark	D
Burton	D
Jackson	D
Douglas	D
Frankfr	D
Reed	
Black	G
Vinson	G

Burns v Wilson
52 422A
346 US 137
Vinson 02/12/53 CCA DC

	CERT 12/13 1952	MERITS 02/09 1953	REPORT 06/15 1953
Minton			A
Clark	G	A	A
Burton		R	R
Jackson	G	A	A
Douglas	G	A	A
Frankfr		A	A
Reed	G	R	R
Black		RQ	A
Vinson	G	A	A

Boortz v American Motorist Insurance Company
52 424A
344 US 897
CCA 5th

	CERT 12/06 1952
Minton	D
Clark	D
Burton	D
Jackson	D
Douglas	D
Frankfr	D
Reed	
Black	G
Vinson	G

Heikkila v Barber
52 426A
345 US 229
Clark 02/12/53 DC ND California

	JURIS 12/06 1952	MERITS 02/09 1953	REPORT 03/16 1953
Minton		A	A
Clark		A	A
Burton	N	R	R
Jackson	N	R	R
Douglas	N		
Frankfr			
Reed	H	R	R
Black			
Vinson	H	A	A

Austrian v Williams
52 431A
344 US 909
CCA 2d

	CERT 12/20 1952
Minton	D
Clark	D3
Burton	D
Jackson	
Douglas	D
Frankfr	D
Reed	
Black	G
Vinson	G

Pennsylvania RR Company v Purvis
52 433A
344 US 898
CCA 3rd

	CERT 12/06 1952
Minton	D
Clark	D
Burton	D
Jackson	D
Douglas	D
Frankfr	G
Reed	D
Black	D
Vinson	

Levinson v Deupree
52 439A
345 US 648 52 631A CCA 6th
Frankfr 02/13/53 CCA 6th

Justice	CERT 12/1952 (1 1)	MERITS 02/09/1953 (1 1)	REPORT 06/01/1953 (1 1)
Minton	D	A	A
Clark	G D	A	A
Burton	G	A	A
Jackson	G D		A
Douglas	G	A	A
Frankfr	G D	A	A
Reed	G	R	R
Black	G	A	A
Vinson	G D	A	A

U.S. v Gilbert Associates
52 440A
345 US 361
Minton 03/17/53 New Hampshire

Justice	CERT 01/03/1953 (1 1)	MERITS 03/14/1953 (1 1)	REPORT 04/06/1953 (1 1)
Minton	D	R	R
Clark	G	R	R
Burton	G	R	R
Jackson	G	R	R
Douglas	G		
Frankfr	G		
Reed	G	R	R
Black	G	A	A
Vinson	G	A	A

Traders Compress Company v Tobin
52 441A
344 US 909
CCA 10th

Justice	CERT 12/1952 (1 1)
Minton	D
Clark	G D
Burton	G D
Jackson	G D
Douglas	G D
Frankfr	G
Reed	
Black	G
Vinson	G D

U.S. v Carroll
52 442A
345 US 457
Douglas 03/17/53 DC WD Missouri

Justice	JURIS 12/06/1952 (1 1)	JURIS 12/13/1952 (1 2)
Minton	S	S
Clark	S	S
Burton	S	S
Jackson	P	N
Douglas		S
Frankfr	P	
Reed	P	N
Black	N	
Vinson	P	P

Orloff v Willoughby
52 444A 52 86M
345 US 83
Jackson 01/22/53 CCA 9th

Justice	CERT 11/08/1952 (1 1)	MERITS 01/17/1953 (1 1)	REPORT 03/09/1953 (1 1)
Minton	D	M	R
Clark	D	M	R
Burton	D	M	
Jackson			
Douglas	G		R
Frankfr	G	R M	R
Reed	GV	R M	R
Black	G	R M	R
Vinson	D	A	A

International Teamsters v Postma
52 446A
345 US 922 52 86A
Michigan

Justice	CERT 01/03/1953 (1 1)	MERITS 04/04/1953 (1 2)
Minton	H	
Clark	H	D
Burton	H	D
Jackson	H	
Douglas	H	G D
Frankfr		
Reed	H	G
Black	H	D
Vinson	H	G D

Allen v Mississippi
52 451A
345 US 901
Mississippi

Justice	CERT 03/07/1953 (1 1)
Minton	D
Clark	D
Burton	D
Jackson	D
Douglas	D
Frankfr	D
Reed	D
Black	G
Vinson	D

Motorola v N.L.R.B.
52 452A
344 US 913
CCA 9th

Justice	CERT 01/03/1953 (1 1)
Minton	D
Clark	D
Burton	D
Jackson	D
Douglas	D
Frankfr	G
Reed	D
Black	D
Vinson	D

Northern Pacific RR Company v Montana
52 455A
344 US 905 52 9A
DC Montana

Justice	JURIS 12/20/1952 (1 1)
Minton	V
Clark	V
Burton	V
Jackson	N
Douglas	V
Frankfr	V
Reed	N
Black	V
Vinson	N

McNish v American Brass Company
52 456A
344 US 913
Connecticut

Justice	CERT 01/03/1953 (1 1)
Minton	D
Clark	D
Burton	D
Jackson	D
Douglas	D
Frankfr	D
Reed	D
Black	G
Vinson	D

Newtex Steamship v U.S.
52 458A
344 US 901
DC SD New York

Justice	JURIS 12/13/1952 (1 1)	REPORT 12/15/1952 (1 1)
Minton	A	A
Clark	A	A
Burton	A	A
Jackson	N	A
Douglas	A	A
Frankfr	A	A
Reed	A	A
Black	A	A
Vinson	A	A

N.L.R.B. v American Thread Company
52 459A
344 US 924 52 97A 52 460A
CCA 5th

Justice	CERT 01/31/1953 (1 1)	MERITS 01/31/1953 (1 1)	REPORT 02/02/1953 (1 1)
Minton	G	R	R
Clark	G	R	R
Burton	G	R	R
Jackson	G	R	R
Douglas	G	R	R
Frankfr	G	R	R
Reed	G	R	R
Black	N		R
Vinson	N	R	R

N.L.R.B. v Nina Dye Works Company
52 460A
344 US 924 52 97A 52 459A
CCA 3rd

Justice	01/31 1953 CERT	01/31 1953 MERITS	02/02 1953 REPORT
Minton	G		R
Clark	G		R
Burton	G		R
Jackson	G	N	R
Douglas	G		R
Frankfr	G		R
Reed	G	N	R
Black	G		R
Vinson	G		R

U.S. v Grower-Shippers Vegetable
52 461A
344 US 901
DC ND California

Justice	12/13 1952 JURIS	12/15 1952 REPORT
Minton	A	A
Clark	A	A
Burton	A	A
Jackson	N	N
Douglas	A	A
Frankfr	A	A
Reed	N	N
Black		
Vinson	N	N

Chicago & Eastern RR Company v U.S.
52 463A
344 US 917
DC SD Indiana

Justice	01/10 1953 JURIS	01/12 1953 REPORT
Minton	A	A
Clark	A	A
Burton	A	A
Jackson	N	N
Douglas	A	A
Frankfr	A	A
Reed	N	N
Black		
Vinson	N	N

Air Transport Associates v C.A.B.
52 465A
344 US 922
CCA DC

Justice	01/17 1953 CERT
Minton	D
Clark	D
Burton	D
Jackson	D
Douglas	G
Frankfr	D
Reed	G
Black	G
Vinson	D

Kelley Glover & Vale v Kramer
52 467A
344 US 914
CCA 7th

Justice	01/03 1953 CERT
Minton	D
Clark	D
Burton	D
Jackson	D
Douglas	D
Frankfr	D
Reed	D
Black	G
Vinson	X

Hall v U.S.
52 471A
345 US 905 52 522A
CCA 2d

Justice	03/07 1953 CERT
Minton	D
Clark	D
Burton	D
Jackson	D
Douglas	D
Frankfr	D
Reed	D
Black	G
Vinson	D

U.S. v Town Of Clarksville Virginia
52 473A
344 US 927
CCA 4th

Justice	01/31 1953 CERT
Minton	D
Clark	D
Burton	D
Jackson	D
Douglas	D
Frankfr	D
Reed	G
Black	D
Vinson	D

Thomas v Chesapeake & Ohio RR Company
52 475A
344 US 921
CCA 4th

Justice	01/17 1953 CERT
Minton	D
Clark	D
Burton	D
Jackson	G
Douglas	D
Frankfr	D
Reed	G
Black	D
Vinson	D

Johnson v U.S.
52 476A
345 US 905
CCA 4th

Justice	03/07 1953 CERT
Minton	D
Clark	D
Burton	D
Jackson	D
Douglas	G
Frankfr	G
Reed	D
Black	G
Vinson	D

L.A. Goodman Manufacturing v Borkland
52 477A
344 US 921
Illinois

Justice	01/17 1953 CERT
Minton	D
Clark	D
Burton	D
Jackson	D
Douglas	G
Frankfr	D
Reed	D
Black	G
Vinson	D

Des Marais v Beckman
52 480A
344 US 922
CCA 9th

Justice	01/17 1953 CERT
Minton	D
Clark	D
Burton	D
Jackson	G
Douglas	D
Frankfr	D
Reed	G
Black	D
Vinson	D

Advertisers Exchange v Hinkley
52 486A
344 US 921
CCA 8th

Justice	01/17 1953 CERT
Minton	D
Clark	D
Burton	D
Jackson	D
Douglas	D
Frankfr	D
Reed	D
Black	D
Vinson	D

Head v U.S.
52 487A
345 US 910
CCA 10th

Justice	03/07 1953 CERT
Minton	D
Clark	D
Burton	D
Jackson	D
Douglas	D
Frankfr	G
Reed	D
Black	G
Vinson	D

Callanan Road Improvement v U.S.
52 488A
345 US 507
Minton 04/15/53 DC ND New York

Justice	04/11 1953 MERITS	05/04 1953 REPORT
Minton	A	A
Clark		
Burton	N	A
Jackson	N	A
Douglas	N	A
Frankfr	R	R
Reed	N	A
Black	A	A
Vinson	A	A

One 1951 Ford Pick-Up Truck v U.S.
52 492A
344 US 928
CCA 3rd

Justice	01/31 1953 CERT
Minton	D
Clark	D
Burton	D
Jackson	D
Douglas	D
Frankfr	D
Reed	D
Black	G
Vinson	G

374

McGuire v Maryland
52 493A
344 US 928
Maryland

Justice	01/31 1953 CERT
	– –
Minton	D
Clark	D
Burton	D
Jackson	
Douglas	D
Frankfr	
Reed	D
Black	
Vinson	D

California Electric Power v F.P.C.
52 495A
345 US 934
CCA 9th

Justice	04/11 1953 CERT
	– –
Minton	G
Clark	
Burton	G
Jackson	
Douglas	G
Frankfr	
Reed	G
Black	
Vinson	G

U.S. v Lane Motor Company
52 499A
344 US 630
CCA 10th

Justice	01/31 1953 CERT	01/31 1953 MERITS	02/09 1953 REPORT
	– –	– –	– –
Minton	G	A	A
Clark	G	A	A
Burton	G	A	A
Jackson	G	A	A
Douglas			A
Frankfr	G		A
Reed		A	A
Black			A
Vinson	G	A	A

Atlantic Coast Line RR v South Carolina
52 502A
345 US 916
South Carolina

Justice	01/31 1953 CERT	03/14 1953 CERT
	– –	1 2
Minton	D	D
Clark	D	D
Burton	D	D
Jackson		D
Douglas	G	D
Frankfr	G	D
Reed	G	D
Black	D	D
Vinson		D

Herrin Transportation Company v U.S.
52 503A
344 US 925
DC ED Louisiana

Justice	01/31 1953 JURIS	02/02 1953 REPORT
	– –	– –
Minton	A	A
Clark	A	A
Burton	A	A
Jackson	A	A
Douglas	A	A
Frankfr	A	A
Reed		
Black	N	N
Vinson	A	A

Malone Freight Lines v U.S.
52 505A
344 US 925
DC ND Alabama

Justice	01/31 1953 JURIS	02/02 1953 REPORT
	– –	– –
Minton	A	A
Clark	A	A
Burton	A	A
Jackson	A	A
Douglas	N	N
Frankfr		
Reed	N	N
Black	N	N
Vinson	A	A

Accinanto v A/S J. Ludwig Mowinckels
52 506A
345 US 992   52 308A
CCA 4th

Justice	06/13 1953 CERT
	– –
Minton	D
Clark	D
Burton	D
Jackson	D
Douglas	G
Frankfr	G
Reed	D
Black	D
Vinson	

U.S. v International Building Company
52 508A
345 US 502
Douglas 04/15/53 CCA 8th

Justice	01/31 1953 CERT	04/11 1953 MERITS	05/04 1953 REPORT
	– –	– –	– –
Minton	G	R	R
Clark	G	R	R
Burton	G	R	R
Jackson	G	R	R
Douglas	G		
Frankfr	G	R	R
Reed	G	R	R
Black	G	R	R
Vinson			

Transcontinental & Western v Koppal
52 509A
345 US 653 51 1A
Burton 04/15/53 CCA 8th

Justice	02/07 1953 CERT	04/11 1953 MERITS	06/01 1953 REPORT
	– –	– –	– –
Minton	G	R	R
Clark	GL	R	R
Burton	GL	R	R
Jackson	GL	R	R
Douglas			
Frankfr	GL		
Reed		R	R
Black	D		
Vinson	G	AQ	A

S.E.C. v Ralston Purina Company
52 512A
346 US 119
Clark 05/11/53 CCA 8th

Justice	03/07 1953 CERT	05/02 1953 MERITS	06/08 1953 REPORT
	– –	– –	– –
Minton	G	R	R
Clark	G	R	R
Burton			
Jackson	D		
Douglas	D		
Frankfr		A	A
Reed	G	R	R
Black	G	R	R
Vinson			

Redwine v Georgia RR & Banking
52 516A
344 US 925
DC ND Georgia

Justice	01/31 1953 JURIS	02/02 1953 REPORT
	– –	– –
Minton	A	A
Clark	A	A
Burton	A	A
Jackson	N	N
Douglas	A	A
Frankfr	A	A
Reed	N	
Black	A	R
Vinson		

Barrows v Jackson
52 517A
346 US 249
Minton 05/11/53 California

Justice	03/07 1953 CERT	05/02 1953 MERITS	06/15 1953 REPORT
	– –	– –	– –
Minton	G		
Clark	G	S	A
Burton	G		A
Jackson	X		A
Douglas	G		A
Frankfr	D		
Reed	X	S	A
Black	D		
Vinson	G	R	R

Central Bank v U.S.
52 521A
345 US 639
Reed 05/20/53 Ct Cls

	03/07 1953 CERT	05/02 1953 MERITS	06/01 1953 REPORT
	1 1	1 1	1 1
Minton		R	R
Clark	D		
Burton	D		
Jackson			
Douglas	G	A	A
Frankfr	G	A	A
Reed	G	A	A
Black			A
Vinson	G	A	A

New York New Haven RR v Nothnagle
52 525A
346 US 128
Clark 05/28/53 Connecticut

	03/07 1953 CERT	05/02 1953 MERITS	06/08 1953 REPORT
	1 1	1 1	1 1
Minton	G	R	R
Clark	G		
Burton	G		
Jackson		A	A
Douglas	G	A	A
Frankfr		A	A
Reed	G		
Black	G	R	A
Vinson	G	A	A

U.S. v United States Cartridge Company
52 526A
345 US 910
CCA 8th

	03/07 1953 CERT
	1 1
Minton	D
Clark	
Burton	D
Jackson	D
Douglas	G
Frankfr	
Reed	G
Black	G
Vinson	G

U.S. v Klinger
52 527A
345 US 979
CCA 2d

	04/04 1953 CERT	05/06 1953 MERITS	06/15 1953 REPORT
	1 1	1 1	1 1
Minton	G	R	R
Clark	G	R	R
Burton	G		
Jackson		A	A
Douglas	D	A	A
Frankfr		A	A
Reed	G	R	R
Black		A	A
Vinson	G	A	A

Duke v C.I.R.
52 528A
345 US 906
CCA 2d

	03/07 1953 CERT
	1 1
Minton	D
Clark	D
Burton	D
Jackson	D
Douglas	D
Frankfr	D
Reed	D
Black	G
Vinson	D

Saulsbury v U.S.
52 529A
345 US 906
CCA 5th

	03/07 1953 CERT
	1 1
Minton	D
Clark	D
Burton	D
Jackson	D
Douglas	D
Frankfr	D
Reed	D
Black	G
Vinson	D

U.S. v W.T. Grant Company
52 532A
345 US 629
Clark 04/15/53 DC SD New York

	01/31 1953 JURIS	04/11 1953 MERITS	05/25 1953 REPORT
	1 1	1 1	1 1
Minton	A	A	A
Clark	A	A	A
Burton	A	A	A
Jackson			
Douglas	N	R	R
Frankfr	N		
Reed	N	R	R
Black	N	R	R
Vinson	A	A	A

Cornett v Nebraska
52 537A
345 US 936
Nebraska

	04/11 1953 CERT
	1 1
Minton	
Clark	
Burton	
Jackson	
Douglas	
Frankfr	
Reed	
Black	
Vinson	G

U.S. v Nugent
52 540A
346 US 1 52 573A
Vinson 05/11/53 CCA 2d

	03/14 1953 CERT	05/06 1953 MERITS	06/08 1953 REPORT
	1 1	1 1	1 1
Minton	G	R	R
Clark	G	R	R
Burton	G		
Jackson	X		
Douglas	D	A	A
Frankfr	G	A	A
Reed	G	R	R
Black	G	A	A
Vinson	G	A	A

McGranery v Vort
52 541A
345 US 911 52 542A
CCA DC

Justice	03/07/1953 CERT
Minton	D
Clark	
Burton	G
Jackson	D
Douglas	D
Frankfr	
Reed	G
Black	
Vinson	G D

Vort v McGranery
52 542A
345 US 911 52 541A
CCA DC

Justice	03/07/1953 CERT
Minton	D
Clark	
Burton	G
Jackson	D
Douglas	D
Frankfr	
Reed	G
Black	
Vinson	G D

Bridges v U.S.
52 548A
346 US 209 52 549A
Burton 05/11/53 CCA 9th

Justice	03/07/1953 CERT
Minton	G X
Clark	
Burton	G
Jackson	G
Douglas	G
Frankfr	G
Reed	
Black	
Vinson	G

Bridges v U.S.
52 549A
345 US 979 52 548A
CCA 9th

Justice	06/13/1953 CERT	06/13/1953 MERITS	06/15/1953 REPORT
Minton	D	A	A
Clark			
Burton	G	R	R
Jackson			
Douglas	G	R	R
Frankfr			
Reed	G	R	R
Black	G	A	A
Vinson	G	A	A

Mid-States Freight Lines v Bates
52 552A
345 US 908
New York

Justice	03/07/1953 CERT	04/04/1953 ENLARGE	05/06/1953 MERITS	06/15/1953 REPORT
Minton	D	B		
Clark		B X	R	R
Burton				
Jackson	D	B	R	R
Douglas	D	B		
Frankfr				
Reed	D	B Y	R	R
Black				
Vinson	D	B	A	A

Brotherhood Locomotive v Central RR
52 554A
345 US 908
CCA 5th

Justice	03/07/1953 CERT
Minton	D
Clark	D
Burton	
Jackson	E
Douglas	D
Frankfr	D
Reed	D
Black	D
Vinson	D

U.S. v Jones
52 556A
345 US 377
DC SD Florida

Justice	04/04/1953 JURIS	04/13/1953 REPORT
Minton	M	M
Clark	M	M
Burton	M	M
Jackson	M	M
Douglas	M	M
Frankfr	M	M
Reed	M	M
Black	M	M
Vinson	M	M

U.S. v American Construction Company
52 559A
345 US 922
Ct Cls

Justice	04/04/1953 CERT
Minton	D
Clark	
Burton	G
Jackson	D
Douglas	D
Frankfr	
Reed	D
Black	G
Vinson	D

Rupert v Empire District Electric
52 561A
345 US 909
CCA 8th

Justice	03/07/1953 CERT
Minton	D
Clark	D
Burton	D
Jackson	D
Douglas	D
Frankfr	D
Reed	D
Black	D
Vinson	D

Joint Anti-Fascist v McGranery
52 563A
345 US 911
CCA DC

Justice	03/07/1953 CERT
Minton	D
Clark	D
Burton	D
Jackson	D
Douglas	D
Frankfr	D
Reed	D
Black	
Vinson	D

Harrison v Bohnen
52 566A
345 US 946
CCA 7th

Justice	03/07/1953 CERT
Minton	G
Clark	G
Burton	G
Jackson	G
Douglas	D
Frankfr	G
Reed	G
Black	D
Vinson	G

F.C.C. v RCA
52 567A
346 US 86 52 568A
Frankfr 05/11/53 CCA DC

Justice	03/07/1953 CERT	05/02/1953 MERITS	06/08/1953 REPORT
Minton	G	RQ	>
Clark	G	R A	>
Burton	G	A	
Jackson	G		
Douglas	G	RQ	>
Frankfr			
Reed	G	R	R
Black	G	R	R
Vinson			V

Mackay Radio & Telegraph v RCA
52 568A
346 US 86 52 567A
Frankfr 05/11/53 CCA DC

Justice	03/07/1953 CERT	05/02/1953 MERITS	06/08/1953 REPORT
Minton	G	RQ	>
Clark	G	R A	>
Burton	G	A	
Jackson	G		
Douglas	G	RQ	>
Frankfr			
Reed	G	R	R
Black	G	R	R
Vinson			V

Harrison v Bohnen (continued)
52 566A
345 US 946
CCA 7th

Justice	05/02/1953 MERITS	05/04/1953 REPORT	06/06/1953 REHEAR
Minton	R	R	B
Clark			B
Burton	R	R	
Jackson		A	Y
Douglas		A	Y
Frankfr		A	Y
Reed			
Black	R	A	B
Vinson			B

Sullivan v California
52 570A
345 US 955
California
05/16 1953 CERT 1 1

Justice	
Minton	D
Clark	D
Burton	D
Jackson	D
Douglas	G
Frankfr	D
Reed	D
Black	D
Vinson	D

U.S. v Packer
52 573A
346 US 1 52 540A
Vinson 05/11/53 CCA 2d
03/14 1953 CERT 1 1
05/06 1953 MERITS 1 1
06/08 1953 REPORT 1 1

Justice	CERT	MERITS	REPORT
Minton	G	R	R
Clark	G	R	R
Burton	G	R	R
Jackson	G D	A	A
Douglas			
Frankfr	G	A	A
Reed	G	R	R
Black	G D	A	A
Vinson		R	R

U.S. (Dolenz) v Shaughnessy
52 576A
345 US 928
CCA 2d
04/04 1953 CERT 1 1

Justice	
Minton	D
Clark	D
Burton	D
Jackson	D
Douglas	G
Frankfr	D
Reed	D
Black	G
Vinson	G

Glyco Products Company v F.S.A.
52 584A
345 US 923 52 610A
CCA 3rd
04/04 1953 CERT 1 1

Justice	
Minton	D
Clark	D
Burton	D
Jackson	D
Douglas	G
Frankfr	D
Reed	D
Black	
Vinson	D

Warner & Swasey v War Contracts Price
52 588A
345 US 924
CCA DC
04/04 1953 CERT 1 1

Justice	
Minton	D
Clark	D
Burton	D
Jackson	D
Douglas	D
Frankfr	G
Reed	D
Black	D
Vinson	D

Mallonee v Fahey
52 591A
345 US 952 52 592A 52 596A 52 658A
CCA 9th
05/02 1953 CERT 1 1

Justice	
Minton	D
Clark	
Burton	D
Jackson	D
Douglas	
Frankfr	G
Reed	D
Black	D
Vinson	D

Wilmington Federal Savings v H.L.B.B.
52 592A
345 US 952 52 591A 52 596A 52 658A
CCA 9th
05/02 1953 CERT 1 1

Justice	
Minton	D
Clark	
Burton	D
Jackson	D
Douglas	
Frankfr	G
Reed	D
Black	D
Vinson	D

Home Investment Company v Fahey
52 593A
345 US 952 52 591A 52 596A 52 658A
CCA 9th
04/04 1953 CERT 1 1

Justice	
Minton	D
Clark	
Burton	D
Jackson	D
Douglas	
Frankfr	G
Reed	D
Black	D
Vinson	D

Utley v Fahey
52 594A
345 US 952 52 591A 52 596A 52 658A
CCA 9th
05/02 1953 CERT 1 1

Justice	
Minton	D
Clark	
Burton	D
Jackson	D
Douglas	
Frankfr	G
Reed	D
Black	D
Vinson	D

Wallis v Fahey
52 595A
345 US 952 52 591A 52 596A 52 658A
CCA 9th
05/02 1953 CERT 1 1

Justice	
Minton	D
Clark	
Burton	D
Jackson	D
Douglas	
Frankfr	G
Reed	D
Black	D
Vinson	D

Title Service Company v Fahey
52 596A
345 US 952 52 591A 52 596A 52 658A
CCA 9th
05/02 1953 CERT 1 1

Justice	
Minton	D
Clark	
Burton	D
Jackson	D
Douglas	
Frankfr	G
Reed	D
Black	D
Vinson	D

Nelson Radio & Supply v Motorola
52 603A
345 US 925
CCA 5th
04/04 1953 CERT 1 1

Justice	
Minton	D
Clark	
Burton	D
Jackson	D
Douglas	G
Frankfr	G
Reed	D
Black	G
Vinson	D

Atlas Powder Company v Ewing
52 610A
345 US 923 52 584A
CCA 3rd
04/04 1953 CERT 1 1

Justice	
Minton	D
Clark	D
Burton	D
Jackson	D
Douglas	G
Frankfr	D
Reed	D
Black	
Vinson	D

Bloch v U.S.
52 612A
345 US 935
CCA 2d
04/11 1953 CERT 1 1

Justice	
Minton	D
Clark	D
Burton	D
Jackson	D
Douglas	G
Frankfr	D
Reed	D
Black	
Vinson	D

Wilson v Reynolds
52 615A
345 US 926
CCA DC
04/04 1953 CERT 1 1

Justice	
Minton	D
Clark	D
Burton	D
Jackson	D
Douglas	G
Frankfr	D
Reed	D
Black	
Vinson	D

District Of Columbia v John R. Thompson
52 617A
346 US 100
Douglas 05/11/53 CCA DC

	04/04 1953 CERT (1 1)	04/11 1953 AMICUS (1 1)	05/06 1953 MERITS (1 1)	06/08 1953 REPORT (1 1)
Minton	G	Y	R	R
Clark	G	Y	R	R
Burton	G	Y	R	R
Jackson	G	Y		R
Douglas	G	Y	R	R
Frankfr	G	Y	R	R
Reed	G	Y	A	R
Black	G	Y	R	R
Vinson	G	Y	R	R

C.I.R. v Golonsky
52 622A
345 US 939
CCA 3rd

	04/25 1953 CERT (1 1)
Minton	D
Clark	D
Burton	D
Jackson	D
Douglas	D
Frankfr	D
Reed	
Black	G
Vinson	D

Sher v DeHaven
52 628A
345 US 936
CCA DC

	04/11 1953 CERT (1 1)
Minton	D
Clark	D
Burton	D
Jackson	D
Douglas	D
Frankfr	D
Reed	
Black	G
Vinson	D

Hiss v U.S.
52 629A
345 US 942
CCA 2d

	04/25 1953 CERT (1 1)
Minton	D
Clark	D
Burton	D
Jackson	D
Douglas	G
Frankfr	D
Reed	
Black	D
Vinson	D

Continental Casualty v The Benny Skou
52 631A
345 US 992 52 439A
CCA 4th

	06/13 1953 CERT (1 1)
Minton	D
Clark	D
Burton	D
Jackson	D
Douglas	D
Frankfr	D
Reed	D
Black	G
Vinson	D

Jensen v Peoples Finance Company
52 633A
345 US 926
CCA 7th

	04/04 1953 CERT (1 1)
Minton	D
Clark	D
Burton	D
Jackson	D
Douglas	D
Frankfr	D
Reed	
Black	G
Vinson	D

U.S. v Grainger
52 634A
346 US 235 52 635A 52 636A 52 750A
Burton 05/11/53 DC ND California

	04/04 1953 JURIS (1 1)	05/06 1953 MERITS (1 1)	06/15 1953 REPORT (1 1)
Minton	N	R	R
Clark	N	R	R
Burton	N	R	R
Jackson	N		
Douglas	N	A	A
Frankfr	N	A	A
Reed	N	R	R
Black	N	A	A
Vinson	N	R	R

U.S. v Clavere
52 635A 52 636A
346 US 235 52 634A 52 750A
Burton 05/11/53 DC ND California

	04/04 1953 JURIS (1 1)	05/06 1953 MERITS (1 1)	06/15 1953 REPORT (1 1)
Minton	N	R	R
Clark	N	R	R
Burton	N	R	R
Jackson	N		
Douglas	N	A	A
Frankfr	N	A	A
Reed	N	R	R
Black	N	A	A
Vinson	N	R	R

Marine Midland Trust Company v McGirl
52 637A
345 US 940
CCA 3rd

	04/25 1953 CERT (1 1)
Minton	D
Clark	D
Burton	D
Jackson	G
Douglas	D
Frankfr	D
Reed	G
Black	D
Vinson	D

Cohen v U.S.
52 646A
345 US 951
CCA 9th

	05/02 1953 CERT (1 1)
Minton	D
Clark	D
Burton	D
Jackson	D
Douglas	D
Frankfr	D
Reed	D
Black	G
Vinson	D

Avery v Georgia
52 648A 52 102M
345 US 559 52 32A
Vinson 05/20/53 Georgia

	10/09 1952 CERT (1 1)	03/07 1953 CERT (1 2)	05/02 1953 MERITS (1 1)	05/25 1953 REPORT (1 1)
Minton	G	G	R	R
Clark	G	G	R	R
Burton	D	D	R	R
Jackson				
Douglas	X	X		
Frankfr		D		
Reed	H	G	R	R
Black	H	G	R	R
Vinson	G	D	R	R

Schennault v U.S.
52 651A
345 US 950
CCA 7th

	05/02 1953 CERT (1 1)
Minton	D
Clark	D
Burton	D
Jackson	D
Douglas	D
Frankfr	D
Reed	D
Black	
Vinson	G

U.S. v Marr
52 **654A**
345 US 956
Ct Cls

	05/16 1953 CERT 1 1
Minton	D
Clark	D
Burton	D
Jackson	D
Douglas	G
Frankfr	D
Reed	D
Black	D
Vinson	D

Odell v Humble Oil & Refining Company
52 **657A**
345 US 941
CCA 10th

	04/25 1953 CERT 1 1
Minton	D
Clark	D
Burton	D
Jackson	D
Douglas	G
Frankfr	D
Reed	D
Black	D
Vinson	D

Willhoit v Fahey
52 **658A**
345 US 952
CCA 9th

	05/02 1953 CERT 1 1
Minton	D
Clark	
Burton	D
Jackson	D
Douglas	D
Frankfr	G
Reed	D
Black	D
Vinson	D

Fargo Glass & Paint v Globe American
52 **659A**
345 US 942
CCA 7th

	04/25 1953 CERT 1 1
Minton	D
Clark	D
Burton	D
Jackson	D
Douglas	D
Frankfr	D
Reed	D
Black	G
Vinson	D

Martin Wunderlich v Secretary Of War
52 **666A**
345 US 950
CCA DC

	05/02 1953 CERT 1 1
Minton	D
Clark	D
Burton	D
Jackson	D
Douglas	G
Frankfr	D
Reed	G
Black	D
Vinson	D

Harvey Aluminum v American Cyanamid
52 **680A**
345 US 964
CCA 2d

	05/23 1953 CERT 1 1
Minton	D
Clark	D
Burton	D
Jackson	D
Douglas	D
Frankfr	D
Reed	D
Black	G
Vinson	G

Cammarata v Ohio
52 **681A**
345 US 998
Ohio

	06/13 1953 CERT 1 1
Minton	D
Clark	D
Burton	D
Jackson	G
Douglas	D
Frankfr	D
Reed	D
Black	D
Vinson	D

Cooper v Peak
52 **682A**
345 US 957
Alabama

	05/16 1953 CERT 1 1
Minton	
Clark	
Burton	
Jackson	
Douglas	
Frankfr	
Reed	
Black	G
Vinson	

Teamsters Local 164 v Way Baking
52 **686A**
345 US 957
Michigan

	05/16 1953 CERT 1 1
Minton	D
Clark	D
Burton	D
Jackson	D
Douglas	G
Frankfr	D
Reed	G
Black	D
Vinson	D

Rosenberg v U.S.
52 **687A** 52 1M
346 US 273 52 111A 52 112A
CCA 2d

	05/02 1953 CERT 1 1	05/16 1953 QUEST 18 1	05/23 1953 CERT 1 2	05/23 1953 QUEST 13 1	06/13 1953 STAY 1 1	06/13 1953 REHEAR 1 1	06/18 1953 STAY 1 2	06/18 1953 HEAR 1 1	06/18 1953 QUEST 13 2
Minton	D	Y	D	Y	B	B	B	B	Y
Clark	D	Y	D	Y	B	B	B	B	Y
Burton	D	B	D	Y	B	B	Y	Y	Y
Jackson	D	B	D	Y	K	B	B	B	Y
Douglas	D	B	G	Y	B	Y	Y	Y	B
Frankfr	GK	B	G	Y	K		X	Y	B
Reed	D	Y	D	Y	B	B	B	B	Y
Black	G	B	G				Y	Y	B
Vinson	D	Y	D	Y	B	B	B	B	Y

Gordon v U.S.
52 **688A**
345 US 968
CCA 10th

	05/29 1953 CERT 1 1	06/01 1953 REPORT 1 1
Minton	GVI	VI
Clark	GVI	VI
Burton	GVI	VI
Jackson	GVI	VI
Douglas	G	VI
Frankfr	GVI	VI
Reed	GVI	VI
Black	GVI	VI
Vinson	GVI	VI

U.S. v Rolland
52 **690A**
345 US 964
CCA 5th

	05/23 1953 CERT 1 1
Minton	D
Clark	D
Burton	D
Jackson	D
Douglas	D
Frankfr	D
Reed	D
Black	G
Vinson	D

Forgione v U.S.
52 **699A**
345 US 966
CCA 3rd

	05/23 1953 CERT 1 1
Minton	D
Clark	D
Burton	D
Jackson	D
Douglas	G
Frankfr	D
Reed	D
Black	G
Vinson	D

Mays v Bowers
52 **706A**
345 US 969
CCA 4th

	05/29 1953 CERT 1 1
Minton	D
Clark	D
Burton	D
Jackson	G
Douglas	D3
Frankfr	D
Reed	D
Black	G
Vinson	D

Scott Publishing Company v Gaffney
52 **707A**
345 US 992
Washington

	06/13 1953 CERT 1 1
Minton	D
Clark	D
Burton	D
Jackson	D
Douglas	D
Frankfr	D
Reed	D
Black	G
Vinson	D

Pockman v Leonard
52 **711A**
345 US 962
California

	05/23 1953 JURIS 1 1
Minton	S
Clark	S
Burton	S
Jackson	S
Douglas	N
Frankfr	N
Reed	S
Black	N
Vinson	S

Amalgamated Association v Southern Bus
52 **716A** 52 717A
345 US 964
CCA 5th

	05/23 1953 CERT 1 1
Minton	
Clark	
Burton	
Jackson	
Douglas	
Frankfr	
Reed	
Black	G
Vinson	

Sobell v U.S.
52 **719A**
345 US 965 52 687A 52 111A 52 112A
CCA 2d

	05/02 1953 CERT 1 1	05/23 1953 CERT 1 2
Minton	D	D
Clark	D	D
Burton	D	D
Jackson	D	D
Douglas	D	G
Frankfr	G	G
Reed	D	D
Black	G	G
Vinson	D	D

James v Shaughnessy
52 722A
345 US 969
CCA 2d
05/29 1953 CERT
1 1

Justice	Vote
Minton	A
Clark	A
Burton	A
Jackson	A
Douglas	N
Frankfr	A
Reed	N
Black	G
Vinson	A

Wales v U.S.
52 723A
345 US 954
DC ND Texas
05/16 1953 JURIS
1 1

Justice	Vote
Minton	A
Clark	A
Burton	A
Jackson	A
Douglas	A
Frankfr	A
Reed	A
Black	A
Vinson	A

Romine v Southern Pacific Company
52 735A
345 US 970
Arizona
05/29 1953 CERT
1 1

Justice	Vote
Minton	D
Clark	D
Burton	D
Jackson	G
Douglas	G
Frankfr	D
Reed	
Black	G
Vinson	D

De Vita v New Jersey
52 732A
345 US 976 52 733A
New Jersey
06/06 1953 CERT
1 1

Justice	Vote
Minton	D
Clark	D
Burton	D
Jackson	D
Douglas	
Frankfr	
Reed	G
Black	G
Vinson	D

Grillo v New Jersey
52 733A
345 US 976 52 732A
New Jersey
06/06 1953 CERT
1 1

Justice	Vote
Minton	D
Clark	D
Burton	D
Jackson	D
Douglas	
Frankfr	
Reed	G
Black	G
Vinson	D

Schneider v Gallagher
52 746A
345 US 993
California
06/13 1953 CERT
1 1

Justice	Vote
Minton	D
Clark	D
Burton	D
Jackson	D
Douglas	D
Frankfr	D
Reed	D
Black	G
Vinson	D

U.S. v Berman
52 750A
345 US 979 52 634A 52 635A 52 636A
DC ND California
06/13 1953 MERITS
1 1

Justice	MERITS	52 634A	52 635A	52 636A
Minton	R			
Clark	R			
Burton	R			
Jackson				
Douglas		A	A	A
Frankfr				
Reed	R	A	R	A
Black	R		R	
Vinson	R	A	R	A

U.S. (Spinella) v Savoretti
52 743A
345 US 975
CCA 5th
06/06 1953 CERT
1 1

Justice	Vote
Minton	D
Clark	D
Burton	D
Jackson	D
Douglas	D
Frankfr	G
Reed	G
Black	G
Vinson	D

Bascom Launder v Telecoin
52 756A
345 US 994
CCA 2d
06/13 1953 CERT
1 1

Justice	Vote
Minton	D
Clark	D
Burton	D
Jackson	D
Douglas	D
Frankfr	D
Reed	G
Black	D
Vinson	G

Skovgaard v U.S.
52 759A
345 US 994
CCA DC
06/13 1953 CERT
1 1

Justice	Vote
Minton	D
Clark	D
Burton	D
Jackson	D
Douglas	D
Frankfr	D
Reed	G
Black	G
Vinson	G

Trenton Chemical Company v U.S.
52 760A
345 US 994
CCA 6th
06/13 1953 CERT
1 1

Justice	Vote
Minton	D
Clark	D
Burton	D
Jackson	D
Douglas	D
Frankfr	D
Reed	G
Black	
Vinson	D

Yglesias v Gulfstream Park Racing
52 752A 52 753A
345 US 993
CCA 5th
06/13 1953 CERT
1 1

Justice	Vote
Minton	D
Clark	D
Burton	D
Jackson	D
Douglas	D
Frankfr	G
Reed	
Black	G
Vinson	D

U.S. v Thomas
52 770A
345 US 994 52 771A 52 772A
Ct Cls
06/13 1953 CERT
1 1

Justice	Vote
Minton	D
Clark	D
Burton	D3
Jackson	D
Douglas	D
Frankfr	D
Reed	
Black	G
Vinson	D

U.S. v Ramsey
52 771A
345 US 994 52 770A 52 772A
Ct Cls
06/13 1953 CERT
1 1

Justice	Vote
Minton	D
Clark	D
Burton	D
Jackson	D
Douglas	D
Frankfr	D
Reed	
Black	G
Vinson	D

U.S. v Frame
52 772A
345 US 994 52 770A 52 771A
Ct Cls
06/13 1953 CERT
1 1

Justice	Vote
Minton	D
Clark	D
Burton	D
Jackson	D
Douglas	D
Frankfr	D
Reed	
Black	G
Vinson	D

Lopez v America-Hawaiian Steamship
52 788A
345 US 976
CCA 3rd
06/06 1953 CERT
1 1

Justice	Vote
Minton	D
Clark	D
Burton	D
Jackson	D
Douglas	D
Frankfr	D
Reed	D
Black	G
Vinson	D

Neal v U.S.
52 791A
345 US 996
CCA 5th
06/13 1953 CERT
1 1

Justice	Vote
Minton	D
Clark	D
Burton	D
Jackson	D
Douglas	D
Frankfr	D
Reed	D
Black	G
Vinson	D

Davis v U.S.
52 792A
345 US 996
CCA 8th
06/13 1953 CERT
1 1

Justice	Vote
Minton	D
Clark	D
Burton	D
Jackson	D
Douglas	D
Frankfr	D
Reed	D
Black	G
Vinson	D

Dart Transit Company v I.C.C.
52 800A
345 US 980
DC Minnesota

Justice	06/13 1953 JURIS 1 1	06/15 1953 REPORT 1 1
Minton	A	A
Clark	A	A
Burton	A	A
Jackson	N	N
Douglas	A	A
Frankfr	A	A
Reed	N	A
Black	N	N
Vinson	A	A

General Motors v Ackermans
52 812A
345 US 996
CCA 4th

Justice	06/06 1953 CERT 1 1
Minton	D
Clark	D
Burton	D
Jackson	D
Douglas	D
Frankfr	D
Reed	D
Black	H
Vinson	D

Cantrall v N.L.R.B.
52 816A
345 US 996
CCA 9th

Justice	06/13 1953 CERT 1 1
Minton	D
Clark	D
Burton	D
Jackson	D
Douglas	D
Frankfr	D
Reed	D
Black	H
Vinson	D

U.S.A.C. Transport v U.S.
52 820A
345 US 997
CCA 10th

Justice	06/13 1953 CERT 1 1
Minton	D
Clark	D
Burton	D
Jackson	D
Douglas	D
Frankfr	D
Reed	D
Black	G
Vinson	D

Robinson v Louisiana
52 6M 51 484M
344 US 904
Louisiana

Justice	06/07 1952 CERT 1 1
Minton	D
Clark	H
Burton	D
Jackson	D
Douglas	G
Frankfr	H
Reed	H
Black	H
Vinson	D

Gresham v California
52 45M
344 US 842
California

Justice	10/09 1952 CERT 1 1
Minton	D
Clark	D
Burton	D
Jackson	D
Douglas	E
Frankfr	D
Reed	D
Black	G
Vinson	D

Gliva v Jacques
52 53M
344 US 843
Michigan

Justice	10/09 1952 CERT 1 1
Minton	D
Clark	D
Burton	D
Jackson	D
Douglas	D
Frankfr	D
Reed	D
Black	G
Vinson	D

Gusik v Schilder
52 67M
344 US 844
CCA 6th

Justice	10/09 1952 CERT 1 1	12/13 1952 CERT 1 2
Minton	D	
Clark	D	
Burton	D	
Jackson	D	
Douglas	G	G
Frankfr	D	
Reed	D	X
Black	D	
Vinson	D	D

Golemon v Texas
52 69M
344 US 847
Texas

Justice	10/09 1952 CERT 1 1
Minton	D
Clark	D
Burton	D
Jackson	D
Douglas	G
Frankfr	D
Reed	D
Black	G
Vinson	D

Sukowski v Ragen
52 72M
345 US 928
Illinois

Justice	10/09 1952 CERT 1 1	04/04 1953 CERT 1 2
Minton	D	D
Clark	D	D
Burton	E	D
Jackson	E	
Douglas	G	G
Frankfr	E	G
Reed	GE	G
Black	D	
Vinson	D	D

Reed v Texas
52 77M
344 US 851
Texas

Justice	10/18 1952 CERT 1 1
Minton	D
Clark	D
Burton	D
Jackson	D
Douglas	G
Frankfr	D
Reed	D
Black	G
Vinson	D

Pierce v U.S.
52 88M
344 US 846
CCA DC

Justice	10/09 1952 CERT 1 1
Minton	D
Clark	D
Burton	D
Jackson	D
Douglas	G
Frankfr	G
Reed	D
Black	G
Vinson	D

Reid v Maryland
52 89M
344 US 848
Maryland

Justice	10/09 1952 CERT 1 1
Minton	D
Clark	D
Burton	D
Jackson	D
Douglas	G
Frankfr	G
Reed	D
Black	D
Vinson	D

Rubino v New York
52 90M
344 US 846
New York

Justice	10/09 1952 CERT 1 1
Minton	D
Clark	D
Burton	D
Jackson	D
Douglas	D
Frankfr	D
Reed	D
Black	E
Vinson	D

Port v Goodman
52 95M
344 US 808

Justice	10/09 1952 MNDMUS 1 1
Minton	D
Clark	D
Burton	D
Jackson	D
Douglas	D
Frankfr	D
Reed	D
Black	G
Vinson	D

Kerr v Teets
52 97M
344 US 846
CCA 9th

Justice	10/09 1952 CERT 1 1
Minton	D
Clark	D
Burton	D
Jackson	
Douglas	G
Frankfr	
Reed	D
Black	D
Vinson	DQ

Crummer Company v DuPont
52 107M
344 US 851 52 240A
CCA 5th

Justice	10/18 1952 CERT 1 1
Minton	D
Clark	D
Burton	D
Jackson	D
Douglas	G
Frankfr	D
Reed	D
Black	D
Vinson	D

Knott v Swenson
52 109M
344 US 847
Maryland

Justice	10/09 1952 CERT 1 1
Minton	D
Clark	D
Burton	D
Jackson	D
Douglas	E
Frankfr	D
Reed	D
Black	G
Vinson	D

Williamson v Oklahoma
52 117M — 344 US 904 — Oklahoma
10/25 1952 — CERT — 1 1

Justice	Vote
Minton	D
Clark	E D
Burton	E D
Jackson	D
Douglas	E D
Frankfr	
Reed	E D
Black	
Vinson	E D

DuBois v Mossey
52 118M — 344 US 869 — CCA 7th
10/23 1952 — CERT — 1 1

Justice	Vote
Minton	D
Clark	D
Burton	D
Jackson	D
Douglas	G
Frankfr	
Reed	D
Black	G
Vinson	D

Vetterli v U.S.
52 128M — 344 US 872 — CCA 9th

Justice	11/10 1952 REPORT	11/08 1952 CERT (1 1)
Minton	V	GM
Clark	V	GM
Burton	V	GM
Jackson	V	GM
Douglas	V	
Frankfr	V	
Reed	V	
Black	V	G
Vinson	V	GM

Paonessa v New York
52 133M — 344 US 860 — New York
10/18 1952 — CERT — 1 1

Justice	Vote
Minton	D
Clark	D
Burton	D
Jackson	D
Douglas	G
Frankfr	
Reed	G
Black	
Vinson	D

Chorak v RKO
52 135M — 344 US 887 — CCA 9th
11/14 1952 — CERT — 1 1

Justice	Vote
Minton	D
Clark	D
Burton	D
Jackson	D
Douglas	G
Frankfr	
Reed	D
Black	G
Vinson	D

Salvaggio v Barnett
52 148M — 344 US 879 — Texas
11/08 1952 — CERT — 1 1

Justice	Vote
Minton	D
Clark	D
Burton	D
Jackson	D
Douglas	G
Frankfr	
Reed	D
Black	D
Vinson	D

Scott v U.S.
52 162M — 344 US 879 — CCA DC
11/08 1952 — CERT — 1 1

Justice	Vote
Minton	D
Clark	D
Burton	D
Jackson	D
Douglas	G
Frankfr	
Reed	D
Black	D
Vinson	D

Bailey v Virginia
52 168M — 344 US 886 — Virginia
11/14 1952 — CERT — 1 1

Justice	Vote
Minton	D
Clark	D
Burton	D
Jackson	D
Douglas	G
Frankfr	
Reed	G
Black	
Vinson	D

Allen v U.S.
52 174M — 344 US 869 — CCA DC
10/25 1952 — CERT — 1 1

Justice	Vote
Minton	D
Clark	D
Burton	D
Jackson	D
Douglas	G
Frankfr	
Reed	D
Black	D
Vinson	D

Fujimoto v Wiig
52 176M — 344 US 852 — DC Hawaii
10/18 1952 — MNDMUS — 1 1

Justice	Vote
Minton	D
Clark	D
Burton	D
Jackson	D
Douglas	D
Frankfr	#
Reed	D
Black	
Vinson	D

Bayne v U.S.
52 202M — 344 US 881 — CCA DC
11/08 1952 — CERT — 1 1

Justice	Vote
Minton	D
Clark	D
Burton	D
Jackson	D
Douglas	G
Frankfr	
Reed	D
Black	G
Vinson	D

Frankfeld v U.S.
52 204M — 344 US 922 — CCA 4th
01/17 1953 — CERT — 1 1

Justice	Vote
Minton	D
Clark	D
Burton	D
Jackson	D
Douglas	G G
Frankfr	
Reed	G
Black	
Vinson	D

Johnson v New Jersey
52 205M — 344 US 894 — New Jersey
11/21 1952 — CERT — 1 1

Justice	Vote
Minton	D
Clark	D
Burton	D
Jackson	D
Douglas	G
Frankfr	
Reed	D
Black	G
Vinson	D

Shelton v U.S.
52 235M — 346 US 270 — CCA 5th

Justice	04/04 1953 CERT (1 1)	06/13 1953 MERITS	06/15 1953 REPORT
Minton		VI	VI
Clark	G	VI	VI
Burton	G	VI	VI
Jackson	G	VI	VI
Douglas	G	VI	VI
Frankfr	G	VI	VI
Reed	G		
Black	G		
Vinson	G		

Clark v Skeen
52 259M — 345 US 918 — West Virginia
03/14 1953 — CERT — 1 1

Justice	Vote
Minton	D
Clark	D
Burton	D
Jackson	D
Douglas	G
Frankfr	G
Reed	G
Black	G
Vinson	G

Woollomes v Heinze
52 274M — 344 US 929 — CCA 9th
01/31 1953 — CERT — 1 1

Justice	Vote
Minton	D
Clark	D
Burton	D
Jackson	D
Douglas	G
Frankfr	D
Reed	G
Black	G
Vinson	D

Knetzer v Schultz
52 276M — 344 US 908
12/20 1952 — HABEAS — 1 1

Justice	Vote
Minton	D
Clark	D
Burton	D
Jackson	D
Douglas	T1
Frankfr	
Reed	T1
Black	T1
Vinson	D

Leyra v New York
52 331M — 345 US 918 — New York
03/14 1953 — CERT — 1 1

Justice	Vote
Minton	D
Clark	D
Burton	D
Jackson	D
Douglas	G
Frankfr	
Reed	G
Black	G
Vinson	G

Christoffel v U.S.
52 341M — 345 US 947 — CCA DC — 05/02 1953 — CERT — 2 1

Minton	Clark	Burton	Jackson	Douglas	Frankfr	Reed	Black	Vinson
D	GV	GV	GV	GV		GV	D	D

Brown v Florida
52 365M — 345 US 913 — Florida — 03/07 1953 — CERT — 1 1

Minton	Clark	Burton	Jackson	Douglas	Frankfr	Reed	Black	Vinson
			G				G	G

Normandale v U.S.
52 382M — 345 US 999 — CCA 5th — 06/13 1953 — CERT — 1 1

Minton	Clark	Burton	Jackson	Douglas	Frankfr	Reed	Black	Vinson
D	D	D	D	D	D		D	D

Grass v Illinois
52 385M — 345 US 999 52 4M — Illinois — 05/04 1953 — REPORT — 1 1

Minton	Clark	Burton	Jackson	Douglas	Frankfr	Reed	Black	Vinson
V	>	>	>	>	>	>		>

Miller v North Carolina
52 391M — 345 US 930 — North Carolina — 04/04 1953 — CERT — 1 1

Minton	Clark	Burton	Jackson	Douglas	Frankfr	Reed	Black	Vinson
D	D	D	D	D			G	D

Miller v Standard Oil Company
52 398M — 345 US 945 — CCA 7th — 04/25 1953 — CERT — 1 1

Minton	Clark	Burton	Jackson	Douglas	Frankfr	Reed	Black	Vinson
D	D	D		G	G		G	G

Kunz v New York
52 402M — 345 US 945 — New York — 04/25 1953 — CERT — 1 1

Minton	Clark	Burton	Jackson	Douglas	Frankfr	Reed	Black	Virson
D	D	D			G		G	D

White v U.S.
52 404M — 345 US 999 — CCA 5th — 06/13 1953 — CERT — 1 1

Minton	Clark	Burton	Jackson	Douglas	Frankfr	Reed	Black	Vinson
D	D	D			G		G	D

Ex Parte International Workers
52 406M — 345 US 915 — 03/14 1953 — MNDMUS — 1 1

Minton	Clark	Burton	Jackson	Douglas	Frankfr	Reed	Black	Vinson
D	D	D			G	G	G	G

Sandro v Graber
52 431M — 345 US 953 — Illinois — 05/02 1953 — CERT — 1 1

Minton	Clark	Burton	Jackson	Douglas	Frankfr	Reed	Black	Vinson
D	D	D		E		D	D	D

Draper v New York
52 442M — 345 US 944 — New York — 04/25 1953 — CERT — 1 1

Minton	Clark	Burton	Jackson	Douglas	Frankfr	Reed	Black	Vinson
D	D	D			G		G	D

Vanderwyde v New York
52 452M — 345 US 959 — New York — 05/16 1953 — CERT — 1 1

Minton	Clark	Burton	Jackson	Douglas	Frankfr	Reed	Black	Vinson
D	D	D			G		G	D

Work v U.S.
52 445M — 345 US 999 — CCA 10th — 06/13 1953 — CERT — 1 1

Minton	Clark	Burton	Jackson	Douglas	Frankfr	Reed	Black	Vinson
D	D	D			G		G	D

Pennsylvania (Baerchus) v Burke
52 467M — 345 US 966 — Pennsylvania — 05/23 1953 — CERT — 1 1

Minton	Clark	Burton	Jackson	Douglas	Frankfr	Reed	Black	Vinson
D	D	D			G		G	D

Livingston v South Carolina
52 443M — 345 US 959 — South Carolina — 05/16 1953 — CERT — 1 1

Minton	Clark	Burton	Jackson	Douglas	Frankfr	Reed	Black	Vinson
D	D	D			G		G	D

Scholla v Scholla
52 464M — 345 US 966 52 721M — CCA DC — 05/23 1953 — CERT — 1 1

Minton	Clark	Burton	Jackson	Douglas	Frankfr	Reed	Black	Vinson
D	D	D		G	G		G	G

Bowen v County Of Los Angeles
52 469M — 345 US 1002 — California — 06/13 1953 — CERT — 1 1

Minton	Clark	Burton	Jackson	Douglas	Frankfr	Reed	Black	Vinson
D	D	D			G		G	D

Petherbridge v County Of Los Angeles
52 470M — 345 US 1002 — California — 06/13 1953 — CERT — 1 1

Minton	Clark	Burton	Jackson	Douglas	Frankfr	Reed	Black	Vinson
D	D	D			G	G	G	G

Elder v U.S.
52 471M
345 US 999
CCA 9th

	06/13 1953 CERT
	1 1
Minton	D
Clark	D
Burton	D
Jackson	
Douglas	G
Frankfr	G
Reed	
Black	GR D
Vinson	D

Pennsylvania (Elliott) v Baldi
52 499M
345 US 976
Pennsylvania

	06/06 1953 CERT
	1 1
Minton	D
Clark	D
Burton	D
Jackson	
Douglas	
Frankfr	
Reed	G
Black	G
Vinson	G D

Collie v Heinze
52 514M
345 US 1000
California

	06/13 1953 CERT
	1 1
Minton	D
Clark	D
Burton	D
Jackson	D
Douglas	D
Frankfr	D
Reed	D
Black	G
Vinson	D

Barnett v Doerfler
52 515M
345 US 1000
Illinois

	06/13 1953 CERT
	1 1
Minton	D
Clark	D
Burton	D
Jackson	E
Douglas	
Frankfr	
Reed	DH
Black	E
Vinson	DH D

Schell v Eidson
52 529M
345 US 1001
CCA 8th

	06/13 1953 CERT
	1 1
Minton	D
Clark	D
Burton	D
Jackson	D
Douglas	D
Frankfr	D
Reed	D
Black	GR
Vinson	D

Sanders v Southern RR Company
52 534M
345 US 1001
CCA 6th

	06/13 1953 CERT
	1 1
Minton	D
Clark	D
Burton	D
Jackson	D
Douglas	D
Frankfr	D
Reed	D
Black	G
Vinson	D

Landgraver v Ragen
52 542M
345 US 1001
Illinois

	06/13 1953 CERT
	1 1
Minton	D
Clark	D
Burton	D
Jackson	D
Douglas	D
Frankfr	D
Reed	D
Black	G
Vinson	D

Appendix I

U.S. Supreme Court
October 1953 Term

Radio Officers' Union v N.L.R.B.
53 5A 52 230A
347 US 17 53 6A 53 7A
Black 01/22/53 Reed 11/16/53 CCA 2d

	10/06 1952 CERT 1 1	10/18 1952 CERT 1 2	01/10 1953 MERITS 1 1	11/14 1953 MERITS 1 2	02/01 1954 REPORT 1 1
Minton	G	G	A	A	A
Clark	G	G	A	A	A
Burton	G	G	A	A	A
Jackson	G	G			A
Douglas	G	G		R	
Frankfr		G	A	A	A
Reed		D	A	R	R
Black		D	A	R	
Warren		D			A
Vinson	G	G	A		

N.L.R.B. v International Teamsters
53 6A 52 301A
347 US 17 53 5A 53 7A
Black 01/22/53 Reed 11/16/53 CCA 8th

	10/18 1952 CERT 1 1	01/10 1953 MERITS 1 1	02/01 1954 REPORT 1 1
Minton	G	R	R
Clark	G	R	R
Burton	G	R	R
Jackson	G		
Douglas	G		A
Frankfr	G	R	R
Reed	G	R	R
Black	G	R	R
Warren		AL	A
Vinson	G		

Gaynor News Company v N.L.R.B.
53 7A 52 371A
347 US 17 53 5A 53 6A
Black 05/11/53 Reed 11/16/53 CCA 2d

	12/06 1952 CERT 1 1	02/07 1953 CERT 1 2	04/11 1953 AMICUS 1 1	05/02 1953 MERITS 1 1	11/14 1953 MERITS 1 2	02/01 1954 REPORT 1 1
Minton	H	G	B	R	R	
Clark	H	G	B	R	R	R
Burton	H	G	B	R	R	R
Jackson	H	G	Y			
Douglas	D	G			A	A
Frankfr	D	G	Y		A	A
Reed	D	G		R	R	R
Black	D	G	B	R	R	R
Warren		G		R	R	R
Vinson	H	G	B			

Brown v Board Of Education
53 1A 52 8A 51 436A
347 US 483 53 2A 53 4A 53 10A
Warren ??/??/5? DC Kansas

	12/31 1951 JURIS 1 1	01/26 1952 JURIS 1 2	06/07 1952 JURIS 1 3	11/14 1952 AMICUS 1 1	05/17 1954 REPORT 1 1
Minton	H	H	N	B	R
Clark	H	H	N	Y	R
Burton	H	H	N	B	R
Jackson	H	H	H		R
Douglas				Y	R
Frankfr	N	H	N	Y	R
Reed	H	H	N		R
Black	N	H	N	Y	R
Warren					R
Vinson	H	NH	N		

Briggs v Elliott
53 2A 52 101A 51 816A
347 US 483 53 1A 53 4A 53 10A
Warren ??/??/5? DC ED South Carolina

	06/07 1952 JURIS 1 1	11/08 1952 AMICUS 1 1	11/14 1952 AMICUS 2 1	05/17 1954 REPORT 1 1
Minton	N	B	B	R
Clark	N	B	B	R
Burton	N	B	B	R
Jackson				R
Douglas	N	B	Y	R
Frankfr	N	B	Y	R
Reed	N	B	B	R
Black	N	B	Y	R
Warren	N			R
Vinson	N	B		

Davis v County School Board
53 4A 52 191A
347 US 483 53 1A 53 2A 53 10A
Warren ??/??/5? DC ED Virginia

	10/07 1952 JURIS 1 1	11/14 1952 AMICUS 1 1	05/17 1954 REPORT 1 1
Minton	N	B	R
Clark	N	Y	R
Burton	N	B	R
Jackson	N		R
Douglas	N	Y	R
Frankfr	N	B	R
Reed	N	Y	R
Black	N	B	R
Warren	N		R
Vinson	N	B	

Bolling v Sharpe
53 8A 52 413A
347 US 497 53 1A
CCA DC

	CERT 11/08 1952 (1 1)	REPORT 05/17 1954 (1 1)	
Minton	G	R	
Clark	G	R	A
Burton	G	R	A
Jackson	G	R	
Douglas	G	R	A
Frankfr	G	R	
Reed	G	R	A
Black	G	R	A
Warren		R	A
Vinson	G		

Maryland Casualty Company v Cushing
53 11A 52 498A
347 US 409
Frankfr 11/16/53 CCA 5th

	CERT 03/07 1953 (1 1)	MERITS 05/02 1953 (1 1)	REPORT 11/14 1953 (1 2)	
Minton	D	RQ	R	AQ
Clark	D	R	R	A
Burton			R	
Jackson	G	X	>	A
Douglas	G		>	
Frankfr	G	A	>	A
Reed				
Black	D	R	RJ	A
Warren	D		>	A
Vinson	G	R	>	A

Irvine v California
53 12A 52 533A
347 US 128
Jackson 12/09/53 California

	CERT 03/07 1953 (1 1)	MERITS 12/05 1953 (1 1)	REPORT 02/08 1954 (1 1)	
Minton	D	R	R	A
Clark	E	R		A
Burton	D			
Jackson		X		
Douglas	G		R	A
Frankfr	G	R	R	A
Reed	G			
Black	G	X	R	A
Warren			R	A
Vinson	D			

Pope & Talbot v Hawn
53 13A 52 535A
346 US 406
Black 10/19/53 CCA 3rd

	CERT 06/13 1953 (1 1)	MERITS 10/17 1953 (1 1)	REPORT 12/07 1953 (1 1)	
Minton	G			
Clark	G	A		A
Burton	G	R	R	
Jackson	G	R	R	
Douglas	G		A	
Frankfr	G	R	R	A
Reed	G		A	
Black	G		R	A
Warren			R	A
Vinson	G			

U.S. v Five Gambling Devices
53 14A 52 558A
346 US 441 53 40A 53 41A
Jackson 10/19/53 DC MD Tennesse

	JURIS 05/23 1953 (1 1)	MERITS 10/17 1953 (1 1)	REPORT 12/07 1953 (1 1)	
Minton	N			
Clark	N	R	R	A
Burton	N	R	R	A
Jackson	N	R		
Douglas	N		A	
Frankfr	N		A	
Reed	N	R	R	A
Black	N			
Warren	N	R	R	A
Vinson	N			

N.L.R.B. v Local Union 1229 IBEW
53 15A 52 609A
346 US 464
Burton 10/19/53 CCA DC

	CERT 04/25 1953 (1 2)	CERT 05/02 1953 (1 3)	MERITS 10/17 1953 (1 1)	REPORT 12/07 1953 (1 1)	
Minton	D	D			
Clark	G	G	R	>	
Burton	G	G	R	>	
Jackson	G	G	R	>	
Douglas	D	D			
Frankfr					
Reed	D	G	R	>	
Black	D	D			
Warren	D	G	R	>	A
Vinson	D	G		>	A

Bankers Life & Casualty v Holland
53 16A 52 614A
346 US 379
Clark 10/19/53 CCA 5th

	CERT 04/11 1953 (1 1)	MERITS 10/17 1953 (1 1)	REPORT 11/30 1953 (1 1)	
Minton	GL	R		S
Clark	GL	A	A	
Burton	GL	A	A	
Jackson	GL	X		S
Douglas	GL	A	A	
Frankfr	GL	A	A	
Reed				
Black				
Warren	D			S
Vinson	GL			

Partmar v Paramount Pictures Theatres
53 17A 52 641A
347 US 89
Reed 10/19/53 CCA 9th

	CERT 05/23 1953 (1 1)	MERITS 10/17 1953 (1 1)	REPORT 02/08 1954 (1 1)	
Minton	G	A	A	
Clark	GL	A	A	
Burton	GL	A	A	
Jackson	GL			
Douglas	GL	A	A	
Frankfr	GL	A	A	
Reed				
Black	G	R	R	
Warren	G	R	R	
Vinson	G			

Toolson v New York Yankees
53 18A 52 647A
346 US 356 52 23A 52 25A
CCA 9th

	CERT 05/23 1953 (1 1)	MERITS 10/17 1953 (1 1)	REPORT 11/09 1953 (1 1)	
Minton	G	R		A
Clark	G			
Burton	G	R	R	A
Jackson	G	D		A
Douglas	G	D		A
Frankfr	G			
Reed	G	R	R	A
Black	G			
Warren	G	D		A
Vinson	G			

Theatre Enterprises v Paramount Film
53 19A 52 649A
346 US 537
Douglas 12/09/53 Clark 12/11/53 CCA 4th

	05/23 1953 CERT	12/05 1953 MERITS	01/04 1954 REPORT	03/06 1954 RETAX
	1 1	1 1	1 1	1 1
Minton	G	A	A	B
Clark	D	A	A	B
Burton	D	A	A	B
Jackson		A	A	X
Douglas		A	A	
Frankfr				
Reed	D	A	R	B
Black				Y
Warren	G	A	A	B
Vinson	D			B

Voris v Eitel
53 20A 52 661A
346 US 328
Warren 10/19/53 CCA 5th

	05/02 1953 CERT	05/16 1953 MERITS	10/17 1953 REPORT
	1 1	1 2	1 1
Minton	GR	A	R
Clark	GR	A	R
Burton	G	A	R
Jackson	X		R
Douglas	G	D	R
Frankfr	GR	D	R
Reed		A	R
Black	GR		R
Warren		A	R
Vinson	G		

Atchison Topeka RR v PUC Of California
53 22A 52 667A
346 US 346 53 43A 52 739A
Minton 10/19/53 California

	05/16 1953 JURIS	10/17 1953 MERITS	11/09 1953 REPORT
	1 1	1 1	1 1
Minton	N	A	A
Clark	S	A	A
Burton	P	R	A
Jackson	P	R	A
Douglas	P	A	A
Frankfr	S	A	A
Reed			A
Black	S	A	A
Vinson	P		

Kowalski v Chandler
53 23A 52 668A
346 US 356 53 18A 53 25A
CCA 6th

	05/23 1953 CERT	10/17 1953 MERITS	11/09 1953 REPORT
	1 1	1 1	1 1
Minton	G	A	A
Clark	G	A	A
Burton	G	R	R
Jackson	G	A	A
Douglas	D	A	A
Frankfr			
Reed	G	R	R
Black	D	A	A
Warren		A	A
Vinson	G		

St. Joe Paper v Atlantic Coast Line RR
53 24A 52 670A
347 US 298 53 33A 53 36A 53 37A
Frankfr 10/27/53 CCA 5th

	05/02 1953 CERT	10/24 1953 MERITS	04/05 1954 REPORT
	1 1	1 1	1 1
Minton	G	Q	A
Clark	G	A	A
Burton	G		
Jackson		R	R
Douglas	D		
Frankfr	GL	R	R
Reed	GL		
Black	X	R	R
Warren			
Vinson	GL		

Corbett v Chandler
53 25A 52 674A
346 US 356 53 18A 53 23A
CCA 6th

	05/23 1953 CERT	10/17 1953 MERITS	11/09 1953 REPORT
	1 1	1 1	1 1
Minton	G	A	A
Clark	G	A	A
Burton	G	R	R
Jackson	G	A	A
Douglas	D	A	A
Frankfr			
Reed	G	R	R
Black	D	A	A
Warren		A	A
Vinson	G		

Olberding v Illinois Central RR
53 27A 52 683A
346 US 338
Frankfr 10/19/53 CCA 6th

	05/02 1953 CERT	10/17 1953 MERITS	11/09 1953 REPORT
	1 1	1 1	1 1
Minton	G		
Clark	G	R	R
Burton	G	RO	R
Jackson	G		
Douglas	G	R	R
Frankfr	G		
Reed	G		A
Black	G	R	R
Warren		R	R
Vinson	G		

F.P.C. v Niagara Mohawk Power
53 28A 52 691A
347 US 239
Burton 12/09/53 CCA DC

	05/16 1953 CERT	12/05 1953 MERITS	03/15 1954 REPORT
	1 1	1 1	1 1
Minton	G		A
Clark	G		A
Burton		X	
Jackson			
Douglas	D	R	R
Frankfr			
Reed	D	A	A
Black	D	A	A
Warren	G	A	A
Vinson	D		

Lober v U.S.
53 30A 52 695A
346 US 335
Black 10/27/53 Ct Cls

	05/29 1953 CERT	10/24 1953 MERITS	11/09 1953 REPORT
	1 1	1 1	1 1
Minton	G	A	A
Clark	G	A	A
Burton		R	R
Jackson	G	A	A
Douglas	D	A	A
Frankfr	D	A	A
Reed	G	R	R
Black	D	A	A
Warren		A	A
Vinson	D		

U.S. v Morgan
53 31A 52 696A
346 US 502
Reed 10/27/53 CCA 2d

	06/06 1953 CERT	10/24 1953 MERITS	01/04 1954 REPORT
Minton	G	R	R
Clark	G	R	R
Burton	G	R A	R A
Jackson	G		A
Douglas	G	V A	A
Frankfr	G		A
Reed			
Black	D	R	R A
Warren	X		
Vinson	G	R	R A

U.S. v Harris
53 32A 52 700A
347 US 612
Douglas 10/27/53 Warren 05/26/54 DC DC

	05/02 1953 JURIS	10/24 1953 MERITS	06/07 1954 REPORT
Minton	N	R	R
Clark	N	R	R
Burton	N	R A	R A
Jackson	N		
Douglas	N	R X	R A
Frankfr	N		
Reed	N	R	R
Black	X	R	R
Warren		R	R
Vinson	N	R	

Lynch v Atlantic Coast Line RR
53 33A 52 702A
347 US 298 53 24A 53 36A 53 37A
Frankfr 10/27/53 CCA 5th

	05/02 1953 CERT	10/24 1953 MERITS	04/05 1954 REPORT
Minton	G	Q	1 A
Clark	G		
Burton	G	R	R
Jackson	D	R	R
Douglas			
Frankfr	GL		
Reed	GL	R	R
Black	X		
Warren			
Vinson	GL		

Howell Chevrolet Company v N.L.R.B.
53 34A 52 703A
346 US 482
Black 11/16/53 CCA 9th

	05/16 1953 CERT	11/14 1953 MERITS	12/14 1953 REPORT
Minton	G		A
Clark	G		A
Burton	G		A
Jackson	G	R	R
Douglas	G		A
Frankfr	G		A
Reed	G		A
Black			A
Warren	G		A
Vinson			

Madruga v Superior Court San Diego
53 35A 52 704A
346 US 556
Black 10/27/53 California

	05/23 1953 CERT	10/24 1953 MERITS	01/18 1954 REPORT
Minton	G		A
Clark	G D		A
Burton	G		AQ
Jackson	G	RQ	A
Douglas	G D	R	R
Frankfr		R	R
Reed	G D		A
Black			A
Warren	G		A
Vinson			

Aird v Atlantic Coast Line RR
53 36A 52 705A
347 US 298 53 24A 53 33A 53 37A
Frankfr 10/27/53 CCA 5th

	05/02 1953 CERT	10/24 1953 MERITS	04/05 1954 REPORT
Minton	G	Q	1 A
Clark	G D		
Burton	G	R	R
Jackson	G D	R	R
Douglas	GL		
Frankfr	GL X		
Reed			
Black			
Warren	GL	R	R
Vinson			

Welbon v Atlantic Coast Line RR
53 37A 52 710A
347 US 298 53 24A 53 33A 53 36A
Frankfr 10/27/53 CCA 5th

	05/02 1953 CERT	10/24 1953 MERITS	04/05 1954 REPORT
Minton	G	Q	1 A
Clark	G D		
Burton	G	R A	R A
Jackson	G D	R	R
Douglas	GL		
Frankfr	GL X		
Reed		R	R
Black	GL		
Warren			
Vinson			

Salsburg v Maryland
53 38A 52 712A
346 US 545
Burton 10/27/53 Maryland

	05/16 1953 JURIS	10/24 1953 MERITS	01/11 1954 REPORT
Minton	S		A
Clark	N		A
Burton	N		A
Jackson	N		A
Douglas	N	S	R
Frankfr			
Reed	N		A
Black	S		A
Warren	N		
Vinson			

Wilko v Swan
53 39A 52 715A
346 US 427
Reed 10/27/53 CCA 2d

	05/29 1953 CERT	10/24 1953 MERITS	12/07 1953 REPORT
Minton	G		A
Clark	G D		
Burton	G D	R	R
Jackson	G	R A	R A
Douglas	G D		
Frankfr	G D		
Reed			
Black	G	R	R
Warren			
Vinson	G D		

U.S. v Denmark
53 40A 52 730A
346 US 441 53 14A 53 41A
Jackson 10/19/53 DC SD Georgia

	05/16 1953 JURIS	10/17 1953 MERITS	12/07 1953 REPORT
Minton	N	R	R
Clark	N	R	R
Burton	N		A
Jackson	H		
Douglas	N	R A	R A
Frankfr			A
Reed	N		A
Black		R	R
Warren	N		A
Vinson			

U.S. v Braun
53 41A 52 731A
346 US 441 53 14A 53 40A
Jackson 10/19/53 DC SD Georgia

	05/16 1953 JURIS	10/17 1953 MERITS	12/07 1953 REPORT
Minton	N	R	R
Clark	N	R	R
Burton	N		A
Jackson	H		
Douglas	N	R A	R A
Frankfr			A
Reed	N	R	R
Black	N		A
Warren	N		A
Vinson			

Southern Pacific v PUC Of California
53 43A 52 739A
346 US 346 53 22A 52 667A
Minton 10/19/53 California

	05/16 1953 JURIS	10/17 1953 MERITS	11/09 1953 REPORT
Minton	P		A
Clark	P	R	R
Burton	P		A
Jackson	P		A
Douglas	P		A
Frankfr	P	R	R
Reed	P		A
Black	P		A
Vinson			

Avondale Marine Ways v Henderson
53 44A 52 744A
346 US 366
CCA 5th

	06/06 1953 CERT (1 1)	10/24 1953 MERITS (1 1)	11/09 1953 REPORT (1 1)
Minton	D	A	A
Clark	G	A	A
Burton	G	A	A
Jackson	G	A	A
Douglas	G	A	A
Frankfr	G	A	A
Reed			
Black	D	A	A
Warren	D	A	A
Vinson	D		

Building Trades v Kinard Construction
53 48A 52 762A
346 US 933 53 56A 52 773A
Alabama

	06/13 1953 CERT (1 1)	01/16 1954 MERITS (1 2)	01/18 1954 REPORT (1 1)
Minton		G	R
Clark	H	G	R
Burton	H	G	R
Jackson	D		
Douglas	G	G	R
Frankfr	H	G	R
Reed	G	G	R
Black	G	G	R
Warren		G	R
Vinson	H		

Pereira v U.S.
53 50A 52 764A
347 US 1
Warren 10/27/53 CCA 5th

	06/13 1953 CERT (1 1)	10/24 1953 MERITS (1 1)	02/01 1954 REPORT (1 1)
Minton	D	A	R
Clark	G	A	R
Burton	G	R	R
Jackson	D		
Douglas	G	A	R
Frankfr		A	R
Reed	G		R
Black	G	A	R
Warren		A	R
Vinson	D		

U.S. v Debrow
53 51A 52 765A
346 US 374 53 52A 53 53A 52 54A 52 55A
Minton 10/27/53 CCA 5th

	06/13 1953 CERT (1 1)	10/24 1953 MERITS (1 1)	11/16 1953 REPORT (1 1)
Minton	G	R	R
Clark	G	R	R
Burton	G	R	R
Jackson	G	R	R
Douglas	G	R	R
Frankfr	G		
Reed			
Black	D	R	R
Warren		R	R
Vinson	G		

U.S. v Wilkinson
53 52A 52 766A
346 US 374 53 51A 53 52A 53 53A 53 54A 53 55A
Minton 10/27/53 CCA 5th

	06/13 1953 CERT (1 1)	10/24 1953 MERITS (1 1)	11/16 1953 REPORT (1 1)
Minton	G	R	R
Clark	G	R	R
Burton	G	R	R
Jackson	G	R	R
Douglas	G	R	R
Frankfr	G		
Reed			
Black	D	R	R
Warren		R	R
Vinson	G		

U.S. v Brashier
53 53A 52 767A
346 US 374 53 51A 53 52A 53 54A 53 55A
Minton 10/27/53 CCA 5th

	06/13 1953 CERT (1 1)	10/24 1953 MERITS (1 1)	11/16 1953 REPORT (1 1)
Minton	G	R	R
Clark	G	R	R
Burton	G	R	R
Jackson	G	R	R
Douglas	G	R	R
Frankfr	G		
Reed			
Black	D	R	R
Warren		R	R
Vinson	G		

U.S. v Rogers
53 54A 52 768A
346 US 374 53 51A 53 52A 53 53A 53 55A
Minton 10/27/53 CCA 5th

	06/13 1953 CERT (1 1)	10/24 1953 MERITS (1 1)	11/16 1953 REPORT (1 1)
Minton	G	R	R
Clark	G	R	R
Burton	G	R	R
Jackson	G	R	R
Douglas	G	R	R
Frankfr	G		
Reed			
Black	D	R	R
Warren		R	R
Vinson	G		

U.S. v Jackson
53 55A 52 769A
346 US 374 53 51A 53 52A 53 53A 53 54A
Minton 10/27/53 CCA 5th

	06/13 1953 CERT (1 1)	10/24 1953 MERITS (1 1)	11/16 1953 REPORT (1 1)
Minton	G	R	R
Clark	G	R	R
Burton	G	R	R
Jackson	G	R	R
Douglas	G	R	R
Frankfr	G		
Reed			
Black	D	R	R
Warren		R	R
Vinson	G		

Garner v Teamsters Local 776
53 56A 52 773A
346 US 485 53 48A 52 762A
Jackson 10/27/53 Pennsylvania

	06/13 1953 CERT (1 1)	10/24 1953 MERITS (1 1)	12/14 1953 REPORT (1 1)
Minton	G	A	A
Clark	G	A	A
Burton	G	A	A
Jackson	G	A	A
Douglas	G	A	A
Frankfr	G	A	A
Reed	G	A	A
Black	G	A	A
Warren		A	A
Vinson	G		

Dickinson v U.S.
53 57A 52 777A
346 US 389
Clark 10/27/53 CCA 9th

	06/13 1953 CERT	10/24 1953 MERITS	11/30 1953 REPORT
Minton			
Clark	G	R	R
Burton	D	R	R
Jackson	D	A	A
Douglas		A	A
Frankfr	G	R	R
Reed		R	R
Black	G	R	R
Warren		A	A
Vinson	G		

Nevada v Stacher
53 61A 52 784A
346 US 906
Nevada

	06/13 1953 CERT	12/07 1953 REPORT
Minton	G	R
Clark	G	R
Burton	G	R
Jackson	G	R
Douglas	G	R
Frankfr	G	R
Reed	G	R
Black	G	R
Warren	G	R
Vinson	G	

PUC Of California v United Air Lines
53 87A 52 823A
346 US 402
Minton 11/16/53 DC ND California

	06/13 1953 JURIS	11/14 1953 MERITS	11/30 1953 REPORT	03/06 1954 RETAX
Minton	P	R	R	Y
Clark	P	R	R	Y
Burton	P	R	R	Y
Jackson	P	R	R	X
Douglas		A	R	X
Frankfr		R	R	Y
Reed		R	R	Y
Black	P	A	R	Y
Warren		R	R	Y
Vinson	P			

Walder v U.S.
53 121A 52 480M
347 US 62
Frankfr 12/09/53 CCA 8th

	06/13 1953 CERT	12/05 1953 MERITS	02/01 1954 REPORT
Minton	G	R	A
Clark	G	A	A
Burton	G	R	A
Jackson	G	A	A
Douglas	G	A	A
Frankfr	G		
Reed	G	R	R
Black	G		
Warren	G	A	A
Vinson	G		A

Scalf v Skeen
53 3M 52 456M
346 US 911
West Virginia

	05/23 1953 CERT	12/05 1953 CERT
Minton	E	D
Clark	E	D
Burton		D
Jackson	E	D
Douglas		D
Frankfr		D
Reed		D
Black		D
Warren	G	
Vinson		D

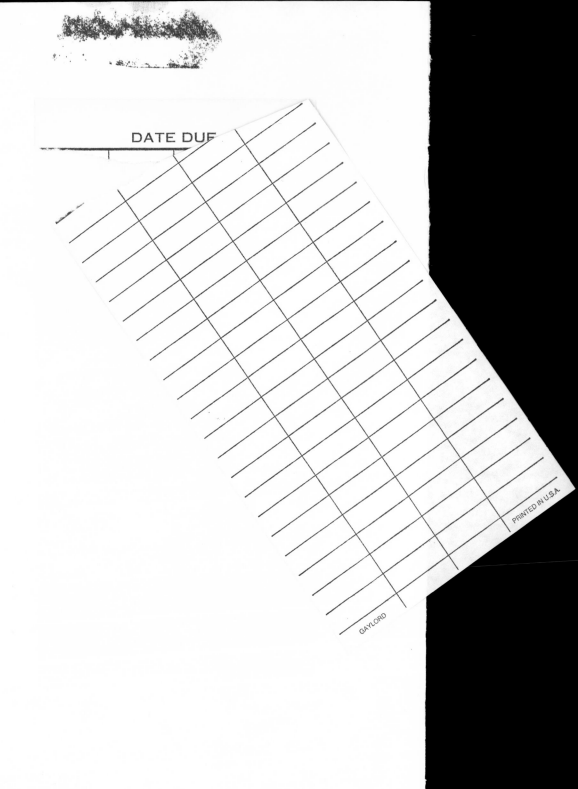

DATE DUE

GAYLORD

PRINTED IN U.S.A.